THE WALTONS GUIDE TO IRISH MUSIC

A COMPREHENSIVE A-Z GUIDE TO
IRISH AND CELTIC MUSIC IN ALL ITS FORMS

HARRY LONG

WALTONS PUBLISHING

Illustrations: Aidan Colgan
Layout and music setting: John Canning
Cover design: Temple of Design

Order No. wm1401
ISBN No. 1 85720 177 9

Exclusive Distributors:

Walton Manufacturing Co. Ltd.
Unit 6A, Rosemount Park Drive, Rosemount Business Park,
Ballycoolin Road, Dublin 11, Ireland

The James Import Company
9 Skyline Drive, Hawthorne, New York, NY 10532, USA

Printed in Ireland by Betaprint

1   3   7   9   0   8   6   4   2

Acknowledgements

Many people have helped with this book in many different ways. Numerous musicians answered queries patiently and promptly and I thank them all for their co-operation. Eamonn Galldubh, Mary Gregg, Sinéad Madden, Michael McInerney, Gloria Mulhall, Mary O'Donnell and Arthur Sealy at Waltons New School of Music all provided valuable information and suggestions, as did the staff of Waltons music shop in South Great George's Street, Dublin, especially Mick Dunphy.

Joan Anderson and Ed Ward of the Milwaukee Irish Fest, Ronan Browne, Jimmy Faulkner, Mick Kinsella, Sarah McQuaid, Brendan Monaghan and Tommy Sands from Co. Down, Seosaimhín Ní Bheaglaoich, Joe O'Donnell in England, Claire O'Regan, Eoin Ó Riabhaigh, Gavin Ralston, Pierce Turner and John Whelan all gave generously of their time and provided me with much useful information on a wide range of specialised subjects.

Fenella Bazin of the Centre for Manx Studies, Douglas gave me valuable guidance on Manx music and was very helpful in answering specific queries relating to my research on this subject. The Galician piper and whistle player Rodrigo Quián Rodríquez taught me much about Galician music and the developments which have taken place in Galicia since the death of Franco. Simon Jones, a Dubliner now resident in Barcelona, also gave me advice on Galicia and Asturias and recordings of music from those regions of Spain. Ciaran Cosgrove of the Department of Spanish and Portuguese at Trinity College, Dublin helped with contacts relating to Argentina. He is a native of Belfast, and conversations with him and Donal McCarthy of Killeavy, Co. Armagh over the years have deepened my understanding of the troubles in Northern Ireland and the relationship between politics and culture. Terry Barry, James Lydon and other members of the Departments of Medieval and Modern History at Trinity College, Dublin gave me a passion for and a grounding in history and archaeology.

Many people loaned me CDs, tapes and books at different stages and drew my attention to recordings or articles that I might not otherwise have seen. In this regard I would particularly like to thank Hugo Camacho-Romero, Brigid McCarthy, Jack McManus and Mick O'Connor for their generosity and enthusiasm.

I made many visits to the Irish Traditional Music Archive in Merrion Square, Dublin where Nicholas Carolan and the staff have always been very helpful. Terry Moylan at Na Píobairí Uilleann made his archives available to me for photographic research. The staff at Gael-Linn, Claddagh Records and Celtic Note were all very helpful at different stages.

The late Seán O'Connell did not play music himself but he and his wife, Cáit, facilitated many wonderful sessions over the years in their guesthouse, Mount Richard, outside Carrick-on-Suir, and later in the Tinvane Hotel. It was he and his son, Robbie, who first encouraged my brother and I to start playing traditional music. The late Bobby Clancy was also a major inspiration in those early days of learning and was filled with a rare passion and enthusiasm for life, music and poetry. He and his wife Máire extended our time in the Tinvane by taking it over after my uncle emigrated to the US and welcoming our continued working holidays there. Many others who frequented the Tinvane were encouraging in those years and gave those who shared time with them a great sense of life and music's importance in it.

My mother and father have always been available to fill in gaps about the music in Mount Richard and the Tinvane. Their stories about the earlier days in Carrick before I was born and the Clancy Brothers and Tommy Makem before and during their rise to fame were always amusing and often hilarious. My cousins, Alice and Robbie, and Tom Nealon of Carrick also tell wonderful stories of the early days of the 'ballad boom'. In Mount Richard and the Tinvane they grew up surrounded by musicians, many of whom would later become musical legends. They provide a fascinating insight into a time which was very different in many ways for traditional musicians than the present day.

Darach de Brún from the Navan Road, Dublin, is a great source of tunes and information on the music and its background. He has taught me much and has always been generous with his time and his own wonderful music.

John Mardirosian and Aideen Walton at Waltons have shown endless patience and attention to detail in editing this book. They have contributed much to its over-all form and made many useful suggestions which improved it. It has been a great pleasure to work with them.

A special thanks to John Canning for the layout and setting of the book and to Niall Walton, without whom this project would not have come to fruition.

A special thanks also to Josephine Boyle at the New School and to the artist Aidan Colgan, who took great care in his drawings of the musical instruments.

My brother, Conor, has been my companion in music since we started to play together. He has helped with this book in too many ways to list them all.

It has been very difficult to find time to work on this book through the last ten years but my wife, Carol, has shown great patience throughout. She also helped with many of the practical details of the research and commented on the writing of different parts of the book. Without her help it would never have been completed.

Many others, too numerous to mention, have provided assistance in different ways, and I am grateful to each one of them.

Introduction

Work on this book began in 1995, when the project was initiated by my brother, Conor, and John Mardirosian at Waltons Publishing. I had been teaching a course on the history of Irish traditional music at Waltons New School of Music and, as with the course, the book was to be inclusive of many different forms and expressions of traditional music.

There had always been music of different kinds around our house when we were growing up, but traditional music assumed a new importance for my brother Conor and I in our early teens, when we started to spend our school holidays at our uncle's hotel outside Carrick-on-Suir. The Tinvane Hotel was an extraordinary gathering place for musicians and singers from all over Ireland and abroad. The 'ballad room' in the basement was the venue for regular Saturday night gigs which included memorable performances by artists such as Bobby Clancy, Robbie O'Connell, the Clancy Brothers, Alice and Seán Rattigan, Colm and Tommy Sands, Paddy Glackin, the Bread and Beer Band (Robbie O'Connell, Tommy Keane, Martin Murray and Paul Grant), Dermot Morgan, Oisín, Shay Healy and local musicians such as Paney Bartley and Gerry Phelan. On Sunday nights there were more informal sessions which often included traditional musicians or folk singers but whose mainstays were Mick Kelly, who played a variety of music on piano accordion; Gerry De Lacy, a great storyteller; Barry Murphy, a guitarist, singer and sometime poet who often sang folk songs but delighted in doing a most impressive Buddy Holly; and Tom Nealon, a local schoolteacher involved in the theatre who was a great seanchaí and also sang. The poet Michael Coady and such fine traditional singers as Mick Forristal and Mariette O'Keefe often came by, and Breda or Anne Mooney brought singers and musicians over from Ring.

Informal sessions could happen at any time in the Tinvane and usually anyone who was present would be asked to contribute something, be it a tune, a song, a recitation or a story. The inclusiveness and the sharing were what mattered most. Annie Roche, an old woman from the town, often came up on Saturday nights to do the door for the gig. She would invariably be up on stage before the night was out, singing 'The Bonny Bunch of Roses' or 'Seven Drunken Nights'. People sang, played or talked, and whether you were professional or amateur, a world-famous musician or simply a lover of music didn't matter. At times, the conversation was as important as the music, songs, story-telling and recitations. The historian and literary scholar Pádraig Power was also a regular at the Tinvane and would talk for hours about history, local characters, the background to a song that had just been sung or his latest expedition to some obscure archeological site. Bobby Clancy, who loved to sing and recite poetry, would at times prefer simply to sit and talk.

The music at the Tinvane was woven into the broader fabric of life, past and present. Carrick-on-Suir at that time was twinned with the town of Tregunc in

Brittany. The visit of people from Tregunc, including musicians who played traditional Breton and Irish music, created an awareness of other traditions which were different in many ways but also shared some of the characteristics of our own music. Occasional visitors came from other parts of continental Europe, Scotland, the United States and other countries. Many of them played or had an interest in music. Their presence created the sense that, while much of the music and song at the Tinvane might be firmly rooted in Ireland or even the immediate locality, it had branches that reached out into a wider world. We might not have consciously traced the connections between the different forms of music and song, but they were there nonetheless. I recall being told of a pub some miles outside Carrick called Delaney's or The Slate Quarries where an unusual dance known as 'The Lancers' was performed. I was told it had been brought to the area by British soldiers during the Napoleonic Wars. It seemed extraordinary to me that this could be the origin of a local traditional dance and that its history could stretch back that far. Then again, wasn't old Annie Roche singing about Napoleon all the time?

To grow up with the music in such an environment, where serious conversations often took place but the sense of fun was never far away, was a great pleasure. Traditional music sometimes suffers from being taken too seriously or played in an overly competitive environment, although competitiveness is part of human nature and has played a significant part in the recent development of traditional music, especially (though not exclusively) through the competitions run annually by Comhaltas Ceoltóirí Éireann. Likewise, the commercialisation of traditional music since the 1920s, by contributing to competition among musicians, has established higher standards of performance and technical ability. It is, however, still important to recognise that many people in Ireland and elsewhere still gather every week simply to sing, play or dance. While it is not possible in a book of this kind to give details of all the singers, musicians and dancers who gather regularly to share and learn from each other, it is important to recognise that this is one of the most vital aspects of our musical tradition. Although, for some time now, music, song and dance have also been passed on in more formal settings, often using written or printed material, it is through more informal gatherings that the tradition has been passed on for centuries. Fashions and tastes in the commercial arena may change, but as long as people still enjoy their music it will survive.

This book aims first to provide an overview of the basic elements of traditional music, song and dance. These include:

- The different types of instrumental music and their connections with dance;
- The history and development of different types of dance;
- The different types of song and styles of singing;
- The main instruments of traditional music and their history in Ireland.

Secondly, the book deals with the musicians, singers and groups who perform the music or, in the case of past performers, made a significant contribution to its development. In this I have been necessarily selective. There have been so many musicians in the past and there are so many performers today that it would be impossible to include them all. I have endeavoured to cover as broad a range of musicians as possible, representing different instruments, different styles and different approaches to the music. Where a musician, singer or group has had a significant influence on the development of the music I have tried to place these developments in context. Such individuals as Seán Ó Riada and Dónal Lunny and bands like the Chieftains, Planxty and the Bothy Band have had such a seminal influence on the development of traditional music that their exclusion would have left a major gap. There may be quibbles about the exclusion of some individuals and groups and the inclusion of others. The selection has been a difficult task, and while I have aimed to be as objective as possible, personal taste and interests were undoubtedly factors in making certain choices. In the case of current or recent performers, the release of commercial recordings is a primary factor in considering whether or not to include them. There are many fine musicians who have not made commercial recordings, but for the interested listener who wants to hear more music the availability of recordings is important.

Many would argue that bands such as Horslips, Moving Hearts and the Afro Celts performed little, if any, music that was traditional and certainly did not play in a traditional style. While there is some basis for these arguments, these bands have undoubtedly been influenced to some degree by Irish traditional music and have certainly stimulated an interest in traditional music among people who might have heard very little of it before. Other musicians like Joe O'Donnell and Pierce Turner may have only an oblique connection with traditional music but have nonetheless done work in this area which is radically different and of considerable interest. In choosing musicians, singers and groups, then, I have included along-side the more purely traditional performers those whose music may not be strictly speaking 'traditional' but is still of interest for some connection with traditional music. The different views on, and relative merits of, more 'progressive' music is discussed under the Fusions entry and more specifically under the individual artists' entries. There are also entries on two television series which dealt with the subject of fusions, *Bringing It All Back Home* and *A River of Sound*. The first Crossroads Conference, organised as a direct result of debate about *A River of Sound*, was the first time that the subject of tradition and innovation had been argued in such an organised and public assembly. It is a subject that is constantly, often heatedly, discussed among musicians themselves.

While most entries on individual musicians give a year of birth (and, where relevant, death), it has not been possible to secure dates for all musicians. Any musician whose year of birth is not given might contact the publishers if he/she wishes it to be included in future editions of the book.

Collectors, cultural organisations, publishing, recording, radio, television and the internet have all played a vital role in the development of traditional music, and a number of entries deal with these subjects. Universities have also played an increasingly significant role in encouraging research during the past two decades, and some of the more significant institutions which have large departments dealing with traditional music are given separate entries.

There are fascinating connections between the musical traditions of Ireland and those of other countries. In some cases the connections are direct and well documented. The entries for Scotland, the United States, Canada, Australia and other countries deal with the historical background and the degree of influence which Irish music has had on the contemporary ethnic music of these places. Regions such as Brittany (France), Galicia (Spain) and Asturias (Spain) also have connections with Ireland. While the musical links between Ireland and these regions has been largely established by musicians themselves in recent decades, there are some historical reasons for the cultural affinity which they share. Argentina has also been included, despite the fact that it does not share a common musical tradition with Ireland. There is, nonetheless, a significant history of Irish emigration to and cultural influence in Argentina. It is in some ways surprising that this influence has not, to date, extended into the field of music but there are signs of a growing interest in Irish music in Argentina which may produce some new form of music in the future.

Some entries deal with people or places which are of historical interest because, for different reasons, they are linked to Irish music. The English monarchs Henry VIII, Elizabeth I, James I, the French leader Napoleon Bonaparte and the Stone Age passage tomb at Newgrange all belong to this group. Terms such as Bard and Minstrel are also examined in their historical context, and some historical events, most notably the Great Famine, are given separate entries because they had such a profound effect on the musicians of the time.

Finally, care has been taken with the cross-referencing of entries to help the reader to follow up various connections among all of these different subjects.

The appendices at the back of the book include a select discography and a select bibliography. Although the original release dates of the albums are not given in the discography, these can be found by consulting the main text under the name of the relevant artist. The inclusion in the main text of catalogue numbers and the names of the labels on which albums were released would have made it too cumbersome. For the purposes of the main text, the date of release was the most significant detail as it places the album in context historically. Anyone seeking a more comprehensive discography should consult *A Short Discography of Irish Folk Music* (Dublin, 1987, edited by Nicholas Carolan) and 'Select Discography (1985-2000)' (edited by Nicholas Carolan, Joan McDermott and Thérèse Smith) in *Irish Folk Music Studies / Éigse Cheol Tíre*, Volumes 5-6 (1986-2001), pp. 137-165. The latter journal also includes an excellent select bibliography of recent publications (1985-2000), edited by Hugh Shields, Maeve Gebruers and Joan McDermott. There are a number of bibliographies dealing with special subjects, but the select bibliography in *The Companion to Irish Traditional Music* (Cork, 1999, edited by Fintan Vallely) is quite extensive and probably the best place to start. The *Companion* also has a good select discography, although unlike the discographies referred to above, it does not give release years for the albums.

The appendices also include a list of specialist record companies, many of which also have their own entries in the main text. There is a list of festivals and summer schools which is as comprehensive and accurate as it could be at the time of publication. Festivals and summer schools sometimes start and are then discontinued after a year or two. I have therefore focused on festivals which are well-established and seem likely to last. However, festival organisers, local tourist offices or other sources should be checked before travelling to any of these festivals.

Albums on vinyl, cassette tape or CD have been the source of much of the material on artists and their music. Interviews in various published sources, from radio and from television have also been used in compiling background information. I have had personal contact with many musicians where information was sparse or details needed to be checked. I thank all of those musicians who took the time to answer my queries. On the subject of song, I gleaned much background detail on particular songs from various sources, but Hugh Shields' *Narrative Singing in Ireland: Lays, Ballads, Come-all-yes and Other Songs* (Dublin, 1993) was very useful in placing the whole subject of song within a broad historical context. Helen Brennan's *The Story of Irish Dance* (Dingle, 1999) is a fascinating and readable account of a complex and highly political subject. Although I had written the initial entries on dance before Brennan's book was published, her work illuminated more clearly certain aspects of the history of Irish dance and quoted from some interesting source material which hadn't come to light before.

Research into various aspects of traditional music, dance and song is progressing at a rapid pace, especially in the last decade or so. Every care has been taken to ensure that the information in this book is accurate and up to date. When ongoing research adds to our knowledge of certain subjects, some of my observations herein may require qualification. Such is the nature of historical research.

Writing this book has been a journey of discovery, and I hope that you enjoy reading it. While it is difficult to capture the spirit of Irish music in words, I hope the book can offer a few pointers and enrich your knowledge.

Harry Long
Slane, June 2005

Note

The appearance of **bold face** in the course of an entry indicates that the subject receives its own separate entry elsewhere in the Guide. Because of their frequency, bold face is not generally used for the most common instruments (accordion, banjo, fiddle, uilleann pipes, whistle, etc.) and dance music forms (jig, reel, etc.), although each receives its own entry.

In this Guide, musicians, collectors and others are alphabetised by surname, although the alphabetisation of some Irish names might confuse non-Irish readers. Note that names such as Darach de Brún, Seán Mac Dhonncha, Maighréad Ní Dhomhnaill and Seán Ó Riada are alphabetised under D, M, N and O respectively.

Accordion (*cairdín* or *bosca ceoil*) One of the **free-reed instruments** played by traditional musicians in a variety of forms, including melodeon (called the 'box'), button accordion (also called the 'box' by some) and piano accordion. Friedrich Buschmann of Berlin patented the earliest model in 1822 and the first manufactured accordion was produced in 1829 under the patent of Cyril Demien of Vienna. It consists of a treble keyboard (with piano keys or buttons) and a casing, connected to a bass keyboard (buttons) by bellows. Shoulder straps help the player to hold the instrument. The right hand plays the treble keyboard while the left controls the bellows' movement and plays the bass. Inside the casing are pairs of free reeds, each producing a single note when air from the bellows causes it to vibrate. The piano keys or buttons open valves allowing the air to flow through to the desired reed. Some accordions have single action (i.e., the reeds are tuned to adjacent pitches on the chromatic scale, such as C and C♯), so that one note sounds when the bellows are pressed and the other when they are drawn. Other accordions have double action (i.e., they produce the same note on the draw and the press as both reeds of each pair are tuned to the same note). Articulation, especially with fast dance tunes, is easier for most players with single-action instruments (melodeon and button accordion).

The melodeon is a single-action button accordion with one row of ten buttons on the right-hand side and two spoon-shaped keys to provide bass on the left-hand side. The original melodeon was usually pitched in C and could sound twenty notes ranging over two diatonic octaves. It grew in popularity among traditional Irish musicians during the 1880s and 90s and its rise coincided with the decline of the **uilleann pipes**. The instrument was more readily available and easier to play and it was not likely to cause the problems posed for the piper by badly made reeds. It was also more suitable for the playing of the **polkas, waltzes, mazurkas, flings** and **barndances** that were popular at the time. It was widely used as an instrument for playing at traditional dances, as the simple style in which it was played and its loud, shrill sound proved ideal for such occasions. The first commercial recording of Irish traditional music (1903) featured the New York melodeon player John J. Kimmel, whose dynamic playing provides a good example of what can be achieved on the melodeon in the hands of the right musician. In 1999 a compilation of recordings of Kimmel's playing, originally released in 1977, was re-released on CD. Other melodeon players who recorded Irish music in the era ca. 1915-1930 were Edward Heborn (born in Boston to an Irish mother) and Peter J. Conlon (born in Co. Galway), one of the first Irish-born melodeon players to record in the **US**. **Brendan Begley**, **Paul Brock** and Johnny Connolly are among the finest contemporary players.

The button accordion is a single-action instrument similar to the melodeon, which it began to replace in the late 1920s. It has a second, outer row of keys pitched a semi-tone above the original notes. It is fully chromatic and comes in a variety of pitches. The C/C♯, C/D and D/D♯ accordions were originally the most popular among traditional players but were replaced by the B/C instrument that involved a smoother legato style, although contemporary accordion players such as **Johnny O'Leary**, **Tony MacMahon**, **Jackie Daly** and **Máirtín O'Connor** prefer the older style. Due largely to their influence since the late 1970s, there has been a

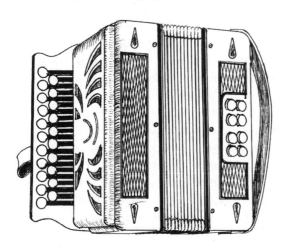

revival of this style, often referred to as 'press and draw' or 'push and pull' because it involves more bellows work than that associated with the B/C accordion. A legendary player of the 'press and draw' style was **Joe Cooley** from east Co. Galway, after whom the popular 'Cooley's Reel' is named.

The B/C accordion can be more difficult to manage than the C/C♯, C♯/D and D/D♯ accordions associated with the 'press and draw' style. **Séamus Begley**, who started on the B/C but later changed over to an E♭ accordion, has commented that the B/C is fine for tunes such as polkas, but some reels simply do not suit it. In order to play in the key of D (the key in which most traditional music is played in sessions), the player has to use cross-fingering (playing on both rows), a problem which the 'press and draw' player does not face. The use of less bellows work generally results in a smooth, legato effect, which can reduce the articulation and staccato effect suited to Irish dance music. Nonetheless, the B/C accordion has enjoyed huge popularity in Ireland, especially since the 1950s. The 1950s and 60s saw the emergence of exceptional players such as Sonny Brogan (who played with **Ceoltóirí Chualann**), **Paddy O'Brien** from Tipperary (who devised a whole new approach to playing B/C accordion) and **Joe Burke**, a Galway player with great technical skill and imaginative style. In 1996 Josephine Marsh made her recording debut. A young player with a sensitive and powerful style from Ennis, Co. Clare, she also plays the concertina. Her second album, *I Can Hear You Smiling* (2001), features an impressive backing group and includes **Mick Kinsella** on harmonica and snare drum.

The button accordion was one of the most popular instruments in traditional Irish music in the 1950s and 60s and has been played by many musicians. Exceptional players include **Joe Derrane** (born in Boston of Irish parents), Kevin Keegan (born in Galway but lived in the US from the late 1950s until his death in the early 70s), Ann Conroy (Galway), **Paul Brock** (born in Athlone), Séamus and **Brendan Begley** (Dingle, Co. Kerry), Dermot Byrne (**Altan**), and a host of players from Co. Clare (Tony MacMahon, **Bobby Gardiner**, Andrew McMahon, P. J. King, Conor Keane and **Sharon Shannon**). Players like Bobby Gardiner and P. J. Hernon play both the legato style (on B/C accordion) and the 'press-and-draw' style (on single-row melodeon). Irish-American player **John Williams** also plays concertina and has recorded with the group **Solas**. Liam O'Connor, who played with the ***Lord of the Dance*** orchestra, is another fine player to emerge recently. Dave Munnelly from Belmullet, Co. Mayo, one of the most promising contemporary players, made a fine solo recording debut with *Swing* (2001), produced by **Gavin Ralston** (who also plays guitars, bass and keyboards on the album).

The piano accordion has been popular with **ceílí bands** for several decades. Unlike the button accordion, it is a double-action instrument and thus produces the same note on the press as on the draw. The double action makes it difficult to produce the necessary articulation for traditional music, and the instrument has other disadvantages: it is large and heavy compared to the button accordion and it can be difficult for the player, especially with fast dance music, to get from one end of the keyboard to the other without accidentally hitting two keys at once. The large range of basses are often used to provide chord accompaniments which some argue do not suit the music. Modern electronic accordions

Piano Accordion

can produce keyboard versions of the sounds of piano, banjo, fiddle and even basic drumbeats, a development viewed with horror by many traditional musicians. Nonetheless, the piano accordion can be an exciting instrument and contemporary players such as Jimmy Keane (see **O'Connell, Robbie**), the Scotsman Phil Cunningham, Englishman Andy Cutting and the young **Alan Kelly** offer excellent examples of what can be achieved. English-born Karen Tweed plays a mixture of styles on the instrument, including Irish and Scandinavian tunes (see **England**). Her CD *Drops of Springwater* (1994) is subtitled '47 Irish session tunes from the repertoire of Karen Tweed', and she has also published a collection of tunes, *Traditional Irish Music: Karen Tweed's Irish Choice* (West Yorkshire, 1994).

Seán Ó Riada was critical of the use of accordions in traditional Irish music, arguing that the player could not vary the volume, tone-quality or intonation of the notes because of the way the instrument was made. This, however, is also largely the case with the uilleann pipes, which many regard as *the* traditional instrument.

The accordion, said Ó Riada, was 'designed by foreigners for the use of peasants with neither the time, inclination nor application for a worthier instrument.' He suggested that the accordion's popularity in the 1950s and 60s was due to 'the laziness that afflicts us as a nation at the moment. We all want to be musicians, but we don't want to take the trouble.' He saw the piano accordion as 'the greatest of all abominations' and criticised many of the techniques used by accordion players, especially 'pointless and random ornament'. Nonetheless, Ó Riada himself recognised that the accordion could be used effectively in Irish music by players who could surmount the limitations of the instrument itself. His own group, Ceoltóirí Chualann, performed and recorded with button accordion (played by Sonny Brogan and Éamonn de Buitléar). See also **Double-Stop**; **Keane, James**; **North Cregg**; **O'Brien, Paddy (Offaly)**; **Wales**; **Whelan, John**.

Afro Celts A group of musicians (originally called Afro Celt Sound System) from Ireland, England, France and Africa. The group's original line-up included **sean-nós** singer **Iarla Ó Lionáird**, **Ronan Browne** (uilleann pipes, flutes, mandolin, harmonium), **James McNally** (bodhrán, low whistle, accordion) and **Davy Spillane** (low whistle, uilleann pipes). It also included the Breton Celtic harpist Myrdhin; Senegalese singers and percussionists; keyboard and drum programmers Joe Buce and Martin Russel; and a number of other musicians, all led by the Englishman Simon Emmerson (guitars, drum and keyboard programming). Their music is an unusual combination of Irish traditional style instrumentals and sean-nós singing with a strong African/electronic backing. The artist Jamie Reid, previously associated with punk music, does drapes and hangings for the group's stage shows and was part of the inspiration behind the concept for the group. His work adorns the cover of their first album, *Afro Celt Sound System, Vol. 1: Sound Magic* (1996). The group performs exciting live shows which often involve dancing on stage, and the visual impact of their performances adds to the weird, otherworldly atmosphere that the music creates.

The sudden death of Joe Buce, one of the group's key members, in October 1997 was a great loss to the group, which had just recorded a slot in the **Gael Force** series of concerts in Dublin a few months earlier. Nonetheless they released a second album, *Afro Celt Sound System, Vol. 2: Release* (1999, with Sinéad O'Connor singing on the title track) and toured extensively in 1999. Ó Lionáird and McNally are still key members of the group, and although Browne performed on the second album, **Michael McGoldrick** played uilleann pipes with the group on their 1999 tour, **Emer Mayock** (flute) filling the slot when McGoldrick wasn't available. By the time of the third album, *Volume 3: Further in Time* (2001), Mayock was a full member of the group, and guests included original member Myrdhin, fiddlers Mairéad Ní Mhaonaigh and Ciarán Tourish of **Altan**, and singers Peter Gabriel and Robert Plant. For their fourth album, *Seed* (2003), they dropped 'Sound System' from their name, calling themselves simply 'Afro Celts'. The African and Irish traditional influences are more to the fore than the electronic in comparison with earlier albums, and there are guest appearances by the singer Mundy from Co. Offaly, as well as fiddlers **Martin Hayes** and **Eileen Ivers**. See also **Fusions**.

Air (*Fonn*) Generally used to describe the melody of a song. Traditional airs fall into two categories, the slow air (*fonn mall*) and airs that have a fixed beat. Many slow airs are derived from old Gaelic songs such as 'Táimse im Chodladh' ('I Am Asleep'), 'Ardaigh Cuan', 'Sliabh na mBan' ('Slievenamon'), 'Casadh an tSúgáin' ('The Twisting of the Rope') and 'Na Connerys' ('The Connerys'). There are also slow airs derived from songs sung in English ('Carrickfergus' and 'Barbara Allen' are two well-known examples). For this reason knowing the original song is often helpful to the player of a slow air. Slow airs require a special sensitivity in the player and are usually performed without strict adherence to a particular time structure. A musician playing a slow air is free to vary the timing, ornamentation and melody of a tune at will, and for this reason the form is best played solo. Accompaniment can be successfully added, but only in a minimal way that does not inhibit the melody player. It is regrettable that many musicians playing in sessions nowadays will rarely, if ever, play slow airs.

The harper **Turlough O'Carolan** and other harpers of the 16th-18th centuries such as **Rory Dall Ó Catháin** composed many of the most popular airs, which are played in a fixed time structure (see also **Carolan**). Like the slow airs, they form a

Ardaigh Cuan

distinct class of music within the traditional repertoire and are not played regularly by all musicians. More recent and contemporary musicians have also composed both types of air, a good example being the popular 'Inisheer'. Some people think it a traditional air, others believe it was composed by **Darach de Brún** (who popularised it through his playing), but in fact it was composed by Dublin musician Tommy Walsh in 1974.

Aisling (Irish for 'vision') The aisling, or 'vision-poem', originated among the Gaelic poets of early 18th-century Munster and was subsequently matched to pre-existing traditional airs to become a popular type of **Jacobite song**. Among the earliest and, in literary terms, most accomplished aislings are the three written in the first two decades of the 18th century by the **Sliabh Luachra** poet Aogán Ó Rathaille (ca. 1675-1729): 'Gile na Gile' ('Brightness Most Bright'), 'An Aisling' ('The Vision') and 'Mac an Cheannaí' ('The Redeemer's Son'). These related to the contemporary hopes of supporters in Ireland that the country would be liberated by the exiled Stuart Pretender. In these semi-erotic poems, Ireland is represented as a beautiful woman awaiting the arrival of her lover (the Stuart Pretender) from across the sea. Art MacCumhaigh (1738-1773), a poet from Co. Armagh, wrote another acclaimed aisling, 'Úr-Chill an Chreagáin' ('The Churchyard of Creggan'), but it was in Munster that the aisling became most widespread as a popular type of song.

In a typical aisling the poet has a vision of a beautiful *spéir-bhean* (literally 'sky-woman') who, after questioning by the poet, reveals that she is not any of the great figures of mythology but Ireland herself, awaiting the return of her lover from exile. A highly polished and technically accomplished aisling from the later 18th century is 'Ceo Draíochta' ('A Magic Mist') by Eoghan Rua Ó Súilleabháin (1748-84), who came from the same area as Ó Rathaille. Closely associated with the aislings however, are those political songs that refer to Ireland using pseudonyms such as 'Droimeann Donn Dílis' ('Beloved Brown White-Backed Cow'), 'An tSeanbhean Bhocht' ('The Poor Old Woman'), or personal names such as 'Caitlín Ní Uallacháin' or 'Cáit Ní Dhuibhir'. One of the most famous of all Irish political songs, 'Róisín Dubh' ('Little Black Rose'), is in the latter category, although it was not originally written as a political song. It was based on a simple love lyric transformed to give the song a new political meaning. The original lover, Róisín, became a pseudonym for Ireland.

The aisling also inspired 18th-century **Nationalist/Republican song**s in English, with **Granuaile** or Grace O'Malley, a 16th-century Gaelic 'pirate', becoming a symbol for Irish nationhood. A song about Granuaile, said to date from the 1750s, was published in 1794. Another 'vision' song in English is the 1803 'Henry's Ghost', a political aisling about Henry Joy McCracken, leader of the United Irishmen who was executed in Belfast on 17 July 1798.

The tradition of portraying Ireland as a woman goes back to medieval bardic poetry and continues into modern times through poets such as P. H. Pearse (1879-1916), **W. B. Yeats** and Seamus Heaney (b. 1939). This tradition has also survived in contemporary folk songs with Tommy Makem's 'Four Green Fields' a well-known example (see **Clancy Brothers and Tommy Makem**). The song was written in 1967, just before Northern Ireland erupted in political violence, and although not strictly an aisling it is very much in the same tradition as 18th-century nationalist songs.

In Daniel Corkery's book *The Hidden Ireland* (Dublin, 1928), a classic study of 18th-century Gaelic Munster, he deals extensively with aislings and the poets who wrote them. Original Irish versions of many of these poems and songs, with excellent English verse translations, can be found in *An Duanaire, 1600-1900:*

Poems of the Dispossessed, edited by Seán Ó Tuama, with translations by Thomas Kinsella (1st ed. Portlaoise, 1981). See also **Ó Héanaí, Seosamh**.

All-Ireland   A term often used to describe the annual **Fleadh Cheoil na hÉireann**, where the All-Ireland finals in numerous categories of traditional music, dance and song take place. It is the climax of a series of smaller competitions held at county and provincial level.

Altan   Donegal group formed in 1986, one of the best-known and highly regarded traditional groups of the last twenty years. Their name derives from a lake in Co. Donegal, and much of the music they play comes from Donegal and other northern counties. As one would expect of Donegal musicians, they play mazurkas and highlands in addition to the other forms of dance music and slow airs. Their songs are in Irish and English, with Mairéad Ní Mhaonaigh's vocals and fiddling central to the group's sound from the earliest days to the present. Together, Ní Mhaonaigh and her husband Frankie Kennedy from Belfast made the album, *Ceol Aduaidh* (1983), before the first group album, *Altan* (1987). The original line-up was Mairéad Ní

Altan (photo: Amelia Stein)

Mhaonaigh (vocals, fiddle), Frankie Kennedy (flute), Ciarán Curran (bouzouki, guitar-bouzouki), Mark Kelly (guitar), with producer **Dónal Lunny** also playing bodhrán and keyboards. Paul O'Shaughnessy (fiddle) joined them for the albums *Horse with a Heart* (1989), *The Red Crow* (1990) and *Harvest Storm* (1992), on which Ciarán Tourish (fiddle, whistle) also played. Tourish is still with Altan.

Flute player Frankie Kennedy's death in September 1994 was a great loss to the group and to the world of traditional music. His playing was an integral part of Altan's sound and he was a master of the slow air, as, for example, in his playing of 'An Feochán' (*Horse with a Heart*). A winter school is held in his honour every year around New Year's Day in Gweedore, Co. Donegal.

Since 1994 the group's line-up has included Dermot Byrne (button accordion), who had guested on *Island Angel* (1993), and Dáithí Sproule from Derry, who replaced Mark Kelly on guitar. In addition to bringing out several compilations, one of which concentrates exclusively on Altan's songs, they also released four new albums between 1995 and 2001: *Blackwater* (1996), *Runaway Sunday* (1997), the country music influenced *Another Sky* (2000) and *The Blue Idol* (2001). The last features guest performances by **Paul Brady** and Dolly Parton. On the opening track Ní Mhaoinaigh and Brady perform a beautiful arrangement of the old folk song 'Daily Growing' (also known as 'The Trees They Grow High' or 'The Bonny Boy'). There are also two different versions of the same song on the album, one (in Irish) sung by Ní Mhaoinaigh and the other (in English) sung by Dolly Parton.

Apart from their outstanding musicianship and singing, Altan are distinguished by their overall sound. The fiddles of Ní Mhaonaigh and Tourish create a distinctly Northern/Scottish feel, with the accordion blended in tastefully and guitar and bouzouki (or guitar-bouzouki) providing a powerful backing. The songs are arranged with great sensitivity, and often feature exceptional guitar accompaniments. The Irish songs and additional forms of dance music played in Donegal and the northern part of Ireland add variety and distinctiveness to the group's repertoire. Website: www.altan.ie. See also **Macalla**.

American Folk Song Folk song in the **US** has been shaped by a variety of different influences, including old English **ballad**s, immigrant music of the Irish and Scots and the blues and African-American spirituals of the south. Because of the associations with immigrants and black slaves, there has always been a strong element of protest in American folk, and it is frequently related to political agitation. During the 1930s, 40s and 50s, singer/songwriters such as Huttie Ledbetter ('Leadbelly'), **Pete Seeger**, **Woody Guthrie** and Cisco Houston formed part of a folk song movement which was highly political and sought to give voice to the American poor. This movement was greatly influenced by the work of the musicologist **Alan Lomax**. In the 1950s Pete Seeger and the Weavers, Oscar Brand and **Jean Ritchie** performed in concerts in New York organised by the **Clancy Brothers and Tommy Makem**. The latter group were themselves strongly influenced by the style of arrangement and presentation of American folk groups. The use of choral singing, guitars and five-string banjo were not common in Irish folk singing before the Clancys, and these elements in Irish music today originated in American folk. This influence went even further, for although **political song** had a long history in Ireland, it was generally dominated by **Nationalist/Republican song** and **Orange/Loyalist song**. Some Irish folk singers, including **Christy Moore** and **Andy Irvine**, were inspired by the views and lifestyle of singers like Guthrie, whose songs of poverty and social protest were of a different type altogether. Folk singers of the 1960s like Bob Dylan (himself influenced by the Clancys) and Joan Baez were also political and influenced emerging musicians and singers in Ireland, including **Paul Brady** and **Mick Moloney**, whose music with the **Johnstons** mixed influences from Ireland, England and America. Many of the most prominent American folk singers and singer/songwriters of the 1960s (as well as some from the 70s and 80s) can be heard on the five-CD collection, *The Best of*

Broadside 1962-1988: Anthems of the American Underground (2000). The words of the 89 songs in this collection were originally published in the radical magazine *Broadside,* and there are contributions from Bob Dylan, Pete Seeger, Phil Ochs, Buffy Saint-Marie, Janis Ian and others. See also **Appalachians**; *Bringing It All Back Home*.

Amhrán   The Irish word for 'song', which can be used to refer to 'song' in general, but is particularly used for **songs in Irish**. See also **Sean-nós Singing**.

Anglo Concertina See **Concertina**.

Anúna   Choral group which performs a variety of different material, including classical, religious, medieval and traditional songs. Anúna started to perform as An Uaithne in 1987 under the leadership of Michael McGlynn, who composes and arranges for the group as well as singing with them. *An uaithne*, from which the name Anúna is derived, is a collective term for the three different types of Irish music found in ancient and medieval times: *suantraí* (lullabies), *geantraí* (happy music), and *goltraí* (laments). Although best known for their performance in **Riverdance** in 1994, Anúna had already made a name for themselves before this. Their first album (*Anúna*) was released in 1993, and up to this they had performed with a variety of musicians, including **Máire Ní Bhraonáin** of **Clannad**, Noel Eccles and **Declan Masterson**, the medieval group Consort of St. Sepulchre and a number of other classical and traditional singers. The *Riverdance* show took many singers from Anúna, but they have continued to perform and compose their own unique blend of music. Up to 2002, they had released a total of eleven albums. *Deep Dead Blue* (1996) includes original material as well as traditional Irish, English and medieval songs. *Behind the Closed Eye* (1997) is a collaboration with the Ulster Orchestra and saxophonist Kenneth Edge. In 1994 they won a National Entertainment award for Classical Music, but much of their work defies conventional categories, spanning a wide variety of styles. *Essential Anúna* (2003) again encompasses material from a range of sources, including a 10th-century dirge, musical settings of poems by Francis Ledwidge and **W. B. Yeats** and medieval Norse music from the Orkney Islands. *Winter Songs* (2003) is a seasonal album, and includes Anúna's versions of Christmas standards such as 'Silent Night' and 'Away in a Manger' as well as more unusual pieces, such as the 16th-century hymn 'Ríu, Ríu' and 'Winter, Fire and Snow' by MacDara Woods and Brendan Graham. Website: www.anuna.ie.

Any Old Time   Trio formed in the late 1970s by **Matt Cranitch** (fiddle), Dave Hennessy (melodeon), and Mick Daly (vocals, banjo and guitar; later with **Four Men and a Dog**). They have recorded several albums and are notable for the unusual combination of fiddle and melodeon, not often heard on recordings, as well as some fine songs.

Appalachians A mountain system in the eastern **US**, which stretches for about 1,600 miles. The northernmost section of the Appalachians is in Canada, but the mountains are largely in the US, where they run from Maine in the north to Alabama in the south. A mass migration from Ireland to America took place in the period 1700-75, when between 200,000 and 300,000 Irish people emigrated, the majority settling in the Appalachians. Most of these settlers came from Ulster and were Presbyterians who had come to Ulster from Scotland in the late 17th and early 18th centuries. Religious persecution and poor economic conditions in Ulster caused them to emigrate from Ireland to America, where they are usually referred to as the Scots-Irish. They were most influential in the Appalachians around Virginia, West Virginia, North and South Carolina, Kentucky and Tennessee, and brought with them a rich tradition of song (ballads sung unaccompanied in English) and dance music. Their musical traditions merged with those of other settlers to become Appalachian music, song and dance. The relative isolation of the Appalachians meant that its unique musical traditions were preserved for generations. In the early 20th century, groups playing instruments such as mandolin, guitar, **autoharp**, fiddle and five-string banjo (see **Appalachian Banjo**) were popular. The advent of radio brought the 'hillbilly' or 'high lonesome' sound of Appalachian music to a wider audience. The musicians themselves began to travel further afield and, with the advent of the Great Depression, the 1930s saw a more widespread demand for 'country' music as the people of the Appalachians migrated to the cities.

American country music originated in Appalachian music, which also contributed many of the hybrid forms resulting from changes wrought by radio and recording, including bluegrass and rock 'n' roll. Interest in the old-time Appalachian music, often referred to simply as 'Old Timey' or 'Hillbilly' music, has increased in recent decades, and even in Ireland groups such as the Lee Valley String Band (with fiddler **Matt Cranitch**) play Old Timey as well as Irish traditional music.

The radio programme ***Bringing It All Back Home*** traced the complex history of Appalachian music in considerable detail, and looked at how versions of Irish, Scots and English songs and melodies can still be found in Appalachian and country music today. Among others, **Jean Ritchie** (b. 1922), from a long line of Kentucky singers, was interviewed. She has researched and written extensively on Appalachian song and visited Ireland and Britain in the 1950s, tracing the roots of Appalachian music back to its source.

The earliest **emigration songs** date from the 18th-century emigration to the Appalachians, and many of them are still sung, including 'Slieve Gallion Braes' and 'The Rambling Irishman' (a memorable version of which was recorded by Scots singer **Dick Gaughan**). Multi-instrumentalist and singer/songwriter Tim O'Brien, a native of Wheeling, West Virginia, initially made his name in the US playing old time Appalachian music and bluegrass. His great-grandfather was from near Kingscourt, Co. Cavan, and in the late 1990s O'Brien began to explore in depth the connections between Irish and Appalachian music. This resulted in two albums, *The Crossing* (1999) and *Two Journeys* (2001), which bring together aspects of the Irish and Appalachian musical traditions. Numerous Irish and Irish-American traditional musicians appear on both albums, including **Kevin Burke**, **John Williams**, **Paddy Keenan**, **Laoise Kelly** and **Michael McGoldrick**. *Traveller* (2003) explores, through twelve songs, O'Brien's experiences of travelling to Ireland and other countries. See also **American Folk Song**.

Appalachian Banjo (*bainseó cúig-shreangach*) An alternative name for the five-string **banjo**, which was eclipsed in many parts of the **US** by the four-string banjo but continued to be popular in the **Appalachians**.

Arcady Group formed by Johnny 'Ringo' McDonagh after he left **De Dannan** in the late 1980s. Their first album, *After the Ball* (n.d.), features McDonagh (bodhrán, bones, percussion), Frances Black (vocals), **Jackie Daly** (accordion), Brendan Larrisey (fiddle, viola), Nicolas Quemenar (guitar, flute, whistles, vocals) and Patsy Broderick (piano, keyboards). It has a large proportion of American material on it, in contrast to their second album, *Many Happy Returns* (1996), which consisted largely of standard Irish dance music and songs. Classic tunes included 'The Bucks of Oranmore', 'The Geese in the Bog' and 'The Boys of Bluehill', as well as songs such as 'The Rocks of Bawn' and 'The Boys of Barr na Sráide'. **Niamh Parsons** replaced Frances Black on this second album, with Conor Keane taking over accordion from Jackie Daly. Guest musicians included **Michael McGoldrick**, **Brendan Power** and the **Voice Squad**. After the second album the group's founder, Ringo McDonagh, joined the *Riverdance* orchestra.

Argentina There is some evidence of Irish arrivals in Argentina as early as the 16th century, when Irishmen are mentioned as early as 1520. John and Thomas Farrel and Isabel Farrel were among a group of colonists led by Pedro Mendoza who founded Buenos Aires in 1536. Other Irish names appear in sources of the 16th, 17th and 18th centuries. In the last quarter of the 18th century, Irishmen in Argentina (still, at this time, part of the Spanish colony of Río de la Plata) were prominent in many walks of life, including trade, the army and the beef industry. The Argentine Navy was founded early in the 19th century by Admiral William Brown from Foxford, Co. Mayo. Argentina declared its independence in 1816, and it was in the 19th century that the most substantial population movements took place. Over 30,000 Irish settlers, many of them from counties Westmeath, Longford and Wexford, settled in Argentina from the 1820s onwards. Many of them worked or became prominent in sheep-rearing and the wool industry. People from Irish communities in Spain, France, Britain, Russia, the **US** and **Canada** also emigrated to Argentina at this time. The Argentine capital, Buenos Aires, still has substantial Welsh and Irish communities who publish their own periodical, *Celtic News*, in English and Spanish. *Southern Cross*, a newspaper for the Irish community in Argentina, was founded in 1875. It is estimated that over half a million people in Argentina today can claim Irish descent.

The Irish-Argentinean Society was set up in 1989 to foster relations and create a greater awareness of the links between the two countries. It has 400,000 members and organises lectures, social evenings and outings, as well as providing advice and contacts for Irish people visiting Argentina. Its committee, which usually meets in Mullingar, Co. Westmeath, is chaired by Mary Egan of Ferbane, Co. Westmeath.

There is a substantial interest in Irish traditional music in Argentina. Irish pubs in Buenos Aires include the Shamrock, the Kilkenny and the Druid. *Plum Pudding*, an Argentinean radio programme presented by Susana Shanahan Atkinson, broadcasts to the Irish-Argentinean community and in ***Irish Music*** magazine (August 1999) sought albums from bands or record companies seeking airplay in Argentina. The six musicians in the Argentinean folk group the Shepherds include a singer/ fiddler, a banjo player, a flautist/tin whistle player, an accordionist/guitarist and a bodhrán player. Collette Cullen in Argentina (*Irish Music*, December 1997/January 1998) compares them to the **Wolfe Tones** and comments that their lead singer sounds like Ronnie Drew, but emphasises that they have no family ties in Ireland. Historian Tim Pat Coogan describes (on a visit in 1997) 'an Irish Christian Brother stepping on to a stage at prestigious Newman College in Buenos Aires to sing Clancy Brothers songs to a huge and rapturous audience' (*Wherever Green Is Worn*, London, 2000, p. 614).

Various groups have facilitated musical links between Ireland and Argentina in recent years, with musicians travelling in both directions between the two countries. In December 1999, a group of Irish musicians and dancers, including fiddler **Frankie Gavin** and **sean-nós** dancer Seosamh Ó Neachtáin, visited Argentina with the help of the Irish Department of Foreign Affairs and the Arts Council. They met members of the Irish community, played in Irish clubs and heard three young Argentineans sing 'Molly Malone' in Buenos Aires. A group from Argentina which plays Irish music and also includes dancers visited Mayo in the summer of 2004. J. J. O'Hara, President of the Admiral Brown Society in Foxford, Co. Mayo, met the group in Argentina and organised their visit to Ireland.

Although there is considerable interest in Irish music and song in Argentina, tango and other forms of roots music and dance which have not been influenced by the Irish tradition are dominant. There are few signs of Irish traditional music fusing with other forms of music in Argentina, but the growing interest may produce something more in the future. One sign of the popularity of Celtic music and culture generally is the fact that the first international Celtic festival, Fest-Celt 2000, was held in Buenos Aires in October 2000. In the following month ***Lord of the Dance*** came to the Argentine capital. Irish accordionist **Sharon Shannon** took the title of her 2003 album *Libertango* from a song of the same name, which is based on a tune by the great Argentinean composer and bandoneon player Astor Piazzolla. Another Irish accordionist, **Máirtín O'Connor**, attempted to fuse Argentinian and Irish traditional styles in the music he composed and performed for the short film *Tango* (2004, directed by Seán Cooney and produced by Ita Kelly), first broadcast on **TG4** on 16 March 2004. The story concerns a couple from the Aran Islands who are living and working in Buenos Aires and return to Inis Meáin to get married. O'Connor's music adds greatly to the warmth and light-heartedness of the film as the couple overcome 27 years of feuding between their families.

Armagh Pipers' Club, The Founded in 1966 by a group of music enthusiasts including Brian and Eithne Vallely to promote the playing of the uilleann pipes and traditional music generally. Although not affiliated to any national organisation, the Armagh Pipers' Club has established a considerable reputation over the years and its members play a variety of instruments in addition to the pipes, including flute, fiddle, tin whistle, concertina and accordion. They have published several tutor books (for uilleann pipes, tin whistle and fiddle) as well as collections of songs for children. They also organise an annual festival (held in November), the William Kennedy Festival of Piping, in honour of an 18th-century blind piper of that name. Website: www.armaghpipers.com.

Asturias Region of Spain located in the northwest Iberian peninsula adjoining **Galicia**. Asturias and Galicia are cut off from the rest of Spain by the Cantabrian mountains and share a common Celtic identity. The music of Asturias has much in common with that of Galicia, and dance tunes like the *muiñeira* (in 6/8 time, like an Irish double jig) are played in both regions. The Asturian pipes (mouth-blown **bagpipes**, usually with two drones) are played with closed fingering unlike the Galician pipes, which use open fingering. The Asturian pipes have a range of 1½ octaves, those of Galicia just over one octave. These bagpipes or *gaita* and a unique type of drum, similar to a snare drum, are the most popular traditional Asturian instruments. The *tonada*, a type of song traditionally popular in Asturias, has been adapted as instrumental music by some groups. One of the finest singers of the Asturian *tonada* today is Mari Luz Cristóbal Caunedo. Among the most prominent Asturian traditional groups of recent decades is Llan de Cubel (formed in 1984), whose repertoire includes Irish dance tunes as well as *muiñeiras*, waltzes, marches and other types of music from their own tradition. Between 1987 and 1999 they made five albums, all available on their own label, Fonoastur, which has also released other Asturian traditional artists. Llan de Cubel have toured extensively in the US and Europe, bringing Asturian music to a wider audience. Lisardo Lombardia have also produced a lot of Asturian traditional music, and Asturian piper José Angel Hevia is a well-known musician throughout Spain. The Irish traditional group **Lúnasa** recorded a set of tunes from Asturias and Galicia on their album *The Merry Sisters of Fate* (2001).

Australia Substantial numbers of Irish rebels and convicts were transported to Australia during the troubled 1790s when Britain faced the real possibility of a French-inspired and French-supported revolution in Ireland (see **Nationalist/ Republican Song**). From this time until the abolition of transportation in 1868, penal colonies in Australia and Tasmania (then known as Van Diemen's Land) received about 45,000 transportees from Ireland, many of them sent there for political activities. Families often followed those transported, but a considerable number of Irish people received some government assistance to emigrate to Australia in the 19th century. Some went in the hope of a better life, some as a result of the **Great Famine** (1845-1849), and some during the Gold Rush of the 1850s.

Only about 5% of the total number of emigrants who left Ireland in the 19th century (see **Emigration Song**) went to Australia, but they made up about a quarter of the immigrant population in that country. Even among those transported for political activities, many were eventually assimilated and contributed to Australian society. Michael Dwyer (1771-1826), for example, was transported for his part in the 1798 rebellion in Wicklow, but became high constable of Sydney in 1815. The song tradition, however, has preserved a memory of Australia that is almost exclusively associated with the harsh conditions of transportation and the social and political circumstances in Ireland that gave rise to it. One of the most famous **sean-nós** songs in the Ring Gaeltacht is 'Na Connerys' which tells the story of the three Connery brothers who were transported to New South Wales in the 1830s for their part in the land war in Co. Waterford (see **Tóibín, Nioclás**). Some Irishmen in Australia became famous as Robin Hood-type characters, the best-known being Ned Kelly (1854-1880), whose legend lives to this day and has been fictionalised in Peter Carey's *True History of the Kelly Gang* (London, 2001). A number of songs commemorate the deeds of similar heroes, including 'Bold Jack Donohue' and 'The Wild Colonial Boy'. The latter was popularised in the 1960s by the **Clancy Brothers and Tommy Makem**, who also had a hit with the sea shanty 'South Australia'.

Outlaw ballads continue to form an important part of the Australian folk song tradition. *The Turning Wave, Poems and Songs of Irish Australia* (Armidale, New South Wales, 2001) is a fascinating collection of material compiled and edited by Vincent Woods. It includes famous songs like 'Na Connery's' and many poems on the Great Famine that were published in Australian newspapers in the mid-19th century. It also includes works by Eliza Hamilton Dunlop from Newry, Co. Down, who arrived in Australia with her husband and children in 1838. She was the first poet to attempt transliterations of Aboriginal song and was also among the first white poets to testify through her art to the massacres of Aboriginal peoples.

Irish dancing and dance music were popular and well organised in Australia in the 19th century. **Francis O'Neill**'s account of the Australian Piper, John Coughlan (1837-1908) is full of interesting insights (*Irish Minstrels and Musicians*, pp. 248-54). Coughlan was born in Co. Cavan but immigrated to the **US** with his family in 1845. From the age of 23, he toured all over the US playing uilleann pipes, but the threat that the American Civil War posed to his career caused him to sail for Melbourne in 1862. It is clear from O'Neill's account that there was a ready audience in Melbourne and Sydney for Irish music and dancing. O'Neill provides details of Coughlan's repertoire, including many jigs and reels that are still popular today. He was also famous for his descriptive pieces, including 'The Fox Chase', 'The Battle of Aughrim' and 'The Old Man Rocking the Cradle'. During the gold rush in New Zealand, he played and organised dancing there, returning to Melbourne in 1883 and to Sydney in 1884, where he performed in an opera 'The Emerald Isle'. In Melbourne what are described as 'noted old time Melbourne dancers' of the 'Irish long set dances' (see **Set Dance 2**) danced to his piping. Although O'Neill laments the decline of this dancing in Melbourne by the time of his writing (1913), he mentions two excellent contemporary Sydney dancers. Elsewhere in his book (pp. 343-44), O'Neill names other Irish uilleann pipers in 19th- and early 20th-century Australia, including 'Charley' McNurney, who played uilleann pipes as part of a vaudeville show with which he toured in the early 20th century. Another fine piper and musician, Denis Duggan from Dunhallow, Co. Cork, played for the dancing competitions. Seán Wayland, founder of the **Cork Pipers' Club**, emigrated to Australia in 1912.

Irish music and dancing continues to be popular and well organised in Australia today. A number of organisations have been active in teaching Irish music and dance since the 1960s revival, including **Comhaltas Ceoltóirí Éireann**. There are sessions in Irish pubs throughout the country and the annual Guinness Celebration of Irish Music Tour brings prominent Irish artists to the larger cities. The one-week Lake School of Celtic Music has been held annually in Koroit since 2000 and has classes on songwriting, dance, drama and a variety of instruments. Singer and multi-instrumentalist **Andy Irvine** spends a considerable amount of time in Australia, and his *Way out Yonder* (2000) features songs dealing with Australia or Irish connections there. *Riverdance* had a huge impact in Australia, as elsewhere, giving a further boost to the already popular Irish dancing schools. *Gaelforce Dance*, Australia's own dance spectacular, is based around a love story involving two brothers and has enjoyed great success. The music, composed by Colm Ó Foghlú, a dancer and multi-instrumentalist who studied composition with **Micheál Ó Súilleabháin** at **University College Cork**, is broadly similar in style and arrangement to that of *Riverdance*, although *Gaelforce Dance* uses a considerable number of traditional tunes as well as original tunes and songs. It can be heard on the CD *Gaelforce Dance* (1999). **Conradh na Gaeilge** also has branches in Australia. See also **Barleyshakes**; **Cooney, Steve**.

Autoharp (*uathchláirseach*) Small stringed instrument consisting of fifteen to twenty strings stretched across a sound-box like a zither. The autoharp has a series of bars, each with its own combination of damper bars. The latter dampen all but the strings required to play a particular chord, which is strummed by using the fingers, fingerpicks or a plectrum. Patented in 1882, the instrument originated in Germany and became popular in the **US** in the late 19th century. Still popular among American folk musicians, it can be heard occasionally in Ireland. Some American singers, such as Thom McCain of Columbus, Ohio, use it to great effect in accompanying Irish folk songs. Other American players, such as Brian Bowers, have taken the instrument to new heights with their virtuoso playing.

B

Bagpipes (*píb mhála* or *na píoba*) A generic term for a range of reed instruments which are thought to have evolved in the Middle East and later spread throughout Europe as well as to India and North Africa. Bagpipes generally consist of a reeded melody-pipe (chanter) with finger holes that sounds when supplied with air from a

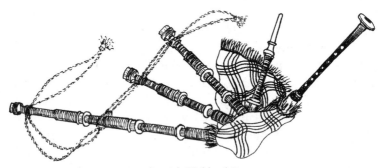

Scottish Highland Pipes

bag held under the player's arm. The player compresses the bag with his arm to provide the level of air-pressure required in order to make the reed vibrate. In the oldest forms the bag is inflated through a blowpipe held in the mouth. In addition to the chanter, many forms of bagpipes have one or more drones. A drone is a pipe that, when supplied with a steady stream of air, sounds a single continuous note.

The best-known form of mouth-blown bagpipes is the Scottish Highland pipes. The chanter consists of eight finger holes, seven in front and one at the back (for the thumb). There are also three drones. It has been used as a martial instrument since the Middle Ages and is now found all over the world. It is still used by bands of pipers who play military music in political marches or on festive occasions. Although the Scottish Highland pipes can occasionally be heard at indoor traditional sessions in Ireland, their volume makes them more suitable for outdoor playing. The mouth-blown *gaita* of Spain (see **Asturias** and **Galicia)** and Portugal, the *biniou* of **Brittany** and the Welsh pipes (see **Wales**) are similar to the Scottish Highland pipes but sometimes have only one or two drones. Other forms of mouth-blown bagpipes include the Irish **war pipes** (*píob mhór*), the German *dudelsack* and the French *cornemuse*.

From as early as the 16th century, a bellows attached to the player's elbow has been used for inflating the bag. This development took place in Europe and bellows-blown forms include the Czech *dudy*, the French *musette*, the English Northumbrian pipes (see **England**) and the Scottish Lowland pipes. The Irish uilleann pipes are also in this class, but differ from other bellows-blown bagpipes in several ways. The chanter or melody-pipe has a range of two octaves, as opposed to a range of only nine notes on other pipes. The use of regulators or closed chanters to provide accompaniment to the melody is also unique.

The CD *Bagpipes of Britain and Ireland* (1996) is an interesting compilation on which the Northumbrian pipes, the Scottish Highland Pipes and the Irish uilleann pipes can all be heard. Although the only English pipes still played today are the Northumbrian pipes, other regional varieties of bagpipes existed in England in the past, including Leicestershire pipes and Yorkshire pipes. Brendan Monaghan from Banbridge, Co. Down plays uilleann pipes, Scottish Highland Pipes and Scottish small pipes (see **Different Drums of Ireland**). See also **Scotland**.

Bakerswell See **Potts, Seán**.

Ballad (*bailéad*) A type of narrative song written in stanzas of four or eight lines, with the same music repeated for each stanza. Although some Irish scholars have studied the **lay** as part of the ballad genre, it seems clear that the Irish lay (although sharing some features of the ballad) is a distinct genre from the European ballad. The earliest texts of recognisable European ballads date from the 15th century, although texts of ballad-like songs do exist from the 12th and 13th centuries. A number of early ballads have internal refrains, very close in style to the **carol** from which they appear to be derived, and were probably associated with dancing. The ballad genre became popular all over Europe (but evidently not in Ireland) in the Late Medieval period and remained popular in many areas, especially England, down to the 19th century. One scholar of the European ballad, the Hungarian Lajos Vargyas, has argued that the ballad originated in the 14th century among the peasants of Wallonia (in modern Belgium) and Picardy (northern France). He relates its development to a more urbanised society, social changes in peasant life and the evolution of a new class-consciousness. This plausible theory could help to explain why we have little evidence of ballads achieving widespread popularity in Ireland before the 18th century. Certainly in Gaelic Ireland, society remained largely rural and sufficiently conservative to maintain the popularity of the heroic lay.

In parts of Ireland colonised by the English, however, there is some evidence that forms of song and dance popular in **England** were finding their way to Ireland in the Medieval period. 'Caroling' was recorded among the colonial population in 1265 and 1413, and the **Ledrede** manuscript (1320s) suggests that songs of possible English origin were popular on the streets of Kilkenny (even if the date is too early for ballads). A version of an English love lyric (not a ballad) survives from the 15th century, but it is not until the 18th century that we find definite evidence of a ballad being sung in Ireland. The few references to 'ballads' (or 'ballets') in the 16th and 17th centuries cannot be taken as definitely referring to the type of narrative song defined as a ballad. In this period, the term 'ballet' was used to describe any popular song or the sheet on which it was printed. There was clearly an active trade in printed 'ballets' in Ireland, but little is known of the actual songs themselves.

Hugh Shields has distinguished 'old ballads' from the 'new ballads' of the Early

Modern period. The old ballads found in Ireland are all of British origin or versions of English and Scots ballads (often referred to as **Child ballads**) derived from European models. The old European ballad was an oral genre, lyric (as opposed to heroic) song which deals with personal relations and not with national or ethnic consciousness. The song tells a story ordered in time like a play and in which events are rationally motivated. Unlike new ballads, old ballads show a preference for third-person narrative and are often fictional.

New ballads share many of the formal and stylistic features of the old ballads, but usually have eight lines, as opposed to four lines, in each stanza. This is partly because they often involve more explaining and documenting of events than the old ballads. Indeed some new ballads are presented as journalistic accounts of real events narrated by a first person 'eyewitness'. The common use of first-person narration in new ballads marks a contrast with the old ballads, and the new type are also more explicit than the old, giving specific details of dates, names and places. New ballads of English origin may have found their way to Ireland on 'ballet' sheets or through singers in the 16th and 17th centuries, and some (such as 'The Blind Beggar's Daughter') are still sung in Ireland today.

The Irish gradually took to composing their own narrative songs in the English language, drawing on old and new ballad models. Shields calls this genre '**come-all-ye**s' and points to the horse-racing song 'Skewball' (1752) as one of the earliest precisely dateable examples which has survived in oral tradition (see **Sporting Song**). Other early come-all-yes include political songs such as 'The Blackbird' or 'Boyne Water'. The former deals with the **Jacobite** cause, the bird itself representing James II (King of England, Scotland and Ireland, 1685-1688); it appeared on an English ballad sheet of around 1718. Although the date of its composition is uncertain, 'Boyne Water' celebrates the victory of the Protestant William III (King of England, Scotland and Ireland, 1689-1702) in 1690 (see **Orange/Loyalist Song**). Both served as prototypes for later varieties of come-all-yes.

Publication of **ballad sheet**s and **chapbook**s was widespread in Ireland from around 1750 onwards, and ballads became an important commentary on political events in the turbulent 1780s and 90s. From this period right down to the present, many ballads have been associated with republican or nationalist politics, the patriotic ballad enjoying a greater popularity than in most countries in Europe (see **Nationalist/Republican Song**). The **Young Ireland** movement developed the ballad as a vehicle for doctrinaire nationalism and their ballads often played an important role in stirring political opinion. The perceived power of the patriotic ballad in contemporary times is evident in **RTÉ**'s deliberate avoidance of patriotic songs on radio or television during the 1980s and early 90s. This policy was perceived as being in line with the spirit of **Section 31** of the Broadcasting Act.

Although the ballad has been strongly associated with political developments, especially nationalism, in modern Ireland, **love song**s remain the largest category in the folk repertoire. See also **Burns, Robbie**; **Comic Song**; **Emigration Song**; **Greig-Duncan Folk Song Collection**; **Scotland**; **Sea Shanty**; **Sea Song**; **Songs in Irish**.

Ballad Boom A term often used to describe the upsurge of interest in Irish folk-song during the 1960s and early 70s. It was initially inspired by the success of the **Clancy Brothers and Tommy Makem** in the late 1950s and early 60s. Numerous groups and solo singers began to emerge, playing in 'singing pubs' around Ireland. Some were merely pale imitations of the Clancys while others had their own unique approach to the music. **Emmet Spiceland**, **Sweeney's Men**, the **Johnstons**, the **Dubliners**, the **Furey Brothers** and Davey Arthur and the **Wolfe Tones** were among the more highly regarded groups to emerge from this period. Although not all of these performers played republican or 'rebel' songs, the ballad boom was associated in the minds of many with republican and/or left-wing politics (see **Nationalist/Republican Song**). A number of solo balladeers also emerged during this period, the most notable being **Danny Doyle**, **Jim McCann**, Paddy Reilly and Johnny McEvoy. Reilly has had several hit singles, including 'The Fields of Athenry', and still performs and records regularly, sometimes with the Dubliners.

Many people now associate the 'Ballad Boom' with the overplaying of certain folk-songs and a plethora of second-rate folk groups playing in loud, smoky bars. Many new and innovative musicians, however, did emerge from this period and **sean-nós** singers such as Joe Heaney (see **Ó Héanaí, Seosamh**) began to find a wider audience for their music. In many ways the ballad boom in Ireland was part of a wider, international folk movement. Many Irish musicians had direct links with folk musicians in other parts of the world, especially the **US** and **England**. Although ballad singing is still popular and many of the above-mentioned artists are still performing, the term 'ballad boom' is usually confined to the 1960s and 70s. See also **Canada**.

Ballad Sheet A sheet on which a ballad was printed, often with a woodcut illustration. Although some modern ballad sheets provide music, in the past this was not standard as few could sing from musical notation. A tune specified by a well-known title might be given, but generally buyers had to rely on their memory of the ballad-seller's rendition for the melody. A reference to the importation of ballad sheets into Ireland as early as 1593 shows that some ballads were already considered seditious and were associated with Catholicism. Protestants were printing ballad sheets in Dublin by 1626, but two references from later in the 17th century indicate that the Gaelic-speaking world viewed ballad sheets and ballad-sellers with suspicion. From the late 17th-century printers of ballad sheets, of different religions, were numerous. Dublin seems to have been the most important centre in Ireland for printing and commercial trade in ballads in the early 18th century, with Mountrath Street (near the Four Courts) being particularly noted for ballad-printing. Cork and Belfast were also important centres.

The National Library in Dublin has a 14-volume collection of ballad sheets under the name of **P. J. McCall**, although the collection may have originated with his father, John, in the second half of the 19th century. The National Library also has a substantial number of sheets that were confiscated by the authorities over a long period. Evidence that many ballads were viewed as seditious, and their sellers often arrested, goes back to the 1790s.

From the 1840s, some songs in Irish and **macaronic song**s begin to appear on ballad sheets, but English remained the main language in which songs were printed. Trade in ballad sheets and **chapbook**s flourished in Ireland in the 17th, 18th and 19th centuries, but newspapers, magazines and anthologies in book form gradually took over from the late 19th century. Nonetheless, ballad sheets were still being used to publish new songs in the late 1950s and early 60s, and old songs printed on a sheet, with music, were available as recently as the 1980s. An example of the latter is the series 'Irish Songs and Balladsheets' published by **Ossian Publications**, Cork in 1980. While many orally transmitted traditional songs that were in wide circulation never appeared on ballad sheets, printed versions of song did play an important role in broadening the repertoire of new ballads and helping many songs to endure for almost 200 years.

Ballet The term **ballad** was often pronounced and written as 'ballet' in the 16th century, when **ballad sheet**s or **broadside**s began to appear for the first time. Like the term 'ballad', 'ballet' could refer to any written or printed text of a popular song, or to the song itself. Early references to ballets or ballads do not necessarily imply traditional narrative song of the old genre, but could refer to any popular song.

Banjo (*bainseó*) Two types of banjo are used in Irish music: the tenor (usually four-string) banjo and the five-string banjo. Both evolved from a long-necked instrument with a gourd sound box brought by black slaves from West Africa to the Caribbean and then on to America. In 17th-century plantation America, this instrument was called the banjar, bangie, banza and other names. It gradually evolved to become (late 18th and early 19th centuries) the modern banjo, which has a body consisting of a round, shallow frame covered with parchment or skin on one side (plastic is often used today). Most plantation banjos had three or four strings, but the American **minstrels** of the early 19th century usually played a five-string banjo. An Irish-American musician, Joel Walker Sweeney (b. 1810) is often credited with this development, although pictures from long before Sweeney's time show five-string banjos on American plantations. He played with the Virginia Minstrels, and their tour of England, Ireland and France in 1843-45 probably saw the introduction of the banjo into Ireland.

The earliest banjos were unfretted, but frets were added in 1878. The five-string banjo became popular as a folk instrument in the **US**, especially in the **Appalachians**. One of the earliest references we have to this instrument in Ireland concerns John Dunne, a singer and banjo player who toured Ireland in the late 19th century with a fiddler called Thompson and the famous uilleann piper Dick Stephenson. At this time it seems that the five-string banjo was used mainly for accompaniment of songs or dance tunes in much the same manner as it is today, although its strings were at this time plucked with the fingers.

The invention of steel strings at the turn of the century heralded changes in the way banjos were made and played. Banjo players, influenced by the mandolin, started to experiment with using a plectrum and tuning their instrument in fifths. Many players removed the short fifth string and eventually manufacturers started to produce four-string banjos. These were originally called 'plectrum banjos' and, like the five-string, had 22 frets. The tenor banjo was invented around 1915 and was also known as the tango, its rise coinciding with a craze for the Latin American dance in the US. It had a shorter neck (17-19 frets) and was played with a plectrum. In the 1920s and 30s it became popular in the US and in Ireland. With only four strings and a shorter neck than the five-string instrument, it is more suitable for playing fast Irish dance tunes. It is usually tuned in fifths and, in Irish traditional music, the tuning g-d-a-e (an octave below the fiddle and mandolin) is commonly used. The players of the early 20th century used tenor banjos which were also tuned in fifths, but the tuning was higher, the top note being tuned to 'b' or 'c' instead of 'e'. Some players, such as Jimmy Kelly of Boston and **Gerry O'Connor** from Co. Tipperary, can still be heard using the older tuning.

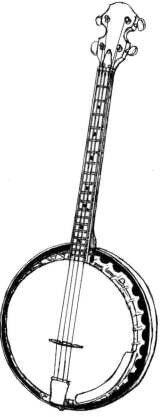

Mike Flanagan of the **Flanagan Brothers** was the most renowned Irish tenor banjo player in the US in the 1920s and 30s, and made numerous recordings. In Ireland from the 1930s the tenor banjo was used in many Irish **ceílí bands**. From this time the ceílí bands also used the banjo-mandolin, a miniature banjo with eight strings (four pairs, with both strings of each pair tuned to the same note), similar in size and tuning to a mandolin. A six-string tenor banjo has also been played by some traditional musicians, including **Mick Moloney**, but is quite rare. Barney McKenna of the **Dubliners** has been the most influential tenor banjo player since the 1960s, but a number of other fine players have emerged since then, including **Kieran Hanrahan**, Gerry O'Connor (who mixes Irish and American styles), Enda Scahill (who composes his own material as well as playing traditional tunes), the late **Johnny Keenan** and **Séamus Egan** of **Solas**. Fiddler **Cathal Hayden** started out playing tenor banjo and has recorded on both instruments. Galway-based banjo player Angelina Carberry has made two fine albums with button accordion players, the first with her father, Peter and the second simply titled *Angelina*

Tenor Banjo

Carberry and Martin Quinn (2003). Another fine player to emerge in recent years is Eamonn Coyne, whose first solo album, *Through the Round Window* (2003) embraces music from diverse traditions, including those of Ireland, Cape Breton and American 'old timey' music.

The five-string (often called 'Appalachian') banjo came to prominence again after World War II, partly through the influence of the American folk singer **Pete Seeger**. The Irish singer Tommy Makem, through Seeger's influence, introduced the five-string banjo into the **Clancy Brothers and Tommy Makem** during the 1950s and Bobby Clancy also became an accomplished player. It has since been used by numerous folk singers and groups for the accompaniment of songs, including Finbar Furey (see **Furey Brothers**), **Luke Kelly** and John Shankey, a fine player from Nobber, Co. Meath. **Margaret Barry** was among the singers who played the unusual six-string banjo-guitar, an instrument that has the body of a banjo but is tuned in the same way as a guitar. It is only rarely seen nowadays but one player is Michael Shannon from Annacurra, Aughrim, Co. Wicklow.

A website dedicated to the banjo is www.irish-banjo.com; it includes information on the instrument in Irish (and other European) traditional music, artist portraits, discography, and how to play, maintain and buy a banjo.

Five-String Banjo

Banjo-Mandolin See **Banjo**.

Bard The Irish word *bard* has passed into the English language as a general term for 'poet', especially one who writes lyric or heroic verse or is of national importance. In the past, the bards were an order of poets found in Celtic societies who composed and often sang or recited verses in praise of chiefs or warriors. Recitations, which in Ireland were usually done by a *reacaire* ('reciter'), were often accompanied by harp music and the term 'bard' is often used to describe poet/harpers of the 17th/18th centuries such as **Turlough O'Carolan**, who is sometimes described as 'the last of the bards'.

In Irish written sources of the Early Medieval period (5th to late 12th century), however, the bards were the lower of two classes of poet, the higher class being the *fili*. The *fili* of Early Medieval times had a more comprehensive, professional training than the *bard*, but during the 12th century the two classes of poet amalgamated to produce hereditary, literate professional praise-poets, the *filidh* or *fir dhána* of the Later Medieval period. These poets produced a substantial body of praise-poems which are generally referred to as 'bardic-poems' and have considerable value as historical sources because of their importance in immortalising the victories of the poet's patrons. The fact that they were an integral part of the politics of Gaelic Ireland from before the late 12th-century Anglo-Norman invasion right down to the 16th century meant that the bards, like the harpers and pipers of the time, were viewed as a threat to the establishment of English 'civility' during the Tudor Conquest of Ireland (see **Elizabeth I**, **Henry VIII**).

The bardic schools taught students history, law and language as well as literature. The most prized form of poetic composition was called *dán díreach* or 'straight verse' and strict rules of metre and rhyme had to be observed. The predominant features of this type of poetry were the number of syllables in each line and in the last word of each line, and it is thus often referred to as 'syllabic poetry'. It contrasts with normal song metres in that the number of stresses, as opposed to the number of syllables, is predominant in songs. Syllabic poetry gradually died out in Ireland during the 17th and 18th centuries, the defeat of the joint forces of Gaelic Ireland and Spain at the Battle of Kinsale (1601) marking the beginning of the demise of the Gaelic society which had supported the bards for centuries. Although many examples of bardic poetry survive, the music to which they were recited or chanted does not.

Barde Canadian-based group formed in 1974 and comprising Irish and Canadian musicians. Their first important gig was at the *Les Veilles de Veilles* festival in Montreal in November 1975. A double album of the music played at this festival featured two tracks by Barde. Their own first album, simply titled *Barde* (1977), had the following line-up: Richard Chapman (mandolin, tenor banjo, dulcimer, guitar, vocals), Toby Cinnsealac (tin whistle, soprano recorder, bones, tambourine), Pierre Guerin (guitar, accordion, English concertina, tenor recorder, vocals), Cris MacRatallaig (fiddle, bodhrán, tambourine, vocals), Ed Moore (bodhrán, tambourine, bones, tin whistle, Anglo-German concertina), Elliot Selick (fiddle, five-string banjo, tin whistle) with guests Joanna Crilly (flute) and Rick McDonagh (viola de gamba). The album comprised a rich variety of instrumentals and songs from the Irish, Scottish and Canadian traditions. There were songs sung in French, English and Irish, including a song version (lyrics in Irish) of **Turlough O'Carolan**'s 'Fanny Power'. Like the supergroups that emerged in Ireland in the 1970s, Barde's music was arranged in a style that made full use of the range of instruments in the group and featured strong rhythmic accompaniment on guitar, bodhrán and other instruments. For example, their second album, *Images* (1978) opens with an intricately arranged rendition of the Irish slip jig 'The Kid on the Mountain'. Barde came to Europe in 1980, touring Ireland and also playing in Switzerland and Scotland. By the time they released their final album, *Voyages* (1980 or 1981), the only original members of the group remaining were Toby Cinnsaelac and Pierre Guerin, who were joined by the jazz fiddler Jacques Joubert. Having brought attention to the rich variety of musical traditions to be found in contemporary Canada with their first two albums, the group offered something different in *Voyages*, which included many of their own compositions. Although Barde disbanded in 1983, they achieved, like Ryan's Fancy (see **Canada**), an almost legendary status in Canada.

Barleyshakes, The Group formed in Dublin in 1992 but based in **Australia** since 2000 who play a mixture of traditional and original material with a sense of wild and joyous abandon. The original line-up featured Ray McCormick (uilleann pipes, tin whistle, low whistle), Alan Kelly (lead vocals, guitars, lute), Dave Hingerty (djembe, congas, bodhrán, cymbals, foot tambourine, floor tom, mandolins, lute, banjolele, backing vocals), Eric Lang (spoons, bodhrán, cymbals, floor tom, backing vocals) and Mark Heffernan (bodhrán, bones, daburka, tambourines, guiro, toys, backing vocals) with guests Kristen Kelly (fiddle) and **Kíla**'s Brian Hogan (double bass, electric bass, backing vocals) among others. Their first album, *Gach Éan*

The Barleyshakes

(1997), includes main original contributions from Alan Kelly, a couple of tunes from McCormick, Con O'Leary's song 'Queen of Galway Town' and **Jimmy Crowley**'s 'Scandinavia'. The line-up changed for their second album, *Jump at the Sun* (1998), with Lang and McCormick gone and Kristen Kelly and Alan Doherty (flute) taking their places. *Jump at the Sun* is a similar mixture of traditional and original material, with Hingerty and both Kristen and Alan Kelly contributing their own compositions. Not all of the traditional tunes are Irish; one is a Romanian polka, and also included is 'Tunnel Tigers' by **Ewan MacColl**.

In 2000 Alan and Kristen Kelly went to Australia where they were soon joined by Alan Doherty. They teamed up with American-born bass guitarist Joe Morris and in 2001 started to record the Barleyshakes' third album. Alan Kelly and Alan Doherty also recorded with film composer Alan Shore and the New Zealand Symphony Orchestra for the soundtrack of *Lord of the Rings*. In 2001, Doherty returned to Ireland and eventually joined **Gráda**, and later that year Randall Matthews (fiddle) became the newest member of the Barleyshakes. *Visions in the Fog* (2003) included some tracks recorded with Alan Doherty before his departure for Ireland. The album is a mixture of traditional and original material. In 2003 the band were joined by Belinda Forde (flute, whistle) and Erin Sulman (percussion), and in 2004 they recorded a new live album at the Wintermoon Festival in Mackay.

Barndance (*damhsa sciobóil* or *rince sciobóil*) A couple dance derived from the **schottische** which originated in America in the 1880s and subsequently became popular throughout Britain and Ireland. In Ireland it is now most frequently danced in the north of the island, although dance historian Helen Brennan has noted barndances being danced in Co. Clare as recently as 1989. The music is in 4/4 time at a tempo similar to that of a **hornpipe**. Musicians who have recorded barndances include **John Doherty**, **Martin Hayes** and the group **Beginish**.

The Kilnamona Barndance

Barry, Garret (1847-1898) Legendary blind uilleann piper from Clare, 'regarded by many', writes **P. J. Curtis**, 'as the father figure of Clare music' (*Notes from the Heart*, p. 141). Barry travelled the countryside, playing at weddings, dances and other festivals; it was considered a great honour to have him stay in one's home. He was a regular visitor to the Lenihan home in Knockbrack, Miltown Malbay, and **Tom Lenihan** had many stories about him. He died in the workhouse in Ennistymon and is buried in an unmarked pauper's grave at Inagh. His repertoire and style were passed on to **Willie Clancy** through Clancy's father, Gilbert. Some tunes still bear Barry's name, including the popular 'Garret Barry's Jig' and 'Garret Barry's Mazurka'.

Barry, Margaret (1917-1989) Along with **Delia Murphy**, one of the first folk singers to achieve a national reputation. Born Margaret Thompson in Peter St. in Cork, she came from a family of **travellers**. Her maternal grandfather, Bob Thompson, was an uilleann piper and won the first **Feis Ceoil** in 1897. Margaret herself took up singing in her mid teens and busked at fairs, football matches and markets, travelling originally by bus and bicycle and later in her own horse-drawn caravan. She taught herself to play five-string banjo as an accompaniment to her songs and sometimes played a six-string banjo-guitar (see **Banjo**). She also played fiddle. Her voice was soulful, strong but subtle. In the 1940s and 50s she lived in England where she formed a long-term musical partnership with fiddler Michael Gorman. The two toured together in Ireland, Britain and the **US**. Barry returned to Ireland in the 1960s where she lived for much of the time with her daughter at Laurencetown, Co. Down, where she is buried. The recently reissued *Her Mantle So Green* (1958, new CD edition 1994) includes many of her own classics such as 'The Cycling Champion of Ulster' and 'Her Mantle So Green' as well as her unique renditions of traditional songs such as 'The Galway Shawl' and 'The Flower of Sweet Strabane'. She can also be heard on *I Sang Through the Fairs* (1998) and *Margaret Barry, Queen of the Gypsies: Come Back Paddy Reilly* (2002). Her singing is featured on several compilations, including *Songs of the Travelling People* (1994).

BBC (British Broadcasting Corporation) A public-service organisation established in 1927, initially to broadcast radio programmes. The BBC opened the world's first television service in 1936. It has played an important role in bringing traditional music to a wider public since 1947, when it first sent collectors to Ireland (north and south) to record singers and musicians. From 1951 to 1958 **Séamus Ennis** worked throughout Britain and Ireland as a collector with this project, and was also a presenter of the radio series *As I Roved Out*. The series, broadcast in the early 1950s, was the first major contribution the BBC made to the broadcasting of genuine traditional music and song. Over 1,500 performances were recorded, an unprecedented field recording achievement at the time. The signature tune was an extract from **Sarah Makem**'s rendition of the traditional song 'As I Roved Out'.

The BBC has continued to make important traditional music programmes and documentaries on both radio and television. Two major projects in the 1990s were *Bringing It All Back Home* and *A River of Sound*, both made by **Hummingbird Productions** for the BBC and **RTÉ** (Raidió Telefís Éireann). See also **Cronin, Elizabeth (Bess)**; **MacColl, Ewan**.

Beginish Group consisting of **Brendan Begley** (accordion, vocals), **Paul Mc Grattan** (flute), **Paul O'Shaughnessy** (fiddle) and Noel O'Grady (bouzouki). Beginish (which means 'small island') is one of the Blasket Islands off the Dingle peninsula in Co. Kerry, from where Begley comes. The group recorded their first album, simply titled *Beginish*, in 1997. The album features a diverse range of jigs, reels, polkas, slides, barndances, songs and a march, and features guest musicians **Arty McGlynn**, **Tríona** and **Maighréad Ní Dhomhnaill** and **Colm Murphy**.

Beginish are notable for their fine musicianship and for the mixture of material they play, incorporating forms of dance music popular in Kerry and Donegal with the more universally popular jigs and reels. On their second album, *Stormy Weather* (2001), they were joined by guitarist **Gavin Ralston**, who tours regularly with the group, and guest artists **Séamus Begley** (vocals) and Colm Murphy (bodhrán).

Beginish

Begley, Brendan (Bréandán Ó Beaglaoich) (b. 1955) Button accordion and melodeon player from Baile na bPoc, Ballyferriter, in the **Gaeltacht** area of Dingle, Co. Kerry and brother of **Séamus Begley**. His first solo album was *Seana-choirce* (1987). From the late 1990s he has toured extensively with the group **Boys of the Lough** and in 1997 released his second solo album, *We Won't Go Home 'Til Morning*, featuring traditional music and song from different parts of Ireland. He is a regular presenter of traditional music programmes with **TG4** and also plays with the group **Beginish**. A third solo album, *Oíche go Maidean – It Could Be a Good Night Yet* (2001) was produced by his nephew **Gavin Ralston**. At a time when so many 'solo' albums feature an array of backing and guest musicians, this album is almost entirely the solo work of Begley. Only five of the thirteen tracks have other musicians providing accompaniment, which in both cases is minimal. Begley plays both melodeon and two-row button accordion on the CD and there are five songs (in both English and Irish), including a fine rendition of the 1798 song 'Sliabh na mBan' and an unusual English-language version of the Irish song 'Níl 'na Lá' ('There's the Day'), which Begley finishes with a verse and chorus in Irish.

Begley, Séamus (Séamus Ó Beaglaoich) (b. 1949) Button accordion player and **sean-nós** singer from the **Gaeltacht** area of Dingle, Co. Kerry. Music, song and dance were an important part of life in the household where Begley grew up. His father, Brendan, owned the local dance hall in Muiríoch, and the céilí dancing nights there were very popular, despite the denouncements of the local clergy. His mother, Mary Ellen, was a dancer and a singer who taught many songs to Séamus and her eight other children. Séamus made two albums with his sister Máire (singer, piano and piano accordion player) and featuring **Steve Cooney** on guitar and piano: *An Ciarraíoch Mallaithe* (1972) and *Plancstaí Bhaile na bPoc* (1989). Begley and

Cooney later released *Meitheal: Working Together* (1993) and were one of the most popular duos in Irish music in the 1990s. The album arose from an excellent documentary about Begley and Cooney, also called *Meitheal*, produced by **Hummingbird Productions**. Their repertoire includes many polkas and slides, and they do much to breathe new life into these forms of dance music with their fiery, energetic arrangements. Begley was initially influenced by **Paddy O'Brien**, who played a B/C accordion in a smooth, flowing style. But in the 1970s he heard **Joe Cooley**, the great 'press and draw' style player (see **Accordion**), playing an E♭ accordion, and preferred the brighter, more penetrating sound. He also uses the wailing sound of the E♭ for slow airs. *Ragairne* (2001), the title of which means 'revelling' is another fine collection of music and song from Begley, accompanied by Jim Murray (guitar) from Macroom, Co. Cork. The album features several guests, including **Mary Black**, **Philip King** and **Tríona Ní Dhomhnaill**. In addition to playing the accordion and singing several songs in Irish, Begley also sings 'In the Early Morning Rain' by Canadian singer/songwriter Gordon Lightfoot. His brother **Brendan Begley** and sisters Eilín and **Seosaimhín Ní Bheaglaoich** are also well-known musicians.

Behan, Brendan (1923-1964) Dublin-born playwright who spent time in prison for IRA activities (1939-1942, in England) and attempting to murder a detective (1942-1946, in Ireland). His experiences in prison eventually led him to write his finest book, *Borstal Boy* (1958). He also collected songs and ballads and often incorporated them into his plays, the most famous of which were *The Quare Fellow* (1954) and *The Hostage* (1958), the latter originally written in Irish as *An Giall* on a commission from **Gael-Linn**. The **Dubliners** played music in Behan's *Richard's Cork Leg* in 1972 at the Abbey Theatre, Dublin and also recorded his popular ballad 'The Auld Triangle'. The latter song was also recorded by the **Pogues** and Behan's work in general has been an inspiration to **Shane MacGowan**. *Brendan Behan Sings Irish Folksongs and Ballads* (1997) includes jokes and anecdotes as well as songs. Brendan was the brother of **Dominic Behan**, and his uncle, Peadar Kearney, wrote the Irish National Anthem.

Behan, Dominic (1928-1989) Dublin-born broadcaster, journalist, novelist, songwriter, collector and singer, and brother of the writer **Brendan Behan**. Dominic lived mostly outside Ireland from 1947, settling eventually in Scotland. In addition to collecting old ballads, he translated songs from the Irish, collected contemporary ballads and wrote or adapted both lyrics and melodies, i.e. 'Liverpool Lou' and 'The Patriot Game'. His *Ireland Sings: An Anthology of Irish Songs and Ballads* (London, 1973) is a mixture of traditional ballads, translations from Irish and songs by 19th- and 20th-century authors, including Behan himself. The book contains an interesting essay, 'Note to Young Singers', in which Behan argues for a fluid, living song tradition instead of an overly academic approach to folk song. 'Notes on Some Song Makers of the Past' gives many interesting details about the background to the songs. Behan, whose politics were Republican, also made clear his dislike of **Thomas Moore**, both for the political act of shunning the United Irishmen and the cultural act of 'bowdlerising' Ireland's folk songs. Behan can be heard singing on *Finnegan's Wake* (ca. 1958) and also recorded an album, *The Singing Streets: Childhood Memories of Ireland and Scotland* (1958), with **Ewan MacColl**. He was instrumental in the rise of the **Dubliners**, who began to make a name for themselves in the late 1960s after Behan introduced them to Philip Solomon of Major and Minor Records and Radio Caroline.

Belfast Harp Festival (1792) This and the **Granard Harp Festivals** of the 1780s attempted to rescue the ancient harping tradition of Ireland from its slide into obscurity. The Belfast Harp Society, founded in 1791 by Dr. James McDonnell, Robert Bradshaw and Henry Joy McCracken, organised the festival. **Edward Bunting** was commissioned to write down all of the music played at the festival and to make notes on the techniques used by the harpers. Eleven harpers attended, one of them from Wales. Of these eleven, seven were blind, harping being one of the few careers open to a blind person. The youngest harper present was William Carr, aged 15, a native of Armagh. The oldest (aged 97) was Dennis Hempson from Derry, also the only harper at the festival who played in the old style, plucking the strings with long, crooked fingernails instead of the flesh of the fingertips. Bunting wrote of Hempson: 'He had been in Carolan's [see **Turlough O'Carolan**] company when a youth, but never took pleasure in playing his compositions. The pieces he delighted to perform were unmixed with modern refinements, which he seemed studiously to avoid; confining himself chiefly to the most antiquated of those strains which have long survived the memory of their composers and even a knowledge of the ages that produced them' (*Ancient Music of Ireland*, Dublin, 1840, p.73). Charles Fanning won first prize (ten guineas), with Arthur O'Neill second (eight guineas) and all other entrants received six guineas. Bunting commented that Fanning was not the best performer but won because he played 'The Coolin', which was much in vogue among pianists of the time.

Although the Belfast Harp Festival could not prevent the further decline of the harp in Ireland, Bunting performed an important service to later generations in writing down the music played at the festival and details on the techniques and lifestyles of the harpers themselves. Much of the music performed there has been recorded on special albums by the **Chieftains** and **Gráinne Yeats**. In 1992, **Janet Harbison** organised a World Harp Festival in Belfast to commemorate the 1792 bicentenary.

Belfast Harp Orchestra Founded in 1992 by **Janet Harbison** with approximately twenty members from different parts of Ireland, but mainly from Northern Ireland. The orchestra learns music by ear and has recorded four albums, which include music by 17th- and 18th-century harpers, traditional airs and dance tunes, as well as original compositions by Harbison. One of their most interesting recordings to date is *The Columban Suite* (1997), composed to mark the 1400th anniversary of the death of St. Columba.

Bell, Derek (1935-2002) Belfast-born musician who was recognised as a child prodigy when he began to play piano at the age of nine. At the age of eleven, he wrote his first piano concerto and subsequently started playing and composing for the **BBC**. In his mid teens he learned to play the oboe, and at sixteen won a scholarship to London's Royal College of Music. In his twenties and thirties he played with orchestras all over the world, including the Royal Philharmonic and the Symphony Orchestras of Moscow, Pittsburgh, Budapest and London. Although most

Derek Bell

famous as a harper, he did not start to play the harp until he was almost thirty years old while, at the same time, managing the Belfast Symphony Orchestra. In 1965 he was employed as principal harpist (and second oboe) by the BBC Symphony Orchestra. He was invited to play with the **Chieftains** for a St. Patrick's Day special in 1972, and subsequently began to play with them whenever other commitments would allow. In 1974 he was forced to choose between the Chieftains and his career in classical music, opting for the former. Right up to the time of his death, he was an important part of the Chieftains' sound, but has also done notable work as a solo performer. He made a special study of the work of **Turlough O'Carolan**, whose music he recorded on the two solo albums *Carolan's Receipt* (1975) and *Carolan's Favourite* (1980). In 1981 he released the ambiguously titled *Derek Bell Plays with Himself*, on which he played a variety of instruments. There were further solo albums in 1982 (*Derek Bell's Musical Ireland*) and 1984 (*From Singing to Swing*). *Ancient Music for the Irish Harp* (1989) included Irish traditional music and pieces composed by the harpers of the 17th and 18th centuries, **Seán Ó Riada**, **Seán Potts** and Bell himself. There were also two tracks from Latin America, one featuring a composition by the Paraguayan harper Sergio Cuevas, the other a set of traditional dances of the Quechua Indians of Peru. Bell played several different types of harp, including the neo-Irish harp and the bardic harp, as well as the piano, oboe and a reconstruction of the medieval Irish **timpán**. His untimely death in 2002 was a great loss to the Chieftains and to Irish music in general.

Bergin, Mary (b. 1949) One of Ireland's finest tin whistle players. She was born in Shankill, Co. Dublin but has lived for many years in Spiddal, Co. Galway. She started the whistle at the age of nine and was greatly influenced by the playing of **Willie Clancy**, whom she visited regularly. A winner of many **Oireachtas** and **Fleadh Cheoil** competitions, as a teenager she played flute with the Green Linnet Céilí Band in Dublin. She later joined **Ceoltóirí Laigheann** and had a brief spell with **De Dannan**. Two members of De Dannan, **Alec Finn** and **Johnny McDonagh**, accompany her on her first solo album, the excellent *Feadóga Stáin* (Irish for 'tin whistle'), released in 1979. She made a second solo album, *Feadóga Stáin 2* (1992) and also plays with the group **Dordán**. She was the TG4 Traditional Musician of the Year in 2000. See also **McKenna, Joe and Antoinette**.

Biddy Boys Biddy boys take their name from St. Brigid (d. 525), an Early Christian saint whose cult was built around that of an earlier pagan goddess. 'Biddy' is a familiar name for Brigid, and St. Brigid's Day (February 1) took over from the pre-Christian Celtic festival of Imbolc, which had strong associations with the pagan Brigid. The festival marks the beginning of the pastoral year. Ancient customs associated with the festival day on February 1 continue to be practised in some parts of Ireland. Biddy balls took place on St. Brigid's Eve (January 31) after a day of making Brigid's crosses and carrying a small straw doll (called a *Brídeog* or 'Little Brigid') through the countryside. Groups of 'biddy boys' or 'biddies' went from house to house and sang, danced and played music in return for small gifts. They wore straw masks like those used by **mummers** and **strawboys**. At the end of the day the biddy boys had a night of music and dancing with porter, tea, bread and butter provided. These biddy balls could go on all night, or even well into the following day. They were often frowned upon and preached against by the Catholic clergy because of what was seen as their markedly pagan character. 'Biddies' or 'biddy boys' can still be seen in some parts of the country, including Ennis, Co. Clare, where they often take part in the **Fleadh Nua**. See also **Wren-Boys**.

Bill the Weaver See Murphy, Bill.

Black, Mary (b. 1955) Singer from Dublin whose work includes a wide range of traditional songs; she is also one of the best known and most popular singers in Ireland. Black made her recording debut with the traditional group General Humbert on the album simply titled *General Humbert* (1976). Black sings in Irish and English on the album, including an English drinking song, a Scottish love song and 'Crazy Man Michael', a contemporary song by the English folk-rock band Fairport Convention. On *General Humbert II* (1982) she sings the **Jacobite Song**

'Mo Ghile Mear' ('My Living Brightness') and the Napoleonic song 'The Isle of St. Helena' (see **Napoleon**), among other traditional songs. Her first solo album, *Mary Black* (1982), included folk songs such as 'Annachie Gordon' as well as contemporary songs. In 1983 she joined **De Dannan**, with whom she recorded the album *Song for Ireland* (1983) and toured for three years. She continued to record solo, releasing *Mary Black Collected* (1984), which included an unusual arrangement of 'She Moved Through the Fair' with sitar, uilleann pipes and synthesiser. *Without the*

Mary Black

Fanfare (1985) was also released during her time with De Dannan and is more modern and electric than her earlier work. From this time Black worked for many years with guitarist and producer Declan Sinnott, developing a name as a fine singer of her own unique style of contemporary music, and showcasing the songwriting talents of Noel Brazil (d. 2001), **Mick Hanly** and **Jimmy MacCarthy**. She still sings traditional songs alongside more contemporary material and performs with her brothers and sister in the Black Family. The latter, made up of Mary, Martin, Shay, Michael and Frances, have recorded two albums together, *The Black Family* (1986) and *Our Time Together* (2004).

The Best of Mary Black, 1991-2001 provides a good sampler of the wide range of material she has performed. In 1992 she recorded the single 'A Woman's Heart' with Eleanor McEvoy (who wrote the song), and the subsequent compilation of female singers performing on the album *A Woman's Heart* became the best-selling album ever in the Irish charts. Website: www.maryblack.net.

Blarge A large-bodied type of Irish **bouzouki** with ten strings instead of the usual eight. It produces a much stronger bass sound than the bouzouki and can be used for both melody and accompaniment. Tunings vary according to the needs of the player. It is quite rare but was played by **Dónal Lunny** with **Planxty** in their later days. Another fine player is Conor Long from Dublin (see **De Brún, Darach**), who has also composed music for the instrument ranging in style from traditional Irish to Greek and Eastern European tinged tunes. The term 'blarge' is said to have been coined by the poet Séamus Heaney.

Blás International Summer School for Traditional Irish Music

A two-week summer school hosted by the Irish World Music Centre at the **University of Limerick**. There are lectures, tutorials, masterclasses, sessions and concerts. A wide range of classes are offered in song, dance and a variety of instruments. Blás started in 1997 and is held annually in June or July. The tutors and lecturers each year are among the best available and there are opportunities for pupils to join in sessions with their tutors each evening. Website: www.ul.ie/~iwmc/Blas.

Bloom, Luka (b. 1955) Singer/songwriter and guitarist born in Newbridge, Co. Kildare, whose first album, *The Treaty Stone* (1978) was released under his birth name, Barry Moore, in 1978. The album is mostly original songs (and one original instrumental) in a contemporary folk style, but also includes the traditional song 'Black Is the Colour'. Moore used several different guitar tunings on the album, which displays his talent for interesting guitar accompaniments as well as an early ability for writing good songs on a variety of themes. Through the late 1970s and 80s, Moore played as a solo artist and with various groups before leaving Ireland for the **US** in 1987. He re-launched his career as a singer/songwriter under the name Luka Bloom, his first album under this name entitled *Riverside* (1990). The album is contemporary rather than folk or traditional and is marked by an unusually full, powerfully rhythmic style of guitar playing (often using **DADGAD** tuning). The influence of traditional music can be heard in some of his material. For example, 'You Couldn't Have Come at a Better Time' has original lyrics and music but also incorporates the traditional tune 'The Kesh Jig' into the arrangement.

Luka Bloom's lyrics uniquely capture his experience of growing up in modern Ireland, falling in love, watching cases like those of the Birmingham Six and the Guildford Four unfold, and emigrating to the US. He can write highly political songs like 'Section 31' (which his brother **Christy Moore** sang; see **Section 31**) and 'Remember the Brave Ones' (recorded by **Moving Hearts**), as well as delicate love songs like 'You', 'Exploring the Blue' (both from *The Acoustic Motorbike*, 1992) and 'True Blue' (from *Turf*, 1994). *Turf* also includes the folk song 'Black Is the Colour' as well as songs set in New York ('Cold Comfort') and the Burren, Co. Clare ('The Fertile Rock'). A fourth Luka Bloom album, *Salty Heaven*, was released in 1998 and *Keeper of the Flame* (2000) is a collection of cover songs from songwriters as diverse as Bob Dylan, U2 and Bob Marley. It features an unusual cover of Abba's 'Dancing Queen' with Christy Moore on bodhrán and traditional fiddler Méabh O'Hare on viola. *Between the Mountain and the Moon* (2002) marks a return to original material and there are some fine songs, including 'Hands of a Farmer', a tribute to whistle player **Micho Russell**. In 2003 he released a live album titled *Amsterdam*, after the city in which it was recorded. The album includes ten of his finest songs, as well as songs by Bob Marley, Mike Scott of the **Waterboys** and Bob Dylan. Hearing Luka Bloom perform this material live underlines his extraordinary ability to create the sound and excitement of a full band with just voice and guitar. *Before Sleep Comes* (2004) is a very different style of album where the normally intense, rhythmic guitar playing is replaced by a softer Spanish guitar style. It suits the material (which combines both original and traditional songs) and the style in which it is sung, softer and gentler that a lot of Luka's previous work.

Although Luka Bloom's music draws on many influences, he has portrayed the political and emotional landscape of Ireland, and in some songs Irish-America, from a unique perspective. While not strictly a folk or traditional musician, he first came to prominence as part of the 1970s and early 80s wave of experimentation in traditional music. His more recent music can be viewed as an extension of this experimentation and certainly reflects many of the social and political concerns of contemporary folk singers. Website: www.lukabloom.com.

Bodhrán A shallow drum consisting of an animal skin (usually goat) stretched over a round wooden frame. It is held vertically with one hand while the other is used to beat the instrument, usually with a beater or stick. Before the late 1950s the bodhrán was little used in traditional music, although with **mummers** and **wren-boys** a type that often had metal plates like a tambourine was popular. The bodhrán's widespread use in traditional music today is due largely to the influence of **Seán Ó Riada**, who preferred its sound to the snare-drum used by **céilí bands** at the time.

Although goatskin is most commonly used in the making of bodhráns, the skins of calves, sheep, dogs, deer, jennet and even buffalo have been used. Ó Riada believed that the bodhrán probably dated back to the Bronze Age or earlier, but the earliest written reference to it comes from the Medieval period. The unlikely source is an Irish translation of a 14th-century English medical text called *Rosa Anglica*. This describes one of the symptoms of dropsy or tympanitis as a 'swelling of the stomach after food, which remains long there; and if the belly resound on being struck like a tympanum (*timpán*) or drum (*bodhrán* or *tabur*) … that is a sign that dropsy is consolidated therein' (*Rosa Anglica,* Irish Texts

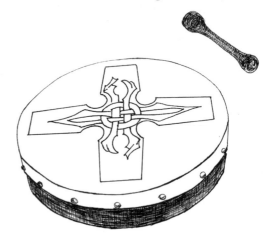

Bodhrán & Beater

Society, Vol. XXV, 1929, pp. 268-69). In some cases bodhrán frames were made from what was originally a sieve or a winnowing drum, used to separate grain from chaff.

Since Ó Riada used the bodhrán in his group **Ceoltóirí Chualann**, it has become widespread among groups and session players. A good player can get a great variety of rhythms from the instrument and can vary the tone by pressing one hand (or the fingers) against the back of the skin. Many players will also beat the stick on the wooden frame from time to time. Other means of varying the tone include beating with the hand as opposed to the stick and using different types of sticks or even brushes as beaters. **Johnny McDonagh** of **De Dannan** and **Arcady** claims to have been the first person to introduce the use of brushes into bodhrán playing and he uses them freely on the albums he made with whistle player **Mary Bergin**.

Other important bodhrán players include Peadar Mercier and **Kevin Conneff** of the **Chieftains**, **Tommy Hayes** and **Colm Murphy**, whose album *An Bodhrán: The Irish Drum* was released in 1996. Mel Mercier, a son of Peadar Mercier, plays bodhrán, bones and other percussion instruments and has featured on the 'Hiberno-Jazz' albums of **Micheál Ó Súilleabháin** as well as with **Stockton's Wing**, **Alan Stivell** and others. Dubliner Eddie McGinn, Brian Fleming of **De Jimbe** and Co. Meath man David Nevin are all accomplished bodhrán players who play a range of other percussion instruments. Some singers, such as **Christy Moore**, have played the instrument as accompaniment to their singing. *Pure Bodhrán: The Definitive Collection* (2000) features many of the above-mentioned players and more, including Gino Lupari of **Four Men and a Dog** and others. Put together by bodhrán player Robbie Harris, it features 19 tracks of different players, encompassing a variety of styles. One track on the album is a 1927 recording from Chicago of John Reynolds playing bodhrán, a rarity indeed given that the instrument did not become widespread in traditional music until decades later.

The bodhrán has developed a poor reputation with some traditional musicians, epitomised by **Séamus Ennis**' famous comment that the best way to play a bodhrán is with a penknife! In Ennis' time the playing of the bodhrán was not as highly developed as it is now, although over-zealous and under-experienced players can still be heard in sessions today.

Beer or water is often used to tone down a bodhrán when the skin is too tight, and it sometimes needs to be left near a heater or fire if the skin is too loose. Tuneable instruments with skin-tightening keys around the frame are now available. The bodhrán and the **lambeg drum** have been used in recent years as symbols of the different political and cultural traditions of Northern Ireland. See also **Different Drums of Ireland**.

Bombarde Small wind instrument played mainly by musicians in **Brittany**. The fingering system is not unlike that of the tin whistle, although the bombarde has a reed and it is difficult for the player to sustain his/her breathing for long. It is therefore normal practice to find the bombarde played in duet with the Breton bagpipes (biniou koz). This allows the player time to recover breath and the bombarde/biniou koz duet is a stylistic feature of Breton music.

Bones (*na cnámha*) An instrument used by many **bodhrán** players and percussionists. Usually made from the rib bones of cows, sheep or goats, wooden or plastic versions are also available. Two 'bones' are held between the thumb, index and middle fingers and played in a similar way to castanets. They provide a clacking, rhythmic accompaniment that can be extremely effective and can be heard in recordings made by groups such as **Ceoltóirí Chualann**, the **Chieftains**, **Stockton's Wing** and solo artists such as **Mary Bergin** and **Tommy Hayes**.

Wooden Bones

Bongos A pair of small, barrel-shaped drums, usually joined together, which originated in Cuba. Although they are not commonly found in Irish traditional music, **Clannad** were one of the first groups to use them extensively. They have also been used by **Moving Hearts**, the **Afro Celts** and **De Jimbe** and can sometimes be heard in sessions.

Bothy Ballads   Ballads composed mainly in farming areas of northeast **Scotland** during the 18th and 19th centuries, some of which are still sung today. Early collectors called them 'ploughman songs' and they were originally sung by travellers and farm labourers. Only about 50 old bothy ballads survive, not all of them in a complete form, and most of them can be found in the **Greig-Duncan Folk Song Collection**. They deal with the experiences of servants or temporary workers on farms and can cover subjects like romance or relationships between fellow servants, the farmer's treatment of those who work for him, working conditions on the farm or even the food. Many were composed for entertainment on the farm itself, were highly localised and were probably never heard beyond the immediate locality where they were composed. Some of the old bothy ballads did survive the social changes of the early 20th century, when many country people migrated to towns, and the concert-hall bothy ballad continues to thrive to this day. **Ewan MacColl** recorded an album entitled *Bothy Ballads of Scotland* in 1961. A good example of a bothy ballad from the repertoire of an Irish folk singer is 'Bogie's Bonny Belle', recorded by **Christy Moore** on *Live in Dublin* (1978). Moore heard different versions of the song in Scotland from traditional journeymen singers such as Davey Stewart and Jimmy McBeath and 'stitched together' his version from these and other sources.

Bothy Band, The   A legendary traditional group of the 1970s who broke new ground with their innovative arrangements. The name came from the rough-built huts, called 'bothies', which were used to house migrant Irish workers in Scotland. Many of the workers played music, hence the term 'bothy band'. The group's line-up was **Paddy Keenan** (uilleann pipes, whistles), **Matt Molloy** (flute, whistles), **Dónal Lunny** (bouzouki, bodhrán, synthesiser, vocals), **Tríona Ní Dhomhnaill** (harmonium, clavinet, electric piano, vocals), **Micheál Ó Domhnaill** (guitar, vocals) and, on fiddle (at different stages) **Tommy Peoples** and **Kevin Burke**. The Bothy Band was preceded by a group called Seachtar (meaning 'the seven'), which had a similar line-up but with **Paddy Glackin** on fiddle and **Tony MacMahon** (accordion) as the seventh member. Their first album, *The Bothy Band*, was released in 1975, with Tommy Peoples on fiddle. They released three further albums, with Kevin Burke on fiddle, before breaking up in 1979.

While all are distinguished musicians in their own right, as evidenced in the group's performances, it was the manner in which the group arranged their material that was startlingly new. Their arrangements of instrumental sets often featured short solos or duets, but the instrumentation was constantly changing and the rhythm and intensity of the music was usually built up towards the end of each set. A prime example of this is the set of a jig and five reels played together as 'Rip the Calico' on their 1977 album *Out of the Wind, Into the Sun*. The variety of changes in instrumentation and rhythm is astounding, with harmonies and counter-melodies played intermittently, while the whole set builds up to a powerful climax. The complexity and driving rhythms of these instrumental arrangements were unlike anything that had been heard before. The Bothy Band also had two fine singers in the siblings Tríona and Micheál. They made many excellent arrangements of traditional songs in Irish, Scots Gaelic and English and famously recorded a piece of mouth music (see **Mouth Music 1**) called 'Fionnghuala' on *Old Hag You Have Killed Me* (1976). Two live recordings of the group are available – *After Hours* (1978), recorded live in Paris, and *The Bothy Band Live in Concert* (re-released by the BBC on CD in 1998), which features recordings made in 1976 and 1978. Although the group's regular piper, Paddy Keenan, can be heard on the 1978 tracks, those recorded in 1976 feature the piping of **Peter Browne**. The group's influence on traditional group playing is still apparent today, and each member of the Bothy Band has had a highly successful career since 1979. They were arguably the most outstanding Irish traditional group to have formed to date. They made a rare appearance at the **TG4** music awards ceremony in 2002 with Molloy, Keenan, Tríona Ní Dhomhnaill, Micheál Ó Domhnaill, Paddy Glackin and Manus Lunny (who played bouzouki instead of his brother, Dónal). See also **Monroe**; **Supergroups; Weldon, Liam**.

The Bothy Band

Bouzouki Member of a family of Near Eastern stringed instruments broadly classified as long lutes. They are all plectrum instruments with long necks and relatively small round-backed bodies and include the Turkish saz (or szaz), the Yugoslav tamborista, and the Arabic buzuk as well as the Greek bouzouki. The design of the modern Greek bouzouki was much influenced by the 19th-century Italian **mandolin**. Like the mandolin, the most common type of Greek bouzouki has four double strings (tuned c-f-a-d), although many older style types have only three pairs of strings (tuned d-a-d).

Johnny Moynihan of **Planxty** is credited with introducing the bouzouki into traditional Irish music in the late 1960s, and two other members of the same group, **Dónal Lunny** and **Andy Irvine**, have been enormously influential in adapting the instrument to Irish music. Although players such as Alec Finn of **De Dannan** still uses the Greek-style round-backed bouzouki (six strings), a flat-backed version, known as the Irish bouzouki, is now more common among Irish musicians. It is more solidly built than the Greek type, has a deeper tone and usually has eight strings, tuned in pairs (see also **Cittern**). One of the most famous Irish bouzouki makers is Joe Foley of Rathfarnham, Dublin, who also makes **blarge**s. Although the standard mandolin tuning (g-d-a-e) is sometimes used for playing melody, tunings can vary according to the taste or requirements of the player. For accompaniment, g-d-a-d, a modal tuning, is often used.

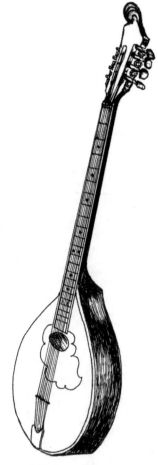

Irish Bouzouki

The bouzouki has been very quickly adapted in design and tuning to suit Irish music and its rise to prominence illustrates how new instruments have brought new and complementary sounds to the music. It can be used either as a melody or accompanying instrument. In the latter role, many traditional musicians find it more suitable to Irish dance tunes, as it does not have as full a sound as the guitar and is less likely to obscure the melody. The modal tunings used by many players are also more suitable for Irish music in the same way as guitars tuned **DADGAD**. Groups such as Planxty, De Dannan, the **Bothy Band**, **Oisín**, **Moving Hearts**, **Devenish**, **Altan**, **Deiseal** and **Tamalin** have all used the instrument to great effect. Former Deiseal bouzouki player Niall Ó Callanáin (also a fine composer of unusual tunes) can be heard with his own band on *Strings and Things* (2001) and *Niall Ó Callanáin and Band Live* (2003). Eoin O'Neill, born in Co. Meath but based in Clare, is a fine bouzouki player who has performed and recorded with many traditional musicians. Bouzouki players often play related instruments, such as the mandolin, **mandola, mandocello**, blarge and cittern. Dónal Lunny even played a specially designed electric bouzouki with Moving Hearts. Both Andy Irvine and Ciarán Curran of Altan have played a twelve-string guitar-bouzouki. Some of the Eastern European music associated with the instrument or its relatives has also been played by Irish musicians, most notably Planxty and Andy Irvine. The bouzouki is also popular in Irish-American music, with the first 'Zoukfest' being held near Kansas City in 1998. Roger Landes' album *Dragon Reels* (1997) consists of both traditional and original tunes played on bouzouki. Some of the tracks are played solo while others illustrate the accompaniment aspect of the instrument, with **John Whelan** (accordion) providing the melody.

Box See **Accordion**.

Boys of the Lough, The Irish/Scottish traditional group formed in 1967 by three Ulstermen – Robin Morton (vocals, bodhrán, guitar), **Cathal McConnell** (vocals, flute, whistle) and Tommy Gunn (fiddle). By the time they recorded their first

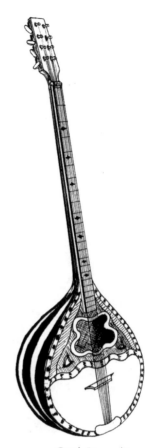

Greek Bouzouki

album, *The Boys of the Lough* (1973), the Shetland Islands' fiddler Aly Bain had replaced Gunn, and Glasgow-born **Dick Gaughan** (guitar, mandolin, vocals) had made the group a foursome. Their debut album was a mixture of songs and instrumentals from Ireland and Scotland, the sleeve-notes emphasising the shared traditions of Ireland (especially the Northern counties), Scotland and the Shetland Islands. There are some memorable tracks, including the slow air/reel combination of 'Caoineadh Eoghain Rua/The Nine Points of Roguery', a Shetland set of two wedding marches and a reel, and Gaughan's powerful renditions of 'Farewell to Whisky' and 'Andrew Lammie'. Gaughan left the group in 1973 and was replaced by Dave Richardson (cittern, mandolin, English concertina, button accordion) from Northumberland.

The group has seen many changes in line-up since it was founded. Although Morton left in 1979, MacConnell, Bain and Richardson remained, joined by Englishman Chris Newman (guitar) and Irishman Christy O'Leary (uilleann pipes, whistle, vocals). This line-up changed again in 1997 when Newman and O'Leary left to be replaced by Irishmen Garry Ó Briain (guitar, mandocello, piano) and **Brendan Begley** (accordion), who also plays with **Beginish**. By the time of their album *Lonesome Blues and Dancing Shoes* (2002), Aly Bain had left and Garry O'Brian was replaced by Malcolm Stitt (guitar). Shetland fiddler Kevin Henderson featured on the album and toured with the band from March 2002.

The Boys of the Lough recorded numerous albums over three decades and have been very successful internationally. Although they sometimes play the odd tune from other sources, their music has always been solidly grounded in the Irish and Scottish traditions. In the mid-1980s, they formed their own recording label, 'Lough', through which they still release their own albums. Their sound has always been traditional, relying on tight ensemble playing and technical virtuosity rather than the high-speed or high-tech approach of some recent groups. Bain, Richardson and McConnell have also written a considerable amount of new material for the group. Website: www.boysofthelough.com. See also **Scotland**.

The Boys of the Lough (photo: Victor Albrow)

Bradshaw, Harry (b. 1947)   Radio producer, record producer, researcher and lecturer who began his recording career in the commercial Eamon Andrews Studio, Dublin in 1965. Three years later he joined Raidió Telefís Éireann (**RTÉ**) where he made many recordings of traditional artists and produced many radio programmes on traditional music. These included (from 1978) the series *The Long Note* and a series featuring recordings of Irish traditional Irish music from the 1920s and 1930s, *The Irish Phonograph* (1983-1986), which was presented by **Nicholas Carolan**. Bradshaw is an expert in remastering old recordings and has produced a number of collections of the music of early recording artists, including those of flute player **John McKenna**, uilleann piper **Johnny Doran** and fiddlers **Michael Coleman** and **James Morrison**. He also remastered recordings of the singer **Elizabeth (Bess) Cronin**. Some of these recordings have been issued on Bradshaw's own label, Viva Voce, which he started in 1989. He remastered 43 early **Gael-Linn** recordings by various artists for a major compilation in 2004. Since the mid-1990s he has been working at the **Irish Traditional Music Archive** on a project which aims to make the vast archive of material recorded by RTÉ more accessible to the public. He also worked as consultant to and first manager (1999-2001) of the

Ceol Centre in Smithfield, Dublin. With Lesley Anderson he put together an exhibition entitled 'Radio 75: From the Wireless to the Web', which has toured throughout Ireland to mark 75 years of radio broadcasting.

Brady, Paul (b. 1947) Singer, guitarist and mandolin player from Co. Tyrone. In 1967, he joined the popular folk group the **Johnstons** and was with **Planxty** in 1974-75. Released in 1976, *Andy Irvine and Paul Brady* became one of the most famous and enduring albums of the 1970s. Brady's playing of melody in the reels 'Fred Finn's' and 'Sailing into Walpole's Marsh' on this album provides one of the earliest examples of how the guitar can sound perfectly natural as a 'traditional' melody instrument. His famous rendition of the ballad 'Arthur McBride' also broke new ground. An intricate guitar rendition of the melody of the song (repeated in the middle and towards the end) sets the style for the accompaniment running throughout the song. Using the guitar in this way, as both melody and accompanying instrument, was rare in the 1970s, and Brady's style was unique and tasteful. *Matt Molloy, Paul Brady, Tommy Peoples* (1978) still stands out as one of the most unique traditional albums of recent decades, not least because of Brady's superb playing. His rhythm playing is exceptional, varying greatly in intensity and highlighting certain parts of the tunes. Sometimes he plays short runs of melody or harmony. One pair of reels ('The Rainy Day/The Grand Canal') features Brady alone playing melody on guitar, with just the drones of the uilleann pipes sounding throughout. On 'Speed the Plough/Toss the Feathers', he plays melody with the fiddle and flute on the first reel, and changes immediately to playing strong rhythms on the second reel.

Brady followed with his only traditional solo album, *You're Welcome Here Kind Stranger* (1978), which includes 'The Lakes of Ponchitrain' sung and played in his own unique style. He also made albums with traditional players Andy McGann, John Vesey and **Tommy Peoples**, but ultimately embarked on a career in rock music, releasing his first album in 1981. A compilation album, *Nobody Knows: The Best of Paul Brady* (1999) features many of his rock songs but also has new recordings of his versions of 'Arthur McBride' and 'The Lakes of Ponchitrain'. *The Missing Liberty Tapes* (2001), a recording of a concert held in Liberty Hall in 1978, harks back to Brady's Planxty days. It features Brady, **Andy Irvine**, **Dónal Lunny**, **Liam O'Flynn**, **Noel Hill** and **Paddy Glackin**. Brady has also released a tutor on DVD titled *The Guitar of Paul Brady Playing Traditional and Contemporary Irish Songs* (2004). Website: www.paulbrady.com.

Breathnach, Breandán (1912-1985) Uilleann piper, collector and scholar of traditional Irish music. Born in Dublin's Liberties, he worked as a civil servant, initially in the Department of Agriculture but later in the Department of Education. He was a founder and chairman of **Na Píobairí Uilleann** and a major force behind the success and development of the organisation. In 1971 he founded the Folk Music Society of Ireland, along with **Hugh Shields**, **Tom Munnelly** and others. He collected numerous tunes, five volumes of which were published as *Ceol Rince na hÉireann* (Dublin, 1963-1999). The fourth and fifth volumes were published after his death, edited by Galway musician, Jackie Small. Taken together, this is the largest published collection of Irish dance music since **Francis O'Neill**'s collections, and there are invaluable notes on the sources of the tunes, with references to other versions and collectors.

Breathnach was also a scholar of Irish music who delved deeply into many aspects of its history. He published fine specialist articles on the history of dancing and piping, collecting Irish music, the use of notation and many other subjects. Several of these articles were gathered together in one volume and published by Na Píobairí Uilleann as *The Man and His Music: An Anthology of the Writings of Breandán Breathnach* (Dublin, 1996). He also published a general history of Irish music, song and dance under the title *Folk Music and Dances of Ireland* (1st ed. Cork and Dublin, 1971), which has been reprinted many times. As a broad-ranging introduction to the subject it has not been rivalled, although the many developments of the last thirty years are better covered in Nuala O'Connor's ***Bringing It All Back Home*** (London, 1991). From the 1960s onwards he edited the journal *Ceol* and was also a regular contributor to the monthly magazine of Na Píobairí Uilleann, *An Píobaire*.

Breathnach was renowned for his generosity of spirit, his organisational abilities and his encouragement of students of the pipes, whether they were young or old, beginners or advanced players. His views were often controversial and he had many reservations regarding certain developments in traditional music and song. He viewed radio and television broadcasts of traditional music, for instance, as a mixed blessing and questioned the idea that a revival was taking place since local tunes and styles were being abandoned. These aspects of his work are of great interest, for they show how a scholarly man, himself a musician, struggled to come to terms with the changes taking place in traditional music in the course of the 20th century. Breathnach was a man of many skills and one of his greatest contributions was to raise the standard of publishing traditional music to a level that not even O'Neill had achieved. His personal collection became the foundation of the **Irish Traditional Music Archive** after his death in 1985.

Breatnach, Cormac (b. 1963) Musician from Dún Laoghaire, Co. Dublin, who started playing traditional music on the flute but has become better known as a low whistle player. He has played with the **Dónal Lunny** group and his jazzy style of whistle playing was central to the sound of the group **Deiseal**. His first solo album, *A Musical Journey* (1999), includes guest appearances by **Mick Kinsella**, **Máire Breatnach**, **Kevin Glackin**, **Steve Cooney**, accordionist Karen Tweed (see **England**), jazz flautist Brian Dunning and his former partner in Deiseal, Niall Ó Callanáin. His playing is highly inventive and passionate, and he is one of the low whistle's finest exponents. *Music for Whistle and Guitar* (2001), with Martin Dunlea (guitar) continues the mixture of different influences. It includes interpretations of the traditional 'Foggy Dew' and 'Down by the Glenside' as well as six original pieces, four of them composed by Dunlea. Breatnach also featured on the ***Riverdance*** and ***River of Sound*** CDs and was one of the organisers of the first **Crossroads Conference** (1996). Website: www.cormacbreatnach.com.

Breatnach, Máire (b. 1956) Fiddle player, composer, producer and arranger from Dublin. Breatnach grew up with both classical and traditional music, going on to study music at University College Dublin as well as ethnomusicology at Queen's University, Belfast. As a producer and arranger she has worked with many singers, including the Black Family (see **Mary Black**), Johnny McEvoy and **Jim McCann**. She has performed and recorded with numerous traditional musicians, including **Sharon Shannon** and Breton musician **Alan Stivell**. The original fiddle soloist with *Riverdance*, she has also worked in film and television. In addition, she has composed and recorded her own music, first the cameo album *Angels' Candles* (1993) and then *Branohm:*

Máire Breatnach

The Voyage of Bran (1994), a concept album inspired by an Irish folk tale. Her third album, *Celtic Lovers* (1996), consists of original compositions inspired by love stories from Celtic mythology. There are many fine tunes composed in a variety of traditional forms such as the jig, reel, polka, waltz and air. Website: www. mairebreatnach.com.

Brennan, Máire/Moya See **Ní Bhraonáin**, **Máire**.

Breschi, Antonio (b. 1950) Italian pianist and singer who employs a blues style of piano playing in his performance of Irish traditional songs and instrumental pieces. He has made a number of albums, but *Bound for America: Irish Meet Blues 2°* (1981) provides the finest examples of Breschi's unique approach, with songs such as 'The Lowlands of Holland' and 'Paddy's Green Shamrock Shore' performed in a style that is varied but often quite bluesy. On 'Paddy's Green Shamrock Shore' Breschi goes into 'Morrison's Jig' and improvises on the original song air after the singing. There are also instrumental tracks on the album: a polka, jigs, a song air and 'Merrily Kiss the Quaker's Blues', a series of variations on a slide. The playing is superb and his style successfully combines Irish traditional and blues styles. He also plays spoons and dulcimer on the album. Breschi has performed and toured with many Irish musicians, including **Ronnie Drew** and the group Al Kamar. In 1998 he released *My Irish Portrait* under the name 'Antoni O'Breskey'. Website: www.ethnicpiano.com.

Brian Boru Harp The oldest surviving Irish **harp**, which is housed in Trinity College, Dublin. Originally thought to date from the time of the High King of Ireland, Brian Boru (d. 1014), but now dated to the 15th or 16th century. It is made of willow, elaborately carved, about 70cm high and originally had jewels inlaid where the neck and fore-pillar meet. The fore-pillar itself is curved, as in all Irish harps. Unlike the modern or neo-Irish harp, it originally had twenty-nine metal (as opposed to gut or nylon) strings. The Brian Boru harp was used as the model for the national emblem appearing on the reverse side of all Irish coins.

Brian Boru Harp
(engraving from Edward Bunting's *The Ancient Music of Ireland*, 1840)

Bringing It All Back Home Five-part series made by **Hummingbird Productions** for **BBC** Television in association with **RTÉ**. Written by Nuala O'Connor and **Philip King**, it dealt with the history of Irish traditional music and the way it has merged with other types of music, especially in the **US** and Britain. The series combined social history, interviews and music. The history of Irish emigration to the US since the 18th century was dealt with in considerable detail, as well as the role Irish music played in the evolution of country music. The series also examined the revival since the 1960s and the way Irish music has influenced – and been influenced by – rock, pop, blues and avant-garde music. Many artists from different musical backgrounds, including the Everly Brothers, Elvis Costello, Van

Morrison and **Pierce Turner**, as well as traditional singers and musicians, recorded special tracks for the series. A double CD of music from the series was also released, as well as a book entitled *Bringing It All Back Home: The Influence of Irish Music* (London, 1991), written by Nuala O'Connor. It was the first major television series to focus on the interaction between Irish and other types of music. In 2000 a revised edition of the book was published and the CD was remastered and released with three new tracks. A DVD was released at the same time, featuring 90 minutes of performances from the original series, interviews and a selected discography.

British Broadcasting Corporation See **BBC**.

Brittany (*Bretagne* in French) A region in northwest France that became known as Britannia Minor as a result of British colonisation in the 5th and 6th centuries. Like many regions of France, Brittany has its own distinct culture, but is especially noted for its strong music and dance tradition and its languages. French is spoken throughout the region, but Gallo (a Romance language, close to French) is also spoken in Upper Brittany and Breton in Lower Brittany. Breton is part of the Celtic language group, more closely related to Welsh and Cornish than it is to Irish, Scottish Gaelic and Manx. Brittany is therefore often considered to be a 'Celtic' region.

There are some historical links between Brittany and Ireland. Churches dedicated to the Irish St. Brendan (484-577) can be found in Brittany and Scotland, and Brendan may have established a confederation of monasteries in Ireland, Scotland, Brittany and Normandy that were linked by sea (see **Shaun Davey**). Despite the fact that there are few real historical links between the traditional music played today in Ireland and that played in Brittany, a strong connection has developed between musicians from these parts of Europe (along with other 'Celtic' regions) since the 1960s. The traditional dances of Brittany were, until recent decades, largely accompanied by singing rather than instrumental music. Most of the dances were danced in a ring or 'round' (*tro* or *ronde*) with the music provided by a leading singer (*kaner*) and a counter-singer (*diskaner*) or singers, in a similar style to the medieval **carol**. Indeed many Breton dances appear to have evolved in medieval times.

Breton musicians regularly play for special occasions such as weddings, but in recent decades they have also tended to replace singers at the dance nights that are a regular feature of the Breton traditional music scene. The use made of the **bombarde** and biniou koz (literally 'old bagpipe', a single-drone variety of **bagpipes**) is one of the most distinctive features of Breton instrumental music. The instruments, played in duos (often for dancing) and in pipe bands, often mirror the functions of the lead singer (bombarde) and counter-singer (biniou koz) in playing for dances. This is partly a practical necessity as well, the bombarde being an instrument requiring a lot of breath that can only be played continuously for short spells.

Since the 1960s, **Alan Stivell** has played a significant role in the instrumentalisation of Breton dance music and in bringing it to international audiences. He has also played an important role in strengthening links between Brittany and other

Celtic countries or regions, including Ireland. During the 1970s some towns in Ireland were twinned with Breton towns, Carrick-on-Suir, Co. Tipperary, for example, being twinned with Tregunc in Brittany. The Carrick-on-Suir/Tregunc twinning involved a bombarde/biniou koz duo, the bombarde player being also an accomplished player of Irish and Breton music on the tin whistle. Through twinnings such as these, as well as continuous traffic in both directions for music festivals (one of the largest being the annual Festival Interceltique Lorient, held in August) and tours, Ireland and Brittany have, since the 1960s, developed strong musical links. It is not uncommon now for Irish musicians to play Breton tunes and vice versa, and they are frequently involved together in recordings or performances. The **Chieftains** made an album of Breton music, *Celtic Wedding* (1997), with Breton guest musicians. The project was partly inspired by Polig Monjarret, a Breton music collector whose *Tonioù Breizh-Izel* ('Traditional Tunes from Lower Brittany', 1995) contains over 3,000 tunes. Stivell has involved Irish musicians in his projects, his album *Brian Boru* (1995) for instance, involving **Máire Breatnach**, **Ronan Browne** and Niall Ó Callanáin of **Deiseal** among others. Breton musicians have also been involved with Irish groups such as **Lá Lugh**, and Breton harpist Myrdhin plays with the **Afro Celts**.

The new, international links which Breton music has established since the 1960s have broadened the repertoire and range of instruments played. There are now a number of accomplished Breton players of the tin whistle and the simple-system flute, both influences from Ireland. The harp enjoys a higher profile in Breton music than ever before and Breton fiddling has developed greatly. Group playing has become more widespread, with some groups, such as Kornog and Gwerz, finding success on the international touring circuit. Kornog were first formed in 1981 and played an important role in bringing Breton music to audiences in the **US**. They broke up in 1988 but re-formed with a new line-up (including ex-**Arcady** member Nicolas Quemener) in 2000, making their fifth album, *Korong* (2000). The superb Breton flute player, Jean-Michel Veillon, also plays with Kornog, who sometimes perform in Ireland. Breton guitarist Dan Ar Baz, who played with Stivell, has had great success with a project called *Heritage des Celtes*, which brings together music and musicians from Brittany, Scotland and Ireland (including **Dónal Lunny** and Ronan Browne). Live performances of the show in Brittany and other parts of France, as well as in **Scotland**, have been very successful, and the first *Heritage des Celtes* (1995) album was the biggest selling album in Brittany. See also **Gráda**; **Lúnasa**.

Broadside (also 'broadside ballad')   In relation to song, a large sheet of paper on one side of which was printed a popular song. Broadsides were sold by hawkers and first appeared in England and Ireland in the 16th century. Although they sometimes carried the 'old ballads' (see **Ballad**) of oral tradition, they were regularly a medium for popularising newly written ballads, forerunners of the 'new ballads' or **come-all-ye**s of Ireland. The term 'broadside ballad' is therefore sometimes used to refer specifically to these new ballads, although in popular usage it tends to have a more general meaning, referring to any type of popular song printed on a broad-side. See also **Ballad Sheets**.

Brock, Paul (b. 1944) Melodeon and button accordion player born in Athlone but living for many years now in Co. Clare. His session performances with fiddler **Frankie Gavin** in the 1970s and 80s are remembered for their unparalleled exuberance. The duo recorded the highly acclaimed *Omós do Joe Cooley* in 1986. *Mo Chairdín*, a solo album, was released in 1992 and Brock is also a founding member of the Moving Cloud Céilí Band. In 2001, he formed the Brock-Maguire Band with fiddler Manus McGuire, pianist Dennis Morrison and multi-instrumentalist Enda Scahill.

Broderick, Vincent (b. 1920) Composer, flute and tin whistle player, born near Loughrea, Co. Galway. His mother was a tin whistle player, and Vincent started to play at the age of twelve. His brother, Peter, was also a fine flute player. Vincent joined the Kincora Céilí Band and, after moving to Dublin in 1951, was a founding member of the Eamonn Ceannt Céilí Band, with which he made two albums. He was an active member of the **Dublin Pipers' Club** in Thomas Street and **Comhaltas Ceoltóirí Éireann**, with which he toured extensively in Ireland, Britain and the **US**. He has recorded two solo albums and has composed ballads and many fine tunes, 69 of which are published in *Traditional Irish Flute Solos: The Turoe Stone Collection* (Dublin, 1990).

Bronze-Age Horns The earliest surviving musical instruments in Ireland, dating from the Late Bronze Age (ca. 700-300 BC). They are trumpets or horns made of cast bronze, and come in two types, end-blow and side-blow. Over 100 of these horns survive, but most of them are incomplete. One of each type from the hoard of four discovered at Drumbest, Co. Antrim survive complete.

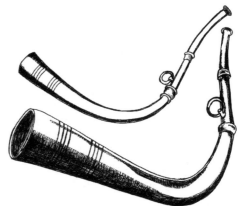

Bronze-Age Horns

For over 200 years, scholars were unable to work out exactly how these horns were played. In 1987-88, a traditional musician, Siomon Ó Duibhir (Simon O'Dwyer), tested a theory developed by Peter Holmes of London which suggested that the Irish Bronze Age horns were similar to the didgeridoo. He had replicas of both of the complete Drumbest horns made from moulds of the originals, and in the summer of 1988 he used didgeridoo techniques to play them. Ó Duibhir found both instruments to be musically compatible, the end-blow producing a backing drone or rhythm for the side-blow, on which melody could be played. The side-blow horn was fully chromatic and could produce a range of almost three octaves. These were important discoveries and have enabled Ó Duibhir to play traditional music on Ireland's oldest musical instrument. *Coirn na hÉireann: Horns of Ancient Ireland* (1994) features Ó Duibhir playing on various Bronze Age horns from the National Museum, Dublin. Perhaps the most effective use yet made of the Bronze Age Horns was in the collaboration between the poet Paul Durcan and composer Michael Holohan on a production of Durcan's 'A Snail in My Prime' (see **Newgrange**). Ó Duibhir, whose wife Maria also plays the ancient horns, can also be heard playing a selection of ancient instruments on the CD *Old and New* (2002).

Brooks Academy A **set-dancing** club founded by uilleann piper Terry Moylan in 1982, based at the premises of **Na Píobairí Uilleann** in Henrietta St., Dublin. It evolved from the set-dancing classes held at the **Willie Clancy Summer School**, at which Moylan started to teach dancing in 1984. Moylan has published three collections of set dances, *Irish Dances* (1984), *The Piper's Set and Other Dances* (1985) and *The Quadrilles and Other Sets* (1988). Teachers from Brooks Academy travel to London and Paris to give set-dancing workshops.

Browne, Peter (b. 1953) A Dubliner who plays uilleann pipes, tin whistle and flute; also a broadcaster and presenter with **RTÉ**. He toured abroad and in 1974-75 was involved with the group 1691 (see **Liam Weldon**), a forerunner to the **Bothy Band**. He toured with the Bothy Band on two occasions and appears on a number of recordings, including *The Bothy Band Live in Concert* (recorded in 1976 and 1978, re-released in 1998). In the early 1980s he also recorded two innovative albums with **Philip King**, both of which were re-released as one album, *Seventeen Minutes to Seven* (2001). It includes Browne's own compositions, 'Rathlin Island' (also recorded by **Sharon Shannon**) and 'Mind the Lighthouse'. Browne is now a senior producer and commissioning editor for RTÉ radio, where he has been involved in many radio series, including *Sounds Traditional*, as well as excellent programmes on **Séamus Ennis** and **Pádraig O'Keeffe** and **Denis Murphy**. He co-produced for radio and performed on uilleann pipes in the unique production of Paul Durcan's poem 'A Snail in My Prime', first broadcast on Christmas Day, 2000 (see **Newgrange**). His *Pipe Maker's Journey* won the top award for a radio documentary at the Deutsche Welle World Music Festival, 2001. It tells the extraordinary story of how Andreas Rogge first became captivated by the sound of the uilleann pipes in a prison in East Germany and ended up coming to Ireland, where he learned to make the pipes.

Browne, Ronan (b. 1965) Uilleann piper, flute and tin whistle player who has been playing the pipes since the age of seven. He has recorded with a number of artists, including **Peadar O'Loughlin**, **Tommy Hayes** and **Alan Stivell** from Brittany. He has also recorded music for films and television and was a member of the **Afro Celts**. He plays with the group Cran (see **Cran 2**). Browne played a superb rendition of the slow air 'Port na bPúcaí' ('Music of the Ghosts') on the pipes as part of the television series ***River of Sound***, also available on CD. He uses the regulators on the pipes to provide a style of accompaniment which is unusual, not the vamping style which most pipers use but chord progressions that follow the tune more closely. His solo album *The Wynd You Know* (2001) has a number of slow airs, including 'An Raibh Tú ag an gCarraig?' ('Have You Been at Carrick?') and 'If I Were a Blackbird', a favourite song of his grandmother, **Delia Murphy**. In an age when fast dance music tends to predominate in sessions and on recordings, it is refreshing to find such an accomplished musician who gives such prominence to slow airs in his playing. He often plays a flat set of pipes, which have a beautiful mellow tone. Browne has also played jazz and classical music and has recorded with Peter Gabriel. Website: www.ronanbrowne.com.

Bumble Bees, The   Young traditional group whose line-up in performance varies, but featured **Laoise Kelly** (harp), Collette O'Leary (piano accordion) and Mary Shannon (banjo, mandolin, fiddle) on their debut album, *Bumble Bees* (1997). The combination of instruments creates an unusual sound, and the album includes new compositions as well as traditional Irish, Scottish, French-Canadian and European music. Since the album was recorded, **Liz Doherty** (fiddle) and John Hoban (vocals) have become members of the group.

Bunting, Edward (1773-1843)   Important collector of traditional Irish music. In addition he collected a wealth of information on the styles and music of the harpers, especially those who attended the **Belfast Harp Festival** of 1792. His father was an English mining engineer who came to work in Dungannon, Co. Tyrone, where he married Mary O'Quin. Edward was born in Armagh city, where he played the organ from an early age. At the age of seven he was sent with his brother Anthony to study music in Drogheda, Co. Louth. A child prodigy, at the age of eleven, he was apprenticed to William Ware, organist of St. Anne's parish in Belfast. While studying organ and piano, he also taught the piano, often to people who were considerably older than himself. In Belfast, Bunting lived with the McCrackens, who were wealthy Huguenot merchants. Henry Joy McCracken (1767-1798) was an early member of the United Irishmen who took a leading part in the 1798 rebellion, for which he was hanged. Bunting had a somewhat bohemian lifestyle in his teenage years, travelling to teach and play music and mixing with high society in Belfast. He often attended dinner parties where Catholic Emancipation and revolution were discussed and was described by Wolfe Tone himself as someone who was opposed to the ideals of the 1798 rebellion. At the age of 19, Bunting was asked to write down the music played at the Belfast Harp Festival. He became fascinated by the harpers and their music, and went on collecting tours between 1792 and 1807, publishing collections of Irish music in 1797 and 1809 (see Bibliography). In 1820 he married Mary Ann Chapman and moved to Dublin, where he continued his profession as church organist. In Dublin he seems to have lost much of the collecting enthusiasm of his early years, and it was only with the encouragement of friends such as **George Petrie** that he published his third and final collection (1840). It included an extensive dissertation on the history and practice of music in Ireland, with details of harps and harp technique, harpers and their compositions. Bunting died suddenly and is buried in Mount Jerome Cemetery in Dublin.

The **Irish Traditional Music Archive** has published a major work on Bunting's manuscripts, *The Irish Music Manuscripts of Edward Bunting (1773-1843): An Introduction and Catalogue* (Dublin, 2000). Compiled by Colette Moloney, it provides a guide to about 1,000 traditional instrumental melodies, of which many are harp tunes, and 500 song texts, mainly in Irish.

Bunting has been criticised for not notating harp music exactly as he heard it and for arranging the tunes in a style more suitable to the piano than to the harp. As recently as 1997 his work provoked controversy when a series of letters-to-the-editor in the *Irish Times* argued for and against the merits of his work. Although the transcriptions of the traditional music he heard do need to be treated with caution, much of what he published would undoubtedly have been lost had he not collected it. He also made an invaluable contribution to our understanding of the styles, techniques and lives of the harpers he met. See also **Harbison, Janet**; **O'Sullivan, Donal**.

Denis Hempson, 'the Harper of Magilligan, County of L'Derry' (engraving from Bunting's *General Collection of the Ancient Music of Ireland*, 1809)

Burke, Joe (b. 1939)   Button accordion player born in Kilnadeema, near Loughrea, Co. Galway. He plays the B/C accordion in the style pioneered by **Paddy O'Brien** (see also **Accordion**). Many musicians and listeners regard him as the finest accordion player alive today, having won two **All-Ireland** Senior titles and influenced many younger players with his relaxed style. He has toured all over the world, living in the US in the 1960s and late 80s to early 90s, and has recorded numerous albums, including *Happy to Meet, Sorry to Part* (1986) and *The Bucks of Oranmore* (1996), on which he plays many traditional standards, accompanied by **Charlie Lennon** (piano). He recorded the classic *A Tribute to Michael Coleman* (re-issued on CD, 1994) with **Andy McGann** and pianist Felix Dolan. He is also an accomplished player of the flute and tin whistle, and his album *The Tailor's Choice*

(1983), with **Máire Ní Chathasaigh**, features just two tracks on which he plays accordion, the rest made up of flute and whistle playing. *The Morning Mist* (2002) features Burke playing accordion on all tracks, with accompaniment again by Charlie Lennon on piano. Burke's wife, Ann Conroy Burke, is also a fine accordion player who often performs with her husband.

Burke, Kevin Fiddler born in London whose family originally came from Co. Sligo. After taking over from **Tommy Peoples** in the **Bothy Band**, Burke became one of the best-known Irish traditional fiddlers. His first solo album, *Sweeny's Dream*, was recorded in 1973 and released in 1977. His smooth, elegant style has been imitated by many young players and his second solo album, *If the Cap Fits* (1978), is one of the best of the decade. Overdubbing allows Burke to play two or three fiddles together on some tracks; there are also fiddle/accordion duets as well as duets with mandolin, bouzouki, piano, guitar, pipes and flute. One 16-minute track consists of a set of eleven reels played by solo fiddle, two fiddles and various combinations with other instruments. After the break-up of the Bothy Band, Burke moved to the **US** and formed a duo with **Micheál Ó Domhnaill** for some time, recording two fine albums, the first called *Promenade* (1979) and the second named after the city where they were based in Oregon, *Portland* (1982). Other work includes a third solo album, *Up Close* (1984), the album *Eavesdropper* (1981) with **Jackie Daly**, many albums with **Patrick Street** and his work with Open House, a group

Kevin Burke

who draw on blues, bluegrass, Scandinavian, Latin-American and French influences. A fourth solo album, *Kevin Burke in Concert* (1999), was recorded in Oregon and features some classic tunes, including 'The Butterfly' and 'The Blackbird', as well as a duet with **Martin Hayes**. Burke was also involved in the innovative Celtic Fiddle Festival with fellow fiddlers John Cunningham (**Scotland**) and Christian Lemaitre (**Brittany**). Website:pws.prserv.net/kevinburke.

Burns, Robert (1759-1796) Known as 'the Ploughman Poet', Burns was born at Alloway, Ayrshire, Scotland. In his relatively brief life, he produced a vast amount of lyric poetry, most of it written in a Scottish dialect. His work included satire, nature poetry and love songs. Some of his work was highly political, and he was a champion of the poor and supporter of the ideals of the French Revolution. His most famous lyrics are probably those of 'Auld Lang Syne', sung in many parts of the world on New Year's Eve. Burns was also a lover of music and song and dedicated himself to rescuing from oblivion many songs without words or with only fragmentary lyrics. He worked, unpaid, to provide words and music for the collections of James Johnson and George Thomas. Many of his lyrics were written to suit known, traditional Scottish melodies.

One four-verse song in the collected works of Burns called 'The Winter Is Past' is very similar to the ballad 'The Curragh of Kildare', well known in Ireland and further afield. **Christy Moore** says that he came across the lyrics of 'The Curragh of Kildare' in the Joyce Collection (see **Joyce, Patrick Weston**) in 1962. Three of the four verses in this version are almost identical to three of the verses in the Burns version. The third verse in Moore's version, however, is not in Burns and is the only

Robert Burns

verse that mentions Kildare. Along with **Dónal Lunny**, Moore worked the last two lines of this verse ('And it's straight I will repair to the Curragh of Kildare/For it's there I'll find tidings of my love') into a chorus. The song appeared on Moore's first solo album, *Paddy on the Road* (1969), although it was a version that Mick Moloney recorded with the **Johnstons** that, in Moore's words, '...established the song as part of the national [Irish] repertoire' (*One Voice: My Life in Song*, London, 2000, p. 126). In *Ancient Irish Music* (1855) **George Petrie** published a melody (identical to the Moore/Moloney melody) and two sets of lyrics (one Scottish, the other Irish) of 'The Winter It Is Past, or The Curragh of Kildare'. Petrie argues convincingly that, while Burns may have added a few touches of his own to the lyrics, it was clearly wrong to ascribe their authorship to him. Some years before two stanzas of the lyrics had been found in Burns' handwriting, a four-stanza version of the song had been published in Johnson's *Scots Musical Museum* (Edinburgh, 1787). Petrie's Irish version of the lyrics, which is based on a version collected by Joyce, has all four verses of the

Moore version (as well as three others) and includes the lines at the end of the third verse which mention Kildare. The Joyce/Petrie version of the song seems to have been collected in Ireland around 1780, and Petrie argues that the song may well be Irish in origin. While this is far from definite, the history of this song provides a fascinating insight into the ways that songs can travel and mutate across borders and time. It seems clear that different versions of the same song were popular in both Ireland and Scotland and that Burns picked up on the Scottish version, adding, as Petrie says, a few touches of his own.

Apart from this interesting link between Burns and Irish folk song, some fine versions of Burns' songs have been recorded by contemporary Irish and Scottish folk singers, including Clare singer/guitarist/bouzouki-player Cyril O'Donoghue, who recorded Burns' 'Ae Fond Kiss' on his album *Nothing But a Child* (2003). Scottish singer **Dick Gaughan** has also recorded Burns' work, and his superb rendition of Burns' 'Now Westlin' Winds' is one of the best and most widely loved of the songs in Gaughan's repertoire. He introduced it as 'one of the most subversive songs ever written' at a concert in Whelan's of Dublin some years ago. The lyrics are an extraordinary combination of love song, nature poem and social/political comment. The Breton singer/harpist **Alan Stivell** and the Irish group the **Voice Squad** have also recorded songs by Burns. The Glaswegian singer Eddi Reader has brought a new freshness and a unique style to the poet's lyrics on her album *Eddi Reader Sings the Songs of Robbie Burns* (2003).

Butcher, Eddie (1900-1980) Singer from Magilligan, Co. Derry. He had a huge repertoire of **come-all-ye**s as well as some old **ballad**s and **chantefable**s, many of them rare or unusual versions. Much of his material was learned orally from his parents and other singers, and he also composed his own songs about local events. Among the latter is 'The New Tractor', about the first tractor ever seen in his parish (ca. 1940). He was often not invited to local parties for fear that he might compose a satirical song about someone who was present. Butcher made an E.P., *Adam in Paradise: Traditional Songs of Courtship* (1969, re-released 1982), and the albums *Shamrock, Rose and Thistle* and *I Once Was a Daysman* (both 1976). He was also included in three compilation albums, *Folk Ballads of Derry and Donegal* (1972), *Shamrock, Rose and Thistle 2-3* (double album, 1983; songs by north Derry singers) and *Early Ballads in Ireland* (1985). All three of these compilations involved the collector **Hugh Shields**, who recorded (in writing or on tape) 237 of Butcher's songs/song fragments. Shields has also done extensive research on many of these songs, some of which was published in his 1981 and 1993 books. Butcher and his repertoire has therefore been the subject of more detailed recording and analysis than most traditional singers of his generation. He sang in English, usually unaccompanied or occasionally with one of his brothers (John, Jimmy and Robert all sang) or his wife Gracie. One of his most interesting songs is a version of 'Our Wedding Day', which the singer himself said was passed on through his family from the 1800s. The song is related to **Pádraig Colum**'s 'She Moved Through the Fair', but there are considerable differences in the stories that each song tells.

Button Accordion See **Accordion**.

Buttons and Bows Group formed in 1984 by **Jackie Daly** (accordion, concertina), Gary Ó Briain (guitar, mandocello, piano) and brothers Séamus (fiddle, viola) and Manus (fiddle) McGuire. They drew their repertoire from a wide variety of sources, playing Scandinavian, French-Canadian, Shetland and original music as well as Irish traditional. They have released three albums: *Buttons and Bows* (1984), *The First Month of Summer* (1987) and *Grace Notes* (1991).

Byrd, William (1543-1623) English composer and organist who wrote church music as well as consort songs, madrigals, music for consorts of viols and keyboard music. He became organist of the Chapel Royal under Queen **Elizabeth I**. After the English victory over the Spanish Armada in 1588, he wrote a suite of twelve pieces entitled *The Battle* to commemorate the event. One of these pieces, 'The Irish Marche', was recorded by the group **Planxty** on *Words and Music* (1983). The group **King's Galliard** recorded another piece from the suite.

Cairde na Cruite Literally 'Friends of the Harp', an organisation founded in 1960 to promote interest in the Irish harp. Cearbhall Ó Dálaigh (President of Ireland, 1974-76) was an inspiration in the 'friends' foundation and served as their first chair-person. With harp schools in Derry, Wexford, Nobber, Co. Meath and Mullingar, Co. Westmeath, teaching is one of the main means by which the harp is promoted. There are also workshops and masterclasses held in Ireland and beyond and a week-long summer school is held at Termonfeckin, Co. Louth every June. Teachers have included **Máire Ní Chathasaigh**, **Kathleen Loughnane** and **Gráinne Yeats**. Cairde na Cruite also commissions music from Irish composers and has published a number of books, including Sheila Larchet Cuthbert's excellent *The Irish Harp Book: A Tutor and Companion* (Cork and Dublin, 1975). The latter includes works by harper-composers such as **Turlough O'Carolan** and contemporary works commissioned by Cairde na Cruite. Website: www.harp.net/cnac/cnac.htm.

Calthorpe, Nancy (1914-1998) During her working life, Calthorpe was perhaps the most respected teacher of Irish harp in Ireland, her work spanning the half-century after the end of World War II. She specialised in the teaching of the solo instrument and the musicological research associated with it. But as a teacher of singing, both classical and Irish, she extended her work into the area of harp-accompanied song, to which her numerous arrangements testify. Calthorpe spent the greater part of her pedagogical career at the DIT College of Music in Dublin, where she became Head of the Singing Department; during that period she also designed the first diploma course for teachers of Irish harp. Her many arrangements for the harp earned her international recognition. **Feis Ceoil** currently has two prizes in her honour, the Nancy Calthorpe Cup for the singing of French Song and the Nancy Calthorpe Memorial Prize for Irish harp performance and arrangement. Her publications include two collections of the music of **Turlough O'Carolan** and the four-volume *Calthorpe Collection: Music for the Irish Harp* (Dublin, 2000).

Canada The earliest major Irish settlements in Canada were established in the 18th century in **Newfoundland**, which still retains a strongly Irish-influenced music, song and dance tradition. Irish fishermen had travelled to the coast of Newfoundland from the second half of the 17th century, a period that also saw the foundation of the Hudson Bay Company (1670). The company built trading stations throughout the Hudson Bay area and many of the trappers who came to trade pelts with the native tribes at these stations were Irish and Scottish people who intermarried with the native Métis people of Manitoba. To this day the Métis live in reservations in Manitoba and play an unusual combination of Irish/Scottish style fiddling and Indian rhythms.

Some Irish immigrants also settled in **Nova Scotia**, although the far larger number of Scottish settlers had a more lasting influence on that province's music, especially on Cape Breton Island. Some Irish soldiers in the French army were given land grants in Québec in the 18th century, but the city's Irish population grew rapidly in the years following the **Great Famine** of 1845-49, reaching over 9,000 by 1851. Throughout the 19th century Irish settlements spread westwards into Ontario. **Gearóid Ó hAllmhuráin** notes how quadrille sets similar to those danced in Ireland were an important part of the social scene in Québec, where a solo dance called the Québecois *gigue* emerged from a fusion of Irish and English dancing. The *gigue* is still danced in parts of Québec today, and the style and Irish traditional repertoire of 20th-century musicians like Jean Carignan (fiddle) and Keith Corrigan (melodeon) still influence musicians in the Irish community of the province. Thomas D'Arcy McGee (1825-1868), a member of the **Young Ireland** movement who fled Ireland after the rebellion of 1848, settled in Montreal in 1857 and played an important role in the foundation of the Dominion of Canada in 1867. McGee had published nationalist ballads in the *Nation* newspaper before leaving Ireland, including 'Feagh McHugh of the Mountain'. He was assassinated in Canada in 1868.

A considerable revival of interest in the Irish- and Scots-influenced traditional music and song of Canada since the 1970s has seen many fine musicians launch successful careers as professional musicians. The group Ryan's Fancy became popular during the **ballad boom** in the early 1970s, initially in Newfoundland but later throughout Canada. Two of the group were Dubliners, Fergus O'Byrne (banjo, mandolin, guitar, concertina, vocals) and Dermot O'Reilly (mandolin, guitar, vocals). Denis Ryan (whistle, fiddle, vocals) came from Newport, Co. Tipperary. They played a mixture of songs and dance tunes from Ireland, Scotland and Canada and became enormously popular in Canada through tours and their own series on CBC TV nationwide. They did many TV series and special shows through the 70s and 80s, and, although they broke up in 1983, they are still renowned in the 21st century and released *Songs from the Shows* in 2001. **Barde**, who emerged in the late 1970s, include native Irish and Canadian musicians in their line-up. La Bottine Souritane ('The Smiling Boot') first came on the scene in the late 70s and their rise coincided with that of the separatist Parti Québecois. They still perform an eclectic mixture of music on a range of instruments, traditional and non-traditional. They have gone through many changes and musical styles, but much of their music is Irish and Scottish, with many of their songs originating in **Brittany**. Bernard Simard, who played with La Bottine Souritane, has become famous for his performances of Québecois foot percussion, and he is also a fine flute player. He now plays with the group Gwazigan, who are based in Brittany and have three Breton members as well as one from Madagascar. They play a mixture of music from different traditions, including Québecois, Cajun, Scottish and Irish, often interweaving elements from some or all of these traditions in more contemporary compositions. Their third album, *Y'avait du Monde* (2000), is an excellent collection of tunes and songs which represents the diversity of the traditions on which they draw.

The late 1990s saw **Leahy** establish a reputation beyond the borders of their native Canada and Seven Nations, Natalie McMaster and Barachois are among the other Canadian artists to establish international reputations in the 21st century. Barachois, from Prince Edward Island, perform a unique blend of music, foot-percussion and bizarre humour and won the 'Best Band' award at the **Milwaukee Irish Fest** in 2001. See also **Ó Lionáird, Iarla**; **Scotland**.

Canny, Paddy (b. 1919) Fiddler from Tulla, Co. Clare and a member of the famous Tulla Céilí Band, with whom he recorded and played all over Ireland, Britain and the **US** (including Carnegie Hall) in the 1940s and 50s. He made the album *All Ireland Champions: Violin* (1959) with **P. J. Hayes**, **Peadar O'Loughlin** and Bridie Lafferty (piano), but it was not until 1997 that he released a solo album, *Traditional Music from the Legendary East Clare Fiddler*. His gentle style, which uses long phrases and slides easily from note to note, is seen by many as typical of the East Clare style of fiddling.

Cape Breton See **Nova Scotia**.

Cappercaillie Enormously successful Scottish group, recording and touring since the 1980s. Their line-up, which has seen only a few changes over the years, now includes Irishman Manus Lunny (bouzouki, guitar, vocals), **Karen Matheson** (lead vocals), Marc Duff (recorder, whistles, bodhrán, wind synthesiser), Charlie McKerron (fiddle), John Saich (bass, guitar, vocals) and Donald Shaw (accordion, keyboards). The inspiration for their music is drawn from *puirt a beul* or mouth music (see **Mouth Music 1**), and they perform songs (in English and Scots Gaelic) and instrumental sets. From the beginning Cappercaillie were distinctive, partly because of Matheson's voice but also because they have managed to create a sound which is modern but clearly rooted in the traditional music of Scotland, Ireland and Cape Breton (see **Nova Scotia**). Over the years they have gradually included more original music in their repertoire.

Karen Matheson and Charlie McKerron of Cappercaille (photo: Bruce C. Moore)

One of their early albums, *Sidewaulk* (1989), included songs by **Dick Gaughan** and John Martyn, instrumentals by Donald Shaw and Charlie McKerron and a substantial amount of traditional material. The first track on the album is a Scottish 'waulking song', 'Alasdair Mhic Cholla Ghasda'. Waulking songs (*Orain Luaidhaidh* in Scots Gaelic), sung throughout the Highlands and Hebrides, were a type of **occupational song** that accompanied the rhythm of beating cloth on a table. This was the method used to shrink tweed or blanket cloth taken from the loom.

Songs by John Saich, Manus Lunny and Donald Shaw make up about half of the material on *Delirium* (1991), with a similar combination of original and traditional material on *Secret People* (1993), blended together very successfully in Cappercaillie's own style. **Dónal Lunny** was involved in the production of all three albums and comparisons have been made to the sound of **Moving Hearts**. While both groups play Celtic music with a modern sound, Cappercaillie have managed to blend the modern with the traditional to a much greater extent than Moving Hearts. *Cappercaillie* (1994) was produced by the writer and keyboard player of Soul II Soul, Will Mowat, and consists mainly of remixes of old material. The majority of the songs formerly appeared on *Secret People*, but the new versions provide an interesting example of how a different producer can alter a group's sound. On *To the Moon* (1995) 11 of the 13 tracks are original but there is still a strong traditional element. This album features 'Rob Roy Reels', which form part of the group's contribution to the Hollywood film *Rob Roy*. *Beautiful Wasteland* (1997) includes **Michael McGoldrick** (uilleann pipes and flute), who toured with the group after the album's release. They subsequently released a compilation CD and a DVD/VHS of their performances.

McGoldrick remained with the group after recording and touring with them in 1997, and by the time of *Choice Language* (2003) another new member, Che Beresford (percussion), had joined. Cappercaillie's albums are usually accompanied by printed lyrics of all songs, with English translations of songs in Scots Gaelic. Website: www.capercaillie.co.uk. See also **Scotland**.

Carol 1 The earliest type of **round dance** known in Ireland, probably brought there by the Anglo-Normans after their invasion in 1169. The first reference to 'caroling' in Irish sources dates from 1265, when a poem describing the building of a wall around the Anglo-Norman town of New Ross refers to the townspeople 'caroling and singing' as they go to work. Another reference to 'caroling' dates from a 1413 description of a visit by the mayor of Waterford to O'Driscoll of Baltimore, Co. Cork. The carol was a dance-song in which a leader sang the verse and the refrain was sung by the rest of the group, who danced behind the leader with simple steps, moving in a circle. The **ballad** form may have derived originally from a type of carol in which there was an internal refrain. Another type of carol had a separate refrain or 'burden'. The carol, like other medieval dance forms, was originally associated with popular fertility rites, and some carols were performed around Christmas in association with pagan survivals of ancient Yule customs.

Carol 2 Christmas carols, or hymns pertaining to Christmastide, originally evolved from the type of medieval dance-song described above. The Franciscans played an important role in transforming the carol from a secular dance-song into a hymn or religious Christmas song, thus using a popular form often associated with ancient pagan customs to spread the Christian message. Carols on both secular and religious (including Christmas) themes survive from 15th-century England. The most famous Irish Christmas Carols are the **Wexford Carols**. The lyrics of these carols, still sung every year in Kilmore, were written in the 17th and 18th centuries, while the airs are traditional. See also **England**.

Carolan, Nicholas (b. 1946) Researcher, music historian, broadcaster and lecturer in Irish traditional music born in Drogheda, Co. Louth. He has served as Director of the **Irish Traditional Music Archive** since its foundation in 1987. His published works include a facsimile edition, with notes and introduction, of **John and William Neal**'s *A Collection of the Most Celebrated Irish Tunes*, originally published in Dublin in 1724 (Dublin, 1986). He has also published *A Short Discography of Irish Folk Music* (Dublin, 1987) and *A Harvest Saved: Francis O'Neill and Irish Music in Chicago* (Cork, 1997), on the life and work of **Francis O'Neill**, which includes a comprehensive list of sources and publications relating to the great collector. Carolan also researched and presented the archival series *The Irish Phonograph* (RTÉ Radio 1, 1983-86) and *Come West along the Road* (RTÉ 1 Television, 1994 to the present).

Carolan A term sometimes used to describe a tune composed by the the harper **Turlough O'Carolan**.

Carolan, Turlough See **O'Carolan, Turlough**.

Carroll, Liz (b. 1956) Fiddler and composer of over 170 tunes, from Chicago. Her father plays the button accordion and comes from Brocca, near Tullamore, Co. Offaly. Her mother, Eileen Cahill, comes from Ballyahill in west Co. Limerick. Carroll played accordion before taking up the fiddle at the age of nine. She learned classical violin and piano but developed her playing of traditional style fiddle through listening to other players and joining in at sessions. In 1975 she won the **All-Ireland** senior fiddle title, the only American fiddler to do so before being Kathleen Collins in 1966. Her first album, *Kiss Me Kate* (1977) also featured Tommy Maguire (accordion) and Jerry Wallace (piano). *A Friend Indeed*, with Marty Fahey (piano) was released in 1979 and featured five of Carroll's own tunes as well as one she composed with Fahey. *Liz Carroll* (1988) has over twenty of her own compositions and she is accompanied by guitarist Dáithí Sproule (see **Skara Brae** and **Altan**). In 1991 she formed the group Trian with Sproule and New York button accordionist Billy McComiskey, releasing albums with them in 1992 and 1995. In 1994 Carroll was awarded a National Heritage Fellowship, the highest accolade that can be conferred on traditional/ folk artists in the **US**. Further solo albums featuring new

Liz Carroll (photo: Dagmara)

compositions followed, guitarist John Doyle accompanying her on *Lost in the Loop* (2000) and *Lake Effect* (2002). Undoubtedly one of the finest fiddlers on either side of the Atlantic, Carroll is also one of the most prolific and accomplished composers of tunes in the traditional style. In addition to her solo recordings and her work with Trian, she has recorded and performed with many other artists, including flautist and whistle player Laurence Nugent and **Robbie O'Connell**. Website: www.lizcarroll.com.

Carson, Ciaran (b. 1948) Writer and flute player from Belfast who, from 1975 to 1998, worked as Traditional Arts Officer with the Arts Council of Northern Ireland, organising many singing festivals throughout the North. He is best known as a poet but his brief guide entitled *Irish Traditional Music* (1986) is an interesting work largely based around the instruments, their history, and styles and musicians associated with them. He also covers such topics as 'Dancing and Music', 'The Song Tradition: Recent Developments' and 'Session Etiquette'. There is a good 'Technical Supplement' which explains **ornamentation** and attitudes to tuning and intonation. *Last Night's Fun* (1996) focuses on traditional music in a very different way, weaving memories and meditations on traditional music around a series of tunes and sessions.

Carthy, Martin (b. 1940) Singer/songwriter and guitarist, one of the major figures in English folk music since the 1960s, born in Hatfield, Hertfordshire, England. His great-great grandfather, George Carthy, was from Ballybunion, Co. Kerry, Ireland and emigrated to England in the wake of the **Great Famine**. George Carthy had changed his name from Timothy McCarthy after emigrating, and his brother, Thomas McCarthy, was a famous uilleann piper. Martin Carthy brought out his first solo album, simply titled *Martin Carthy*, in 1965. He has had a musically varied career, performing with the electric folk group Steeleye Span, in a duo with Dave Swarbrick, experimenting with brass in the group Brass Monkey and singing *a capella* with the **Watersons**. He married Norma Waterson in 1972 and they have performed and recorded together extensively. Their daughter, Eliza (fiddle, singer/songwriter), has also toured with them.

Martin Carthy is renowned for his intricate style of accompaniment and sings a mixture of old English or **Child ballads** and newer material, much of which he composes himself. Paul Simon recorded Carthy's arrangement of the traditional song *Scarborough Fair*, for which he was forced to make a legal settlement in 1970. Carthy has made numerous albums since the 1960s and recently released *The*

Carthy Chronicles (2000), a four-CD boxed set. It includes 83 tracks divided into four sections, Classic Carthy, Carthy in Company, Carthy Contemporaries and Child Carthy. There are previously unrecorded tracks included, as well as a biography and a detailed discography. Carthy has performed many times in Ireland, often with his wife, Norma Waterson.

Carty, John (b. 1962)   Fiddler and banjo player born in London who moved to his father's home town of Boyle, Co. Roscommon in 1991. His father, John P., is a fine flautist and multi-instrumentalist, and from an early age John Carty was influenced by the playing of Sligo fiddlers such as **Michael Coleman**, **James Morrison** and **Paddy Killoran**. His first album, *The Cat that Ate the Candle* (1994) was followed by *Last Night's Fun* (1996) and *At It Again* (2003). Carty has toured extensively in Europe and the **US** and was the TG4 Traditional Musician of the Year in 2003.

Carty, Paddy (1929-1985)   Flute player born in Rafford, Co. Galway who started playing tin whistle at the age of six, graduating to fife and flute. Self-taught, he was unusual among traditional players in that he used a keyed flute rather than the open-holed, simple-system flute used by most traditional players (see **Flute**). He played in a flowing style at a relatively slow tempo, his breathing barely noticeable. He often played in unusual keys, sometimes the same tune consecutively in different keys. He won five **All-Ireland** titles, three as a solo flautist and two with the Leitrim Céilí Band. He recorded one album, *Irish Traditional Music* (1972) with London tenor banjo player Mick O'Connor. The album was re-released on CD in 1997.

Casadh ('Turn')   Sometimes called 'double grace note' or 'double cut'. A form of ornamentation similar to the **cut** but slightly more complex. It involves playing the main note as a grace note, followed by a higher note and a return to the main note. As with the cut, the higher grace note and the way it is fingered will vary according to the instrument or the desired effect. The two grace notes used in a turn are sometimes notated as a pair of small quavers (eighth notes) with a line through them, sometimes as a pair of small semi-quavers (sixteenth notes), but in either case they have no time value.

Casadh

Casey, Bobby (1926-2000)   Fiddler born at Annagh, near Miltown Malbay, Co. Clare. His father, Scully, was also a highly regarded fiddler and taught **Junior Crehan** to play. Crehan in turn passed on to Bobby many of the tunes he had learned from Scully. Bobby played fiddle from a young age and played with **Willie Clancy**, with whom he went to Dublin and then on to London in the 1950s. Clancy eventually returned to Clare, but Casey stayed in London, becoming part of a vibrant traditional music scene that involved musicians such as **Séamus Ennis**, **Paddy Taylor** and Tommy McCarthy (see **McCarthy Family**). In 1959 he recorded a tribute to his father Scully at Junior Crehan's farm, released on tape as *Casey in the Cowhouse*. He can also be heard (with Junior Crehan and others) on *Ceol an Chláir* (1979) and released a solo album, *Taking Flight* (1979). See also **England**, **Topic Records**.

Casey, Karan (b. 1968) Lead vocalist with the Irish-American group **Solas** from 1995 to 1999. Even during her time with Solas Casey toured as a solo singer and in 1997 released her first solo album, *Songlines*. Born in Ballyduff Lower, Co. Waterford, she has been singing since childhood. She studied music at University College Dublin and plays classical piano and sings jazz as well as traditional songs. Traditional singers **Frank Harte** and **Sarah Makem** are cited as sources for Casey's songs, while she also performs material by American singer/songwriters such as Peggy Seeger and **Woody Guthrie**. *The Winds Begin to*

Karan Casey
(photo: Colm Henry)

Sing (2001) has nine traditional songs and two songs written by **John Spillane** and Louis de Paor. The latter two writers contributed further new material to Casey's *Distant Shore* (2003) which also includes original songs by **Ewan MacColl**, Casey herself and others. There are only two traditional tracks on the album, which has a host of talented guest artists including **Michael McGoldrick** and **Dezi Donnelly**. Karen Matheson (vocals) and Donald Shaw (producer), both of **Cappercaillie**, also contributed to the album. Casey is one of the most promising young traditional singers to emerge from the 1990s. See also **Mad for Trad**. Website: www. karancasey.com.

Casey, Nollaig See **Ní Chathasaigh, Nollaig**.

Céilí The word *céilí* was originally used to describe a gathering of friends or neighbours in someone's house, usually in the evening, to talk and gossip. It could also mean simply a friendly call or visit. The use of céilí to describe 'an Irish dancing session' did not evolve until the closing years of the 19th century (see **Céilí Dancing**) and was initially promoted by **Conradh na Gaeilge**, in much the same way as they promoted the use of the term **sean-nós singing**.

Céilí Band A band that plays for a céilí or dance night. Originally this type of band was particularly associated with **céilí dancing**, but in recent decades *céilí* has come to be used for a night of **set dancing**, or a mixture of set and céilí dancing. The Kilfenora Céilí Band traces its history to the year 1907, although it is not clear that they called themselves a 'céilí band' at this early stage. **Gearóid Ó Hallmhúráin** suggests that the term itself may have been coined by Frank Lee's Tara Céilí Band, who came together to play for a Saint Patrick's Day dance in London's Notting Hill in 1918. The Irish radio station 2RN, under its first director, Séamus Clandillon, had céilí trios and bands doing radio series and recitals in the late 1920s and 30s (see **RTÉ**), and some of these bands became very popular. The Ballinakill Céilí Band (from Co. Galway) were highly influential in this period, achieving widespread popularity and making numerous radio broadcasts and 78 rpm recordings. The era of the big céilí bands, however, did not begin until about twenty years later. In the wake of the **Public Dance Hall Act** (1935), the popularity of céilí bands grew and they pulled huge crowds in the 1940s and 50s. One of the most famous bands of this era, which celebrated its 50th anniversary with an album released in 1997, was the Tulla from East Clare. In 1958, they played Carnegie Hall in New York and in the same year played in London to an audience of 5,000.

Although there were, at one stage, fourteen céilí bands in Co. Clare alone, the Tulla and the Kilfenora were always the most prominent, partly due to showdowns in the céilí band competition at the fleadh (see **Fleadh Cheoil Na hÉireann**). Thousands of supporters in both camps watched the Tulla and Kilfenora battle for the title of **All-Ireland** champions, although there were always good relations between the two bands despite the competition. The Kilfenora won three titles in a row (1954 to 1956), and the Tulla won the first of three titles in 1957. There were numerous bands throughout Ireland in the 1940s and 50s, including the Gallowglass, the Austin Stack and the Aughrim Slopes. This decade even saw the establishment of the New York Céilí Band. In the 1960s several new bands emerged, including the Lough Gamhna and the Castle. Although the boom days had passed, there was (and still is) a demand for good bands to play at céilí dances. The Táin Céilí Band from Dundalk is one of the more prominent bands to emerge in recent years, winning three All-Ireland titles in a row (1998-2000). The Ennis Céilí Band also won the 'three-in-a-row', in 2001-2003.

The original Ballinakill Céilí Band had two flutes, two fiddles and an accordion. The typical line-up of a céilí band, however, would also include drums and piano. Other instruments – including banjo, concertina, saxophone and double bass – could also be found in the line-up. Modern bands usually have eight to ten musicians and aim at producing a big sound with a clearly defined rhythm for dancers to follow.

Céilí bands have been criticised by many, most famously by **Seán Ó Riada**, who abhorred the way the entire band would simply belt away at a tune without stopping, abandoning variation and personal utterance. 'The result', he commented in 1962, 'is a rhythmic but meaningless noise with as much relation to music as the buzzing of a bluebottle in an upturned jam jar' (*Our Musical Heritage*, Mountrath,

1982, p. 74). Ó Riada thought that variation and personal utterance were the most important principles of traditional music, but defenders of the céilí bands have argued that the fundamental role of traditional musicians is to provide a solid rhythmic base for dancers. The debate highlights different ideas of what traditional music is or should be, a subject frequently provoking heated argument.

Interestingly, some of the most innovative traditional musicians have played with céilí bands. **Martin Hayes**, one of the masters of 'variation' and 'personal utterance' in the 1990s, played, from the age of 13 or 14, with the Tulla Céilí Band. So too did **Willie Clancy**, acknowledged as one of the most stylistically innovative pipers of the 20th century. Céilí bands were, in many ways, a response to the demands of their time. It was the era of big dance bands and in order to compete with these, the céilí bands borrowed from them; hence the drums and piano to provide rhythm and the suits and bow ties for presentation. See also **England**.

Céilí Dancing A form of Irish dancing which often involves long lines of dancers – girls on one side, boys on the other – dancing steps to Irish **dance music**, as in the dances called 'The Bridge of Athlone', 'The Waves of Troy' and 'The Haymakers Jig'. Figures involving the linking of arms or other movements can also be an important part of these dances. Céilí dancing tends to be slightly stiffer and more formal than the **quadrille**-based **set dancing**, although both types may use similar steps. Some figure-dances in vogue before set dancing, such as the eight-hand jig and the eight-hand reel, also bore a close resemblance to the quadrilles on which set dancing was based. These eight-hand dances were also incorporated into the official céilí-dance repertoire.

Although the word *céilí* originally had no association with music or dancing, it was first used by **Conradh na Gaeilge** to describe an organised dance in October 1897. The céilí was held in London's Bloomsbury Hall and was organised by the secretary of Conradh na Gaeilge in London, Fionán MacColum, from Scotland. There was a league ban on its members dancing 'English' or 'foreign-influenced' traditional dances, including **round dances** and quadrilles. Despite this, **set**s, quadrilles and **waltz**es were danced to Irish music at this first céilí.

Conradh na Gaeilge sought to develop céilí dancing as something purely Irish, and its ban on many 'foreign-influenced' traditional dances caused those dances to decline. The Irish **Dancing Commission**, formed in 1929, attempted to revive some of the dances that had disappeared. When they failed to do so, they composed other dances instead. Thus the secretary of Conradh na Gaeilge in Munster was said to have composed 'The Siege of Ennis' and 'The Walls of Limerick', both group dances where the dancers face each other in long lines. Other dances were put together by Scottish officials in Conradh na Gaeilge such as Fionán MacColum. Céilí dancing developed in a strict and formal style, in contrast to the relaxed, informal style of the older set dancing. Despite the ban, however, set dancing survived in all areas where dancing had been popular.

In the wake of the **Public Dance Hall Act** (1935), the clergy generally favoured céilí dancing over set dancing, praising the former for its modesty and strict formality.

The increased number of dancehalls, often controlled by the clergy, gave a new impetus to what became a phenomenon in traditional music, the **céilí band**. Although céilí dances themselves were held to be more Irish than set dances, the latter continued to survive and in some parts were even danced in the dancehalls. After the founding of **Comhaltas Ceoltóirí Éireann** in 1951, a revival of set dancing began. More people began to take an interest in their own local sets and the 1980s and 90s have seen further developments in the spread of set-dancing workshops and céilís.

Although many people still distinguish between the different styles of set dancing and céilí dancing, the term céilí is often used now to describe a session of Irish dancing in which sets are danced. At the annual **Fleadh Cheoil Na hÉireann**, the distinction between set and céilí dancing is rigorously maintained, although the term 'fíor céilí' or 'real céilí' is used to distinguish dancing sessions exclusively devoted to céilí dancing from those which mix both types of dancing. See also **England** and **Scotland**.

Celtic Note   Record shop in Nassau Street, Dublin that specialises in traditional music and music by Irish artists. Owned by Senator Donie Cassidy, manager of **Foster and Allen**, it was opened in 1996 and has livened up the music shop scene in Dublin by holding free gigs in the shop itself, often featuring the latest traditional groups. Website: www.celticnote.com.

Celtic Rock   See **Fusions**.

Ceol   Periodical, subtitled 'A Journal of Irish Music', edited by **Breandán Breathnach** and **Nicholas Carolan**. It included articles in English and Irish on subjects relating to traditional music and song as well as reviews of books and recordings. Transcriptions of songs and tunes were also included. A total of 22 numbers in eight volumes were issued at irregular intervals between 1963 and 1986.

Ceolas   Set up in 1994, Ceolas – the name combines *ceol* (music) and *eolas* (knowledge) – is a website housing the largest online collection of information on Irish and Celtic music, with links to hundreds of related sites. Information is researched and sourced from official bodies, commercial interests and other individuals on the net. The developers have been careful to 'filter' commercially-supplied information, in order to avoid the bias and advertising hyperbole of many web services. The Ceolas site includes an overview of Celtic music, as well as information on artists (profiles, links and discographies); instruments; resources (books, magazines, mail order sources, etc.); tunes (several hundred traditional tunes in various formats, including software and tune indexes); and extensive live music and regional guides for Ireland, Europe and North America. Address: www.ceolas.org/ceolas.html.

Ceoltóir   The Irish word for 'musician' or 'singer', used as a working title for a two-year course run by the Senior College, Ballyfermot, Dublin which leads to a

Higher National Diploma in Professional Traditional Music Performance. The course aims to help young traditional musicians to make their way into professional employment and to provide a network of European venues for performers. It offers training in a wide range of areas, including instrumental and vocal tuition, composition, recording technology, computer sequencing, gig production, and the music industry in Ireland and Europe. Musicians are also taught to locate and arrange original source material, concentrating in the first year on Irish traditional music and in the second year on traditional music from around the world. The course director is **Paul McGrattan**. Patrick Daly (composer, sound engineer, producer) and harper Mary O'Donnell (music theory, traditional performing arts, traditional music from around the world) are regular teachers. **Niamh Parsons** (singing) and Paul Kelly (mandolin) have also contributed frequently to the vocal and instrumental classes, and guest contributors have included many prominent traditional musicians, such as accordionist **Brendan Begley** and banjo player **Gerry O'Connor**.

Ceoltóir started in 1996-7, initially as a one-year course, and in 1998 the CD *Triad: Three from Trad* was released, featuring three of the musicians who took part in the course: Eamonn **Galldubh** (uilleann pipes, whistles), Dave Munnelly (button accordion) and singer Tina Price. Over twenty places are available on the course each year and preference is given to people under twenty years of age who are unemployed. Ceoltóir has provided practical and creative assistance to many young musicians and encourages a progressive approach to traditional music. Contact: The Project Manager, Ceoltóir, Senior College, Ballyfermot, Dublin 10.

Ceoltóirí Chualann

Ceoltóirí Chualann Group formed by **Seán Ó Riada** after he was asked to provide music for the play *The Golden Gypsy* in the Abbey Theatre Festival in 1959. The original line-up for the play included Ó Riada (harpsichord, bodhrán), **Paddy Moloney** (uilleann pipes, tin whistle), **Seán Potts** (tin whistle), Éamonn de Buitléar (accordion), Sonny Brogan (accordion), **John Kelly** (fiddle) and **Vincent Broderick** (flute). **Michael Tubridy** replaced Broderick on flute when the group began rehearsals after the production closed; other musicians who joined at this stage were Ronnie McShane (bones) and Martin Fay (fiddle). **Seán Keane** (fiddle), Seán Ó Sé (vocals) and **Darach Ó Catháin** (vocals) joined later.

Ó Riada presented the group as a small orchestra, and his arrangements, in which solos and duets were interspersed with ensemble playing, were markedly different from those of **céilí band**s (in which everyone started and finished together). He also made use of harmonies and more subtle percussion instruments (bodhrán, bones) than the typical drums of the céilí bands. In addition to playing tunes from the standard traditional dance music repertoire, Ó Riada paid considerable attention to the neglected music of **Turlough O'Carolan**, as well as to **sean-nós singing**. It was, however, the overall sound and presentation of the group that won public and critical acclaim, providing a new vision of how traditional music could be performed.

During the early 1960s it was through radio programmes more than concert performances that Ceoltóirí Chualann's fame grew. The group did two series of radio programmes, *Reacaireacht an Riadaigh* and *Fleadh Cheoil an Raidió*. Their first album, *Reacaireacht an Riadaigh* (1962), took its title from the first radio series. The arrangement of the jig, 'An Long fé Lán-tSeol' ('Ships in Full Sail') on the album in many ways typifies the group's approach. It begins with solo flute, with bodhrán and tin whistle joining in before the first round of the tune is completed. The lead instruments are changed around as the tune progresses and there is one round of the tune in the middle with two tin whistles playing in harmony to bodhrán accompaniment. Most of the songs on the album are unaccompanied, and although Darach Ó Catháin sings on this first album, Seán Ó Sé took over on subsequent recordings.

Ó Riada's score for the film version of Synge's *The Playboy of the Western World*, performed by Ceoltóirí Chualann, was released in 1963. Further recordings of the group include *Ó Riada sa Gaiety* (1964, re-released 1988) and *Seán Ó Riada and Ceoltóirí Chualann* (1971), a live recording. Although the group did not formally disband until 1970, they didn't play together regularly after Ó Riada moved to West Cork in 1964.

With Ceoltóirí Chualann, Ó Riada applied the concepts for ensemble playing, so clearly articulated in his radio series *Our Musical Heritage* (1962), in which he denounced the céilí bands for their choice of instruments and the way they 'flog away all the time, with all the instruments going at once.' He sought to develop an approach in which variety, a keystone of traditional music, was of primary importance. He also gave careful consideration to instrumentation, seeing wind instruments (uilleann pipes, tin whistle, flute) and fiddles as central to the sound, with accordions filling out the sound where the whole group was playing. The bodhrán he viewed as more suitable than drum kit as a percussion instrument, because of its subtlety and its long history in traditional music. Ó Riada had little time for the soft, blurred sound produced by contemporary harp players and believed that the sound of the old Irish steel string harp, plucked with the finger-nails, could be better represented in modern times by the harpsichord. He saw no place at all for the piano, double bass, saxophone, guitar and banjo as they were used by céilí bands. These ideas were based on Ó Riada's belief that the céilí band approach was harmful to the spirit of traditional music.

Ceoltóirí Chualann's achievement at a time when traditional music was treated with contempt or indifference by most of the urban Irish population is best summed up by the poet Thomas Kinsella. Ó Riada 'identified a number of players who were masters in the tradition, grouped them together in a manner that had never been attempted before, got them to play in a way that astonished even themselves, and revealed their music to the country as a whole' (Kinsella's introduction to *Our Musical Heritage*, p. 9). Ó Riada himself described Ceoltóirí Chualann as 'the parent group' of the **Chieftains**, and it is this group that most closely resembles the 'parent' in style and sound today. Ó Riada's experimentation marked the beginning of a new era in traditional music, opening up infinite possibilities for new approaches subsequently explored by groups such as **Horslips**, **Planxty** and the **Bothy Band**, each in its own unique way.

Ceoltóirí Laighean Group formed by Éamonn de Buitléar (accordion) after the death of **Seán Ó Riada** in 1971. De Buitléar had been a member of Ó Riada's **Ceoltóirí Chualann** and, with many of that group's members then performing with the **Chieftains**, he decided to form a new group when Ó Riada died. Another former member of Ceoltóirí Chualann, **John Kelly** (fiddle), joined Ceoltóirí Laigheann. Other members included **Paddy Glackin** (fiddle), **Paddy O'Brien** of Offaly (accordion), **Mary Bergin** (whistle) and **James** (son of John) **Kelly** (fiddle). Sean-nós singer **Diarmuid Ó Súilleabháin** sang with the group, which lasted into the 1980s and released two albums, *An Bothár Cam/The Crooked Road* (1973) and *The Star of Munster* (1975). They had considerable success and toured France and Germany.

Chantfable Term used by **Hugh Shields** (lecturer in French at Trinity College, Dublin) to describe a narrative consisting of a combination of recited prose and verse, closely associated with many songs in Irish. Some of these chantfables (or 'cantfables') are spoken folk tales in which ballad verses are sung for embellishment; others provide commentaries on songs, perhaps explaining the meaning or background to a song. Shields argues convincingly that the hybrid chantfable was the means by which the Irish adapted the unfamiliar narrative form of the **ballad** to native practices. Although the ballad form did not have a strong influence on songs in Irish, many of the tales found in imported ballads became chantfables or ordinary prose folk-tales. Sean-nós singer **Seosamh Ó Héanaí** recorded two chantfables.

Chapbook A small book of ballads, generally of eight pages, which was sold by chapmen or hawkers. Chapbooks became popular in Ireland from around the middle of the 18th century when they contained many 'old ballads' (see **Ballad**) or **Child ballads**. From that time and into the 19th century there was a tradition of 'Robin Hood' ballads printed in chapbooks, with a comprehensive collection published under the title *The English Archer* in three volumes between 1744 and 1796. Chapbooks and **ballad sheets** played an important role in spreading the 'new ballads' or **come-all-ye**'s during the 19th century. Chapbooks survive from many cities and towns in Ireland and remained popular until the 1840s. They rarely included songs in Irish. James Boswell collected many early chapbooks and his collection is today kept in Harvard University. See also **Ballad Sheet**; **Broadside**; **Ballads**; **Garland**.

Cherish the Ladies All-female Irish-American group, based in New York, which released its first album, *Cherish the Ladies (Irish Women Musicians)* in 1985. Their name derives from the title of a well-known traditional jig. They combine songs and airs with hard driving dance tunes, and step dancers were a regular part of their shows and recordings long before the emergence of *Riverdance*. Winnie Horan (fiddler and dancer), now with **Solus**, was with the group for some time. The line-up of musicians and dancers has changed considerably over the years. Founder-members **Joanie Madden** (whistle, flute, backing vocals) and Mary

Coogan (guitar, mandolin, banjo) are still central to the group's success, and the 2001 line-up included Donna Long (keyboards, fiddle, harmony vocals), Mary Rafferty (button accordion, concertina, low whistle, flute), Liz Knowles (fiddle) and Deirdre Connolly (lead vocals, whistle, flute). Former members include Winnie Horan (fiddle and dancer), who left to join **Solas**, Maureen Doherty-Mahon (button accordion, whistle) and Siobhan Egan (fiddle, bodhrán). Cathy Ryan (lead vocals) and **Aoife Clancy** (lead vocals, guitar, bodhrán) are now highly successful as solo artists after spells with Cherish the Ladies. The group's most recent albums are *The*

Back Door (1992), *Out and About* (1993), *New Day Dawning* (1996), *Threads of Time* (1998, which includes eight tunes composed by members of the group), *One and All* (1998, a compilation), *Cherish the Ladies at Home* (1999) and *The Girls Won't Leave the Boys Alone* (2001). The last includes guest appearances by singers Liam Clancy, Brian Kennedy and **Luka Bloom**, among others. **Pete Seeger** also guests on the album, playing banjo. Among those who have danced with the group are Cara Butler (a sister of Jean), Eileen Golden and Donny Golden. In 2003 the line-up still included Madden,

Cherish the Ladies
(Clockwise from left: Mary Coogan, Joanie Madden, Mirella Murray, Heidi Talbot, Roisin Dillon)

Long and Coogan along with Marie Reilly (fiddle, whistle) and Heidi Talbot (lead vocals, bodhrán). Website: www.cherishtheladies.com.

Chieftains, The Internationally renowned group (formed in 1962) who have had phenomenal success in their recordings, performances and collaborations with musicians from different musical backgrounds, as well as in composing and performing film scores. The core members of the original Chieftains were also members of **Seán Ó Riada**'s groundbreaking **Ceoltóirí Chualann** and, like the latter, they explored new approaches to the arrangement and presentation of Irish traditional music. Unlike Ceoltóirí Chualann, however, **sean-nós singing** has not featured as a major element in the Chieftains' repertoire, which consists largely of instrumental music with the occasional song. The line-up for their first album, *The Chieftains*

(1963) was: Dubliners **Paddy Moloney** (uilleann pipes, tin whistle), **Seán Potts** (tin whistle), and Martin Fay (fiddle); **Michael Tubridy** (flute, tin whistle, concertina) from Clare; and Davy Fallon (bodhrán) from Westmeath. In the years immediately after the first album, the Chieftains began to develop something of a cult status among other musicians, including Mick Jagger and members of the Rolling Stones. John Peel, the BBC Radio 1 disc jockey, started to play *The Chieftains* on his show and the English rock/pop magazine *Melody Maker* did a profile of the group. It was rare at the time for the British music media to take such interest in Irish traditional music.

By the time *Chieftains 2* (1969) was made, Davy Fallon had been replaced by Peadar Mercier on bodhrán and **Seán Keane** had also joined. The group was still part-time when it recorded *Chieftains 3* (1971) and *Chieftains 4* (1974), on which

The Chieftains today

Derek Bell (harp) appeared for the first time. With an ever-growing popularity, on St. Patrick's Day, 1975 the group played to a capacity crowd of 6,000 at the Royal Albert Hall in London. The success of the concert, organised by the American pro-moter Jo Lustig, convinced the group to become full-time professionals. Their next album, *Chieftains 5*, opened with Derek Bell playing, for the first time, a reconstruction of a medieval Irish **timpán**. The album also included a tune from **Brittany**, making them one of the first Irish groups to record traditional Breton music.

The Chieftains' success continued to grow, at home and internationally. They recorded the first of many film scores for Stanley Kubrick's *Barry Lyndon* (soundtrack released 1976), for which they won an Oscar. **Kevin Conneff** (bodhrán, vocals) replaced Peadar Mercier in 1976 and recorded the concept album *Bonaparte's Retreat* (1976) with the group (see **Napoleon**). Dolores Keane (see **Keane Family**), only seventeen at the time, sang on the album, and a chorus (led by Moloney) was inserted into the set of Kerry slides 'Around the House and Mind the Dresser'. Singing and lilting now formed a regular, if relatively small, part of the group's repertoire. Further changes in line-up took place in 1979, when Seán Potts and Michael Tubridy left to be replaced by **Matt Molloy** (flute and tin whistle). The line-up of Maloney, Keane, Fay, Bell, Conneff and Molloy remained unchanged from 1979 until Derek Bell's death in 2002.

The Chieftains' work since 1979 has been as diverse as it is voluminous. They have done numerous film scores, including *Treasure Island, Tristan and Isolde, The Year of the French* and *Far and Away*. They have released two albums of selections from their film music, *Reel Music: The Film Scores* (1991) and *Film Cuts* (1995) and recorded albums with musicians from China (1985), Brittany (1987) and **Galicia** (1997). Collaborations with classical musicians include *Over the Sea to Skye: James Galway and the Chieftains* (1990) and there have been numerous collaborations with rock artists. *Irish Heartbeat: Van Morrison and the Chieftains* (1988) featured Van Morrison singing his own unique versions of classic Irish songs such as 'Star of the County Down', 'She Moved Through the Fair', 'My Lagan Love' and others. *The Bells of Dublin* (1991), a Christmas album, featured performances by Elvis Costello, Jackson Browne, Rickie Lee Jones and other international artists. Nineteen ninety-two saw the release of both *An Irish Evening: Live at the Grand Opera House, Belfast, with Roger Daltrey and Nanci Griffith* and *Another Country*, which featured Don Williams, Willie Nelson, EmmyLou Harris, Ricky Scaggs and other Nashville stars. Both albums won Grammy Awards in 1993. On *The Long Black Veil* (1994) a host of famous rock stars performed mostly Irish songs with the Chieftains, including Sting ('Mo Ghile Mear'), Sinead O'Connor ('The Foggy Dew' and 'She Moved Through the Fair'), Mark Knopfler ('The Lily of the West'), Ry Cooder ('Coast of Malabar' and 'The Dunmore Lassies'), Tom Jones ('The Tennessee Waltz'), Mick Jagger ('The Long Black Veil') and the Rolling Stones ('The Rocky Road to Dublin'). Marianne Faithfull, who also appeared on *The Bells of Dublin*, sang 'Love Is Teasin''. The version of 'Have I Told You Lately that I Love You', with Van Morrison, won a Grammy Award in 1996 for 'Best Pop Collaboration with Vocals'. It was the fourth Grammy for the Chieftains (they had won a third in 1994 for *The Celtic Harp*), and they were awarded a fifth in 1997 when *Santiago*, their Galician collaboration album, won 'Best World Music CD'. They returned to collaboration in 2002 with *Down the Old Plank Road: The Nashville Sessions*, which includes tracks with Lyle Lovett, Alison Kraus, Ricky Scaggs and others. This was followed by *Further down the Old Plank Road* (2003).

In addition to these collaborations, the Chieftains have continued to produce more strictly traditional albums and released eight videos between 1982 and 1995. With *Tears of Stone* (1999) the group returned to international collaboration, this time with female artists, including Joni Mitchell (singing her own 'The Magdalene Laundries'), Akiko Yano ('Sake in the Jar'), Sinead O'Connor ('The Factory Girls') and others singing Irish songs or songs related to Ireland. On it Brenda Fricker reads the W. B. Yeats poem 'Never Give All the Heart' with musical backing from the Chieftains and vocal backing from **Anúna**. *Water from the Well* (2000) saw a return to the group's roots in traditional music and *The Wide World Over: A 40-Year Celebration* (2002) marked an extraordinary four decades in the music business.

The Chieftains: The Authorised Biography (London, 1997), by the English music journalist John Glatt, tells the story of the group's rise to the status of international superstars. It reveals the tensions that success brought, providing an interesting insight into the lives of the various members of the group as individuals and their different reactions to the demands of show business at the highest level. The Chieftains have had their critics, but they have proved remarkably resilient for four decades. They have brought Irish traditional music to people all over the world. Their collaborations with other artists have brought them an even wider audience, as well as commercial success. Their more traditional albums of recent years, however, have shown that they remain true to their musical roots. Despite the experiments with rock and pop artists, much of their own music remains remarkably close in style and spirit to their earliest work. Even the sound and arrangement style of Ceoltóirí Chualann still echoes in their more traditional albums of the last two decades. Website: www.thechieftains.com.

Child Ballads Traditional ballads of English and Scottish origin which are named after their literary editor Francis James Child (1825-1896). His *English and Scottish Popular Ballads* (1882-1898) contained 305 songs, which are usually referred to by the numbers that Child gave them. Although the term 'Child ballads' is widely used by singers and commentators, **Hugh Shields** refers to them as 'old ballads' (see **Ballad**). A number of these ballads were brought over to Ireland (in many cases before Child published them), and versions of them, passed on orally, are still sung today.

   Oliver Goldsmith (1728-1774) provides one of the earliest references to ballads being sung in Ireland when he describes a childhood memory of a dairy-maid singing him to tears with 'Johnny Armstrong's Last Good Night' (Child 169) and 'The Cruelty of Barbara Allen' (Child 84). 'Barbara Allen' was and remains the most popular Child ballad in Ireland, Britain and the **US**. Versions of a number of other old ballads are known to have been sung in Ireland in the 18th and 19th centuries. Among those still sung today and available on commercial recordings are: 'The Creel' (Child 281), sung by **Tríona Ní Dhomhnaill** on *The Bothy Band* (1975); 'The Two Sisters' (Child 10), sung by **Máire Ní Bhraonáin** with **Clannad** on *Dúlaman* (1976); 'The Jolly Beggarman' (Child 279), sung by **Andy Irvine** with **Planxty** on *Planxty* (1972); 'The Raggle Taggle Gypsy' (Child 200), sung by **Christy Moore** on *Prosperous* (1971) and also on Planxty's *The Well Below the Valley* (1973). These versions of the songs were all passed on orally from singer to singer rather than being learned from Child's collection, and some of them have considerable melodic or lyrical differences to the Child versions.

   Christy Moore has also recorded two long ballads which are exceptional for their old-world atmosphere and the drama of the stories they relate: 'Little Musgrave' (Child 81, with the title 'Little Musgrave and Lady Barnard'), which appears on *Christy Moore* (1976), Planxty's *The Woman I Loved So Well* (1980), *Planxty Live, 2004*; and 'Lord Baker' (Child 53 as 'Lord Bateman'), which appears on Planxty's *Words and Music* (1982). Both songs provide interesting examples of how old ballads can be adapted in the modern age. Moore added some lyrics of his own to an old version of 'Little Musgrave' and put them together with a melody from the singing of Nick Jones. Moore learned 'Lord Baker' from the traditional singer John Reilly of Boyle, Co. Roscommon (see **Travellers**), although he rewrote certain verses that didn't make sense in Reilly's version. This is a good example of an English song with a long history that seems to have survived better in the Irish oral tradition than it did in the English. **Sam Henry** published a version of it in 1932 called 'Lord Beichan', which he collected from a 90-year-old woman in the Bushmills district. Although his version has 13 stanzas, Henry noted that in a radio broadcast to celebrate the coming-of-age of the **English Folk Song and Dance Society** (10 December 1932), a traditional singer sang 'Lord Bateman' (an English version of 'Lord Beichan') but the air was different and only five stanzas were sung. Christy Moore's 'Lord Baker' has eighteen stanzas. Henry also noted that, in England, the song is linked with Gilbert, son of Thomas Beckett, the Archbishop of Canterbury who was murdered at his cathedral in 1170 by knights acting for King Henry II. The song is sometimes called 'Young Bekie' (thought to be a form of Beckett) and Gilbert was apparently imprisoned by a Saracen Prince Admiraud, just as Lord Baker/Lord Beichen is imprisoned by a Turk. The song is also known under other titles, some with different versions or corruptions of the name 'Becihen' or 'Bateman'. Henry describes it as a variant of a ballad well known throughout Western Europe.

Although the number of Child ballads/old ballads which are sung in Ireland today is small compared to the number of 'new ballads' (see **Ballad**), those which do survive provide important evidence of English and Scottish influence on the development of ballad singing in Ireland. See also **England**; **Scotland**.

Cinnamond, Robert (1884-1968)   Singer from Aghadealgan, near Lough Neagh, Co. Antrim. Cinnamond's repertoire had a remarkable number of old traditional songs, especially versions of **Child ballads**. He sang a song called 'I'm in Deep Love with My Love' which was a version of the traditional song on which **Padraig Colum** based his famous lyrics 'She Moved Through the Fair'. Cinnamond also sang a version of 'You Rambling Boys of Pleasure', the traditional song of which **W. B. Yeats** wrote his own version, 'Down by the Sally Gardens'. The singer was renowned for his high-pitched singing style, and was recorded by the **BBC** during the early 1950s. An album of his singing, *You Rambling Boys of Pleasure*, was released in 1975. **Ciaran Carson** wrote of the album: 'Those wishing to find some antecedent for the "high lonesome" singing of the **Appalachians** could well use this record as a text' (*Irish Traditional Music*, p. 71).

Cittern (*siotaran*)   A stringed instrument which traces its history back to the Kithare of Ancient Greece. In England up to the early 19th century a form of cittern called the 'English Guitar' was played. It had ten strings, with two single bass strings (tuned c-e′) and four pairs (tuned g-c-e-g′). The instrument has been revived recently by the instrument-maker Stefan Sobell of Northumberland. He makes them with four or five courses of double strings and the Irish **bouzouki** is very similar in shape to these citterns. Indeed **Andy Irvine** has worked with Sobell on the design of bouzoukis. See also **Blarge**.

Claddagh Records   Company founded in 1959 by Garech Browne to record Irish and Scottish traditional players and singers, as well as some spoken arts. Its first album was **Leo Rowsome**'s, *Rí na bPíobairí (King of the Pipers)* (1959). *The Chieftains* (1963) was the second Claddagh album, and the first of many that the group made with Claddagh. This was followed by *Almost Everything* (1964), a recording of Patrick Kavanagh reading his poetry and talking about his life. **Paddy Moloney** worked as Managing Director of the company in its early years, and many individual members of the **Chieftains** released solo albums on the label. Claddagh also released recordings by **Tommy Potts**, **Willie Clancy**, **Skylark**, the mainly Scottish group the Whistlebinkies and many others. It played an important role in preserving and publicising traditional music and song at a time when the commercial side of traditional music was under-developed. The company opened a shop at 2 Cecilia Street, Dublin 2 in 1984 where practically every Irish traditional album currently available is stocked. It also carries a substantial stock of world music and runs a mail order service. On the recording side, one of Claddagh's most recent discoveries is the group **Cran**. Website: www.claddaghrecords.com. See also **Gael-Linn**.

Clancy, Aoife (b.1966) Singer and guitarist from Carrick-on-Suir, Co. Tipperary, daughter of Bobby Clancy (see **Clancy Brothers and Tommy Makem**) who has established herself as one of the finest Irish singers on the **US** circuit. Her father gave her a guitar at the age of ten and by the age of fourteen she was performing with him at sessions in local pubs. Her mother, Máire Mooney, is from the **Gaeltacht** area of Ring in Co. Waterford where her family has run a pub for seven generations. Mooney's pub has been famous for traditional music since the 1960s. Here Aoife developed a love of traditional music and song from an early age, participating in sessions with her father, her uncle, Liam Clancy and many other musicians. She studied drama at the Gaiety School of Acting but later started to tour as a singer, sharing stages with **Christy Moore** and the **Furey Brothers** in Australia and performing in the US and the Caribbean with the Clancy Brothers. By the mid-1990s she was settled in the US and her first solo album, *It's About Time* (1994), included traditional favourites such as 'Factory Girl', 'Go Lassie Go' and 'Mrs. McGrath'. She joined **Cherish the Ladies** in 1995 and made several albums with them between 1995 and 1999. Her second solo album, *Soldiers and Dreams* (1996), combined contemporary and more traditional songs. Among the latter are fine renditions of 'High Germany', 'You Rambling Boys of Pleasure' and 'The Gartan Mother's Lullaby'. *Silvery Moon* (2002) features musicians from **Solas** and **Mary Black**'s band and has more contemporary songs than her previous albums. There is also a duet with her father, 'Kisses Sweeter than Wine'. Aoife and her brother Finbarr (guitar, flute, vocals) made two albums with their father, *The Quiet Land* (1998) and *Make Me A Cup* (2000). On the latter album she sings a fine version of **W. B. Yeats**' poem 'The Lake Isle of Inishfree' for which she herself wrote music. A naturally gifted singer, she has a warm and expressive voice. Website: www.aoifeclancy.com.

Clancy Brothers and Tommy Makem, The A group of ballad singers who rose to prominence during the 1960s in the **US** and had a profound influence on folk song and traditional music on both sides of the Atlantic. Economic circumstances in Ireland caused Tom (1923-1990) and Paddy (1922-1998) Clancy, brothers from Carrick-on-Suir, Co. Tipperary, to emigrate in 1947. After spending some time in Canada, they eventually settled in New York, where they were involved in theatre. From 1953 they staged concerts to support their theatre activities, but were so successful at singing that they continued with it. Their brother, Bobby (1927-2002), was in the original Clancy Brothers line-up but returned to Ireland before their first recording.

For their first album, *Irish Songs of Rebellion*, recorded in New York in 1956, Tom and Paddy were joined by their younger brother Liam and Tommy Makem (b. 1932) from Keady, Co. Armagh (see **Makem, Sarah**). The Clancys and Makem had been brought together initially through the work of the American song collector, Diane Hamilton (Guggenheim). Hamilton had also brought Liam Clancy (b. 1935) to the US to help him to pursue a career in acting. She then founded and funded the recording company Tradition Records, which released *Irish Songs of Rebellion* and served as a launching pad for the musical careers of the Clancy Brothers and Tommy Makem. All four members of the group sang, often in harmony, with Paddy playing harmonica and Tommy Makem on tin whistle. The first album also had accompaniment on guitar (Jack Keenan) and Irish harp (Jack Melady). On later albums Liam played guitar and Tommy Makem, strongly influenced by the American folk singer/banjo-player **Pete Seeger**, played five-string banjo. The group's approach was influenced by American folk music, particularly the Weavers (of whom Seeger was a member). Most of their repertoire was Irish and the group was popular with American audiences during a period when there was a considerable revival of interest in folk music generally. They also popularised some songs by the radical British songwriter **Ewan MacColl**, most notably 'The Shoals of Herring', which they recorded on their album *The Boys Won't Leave the Girls Alone* (1962).

The real turning point for the Clancy Brothers and Tommy Makem came in 1961 when they appeared on 'The Ed Sullivan Show'. This was one of the most popular television shows in the US at the time, broadcast live on Saturday nights and viewed every week by up to 80 million people. The group played on the occasion of their appearance for a full eighteen minutes. Their fame grew after this and a professional career in music, which lasted over a quarter of a century, was assured. Aran sweaters became a trademark of the group, and throughout the 1960s they released numerous albums and played to huge audiences in both Ireland and the US. What is often referred to as the **Ballad Boom** began as a result, with a plethora of 'Clancy-style' groups springing up in Ireland and America. Songs made famous by the Clancys, such as 'I'll Tell My Ma', 'The Holy Ground', 'The Wild Colonial Boy' and 'The Old Woman from Wexford', were sung by numerous groups whose imitations of the Clancys were often inferior.

In the 1970s Tommy Makem went his own way and made two solo albums before getting together with Liam Clancy to form a highly successful duo. They made a number of albums together, one of the most famous being *The Makem and Clancy Concert*, recorded at the Gaiety Theatre, Dublin in July 1977. It featured some old standards from the 1960s such as 'O'Donnell Abu', as well as new songs, poetry and a unique story, told with musical backing and some singing, called 'Peter Kagan and the Wind'. Meanwhile Tom and Paddy Clancy re-formed The Original Clancy Brothers with their brother Bobby (vocals, guitar, five-string banjo, bodhrán and harmonica) and their nephew **Robbie O'Connell**.

The Clancy Brothers & Tommy Makem, 1964
(photo: Don Hunstein)

Bobby performed and recorded in the 1960s with his sister Peg and was a great solo performer, a reciter of poetry as well as a fine singer, lilter (see **Lilting**) and multi-instrumentalist. He made numerous albums with his brothers, including three which featured both the Clancy and the **Furey Brothers**, one of them a Christmas album. Bobby also recorded several solo albums. His *Make Me a Cup* (2000) is a fine collection of songs, humorous verses and poetry, including nine tracks of songs or poems by **W. B. Yeats**. He is joined on the album by his son Finbarr (flute, guitar, vocals) and his daughter **Aoife Clancy** (vocals, guitar).

Liam Clancy is still touring and making albums with Robbie O'Connell and his son Dónal (see **Solas**), who plays guitar, mandola, cittern, bouzouki, five-string banjo and whistle. In 1997 they appeared on the official 1798 commemorative album *Who Fears to Speak* and also released *Clancy, O'Connell and Clancy*. In 1998 they recorded (with Warp Four) *The Wild and Wasteful Ocean*, a collection of sea shanties and tunes associated with the sea. Liam also recorded with **Cherish the Ladies** in 2001. The first part of his autobiography, *The Mountain of the Women: Memoirs of an Irish Troubadour* (New York, 2002), covers his childhood and early adult years and a companion five-CD set has many reworked Clancy Brothers tunes and songs. Tommy Makem has also continued to perform and record (including one spoken word collection), and his sons Connor, Rory and Shane perform regularly in the US as The Makem Brothers.

There can be no doubt that the Clancy Brothers and Tommy Makem played an important role in popularising Irish music. They were the first Irish group of folk or traditional musicians to achieve international recognition and have influenced many groups since the 1960s. Such contemporary folk/rock artists as Bob Dylan, who adapted some of their songs, have acknowledged their influence. Among the many awards which various members of the group have received are Honorary Doctorates in Letters from the **University of Limerick** for Liam Clancy and Tommy Makem (December 2001). The university recognised the enormous role both have played in transforming Irish music, particularly song, and bringing Irish culture generally to a wide international audience. See also **Scotland**; **Song, General**.

Clancy, Willie (1918-1973) Famous for his singing, story-telling and playing the whistle, the flute and, above all, the uilleann pipes. He was born in Miltown Malbay, Co. Clare and began to learn the whistle at the age of five. His father, Gilbert, provided Willie with a direct link to the legendary 19th-century Clare piper **Garret Barry**. Willie also knew the famous travelling piper **Johnny Doran** and his brother, Felix. Felix himself played the pipes and helped Clancy to obtain a practice set in

1938. In 1947, Clancy won the uilleann pipes competition in the **Oireachtas**. In the 1930s and 40s his playing was strongly influenced by the legato or open-fingering style of Johnny Doran, as well as the West Clare fiddler Scully Casey, father of **Bobby Casey**. In the 1950s he left Miltown Malbay, spending some time in Dublin before moving on to London. In Dublin he met pipers who favoured the staccato or close-fingering style, including **Séamus Ennis**, John Potts (see **Potts, Seán**) and Tommy Reck. Clancy's blending of their techniques with his own legato playing produced a unique new style. During the 1950s, he worked as a carpenter in London, which had a vibrant Irish music scene at the time. In 1957 his father died and he returned to

Willie Clancy

Miltown Malbay, where he remained until his own death in 1973. By the 1960s,

Clancy's style was recognised and admired by musicians throughout Ireland. Among these were **Liam O'Flynn** and Pat Mitchell, who subsequently published *The Dance Music of Willie Clancy* (Mercier Press, 1976), a collection of tunes transcribed as they were played by Clancy, with a detailed account of the piper, his style and his music. In the 1950s he recorded several 78s with **Gael Linn** and after his death Claddagh Records released *The Piping of Willie Clancy, Vol. 1* (1980) and *Vol. 2* (1983). Clancy was undoubtedly one of the greatest pipers of this century, and it is a fitting tribute to him that the largest traditional music summer school in Ireland is held every year in his honour. See **Willie Clancy Summer School**.

Clannad Group from Gweedore in the Donegal **Gaeltacht**. Founded in 1971, they recorded the first of many albums in 1973 after winning the Letterkenny Folk Festival in 1970. The original line-up was **Máire Ní Bhraonáin** (harp, vocals), her bothers Pól (flute, bongos, guitar, piano, vocals) and Cíarán (double bass, guitar, piano, vocals) and their uncles Noel Ó Dúgáin (lead guitar, vocals) and Pádraig Ó Dúgáin (guitar, mandola, vocals). The group's name is an abbreviated form of 'Clann as Dobhair', the Irish for 'the family from Dobhair/Gweedore'. They originally established their reputation with unusual arrangements of songs (many sung in Irish) and instrumental pieces centred around the harp and flute. Their most famous piece in the early years was a traditional drinking song called 'Níl Sé'n Lá' which the group extended and developed, with long improvisations on flute, guitar, double bass and vocals. Their approach was decidedly original, and they quickly attracted a large following both in Ireland and abroad. Their 1982 album *Fuaim* led to a commission to write the theme music for the television series 'Harry's Game', which was subsequently released as a single. It was the first song in Irish to become a major hit in the British pop charts, reaching No. 5. In 1984 they released *Legend*, an album of music composed for the TV series *Robin of Sherwood*. The ethereal quality of much of their soundtrack material, particularly its rich vocals successfully blended with synthesiser, won the group many new admirers. They had always been experimental in their arrangements and use of instruments, but they were now composing more of their own material than previously. Of the ten tracks on their 1985 album, *Macalla*, only one is traditional and many of the songs are better classified as pop. The hit single, 'In a Lifetime', on which Bono of U2 shares the lead vocals with Máire, is included on this album.

Clannad have recorded a wide variety of material since 1973. Earlier albums such as *Dúlamán* (1976) and *Clannad in Concert* (1978), featuring 'Níl sé'n Lá', are predominantly traditional and acoustic, while later albums, including *Sirius* (1987), are essentially pop/rock. In many ways the group defy classification. Some of their material successfully combines elements of traditional singing with a more modern sound, as on albums such as *Magical Ring* (1983), which includes 'Harry's Game', and *Anam* (1990). Pól left the group in 1990 to pursue a solo career and has recorded and produced with Peter Gabriel. The other four original members continued for some time as Clannad, which had another family member, **Enya**, from 1979 to 1982. They have had many guest members, but saxophonist Mel Gibson

Clannad, 1979 (courtesy of Tara Music)

and keyboard player Ian Parker have been with them since the late 1980s. In 1998 they released *Landmarks*, an album marking a quarter century of recording. *The Clannad Anthology* (2002) is a two-CD retrospective with 34 tracks taken from fourteen albums released between 1973 and 1998.

Clannad have captured the imagination of a huge international audience with their unique sound. The Irish language has always featured prominently, even in their own compositions, and their contribution to Irish music has been highly original and imaginative. Máire continues to pursue a highly successful career with her own group. Website:. www.clannad.ie. See also **Newgrange**.

Clarke, Eddie (1945-2004) Harmonica player born in Virginia, Co. Cavan who started to play **harmonica** while still at school in the 1950s. He came to prominence in the late 1960s and early 70s, when he played in many sessions around Dublin and developed his technique through contacts with such players as Seán Walsh and Paddy Bán Ó Broin. Like Paddy Bán, he plays the chromatic as opposed to the tremolo harmonica, which is more commonly used by traditional players. He generally plays with the slider button in, but can get semitones and a variety of ornaments and passing notes by releasing the slider. As a result of playing with the slider in,

Clarke plays in keys like A♭, E♭, A♭ minor and E♭ minor, unusual for traditional music. He recorded the album *Sailing into Walpole's Marsh* in the late 1970s with Maeve Donnelly (fiddle) and Seán Corcoran (bouzouki), playing 'The Morning Star' as a harmonica solo. With Clare fiddler Joe Ryan he won the **Oireachtas** duet competition twice in the 1970s and recorded the album *Crossroads* (1981). The album consists of a selection of traditional tunes, including an old time waltz, most of which are played as duets. Clarke does play one solo on the album, 'Johnny Leary's Polkas', displaying his great talent for playing highly ornamented dance tunes at speed on the chromatic harmonica. In his heyday Clarke was an exceptional talent among Irish harmonica players, vamping and displaying a mastery of variation in his playing. His style has influenced a number of other players of traditional music on the chromatic harmonica, most notably Joel Bernstein and **Mick Kinsella**.

Clavinet   Electronic version of a clavichord, manufactured by Hohner and often played by **Tríona Ní Dhomhnaill**. See also **Keyboard Instruments**.

Clifford, Julia (1914-1997)   Fiddler from **Sliabh Luachra**. Her father, **Bill Murphy** and brother, **Denis Murphy** are also renowned as fiddlers. In 1952 she recorded what later became the album *Kerry Fiddles, Vol. I* (LP 1977, CD 1993) with **Pádraig O'Keeffe** and her brother, Denis. *The Star of Munster Trio* (1977) features Julia with her husband, John (accordion) and son, Billy (flute). She recorded *The Star Above the Garter* (1969) with Denis Murphy and *Ceol as Sliabh Luachra* (1982) with her son Billy, who has made his own solo album, *Billy Clifford* (1989). Julia spent much of her life in Britain and died in Norfolk, England in her eighties. A number of Sliabh Luachra tunes are named after the Cliffords. See also **Topic Records**.

Cló Iar-Chonnachta   Publishing and recording company based at Indreabhán in the **Gaeltacht** of Connemara, Co. Galway. The company was founded in 1985 by the writer Micheál Ó Conghaile and is a patron of Irish language and Gaeltacht culture. Most of the books they publish are in the Irish language and include poetry, short stories, novels, songs, children's books and history books. Their original aim with the release of music recordings was to concentrate on the traditional music of Connemara, especially **sean-nós singing**. While this remains a priority, the company now also produces traditional music and sean-nós singing from all over Ireland as well as Cajun, country and Cape Breton (see **Nova Scotia**) music. Among the many albums of Connemara sean-nós singing released by Cló Iar-Chonnachta is a double-CD of **Seosamh Ó Héanaí**, a co-production with the English company **Topic Records**. In 2002 Cló Iar-Chonnachta published a book by **Lillis Ó Laoire** on the song, music and dance of Tory Island, Co. Donegal, with a companion CD. These releases and publications have been produced to the highest of standards and have done much to raise the profile and availability of sean-nós singing material. Their releases of traditional instrumental music have been equally well produced, usually with detailed background information on the musicians and tunes. Among the considerable number of instrumental music releases are two fine albums by flute players **Marcas Ó Murchú** and **Catherine McEvoy**. Website: www.cic.ie.

Clog Dancing Although the term 'clog dancing' usually refers to an English style of dancing, it has also been used by observers to describe a regional style of Irish **step dancing** that is found in the northern part of the island. The distinguishing characteristic of this style is the use of a persistent drumming action on one foot, achieved by executing a constant heel-and-toe movement on that foot, while the other performs the more elaborate features of a particular step. It gives the dance a significant percussive element and led observers in the early 20th century to compare this style with English clog dancing, in which a similar heel-and-toe movement is used. Such regional varieties of dance (especially given the comparison to English dance) did not find favour with **Conradh na Gaeilge** in their pursuit of purely Irish dances. Despite this, 'clog dancing' survived for many decades in northern counties such as Donegal, Cavan, Fermanagh, Leitrim and Tyrone, although there are few dancers who still perform in this style today.

Coimisiún Bhéaloideas Éireann See **Irish Folklore Commission**.

Coleman, Michael (1891-1945) Legendary fiddler from Co. Sligo who emigrated to the **US** in 1914. Coleman was based there for much of his career but his influence filtered back to Ireland through his recordings. Made in the 1920s and 30s, these recordings have exerted an enormous influence on traditional Irish music right down to the present day. Coleman had a particular talent for improvisational variation and arrangement. Many of his arrangements and repertoire have come to be considered as 'standard', and the imitation of his essentially Sligo style is still widespread. Most of his recorded material used a style of **piano** accompaniment fashionable in Coleman's day but unpleasant to the ears of many modern musicians and listeners. He is buried in St. Raymond's cemetery in the Bronx, New York, just yards away from **James Morrison,** another Sligo fiddler who made a big name for himself in the US in the 1920s and 30s. A double CD of Coleman's recordings is now available, remastered by **Harry Bradshaw**. Titled *Michael Coleman 1891-1945*, it was first released on cassette in 1991. The Coleman Traditional Festival takes place on the first weekend in September in Gurteen, Co. Sligo, where there is also a Coleman Heritage Centre. See also **McGann, Andy**.

Colum, Padraig (1881-1972) Poet, playwright and collector of folklore and song. Born in Longford, reared in Cavan, he later moved to Dublin. His lyrics to 'She Moved Through the Fair', based on an old folk song, were written when he was about 30 years old and have since become the standard version. Colum moved to the **US** in 1914, where he lectured in comparative literature. He also studied the folklore of Hawaii and Ireland, producing the first edition of *A Treasury of Irish Folklore* (New York) in 1954. The book contained a section of ballads and songs in addition to legends and other folk material. Colum died in Enfield, Connecticut and is buried in Sutton, Co. Dublin. See also **Butcher, Eddie**.

Come-All-Ye Term used by the historian of Irish song **Hugh Shields** for the 'new' type of ballad written in Ireland in the English language from the 18th or possibly even 17th century on. The term is derived from the fact that many of these songs open with the words 'Come all ye...' The development of the come-all-ye is discussed in more detail under **Ballad**.

Comhaltas Ceoltóirí Éireann (CCÉ) Organisation founded in 1951 to promote and preserve the integrity of Irish traditional music, dance and song. It was founded when members of the old **Dublin Pipers' Club** travelled to Mullingar in January 1951 to help set up a pipers' club there. Instead they decided to set up an organisation that would embrace all Irish traditional instruments, initially calling it Cumann Ceoltóirí Éireann, which became Comhaltas Ceoltóirí Éireann ('Musicians Organisation of Ireland') in 1952. The original group included Cáit Bean Uí Mhuineacháin, Paddy McElvanny, Jim Seery, Eamon Ó Muineacháin, **Leo Rowsome** and his brother Tom. **Fleadh Cheoil Na hÉireann** was held that year for the first time, and membership of Comhaltas boomed in the 1950s and 60s. Its organisational structures are modelled on those of the Gaelic Athletic Association (GAA) with local branches, county and provincial boards and a national *ard-chómhairle* or 'supreme council'. Since 1968 the *ard-stiúrthóir* or director of the organisation has been Labhrás Ó Murchú, now also a Fianna Fáil senator.

CCÉ's approximately 400 branches (including 80 in the **US**, **Australia**, Britain, Europe and Japan) hold regular music classes, sessions, concerts, *céilithe*, summer schools, festivals and competitions. CCÉ also organises concert tours, mainly to the US, and brings out a quarterly magazine called *Treoir*. A number of its branches also have substantial archives of audio and video material. The organisation runs a teacher's diploma course for teachers of traditional instruments and graded exams in traditional music. It has 35,000 registered members (with a family counting as a single registration); its headquarters are in Monkstown, Co. Dublin.

CCÉ has sometimes been criticised for its conservative attitude towards Irish traditional music, its playing and its presentation. In the 1970s and 80s it was often embroiled in controversy over its involvement in political issues, especially in relation to Northern Ireland. However, Comhaltas has undoubtedly done more than any other single organisation to teach and promote traditional music and the All-Ireland Fleadh continues to be one of the most important and popular events in Ireland's cultural calendar. Website: www.comhaltas.com. See also **Fleadh Nua**.

Comic Songs Comic songs in the Irish tradition appear in a variety of styles and deal with a considerable range of subjects. Many are well-known **ballad**s with rousing choruses, such as 'Whiskey in the Jar' or 'The Wild Rover', which provide a good opportunity for communal singing and general merriment in a **session**. Many comic songs are on the theme of love (or the lack of it!), including 'The Old Woman from Wexford', 'I'll Forgive Him' (recorded by the **Bothy Band** as 'Do You Love an Apple?') and 'Biddy McGrath's Bra'. There are a number of traditional ballads about *poitín* (Irish moonshine), including 'The Moonshiner', 'The Rare Oul' Mountain Dew' and 'The Black Stripper', as well as the more recently composed 'McIlhatton' (written by the IRA prisoner/British MP, Bobby Sands). 'The Finding of Moses' is a classic comic ballad set in ancient Egypt and passed down from the blind 19th-century Dublin ballad-maker **Zozimus**. Other unusual comic ballads include 'The Chinaman' (about an Irishman who becomes a Chinaman), 'The Glendalough Saint' (about the attempted seduction of the Irish 6th-century saint, Kevin) and 'The Man from Kinsale' (an extraordinary song about what a fisherman does with various parts of a fish). A number of **sea songs** are comic, including 'The Holy Ground' (first popularised by the **Clancy Brothers and Tommy Makem**) and 'The Irish Rover' (a chart success for the **Pogues** with the **Dubliners**). In many parts of Ireland, rural and urban, there are locally composed and locally famous songs about particular incidents or personalities. Good examples are the ballads 'Bobby's Britches' and 'Ham Sunday', composed by **Robbie O'Connell** in the 1970s. The latter tells of events in Carrick-on-Suir in 1932, when a GAA Munster Final was held in the town. Newly written satirical songs, often using older melodies, are very popular and have a long tradition in Ireland. **Fintan Vallely** has recorded three albums of satirical songs, two with Tim Lyons from Cork. See also **Sands Family.**

Concertina (*consairtín*)   One of the **free-reed instruments**, in many ways similar to the **accordion**. The concertina was first patented by Charles Wheatstone in London in 1829 and arrived in Ireland during the second half of the 19th century. Smaller than the accordion and hexagonal in shape, it also differs from the accordion in having no bass and in the fact that its keyboard is extended across the casing on both sides of the bellows. There are two main types of concertina in use among Irish players today. The English concertina has double action (i.e., it produces the same note when the bellows is compressed as when it is extended). The more common Anglo- or German concertina has single action (i.e., it produces a different note when the bellows is compressed to that which is produced when the bellows is extended). The number of keys on a concertina can vary, but the instrument often consists of thirty keys or buttons arranged in six rows of five keys each. There are three rows on the left-hand side and three on the right. The main row on each hand is often tuned in C and G, so cross-fingering is required to play the scale of D. Other systems of tuning, such as A♭/E♭ and B♭/F, can also be found.

The concertina is a lighter and more portable instrument than most types of accordion. Fingering can be achieved without moving the basic position of the hands and the bellows' work requires relatively little effort. The tone of the concertina is light and sweet, and it blends well with other instruments such as **uilleann pipes** and **fiddle**. It is not unusual to find concertina players who are also accomplished on the button accordion.

Concertina players are numerous in Co. Clare and some neighbouring areas. One of the few female traditional musicians to achieve fame throughout Ireland in the 1950s was the Clare concertina player **Elizabeth Crotty**. The most renowned player of the last twenty years is **Noel Hill** from Caherea, near Ennis, Co. Clare. Another well-known player is Jacqueline McCarthy (see **McCarthy Family** and **Keane, Tommy**). She was born in London but her father, Tommy, was from Clare and also played the concertina. Her father bought her a concertina when she was only nine years old, a Wheatstone which she continues to play today. Other fine players include John Kelly, Tom Carey, Paddy Murphy, Bernard O'Sullivan, Sonny Murray, Chris Droney, Packie Russell (brother of **Micho Russell**), Mary McNamara, Miriam Collins, Dympna O'Sullivan, Terry Bingham and **Gearóid Ó hAllmhuráin**, all from Co. Clare. Among the finest young players to emerge in the 1990s are Ernestina Healy from Co. Mayo, Aogán Lynch (who has recorded with the group **Slide**) and Armagh-born Niall Vallely (of **Nomos**), whose first solo album, *Beyond Words* (1999), consists of both traditional and original tunes. *The Nervous Man* (2001) is the title of the debut album of Micheál Ó Raghallaigh, a young Co. Meath player of great promise. See also **Double Stop**; **Wales**.

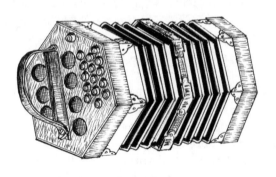

Concertina

Congas Large Afro-Cuban barrel drums which, like the smaller **bongos**, are usually played in pairs, using the hands. They are not widely used in traditional music but have been played by groups such as **Moving Hearts**, **Kíla**, the **Barleyshakes**, the **Afro Celts** and **De Jimbe**. Harmonica virtuoso **Mick Kinsella** also plays them occasionally.

Conneff, Kevin (b. 1945) Singer and bodhrán player from the Liberties in Dublin. His interest in traditional music didn't begin until his late teens when, after attending the 1964 **All-Ireland Fleadh Cheoil** in Mullingar, he started to pick up **sean-nós** songs and play bodhrán. From the mid 1960s, he was involved in running the Listener's Club, a folk club based in Slattery's of Capel Street, Dublin, which became the famous Tradition Club. He featured on **Christy Moore**'s seminal album **Prosperous** (1972) and in 1976 went to London to record with the **Chieftains** on their album *Bonaparte's Retreat* (1976). He has been with the Chieftains since then and although initially taken on as a bodhrán player, his singing has come to play an increasingly important role. He has released one solo album, *A Week Before Easter* (1988), on which there are traditional songs in English and some instrumental tracks.

Conradh Na Gaeilge (The Gaelic League) Founded in 1893 to recreate a separate 'cultural' Irish nation primarily through attempting to revive the declining Irish language. Attention was gradually turned to other aspects of Irish culture, including literature, music and **céilí dancing**. The league played a role in the founding of **Feis Ceoil** in 1897 and established the **Dancing Commission** in 1929. It operates mainly through a network of over 200 branches throughout Ireland and there are also branches in the **US** and **Australia**. These branches provide language classes and organise social events which provide an opportunity for people to speak Irish. Another key vehicle is a string of clubs which are scattered around the Conradh's seventeen premises nationwide. These are pubs which provide a relaxed atmosphere and regular music sessions. The largest is 'Club na Conartha' in the basement of Conradh's offices in Harcourt Street, Dublin, but similar clubs in Galway, Cork and other locations are popular centres of music and social life. Conradh na Gaeilge also has an important lobbying role and was actively involved in the campaigns which led to the establishment of **Raidió na Gaeltachta** and the television channel **TG4**. The organisation's website supplies information about its activities and its offspring, **An tOireachtas** and Seachtain na Gaeilge. Website: www.cnag.ie.

Conway, Zoë (b. 1981) Fiddler born in Dundalk, Co. Louth, one of the most talented musicians to emerge in recent years. She started playing the fiddle at the age of eight, having already learned tin whistle, banjo and piano. At the age of nine she started to learn classical violin and has continued to maintain her interest in both classical and traditional music. In 2001 she won the **All-Ireland** Senior Fiddle title but has also been a member of the Junior and Senior Youth Orchestras of Ireland and has guested as a soloist with the Irish Chamber Orchestra. She has performed with **Riverdance** and the traditional band Dal Riada. Her début album, *Zoë Conway* (2002) was produced by **Bill Whelan** and features a number of guests, including **Dónal Lunny** and **Micheál Ó Domhnaill**. The album displays Conway's virtuosity in playing traditional music and her considerable talent for composition. She has also toured with the Mexican guitar duo, Rodrigo y Gabriela and recorded with them on their album *Re-Foc* (2002). Website: www.zoeconway.com.

Zoë Conway
(courtesy of Tara Music)

Cooley, Joe (1924-1973) Great 'press-and-draw' style (see **Accordion**) button accordion player from Peterswell, in east Co. Galway. He played with the Tulla Céilí Band for a while before emigrating from Ireland to the **US** in 1953 (he returned to Ireland in the early 1970s). His style was energetic and rugged and he has many admirers among contemporary players, most notably **Paul Brock** and **Frankie Gavin**, who released the tribute album *Omós do Joe Cooley* in 1986. In spite of his fame, Cooley himself never made an album during his career, although the album *Cooley* (1975) was posthumously released. It is compiled from various recordings of sessions dating from the 1960s up to the month before his death.

Cooney, Steve Guitar, didgeridoo, bass and keyboards player who has been influential in traditional Irish music since the early 1980s, when he came to Ireland

Steve Cooney

from **Australia**. Born in Melbourne to an Irish father, he learned didgeridoo from aboriginal tribesmen in Northern Australia. After coming to Ireland, he played bass with **Stockton's Wing** before teaming up with **Séamus Begley** to form one of the most famous duos in Irish music. His style is unique among guitarists in Irish music, and he has an extraordinary ability to switch from a driving, fiery rhythmic accompaniment to a gentle, almost classical rendition of an Irish slow air. He also composes his own material and is one of the most sought-after producer/arrangers in traditional music. Cooney has made some interesting arrangements of Irish tunes with didgeridoo backing and has even evolved his own system of **music notation**. Settled for many years in Dingle, Co. Kerry, he has described the community there as an aboriginal society that shares many of the values of Australian aboriginal culture. He has also worked with children, arranging and performing music for the CD *Rabhlaí, Rabhlaí* (1998), a collection of 31 traditional rhymes for children in Irish.

Cork Pipers' Club, The The oldest pipers' club in the world, founded in 1898 by Seán Wayland, a native of Cashel, Co. Tipperary. (Wayland emigrated to **Australia** in 1912, when the club was at its height.) Members played not only all over Ireland but also throughout Britain. Wayland was also instrumental in the founding of the Brian Boru Pipe Band, the first of its kind to wear kilts in Ireland. Another notable aspect of the Cork Pipers' Club was the number of women pipers involved (two of whom are mentioned by **Francis O'Neill** in his *Irish Minstrels and Musicians*). The First World War (1914-1918), the Irish War of Independence (1919-1921) and the rise in popularity of accordions all contributed to the decline of piping in Cork, and the club no longer existed by 1930.

The piper Micheál Ó Riabhaigh revived the club in 1963, starting a great period of piping in Cork that lasted well into the 1970s. His personal inspiration was central to the success of the club, which closed again just five years after Ó Riabhaigh died in 1974. In this period, Ó Riabhaigh initiated an annual pilgrimage to Tralibawn, the birthplace of Francis O'Neill.

The Cork Pipers' Club was revived again by piper and pipe-maker Sylvester Ryan in 1986 and is still thriving. There are uilleann-piping classes for beginners and advanced pupils and an annual uilleann-piping and reed-making weekend is held in conjunction with **Na Píobairí Uilleann** of Dublin. The club is based at the Aras, 13 Dyke Parade, Cork City. See also **Phairs Pipes**; **Ó Riabhaigh, Eoin**.

Cotillion (*coitileán*) A French country dance of the 18th century adapted in Ireland by **dancing masters** to form the basis for the earliest Irish **set dancing**. The cotillion was said to be inspired by or derived from English country dancing, and is first mentioned in Ireland by Arthur Young in his book *A Tour of Ireland* (London, 1780). It was a forerunner of the **quadrille**, and usually involved four couples starting in square formation. Many of the movements were similar to those found in the quadrille and in modern Irish set dances influenced by the quadrille.

Coulter, Phil (b. 1942) Singer/songwriter and pianist from Derry who, despite being associated with showbands and light entertainment has made a significant contribution to folk music since the 1960s. He worked as a producer, musician, arranger and songwriter with a number of folk groups, including **Planxty** (for whom he produced their first three albums), the **Dubliners** and the **Furey Brothers**. Some of his compositions have become widely popular and are often performed in sessions alongside older traditional songs. 'The Town I Loved So Well', written in 1972, is his best-known song. Dealing with the effects which political strife and violence have had on his native Derry, it has struck a chord with many people since the early 1970s. The song underlines the role newly composed songs dealing with contemporary issues have played in keeping the folk tradition alive. 'The Town I Loved So Well' is often sung in sessions where most of the material is much older. It was composed with the singer **Luke Kelly** of the Dubliners in mind, as were Coulter's 'Scorn Not His Simplicity', 'Donegal Danny' and 'Ronnie's Mare'. 'Hand Me down the Bible' also came from Coulter's collaboration with the Dubliners, a song 'dedicated' to the Northern Ireland Unionist politician, Dr. Ian Paisley. Coulter also contributed significantly to the repertoire of the Furey Brothers and Davey Arthur, writing 'The Old Man' as a tribute to the Fureys' father, Ted. 'Stealaway' and 'Katriona' were also written by Coulter and recorded by the Fureys. More recently Coulter himself recorded some of the above-mentioned songs with other compositions of his own on *The Songs I Love So Well, Phil's Vocal Album* (2000). His *Highland Cathedral* (2000) included three tracks with **Different Drums of Ireland**, with whom he also toured in the **US** in 1999. He has made numerous albums of instrumental music and has collaborated with many traditional musicians and singers as well as with pop artists. He composed the anthem, 'Ireland's Call' for the Irish rugby team. Website: www.philcoulter.com.

Cran 1 A form of ornamentation which was originally used by uilleann pipers on the bottom two notes of the chanter (usually E and D). It is now also used by flute and whistle players, and sometimes by fiddlers. Similar to a **roll**, but of greater complexity, it is usually played on a D or E dotted crochet (quarter note) and consists of a series of grace notes which link a series of E or D notes, all played in rapid succession. It is not necessary for the grace notes to finger full notes but simply to give a quick flick of the finger. The main note must be returned to between each grace note, and the speed at which this must be done makes the cran a difficult ornament to execute correctly. Like the grace notes used for **cuts** or other forms of ornamentation, the grace notes used in a cran have no time value and are therefore normally written in notation as a small quaver (eighth note) with a line through it.

Cran

Cran 2 Traditional group with **Ronan Browne** (uilleann pipes, bansari, flute, vocals), Desi Wilkinson (flute, bamboo flute, whistle, vocals) and Seán Corcoran (bouzouki, vocals), three top class musicians who play a fine mixture of songs and instrumentals. Their first album, *The Crooked Stair* (1993) was followed by *Black, Black, Black* (1998), which also features guest performances by **Tríona Ní Dhómhnaill** (clavinet, harmonium), Conan Doyle (bass), Michael Holohan (strings), **Anúna** (vocals) and **Kevin Glackin** (fiddle). The title *Black, Black, Black* comes from the traditional air 'Black, Black, Black Is the Colour of My True Love's Hair' which is beautifully played on the album by uilleann pipes (with regulators overdubbed), flute and Anúna providing vocal accompaniment. The three members of Cran are also fine singers, as shown on the *a cappella* rendition of the ballad 'Willie Taylor', which alternates between solo verses and harmonised choruses. All three also provide vocals on the old Irish religious song 'Seacht Suáilcí na Maighdine Muire' ('The Seven Virtues of the Virgin Mary'), which has an appropriately medieval sound, arranged with harmonium accompaniment and an instrumental break on whistle. Another song in Irish, 'Staimpí' ('Boxty'), is also beautifully arranged with the singing accompanied for most of the track but going unaccompanied for one chorus just after an unusual instrumental break in the middle of the song. There are some powerfully arranged sets of jigs and reels with excellent bouzouki accompaniment and the uilleann pipes regulators often featuring in the full group arrangements. Cran are equally at ease, however, on the unaccomapanied track of two reels, 'The Dunmore Lassies/ The Dublin Reel', played at a moderate tempo on bamboo flute and bansari. On another track the march 'The Return from Fingal' is played on just pipes (with regulator accompaniment) and flute before changing into two jigs where the instrumentation builds to the group in full swing with bouzouki and keyboard accompaniment. The one original track on the album, Duncan

Johnstone's 'Farewell to Nigg', is subtly arranged with flute, pipes (sometimes with regulators) and a delicate string arrangement by Michael Holohan. *Lover's Ghost* (2001) again featured guest appearances by Ní Dhomhnaill and Glackin and *Music from the Edge of the World* (2002) confirms the group's talent for choosing and arranging their material.

Cranitch, Matt Renowned Cork fiddler who has played both Irish traditional and music from the **Appalachians** (with the Lee Valley String Band), lectured on traditional music and done workshops in Ireland and abroad. A founder member of **Na Filí**, he has also played with **Any Old Time**. In addition to recording with these groups he has made a number of solo albums. His album *Give It Shtick!* (1988, re-released 1996) includes **Sliabh Luachra** slides and polkas as well as other forms of dance music and two airs. It includes both fine solo playing and fiddle/melodeon duets (with Dave Hennessy, also of Any Old Time). All of the tunes on the album appear in Cranitch's comprehensive fiddle tutor, *The Irish Fiddle* (Cork 1988, new edition 2001 with demonstration CD). More recently he has played with the group **Sliabh Notes**. Cranitch has carried out extensive research on the music of Sliabh Luachra and is working on a Ph.D. thesis about the fiddler **Pádraig O'Keeffe**. See also **Ó Canainn, Tomás**.

Creagh, Séamus (b. 1946) Influential fiddler from Kilucan, Co. Westmeath. He started to learn fiddle at the age of twelve, moved to Dublin in the 1960s and settled in Co. Cork in 1968. He recorded·a famous album with accordionist **Jackie Daly** in 1977, after which the duo toured extensively. He also featured with **Seán Keane** and **Kevin Burke** on the fiddle compilation *An Fhidil II* (1980). In 1988 he travelled to St. John's, **Newfoundland**, where he researched songs and tunes, staying there for over five years and releasing a solo album, *Came the Dawn* (1993). *Traditional Music from Ireland* (1999) is a duo album with **De Dannan** accordionist Aidan Coffey from Bunmahon, Co. Waterford. They are accompanied by Seán Ó Loinsigh on bouzouki. *It's No Secret* (2001), with **Colin 'Hammy' Hamilton** and **Con Ó Drisceoil** is an unusual mixture of solo, duo and trio performances of tunes and songs. As well as playing fiddle on this album, Creagh gives fine renditions of the songs 'In Praise of the City of Mullingar' and 'The Plains of Drishane'.

Crehan, (Martin) Junior (1908-1998) Fiddler, concertina player, composer of tunes and songs from Bonavilla, Mullach (near Miltown Malbay) Co. Clare. Crehan came from a musical family. His mother, Margaret Scanlon, was a concertina player who passed on music from the 19th century to her children. Her father was a fiddle maker and her cousin was married to the legendary piper **Garret Barry**. Crehan learned tin whistle at the age of six and later took up the fiddle, which he learned from Scully Casey, father of **Bobby Casey**. In his earlier years of playing, traditional music was centred on house dances, which ended after the **Public Dance Hall Act** (1935). In an interview in *Dal gCais*, Vol. 3 (1977), Junior Crehan lamented the fact that 'the Dance Hall Act had closed our schools of tradition.' 'The dance halls,' he remarked, 'were not places for traditional music, story-telling and dancing; they were unsuitable for passing on traditional arts.' Among Crehan's best known compositions is 'The Lament for the Country House Dance'.

One of the most remarkable aspects of Junior Crehan's contribution to traditional music is the way in which he bridged the gap between the very different era of the first three decades of this century and the later decades. He adjusted to the many social changes that took place in Irish society and had a profound influence on traditional musicians, contributing to the survival and development of the music through organisations such as **Comhaltas Ceoltóirí Éireann** and the committee of the **Willie Clancy Summer School**, which he was instrumental in founding. He was a close friend of Clancy's and gave workshops in West Clare fiddling at the summer school from the time of its foundation.

Despite his fame, Crehan never made a commercial recording, although he was featured by **Seán Ó Riada** on the radio series *Our Musical Heritage* (1962) and can be heard playing his own jig, 'The Mist-Covered Mountain' with 'Scully Casey's Jig' on the records from the series that were released in 1982. He can also be heard on *Ceol an Chláir Vol. 1* (1979). His special contribution to Irish music was acknowledged by the Arts Council on his 80th and 90th birthdays. At his funeral in August 1998 many famous musicians played, including **Liam O'Flynn** and **Seán Keane**.

Junior Crehan's grandson, Kevin, made the CD *An Bhábóg sa Bhádóg* ('The Baby in the Boat', 2001) as a tribute to his grandfather's playing. Kevin learned and recorded many of Junior's tunes in an attempt to preserve his grandfather's style, spending the summer of 1998 working on the music with him in Clare. A fine fiddler in his own right, Kevin settled in Cincinnati, Ohio, and set up his own studio, eventually producing the 2001 CD from the vast repertoire of tunes which he had worked on and recorded with his grandfather.

Cronin, Elizabeth (Bess) (1879-1956)

Singer from Ballyvourney, Co. Cork who had a great repertoire of songs in Irish and English, many of them rare or unusual. Her repertoire included **Child ballads**, lullabies, local songs and some fine examples of the **aisling** or vision-poem. She sang in both English and Irish. Her version of the famous Child ballad 'Lord Gregory' excited collectors as the many versions collected in Britain did not have an accompanying tune but Bess Cronin's did. One of the rarest and most famous of her songs was 'On Board the Kangaroo' which, as 'The Good Ship Kangaroo', was sung by **Christy Moore**

Bess Cronin

on the **Planxty** album *After the Break* (1979). She was visited by many song collectors in the 1940s and 50s, including George Pickow, **Jean Ritchie**, **Alan Lomax** and **Séamus Ennis**. Although she only rarely performed in public, she has been highly influential because of the wealth of her repertoire. Her grandson, Dáibhí Ó Cróinín, collected almost 200 of her songs and published them as *The Songs of Elizabeth Cronin* (Dublin, 2000). The book is accompanied by two CDs of recordings of Bess singing which were made in the 1950s, and it includes background material on the life and times of the singer, the sources of the songs and alternative or variant versions of them. The first CD (30 tracks) is compiled from acetate recordings made by the **Irish Folklore Commission** in 1947 and 1951 and the **BBC** (1947, 1952 and 1954), while the second (29 tracks) comes from magnetic tape recordings made by American collectors Lomax (1951), Pickow and Ritchie (1952) and Diane Hamilton (1955).

Crossroads Conference   The first Crossroads Conference was held at the Temple Bar Music Centre, Dublin over the weekend of 19-21 April 1996; the full title was *Crosbhealach an Cheoil / The Crossroads Conference 1996: Tradition and Change in Irish Traditional Music*. The latter was also the title of a book comprising most of the papers given at the conference and edited by **Fintan Vallely**, **Colin 'Hammy' Hamilton**, Eithne Vallely and **Liz Doherty** (Dublin, 1999). The Conference was initiated by **Cormac Breatnach** and Fintan Vallely and invited participants from 'within the music, song and dance community in Ireland and abroad, and from academics and specialists in other music fields.' As a result of the debate that had taken place on **RTÉ**'s *Late Late Show* special to mark the launch of the TV series *A **River of Sound***, **Tony Mac Mahon** and **Micheál Ó Súilleabháin** were invited to give keynote addresses to the conference.

MacMahon had been heckled and derided with shouts of 'begrudger' on the *Late Late Show* for criticising the series theme tune as having little to do with Irish traditional music. In his conference address he made an impassioned plea for traditional music, saying that he had received 168 phone calls and letters from traditional musicians after the *Late Late Show*, all in agreement with what he had said and adding their own views. He described the anger and frustration that many musicians felt at some of the changes taking place in traditional music, especially in the way that the music and musicians were being manipulated by vested interests in the media who understood or cared little for 'the wonder and beauty of the music that has been given to us'. He spoke of the music as something spiritual which carried the 'footprint of generations', a deep personal experience charged with passion and emotion. He named many of the great musicians of the last 90 years who had not been acknowledged by the series and decried the commercialism which resulted in the music being 'reduced, drained of the veiled voices of Ireland, electronically scrubbed clean, packaged and presented as a commercial commodity whose value is measured in record sales, TV Tam Ratings.'

Ó Súilleabháin's address was titled 'Crossroads or Twin Track? Innovation and Tradition in Irish Traditional Music' and argued for the importance of innovation. It was his view that traditional musicians could not recreate the music of past masters because they belonged to a different era and mindset. He used case studies of the development of the bodhrán and the playing of fiddler **Tommy Potts** to illustrate innovation at work and argued that his inclusion of many performances by younger musicians in *A River of Sound* horrified certain members of the traditional music community because: 'Suddenly the subversion which had remained hidden beneath the ground, entombed and casketed within the vinyl of Potts' *The Liffey Banks* album, broke ground and surfaced. For some it was as if the tradition had been bypassed.'

Musicians, singers, dancers, collectors, educators, and academics were among the many other contributors to the 'first' Crossroads Conference, which, in addition to its focus on many aspects of the Irish tradition, also included papers dealing with Manx, Breton, Canadian and American folk music. As a whole the papers represent a wide variety of perspectives on tradition and change. It was the first time that a major conference debated the development of Irish traditional music and threw open many questions about the music that will be argued over for some time to come. The tension between 'preservation' and 'innovation' is, in itself, a sign of a healthy, vibrant tradition. Irish traditional music of the past few decades has developed in an atmosphere of commercialisation and international popularity that has never existed before; the entire social structure in which traditional music once flourished has also changed. These changes are so great that it will take time for people to come to terms with them, and in many ways the Crossroads Conference was an important part of this process. Even the most enthusiastic innovators, however, would surely acknowledge that Tony MacMahon's contribution to the conference clearly articulated many of the problems and questions that change and innovation pose. 'In the course of my work and travels around the country', MacMahon said, 'my eyes have been opened to the distance that has opened up, countrywide, between the main body of traditional performers whose music and song give us unique reflections of the spirit and character of this country and the smaller group of performers who regard this music as a convenient mode of joy riding to the glitzy heights of commercial popularity and success.'

A second Crossroads Conference took place on 25-27 April 2003 at the University of Ulster, Derry. The title of the conference was 'Education and Traditional Music', a reflection, perhaps, of the extent to which traditional music had become a greater part of educational institutions (especially third level) since 1996. Keynote addresses were given by Philip Bohlman of the University of Chicago (author of *Folk Music in the Modern World*) and Caomhín MacAoidh of Cairdeas na bhFhidléirí, Donegal (author of *Fiddling in Donegal*). Other speakers came from Ireland, Norway, **Scotland**, **England**, **Brittany** and the **US**, and the conference examined in detail the different approaches to folk/traditional music education in these diverse places.

Crotty, Elizabeth (1885-1960) Concertina player born Elizabeth Markham near Cooraclare in west Co. Clare. She grew up in a musical household, her mother playing fiddle and her older sister concertina. In 1914 she married into the Crotty family and moved to Kilrush where she ran a pub with her husband. In the 1940s and 50s Crotty's of Kilrush became a famous pub for traditional music. The fame of Mrs. Crotty as an exceptional player of the concertina spread in the 1950s with her involvement in **Comhaltas Ceoltóirí Éireann** and the nationwide broadcasting of **Ciarán Mac Mathúna**'s recordings of her playing. She became the first president of Comhaltas in Co. Clare (1954) and held the position until her death. Although she never made any commercial recordings in her own lifetime, her fine playing can be heard on the CD *Concertina Music from West Clare* (1999). This includes her renditions of 'The Wind that Shakes the Barley/The

Mrs. Crotty
(courtesy of Rebecca Brew)

Reel with the Beryl', 'The Green Groves of Erin', 'The Flogging Reel' and many other great dance tunes as well as one song, a rendition in English of the old Irish song 'An Droighneán Donn' ('The Blackthorn'). Since 1998 an annual festival in her honour, Éigse Mrs. Crotty, has been held in Kilrush over a weekend in mid-August (website: www.eigsemrscrotty.com).

Crowley, Jimmy (b. 1950) Singer/songwriter from Co. Cork who, since the 1970s, has developed a reputation as a fine singer of **sea songs** and Cork songs, especially urban ballads. He also plays bouzouki, guitar, mandolin, mandola and harmonica. Crowley has played and sung with a number of different groups, including Stoker's Lodge, and has also toured extensively as a solo artist. He has recorded many albums, including one of songs in Irish, *Jimmy Mo Mhile Stór* (1985). More recently he has released *My Love Is a Tall Ship* (1997), consisting entirely of his own songs, and *Uncorked* (1998), which includes 'The Boys of Fairhill', 'Salonika', 'Johnny Jump Up' and other songs for which he is renowned. *The Coast of Malabar* (2000) is subtitled 'Romantic songs of Ships and the Sea from Ireland, England, Scotland and America' and includes traditional and original material. He studied folklore at University College Cork, graduating in 1997, and did a special study of Seán O'Callaghan, who wrote 'The Boys of Fairhill' and other ballads. Crowley also published *Jimmy Crowley's Irish Songbook* (Cork, 1986). Website: www.jimmycrowley.com. See also **Ó Drisceoil, Con**.

Curtis, P. J. Award-winning record producer from Co. Clare who has produced albums for many of the most famous Irish traditional artists, including **Stockton's Wing**, **Altan**, **Davy Spillane**, **Mary Black** and Dolores Keane (see **Keane Family**). He has also worked with **RTÉ** radio and published a book, *Notes From the Heart: A Celebration of Traditional Irish Music* (Dublin, 1994). The book is divided into two parts. The first covers the history of Irish traditional music since 1900, music of the Irish emigrants and a brief history of Irish **set dancing** since the 17th century.

In the second part, Curtis gives a series of colourful, often quite personal, portraits of famous musicians from Co. Clare or with strong Clare associations, including **Tommy Peoples**, **Willie Clancy**, **Johnny Doran** and others. There is an interesting chapter on **Doolin** and one on the Kilfenora Céilí Band.

Custy Family Frank Custy, fiddler and music teacher from Toonagh, Co. Clare has, since the 1960s, taught many famous players, including his own daughters Frances, Catherine and Mary, his son Tola, **Tony Linnane**, **Noel Hill**, Síobháin Peoples and **Sharon Shannon**. His daughter Mary has built a reputation as a fine fiddler, spending much of her time in **Doolin**, Co. Clare. She has played with the **Sharon Shannon** band and has also recorded a number of albums of her own. *The Mary Custy Band* (1996) features traditional fiddle tunes from diverse sources, including Appalachian, reggae and Yiddish tunes. The sound is quite modern, with drums, guitar, bass and bouzouki (played by Eoin O'Neill) backing the raw, energetic fiddle playing. Her brother, Tola, is among the best young fiddlers to emerge in the 1990s. His debut solo album, *Setting Free* (1994), included his own compositions, as did *Three Sunsets* (2002), his duo recording with piano accordion player Mirella Murray. Although the latter CD includes music from the Irish tradition, there is also a strong European feel to much of the music, with the influence of **Brittany** particularly evident.

Cut A form of **ornamentation**, sometimes referred to as single grace note. It can be used to separate two notes of the same pitch, or to emphasise an accented note. A player will 'cut' into a note by playing a grace note before the main note. The grace note is usually higher in pitch but the exact note used, and the way it is fingered, can vary according to the instrument or the effect desired. The cut should be light and unobtrusive and on many instruments this is better achieved by not fingering it as a full note. It has no time value and is often written in notation as a small quaver (eighth note) with a line through it.

D

DADGAD A system of tuning used by some guitarists and devised by the English guitarist Davey Graham. It involves tuning the first (highest) and sixth (lowest) strings down one tone, from E to D, and tuning the second string down one tone from B to A. Players who use DADGAD tuning argue that it suits the **modes** in which Irish music is played better than standard tuning, with sympathetic vibrations of the strings more likely to suit the music than with standard tuning. The lowered bass also adds to the depth of sound. *The Irish DADGAD Guitar Book* (Cork, 1995) by **Sarah McQuaid** provides an excellent guide, covering backing and playing melody, as well as providing comprehensive explanations of modes, key signatures and chord sequences. Players who use DADGAD tuning include Sarah McQuaid herself, **Luka Bloom**, Donagh Hennessy of **Lúnasa** and, occasionally, John Doyle of **Solas** and the **Eileen Ivers** Band.

Daly, Jackie (b. 1945)   Button accordion and melodeon player from Kanturk, Co. Cork who has been a central figure in some of the major traditional groups of the last 30 years. He won the senior accordion title in the 1974 **All-Ireland Fleadh Cheoil**. His first album was the sixth volume of **Topic Records**' *Music from Sliabh Luachra* series (released 1977) and offers fine examples of the music of **Sliabh Luachra**. He was a founder-member of **De Dannan** and has also played with **Patrick Street**, **Buttons and Bows** and **Arcady**. Daly has also been involved in some dynamic duos, including *Jackie Daly agus Séamus Creagh* (1977), an album of fast, energetic playing on box and fiddle that has been influential among young traditional players. This album introduced a new sound to Irish accordion playing, with Daly using mellower, more closely tuned reeds than the old-style loud, widely tuned reeds. This sound has been imitated by many younger players and Daly went on to experiment further

Jackie Daly

with the sound of the accordion. He also made *Eavesdropper* (1981) with fiddler **Kevin Burke**, and on a more recent solo album, *Many's a Wild Night* (1995) returned to his roots in Sliabh Luachra music.

Dance Halls Act See **Public Dance Halls Act.**

Dance Music Term used to describe the various types of traditional tunes originally played for dancing. Most of the instrumental music played today is dance music, apart from **airs** and **marches**. The most popular forms of dance music are the **reel** and the **jig**. Other forms include the **hornpipe, polka, waltz, slide, barndance** and **schottische**. Right up to the early years of the 20th century it was rare for dance music to be played without dancers. The invention of the gramophone in the 1920s and the availability of mass-produced recordings began the process of separating the music from the dance itself, and the playing of dance music solely for listening is now common. Many contemporary traditional musicians would only rarely, if ever, play for dancers.

Dancing The modern Irish words for dancing, *damhsa* and *rince*, are both loan words. *Damhsa* is derived from the French *danse* or the English 'dance' and is first attested in written Irish in 1520. *Rince* comes from the English 'rink' ('to skate') and is found in Irish from 1609. Although there are few specific references to dancing in early Irish literature, there can be little doubt that, as in other ancient societies, dance played an important role in many areas of life. Dancing is likely to have taken place in ritual ceremonies, in association with work, courtship or battle and to mark special events such as births, deaths or marriages.

The earliest specific reference to dancing in Ireland is to the **carol**, in 1413. From the 16th century onwards, other types of dance are mentioned, including the Irish *hey*, the ***rince fada*** or long dance (from the 17th century), the ***rince mór*** or big dance and various types of **pantomimic dances**. The 18th century saw the development of solo **step dancing**, principally the **jig**, **reel** and **hornpipe**. There were also group or round dances based on the solo jig and reel. Modern Irish **set dancing** developed in the 18th and 19th centuries from the French **cotillion** and **quadrille**. The latter types of dance were adapted in Ireland by the **dancing masters** and were very popular. With the development of **céilí dancing** (encouraged by **Conradh na Gaeilge**) from the late 19th/early 20th century, set dancing was denounced as 'foreign', although some céilí dances seem to be based on (or certainly share common features with) set dances. Despite the work of the League's **Dancing Commission** in bringing in strict rules governing the movements, costumes and footwear to be used in Irish dancing, less formalised group (see **Set Dancing**) and solo (see **Clog Dancing** and **Sean-nós Dancing**) dances survived. Other forms of European dance and **dance music** – such as **polkas, mazurkas, waltzes** and **schottisches** – were also adopted by Irish dancers and musicians. Recent years have seen the phenomenal rise of Irish-style dancing to an international stage, with the commercial productions of ***Riverdance*, *Lord of the Dance*** and others, and the revival of interest in Irish dancing owes something to the huge popularity of these shows. It was, however, already under way in the 1980s, when modern dancing masters began to spread a new enthusiasm for set dancing through an increased number of classes and workshops throughout Ireland.

Alan Gilsenan's documentary, *Emerald Shoes* (1999), was commissioned by Ulster Television (UTV) and provides an interesting range of perspectives on the development of Irish dance in the last 100 years. Incorporating views that are often cynical and humorous, the documentary also includes interviews with established dance teachers and dancers. The *Riverdance* phenomenon is examined and the sharply competitive edge of the dance scene is brought to light.

The history of Irish dance in all its forms is treated in a highly readable style by Helen Brennan in *The Story of Irish Dance* (1999). Covering the subject from medieval times right up to the present, the book is excellent on subjects like the politics of Irish dance in the 20th century and the different forms of dance and dance music. There are some wonderful stories about the experiences of individual dancers, and the author makes great use of material collected by the **Irish Folklore Commission** and articles from the newspapers. See also **Dancing and Religion**.

Dancing and Religion Tension between religious authorities and those involved in dancing has existed all over the world since the earliest times. In the early Christian world, dancing was associated with pagan ritual and condemned as immoral. In Ireland, the hostility of church authorities to dancing is well documented for the last four centuries. In 18th- and 19th-century Ireland, music, dancing and drinking were seen as resulting in inappropriate behaviour at wakes, festivals, pattern days (held in honour of local saints) and other gatherings. Dancing was condemned by priests and bishops, and many punishments, including excommuni-cation, were threatened. Musicians who grew up in the first decades of the 20th century can still remember incidents in which zealous clergy were involved in physical assaults on the musicians whom they held responsible for the sin and debauchery which, in their opinion, could result from dancing. Dances held in houses, at cross-roads or in other locations were often broken up by clergymen promising hellfire and damnation to all present. Numerous incidents are related of musicians having their instruments broken or destroyed. Musicians and dancers were often condemned at Sunday masses, and the Lenten pastorals of 1925 warned parents of their responsibilities in preserving the 'chivalrous honour of Irish boys and the Christian modesty of Irish maidens.' The pastoral continued: 'It is nothing new, alas, to find Irish girls now and then brought to shame and retiring to the refuge of institutions or the dens of great cities. But dancehalls, more especially in the general uncontrol of recent years, have deplorably aggravated the ruin of virtue due to ordinary human weakness' (quoted in Pat Murphy, *Toss the Feathers*, Cork 1955, pp. 35-36).

In the following years there were calls for tighter controls over commercial dance halls, leading eventually to the infamous **Public Dance Halls Act** of 1935. In the years after its introduction, this act was used not just against commercial dance halls but also against house dances and dances held in other locations. Its effects were severe, but more recent decades have seen a revival of many of the old **set dances** that had declined in the late 1930s. The secularisation of Irish society and the decline in influence of the Catholic Church in the latter part of the 20th century have meant that the age-old tension between religion and dancing no longer manifests itself in the extreme attitudes and actions so common in the 1920s and 30s.

Dancing Commission, The Irish (*An Coimisiún Le Rincí Gaelacha*) A regulatory body set up by **Conradh na Gaeilge** in 1929 which still exercises considerable control over the teaching of formalised Irish dancing. Conradh na Gaeilge had previously played a vital role in developing and promoting **céilí dancing**. By 1930, its Dancing Commission had established dancing competitions, strictly codified through regulations concerning group and solo dances, costumes and the proper type of music required for dancing. It standardised the teaching and adjudication of Irish dancing, which was to be purged of all 'foreign' influence. This was part of the broader Conradh na Gaeilge policy of developing a uniquely Irish cultural identity in line with the political nationalism of the late 19th and early 20th centuries. The Commission brought out a description of thirty of the céilí dances in three volumes of *Ár Rinncidhe Foirne,* published originally in 1939, 1943 and 1969. Despite the fact that the Dancing Commission favoured a style of **step dancing** that was based largely on the Munster style, other regional styles such as the **sean-nós dancing** of Connemara and Rathcairn and, to a lesser extent, the **clog dancing** of the northern part of the island survived.

Dancing Masters The Englishman Arthur Young, who travelled around Ireland in the years 1776-1778, wrote: 'Dancing is very general among the poor people, almost universal in every cabin. Dancing masters of their own rank travel through the country from cabin to cabin, with a piper or blind fiddler, and the pay is 6d. a quarter. It is an absolute system of education' (A. Young, *A Tour of Ireland* edited by Constantia Maxwell, Cambridge, 1925, p. 153). Itinerant dancing masters, in fact, were found not just among the poor but at all levels of Irish society in the 18th and 19th centuries. At the highest level were those who claimed to have been trained in France, where many of the fashionable dances of the time originated; they taught the latest dances to the upper classes in the big houses. There were also dancing masters, however, who brought the dances from the big houses to the general public, teaching their own versions to people dancing at house and crossroads' dances, at pattern days (held in honour of local saints) and celebrations. Many of the dancing masters also taught fencing and social etiquette. This is what Arthur Young meant by 'an absolute system of education.'

The dancing masters are thought by most historians to have created **step dancing**, various **round dances** and later **set dancing**. They appear to have had more influence in Munster than they did in the west or north, where regional variations of step dancing have survived (see **Sean-nós Dancing** and **Clog Dancing**). They based the group dances on the solo dances and steps that were known to the people of the locality, adapting dances such as the **cotillion** and **quadrille** in this way to suit the ability and tastes of their pupils. Many of the solo dances were too difficult for all but the best of dancers, and the invention of round and set dances by the dancing masters enabled a greater number of people to partake in what was a major and widespread pastime. Traditional tunes already known and played in an area were used for the dances.

By the early 20th century, the greatest years were gone for the old dancing masters. Prof. Patrick D. Reidy, a native of Co. Kerry who came from a family steeped in the traditions of the dancing masters, spent much of his life in London. Here he was involved in **Conradh na Gaeilge** and contributed dances to the 1902 book, *A Handbook of Irish Dances*. He lamented the decline of music and dancing in Ireland, commenting: 'It is really a miracle that there is any Irish music or dancing in existence. The parish priests, and sometimes the curates, finished the work of Lord Barrymore [see **Elizabeth I**]. It is like visiting a churchyard to visit the villages now, which were formerly alive with music and dancing' (quoted in O'Neill, *Irish Minstrels and Musicians*, p. 423). Conradh na Gaeilge, however, did much to generate a new interest in Irish dancing, especially through its **Dancing Commission**. Although its attitude towards set dancing was somewhat hostile, this and **céilí dancing** continued to co-exist throughout the first half of the 20th century.

The revival of set dancing in the last two decades has seen new dancing masters come to prominence, most notably **Connie Ryan**, **Joe O'Donovan**, **Timmy 'The Brit' McCarthy** and Pat Murphy (see **Set Dancing**). Dancing masters all over the country now give regular classes and teach at special summer schools such as the **Willie Clancy Summer School**.

Danú Young seven-piece group; their name is that of the mythological goddess who was mother of a divine people, the Tuatha Dé Dannan. With members from Waterford and Dublin, they formed in 1995, when they won the group competition at the *Festival d'Interceltique* in Lorient, **Brittany**. Dónal Clancy (guitar, bouzouki) had played with the group originally but the line-up at the time of their first album was Cathach MacCraith (vocals), Donnachadh Gough (uilleann pipes, bodhrán), Brendan McCarthy (accordion), Daire Bracken (fiddle), Tom Doorley (flute) and brother Eamonn (bouzouki), and Timmy Murray (guitar). Their repertoire consists of sean-nós songs

Danú

from the Ring **Gaeltacht**, folk songs sung in English and dance music. Their drive and energy has been favourably compared to that of the the **Bothy Band** and **Dervish**. Their first album, *Danú*, was released to critical acclaim in 1997, and they have a reputation for fine live performances. A second album, *Think Before You Think* (2000), has a similar style and range of material to the first, with two new members, Ciarán Ó Gealbháin (vocals) and Jesse Smith (fiddle and viola) replacing MacCraith and Bracken. The American Jesse Smith was replaced on fiddle by Donegal's Oisín MacAuley (who also plays guitar) in 2001, although both play on the third album, *All Things Considered* (2002). In 2003, Ciarán Ó Gealbháin was replaced on vocals by Muireann Nic Amhlaoibh from the west Kerry Gaeltacht of Dún Chaoin, and Dónal Clancy rejoined the group, replacing former guitarist Noel Ryan. The first album with this new line-up, *The Road Less Travelled* (2003), is a fine collection of songs in English and Irish, fast dance tunes (including slides and polkas as well as jigs and reels) and slower instrumentals. The guests on the album include **John Sheahan** (fiddle), who plays one of his own compositions with the band on the album, and James Blennerhasset (bass). The album *Up in the Air* (2004) is a novel collection of solo performances by the various band members. Website: www.danu.net. See also **Shanachie Records**.

Davey, Shaun (b. 1948) Composer who broke new ground in 1980 with *The Brendan Voyage*, the first suite of music for orchestra and uilleann pipes (played by **Liam O'Flynn**). It was inspired by Tim Severin's book of the same name (see **Newfoundland**), which recounts how the author reconstructed a leather boat and undertook a voyage across the Atlantic to establish that the 6th-century Irishman, St. Brendan (484-577), could have sailed to North America. There are ten parts to the suite, with the uilleann pipes representing the boat as it battles with the forces of nature and finally arrives in Newfoundland. Within the structure of the melody line composed for pipes, O'Flynn was able to use ornamentation in the traditional way. Davey subsequently produced further new works blending elements of traditional and orchestral music, including *The Pilgrim* (1983), *Granuaile* (1985; see **Granuaile**) and *The Relief of the Siege of Derry* (1989). The latter was commissioned by Derry City Council to commemorate the 300th anniversary of the 1689 Siege of Derry during the Williamite/Jacobite War (see **Jacobite Song**). Shaun Davey's works have been performed not only in Ireland but also in Britain, the US, Canada and Australia. In 1989 he received a 'People of the Year' award for his contribution to Irish culture. A special performance of *The Brendan Voyage* and *Granuaile* in the Waterfront Hall, Belfast on St. Patrick's Day, 2001 featured singer Rita Connolly, **Peter Browne**, **Nollaig Ní Chathasaigh**, **Michael McGoldrick** and the Ulster Orchestra. Davey also composed 'May We Never Have to Say Goodbye', the anthem for the 2003 Special Olympics (held in Ireland), on which the lead parts were sung by Rita Connolly and Ronan Tynan. Website: www.shaundavey.com.

De Brún, Darach (b. 1948) Tin whistle player, uilleann piper and composer born in the Navan Road area of Dublin. De Brún's exceptionally large repertoire of tunes, some of them extremely rare, includes many he wrote himself. Four of these – 'The Maple Leaf', 'The Man of Aran', 'Terry's Travels' and 'The Walk of the Fiddler's Bride' – he recorded with the group **Oisín** on their first album, simply titled *Oisín* (1976). 'The Man of Aran' has been recorded on at least a dozen albums, in some cases described as 'traditional' – a remarkable testament to its popularity and the rapidity with which it has been absorbed into the tradition. More recently De Brún has composed and recorded a selection of thirty tunes that are linked thematically and together comprise *The Beehive Suite* (due for release in 2005). The tunes are arranged in an order that follows developments in the beehive from spring through summer and on into winter. Although linked thematically by their titles, the tunes themselves are arranged as separate tracks, including sets of jigs, reels and hornpipes as well as a waltz (intriguingly titled 'The Waggle Dance'), three slow tunes and a slow march. De Brún worked on the arrangements with producer Conor Long (who also plays **blarge** on the album), and additional musicians include Sinéad Madden (fiddle), Gerry Byrne (classical flute) and Harry Long (low whistle). De Brún himself plays uilleann pipes and tin whistle on the album and carried out for it extensive research on the subject of bees and bee-keeping.

De Dannan   One of the best-known and longest-lasting traditional groups, formed in 1974. There were numerous changes in line-up, but the core members of the group were always **Frankie Gavin** (fiddle, flute) and **Alec Finn** (bouzouki, guitar). The original line-up also included Charlie Piggot (banjo, whistles), **Jackie Daly** (accordion), **Johnny 'Ringo' McDonagh** (bodhrán, bones, percussion) and Dolores Keane (see **Keane Family**, vocals). Other singers with the group were **Andy Irvine**, **Johnny Moynihan**, Maura O'Connell, **Mary Black**, **Eleanor Shanley**, Seán Ó Conaire and Tommy Fleming. **Colm Murphy** replaced McDonagh on bodhrán while **Máirtín O'Connor** took over from Daly on accordion and was himself replaced by Derek Hickey. Box player Aidan Coffey from Bunmahon, Co. Waterford joined the group in their latter years. Charlie Piggot left the group after his hands were seriously injured in an accident but he now plays the button accordion and can be heard on *The New Road* (2000) with Gerry Harrington (fiddle). Gavin's fast and fiery fiddle playing, along with Finn's delicate bouzouki accompaniments, were central to the group's sound throughout all of these changes.

De Dannan rapidly developed a reputation for virtuoso playing and lively arrangements of dance tunes. Most of the material on their numerous albums is traditional, but they also dabbled in other types of music. 'My Irish Molly O', an Irish-American dance-hall song originally released by the **Flanagan Brothers** in 1928, was a popular hit for them in 1981. They also experimented with 'traditional Irish' interpretations of Beatles' songs, most famously with the 1980 single 'Hey Jude', as well as Jewish Klezmer, Black Gospel and Classical music. Their 1996 album *Hibernian Rhapsody* features as its title track De Dannan's instrumental version of the classic Queen song 'Bohemian Rhapsody', although the rest of the album is traditional. 'Hibernian Rhapsody' and 'Hey Jude' both reappear on *Welcome to the Hotel Connemara* (2000). De Dannan released a double-CD, *How* *the West Was Won*, in 1999 to celebrate the group's twenty-fifth anniversary. They broke up in 2002.

De Hóra, Seán   **Sean-nós** singer from Ballferriter in the Dingle **Gaeltacht** in Co. Kerry. His style is highly nasal compared to that of Connemara singers such as **Seosamh Ó Héanaí**. He recorded an album of songs in Irish, simply titled *Seán De Hóra* (1977).

Brian Fleming of De Jimbe

De Jimbe   Group which combines Irish traditional music with drumming and rhythms from West Africa and the Caribbean. The group originated as a percussion ensemble, led by Brian Fleming, that explored different traditions in drumming and were especially interested in the West African djembe and related instruments. While most of the musicians are Irish, the Nigerian-born percussionist Bisi Adigun is an important part of the line-up, playing djembe, talking drum and rhumba. Brian Fleming plays bodhrán, djembe, djoun djoun, sangban, darabuka, sagaat, congas, bongos, bells and chekere. Hugh O'Byrne plays drum kit, djoun djoun, kenkeni, sang ban, bells, maracas and timbales. In addition to this strong percussion section is Pádhraic Ó Láimhín (uilleann pipes), Muireann Nic Amhlaiobh (vocals, flute, whistle, low whistle), Brian O'Toole (bass), Des Charleson (guitar) and Tony Byrne (guitar). They have been involved in projects with **Kíla**, **Anúna** and singer **Iarla Ó Lionáird** of the **Afro Celts**. Their first album, *De Jimbe* (2001), invites comparisons with the Afro Celts, although De Jimbe rely on percussion rather than the programmed sounds and loops which are a strong element of the Afro Celt's music.

One of the most interesting projects that De Jimbe has been involved in was the ESB Millennium Drum Carnival at which a group of 50 musicians played, centred on De Jimbe and directed by Brian Fleming. Fleming played an enormous drum designed to symbolise harmony between the Protestant and Catholic communities in Ireland by appearing to be a bodhrán on one side and a **lambeg drum** on the other. This drum is in the Guinness Book of Records, 2001 as the largest drum in the world. De Jimbe have performed in many parts of the world including **Brittany**, Gambia, Cuba, Korea and the **US**. Website: www.dejimbe.com.

Deiseal Dublin-based experimental group (*deiseal* means 'direction of the sun'), consisting of **Cormac Breatnach** (whistles, backing vocals), Niall Ó Callanáin (acoustic and electric bouzouki, acoustic guitar) and Paul O'Driscoll (double and fretless bass). The group, who made two albums, played an interesting combination of traditional and original material in a style that was strongly influenced by jazz. Breathnach's whistle playing, even on the traditional tunes, is highly improvisational. The title track of their first album, *The Long, Long Note* (1992) is based around sections from two traditional dance tunes married together and arranged in a jazz style, with the whistle improvising in the middle. The album also has an unusual, up-tempo version of the **Turlough O'Carolan** air 'Sí Bheag, Sí Mhór' and **Seán Ó Riada**'s slow air 'Mná na hÉireann' ('Women of Ireland'). There are compositions by Breathnach, Ó Callanáin and three musicians from the **US**, and a fine rendition of the traditional hornpipe 'The Rights of Man'.

For their second album, *Sunshine Dance* (1995) the trio were joined by jazz musicians Mirabelle de Nuit (vocals), Richie Buckley (saxophone) and Conor Guilfoyle (drums, tablas and percussion; see **Khanda**). The album was a similar mixture of traditional and original material (including a composition by O'Driscoll). The traditional 'O'Neill's March', 'The Flowing Tide/Biddy Walsh's' and 'The Wise Maid', as well as the jazzy original title track, include vocals worked into the melody in an unusual way, an experiment tried in a less pronounced way on *The Long, Long Note*. The only song recorded by Deiseal is also on the album, sung by de Nuit with French lyrics and arranged in a vaguely Afro-Caribbean style. The group broke up in 1996.

Derrane, Joe (b. 1930) Bostonian accordion player whose father was born on Inis Mór, largest of the Aran Islands, Co. Galway. Derrane was a legend among box players in the 1940s and 50s, but in the 1960s took up the piano accordion and started to play whatever kind of music at which he could make a living. He gradually drifted away from the traditional scene but made a remarkable comeback in the 1990s, when he returned to Irish traditional music on the button accordion, appearing on stage in 1994. A 1950s recording, *Irish Accordion Masters*, made with his teacher, Jerry O'Brien and his brother, George (banjo) was re-released in 1995. Three new albums then followed. The first two, *Give Us Another* (1995) and *Return to Inis Mór* (1996), have piano accompaniments by Felix Dolan and Carl Hession respectively. The third album, *The Tie that Binds* (1998), has guest performances by **Frankie Gavin** (fiddle), **Séamus Egan** (guitar, banjo) of **Solas** and others – musicians who bring out the best in Derrane's playing.

Dervish One of the finest acoustic traditional groups to emerge in the 1990s. Initially called the Boys of Sligo, their first album was entitled *Dervish* (1989). The album is entirely instrumental and features Sligo musicians Liam Kelly (flute, tin whistle), Shane Mitchell (accordion) and Michael Holmes (guitar, bouzouki), with Martin McGinley (fiddle, viola) from Donegal and Brian McDonagh (mandola, mandolin and bouzouki) from Dublin. Most of the music is traditional jigs and reels, with some original tunes, including 'The World's End' (Holmes and McDonagh) and **Darach de Brún**'s reel 'The Man of Aran'.

For their second album, *Harmony Hill* (1993), the group adopted Dervish as their name. The dervish is a Muslim ascetic, and whirling dervishes are noted for a frenzied, ecstatic, whirling dance. This is the first album on which the Roscommon singer Kathy Jordan joined the group. Her singing became an integral part of the group's performances, and she also plays spoons and bodhrán on instrumental tracks. Shane McAleer from Tyrone also joined at this stage, replacing McGinley on fiddle. Two further CDs, *Playing with Fire* (1994) and *At the End of the Day* (1996), were followed by a double CD, *Live in Palma* (1997). Recorded in the 'Teatre Principal' at Palma on the Spanish island of Mallorca in April 1997, the album captures the atmosphere of this live performance superbly. The music has great energy and vitality and epitomises all that is best about Dervish. The songs (in both English and Irish) are beautifully arranged, with the stringed instruments (bouzouki, mandola and mandolin) dancing delicately around Jordan's vocals and other instruments coming and going between verses. The instrumental tracks have an exceptional power, well arranged with the stringed instruments again playing a major role. Sometimes they play melody, sometimes a light, delicately woven accompaniment, often developing into powerful, driving rhythms. There are few groups in which the mandolin, mandola and bouzouki are used in such varied and striking ways. The style is reminiscent of an earlier group, **Oisín**, of which Brian McDonagh was also a member. In 1998 Shane McAleer left the group, which was then joined by Séamus O'Dowd (guitar) and Tom Morrow (fiddle). With this line-up they made their sixth album, *Midsummer's Night* (1999). *Decade* (2001) is a compilation of material from the group's previous albums.

Spirit (2003) marks a new departure for the group in many ways. It incorporates, for the first time, a newly composed song ('The Fair-haired Boy' by Brendan Graham) and further songs by Scotttish poet **Robert Burns**, **Ewan MacColl** and Bob Dylan ('Boots of Spanish Leather'). There is also an unusual arrangement of a triad of traditional songs in Irish, collectively titled 'Jig Songs', and seven of the album's thirteen tracks are instrumentals. Séamus O'Dowd provides lead vocals on two tracks and plays electric as well as acoustic guitar, bodhrán, harmonicas, tarabuka,

Dervish

bass, tiple and tambourine. Guests on the album include the West Ocean String Quartet, Chris Hinderyckx (sitar), Dave Carthy and Eddie Lee (both playing bass) and the Israeli Avshalom Farjun, who plays the *qanoun*, an Arab harp. The latter instrument is used to great effect on the album's closing track, with the second jig in the set, 'Whelan's', arranged with an long section of improvisation in the middle. Website: www.dervish.ie.

Different Drums of Ireland

Different Drums of Ireland   Innovative group formed in 1992 whose initial inspiration was the brilliant Kodo drummers from Japan. Taking the **lambeg drum** and the **bodhrán** as symbols of the Protestant and Catholic communities, the group has attempted to play a music that respects the diversity of different musical traditions within Northern Ireland. At a time when the lambeg drum was internationally associated with political tension and Orange intimidation in Northern Ireland, the group's idealism met with some outraged responses but was increasingly admired and respected. Founder members Roy Arbuckle and Stephen Matier, both from Derry, had a strong background in community arts and cross-community projects. As Northern Ireland strove to establish a lasting peace process through the 1990s, Different Drums of Ireland captured the spirit of the times through their music.

After numerous appearances at festivals and on television throughout Ireland, a major breakthrough was the group's inclusion in the 'Both Sides Now' tour of the **US** in 1999. The tour involved **Phil Coulter**, classical flautist James Galway, actors Gregory Peck and Aidan Quinn, writer Edna O'Brien and others. Different Drums performed in St. Patrick's Cathedral, New York and, on St. Patrick's Day, for President Clinton in the White House. They had also performed the previous year for the Irish Presidents Mary Robinson and Mary McAleese. Stephen Matier (lambeg) and Brendan Monaghan (bodhrán) played with Tommy Sands (see **Sands Family**) outside Stormont Castle in the days just before the Good Friday Agreement (1998) was signed.

Arbuckle and Matier both play bodhrán and lambeg with the group, and Arbuckle is their main singer. Matier also plays bones and tarbuca and provides additional vocals. The multi-talented Brendan Monaghan played uilleann pipes, Scottish small pipes, Highland pipes, whistles, bodhrán and contributed significantly to the group's vocals. A native of Banbridge, Co. Down, he has won many **All-Ireland** titles and was the mainstay of Irish traditional music in the group. Kevin Sharkey from Derry plays djembe, bodhrán, lambeg, tabla and snare drum. Rory McCarron, who joined Different Drums in 1998, plays bodhrán, djembe, snare drum, lambeg and long drum. The latter is a new, single-headed drum designed by the group. It is like a cross between a snare drum and a bodhrán, consisting of an elongated cylinder about sixteen inches in diameter and two feet deep. The top is covered in goatskin and can be played with soft sticks or drum sticks.

The group's first CD, *Different Drums of Ireland* (1999) includes 'Shanghai Lil', a version of an Orange marching tune called 'The Orange Lily-O', which was in turn derived from the traditional reel 'The Swallow's Tail'. There are just five tracks on the CD, which also includes the group's 'Millennium Theme'. Their second CD, *New Day Dawning* (2001) has nine tracks which encompass a variety of traditional and original material. There is an interesting version of the traditional reel 'My Love Is in America' with a funky bass line and sections of pure percussion. 'Lilty Reels' features the excellent **lilting** of Brendan Monaghan with percussion backing, interspersed with a reel played on uilleann pipes and whistle as well as percussion breaks. 'Biddy McDole' comes from the lambeg drumming tradition and incorporates two pieces in which rhymes are used to teach rhythmic patterns. It an interestingly arranged piece in which the two rhymes used to teach lambeg patterns are eventually overcome by the words 'dancing to the rhythm of a different drum, a different drum, a different drum'. There are also three songs, two by Roy Arbuckle and one by Peter O'Hanlon and an interesting track entitled 'Beannat', which begins with Arbuckle reciting words from John O'Donoghue's *Anam Cara* (London, 1997) to a sparse musical backing. Brendan Monaghan left Different Drums in 2002 and was replaced by Dolores O'Hare (uilleann pipes, whistles). Website: www.differentdrums.co.uk.

Dillon, Cara (b. 1975)   Singer born in Dungiven, Co. Derry who won the **All-Ireland** singing trophy at the age of 14. In the mid-1990s she replaced Kate Rusby (see **England**) in the folk band Equation and after a frustrating spell with a major recording label eventually released her first solo album, *Cara Dillon* (2001). The album won a number of awards, including two BBC Folk Awards. Dillon mixes traditional songs and original material, and her second album, *Sweet Liberty* (2003) includes traditional songs from Co. Derry as well as some fine original songs, including a cover of Tommy Sands' (see **Sands Family**) excellent song 'There Were Roses'.

Dirty Linen   The best-known American folk magazine, published bi-monthly. Covering a wide range of music, from world music to folk-rock and including articles, interviews, reviews and listings relating to Irish, Irish-American and other Celtic music, it is available by subscription worldwide. Website: www.dirtylinen.com.

Djembe   Single-headed African drum which since the 1990s has been used in Irish music by some of the more experimental groups, most notably **Kíla**, the **Afro Celts,** the **Barleyshakes** and **De Jimbe. Tommy Hayes** also plays the instrument. Like the **bongos** and **congas**, it is played with the hands.

Doherty, John (ca. 1895-1980)   Fiddler born in Ardara, in southwest Donegal. His family were travelling tinsmiths (see **Travellers**) and had been musicians (pipers and fiddlers) for generations. His father and brothers were all fiddlers and John was renowned as a virtuoso player by the time he was in his twenties. He spent most of his life travelling around Donegal, tinsmithing and fiddling, and was an honoured guest in the homes of many. He left Donegal on just two occasions, going to Belfast for a television appearance and to Dublin to win a gold medal for fiddling at the **Oireachtas** during the early 1950s. He came to prominence during the 1940s and was sought out by many collectors. **Paddy Glackin**'s father, Tom, set up a famous recording involving the Dohertys and **Breandán Breathnach** at Reelin Bridge, Co. Donegal in 1965. Other collectors attempted to approach him, and he is reported to have hidden from them on occasions in friends' houses. He made a number of albums throughout his career and UTV made a documentary film about him entitled *Fiddler on the Road*.

Doherty's unique style includes a powerful attack, clear, staccato triplets and double-stopping (a technique imitative of piping). He frequently played tunes in difficult keys that might involve moving beyond the first position at great speed. He also used a number of bowing techniques for which he had his own terms, including one used as the title for a recent compilation of Doherty recordings, *The Floating Bow* (1996). The term describes a slow use of the whole bow across the strings, playing chords and often slowing the rhythm of a tune. Doherty's playing of 'Miss Paterson's Slipper' and 'The Lancer's Jig/The Silver Slipper' on this album displays the breathtaking effect of his technique. The companion booklet provides valuable background information on the Dohertys by Alan Evans. John was renowned as a storyteller as much as a fiddler and often told strange tales about the tunes he played.

Another excellent Doherty recording, *Taisce: Celebrated Recordings from a Legendary Fiddle Player* (1978) was re-released on CD around the same time as *The Floating Bow*. *Taisce* means a 'store', 'hoard' or 'treasure', and the Doherty family were renowned for the wealth of their musical repertoire. The album includes **strathspey**s, **highland**s and **schottische**s, as well as marches, airs, hornpipes, jigs, reels and a song. John Doherty was influenced by many players, but had a special affection for the playing of the Scots fiddler John Scott Skinner, to whom the hard edge and precision of much of his playing has been traced. Many have erroneously identified Doherty's as *the* Donegal style, but despite his influence, his style is but one of a number of styles of fiddling within Donegal (see **Regional Styles**).

John's brother, Mickey (1894-1970), was also a fine fiddler who was recorded by members of the **Irish Folklore Commission** in 1949. These recordings were later edited and released as the album *The Gravel Walks: The Fiddle Music of Mickey Doherty* (1990).

Doherty, Liz (b. 1970) Fiddler born in Buncrana, Co. Donegal who learned fiddle and dancing in her childhood from the renowned teacher Dinny McLaughlin. She studied music at **University College Cork**, where she played with **Nomos** in the mid-1990s and eventually became head lecturer in Traditional Music. Although she left UCC in 2001 to devote more time to playing, she still does guest lectures in places as far away as the **US** and **Australia**, and also does consultation work in music and education. She was awarded a Ph.D. by the **University of Limerick** in 1996 for her thesis *The Paradox of the Periphery: Evolution of the Cape Breton Fiddle Tradition, 1929-1995*. In autumn 2003 she was appointed to a part-time post lecturing in Irish Traditional Music at the University of Ulster, Magee Campus, Derry. Her solo recordings, *Last Orders* (1999) and *Quare Imagination* (2002) display her remarkable ease in playing traditional music from Ireland, **Scotland** (especially the Shetland Islands), Cape Breton (see **Nova Scotia**) and even Finland. She has also recorded with the **Bumblebees** and the 16-piece fiddle orchestra, Fiddlesticks, whose *Racket in the Rectory* was released in 2000. She is among the most notable examples of the increased tendency among Irish musicians to show an interest in playing the music of other traditions which are historically linked to Ireland. Website: www.lizdoherty.ie. See also **Crossroads Conference**.

Donnelly, Dezi (b. 1973) Young Manchester-born fiddler who has won the **All-Ireland** and All-British Championship titles. His uncle, also Des Donnelly (1933-1973), was a renowned fiddler from Co. Tyrone. Dezi has a wild, innovative style with great drive and rhythm on dance tunes as well as an ability to handle slow airs with great sensitivity. He played in the folk-rock band Toss the Feathers with **Michael McGoldrick**, with whom he recorded the album *Champions of the North* in 1989-90 (re-released in 1996). His excellent performances with **Skirm** can be heard on the live album *Welcome* (1995) and on *Familiar Footsteps* (1998) he is accompanied by Andy Jones (guitar). He has also toured extensively with **Stockton's Wing**. Donnelly won the 'Young Traditional Musician of the Year' award in Dublin in 1999 and in the same year released a new solo album, *Handed Down*. See also **England**.

Doolin Area on the west coast of Co. Clare that has, since the 1970s, become a mecca for traditional music enthusiasts. It consists of two tiny villages, Roadford and Fisherstreet. It was part of the **Gaeltacht** up to the 1940s, and even before its rise in popularity in the 70s, its old-world atmosphere attracted writers, artists and musicians. George Bernard Shaw, J. M. Synge, Oliver St. John Gogarty and Dylan Thomas were among the many writers to be attracted there in the 1930s and 40s. **Séamus Ennis** visited in the mid 1940s to collect music and songs and **Ciarán Mac Mathúna** has been a frequent visitor since the 1950s.

A major hub of activity for visitors to Doolin since the earliest decades of the 20th century has been O'Connor's pub in Fisherstreet, licensed since 1832. O'Connor's was a regular haunt of the famous local musician **Micho Russell**, who often played there with his brothers, Packie and Gussie. Micho Russell's rise to fame in the 1960s and 70s undoubtedly contributed to the phenomenal rise of Doolin during the same period. People travelled from all over the world to hear the Russell brothers and other local musicians such as Paddy and John Killourhy performing in sessions which regularly featured famous musicians from other parts of Ireland and beyond. O'Connor's was owned and run from 1956 to 1998 by Gus O'Connor (1926-2003) and his wife Doll. Many sessions (including regular broadcasts of **RTÉ**'s *Céilí House* programme) were recorded in the pub, the earliest being *Behind the Cliffs of Moher* in 1949.

The isolated, wind-swept Doolin became a major tourist attraction. New restaurants opened as well as an international hostel, a craft shop, a record shop specialising in traditional music and also numerous 'bed and breakfast' houses. A regular daily bus service between Doolin and Dublin was established. The boom has undoubtedly brought great benefits to the local economy, but there are local musicians who dislike the congestion and the crowds seeking to join sessions. Some have sought quieter places for playing their music, although Doolin still attracts musicians and tourists from all over the world. Some musicians have moved there and settled from other parts of Ireland. Developments such as the Magnetic Music shop/restaurant provide a tasteful addition to Doolin's music scene. Here one can browse through the CDs on sale and listen to them on headphones or while eating in the restaurant. The restaurant also features some of Ireland's finest traditional musicians in its concert series. The Clare-born music producer **P. J. Curtis** wrote affectionately in 1994 of the unique spirit of place that attracts people to Doolin. Nonetheless he warned that 'if it is over-exploited or tampered with in an insensitive way, it may yet destroy that spirit, that special magic that lies at the heart of Doolin's appeal' (*Notes from the Heart*, p. 156). Development to date has, however, been slow and largely unobtrusive, and John Doorty, author of *A Place Called Doolin* (2002), has expressed amazement at the way Doolin has developed without any conscious effort or entrepreneurial vision. The CD *Doolin Point: The Best of Divers Nights 1992-1999* (2002) underlines the extent to which Doolin has retained its popularity among the best of traditional musicians, with performances from **Martin Hayes**, Dónal Clancy of **Solas**, Kevin Crawford of **Lúnasa**, **Matt Molloy**, **Jackie Daly** and others.

Doran, Felix (1914-1972) Younger brother of **Johnny Doran**, Felix started to learn the uilleann pipes from his brother in 1932 and, like the latter, travelled around the country playing. He won the All-Ireland uilleann piping title in 1963. It was from Felix that the Clare piper **Willie Clancy** bought his first set of practice pipes. Felix, although not as famous as his brother, became a fine piper in his own right and recorded a highly evocative and entertaining version of the descriptive piece 'The Foxhunt'. This, along with other recordings of Doran's playing made between 1965 and 1967, can be heard on *The Last of the Travelling Pipers*, initially released by **Topic** and later by **Ossian**.

Felix Doran

Doran, Johnny (1907-1950) Uilleann piper born into a family of travelling pipers (see **Travellers**) related to the legendary John Cash (1832-1909). In the 1930s

Doran started to travel the country in a horse-drawn caravan and made his living by trading horses and playing the pipes at fairs, sporting occasions and other gatherings. He played in the legato style, but sometimes incorporated staccato runs into a tune. He had an exceptional control over all parts of the uilleann pipes, chanter, drones and regulators and used the instrument to an extent not commonly heard among pipers today. On surviving recordings, Doran uses the drones and regulators throughout most of the tunes. He often switches off the drones and stops playing the regulators in the middle of a set, changing the whole texture of the piece and allowing him to display his virtuosity on the chanter. He is said to have done most of his playing outdoors and in a standing position, his leg placed in a T-shaped rest. During the 1930s and 40s, Doran spent long periods in Co. Clare, where he knew and influenced the young **Willie Clancy**. Certain tunes are still particularly associated with his playing, such as the reels 'Colonel Fraser', 'My Love Is in America' and 'Rakish Paddy'; the jigs 'Copper and Brass' and 'The Rambling Pitchfork'; and the slow air 'An Chúileann' ('The Coolin'). *The Bunch of Keys* (1988) features recordings made on acetate discs by Kevin Danaher of the **Irish Folklore Commission** in 1947, remastered by **Harry Bradshaw**. *The Master Pipers Vol. 1: Johnny Doran*, released in 2003, is another selection of tunes from the 1947 recordings remastered by Bradshaw. Many contemporary pipers were strongly influenced by Doran, including **Finbar Furey**, **Paddy Keenan** and **Davy Spillane**. See also **Felix Doran**.

Dordán All-female group who play Irish traditional and baroque music. *Dordán* is the Irish for 'hum, buzz, drone'. They started as a trio in 1990 with **Mary Bergin** (whistles), **Kathleen Loughnane** (harp) and Dearbhaill Standún (violin, viola). The singer Martina Goggin later joined the group and appears on their third album, *Christmas Capers: Oíche Nollaig* (1996), an interesting collection of Irish traditional and original material associated with Christmas. The album was released (with additional tracks) in the **US** as *The Night Before...A Celtic Christmas: Celtic Aire* (1999) and includes original songs, traditional airs and dance tunes and arrangements of **O'Carolan**, Handel and Mozart.

Double Cut See **Casadh**.

Double Jig See **Jig**.

Double Stop A type of ornamentation originally associated with the **fiddle** which involves playing two strings at once. It is often used at the end of a phrase, or sometimes at the beginning. A similar technique, involving the simultaneous sounding of more than one note, is now used by many **accordion** and **concertina** players.

Doyle, Danny Singer/guitarist from Dublin who emerged during the **Ballad Boom**. He had a number of hit singles in the 1960s, including 'Whiskey on a

Sunday', and has always sung **rebel songs**, part of a family tradition that he traces to his grandmother. Doyle has made many albums and has recently written three shows dealing with themes from Irish history through song. Material from one of the shows was released on a CD entitled *The Gold Sun of Freedom: 1798 in Song and Story* (1998), and a book of the same title was also published. Doyle was assisted in the project by **Frank Harte** and like the latter has dedicated much time to researching the historical background of Ireland's ballads. Doyle has been living in the **US** since 1982.

Draíocht   The word 'draíocht' in the Irish language has a range of meanings and can be used to refer to 'druidism' or 'druidic arts'. It also means 'magic' or 'enchantment' and the phrase 'ceol draíochta' is used to describe 'magical or enchanting music'. Musicians of the 20th and 21st century use it to describe a magical, lonesome sadness which can be expressed by playing traditional music in a certain way. Although not confined to any particular area, it is often associated with the music of Galway and Clare. Musicians like the fiddler/composer **Paddy Fahy** from east Galway are often said to have this strange, lonesome quality in their music. Among the older players the names of **Séamus Ennis** and **Joe Cooley** are often mentioned in connection with 'draíocht'. The enchantment is often associated with certain tunes as well as certain players. These tunes are often in minor keys and their magic can be brought out more effectively by being played in a slower tempo than normal. Among the younger contemporary players, **Martin Hayes** is a good example of a player who has 'draíocht' in much of the music he plays. On *The Lonesome Touch* (1997), airs, reels, jigs and hornpipes are all suffused with a wistful delicacy. In an interview with the *Irish Times* (29 August 1998) after the release of *The Lonesome Touch*, Hayes spoke of how 'a lot of the older players kept talking to me about that sadness in the music, that *draíocht*, that touch.'

Drennan, William (1754-1820)   Belfast-born Presbyterian who was a founding member of the Dublin Society of United Irishmen. He was a poet and his 'The Wake of William Orr' became a popular song in 1798. Orr (1766-1797) was a Protestant farmer in Co. Antrim and the first United Irishman to be hanged for treason under the new insurrection act. 'Remember Orr' became a rallying cry for many of the rebels of 1798, and Drennan's song did much to spread Orr's fame. Drennan also published the poem 'When Erin First Rose' (1795), from which the phrase 'the emerald isle' was coined. See **Nationalist/Republican Song**.

Drew, Ronnie (b. 1934)   Dublin-born singer and guitarist who was a central figure in the group the **Dubliners**, known as the 'Ronnie Drew Group' in their early days. Before forming the group, he spent three years in Spain, where he taught English and learned to play flamenco guitar. His unique, gravelly voice was part of the Dubliners' unique sound from 1962 to 1995, with the exception of 1974-1978, when he pursued a solo career. He again went solo in 1995, producing his own album and touring with a wide range of artists, including the **Dónal Lunny** Band, **Antonio Breschi** and **De Dannan**. He still appears with the Dubliners occasionally.

Dublin Pipers' Club   Founded in 1900, two years after the **Cork Pipers' Club**. Its secretary, Michael O'Duibhginn, brought the unprecedented number of seventeen pipers to the **Oireachtas** in 1912. Only twenty years later, however, the uilleann pipes were declining in popularity, due partly to the availability of mass-produced accordions, and the original Dublin Pipers' Club became defunct in 1925. In the late 1930s, however, **Leo Rowsome** led an attempt to revive piping in Dublin by reforming the Dublin Pipers' Club. The club was located at Molesworth Place from 1940 and from 1946 at Áras Ceannt, in Thomas Street. It became a gathering place for many famous musicians and inspired the foundation of other clubs, including one in Walterstown, Navan, Co. Meath (under Willie Reynolds). The involvement of Leo and Tom Rowsome in the founding of **Comhaltas Ceoltóirí Éireann** gradually led the Dublin Pipers' Club members into the broader, nationwide organisation of CCÉ, and the club itself became a branch of CCÉ in 1976. A new pipers' club, **Na Píobairí Uilleann**, was founded in Dublin in 1968.

Dubliners, The   Enormously successful traditional group formed in 1962 by **Ronnie Drew** (vocals, guitar), **Luke Kelly** (vocals, five-string banjo), Ciaran Bourke (tin whistle, vocals, guitar), **Barney McKenna** (tenor banjo, mandolin, vocals), and soon joined by **John Sheahan** (fiddle). They played a combination of songs and traditional dance music that was quite rare among the performers who had emerged during the **ballad boom**, who tended to concentrate exclusively on songs. In McKenna they had the most accomplished player of Irish traditional music on the tenor banjo, with Sheahan and Bourke strengthening the group's instrumental section. The main singers, Drew and Kelly, both had strong, earthy voices which were very much part of the Dubliners' sound from the beginning. Although Kelly left in 1964 and was replaced by Bob Lynch (d. 1982), he was back with the group about two years later. They were popular throughout Britain and Europe in the 1960s, their album *The New Dubliners* (1967) selling 25,000 copies in less than three weeks. This broke all records for folk music, and in the same year the single 'Seven Drunken Nights' (learned from **Seosamh Ó Héanaí**) reached No. 5 in the British charts. This was a major breakthrough not only for the Dubliners but for Irish music generally, which had never known such chart success before. The song was banned by **RTÉ** as offensive to public decency.

The group went from strength to strength, touring major concert venues throughout Europe and Britain. In 1974, however, Ciaran Bourke suffered a massive brain haemorrhage that effectively ended his career with the group. He made a partial recovery, but died in 1988. Ronnie Drew left in 1974 to be replaced by **Jim McCann**, who toured and recorded with the group until the end of 1978. Drew returned at the start of 1979 and Galway-born Seán Cannon (vocals, guitar) joined in 1982. Luke Kelly, who had been suffering from cancer, died in 1984, but the Dubliners continued, touring the **US**, **Canada**, **Australia** and New Zealand. In 1987 they marked 25 years together with a double album, *The Dubliners Celebration*, with guest appearances by **Christy Moore**, **Paddy Reilly**, Jim McCann, **Kevin Conneff**, **Stockton's Wing** and **Finbar Furey**. The **Pogues** also guested on this album, and their single with the group, 'The Irish Rover', reached No. 8 in the British charts. Eamonn Campbell (guitar, mandolin, tambourine, backing vocals), who produced the album, joined the group full-time after its release. RTÉ's *Late Late Show* did a special on their 25th anniversary, and in 1988 *Dubliners' Dublin* (a special collection of Dublin songs on album and video) was released to mark the city's millennium. On the first entry of the Republic of Ireland soccer team into the Word Cup Finals in 1990, the group released a single and video, 'Jack's Heroes', with the Pogues. Their double CD collection, *30 Years A-Greying* (1992) is a fine collection of songs and dance music, with special guests Billy Connolly, **De Dannan**, Hot House Flowers, the Pogues and Rory Gallagher. It contains a booklet with an excellent history of the group. Ronnie Drew left in 1995 to pursue a solo career, but still appears with the group from time to time. *The Dubliners: 40 Years* (2002) is partly

The Dubliners, 1960s

a compilation, but eleven of the twenty tracks are new. The group toured throughout Europe in 2002 with a line-up that included McKenna, Sheahan, Cannon, Campbell and the most recent member, Paddy Reilly. The Dubliners have played an important role in bringing Dublin into a central position in the traditional music revival, giving a new credibility and popularity to street ballads and (especially in the days of Luke Kelly) songs that have a relevance to contemporary social and political issues. See also **Dominic Behan**.

Dulcimer (*téadchlár* or *dulcaiméir*)   A stringed instrument of the zither family of which there are two main types, the hammer dulcimer and the Appalachian dulcimer. The word 'dulcimer' came into English in the 15th century and is ultimately derived from the Latin *dulce melos* ('sweet song'). The hammer dulcimer consists of a flat, shallow sound box which comes in a variety of shapes but is often trapezoidal. Ten or more pairs of strings, stretched over two bridges, are struck with hammers, usually made of wood. The instrument originated in Western Asia and came to Western Europe in the 15th century, possibly from Byzantium. It is interesting to note, however, that a very similar instrument, called the **timpán**, existed in Ireland as early as the 12th century. The modern hammer dulcimer, however, seems to have arrived in Ireland around the 18th century, probably from Britain. There is no evidence to link it directly to the medieval timpán. In modern Ireland the hammer dulcimer is quite rare, and is mostly played in the northeastern counties of Antrim and Down. The most famous player in recent times was John Rea (d. 1983), an Antrim man, who made two albums and is the subject of **Colin 'Hammy' Hamilton's** study *John Rea: Profile of a Hammer Dulcimer Player* (1977). Rea played mostly traditional Irish and Scottish tunes, including many of those attributed to **Walker Jackson**.

The Appalachian dulcimer is only rarely played in Ireland. It is more popular in the **US**, where it is usually used by singers like **Jean Ritchie** to accompany songs. It was originally made in the 18th century in the southern **Appalachians** by people of Scottish origin. It consists of a long, narrow, oval frame about one metre long and 70 centimetres wide over which are stretched three metal strings. One of the strings is fretted and used for playing melody while the other two are drones which sound almost continuously. The instrument is held flat on the lap or placed on a table, and the strings are sounded with a plectrum or finger-picks.

One of the most interesting and unusual dulcimer players is Frenchman John Molineux, who made an album with the Irish company, **Claddagh Records**. *Douce Amère/Bitter Sweet: Music Divers for the Dulcimer Family from Ireland, England and France, with Tablatures* (1978) includes three instrumental tracks played on the Appalachian dulcimer. Molineux started by playing the Appalachian dulcimer but wanted more basses. Initially he added two more strings to the three normally found on the Appalachian instrument. Later he made a new, larger instrument called a 'dulcichord', which has a range of four octaves and a wider tonal range. Much of the music on the album (which includes Irish traditional dance tunes) is played on the dulcichord, Molineux displaying exceptional skill on the instrument.

Egan, Séamus (b. 1959)   Multi-instrumentalist born to Irish parents in Philadelphia who lived in Co. Mayo for much of his childhood. While living in Mayo, he learned to play tin whistle and started to learn flute. He won four **All-Ireland** under-14 titles (whistle, flute, mandolin and tenor banjo) and made his first solo album, *Traditional Music of Ireland* (1986) at the age of 16. In the **US** he played tenor banjo with **Mick Moloney**, **Robbie O'Connell**, **Eileen Ivers** and Jimmy Keane (accordion) in the Irish-American group, the Green Fields of America. On his solo albums *A Week in January* (1990) and *When Juniper Sleeps* (1996) he experimented with music from different traditions, including those of Sweden, **Newfoundland** and **Cape Breton**, and used backing musicians from a variety of different backgrounds. He also recorded the soundtrack for the award-winning film *The Brothers McMullen,* three tracks from it featuring on *When Juniper Sleeps*. On his fourth solo album, *In Your Ear* (1998), he plays sets of traditional reels, jigs, hornpipes and planxties, mostly on banjo. In the early 1990s he played with **Susan McKeown**, Eileen Ivers and John Doyle in the New York-based band Chanting House. In 1995 he was a founder member of the group **Solas**. See also **Mad for Trad**.

Elizabeth I   Queen of **England** and Ireland (1533-1603). Her reign saw a comprehensive attempt at completing the military conquest and colonisation of Ireland. As part of this policy, the importation into Ireland of Papist 'books, ballets [ballads], songs, sonnets, works, treatises, rymes or writings' could incur a fine or imprisonment. Pipers and harpers (as well as bards), closely associated with the Gaelic Irish nobility, were targeted by severe legislation that could, in times of war, mean imprisonment or hanging. Hence the infamy of Lord Barrymore, ordered by Elizabeth 'to hang the harpers, wherever found, and destroy their instruments' (F. O'Neill, *Irish Minstrels and Musicians*, p. 27). At times when Gaelic-Irish resistance to the conquest was less marked, however, the pipers and harpers were often pardoned. In 1601, for example, after the English had brought the Nine Years War to an end with their victory at the battle of Kinsale, a total of 11 harpers and (between 1601 and 1603) over twenty pipers were pardoned by the queen. Ironically, Elizabeth herself was renowned for her love of Irish music and dancing. She had an Irish harper, Cormac McDermot, at her court from 1590 until the time of her death. McDermot continued in favour with Elizabeth's successor, **James I**. See also **Bard**; **England**; **Granuaile**; **Harp**; **Henry VIII**; **War Pipes**, **Irish**.

Emmet Spiceland   Group that emerged during the 1960s **ballad boom** with **Dónal Lunny**, Brian Bolger and the Byrne brothers from Yorkshire, England. Lunny and Bolger had been members of the Emmet Folk Group (with **Mick Moloney**), and the Byrnes had been in a group called Spiceland. The four got together just before the Wexford Ballad Contest in 1967. After winning the contest they went on to have a number one hit in Ireland with their single 'Mary of Dungloe', which was also included on their only album, *Emmet Spiceland* (1968, reissued 1977). The album consisted mainly of songs, among which were 'The Curragh of Kildare' and 'Lagan Love', but there were also instrumental tracks, including 'Carolan's Concerto', composed by the blind harper **Turlough O'Carolan**. Noted for their harmony singing and interesting arrangements, Emmet Spiceland had a more subtle approach to traditional music and song than some of the groups which performed during the ballad boom.

Emigration Song Songs about emigration became popular during the 19th century and are still widely sung and composed. Although emigration had taken place on a considerable scale in the 17th and 18th centuries (especially to the **Appalachians**) and the earliest decades of the 19th century, the years of the **Great Famine** (1845-1849) and the following decades saw a massive exodus, with millions of Irish people leaving the country. Emigration continued to take place – especially to the **US**, **Canada**, **Australia** and Great Britain (see **England**, **Scotland**, **Wales**) – throughout the 20th century and remains an important theme in traditional song. Emigration songs have treated the theme in different ways. In some songs, the land of Ireland or a particular locality is simply praised, but in others the love of a place left behind is closely tied to the love of a man or woman. Other songs place more emphasis on social comment, as in 'Lone Shanakyle', which deals with the horrors of the Great Famine in Co. Clare. Some songs combine several of these elements, as in 'Paddy's Green Shamrock Shore', lamenting the leaving of Ireland and a 'lassie' but also describing in considerable detail the conditions on board a ship bound for New York from Derry. More contemporary songs on the theme of emigration have been written by songwriters such as **Robbie O'Connell** and members of the **Pogues**. See also **Argentina**; *Bringing It All Back Home*; **Moloney, Mick**.

England England frequently appears in Irish traditional and folk song as the 'old enemy' because of her involvement in Ireland as a colonial power since the late 12th century. The history of musical connections between Ireland and England, however, is complex. English monarchs such as **Henry VIII** and **Elizabeth I** employed Irish musicians, despite the fact that in Ireland itself they legislated against them. It was through English settlers, merchants and travellers that forms like the **carol** and the **ballad** (see also **Child Ballads**) came to Ireland. Settlers from **Scotland** also had an enormous influence on the growth in popularity of ballads from the 17th century. **Breandán Breathnach** also noted that some Irish jigs are undoubtedly of English origin, and the hornpipe is also a dance or dance tune which originated in England. Even in the Middle Ages emigrants from Ireland went in considerable numbers to England, and Irish emigration to all parts of Britain since the **Great Famine** (1845-1849) has been considerable. These emigrants brought their music with them, and traditional Irish music has enjoyed considerable popularity in England for the last century.

The first céilí dance was held in London in 1897 (see also **Céilí Dancing** and **Conradh na Gaeilge**) and **céilí bands** were popular in Britain in the 1950s, many being formed among emigrant communities in Britain itself. The **BBC** undertook the collection of folk music in Ireland (as well as Britain) in the 1940s and 50s; **Séamus Ennis** was among those employed by the organisation to do so. Musicians such as **Bobby Casey**, **Julia Clifford**, **Catherine McEvoy** and many others spent much of their lives in England, and traditional music has been popular and well organised in English cities like London, Birmingham and Liverpool since the 1950s. In the 1960s singers such as Peggy Seeger and **Ewan MacColl** had a profound influence throughout Britain and on some Irish singers like **Luke Kelly**, and the **Dubliners** enjoyed great success in England. The early 1980s saw the emergence of the **Pogues**, a group that was in many ways a unique product of the Irish community in England. More recently **Afro Celts**, a group with members from Ireland, **Brittany**, Africa and England, has emerged through the inspiration of Simon Emerson from Stoke Newington, England. English-born **James McNally** has played with the Pogues and is now with Afro Celts. Many other exceptionally talented young traditional musicians have emerged from the Irish community in England, including **Michael McGoldrick**, **Dezi Donnelly** and the group Céile, all from Manchester.

English dance music was far more widely played in the late 19th and early 20th centuries than it is now. Even at the beginning of the 20th century, musicians in the countryside all over England could be found playing jigs, hornpipes, double-hornpipes (in 9/4 time), reels and **schottische**s. In an interview in the *Irish Times* (13 July 1999), **Martin Carthy** and Norma Waterson (see **Watersons**) remarked that the decline of English dance music was caused by the dances being suppressed by the Church. They claimed that, although the Catholic Church attempted to control or wipe out country dance all over Europe (for Ireland see **Dancing and Religion**), the Protestant churches were more effective. Carthy noted that they always had the best audiences in Catholic countries when on tour in Europe.

Although English dancing and dance music do not now have the same variety, vigour and international appeal as their Irish counterparts, some English folk singers and groups have been popular and influential in England, Ireland and elsewhere since the 1960s. The Copper Family from Sussex enjoyed considerable popularity on the English folk circuit in the 1960s and 70s, singing *a cappella* with warm, delicately woven harmonies. They influenced the singing of the Irish group the **Voice Squad**. Other significant English acts include the Watersons, singer/songwriter Ralph McTell (whose song 'Clare to Here' was a big hit for the **Furey Brothers**), **Pentangle**, the folk/rock groups Fairport Convention, Steeleye Span, the Albion Band and the Oyster Band, Martin Simpson, singer/songwriter Martin Carthy and his wife Norma Waterson. Richard Thompson (singer/songwriter, guitarist), who played with Fairport Convention up to 1971, has established a reputation as one of the finest contemporary folk songwriters of the past 30 years. The virtuoso guitarist Chris Newman plays Irish, Scottish and other types of music superbly on guitar and has formed a unique partnership with Irish harpist **Máire Ní Chathasaigh**. Since the mid-1980s Londoner Billy Bragg has provided a sharper edge to the English contemporary folk scene, performing his own highly political songs in a style often bordering on punk. One of his most interesting projects involved collaboration with the American band Wilco in the late 1990s on a collection of newly discovered **Woody Guthrie** songs, released on two albums, *Mermaid Avenue I* and *Mermaid Avenue II.*

English folk music seems, in many respects, to be in a healthier state at the start of the 21st century than at any other time since the 1960s. Chris Wood (vocals, fiddle, guitar) has played with many of the finest English folk singers and traditional musicians and performed and taught throughout Britain and Ireland. Singer Beth Orton has developed a unique style of music which is based in folk but fused with more contemporary influences. The Northumbrian piper and fiddler Kathryn Tickell (see **Bagpipes**) and melodeon/button accordion player Andy Cutting (from Middlesex) have both made a considerable impact internationally. Cutting has recorded and performed with Kate Rusby, one of the finest singers of English, Irish and Scots song to emerge from England in decades. He also made a fine album, *One Roof Under* (2002), with Northamptonshire-born piano accordion player Karen Tweed. Tweed is a highly accomplished player who mixes traditional, jazz and classical styles and plays music from Ireland (see **Accordion**), England, Scandinavia and Europe. She was a founder member of the Poozies and can be heard on *May Monday* (2001). She and Kathryn Tickell are also among the core staff on the Folk Music degree course at the University of Newcastle-upon-Tyne. This course, which began in September 2001, covers folk and traditional music and song of Britain and its islands and is the first course of its kind in England. The course is perhaps a sign of the times, with a seemingly greater tendency for traditional musicians from throughout Britain and Ireland to perform and record with each other. Much of the music recorded as a result underlines the extent to which some of the music of England, Scotland and Ireland has common roots. Listening to Kate Rusby's excellent first album, *Hourglass* (1997), for example, one is struck by the extent to which she is equally at home singing traditional songs from Ireland, Scotland and England as she is with contemporary material. Rusby, a native of Barnsley, Yorkshire, has since released *Sleepless* (1999), *Little Lights* (2001) and *Underneath the Stars* (2003), and has played in Ireland to great critical acclaim.

The collector Reg Hall has gathered together a great variety of folk music and song from England, Scotland, Wales and Ireland for a 20-volume anthology, a sampler of which has been issued as *The Voice of the People: A Selection from the Series of Anthologies* (2000). See also **English Folk Dance and Song Society**; **fRoots**; **Newfoundland**.

English Concertina See **Concertina**.

English Folk Dance and Song Society Founded in London as the English Folk Song Society in 1898. The society collected and published folk songs,

ballads and tunes, and from its earliest days looked far beyond purely English material. It published the *Journal of the Folk Song Society* (8 vols, 35 parts) from 1899 to 1931, including Irish, Scots Gaelic, Manx, French and Canadian songs as well as English material. In 1932 the English Folk Song Society amalgamated with the English Folk Dance Society to form the English Folk Dance and Song Society. Their publication, the *Journal of the English Folk Dance and Song Society* (9 vols, 1932-63) continued to publish material from a wide variety of sources within and beyond England. The society also held international dance festivals and published articles on dance from such diverse places as Poland, Catalonia and the **Isle of Man**. It is indicative of the continued international interests of the society that it changed the name of its journal in 1965, calling it simply *Folk Music Journal*. This has been published annually since 1965 and the society's work continues to the present day. It also publishes (more or less quarterly) *English Dance and Song* for its members. In addition to the various journals and quarterlies over the years, the society also published two major reference works: *An Index of English Songs Contributed to the Journal of the Folk Song Society, 1899-1931, and its continuation the Journal of the English Folk Dance and Song Society to 1950* (London, 1951), compiled by E.A. White and edited by Margaret Dean-Smith; and *A Guide to English Folk Song Collections, 1822-1952* (Liverpool, 1954) by Margaret Dean-Smith.

Ennis, Séamus (1919-1982) Uilleann piper, singer, collector and broadcaster

born in Jamestown, Finglas, Co. Dublin. His father, Jimmy, was a prize-winning musician in several instruments, including the pipes. At school, the young Ennis excelled at English, Irish and Scots Gaelic, all of which would benefit him as a collector in later years. He picked up the uilleann pipes from about the age of 13, listening to his father, who also taught him to read music. **Colm O Lochlainn** of the Three Candles Press employed him for four years and he learned how to notate song airs, another invaluable skill that served him well in later years.

Ennis is considered to have been one of the greatest

Séamus Ennis & Colm Ó Gaodháin
Glinsk, County Galway
(courtesy of the Department of Irish Folklore,
University College Dublin)

uilleann pipers of the 20th century, with his own unique tone and style of varying tunes. He used all parts of the pipes – chanter, drones and regulators – although his use of the regulators was not as constant as in the playing of his contemporary, **Johnny Doran**. He developed unique playing techniques and could play several notes in the third octave of the chanter, a rare feat in piping. Many tunes in his large repertoire were learned from his father.

From 1942 to 1947 Ennis worked for the **Irish Folklore Commission** as a folk music collector, travelling to different parts of the country as well as to the Hebrides, off Scotland, to collect over 2,000 songs and tunes. From 1947 to 1951 he worked for Raidió Éireann (see **RTÉ**) and recorded music for broadcast from many musicians, including **Johnny Doherty**, **Micho Russell**, **Willie Clancy** and **Pádraig O'Keeffe**. The **BBC** set up a scheme in 1947 to record in detail the surviving folk culture of Britain and Ireland, and in 1951 Ennis left Raidió Éireann to work for the BBC on this scheme. He travelled extensively throughout Ireland, **England**, **Scotland** and **Wales** and was one of the presenters of the famous folk music programme *As I Roved Out* on BBC radio. He worked with the great American collector **Alan Lomax**, whom he introduced to many Irish musicians, including the singer **Elizabeth Cronin**. In 1952 he married and had two children, Catherine and Christopher. The BBC scheme came to an end in 1958, and Ennis eventually returned to Ireland.

Raidió Telefís Éireann, the newly established radio and television authority, provided Ennis with the opportunity for freelance work in Ireland. He worked for radio and on television programmes such as *Tales of Wonder: An Ceoltóir Sidhe* (*The Enchanting Musician*) and *Séamus Ennis sa Chathaoir* (*Séamus Ennis in the Chair*). In 1968 he was involved in founding **Na Píobairí Uilleann**, and his all-night sessions of piping were for many years a highlight of their annual assembly. He continued to tour Ireland, and sometimes England, eventually settling in Naul, Co. Dublin in 1975. He had a small plot of land on which he put a mobile home which he called 'Easter Snow' and it was there he died on 5 October 1982 after performing at both the **Willie Clancy Week** and the **Lisdoonvarna** Festival during the summer. There is now a Séamus Ennis Centre in Naul outside of which is a life-sized sculpture of the piper playing under a tree. The villages of Naul and Ballyboughal host Scoil Shéamuis Ennis every year in October.

A number of recordings of Ennis's playing are still available. *The Return from Fingal* (1997), is a collection of recordings from the RTÉ archives, some of which date back to 1940. This collection is of particular interest as most of the other recordings date from the 1970s. Of the latter, one of the finest is *The Best of Irish Piping* (1984), a reissue of two Ennis albums in one, *The Pure Drop* (1973) and *The Fox Chase* (1978). *Irish Pipe and Tin Whistle Songs* (1977), with Tommy Makem (see **Clancy Brothers and Tommy Makem**) and the **Dubliners**, was also re-released in 1989. Another valuable Ennis collection, originally released in the 1970s but now on CD, is *Forty Years of Irish Piping* (2000). *Séamus Ennis, Master of the Uillenn Pipes* (1985) and the double album from RTÉ, *The Séamus Ennis Story* (1988), were released on cassette tape. **Robbie Hannan** and Wilbert Garvin edited an uilleann pipes tutor by Ennis which was published in 1998.

Enya (Eithne Ní Bhraonáin, b. 1961)   Singer/keyboard player from the **Gaeltacht** area of Gweedore, Co. Donegal. Irish was her first language and she grew up surrounded by traditional music, although she was trained classically on the piano. A sister of **Máire Ní Bhraonáin**, Enya was vocalist and keyboard player with the group **Clannad** between 1979 and 1982 and performed one track on *Ceol Aduaidh* (1983), the first album of the group that subsequently became famous as **Altan**. She left Clannad to pursue a solo career, working on her own compositions with former Clannad manager Nicky Ryan and his wife, Roma. Her first solo album, *Enya* (1986), is a selection of music composed for the BBC series *The Celts*. Guest musicians on the album include **Arty McGlynn** and **Liam O'Flynn**. On *The Celts* Enya established the sound that was to make her internationally famous, using multi-layered vocals (often non-verbal) and synthesisers to create what is best described as mood music. While she has occasionally used traditional material (as in the lyrics, for example, of 'St. Patrick' on *The Celts*), the majority of her music is original but is perceived by many as Celtic New Age music. She has made numerous albums since *The Celts*, including *Watermark* (1988), from which her popular single 'Orinoco Flow' was taken. *A Day Without Rain* (2000) enjoyed phenomenal success in the **US** after the attacks of September 11th, 2001. The album sold 250,000 copies in two weeks and became the biggest selling album in the world for 2001. In 2002 she was nominated, along with Nicky and Roma Ryan, for an Oscar (Best Original Song) for 'May It Be', composed for the film *Lord of the Rings*. Enya has achieved her remarkable success without ever playing live shows and she rarely gives interviews. Website: www.enya.com.

F

Fahy, Paddy (b. 1926)   Fiddler and composer from Kilconnel, County Galway. Although Fahy has not recorded to date, some of his tunes are published in **Breandán Breathnach**'s *Ceol Rince na hÉireann* and many of them are widely played. **Matt Molloy** recorded a beautiful, slow version of a 'Paddy Fahy's Reel' on the **Planxty** album *The Woman I Loved So Well* (1980). His tunes have also been recorded by **Seán Tyrrell** and others.

Famine (1845-1849)   See **Great Famine, The**.

Faulkner, Jimmy (b. 1950)   Guitarist born in Dublin who has performed and recorded with some of Ireland's top rock and blues – as well as folk and traditional – musicians. Faulkner's work with folk and traditional musicians has often brought a unique feel to their music which couldn't have been provided by a guitarist from a purely traditional background. In the mid-1970s Faulkner started to perform with **Christy Moore**, with whom he has toured extensively and made several albums. His playing was a significant part of the contemporary, electric sound of Moore's *Whatever Tickles Your Fancy* (1975). *Live in Dublin* (1978) remains one of the latter's finest albums, largely because of the superb intertwining of Faulkner's guitar and **Dónal Lunny**'s bouzouki around Moore's singing. Moore includes Faulkner among those artists 'who have chilled me and uplifted this heart of mine' (*One Voice*, London, 2000, p. 208) and in the same book writes that Jimmy Faulkner 'is my favourite guitarist' (p. 44). They still perform together from time to time, and Faulkner appeared in the TV series *Moore Uncovered* (2001).

Faulkner also recorded with **Máirtín O'Connor** on *Perpetual Motion* (1990) and *Chatterbox* (1993). O'Connor plays a wide range of music on both albums which is not Irish traditional, and on *Perpetual Motion* Faulkner plays a significant part in tracks of Spanish and Bulgarian tunes. Faulkner's playing with O'Connor embraces a diversity of styles and different types of music that fully display his versatility. He has also recorded with fiddler Seán Smyth on *The Blue Fiddle* (1993) and with Finbar Furey (see **Furey Brothers**).

Feeley, John   Perhaps Ireland's best-known classical guitarist who has made recordings of Irish music for guitar, including slow airs, Carolan tunes (see **O'Carolan, Turlough**) and the occasional traditional dance tune. *Celtic Classics* (1993) includes interesting arrangements of **Finbar Furey**'s 'The Lonesome Boatman' and 'Carolan's Concerto' as well as many slow airs.

Feis Ceoil An Irish music festival inaugurated in 1897 by a committee made up of members of the Irish National Literary Society and **Conradh na Gaeilge**. The Feis involved competitions in different types of music and included among its stated aims the collection and preservation, by publication, of the old airs of Ireland and the promotion of Irish music study. Although these aspirations are still part of the festival, the Feis is now almost entirely concerned with Western European art music (with the exception of such competitions as the **Nancy Calthorpe** Memorial Prize for Irish harp performance and arrangement). The earliest years of the competition, however, were significant because they provided the first recordings of traditional music (see **Recording**).

At the first Feis, held in Dublin in May 1897, there were three competitions in traditional music, described as 'Competitions of Archaeological Interest'. Two were for performance on specific instruments, the Irish Wire Strung Harp and the Irish Pipes (uilleann pipes), while the prize in the third competition was 'for the discovery of vocal or instrumental performance of ancient Irish melodies hitherto unpublished.' Although seven pipers entered both the piping and the unpublished airs' competitions in the first Feis, there were no entrants for the harp competition. Six of the pipers were, interestingly, described as professionals, and among them was Thomas Rowsome, an uncle of **Leo Rowsome**. He came third in the 1897 piping competition to Turlough MacSweeny of Donegal (second) and Robert Thompson of Cork (first) but won first prize in 1899.

In 1898 and 1900 the Feis was held in Belfast, but has been held in Dublin every year since. The initial enthusiasm for traditional music, which was evident at the beginning, quickly faded, but in addition to the recordings, the earliest *feiseanna* have left some interesting accounts of traditional musicians and their repertoires at the turn of the century. *The Feis Ceoil Collection of Irish Airs* was published in 1914, edited by Arthur Darley and **P. J. McCall** (reprinted by Ossian, Cork, 1985). It consists of 43 song airs, 35 dance tunes and eight marches, many of which came from the unpublished airs competition. **Breandán Breathnach** published an excellent article on 'The Feis Ceoil and Piping' in 1986, now available in *The Man and His Music: An Anthology of the Writings of Breandán Breathnach* (Dublin, 1996, pp. 138-50). Website: www.siemens.ie/feis.

Fiddle (*fidil*) A four-string, bowed instrument, usually (although not invariably) tuned g-d-a-e'. Traditional Irish musicians, like folk musicians in other parts of the world, use 'fiddle' as the name of the instrument which classical musicians call the violin. The fiddle has been one of the most popular traditional instruments since the late 17th century, when the modern instrument became widespread in Ireland. Earlier forms did exist throughout Europe, where neither the shape nor size of the medieval fiddle was standardised. It was usually flat-backed and lacked the well-defined waist of the modern fiddle. Medieval fiddles, popular in Europe from the 12th to the 15th century, were also found in Ireland. A poem on the Fair of Carman in the 12th-century *Book of Leinster* refers to fiddles (called *fidlí*) being played with other instruments, including pipes and **bones**. A fragment of a bow, dated to the mid-11th century, was also found in Christchurch Place, Dublin. It has a terminal carved in the shape of an animal head, executed in the Scandinavian Ringerike style. It is difficult to assess how widespread and popular the fiddle was in Ireland before the 17th century as evidence is lacking.

The modern violin, developed in Europe from around 1550, was an amalgam of three instruments. The rebec, which was a bowed, stringed instrument of 10th-century origin, was usually pear-shaped or straight and narrow. The Renaissance fiddle was the second, and the *lira de braccio* – an instrument popular in the 15th and 16th centuries – had a body like a violin, a wide fingerboard, a relatively flat bridge, a leaf-shaped peg box and normally seven strings. Violin making reached a peak of excellence in the period 1650-1750 with famous makers such as Stradivarius of Cremona. It is also in this period that we begin to find evidence of the popularity of the fiddle in Ireland. In *A Western Wonder* (1674) Richard Head, an English tourist, noted of Sunday amusements in Ireland: '...in every field a fiddle and lasses footing it till they were all of a foam' (quoted in B. Breathnach, *Folk Music and Dances of Ireland*, p. 55). It is likely that many of these fiddles were modern violins, although more primitive or less costly fiddles also existed. In Co. Donegal, for example, metal fiddles (usually of tin but there is evidence of one made of brass) were made, originally by itinerant craftsmen (often professional fiddlers themselves) of the late 19th century. The low cost of these instruments was a major factor in their development, and a metal fiddle was made as recently as 1984. The fiddle, unlike the uilleann pipes, never seems to have waned in popularity during the 19th and 20th centuries, probably because the instrument was easier to secure and maintain than the pipes. The flexibility of fingering, the possibilities for developing a variety of bowing techniques and the fact that the fiddle can accommodate all forms of ornamentation were undoubtedly factors contributing to the instrument's popularity.

The words 'fiddle' and 'violin' are etymologically related, both derived from the Latin *vitulari* ('to rejoice') or Vitula, the Roman goddess of victory or jubilation. Although both words are used for the same instrument, the techniques used by traditional fiddlers are considerably different to those used by classical violinists. A traditional fiddler might choose to hold his instrument like a classical player (tucked under the chin), but this is not essential as most traditional music can be played in the first position. Traditional players, therefore, might hold the fiddle against the upper arm, chest, shoulders or even the waist. Bowing styles and holds vary greatly in different regions or among individual players. What matters most to the traditional fiddler is the music that he produces rather than a rigidly defined concept of correct technique.

Regional styles of fiddling tend to be quite marked and are usually defined in terms of bowing technique, ornamentation and rhythm. Some Donegal fiddlers often lean heavily on the bow, producing a loud, even harsh tone, and the rhythm tends to be quite evenly spaced, with a more sparing use of ornamentation than in areas like Sligo. Donegal fiddlers also, on occasion, attempt to imitate the drones of the uilleann pipes. The Sligo style tends to be more flowing and ornamented, with the bowing generally slurred and the rhythm slightly accentuated. The fiddlers of

Sliabh Luachra are generally renowned for the rhythmic vitality and relative simplicity of their style. In most areas, however, mass-produced recordings and styles heard through radio and television exert an influence on individual styles that can be just as significant as the local style.

It is difficult to generalise about styles. A young fiddler growing up in Sliabh Luachra, for example, could be more influenced by the flamboyant style of the Irish-American recording artist **Eileen Ivers** than by the local style. On the other hand, some fiddlers might strive to incorporate elements of the Donegal style although they are not from that region at all. A variety of factors, not always easy to identify, can influence the style of individual players. It is true, however, that regional characteristics are more pronounced in fiddling then they are, for example, in piping. Certain recording artists have also had a great influence, cutting across regional distinctions. The brilliant Sligo fiddler **Michael Coleman** (and to some extent his contemporaries **James Morrison** and **Paddy Killoran**) has influenced fiddlers from the 1920s right down to the present day. **Andy McGann** learned directly from Coleman, and many others have tried to imitate the latter's smooth, elegant and highly ornamented style. Coleman's settings of tunes would be considered as 'standard' by many. The idea of standard settings and model styles, however, is in many ways alien to what is best in traditional music. Each individual and regional style forms part of a colourful and varied patchwork of music in which technical brilliance is not necessarily vital to expression. Standardisation can only diminish the colour and variety of styles, especially in fiddle music.

Medieval Fiddle

Francis O'Neill wrote sketches of numerous fiddlers of the 18th, 19th and early 20th centuries for his *Irish Minstrels and Musicians* (1913). Important players of recent years include **John Doherty**; **Tommy Potts**; **Seán Maguire, Martin Fay** and **Seán Keane** of the **Chieftains**; **Paddy Glackin, Tommy Peoples** and **Kevin Burke**, all of whom played with the **Bothy Band**; **Frankie Gavin** of **De Dannan**; **Matt Cranitch**; **Máire Breatnach**; Seán Rattigan of Wexford; **Antóin Mac Gabhann** and Gerard Doggett, both living in Co. Meath; **Nollaig Ní Chathasaigh**; **Cathal Hayden** and **Martin Hayes**. Donegal-born **Liz Doherty** is a player of exceptional interest who plays music from different traditions and has led the innovative 16-piece fiddle orchestra called Fiddlesticks. Among the most exciting young talents to emerge in recent years are Brendan O'Sullivan of the group **Gráda**, Daire Bracken of **Slide**, Méabh O'Hare (winner of the **TG4** 'Young Musician of the Year' award in 2000), **Zoë Conway**, Michelle O'Brien (see **Ralston, Gavin**) and Sinéad Madden from Co. Mayo, who plays with **Máire Ní Bhraonáin**'s band and composes tunes of her own. The American-based **Brendan Mulvihill** and his father **Martin Mulvihill** have also made significant contributions to Irish music.

Chicago-born **Liz Carroll** is also a fine fiddler and a renowned composer of tunes. She has performed and recorded with many Irish and Irish-American musicians, including **Mick Moloney** and **Robbie O'Connell**. Jim McKillop of Antrim is a fine composer and fiddler equally at home with American bluegrass and Irish traditional music. He has recorded solo (most recently *The Road from Ballybrack*, 2003) and with flute player **Séamus Tansey**. The talented young fiddle duo, Liz and Yvonne Kane from Letterfrack, Co. Galway, in addition to performing with **Sharon Shannon**'s group, the Woodchoppers, have released two fine albums, *The Well-Tempered Bow* (2002) and *Under the Diamond* (2004).

There are many other fine fiddlers throughout Ireland and, unlike some instruments, the fiddle is popular almost everywhere in Ireland. See also **Altan**; **Canada**; **Carty, John**; **Double-stop**; **Newfoundland**; **North Cregg**; **Nova Scotia**; **O'Donnell, Joe**; **O'Shaughnessy, Paul**; **Solas**.

Fife (*fīf*) Small, cylindrical or cigar-shaped transverse flute which is louder and shriller than a full-sized flute because of its narrower bore. Generally made from a single piece of wood, it has (like the whistle) six finger-holes and no keys. The lowest note is pitched between E♭ and B♭, making the fife incompatible with the standard whistle, flute or uilleann pipes used in traditional sessions, where the bottom note is D. The fife has been associated with side drums in military use since the 14th century or earlier and continued in use among the armies of Europe and America into the 19th century. In 20th-century Ireland it was often used by marching bands with **lambeg drum**s, especially among members of the Orange Order (see **Orange/Loyalist Song**) and the Ancient Order of Hibernians. It has now been largely replaced in marching bands by short flutes pitched in B♭, and although some players can be found in parts of Ireland (especially the North) and the **US**, the fife is rare nowadays.

Filí, Na Trio formed in Cork in 1968 whose name literally means 'The Poets'. **Tomás Ó Canainn** (uilleann pipes, accordion, vocals), **Matt Cranitch** (fiddle) and Reamonn Ó Sé (later Tom Barry) on whistle won the **All-Ireland** trio competition in 1969 and made six albums together, some of them now available on CD. They toured in Europe and the **US** and appeared regularly on **RTÉ** television before disbanding in 1979.

Finn, Alec (b. 1944) Guitarist and bouzouki player best known for his central role in the group **De Dannan**. He was born in Yorkshire to an Irish family and initially played country and blues music. He moved to Dublin in the 1960s and eventually to Spiddal, Co. Galway where he began to play Irish music. He was given a six-string Greek **bouzouki** and, inspired by **Andy Irvine** and **Johnny Moynihan**, began to develop his own style of accompanying Irish music on the instrument. In 1974 he formed De Dannan with **Frankie Gavin** and remained with the group until it broke up in 2002. He has also played as an accompanist on a number of other musicians' albums, including two with **Mary Bergin**. His style on the bouzouki combines delicate counter-melodies and chords with a limited amount of rhythm playing. On his own solo album, *Blue Shamrock* (1994), he uses guitar as the main solo instrument, performing many well-known airs such as 'Down by the Sally Gardens' and 'The West's Awake'. *On Inisfree* (2003) he plays traditional and original slow tunes on both guitar and bouzouki. He has also recorded with the Scottish banjo and mandolin player Kevin Macleod on *Springwell* (1999), which features Frankie Gavin, and *Polbain to Oranmore* (2003), on which Macleod's mandolin and Finn's bouzouki are the main instruments.

Flanagan Brothers, The   Raised in a musical household in Waterford city until 1911, when the family moved permanently to the **US**, Joe (1894-1940; piano accordion), Louis (1896-ca. 1936; banjo, guitar) and Mike (1897-1990; tenor banjo) were successful recording and music hall artists. Their first disc was released in December 1921 and their last recording was made in 1933, the Great Depression (1929-1934) effectively ending a highly successful career. They were innovators in many ways, using accordion and banjo together as lead instruments in a way not heard before. Their use of guitar in accompanying Irish music was also new, and they broke new ground by using clarinet in a number of arrangements. Their recording of 'My Irish Molly' in 1928 included a brass and wind ensemble.

The Flanagan Brothers' unique arrangements of Irish songs, often with harmony singing, have a distinct flavour of the American music halls of the Jazz Age, best exemplified in recent times by **De Dannan**'s 1981 recording of the old Flanagan's song, 'My Irish Molly O'. They also played instrumentals, not always confining themselves to Irish traditional tunes, and did comedy sketches in the vaudeville style of the day. Harry Bradshaw remastered their recordings for *The Flanagan Brothers: 'The Tunes We Like to Play on Paddy's Day'* (1996), which provides a wealth of historical material in the notes. Although the term was not used at the time, the Flanagans were in many ways the first of the Irish **Supergroups**, gaining status as musical stars and using instruments (like guitar) and arrangement in a style that had never been heard in Irish music before.

Flatley, Michael (b. 1958)   Dancer and flute player born in Chicago to Irish parents. He appeared with the **Chieftains** on a number of international tours in the 1980s. His flute playing, for which he won two **All-Ireland** titles, has been released on CD (see *Michael Flatley*, 1995, for example), but it is as a dancer that he is best known. He is recorded in the *Guinness Book of Records* as having danced 28 taps per second in Chicago in 1989, making him the fastest dancer documented. It was, however, his roles in the shows ***Riverdance, Lord of the Dance*** and *Feet of Flames* that brought him worldwide fame.

Fleadh Nua   A festival run annually over a long weekend in late May by **Comhaltas Ceoltóirí Éireann**. Unlike the same organisation's **Fleadh Cheoil na hÉireann**, Fleadh Nua concentrates mainly on non-competitive events. It began in Dublin in 1970, but in 1974 moved to Ennis, Co. Clare where it is still held every year. Renowned for its outdoor entertainment and street festival atmosphere, it includes performances by singers, musicians, dancers, **wren-boys**, **strawboys** and **biddy boys**. Fleadh Nua attracts thousands of people annually from all over Ireland and from abroad. Website: www.fleadhnua.com. See also **Mac Gabhann, Antóin**.

Fleadh Cheoil Literally 'music festival', the term 'Fleadh' or 'Fleadh Cheoil' is often used as a shorter term for **Fleadh Cheoil na hÉireann**. There are, however, a whole series of *fleadhanna* or festivals held annually at county and provincial level in Ireland, and also in the UK and the **US**. *Fleadh Cheoil na hÉireann* is simply the culmination of all these regional *fleadhanna*.

Fleadh Cheoil Na hÉireann An annual festival held over one week in August by **Comhaltas Ceoltóirí Éireann** at which the **All-Ireland** competitions in traditional music, song and dance are held. The competitions are the culmination of a series of about 47 smaller *fleadhanna* held at county and provincial level. Like the organisation of Comhaltas itself, the organisation of the *fleadhanna* is modelled on the GAA All-Ireland Football and Hurling championships. Competitions on numerous instruments take place in many different age groups and there are also dancing, singing and **lilting** categories. The **céilí band** competition is often seen as *the* major attraction, but an All-Ireland medal in any category is a treasured prize for many musicians. Entrants come not just from the Republic of Ireland and Northern Ireland, but also from Comhaltas 'provinces' in Britain, Europe, **Australia** and the **US**. In addition to the competitions, numerous sessions and dances take place, many of them informally. Up to 100,000 people attend each year and although the *Fleadh* moves around to different venues, it does tend to stay in a particular town for a few years. Recent venues include Clonmel, Co. Tipperary, Listowel, Co. Kerry, Ballina, Co. Mayo and Enniscorthy, Co. Wexford. In 1971 the *árd-chomhairle* of CCÉ cancelled the *Fleadh* after the introduction of internment in Northern Ireland. This move was criticised by many people within and outside of the organisation, as CCÉ is defined in its own constitution as a non-political organisation.

Fleischmann, Aloys (1910-1992) Professor of music in **University College Cork** who published many articles on the history of music in Ireland. From the early 1950s until the time of his death, he undertook research to compile a list of every traditional tune in Irish manuscripts or printed collections. He also delved into related material in Scottish, Welsh and English collections. Over 7,000 tunes were collected and annotated. Although most of the work had been completed by the time of Fleischmann's death, **Micheál Ó Súilleabháin** and Paul McGettrick of the Irish World Music Centre, **University of Limerick** completed the preparation of Fleischmann's work for publication. *The Sources of Irish Traditional Music 1583-1855* (New York and London, 1998) marks a major development in the study of Irish music and will be of great assistance to researchers, bringing together for the first time the full range of sources.

Fling (*flaing*) A term used for the highland or **schottische**, which is popular in Donegal and other Ulster counties as well as in Co. Clare. 'Fling' is sometimes used in the south and west of Ireland, where these tunes and the associated dance are less common.

Flook Group which originally had the unusual line-up of three flutes (**Michael McGoldrick**, Sarah Allen and Brian Finnegan) and guitar (Ed Boyd). In 1997 they released their first album *Flook! Live at Sidmouth*, recorded at the 1996 Sidmouth festival. Original tunes (usually composed by Finnegan and/or Allen) have always been part of their repertoire, and *Flatfish* (1999) has six original compositions. Their third album, *Rubai* (2002), has twelve of their own tunes. Although McGoldrick is no longer with the group, the playing of John Joe Kelly (bodhrán and mandolin) has added a different dimension to their sound. They have played traditional Irish, Scottish, Breton, Spanish, Swedish, Greek and East European music, and they combine both traditional and jazz styles of playing, often improvising and even changing the rhythms of traditional tunes. Highly original in their approach to composing and playing traditional material, they are one of the more innovative and dynamic groups to emerge in the late 1990s. Website: www.flook.co.uk.

Flute (*fliúit*) The most common type of flute in Irish traditional music today is the 'simple-system' wooden flute. This consists of a tube (plugged at one end and usually having a conical bore) with six finger-holes and an *embouchure* or mouth-hole. Some wooden flutes have extra metal keys (in some cases up to eight) for accidental notes, but these are not necessary for most traditional tunes. On the most common flute, where the lowest note is pitched to D, the player can obtain C by cross-fingering and F by half-covering the second hole from the bottom (similar techniques are used by players of the tin whistle and the low whistle). It is, therefore, possible to get any accidentals that might be required without having additional keys on the flute. Indeed some flute-makers argue that the addition of metal keys takes away from the sound of the wooden flute. Hardwoods such as African blackwood, ebony, grenadilla or cocus are generally used. These flutes usually have a range of two octaves, although the classical, keyed flute, which has a range of three octaves, is sometimes used for playing traditional music. Pól Ó Braonáin, **Clannad**'s flute-player, plays the classical flute. This type of flute, with padded keys over all the holes, is not as well suited to Irish traditional music as the simple-system flute. Exceptional players such as

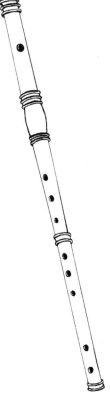

Open-Holed or
Simple-System Flute

Paddy Carty did experiment with various types of flute, eventually settling for a wooden flute with holed keys, a compromise between the padded keys of the metal classical flute and the open holes of the wooden simple-system flute. In the latter type, the fact that the fingers are directly covering the holes makes it easier to achieve traditional forms of ornamentation such as cuts, rolls and slurring.

Keyed Wooden
Flute

In 18th-century collections of Irish music, the instrument was usually called the 'German flute'. This was to distinguish it from the *flauto* (Italian for flute), which then meant 'recorder' as opposed to 'transverse flute'. Thus in the title of the **Neale** collection of 1724, and even in the **O'Farrell** collection (ca. 1800) we find mention of the German flute. This was the same instrument used by classical players at the time. The 'Boehm system' flute (using keys instead of open holes) developed in the 1830s and 1840s. Although classical musicians were playing the flute in early 18th-century Ireland, and the Neale collection was arranged for German flute, it is not clear how popular the instrument was in the 18th century. It seems likely that its popularity spread gradually after the simple-system flute was abandoned by classical players in favour of the Boehm system flute. The collector, **Francis O'Neill**, for example, learned to play the flute from a gentleman farmer in Co. Cork in the mid-19th century, but most of the professional traditional musicians of the time played fiddle or uilleann pipes. O'Neill's account of flute-players (in Chapter 27 of his *Irish Minstrels and Musicians*) is far shorter than his accounts of harpers, pipers and fiddlers. With the exception of **Oliver Goldsmith**, the earliest flute players he mentions would have been playing in the period around 1830-1880. 'Flutes' were popular in the Inishowen Peninsula in Co. Donegal in the 1820s, but the term seems to have been used for **fife**s played in military bands rather than the larger 'concert flute'.

In the 1920s and 30s, when the commercial recording scene in the **US** was dominated by fiddlers such as **Michael Coleman** and **James Morrison**, and pipers such **Patrick J. Tuohey**, **John McKenna** was one of the few Irish flute players to make a name for himself. McKenna came from Co. Leitrim and the Sligo/Leitrim/Roscommon area has particularly strong associations with the flute. Josie Mc Dermott (1925-92, also a composer of many tunes) and **Matt Molloy** also come from this area, although Molloy's highly ornamented style is considerably different from the more sparse style of McKenna. **Regional styles** of flute playing have been identified but are not as marked as regional fiddle styles. Although good flute playing can be heard in most parts of Ireland, the flute is probably not played by as many musicians today as the fiddle or the uilleann pipes. There are, however, a considerable number of craftsmen now making flutes in Ireland, an improvement on the earlier decades of the 20th century when flutes made in England, Germany or other countries could be difficult to obtain.

Stylistic factors that vary in flute playing include the way tunes are broken up (long or short phrases), the extent to which tonguing is used, the degree of breathiness in the playing, the degree of rhythmic emphasis and the way ornamentation is used. **Fintan Vallely** has published a tutor for the simple-system wooden flute. **Colin 'Hammy' Hamilton's** *The Irish Flute Player's Handbook* (originally published in 1990) includes sections on the history of the flute and flute making as well as a tutor. Other well-known players of recent decades include Roger Sherlock, **Vincent Broderick** (who wrote a number of original tunes for the instrument), **Paddy Taylor**, **Michael Tubridy** of the **Chieftains**, **Séamus Tansey**, **Frankie Gavin** of **De Dannan**, Frankie Kennedy of **Altan**, **Michael Flatley**, **Paul McGrattan** of **Beginish**, Kevin Crawford of **Lúnasa**, Laurence Nugent, Conal Ó Gráda, Séamus Egan of **Solas**, **Michael McGoldrick**, **Joannie Madden**, **Catherine McEvoy**, **Marcas Ó Murchú**, Tom Doorley of **Danú** and **Emer Mayock**. Eamonn De Barra of **Slide** and Conor Byrne are among the most talented of young players to emerge in recent years. Although best known as a box (button accordion) player, **Joe Burke** is also a fine flute player and plays mainly flute on his album *The Tailor's Choice* (1983). Among the more innovative players to emerge in recent years are Alan Doherty (who plays with the group **Gráda**) and Niall Keegan, who mixes jazz, classical and traditional influences and released his first solo album, *Don't Touch the Elk*, to wide critical acclaim in 1999. The playing of Harry Bradley from Belfast is influenced by John McKenna's style and he released his second album, *As I Carelessly Did Stray*, in 2002.

A website dedicated to the Irish flute is www.firescribble.net/flute; it includes information on the instrument, a directory of flute makers, and recommended players. See also **McConnell, Cathal** and **McDermott, Josie**.

Concert or Classical Flute based on a design developed by Boehm in the 1840s

Folk Music Society of Ireland (*Cumann Cheol Tíre Éireann*) Organisation founded in 1971 to encourage an informed interest in traditional music through lectures, the publication of a journal and other activities. The founders of the society included **Breandán Breathnach**, **Seán O'Boyle**, **Hugh Shields** and **Tom Munnelly**. Since 1973 it has published a newsletter, *Ceol Tíre* and a journal, *Irish Folk Music Studies/Éigse Cheol Tíre*, Volumes 5-6 (1986-2001) of which were published in one volume in 2001. The Society has also published three works by Hugh Shields, *A Short Bibliography of Irish Folk Song* (1985), *Ballad Research: The Stranger in Ballad Narrative and Other Topics* (1986) and *Old Dublin Songs* (1988). Other publications include two works by **Nicholas Carolan** (secretary, 1977-1992), *A Short Discography of Irish Folk Music* (1987) and *Popular Music in 18th-Century*

Dublin (1985). The latter work was published in conjunction with **Na Píobairí Uilleann** with which the Folk Music Society of Ireland also shares the building at 15 Henrietta Street, Dublin 1. The society is also involved with the Dublin annual festival Sean-nós Cois Life ('Sean-nós by the Liffey') and hosts seminars and conferences on subjects dealing with traditional music and song. Website: homepage eircom.net/~shields/fmsi.

Forde, William (1795-1850) Cork collector and musician who had a broad range of musical interests and lectured on the music of many countries, including China and Peru. From 1840 to 1850, he collected Irish music in Munster as well as in Co. Leitrim and its adjoining counties. He built up a collection of over 1800 tunes, which are housed with his writings and lectures in the Royal Irish Academy, Dublin. While the tunes in the collection were mostly song airs, there were also dance tunes, airs by **Turlough O'Carolan**, marches, laments and the airs of some Ossianic **lays**. In addition to music from Ireland there were traditional tunes from **England**, **Scotland** and the **Isle of Man**. Forde's material came from printed and manuscript sources as well as his own transcriptions from traditional musicians, including Hugh O'Beirne, a piper whom Forde met in Co. Leitrim. **Patrick Weston Joyce** included over 80 of the tunes Forde had collected from O'Beirne in his *Old Irish Music and Songs* (1909). Although Forde had intended to publish his collection, along with a dissertation on the nature and historical importance of Irish music, he never managed to raise sufficient funds for the project. His collection (which passed into the hands of **John Edward Pigot**) is still of considerable interest and **Breandán Breathnach** noted that he was the first collector to use a systematic approach to the material he amassed.

Foster and Allen Duo who formed in 1975, having played together in various bands in the 1960s and early 70s. Mick Foster plays piano accordion and was an **All-Ireland** champion in 1964, 1968 and 1970. He made his first traditional album in 1972, but it is no longer available. Initially in his duo with Tony Allen (guitar), they played traditional ballads, with both men singing. Although many ballads are still incorporated into their repertoire, they gradually began to include any material that they could adapt to their sound, including country, pop and classical. Their recording of 'A Bunch of Thyme' made it to No. 18 in the British Charts in 1982, and they appeared on *Top of the Pops* in what was famously described as 'leprechaun suits'. They have sold over eighteen million albums world-wide and were in the Guinness Book of Records for having fifteen consecutive albums in the British charts at Christmas time (a record equalled only by the Rolling Stones). They tour around the world and have also made numerous videos. Their phenomenal success is due largely to their easy listening, middle-of-the-road style.

Four Men and a Dog Group whose first album, *Barking Mad* (1992), is a mixture of traditional Irish, Cajun and acoustic rock styles. The album won them the 'Folk Roots Album of the Year' award. In 1993 they released a second album,

Shifting Gravel, produced by the renowned guitarist, **Arty McGlynn**. The album shifted them towards a country-rock style, and also saw a new singer/songwriter, Kevin Doherty, replace founder-member, Mick 'Black Dog' Daly, the inspiration behind the group's name. They have seen many changes in line-up, but by the time of their third album, *Doctor A's Secret Remedies*, in 1995 the line-up was Kevin Doherty (guitar and vocals), **Gerry O'Connor** (banjo and fiddle), Gino Lupari (percussion) and **Cathal Hayden** (fiddle). *Long Roads* was released in 1996, and although the group did not perform together on a regular basis in the late 1990s, Doherty, Lupari, Hayden and O'Connor played a number of gigs in 2002, including Castlewellan's Celtic Fusion Festival and Dublin's Cobblestone. They also recorded as part of a 2002 Christmas special of the series *Geantraí* for **TG4**. At the end of the year they released a new album, *Maybe Tonight* (2002) with Donal Murphy of **Sliabh Notes**, **Máirtín O'Connor** and **Arty McGlynn** guesting. Website: www.tradcentre.com/fourmen.

Four Men and a Dog

France France has had a considerable influence on the evolution of Irish traditional song and dance. In the Middle Ages the influence of the French *chanson courtois* (courtly love song) and *chanson populaire* (folk song) began to spread all over Europe. Developed in Provence in the 12th century and used by medieval troubadors, *chanson courtois* employed a sophisticated poetry and was more subjective than *chanson populaire*.

Robin Flower, a scholar of medieval Irish literature, has claimed that the Gaelic poetry of Gearóid, 3rd Earl of Desmond (d. 1398), was influenced by the Provençale songs of *amour courtois*, although this has been challenged by more recent scholars. Other French influences are clearly traceable in songs that are still sung today. These derive from literary imitations of certain types of folk song which the Northern French began to produce in the 13th century: the song of the lovers' separation at dawn; the *pastourelle*, originally a song narrating the attempted seduction of a shepherdess; the *reverdie*, which celebrates the return of spring; the *malmariee* or song of the unhappily married wife and others. Many of these song types became popular in folk song throughout Europe and can still be heard in Irish **ballad**s and **songs in Irish**. Ballads such as 'The Raggle Taggle Gypsy', found in Ireland in many variants, is an example of a later style of *pastourelle*, and such songs of attempted or successful seduction have been popular among ballad singers in Ireland. Although the *pastourelle* usually has a rural setting, 'The Factory Girl' provides an example with a more modern, urban setting. Examples of this type of song, such as 'Cailín Deas Crúite na mBó ('The Pretty Girl Milking the Cows'), are also sung in Irish. 'Night-visit' songs, similar to the old dawn songs, can also be found among Irish ballads, although few are sung in Irish. One exception is 'An Rábaire' ('The Dashing Fellow'), a comic night-visit song about a lodger visited by the daughter of the house. Some of the most famous songs in Irish are more serious expressions of a girl's grief at the loss of – or desertion by – a lover, including 'Dónal Óg' ('Young Donal') and 'Fear a' Bhata' ('The Boatman'). This is one of the oldest of the European lyric types, but the examples found in Irish often have a greater intensity and lyric density than their medieval counterparts.

Other types of song that find parallels in French medieval lyrics, such as the song of the *malmariee*, can be found in Ireland. At times it is difficult to tell how directly a part French music has played in the form of particular Irish songs. Much French influence undoubtedly came to Ireland through **England** and **Scotland**, and some of the motifs and forms used are part of a broader European tradition. It is clear, however, that France has had a huge influence on the evolution of folk song throughout Europe, including Ireland, where songs in Irish and English still bear traces today. It was also in medieval France that the **carol**, originally a song dance, became popular, and remained so into the 18th and 19th centuries. Seán Ó Tuama carried out a detailed study of the influence of French song types and motifs in Ireland (see **Sean-nós Singing**).

In addition, France had a major impact on Irish **set dancing**, based on the popular French **cotillion**s and **quadrille**s. The Irish **dancing masters** of the late 18th and early 19th centuries were strongly influenced by French culture, and indeed that country's influence on Ireland as a whole was marked from the 17th to the 19th century. The Penal Laws forced many Irish Catholics abroad, and France was one of the main European countries where they found sympathy. By 1700 there were 20,000 Irish soldiers in the French army and the **macaronic song** 'Siúil a Rún' ('Walk, My Love') is a beautiful evocation of a woman's loss of her lover to the French army during this period. The French Revolution (from 1789) had a profound impact in Ireland, and this is reflected in **Nationalist/Republican song** and in tunes and songs relating to **Napoleon Bonaparte**.

In modern times, there are strong cultural links between Ireland and France, especially **Brittany**, where music from 'Celtic' regions (including Ireland) has grown in popularity since the 1960s.

Free-Reed Instruments A free reed is a metal strip fastened at one end, free at the other, which produces a sound when air pressure is applied to it from the player's breath or a bellows. Each reed provides a single note, the precise pitch depending on the length and thickness of the reed. Instruments using free reeds include **harmonica**, **accordion** and **concertina**, all of which were developed in Europe in the early 19th century.

French, Percy (1854-1920) Songwriter born in Cloonyquin House, not far from Roscommon town. French is best remembered for songs such as 'The Mountains of Mourne', 'Phil the Fluther's Ball', 'Come Back Paddy Reilly' and 'The Darlin' Girl from Clare'. Despite the fact that he was the son of a landlord and was educated at Trinity College, Dublin, French pursued a stage career that became his livelihood from 1891 until his death. He sang and played banjo as well as telling stories and painting pictures on the stage. He did not write overtly political songs and while many folk singers today would find his material somewhat 'stage Irish' in style, **James N. Healy**, who has edited French's songs, considers them to be 'firmly entrenched in the folklore of Irish song'. 'While humorous and ironic', Healy continues, 'they never ridicule and show a genuine love for the Irish country people about whom he wrote.' Healy's *The Songs of Percy French* (Cork, 1996) is a selection of 44 songs from a larger collection of French songs that Healy had published previously.

fRoots English-based folk and world music magazine covering a wide range of music, including Irish, Scottish, American and other types of folk music. It is available in some music and bookshops in Ireland and the **US** as well as by subscription worldwide. Website: www.frootsmag.com.

Furey Brothers, The Sons of Ted Furey (fiddler, music collector and teacher), a traveller who lived in Ballyfermot, Dublin for some time (see **Travellers**). Ted Furey can be heard on the CD *Toss the Feathers* (1998, recorded 1967) with Brendan Byrne (bodhrán), and his 1975 book *The Ted Furey Collection of Irish Traditional Tunes* was republished in a new edition (Dublin, 1992). His sons have played together in various combinations but were perhaps at their peak as the Furey Brothers and Davey Arthur. Finbar (the second eldest son) was taught the uilleann pipes by Johnny Keenan, father of **Paddy Keenan**, and as a teenager won three **All-Ireland** championships for his piping. With his older brother Eddie (vocals, guitar, mandolin) he formed a highly successful duo, recording and touring throughout Ireland, England and Germany in the 1960s. It was on their album *The Town Is Not Their Own* (1969) that 'The Lonesome Boatman', the famous tune composed by Finbar and played on the **low whistle**, was first heard. They recorded with the

Clancy Brothers (see **Clancy Brothers and Tommy Makem**) in the early 1970s. In the late 1970s the duo expanded to include brothers George (vocals, guitar, mandolin, banjo) and Paul (button accordion, bodhrán, spoons). Davy Arthur (mandolin, banjo), whom Finbar and Eddie had met in Edinburgh in 1967, made up the fifth member of the Furey Brothers and Davy Arthur, who for the best part of two decades had great international success. Finbar did most of the group's arrangement and became their lead singer, as well as playing pipes, low whistle and five-string banjo. They played a mixture of songs and instrumental pieces with a considerable amount of original material written by Finbar, Eddie and George. One of their best-known songs is 'The Green Fields of France', an anti-war song written by Eric Bogle, a Scotsman who settled in Australia. They had a number of chart successes with singles, including Gerry Rafferty's 'Her Mother Didn't Like Me Anyway' and Ralph McTell's 'Clare to Here'. 'Sweet Sixteen' reached No. 1 in several countries and No. 5 in the British pop charts, earning the Furey Brothers and Davy Arthur an appearance on *Top of the Pops*, a rare achievement for an Irish folk group.

The Fureys are still a big name in traditional music, although Davy Arthur and Finbar (who is pursuing a solo career) are no longer members of the group. The youngest of the Furey brothers, Paul, died in 2002. In 2003, Finbar appeared in the film *Gangs of New York* and also recorded the song 'New York Girls' for the film's soundtrack. In the same year he released a solo album, *Chasing Moonlight: Love Songs of Ireland*, which featured old favourites such as 'The Lonesome Boatman' and 'The Green Fields of France', as well as three new songs by Finbar himself. After a reunion concert in 2003, Davey Arthur rejoined the Fureys. See **Coulter, Phil**.

Fusions   'Fusion' is a term often used in recent years to describe the mixing of Irish traditional music with influences from outside the tradition. It can, however, be argued that 'fusions' with other musical traditions have always been part of the development of Irish traditional music, song and dance. In dance, for example, the introduction of **cotillions** and **quadrilles** from France formed the basis of Irish **set dancing** in the 19th century. Certain forms of dance music, for instance **polkas** and **mazurkas**, apparently came to Ireland with the quadrilles, and Irish musicians began to compose their own tunes in these forms. The dances themselves were, in many cases, adapted by the Irish **dancing masters** to suit the pre-existing dance tunes. The evolution of set dancing can therefore be viewed as a fusion of different cultural traditions. In song one only has to look at the development of the **ballad** in Ireland to realise that here, too, external influences were at work.

In modern times 'fusions' of Irish music, song and dance with the music, song and dance of other traditions are viewed by some with scepticism and even distaste. Fusions have, however, played an important role in bringing Irish music to a wider audience in the 20th century. The earliest recordings of fiddlers such as **Michael Coleman** fused Irish traditional fiddling with a style of piano accompaniment that had not been heard before in Irish music but made it more palatable to ears not used to Irish solo fiddling. The **Flanagan Brothers**, contemporaries of Coleman, went even further, developing new styles of arrangement using accordion, banjo and guitar, as well as playing a repertoire that married Irish dance music and song with American vaudeville of the 1920s and 30s. They even did comic sketches that incorporated music from Ireland, Italy and the **US**. Some of their arrangements included clarinet, which gave the Irish tunes a sound somewhat reminiscent of eastern European Jewish Klezmer music.

The style of piano playing pioneered in the recordings of Coleman and other Irish musicians has long been accepted by many in Irish music as an integral part of the tradition. The Flanagan Brothers' renditions of Irish music and song in a style which owed much to the contemporary American music scene was paralleled in the 1960s by the influential **Clancy Brothers and Tommy Makem**. Other developments in the 60s include **Seán Ó Riada**'s **Ceoltóirí Chualann**. Groups such as **Planxty** and the **Bothy Band** included new instruments such as the bouzouki with more traditional instruments and broke new ground with superb arrangements of traditional music and song. **Clannad** initially brought classical and jazz influences to their music, and later used modern electronic keyboards and modern recording techniques such as overdubbing of voices to great effect. The 1970s also saw the emergence of the first 'Celtic Rock' group, **Horslips**, and in 1973 Thin Lizzy had a big hit with the ballad 'Whiskey in the Jar' in Ireland and Britain (where it reached No. 6 in the charts). In the 1980s **Moving Hearts** brought traditional, rock and jazz musicians together to produce music (much of it original) that fused many influences into a unique new sound, and composer **Shaun Davey** launched the first of a series of compositions for orchestra and uilleann pipes or uilleann pipes and voice, *The Brendan Voyage* (1980) marking a new departure in this area. Similar works for orchestra and traditional instruments followed from composers such as **Charlie Lennon** and **Bill Whelan**, the latter incorporating rhythms from other musical traditions into his compositions. **Micheál Ó Súilleabháin** has used chamber orchestras for his work, which incorporates both traditional and original material, and has also experimented with a traditional/jazz style which he calls 'Hiberno-Jazz'. Groups such as **Deiseal** have played traditional music with a strong jazz flavour, while more recently **Khanda** have experimented with Irish/Jazz/Indian fusions. The **Afro Celts** have, as their name suggests, brought together musicians from Africa, Ireland, Brittany and England to produce a unique style of music that draws on a variety of influences. The original music of **Kíla** also draws on diverse influences, with traditional music remaining very strong. The Corrs played a number of traditional tunes on their first album in 1995, but on albums in 1998 and 2000 the mainstream pop element in their music became more dominant.

The extent to which fusion with other traditions has become part of the Irish traditional music scene is reflected in two major television series of the 1990s, ***Bringing It All Back Home*** and *A **River of Sound***. The latter provoked much controversy and debate that was continued at the 1996 **Crossroads Conference**. In fact, among the more commercially successful groups, fusion is now the rule rather than the exception – a fact that might explain the stagnancy in much of the traditional material released in the 1990s and at the start of the new millennium. The style of ensemble playing pioneered by groups such as Planxty, the Bothy Band and

De Dannan in the 1970s was new and exciting then but has been imitated more recently by so many groups seeking commercial success that it has often become dull and formulaic.

Fusions remain a controversial subject among traditional musicians, and there have always been critics of any form of experimentation. Many who listen now to traditional music, however, might never have come to it if it wasn't for hearing it initially through groups such as Horslips and Moving Hearts. It is also important to recognise that many musicians playing 'fusion' do not see themselves as playing traditional music at all. Thus Simon Emerson of the Afro Celts, for example, has stated that he was interested not in playing traditional music but in making new music. See also **Galldubh**; **Supergroups**; **McKeown, Susan**; **O'Donnell, Joe**; **Solas**.

G

Gael Force A unique musical event in Irish music which involved a series of six concerts at the Point Depot, Dublin between September 8th and 13th, 1997. The aim was to bring together the best Irish musicians on one stage over the six nights. The series was recorded for American and Irish television, and a video and CD of highlights from the concerts were released. Although not all of the acts were traditional, many of the best traditional, folk and fusion artists were included in the series. Among them were **Altan**, the *Riverdance* Irish troupe, **Sharon Shannon**, the **Afro Celts**, **Nomos**, **Stockton's Wing**, **Christy Moore**, **Liam O'Flynn**, **Mary Black**, **De Dannan**, the **Chieftains**, **Leahy** and **Clannad**.

Gaelforce Dance See **Australia**.

Gaelic League See **Conradh na Gaeilge**.

Gael-Linn Founded in 1953, Gael-Linn was one of the most successful of a number of organisations established by Irish language revivalists during the 1940s and 50s. Dónal Ó Móráin was a key figure in the founding of the organisation. Part of its success lay in the use it made of modern media and, although involved in many areas of Irish language promotion, it made an important contribution to the commercial **recording** of Irish traditional music and song from 1957. Its first releases were on 78s (1957-61) and featured musicians such as fiddlers **Dennis Murphy** and **Paddy Canny**, pipers **Willie Clancy** and **Tommy Reck** and singers from the **Gaeltacht**, including the famous **sean-nós** singers **Seosamh Ó hÉanaí** and **Seán Mac Dhonncha**. Around this time the first LPs of traditional music were being made in Ireland by Gael-Linn and **Claddagh Records**. In 1959 the Gael-Linn film on Irish history, *Mise Éire* ('I Am Ireland') brought the music of **Seán Ó Riada** to national attention for the first time. Gael-Linn made two further films on Ireland's history in 1960 and 1966 and released Ó Riada's famous scores for the films on *Mise Éire* (1979). The company has released some of the finest Irish singers and musicans on albums over the past few decades, including **Clannad**, **Mary Bergin**, **Joe Cooley**, duo **Jackie Daly** and **Séamus Creagh**, **Séamus Ennis**, Willie Clancy, **Paddy Keenan**, **Paddy Glackin**, Dolores Keane (see **Keane Family**) and many sean-nós singers.

Gael-Linn announced in 2001 that their music recording operation was to be wound up, a great loss to traditional music. The label continues to issue recordings from its back catalogue and is also involved in distribution. *Seoltaí Séidte/Setting Sail* (2004) is a fine collection of Gael-Linn recordings originally made between 1957 and 1961, digitally remastered by **Harry Bradshaw**. An accompanying dual-language book by **Nicholas Carolan** provides a wealth of historical information on the role of Gael-Linn in recording and biographies of all the musicians as well as words and background information on all of the songs. There are 43 recordings on the two CDs, including performances of the aforementioned Gael-Linn recording artists of 1957-1961.

From 1969 to 2001, Gael-Linn ran an important youth competition called Slógadh, which included competitions in **set dancing** and music ensemble performance. There are now two youth competitions run by Gael-Linn, Siansa and Coirm. Siansa, a competition for new traditional music groups, is aimed at teenagers. There are three rounds of the competition, which includes workshops (held in January and February) and finals (in March or April). Coirm is a one-day talent contest for National Schools held annually in February. Each school puts on a show which includes music and drama. See also **Behan, Brendan** and **Topic Records** Websites: www.gael-linn.ie/www.gael-linn.com.

Gaeltacht The Irish word for an area where Irish is the main spoken language, also used to describe these areas collectively. In 1922, when the Irish Free State became independent of Britain, Irish was still the main language spoken in parts of counties Donegal, Mayo, Galway, Kerry, Cork and Waterford, and there were also scattered communities of Irish speakers in Clare, Kilkenny and Louth. The new State established Coimisiún na Gaeltachta in 1925 to define the Irish-speaking districts and make recommendations about how to promote the language within the Gaeltacht. Official government policy since that time has been to preserve the Gaeltacht and try to spread the use of the Irish language outside it. The Gaeltacht has been given preferential treatment, including special employment grants and (since 1979) its own development authority. Despite this, there has been a continuous decline in the use of Irish since the 1920s. Lack of employment and opportunities for advancement have been a major problem, leading to high levels of emigration. Some Irish-speaking communities from Donegal, Kerry, Mayo and Galway were resettled in Leinster in the 1930s; among those who made the move was Aodh Ó Domhnaill, father of **Maighréad and Tríona Ní Dhómhnaill** and **Micheál Ó Domhnaill**. The only one of these communities which is still reasonably vigorous in terms of language and culture is that at Rathcairn, Co. Meath. In some of the areas still officially designated as part of the Gaeltacht there is little Irish spoken on a regular basis.

The status of Gaeltacht areas is currently under review. In 2002 a special report was presented to the government by Coimisiún na Gaeltachta. This proposed that Gaeltacht boundaries should be redrawn after the next census data becomes available in 2006 or 2007. The criteria suggest that Gaeltacht status should relate to areas where 50% of the population of the district electoral division (DED) use Irish every day. Coimisiún na Gaeltachta also advised that other indicators be taken into account when redrawing boundaries. It was proposed that areas where 40-50 percent of the population used Irish daily should be given seven years to reach the required percentage. It is far from clear, however, how rigidly these proposals will be implemented. The Minister for Community, Rural and Gaeltacht Affairs Eamon Ó Cuív, in a radio interview on 8 July 2004 said that no Gaelatcht area would be excluded in a boundary revision as long as Irish was still being promoted there and its population showed the right attitude.

The current Gaeltacht area has a population of 90,000 people. Donncha Ó hÉallaithe, a maths lecturer and resident of the Connemara Gaeltacht for 30 years, carried out an analysis of Gaeltacht areas based on the 2002 census figures. He estimates that, according to the Coimisiúin na Gaeltachta proposal that areas where 50 percent of the population use Irish daily should retain Gaeltacht status, the current Gaeltacht area would shrink from 90,000 people to 27,000 people. Glencolumcille, Co. Donegal, Galway city and Furbo, Co. Galway are among the many areas that would lose their Gaeltacht status. While the review of Gaeltacht boundaries is unlikely to be so rigorously enforced, Ó hÉallaithe's research points to the stark reality facing the Irish language and its survival. He has contributed to a collection of eassys in English entitled *Who Needs Irish?: Reflections on the Importance of the Irish Language Today* (Dublin, 2004), edited by Ciarán Mac Murchaidh. This important book covers many aspects of the Irish language today and should help to stimulate debate on the future of the language and Gaeltacht areas.

All of the most important areas for **sean-nós singing** are within the Gaeltacht, and this particular style of traditional singing would certainly not have survived if the Irish language had died out. There have been some notable singers from outside Gaeltacht areas (especially Dublin) in recent years, but the Gaeltacht remains the heartland for sean-nós singers. Instrumental music is strong in many – but not necessarily all – Gaeltacht areas. Southwest Donegal, south Connemara and the western part of the Dingle peninsula provide some examples of Gaeltacht areas where instrumental traditional music *is* particularly strong. The founding of **Gael-Linn** in 1953 added a new impetus to the promotion and development of both singing in Irish and traditional instrumental music, particularly through the release of commercial recordings.

The opening of **Raidió Na Gaeltachta** (1972) and **TG4** (1996, originally Teilifís na Gaeilge) have certainly been a boost to the Gaeltacht, providing more regular programmes in Irish than ever before and bringing together isolated communities around the country. These new broadcasting services also give over a considerable amount of time to programmes on traditional music.

Many people in Ireland, however, feel that successive governments since 1922 have unrealistically attempted to prevent the decline of the Irish language by giving special treatment to Gaeltacht areas and maintaining a special status for the Irish language in all government and civil service business. Within the Irish-speaking communities, some (such as Donncha Ó hÉallaithe) are highly critical of the ineffectiveness of state policy in halting the decline of Irish. These issues, fraught with complexities and controversy, are not unrelated to some important aspects of traditional music. For sean-nós singing to survive as a living art form, it is clearly essential that the Gaeltacht communities survive. Although the survival of instrumental music is not dependant upon the survival of the Irish language, there are some who would argue, as **Tomás Ó Canainn** does, that 'no aspect of Irish music can be fully understood without a deep appreciation of sean-nós singing. It is the key that opens the lock' (*Traditional Music in Ireland*, London 1978, p. 49). There is certainly an important relationship between sean-nós and the instrumental playing of slow **air**s. It could also be argued that, while an understanding of sean-nós is not *essential* to the playing or understanding of dance music, it can deepen our appreciation of it. In a more general sense, it is clear that much of the folklore relating to tunes and songs, orally transmitted through Irish, has already been lost through the decline of the language. For many, the Irish language also represents a different way of viewing the world, a different mode of expression that is closely related to the traditional forms of musical expression.

The Irish Gaeltacht has some well-established contacts with the Gáidhealtachd of **Scotland**, including Turas na BhFilí, The Poet's Tour. Originally aiming to recreate the 'poetic courts' of the 18th century, this artistic exchange between the two Gaelic-speaking areas began in 1971. Musicians, singers and dancers as well as poets have been involved in the exchanges in recent years. In 1999, for example, Róisín Elsafty (sean-nós singer), Sonaí Ó Conghaile (accordion player) and his daughter Eileen (sean-nós dancer) from Connemara accompanied poets Colm Breathnach and Collette Ní Ghallchóir on the trip to Scotland.

Pobal na Gaeltachta: a scéal agus a dhán, published by **Cló Iar-Chonnachta** in 2000, provides a wide range of views on the present state and future prospects of the Irish language from those who live in the Gaeltacht. There are 52 essays which cover various aspects of life in different Gaeltacht areas, including history, folklore and literature. The essays were originally commissioned by Raidió na Gaeltachta as a series of lectures. Like the more recent *Who Needs Irish?* this work brings to light the uneven survival of Irish within the Gaeltacht. Areas like west Galway and the Aran Islands, that part of Donegal around Gweedore, and west Kerry still have strong Gaeltacht communities. In other areas, like Ring in Waterford and West Cork, the number of homesteads that speak Irish on a regular basis has shrunk considerably.

It may be the case, as some believe, that the true Gaeltacht is facing extinction. It is, however, of primary importance to appreciate what the survival of the Irish language means to those who grow up speaking it. Some musicians from Gaeltacht areas, such as members of **Clannad** and **Altan**, have tried to promote awareness of the Irish language through their music. They and many other less famous musicians, singers and storytellers in Gaeltacht areas are the carriers of a rich tradition in words and music which is an essential part of life. Vigorous attempts to pass on the living traditions of the Gaeltacht to the younger generation are nowhere more apparent than in the annual Cumar (meaning 'channel' or 'ravine') school. Started in 1999, the school is aimed at teenagers and takes place in a different part of the Connemara Gaeltacht every year. There are intensive music classes and workshops in traditional music, sean-nós singing, **sean-nós dancing** and oral tradition. The school, usually run over a week in April, celebrates the traditional aspects of contemporary Gaeltacht arts and released a CD of various young people performing traditional music and song, simply titled *Cumar* (2000). Overall, there has been considerable growth in gaelscoileanna and gaelcholáistí in recent years. Even in places as far away as the **US**, interest in learning Irish has grown with summer schools such as the annual **Milwaukee Irish Fest** witnessing a phenomenal increase in the number of people enrolling for Irish language courses at all levels. The Irish language radio and television stations as well as newspapers such as *Foinse* and *Lá* have been positive developments. Another development is the government's Official Languages Act (2003), which protects the rights of Irish speakers. Many Irish speakers are determined and hopeful about the long-term survival of the language, but the coming decades will be crucial in terms of the kind of government policies and other initiatives which are developed to support the continued survival of Irish as a living language. See also **Gael-Linn**.

Galicia A region of northwest Spain, north of Portugal. Although most people in Galicia can speak Spanish, Gallego or Galician, a language which, with Portuguese, forms a branch of Romance language distinct from Castilian Spanish, is widely spoken in rural areas and smaller towns. Galicia, along with **Asturias** to the east, is isolated from the rest of Spain by an extensive mountain range and has always had a distinct identity. Although the Iberian Peninsula was extensively settled by the Celts in prehistoric times, Galicia (and to some extent Asturias) has retained a strong Celtic identity to the present day. While archaeologists in Ireland still debate the possibility that the Celts came to Ireland from Spain, direct Celtic links between Galicia and Ireland are difficult to find. Medieval pilgrims from Ireland certainly travelled to the famous Santiago de Compostela in Galicia (still the region's capital), where the apostle St. James is reputedly buried.

For many people in Galicia today, the Celtic link established by the bishop Maeloc in the 5th or 6th century seems to have great significance. Maeloc was a bishop from **Brittany** who came to Galicia with a group of monks and established a cathedral. The Galician group Milladoiro titled their second album *A Galicia de Maeloc* (*The Galicia of Maeloc*, 1979) and the album's sleeve notes mention how the 'Celtic Breton' monks brought with them a whole new lifestyle, religious organisation and music. The Galician piper Carlos Nuñez also pays tribute to Maeloc with a track on his album *Irmandade das Estrellas* (*Brotherhood of Stars*, 1997) called 'Villancico para la Navidad de 1829'. A *villancico* is a popular poetic composition with a refrain which is sung in churches at Christmas. The 'Villancico for the Christmas of 1829' was composed by the master of the cathedral of Mondoñedo, the latter having been founded by bishop Maeloc. In the 19th century, Christmas was the only time when the playing of traditional instruments and the speaking of the Galician language were allowed inside the cathedral. Nuñez plays the *villancico* as an instrumental piece, and the additional musicians include the Irish uilleann piper **Paddy Moloney**.

Many Galicians are proud of their Celtic identity and feel a stronger cultural affinity with places like Ireland, **Scotland** and Brittany than they do with the rest of Spain. Their language and culture have been repeatedly threatened through

153

attempts to establish a linguistically and culturally uniform Spain – most recently under General Franco, who ruled Spain from 1939 until his death in 1975. Since Franco's death, many of Galicia's unique cultural traditions, including its music, have been revived and developed.

Galicia has a rich tradition of dance music, and some of the most popular types of dance tunes have parallels in Irish music. The *muiñeira*, in 6/8 time, is the most popular type of Galician dance tune and is very like the Irish double jig. The *polca* (polka) also enjoys considerable popularity. A number of dance tunes in 3/4 time are played, including the *valse* (waltz), the *foliada* (often danced at festival times), the *xota* (a very fast dance, typical of central Spain, but also played in Galicia) and some *danzas*. The *pasodoble* is a slow, simple dance tune in 2/4 time. Marches are also played in a variety of time signatures. As in Ireland, dance music is both for dancing and listening.

The most popular and unique form of traditional singing in Galicia is performed by groups of women who sing accompanied only by their own tambourine playing. These singing groups are called *pandereteiras*, from *pandeireta*, 'tambourine'. The gaita, a variety of **bagpipes**, is among the most popular Galician traditional instruments. The gaita has a range of just over an octave and is usually tuned to C. It is not chromatic but some semitones can be played, allowing the piper to play in keys such as F and D minor as well as C. The gaita can have a single drone, but typically has two, one of them tuned to C, two octaves below the bottom C of the chanter, the other tuned to C an octave below the chanter. Occasionally a gaita with three drones can be heard. The zanfona or **hurdy gurdy** is also very popular, and like the gaita is made by a number of Galician instrument makers. The fiddle, the Celtic harp (with nylon strings, like the neo-Irish **harp**) and various types of whistle, flute and ocarina (a small, potato-shaped wind instrument) are also played. Piano, stringed instruments (including guitar and bouzouki), soprano saxophone and clarinet are also played. Percussion instruments include the bombo (a bass drum played with a single stick), the metal-frame caja and the wooden-frame tamboril, both played with two sticks. Culleres, **spoons** made of wood, are also used, and the tarrañolas are played in a style very similar to Irish **bones**, although they are made from wood. The use of tambourine is not confined to *pandereteiras*.

The revival of Galician music since the death of Franco is exemplified by the group Milladoiro, formed in the late 1970s. Their earlier albums include some Irish traditional tunes as well as Galician dance music and several original compositions played on traditional Galician instruments. *A Galicia de Maeloc* includes traditional Galician *muiñeiras*, *danzas* and *pasodobles* as well as some Irish tunes. **Turlough O'Carolan**'s 'Sí Bheag, Sí Mhór' is played with 'John Ryan's Polka' and an Irish jig is included in a set that includes a Galician *muiñeira*. Group member Antón Seone's composition 'A Bruxa' ('The Witch') is among the original compositions on the album (the Irish group **Lá Lugh** also recorded this tune). The group is still together but now play more original compositions with orchestral arrangements. More recent groups include Na Lúa ('In the Moon') and Berrogüeto, who combine traditional

Galician and original music. Both Milladoiro and Berrugüeto have recorded with *pandeiriteras*.

Important Galician solo artists include gaita player Carlos Nuñez, an internationally renowned artist who has recorded and performed with a number of Irish musicians, including **Liam O'Flynn** and the **Chieftains**. Nuñez first worked with the latter on their film score for *Treasure Island* in 1990 and featured on *The Long Black Veil* (1994). He also played on *Santiago* (1996), the Chieftains' album of Galician and Galician-Cuban music, and helped Paddy Moloney in selecting material for the album. His *Irmandade das Estrellas* (1997) includes guest appearances by **Micheál Ó Domhnaill** and **Tríona Ní Dhomhnaill**, the Chieftains, American guitarist Ry Cooder and Cuban musicians. Nuñez has more recently experimented with mixing Galician and flamenco music on *Os Amores Libres* (1999). The latter album includes guest performances from a host of Irish musicians, including **Dónal Lunny**, **Sharon Shannon** and **Paddy Keenan**. Another fine gaita player is Xose Manoel Budiño; Budiño composes his own tunes as well as playing traditional music and the uilleann pipes.

Many Irish traditional musicians have performed in Galicia, where there are numerous Celtic music festivals, especially in the summer. The best of these festivals, which has been running for about two decades, is held annually at Ortigueira, a village in the north of Galicia, in mid-July. It usually features musicians from Ireland, Scotland, Brittany and Galicia. Although the **session** is not traditionally an important part of the Galician music scene, it is becoming more popular. This is especially true in the case of Irish bars, of which Vigo has a number, including the Dublin. Vigo is also the centre of the Universidad Popular, which teaches Galician music on gaita, fiddle, zanfona and Celtic harp. There are also courses in the making of various instruments, including gaita, zanfona, wooden flute, harp and various other stringed instruments such as the císther and cítaras.

Even if direct historical links between Irish and Galician music are vague, there are now strong bonds, as in the case of Brittany, between the musicians of Galicia and Ireland, and a musical dialogue benefitting both traditions continues to take place. See also **Ní Chathasaigh, Nollaig**.

Galldubh Dublin-based group which mixed traditional, rock and jazz influences. The name is derived from that of Eamonn Galldubh (uilleann pipes, whistles, soprano saxophone), the central figure in the group. Eamonn took part in Ceoltóir, a project in traditional music performance at Ballyfermot Senior College, Dublin. Part of the project involved the recording of a CD called *Triad: Three from Trad* (1998), which featured tracks by Eamonn Galldubh, Dave Munnelly (button accordion) and singer Tina Price. The piper's tracks on this CD were markedly experimental and his backing group included Fionán de Barra (guitar) and Eugene Wogan (bass), both of whom went on to record the first CD under the name Galldubh, *Two Little Ducks* (1999). The line-up also included fiddler **Zoë Conway**, Ruairí de Barra (electric guitar, vocals), Paul Byrne (bodhrán, percussion) and Eamonn de Barra (flute). The group's mixture of different influences made them a popular act at the L'Orient

Festival in Brittany in 1998, and they afterwards played throughout Europe and in the Middle East. The line-up for their second CD, *The Seventh Step* (2001), included Carmel O'Dea (fiddle) and Aideen Curtin (vocals, flute) instead of Zoë Conway and Eamonn de Barra.

Most of the material on *The Seventh Step* is original, with tunes by Eamonn Galldubh, Carmel O'Dea and others, and three songs co-written by different combinations of group members. Many of the tunes are jigs and reels arranged in a style that can shift between different moods, even within individual tracks. At times the accompaniments are sparse, as on 'Nice and Easy/Spraoi/Lománach', a set of reels played on fiddle with acoustic guitar accompaniment. 'Hob Nobs' (composed by brothers Cormac and Fionán de Barra) is a delicately arranged slip jig involving harp (played by guest Cormac de Barra) acoustic guitar, fiddle and whistle. There are other instrumental tracks which have a much more rock-influenced, big band sound, such as 'The Well Fed Reel/The Fruit Pastille Reel'. Here the drums and bass play a prominent role and the pipes and flute break into a jazzy improvisation in the middle of the second tune. In stark contrast, 'Paddy's Rambles Through the Park' is a tune from Donegal fiddler **John Doherty**, played solo on acoustic guitar. There are some traditional tunes and a track of Breton style tunes, one composed by flute-player Jean-Michel Veillon (see **Brittany**). The songs lean more towards contemporary folk, or even blues in the case of 'Touch of the Tune', but like the instrumentals cannot be easily categorised.

The music of Galldubh incorporates a range of musical influences and a wealth of talent in playing, composition and arrangement. They were one of the more interesting young groups to emerge in recent years and, like **Kíla**, represent a new

Galldubh

generation of musicians who have strong roots in traditional music but are not afraid to experiment and compose original music. The group broke up in 2004.

Gardiner, Bobby (b. 1939)   Renowned button accordion and melodeon player born in Aughdarra, near Lisdoonvarna, Co. Clare. During the 1950s, he played with the Kilfenora Céilí Band before emigrating to the **US** in 1960. He made his first recording there in 1962 and played with the legendary accordionist **Joe Cooley** in sessions in the Catskill Mountains. He returned to Ireland in 1970. His playing can be heard on *Traditional Music of Ireland* (1989) and *The Master's Choice* (1993). His clear, uncluttered style, with light ornamentation, distinguishes his playing and he is famous for use of the single button triplet. On *The Clare Shout* (1998) he does some **lilting** as well as playing accordion.

Garland   A term which often describes an eight-page chapbook containing the words of one long song, although it can also be used of a chapbook containing several songs. Garlands in the former sense were popular in Ireland around the middle of the 18th century. Most of the garlands printed in Ireland were reprints of English garlands. They contained long verse narrations with titles like 'The Children in the Wood', 'The Wanton Wife of Bath' or 'Sir Guy of Warwick'. Irish-composed garlands are rare, but Hugh Shields mentions three in his *Narrative Singing in Ireland* (Dublin, 1993): the 'Waterford Tragedy', the 'Dublin Tragedy' and the 'Ulster Tragedy' (which dates from around 1750). Although most of the 'garland ballads' seem far too long to be sung from memory, Shields notes that some, such as the 'Lancashire Cuckold', did survive orally by being drastically pruned. An earlier and different use of the term 'garland' can be found in the titles of the original works that contained the songs now known as the Kilmore or **Wexford Carols**. These were *A Garland of Pious and Godly Songs* (Ghent, 1684) and *A New Garland Containing Songs for Christmas*, a manuscript collected in Wexford in 1728.

Gaughan, Dick (b. 1948)   Singer/songwriter and guitarist born in Glasgow who grew up in Leith, near Edinburgh. His paternal grandparents came from Ireland and much of Gaughan's material derives from, or concerns, Ireland. His mother was from the Scottish highlands and spoke Scots Gaelic. Gaughan began as a singer of unaccompanied ballads and moved on through bluegrass, jazz and pop during the 1960s. He released a solo album, *No More Forever*, before joining the **Boys of the Lough** in 1972 and features strongly in the Scottish/Irish group's first album, *The Boys of the Lough* (1973). Before the end of 1973, however, Gaughan had left the group and went on to pursue a solo career. On *The Boys of the Lough*, he shows great flair in his use of the guitar as a melody instrument; this was also evident in 1977 when he released *Coppers and Brass: Scots and Irish Dance Music on Guitar*. The album illustrates Gaughan's rare ability to use the guitar successfully to play reels, jigs, marches and hornpipes; his melody playing and ornamentation are outstanding. In subsequent albums – including *Gaughan* (1978), *Handful of Earth* (1981) and *A Different Kind of Love Song* (1983) – subtle guitar-playing supports his

Dick Gaughan

strong, earthy voice. Few solo performers have combined such a unique style of singing (which Gaughan himself says is greatly influenced by traditional singers of Northern Ireland) with such sophisticated guitar accompaniment. Songs such as 'Erin-Go-Bragh' and 'Now Westlin Winds' on *Handful of Earth* are good examples. His material is derived from a range of sources, including the music and song traditions of Ireland and Scotland as well as more contemporary songwriters. Gaughan has never hidden his socialist views and many of his songs are thought-provoking commentaries on historical or political events.

While acknowledging that the Jacobite risings (see **Jacobite Song**) of the 17th and 18th centuries brought out hopes and loyalty in many Scottish people and produced numerous songs, he has little sympathy for the Jacobites. His song 'No Gods and Precious Few Heroes' talks of 'the lies of a past that we know was never real'. He argues that the 'young pretender', Charles Stuart (1720-1788), defeated at Culloden (1746), did not have the interests of Scotland and her people at heart but only wished to restore Jacobite control over the English throne. He asks 'will we never hear the end' of Charles Stuart and Culloden and describes how Charles 'ran like a rabbit from the glen, leaving better folk than him to be butchered'. Gaughan places the Jacobite cause in a contemporary context, singing:

> So don't talk to me of Scotland the Brave,
> When if we don't fight soon there'll be nothing left to save,
> Or would you rather stand and watch them dig your grave,
> While you wait for the tartan messiah.

The title track on *A Different Kind of Love Song* is his own response to those who criticise him for being 'too political', and is a direct and moving defence of political song. The album includes songs written by the great political songwriters Peggy Seeger and **Ewan MacColl** as well as the extraordinary 19th-century American poem 'Revolution' (sung to a tune by Gaughan). *Live in Edinburgh* (recorded in 1984) was Gaughan's first performance after a long illness that had threatened his ability to sing. Again the songs are political, including a strikingly meditative and understated rendition of Tommy Makem's song about Northern Ireland, 'Four Green Fields'. The album captures the wit and the sharp political comments with which he sprinkles his introductions. *Sail On* (1996) includes **Pete Seeger**'s Vietnam War song 'Waist Deep in the Big Muddy', 'The Sist (Highland) Division's Farewell to Sicily', 'Geronimo's Cadillac' and Gaughan's own 'No Cause for Alarm'. *Redwood Cathedral* (1998) is dedicated by Gaughan to fellow songwriters. It includes renditions of the Brian McNeill songs 'Ewan and the Gold' and 'Muir and the Master Builder', and Pete Seeger's classic 'Turn, Turn, Turn'. *Outlaws and Dreamers* (2001) is another fine collection of songs, including Woody Guthrie's 'Tom Joad' and Si Kahn's 'What You Do With What You've Got'. Gaughan is accompanied on some tracks by Brian McNeill (fiddle, concertina). *Prentice Piece: The First Three Decades* (2002) is a two-CD compilation with 21 tracks and a comprehensive accompanying booklet. Website: www.dickalba.demon.co.uk. See also **Scotland**.

Gavin, Frankie (b. 1956) Multi-instrumentalist born into a musical family at Corandulla, Co. Galway. He started playing at a very young age and was greatly influenced by the early recordings of Irish musicians in America, especially those of fiddlers **James Morrison** and **Michael Coleman**, and piper **Patsy Tuohey**. Although best known for his fiddling, Gavin can play a number of instruments and is a fine flute and whistle player. Gavin and **Alec Finn** were central to the group **De Dannan**'s success, but Gavin has also done a lot of work outside De Dannan; *Frankie Gavin and Alec Finn*, originally recorded in 1977, was re-released

Frankie Gavin
(courtesy of Tara Music)

on CD in 1994. The album *Ómós do Joe Cooley* (1986), with Paul Brock (accordion) and **Charlie Lennon** (piano) is regarded as a classic. Gavin plays many different types of music, from Jewish Klezmer to jazz, and has recorded with Stephan Grapelli, Yehudi Menuhin and The Rolling Stones. A selection of his recordings, from 1977 up to 1995, can be heard on *The Best of Frankie Gavin* (n.d.). On *Fierce Traditional* (2001) he harks back to the music recorded in the 1920s and 30s by musicians like Coleman, Morrison and the **Flanagan Brothers**. Website: www.frankiegavin.com.

German The name used in Donegal for a **barndance**.

German Concertina See **Concertina**.

German Flute See **Flute**.

Glackin, Paddy (b. 1954) Fiddler and broadcaster born in Dublin. His father, Tom (a fiddler from the Rosses, Co. Donegal) and **John Doherty** were both important influences on his playing from his youth. Glackin was a member of **Ceoltóirí Laigheann** and was the **Bothy Band**'s first fiddler. He was also the first Traditional Music Arts Officer with the Irish Arts Council until he left this post to join **RTÉ**, where he presented the radio programme *The Long Note* and the television programme *The Pure Drop*. He has recorded a number of albums, including *Ceol ar an bhFidil* ('Music on the Fiddle', 1977), *Doublin* (1978) with **Paddy Keenan** and further albums with **Robbie Hannan**. In 1980 he made *Hidden Ground* with the late Jolyon Jackson. The album is an extraordinary achievement, using multi-track recording techniques to allow Jackson to play a number of instruments on each selection. The arrangements are daring and innovative, using synthesisers, harmonica, whistles, mandolin, cello, bottles and other instruments to great effect. Their arrangements of 'The Butterfly', 'The Drunken Sailor' and 'The Japanese Hornpipe' (from the playing of Johnny Doherty) are of particular interest. Unfortunately, when the great days of experimentation and the **supergroups** are discussed, this fine album is rarely mentioned. More recently Glackin released *Athchuairt/Reprise*, (2000) with former Bothy Band member **Mícheál Ó Domhnaill** (guitar), and the guests include two other Bothy Band musicians **Tríona Ní Dhomhnaill** (vocals, bodhrán) and Paddy Keenan (pipes, low whistle). Among the other guests are **Noel Hill** (concertina), **Máirtín O'Connor** (button accordion), Philip Begley (bass, harmonium) and jazz flautist Brian Dunning.

Glackin's younger brothers, Séamus and Kevin, are also accomplished fiddlers. Together they recorded the album *Na Saighneáin: Northern Lights* (1988); Séamus also recorded an album with his brother Paddy, *An Bóthar Cam* ('The Crooked Road'). Kevin's album with **Davy Spillane**, *Forgotten Days* (2001), won *Irish Music* magazine's 'Best Album' award in 2001. Kevin was also involved in setting up the internet traditional music school, **Scoiltrad**.

Glór Irish Music Centre Located in Ennis, Co. Clare, this national performance centre for Irish traditional music opened in November 2001. The Irish word *glór* means 'voice' and can be used of the human voice in particular or, in a more general sense, as 'sound'. The centre is funded by the Exchequer (central government), local authorities and the European Regional Development Fund. Its facilities include a 500-seat auditorium, a gallery space, a café and a bar.

The Glór Summer Festival has an extensive programme of events from April to September. This includes regular evenings of **set dancing**, traditional music of Co. Clare, a musical journey through Irish folklore and mythology and a performance which shows how Irish traditional music and dance have influenced or been influenced by the traditions of America, Europe, Africa and Asia. There are daily lunchtime performances of traditional music, and other daily events in the Summer Festival include a film on traditional music in Co. Clare and an interactive exhibition of contemporary recordings of Irish music.

The centre is open all year round and in autumn and winter hosts a wide range of events including concerts by some of the top performers in classical and jazz – as well as Irish traditional – music. There are also plays performed by the Druid Theatre Company (and occasionally visiting theatre groups), dance and children's events, and a cinema club. The centre plays host to many events during the **Fleadh Nua** in May each year and offers its facilities for conferences. The gallery hosts various art and craft exhibitions.

Katie Verling was contracted in 2001 to work as the full-time director of the Glór centre for its first three years. A niece of **Seán Ó Riada**, she was involved in developing the idea for the centre while working with Telegael in Spiddal, Co. Galway. In a relatively short time, she established Glór as one of the most important venues for live music in Ireland. Website: www.glor.ie.

Goldsmith, Oliver (1728-1774)   Poet, novelist and dramatist, born in Pallas, Co. Longford. His most famous works include the poem *The Deserted Village* (1770) and the novel *The Vicar of Wakefield* (1766). His works have been studied by **Hugh Shields** for the invaluable light they shed on the oral tradition of old **ballad**s in Ireland in the first half of the 18th century (see also **Child Ballads**). Goldsmith also played the flute, and is the earliest player of this instrument to be mentioned by **Francis O'Neill** in *Irish Minstrels and Musicians*. Often neglecting his studies in Trinity College, Dublin to play the flute, Goldsmith brought his instrument along with a guinea and 'the shirt on his back' when he began his extensive travels around Europe in 1755. He also wrote an interesting essay on 'Carolan, the Irish Bard' in 1760 (see **O'Carolan, Turlough**).

Goodman, James (1828-1896)   Uilleann piper, flautist and collector born in Ventry on the Dingle peninsula, Co. Kerry. He studied Arts and Divinity in Trinity College Dublin and was ordained in 1853. A native speaker of Irish, he was Professor of Irish at Trinity College for the last twelve years of his life. He played the flute from an early age and although he didn't take up the pipes until he was over 30, was renowned as an excellent piper. His renditions of 'The Fox-chase' and old Irish airs were particularly remarked upon by those who heard him play, and he also used to sing in Irish while accompanying himself on the uilleann pipes. His work as a collector took place mainly from 1860 to 1866 while he was at Ardgroom on the Beare peninsula, Co. Cork. Although some of his airs were copied from printed sources (including **Bunting** and **O'Farrell**), he also collected many airs and dance tunes from the playing of pipers in Munster. Many of the dance tunes came from the playing of Thomas Kennedy, a blind piper from Dingle, Co. Kerry, who was in Ardgroom with Goodman. **Francis O'Neill** gave an interesting account of

Goodman in his *Irish Minstrels and Musicians*, remarking on his great charity to the poor and his willingness to repair sets of pipes for all comers free of charge. O'Neill (pp. 174-6) described how Goodman's funeral on January 21, 1896, was attended by many, 'the procession composed of all classes and creeds in the community'. He concludes that the reverend piper's 'generosity to the poor left him without wealth in the end. Yet he died rich, for money could not buy the esteem and respect of his countrymen which were his without limit or reserve.' **Breandán Breathnach** also took a great interest in Goodman, whom he regarded as particularly well equipped to collect Irish music. After Breathnach's death, **Hugh Shields** continued to work on the Goodman manuscripts, housed in TCD. In conjunction with the **Irish Traditional Music Archive**, Shields published *Music of the Munster Pipers: Irish Traditional Music from the Goodman Manuscripts, Vol. 1* (1998), which contains over 500 song airs, dance tunes and other forms of music. All of the tunes in the book were taken by Goodman from the living tradition rather than from any previously published sources.

Grace Note Term used to describe ornamental notes written or printed smaller than the main text in notation, which have no time value within the written bar length. In Irish traditional music, various forms of ornamentation use one or more grace notes. The term 'single grace note' is sometimes used for what is here described as a **cut**, while 'double grace note' can be used for **casadh**. See also **Cran** and **Roll**.

Grace Note

Gráda Innovative group formed in 2001 by Kilkenny-born Brendan O'Sullivan (fiddle, viola), Dubliner Alan Doherty (flute, whistles, vocals) and Mayo singer Anne-Marie O'Malley (vocals, bodhrán), along with Irish-New Zealander Gerald Paul (guitar, bouzouki) and New Zealander Andrew Laking (double bass). Their first album, *Endeavour* (2002), was co-produced by Gráda and Trevor Hutchinson of **Lúnasa**. The album is a mixture of traditional and original material, with six instrumental tracks and six songs. Dave Hingerty plays percussion on various instruments throughout the album. The songs include a fine, percussion-driven arrangement of Rónán Ó Snodaigh's (see **Kíla**) Irish-langauge song 'Cathain' ('When') and the traditional song 'She Is Like a Swallow', given a contemporary feel with guitar/percussion/bass accompaniment and some inventive instrumental breaks on flute and fiddle. The traditional tunes include the slow air, 'Cailín na Gruaige Doinne' ('The Girl with the Brown Hair'), and a tune from **Brittany** which is played in the middle of a set that starts with a composition by Diarmiud Moynihan (piper and whistle-player with Calico and, more recently, the Red Hat Band) and ends with an original tune by Gráda. Other tunes on the album are original compositions by the members of Gráda and display a wealth of talent in composing and arranging in different rhythms. 'Pint of Reference' starts with a slip jig and then changes into a fast reel with a distinctive, almost oriental quality, continuing in the same rhythm for 'Men of Destiny' (composed by Diarmuid Moynihan). 'Biodegrádable' consists of two moderate-tempo Breton-style tunes, the first composed by Gráda and the second, 'Kishor's Tune', by Breton guitarist Soïg Sbéril. As with the songs, the instrumentals are well arranged, with short bridges often linking tunes of different rhythms and some inventive playing on fiddle and flute, both of which interchange between melody and harmony on many tracks. The Group's second album, *The Landing Step* (2004), again with Trevor Hutchinson in production, displays a further expansion of their sound, with additional guests playing percussion, cello, trumpet and piano. Gráda is a fine example of how a contemporary traditional band can successfully combine traditional and original material, and is one of the most talented young bands to emerge in recent years. Website: gradamusic.com.

Graham, Len (b. 1944)   Antrim-born singer, lilter (see **Lilting**) and collector. From his early twenties, he was a close friend of the great Derry singer, **Eddie Butcher**, from whom he learned a number of his songs. He also developed a close relationship with another Ulster singer, **Joe Holmes**, with whom he recorded two albums (in 1976 and 1979). On Graham's first solo album, *Wind and Water* (1977), he sings songs and ballads as well as lilting, some of the time unaccompanied. Two further solo albums followed before Graham joined the group **Skylark**, with whom he made four albums. He has also worked as a collector of songs and, in conjunction with the Arts Council of Northern Ireland, released *It's of My Rambles...* (1993), a collection of field recordings. With his wife **Pádraigín Ní Uallacháin** he made an album of children's songs in English and Irish, *When We Were Young* (1996). He continues to perform solo and is featured on the official 1798 commemoration album, *Who Fears to Speak?* (1997). See also **Nationalist/Republican Song**.

Granard Harp Festivals   Three harp festivals, or 'Grand Balls', as they were called, held at Granard, Co. Longford in 1781, 1782 and 1783. The festivals were initiated by James Dungan, an Irishman living in Copenhagen, and monetary prizes were offered for those placed first, second and third in the competition. In the first year these prizes were awarded respectively to Charles Fanning, Arthur O'Neill and Rose Mooney; the prize-winners were the same in 1782 and 1783. Jealousies and animosities among the harpers finally prompted Dungan to abandon the idea of holding more competitions. Many of the harpers who played at the Granard festivals also played in the **Belfast Harp Festival** (1792). The latter festival, however, is better known because **Edward Bunting** transcribed much of the music played and wrote additional material on the techniques and lifestyles of the harpers themselves. No such transcriptions or details on the harpers were recorded at Granard.

Granuaile (ca. 1530-1603)   Otherwise known as Gráinne Ní Mháille or Grace O'Malley, Gaelic 'pirate queen' of Connacht who was celebrated in popular tradition as a nationalist heroine and, more recently, as a feminist. She fought against, and eventually met, **Elizabeth I** of England. In 18th-century song, she was celebrated as a symbol of Irish nationhood in verses written in English and inspired by the Gaelic political **aisling** or vision poem. These songs were very popular in the 18th and 19th centuries and their lyrics can be found in *Granuaile: The Life and Times of*

Grace O'Malley by Anne Chambers (new edition, Dublin, 1988). More recently, the pirate queen again became the focus of public interest when **Shaun Davey** composed his *Granuaile* (1985), a suite for orchestra, uilleann pipes (played by **Liam O'Flynn**) and voice (Rita Connolly).

Great Famine, The (1845-1849) Approximately one million died, and even more emigrated, as a result of the Great Famine, caused by the failure of the potato crop in 1845, 1846 and 1848. In 1847, the worst year of the famine, potato yields were average, but little had been sown because of the scarcity of seed potatoes. More people died from disease than hunger and many survived by emigrating, mainly to the **US** and Britain (see **England**, **Scotland**, **Wales**), and some to **Australia**. **Francis O'Neill** wrote in 1913: 'To no class in the community did the terrible famine years prove more disastrous than to the pipers. Those who lived through plague and privation found but scanty patronage thereafter' (*Irish Minstrels and Musicians*, p. 208). O'Neill goes on to relate the story of the travelling piper John McDonagh from Annaghdown, Co. Galway, 'who died [in 1857] neglected and ignored in the Gort poorhouse' (p. 209). His widow held on to his pipes for seven years after his death but was eventually forced to sell them for a fraction of their true value.

O'Neill also gives a profile and photograph of the professional piper Thomas McCarthy from Ballybunion, Co. Kerry. McCarthy (1799-1904) was among the most celebrated musicians of his time, not least because his life spanned three centuries. Although he spent his whole life in Co. Kerry, his brother, Timothy, emigrated from Ireland to England in the wake of the Great Famine and changed his name to George Carthy. His great, great grandson is the famous English folk musician, **Martin Carthy**.

The Great Famine certainly caused, directly or indirectly, the deaths of many musicians and **dancing masters**. Those who emigrated in the late 1840s and the decades that followed (including Francis O'Neill) formed large Irish communities in many foreign cities (including Québec, New York, Boston, Chicago, Glasgow, London and Liverpool), where traditional music often flourished. In the US, Canada and Britain there were numerous musicians, some of whom played professionally or semi-professionally in the late 19th and early 20th centuries. Between 1856 and 1921 over four million Irish people emigrated, strengthening many of the communities that had been formed during the Famine years.

Only a few contemporary famine songs written in Irish survive. These include 'Na Prátaí Bána' ('The White Potatoes'), 'Soup House Mhuigh-Iorrais', 'An Droch-Shaoghal' ('The Bad Life'), 'Amhrán na bPrátaí Dubha' ('Song of the Black Potatoes') and 'Dúchan na bPrátaí ('The Blighting of the Potatoes'). These songs, like those written in English at the time, are rarely heard today. One exception is 'Skibbereen', a song set in America, where a son asks his father why he left Ireland. Known in the US today as 'the granddaddy of all Irish famine songs', it had been recorded by **Mick Moloney,** who has done much research and recording in the area of Irish songs in the US. 'Lone Shanakyle', which deals with the effects of the famine in Co. Clare, is another song which is still sung. Many of the songs in English were written by nationalists like the **Young Irelanders**, but despite the fact that a number of their political songs are still sung, most of those relating to the famine are not. Nonetheless, more recent songs on the subject, sung by **Christy Moore** ('City of Chicago') and **Paddy Reilly** ('The Fields of Athenry') have become popular. **Frank Harte** (accompanied by **Dónal Lunny**) has made a major contribution to the memory of the Famine in song with his *The Hungry Voice: The Song Legacy of Ireland's Great Famine* (2004). Like other works by Harte, it is masterly not just in the performance of the songs but in the research and background information, provided in the accompanying 50-page booklet. Harte subscribes to the idea that the hunger of the Great Famine was simply too horrific to be recorded in song, but points out that its effects – in terms of eviction, emigration, an enduring memory of hardship and a sense of injustice – have been recorded in song. Another major contribution to music commemorating the Great Famine is **Charlie Lennon**'s *Flight from the Hungry Land* (1996), composed for a traditional ensemble and concert orchestra to mark the famine's 150th anniversary. See also **Emigration Songs**.

Green Linnet

Green Linnet American recording label based in Connecticut which started in 1973 and specialises in traditional music from Ireland, **Scotland**, **Brittany**, **Galicia**, **England** and the **US**. Wendy Newton joined the company in 1975 (becoming sole owner in 1978) and turned it into one of the most significant specialist labels involved in music from the Celtic nations. **Séamus Ennis** was among the first Irish musicians whose work was released on Green Linnet, and the label has played a major role in launching and developing the careers of many Irish artists and groups including **Robbie O'Connell**, **Mick Moloney**, **Altan** and **Lúnasa**. They first recorded the Irish-American fiddler **Eileen Ivers** at the age of 13 and played a major role in launching and promoting the Irish-American group **Cherish the Ladies**. Scottish artists and groups like Silly Wizard, **Cappercaillie** and Old Blind Dogs have also been recorded and promoted by Green Linnet, as well as the excellent Irish/Scottish group **Relativity**. Breton musicians who have recorded with the label include guitarist Dan Ar Bras and the group Kornog. The company has also bought some recordings that were originally made with other labels, including those of the **Bothy Band**, originally released by the Irish label Mulligan Records.

Green Linnet has enjoyed remarkable success as a specialist label within America and in other parts of the world. Its continued survival through the 1990s and into the 21st century is all the more remarkable in an era when large, multi-national recording labels have tended to push smaller, specialised labels out of the market. Website: www.greenlinnet.com.

Greig-Duncan Folk Song Collection

Greig-Duncan Folk Song Collection A major collection of over 3000 Scottish folk songs amassed in the first two decades of the 20th century. Work on the project began in 1903 when Gavin Greig, a schoolmaster, musician and writer, started collecting songs in Aberdeenshire. Around 1905, the Reverend James Bruce Duncan, a noted musicologist, became involved with Greig and the project was expanded through lectures, a newspaper column and correspondence with people interested in folk song. Greig published *Folk Song in Buchan* (1906) and a number of articles on folk song in the *Buchan Observer* between 1907 and 1911. The amount of material he and Duncan had gathered was, however, so great that years of work would have been required to sort all the songs for publication. Although they had begun to work on a volume of classical or **Child ballads**, neither Greig (d. 1914) nor Duncan (d. 1917) lived to bring this work to publication. It was completed and edited by Alexander Keith and published as *Last Leaves of Traditional Ballads and Ballad Airs Collected in Aberdeenshire by the late Gavin Greig* (1925), although this consisted of only about one eighth of the material which had been collected. In the 1960s work began at the universities of Aberdeen and Edinburgh to sort and publish the complete collection. The first of a projected eight volumes was published by the Aberdeen University Press in 1981 as *The Greig-Duncan Folk Song Collection*, edited by Patrick Shuldham-Shaw and Emily B. Lyle. Volume 2 was published in 1983 and the latest, Volume 7, in 1997. Shuldham-Shaw also edited Duncan's *Folk Songs of Aberdeenshire* (London, 1967), published in conjunction with the **English Folk Dance and Song Society**. The Greig-Duncan collection includes many Child ballads, but also contains **bothy ballads** unique to the northeast of Scotland and 19th-century ballads.

Griallais Family From Carraroe in Connemara, Co. Galway. There are eleven Griallais sisters, all of whom sing, but Nan, Sarah and Nora are the best-known of this **sean-nós singing** family. Their parents and aunts, from whom they learned many of their songs, sang regularly at home. Nan, Sarah and Nora participated in the **Oireachtas** sean-nós competition, *Corn Uí Riada*, for many years and Nora won it three times. *Nora Griallais: Native Connemara Irish Singing* was released on CD in 1993. Sarah, who won Corn Uí Riada in 1984, released *Connemara Sean-nós* in 2000.

Guitar A stringed instrument of the lute family. In the 19th century it existed in two forms, the 'English guitar' or **cittern** and the 'Spanish guitar', which developed into the modern guitar. The guitar is a relatively recent addition to Irish music. Its use in accompanying Irish dance tunes and songs was charted by the **Flanagan Brothers** in the **US** in the 1920s, but it was not until the 1950s and 60s that it became popular in Irish music on both sides of the Atlantic. The **Clancy Brothers and Tommy Makem** incorporated guitar (and Appalachian banjo) into their arrangements of Irish songs, and the use of the guitar by ballad singers became widespread during the **ballad boom**. Gradually the guitar became more commonly used in accompanying instrumental music, but some musicians criticised its use as an impediment to the strong melodies of traditional music. There have, however, been many interesting developments in the use of guitar in traditional music since the 1960s. **Micheál Ó Domhnaill** provided fine accompaniments to both songs and instrumentals through his work in the 1970s with groups such as **Monroe**, **Skara Brae** and the **Bothy Band**. Also in the 1970s, **Paul Brady** made outstanding contributions to the development of accompaniment (of both songs and instrumental music) and the playing of melody on guitar. Scotsman **Dick Gaughan**'s *Coppers and Brass: Scots and Irish Dance Music on Guitar* (1977) was a milestone in the use of the guitar as an instrument for playing dance music. Three years later **Arty McGlynn** released *McGlynn's Fancy*, another seminal album comprising mostly jigs, reels, Carolan tunes and slow airs – the melodies (and often accompaniment as well) played with rare artistry by McGlynn on guitar. Both Gaughan and McGlynn have a natural ability and sensitivity to the music that is quite rare in using the guitar as a melody instrument, and few have come close to emulating their achievements in recording albums made up entirely, or largely, of Irish traditional music played on guitar. Since the late 1980s English guitarist Chris Newman has done excellent melody work solo and in his duo with harpist **Máire Ní Chathasaigh**, playing Irish and Scottish music as well as music from other traditions. A veteran of the jazz scene, Newman has a great sense of the depth of the Irish musical tradition and he has made three solo albums, the most recent being *Fretwork* (1998). Scottish guitarist Tony McManus also plays music from different traditions, including Irish, Scottish, Breton and French-Canadian tunes.

Both McGlynn and Gaughan generally use steel-string guitars, but since the 1980s a number of classical guitarists have released albums of Irish music played in a classical style on the nylon-string guitar. These include **John Feely**, English guitarist Gerald Garcia and **Simon Taylor**. Much of the material recorded by these artists consists of slow airs and Carolan tunes, with very few of the faster dance tunes.

In terms of accompaniment, there are now many good guitarists with different styles who often use different tunings. Australian **Steve Cooney** has developed his own highly percussive style of accompaniment for dance music, and can also play subtle versions of Irish slow air melodies on the guitar. **Jimmy Faulkner** has brought rock and blues influences to traditional playing. Chicago-based Dennis Cahill, best known for his work with **Martin Hayes**, has developed a delicate, minimalist approach to accompaniment. While Cahill generally uses standard guitar tuning (e-a-d-g-b-e″), Cooney uses 'dropped D' tuning (lowering the bass E string to D). **Gavin Ralston**, who has produced a book and video on Irish traditional guitar accompaniment, also uses dropped D tuning. Some players, however, find that alternative tunings such as 'open D' (d-a-f♯-d′-a-d″) or d-a-d′-g-a-d″ (see **DADGAD**) are more suited to the modal nature of most traditional music, allowing the guitar to resonate more naturally and often providing the effect of a drone. A variety of other tunings are used. For example, John Doyle of **Solas**, who generally uses dropped D tuning for accompanying dance tunes, will occasionally use DADGAD or open G (where the strings are tuned to a G-major chord when played open) with a C bass. He also employs a 'high strung' guitar (basically, using the four-octave and two unison strings from a twelve-string guitar set on a six-string guitar) and a variety of other tunings for songs.

The Algerian-born guitarist Pierre Bensusan has absorbed a diverse range of influences, including jazz, African and traditional French music. Irish music has also been a strong influence, and on albums such as *Pres De Paris* (1975) and *Pierre Bensusan 2* (1977) he can be heard playing Irish and French traditional music. The Irish tunes on these albums include the reels 'The Flax in Bloom' and 'The Ashplant', the march 'The Return from Fingal' and the slide 'Merrily Kiss the Quaker'. Bensusan favours DADGAD tuning for the playing of Irish music. He has also composed original music for the guitar, some of it Irish-influenced in form and style, including 'The Last Pint', recorded by **Lúnasa** on their first album.

Guitar playing has come a long way since the 1950s, and the guitar can be heard played percussively (almost like a bodhrán), with a rock-style rhythm, as a harmony instrument or, occasionally, as a melody instrument. Much experimentation and adaptation has taken place to make the guitar more suitable to the playing of traditional music. There are now three tutors dealing specifically with 'Irish Guitar': Paul de Grae's *Traditional Irish Guitar* (revised edition, Cork, 1997); **Sarah McQuaid**'s *Irish DADGAD Guitar Book* (Cork, 1995); and Gavin Ralston's *Irish Traditional Guitar Accompaniment* (Dublin, 1998). In the US, Glenn Weiser has published some significant books of Irish/Celtic music for guitar, including arrangements of Carolan tunes and *Celtic Guitar* (2001), a book of 40 traditional (Irish and Scottish) and Carolan tunes with a CD. The guitar is now an integral part of the traditional music scene – not in all areas perhaps, but certainly for ensemble playing and also in many sessions.

Guthrie, Woody (Woodrow Wilson Guthrie, 1912-1967) American folk singer/ songwriter, harmonica player and fiddler born in Okemah, Oklahoma, who came to prominence for his singing and songwriting around the time of the Great Depression (1929-34). Initially he sang and played in small towns and farms and during World War II (1939-45) had a sticker on his guitar that read 'This Machine Kills Fascists'. Some of his songs were new arrangements, with new words, of older folk songs; his own songs were often bitter comments on America's social, economic and political problems. **Alan Lomax** played a major role in bringing Guthrie to a wider audience, having him on radio shows in 1939 and in the early 40s. It was with Lomax at the Library of Congress that Guthrie recorded seriously for the first time in March 1940. The writer John Steinbeck (1902-68) was a fan of his music, and Woody wrote a ballad based on Steinbeck's famous novel *The Grapes of Wrath* (1939). The album *Dust Bowl Ballads* (1940) enjoyed considerable popularity, partly because of its association with a 'Grapes of Wrath' show in which Guthrie was involved. *Dust Bowl Ballads* was ultimately recognised as a one of the most influential American recordings of the 20th century. It was also at this time that Lomax, Guthrie and **Pete Seeger** put together the collection *Hard-Hitting Songs for Hard-Hitting People*, although it was not published until 1962. Steinbeck wrote an introduction to the book, which included a profile of Woody and the significance of his music.

In 1941 Guthrie joined the Almanac Singers (which included Pete Seeger), a group strongly associated with workers' rallies and left-wing politics. In subsequent years he played and recorded with many musicians, including the famous singer

Leadbelly, Cisco Houston and Sonny Terry. Guthrie's most famous song – later popularised by Seeger and recorded in an Irish version by the **Waterboys** – was 'This Land Is Your Land'. The song started as Woody's response to the patriotic song 'God Bless America', a song he despised. Working on his song in 1940, Guthrie originally had 'God blessed America for me' at the end of each verse. This line was replaced in 1944 by 'This land was made for you and me'. The tune was taken from an old Carter family song, 'Little Darlin', Pal of Mine', which in turn had come from an old Baptist hymn, 'Oh My Lovin' Brother'. The change of the song title from 'God Blessed America' to 'This Land Is Your Land' in 1944 took place during Guthrie's famous record-ing sessions with producer Moses Asch, which also involved Cisco Houston, Leadbelly, Sonny Terry and Bess Lomax (sister of Alan Lomax). Guthrie also wrote and recorded many children's songs.

Woodie Guthrie

Guthrie influenced many con-temporary singers, including Bob Dylan, Bruce Springsteen and Billy Bragg (see **England**). In the late 1990s, Bragg collaborated with the American band Wilco and Woody's daughter Nora on a project which involved the recording and release on two albums of songs which Guthrie himself had written but never recorded. Woody Guthrie's music has been a major influence on a number of Irish folk singers since the 1950s and 60s, including **Christy Moore** and **Andy Irvine**, as well as Scottish singer **Dick Gaughan**. Moore has recorded several Guthrie songs, including 'Sacco and Vanzetti' on his album *Christy Moore* (1976) and 'Pretty Boy Floyd' on *Live in Dublin* (1978). Irvine wrote a song about the American singer entitled 'Never Tire of the Road' (on *Rude Awakening*, 1991).

Guthrie was hospitalised in 1952 with Huntington's chorea, a disease he died of fifteen years later. He published an autobiography, *Bound for Glory*, in 1943 and Joe Klein's classic biography, *Woody Guthrie: A Life* (1980), provides a comprehensive and balanced view of a fascinating life which was often lived amidst chaos and tragedy. See also **American Folk Song**.

Half Set A form of **set dancing** which involves only two couples instead of the usual four. See also **Set 1**.

Hamilton, Colin 'Hammy' (b. 1953) Belfast-born flautist and singer who has also established himself as a flute-maker, researcher, writer and composer. He became interested in traditional music during the folk revival of the 1960s. After studying Science at Queen's University, Belfast, he went on to research an M.A. thesis on the traditional **session**. As part of this research, he went to the Co. Cork **Gaeltacht** of Cúil Aodha in 1976, settling there in 1979. He set up a flute-making workshop and is among the most highly regarded flute makers in Ireland today. In 1990 he published *The Irish Flute Player's Handbook* (see **Flute**) and a twelve-track tape, *The Moneymusk*. *The Moneymusk* was re-issued on CD in 2001 with six additional tracks and includes jigs, reels, polkas, barndances, highlands and slow airs. Among the guests on the album is another fine flautist, **Paul McGrattan**. Hamilton has published many articles

Hammy Hamilton

on a variety of topics related to traditional music and was one of the organisers of the first **Crossroads Conference** (1996). He also gave a paper there (entitled 'Innovation, Conservatism and the Aesthetics of Irish Music'), which was full of insights into the origins and evolution of traditional music. See also **Creagh, Séamus**; **Ó Drisceoil, Con**; **Dulcimer**.

Hammer Dulcimer See **Dulcimer**.

Hammond, David (b. 1928) Singer, song collector and producer of radio programmes and films who was born and reared in Belfast. In the 1950s he produced the ground-breaking series *As I Roved Out* for the **BBC** and went on to produce films for television on a variety of topics relating to traditional music, dance and song. In addition to recording albums of his own singing, he has produced albums of other musicians' playing, including a double LP of the Donegal fiddler **John Doherty**. His collection *Songs of Belfast* (Dublin, 1978) includes children's songs, working songs (including a special section devoted to the linen mills), and songs of love, soldiers and sailors, among the last 'The Titanic', a ballad about the famous ship which was built in Belfast and sank on her maiden voyage to New York in 1912.

Hanly, Mick   Singer, guitarist and songwriter who played with **Monroe** and **Moving Hearts**. He has recorded several solo albums of ballads and contemporary folk songs, including *A Kiss in the Morning Early* (1976) and *As I Went over Blackwater* (1980), both of which were re-released in 1982, *All I Remember* (1989), *Warts and All* (1991), *Happy Like This* (1993), *Live at the Meeting Place* (1998) and *Wooden Horses* (2000). Hanly has written many fine songs, which have been recorded by Moving Hearts and **Mary Black**, who in 1988 recorded his 'Past the Point of Rescue' before it became a country music hit. Website: www.mickhanly.com. See also **Pentangle**.

Hannan, Robbie (b. 1961)   Belfast-born uilleann piper and broadcaster who grew up in Hollywood, Co. Down, where he now works as curator of musicology in the Ulster Folk Museum. Hearing **Planxty** and the **Chieftains** in the 1970s fired his interest in traditional music and he started playing accordion. He soon changed to uilleann pipes, learning from the Belfast piper Seán McAloon. He recorded a couple of tracks on *The Piper's Rock: A Compilation of Young Uilleann Pipers* (1978). On his solo album, *Traditional Irish Music Played on the Uilleann Pipes* (1990), he plays a 'flat set' (see **Uilleann Pipes**) pitched in B. The album is a fine collection of jigs, reels, hornpipes and airs played exclusively on the pipes with a selective and tasteful use of drones and regulators. Hannan has studied the fiddlers of Donegal and adapted their tunes to suit the pipes, as well as studying the great 20th-century pipers, of whom he says **Séamus Ennis** probably had the greatest influence on his playing. With Wilbert Garvin he edited Ennis' *The Master's Touch: A Tutor for the Uilleann Pipes* (Dublin, 1998). Hannan has also performed with **Paddy Glackin**, with whom he made two albums, *Rabharta Ceoil: In Full Spate* (1991) and *Séidean Sí* (*Swirling Gust of Wind*, 1995).

Hanrahan, Kieran (b. 1957)   Tenor banjo and mandolin player and broadcaster born in Ennis, Co. Clare. He won an **All-Ireland** Senior title at the age of 19 and was a founder member of **Stockton's Wing** in 1978. He left the group in 1991 to play with the Temple House Céilí Band, which he had set up in 1989. In 1992 he began broadcasting on the **RTÉ** Radio One programme 'Fleadh Club' and since 1995 has been presenting *Céilí House* on Saturday evenings. He has guested on some albums with other musicians, including **Tommy Hayes**' *An Rás* (1991), and released a solo album, *Kieran Hanrahan Plays the Irish Tenor Banjo* in 1997.

Harbison, Janet (b. 1955) Dublin-born harpist who studied harp with Máirín Ní Shé at Sion Hill, Blackrock, Co. Dublin and composition at Trinity College Dublin. In the mid-1980s she wrote a masters degree thesis on **Edward Bunting** under the supervision of **Micheál Ó Súilleabháin** at **University College Cork**. She subsequently worked as Curator of Music at the Ulster Folk and Transport Museum and has been involved in the organisation of various summer schools and harping groups, including the **Harp Foundation**. In 1992 she organised a World Harp Festival in Belfast to celebrate the bicentenary of the **Belfast Harp Festival**, and this led to the foundation of the Belfast Harp Orchestra in the same year. She has recorded a number of albums, including *O'Neill's Harper* (1993) and *Colmcille* (1997), and plays traditional dance tunes, pieces by **Turlough O'Carolan** among others and her own compositions.

Hardebeck, Carl Gilbert (1869-1945) Organist, pianist, composer and collector born in London to a German father and a Welsh mother. Blind from birth, he had obtained diplomas as an organist, pianist and music teacher by 1892. In 1893 he went to Belfast and gradually became interested in traditional music, studying the collections of **Edward Bunting**, **George Petrie** and **Patrick Weston Joyce**. He won first prize for a composition he sent to the Dublin **Feis Ceoil** in 1897 and continued to send his works to the Feis until 1908. After hearing unaccompanied singing by a native Irish speaker at a **Conradh na Gaeilge** concert in Belfast in 1900, he went to the Donegal **Gaeltacht** where he studied Irish language and poetry. He invented a Braille alphabet in Irish and took down many traditional airs from singers on his Braille frame. He was a friend and admirer of the writer, educationalist and revolutionary, Patrick Pearse (1879-1916), both men sharing the belief that the Gaeltacht 'kept Ireland's soul'. Hardebeck's instrumental collection *Gems of Melody/Seoda Ceoil* (Belfast, 1908) received great critical acclaim, and from 1918 to 1923 he held the Chair of Music in University College Cork. From 1923 until his death, he continued his work on collecting, transcribing and arranging traditional music, first in Belfast and, from 1933, in Dublin.

Harmonica (*armónach* or *orgán béil*) Harmonicas, also called mouth organs, are the simplest of the family of **free-reed instruments**. There are four types (each quite a different instrument) used in traditional music: diatonic, tremolo, octave and chromatic. The invention of the diatonic harmonica in 1821 is credited to the German C. F. L. Buschmann (1805-64). Its development may, however, have been influenced by the ancient Chinese mouth organ called the *sheng*.

The diatonic harmonica, sometimes called the blues harp, consists of a flat metal box containing pairs of free reeds. A series of holes in one of the long sides of the box convey the player's breath to each pair of reeds. One reed sounds when the player exhales, the other when inhaling. The reeds of each pair are normally tuned to adjacent pitches so that exhaling, for example, will produce the note A while inhaling will produce G. Diatonic harmonicas come in a range of pitches and a player wishing to play in different keys would either have a range of harmonicas or use a technique known as 'note bending' in order to get notes not normally occurring in the key in which the harmonica is pitched. Bending, a difficult technique to master, is like whistling backwards and can also be used to get passing notes.

The tremolo and octave harmonicas are similar to the diatonic but in both cases have a double pair of reeds for each note. In the tremolo, the second set is tuned slightly above the pitch of the main set, while in the octave the double reeds are pitched an octave apart, giving a very full sound. The chromatic harmonica was developed in the 1920s by adding a slider stop, which gives access to a second set of reeds tuned a half tone higher than the first set.

The tremolo is the most widespread type of harmonica used by traditional players, including Noel Battle, Austin Berry, Tom Clancy, Rory Ó Leoracháin and Phil Murphy (see **Murphy, Phil, John and Pip**). In **Fleadh Cheoil na hÉireann** only tremolo players are allowed to enter in the harmonica category; players of other types of harmonica must enter in the miscellaneous instrument section. Although Phil Murphy played tremolo, he also experimented with chromatic and his son John uses diatonic as well as tremolo. The Murphys are among a growing number of players who, since the 1960s, have developed new and often highly individual approaches to using different harmonicas for playing traditional music. Different harmonicas require different techniques and because Irish traditional tunes do not always use scales and modes easily played on all harmonicas, a considerable amount of thought can go into which harmonica best suits a particular tune. **Eddie Clarke** developed a style of playing the chromatic harmonica that has influenced players such as **Mick Kinsella** and the American Joel Bernstein. Mark Graham, who plays in the group Open House with **Kevin Burke**, is another significant American player; he plays both diatonic and chromatic harmonicas. Rick Epping from the **US** visited Ireland and lived in Sligo, learning from the Irish traditional player Joe O'Dowd. He played with the group Pumpkinhead in the 1970s and is a fine player of diatonic and octave harmonicas. He often uses a rack to hold the instrument, leaving him free to play concertina or mandolin as well as harmonica. Epping is also a master technician and works for the largest harmonica manufacturer, Hohner, experimenting with new designs.

Very large bass and chord harmonicas, usually coming in pairs attached to each other, are rare in Irish traditional music. These are used only to provide bass or chord accompaniments and are generally played by harmonica trios. An Irish group of the 1960s and 70s who made their name as The Bachelors started out as The Harmonichords and used both bass and chord harmonicas.

Several interesting players have emerged in recent years, most notably Mick Kinsella and **Brendan Power**. Although the harmonica is still a minority instrument in Irish traditional music, Kinsella and Power have both, in different ways, contributed to raising the profile of the instrument and introduced new approaches to playing it.

Harp (*cláirseach* or *cruit*)   The triangular frame-harp evolved from more ancient stringed instruments such as the lyre and the cithara, possibly in the 8th or 9th century. It consists of three main parts: the neck (the curved top of the frame), the pillar or upright part, which is straight in a modern orchestral harp but curved in Irish harps, and the lower part connecting the pillar and the neck, which contains the soundboard of the instrument. Most depictions of King David playing the 'harp' on the Irish high crosses of the Early Christian period show earlier lyre-type instruments rather than triangular frame-harps. It is interesting to note, however, that the Cross of Patrick and Columba at Kells, Co. Meath and Muiredach's Cross at Monasterboice, Co. Louth (both dated to the early 10th century) have carvings of harps which were described by the scholar Helen M. Roe as 'triangular'. Although there appears to be a short fourth side to the frame of these harps, lying horizontally at the base, the harps do bear a close resemblance to triangular frame harps and are clearly different from 'harp' carvings on other Irish high crosses. The depiction of a harp on the 11th-century metal book-shrine known as the *Breac Maedóc* is clearly triangular. The 12th-century Ardmore Cathedral, Co. Waterford has a stone carving of what appears to be a triangular harp, but like the carvings at Kells and Monasterboice there is a short fourth side to the frame where the instrument rests on the harper's knee. The triangular frame-harp may have originated in Early Christian Ireland, although some scholars argue that there is a stronger case to be made for **Scotland** as the place where the instrument was first made.

The oldest surviving Irish harp is the 15th/16th-century **Brian Boru Harp**, which has 29 strings and is about 70 cm tall. Like all of the Irish 'Bardic' harps of the Middle Ages, this had metal (as opposed to gut) strings. The Dubliner Richard Stanihurst wrote in 1583 of the strings being 'woven from iron or bronze threads and not from sinews as other strings'. The harper, he said, 'produces sounds by his curved fingernails and not with a plectrum' – in contrast to the modern gut or nylon-strung harp, which is played with the fingertips and requires short nails. At the **Belfast Harp Festival** (1792) Dennis Hempson was the only harper who played in the old style, with long, crooked fingernails. His harp, known as the Downhill Harp, still survives and is somewhat taller than the Brian Boru Harp. Another famous harp of the 18th century is the Sirr Harp, taller again (143 cm) than the Downhill Harp but still strung with metal strings (36). From the Brian Boru Harp, through the Downhill and Sirr Harps, a gradual evolution away from a thick-walled, stout construction towards a more slender and taller instrument can be seen. The old metal-string harp had declined by the early 19th century but much of the music played on the instrument, as well as the techniques used by the harpers, were noted by **Edward Bunting**.

The neo-Irish harp is different in several respects to the old 'Bardic' harp. It is more slender and less robust in its construction, with a round (as opposed to a squared) sound box. It has nylon instead of metal strings, usually numbering 34. It is played with the fingertips as opposed to the fingernails. A portable harp made by John Egan of Dublin ca. 1820, which can be seen in the Horniman Museum in London, has the same basic design as the neo-Irish harp. It has nylon strings (only

30) and is 91 cm high. Egan's harp also has a lever mechanism not found on more recent harps. In the neo-Irish harps there is usually a series of brass blades along the neck that can raise the pitch of each string independently by a semitone.

In Early Medieval Ireland, harpers (who often played the **timpán** as well) had a far higher social status than other musicians. They were closely associated with the poets, who played an important part in the political life of early Irish society. Harpers were the only musicians mentioned in the Brehon Laws who had independent legal status, and their rank in society was close to that of the lower aristocracy. Gerald of Wales, in a late 12th-century book on Ireland, infamous for its depiction of the Irish as barbaric and lazy, nonetheless wrote: 'It is only in the case of musical instruments that I find any commendable diligence in this people. They seem to me to be incomparably more skilled in these then any other people I have seen.... It is remarkable how, in spite of the great speed of the fingers, the musical proportion is maintained. The melody is kept perfect and full with unimpaired art through everything' (*Topography of Ireland*, translated by J.J. O'Meara, Dundalk, 1951, p. 87). The English and Welsh invaders with whom Gerald arrived in Ireland were similarly taken with Irish music, but these colonists' gradual adoption of Irish customs and culture led eventually to apartheid legislation. The Statutes of Kilkenny (1366) attempted to keep the English and Gaelic worlds apart and included legislation against harpers, 'tympanours' and other entertainers. By the 16th century, even more severe laws against harpers were instituted by **Henry VIII** and **Elizabeth I**. The final collapse of Gaelic society in the wake of the defeat at the Battle of Kinsale (1601) had serious consequences for harpers as the entire system of patronage that had supported them disappeared. The next 200 years saw a serious decline from which harping has never fully recovered. Harpers such as **Turlough O'Carolan** (1670-1738) barely eked out a living by travelling the countryside and securing some patronage from the landed gentry. By the time of the **Granard Harp Festivals** (1781-83) and the **Belfast Harp Festival** (1792), the Irish harping tradition was barely surviving. Throughout the 19th century the harp had little significance in traditional music compared to the **uilleann pipes** and **fiddle**, and its decline was accelerated by the rise in popularity of the **piano**.

The second half of the 20th century saw something of a revival in harping. Singer/harpists such as Kathleen Watkins, Deirdre O'Flynn and the internationally acclaimed Mary O'Hara emerged in the 1960s. A new society called **Cairde Na Cruite** ('Friends of the Harp') was founded in Dublin in 1960 and still pursues its stated aim, 'to restore the harp to its former place of honour and to further interest in harp playing and composition'. The 1960s and 70s also saw the emergence of traditional groups in which the harp was a central element, either playing melody or acting as an accompaniment instrument for dance music. These groups included the **Chieftains**, **Clannad** and **King's Galliard**, as well as Breton harper **Alan Stivell** and his group. In the 1970s and 80s, **Máire Ní Chathasaigh** developed new techniques for playing dance music on the harp and has even played bluegrass on the instrument. **Janet Harbison** has also played a crucial role in developing and teaching new techniques for playing dance music on the harp. Both Ní Chathasaigh and Harbison, as well as the Chieftains' **Derek Bell**, recorded albums devoted exclusively to the work of Turlough O'Carolan, whose compositions have played an important role in the harping revival.

The work of **Gráinne Yeats** as both performer and researcher has done much to shed new light on the harpers of the 17th and 18th centuries and their music. Talented young harper/composers such as **Laoise Kelly** and Patrick Cassidy are beginning to take the instrument in new directions.

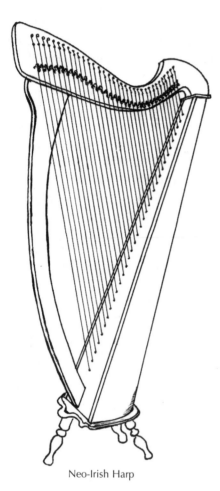

Neo-Irish Harp

Despite these developments, many traditional musicians would not see the harp as a traditional instrument. It is only rarely found in pub sessions, largely because of the problem of portability. For many, the harp still carries associations both with an ancient, aristocratic past and a repertoire, by Carolan and others, which is quite different to the dance music of the last two centuries. Paul Dooley's *Rip the Calico* (1996) is a fine response to this argument. This album combines material from the standard traditional dance repertoire with slow airs, Carolan tunes and original compositions, all played with extraordinary skill on a wire-strung harp. Dooley has mastered difficult techniques and shown that traditional jigs and reels composed *after* the demise of the 'Bardic' harp can be played on this instrument as effectively as on the fiddle, uilleann pipes or other traditional instruments. Dooley's album gives a new impetus to the growing interest in the 'Bardic' harp and this instrument may well have a more prominent place in coming decades. Even if the music Dooley plays is not medieval, his rapid finger work and delicate ornamentation certainly echo Gerald of Wales' laudatory description.

The foundation of the Historical Harp Society of Ireland by Siobháin Armstrong in 2002 has provided an organisational structure through which the revival of the wire-strung harp can be developed. Armstrong studied the neo-Irish harp under the great teacher **Nancy Calthorpe** at the College of Music in Dublin. A fascination with Baroque musical instruments led her to the Irish wire-strung harp and the foundation of the Historical Harp Society is part of a concerted effort to revive the instrument. The Society held its first Summer School in 2003, attracting students from as far away as Italy and Hungary. One of the teachers and concert performers at the school was the virtuoso player Ann Heymann from the **US**.

Irish harping is certainly in a far healthier state at the start of the 21st century than it has been for many years. There are many talented young harpists playing now, Anne-Marie O'Farrell, Mary Gregg, Cormac de Barra, Dearbhail Finnegan, Mary O'Donnell, Teresa O'Donnell, Michael Rooney and Helen Gilsenan, to name but a few. Many of the players of the past thirty years have taken harping in new directions while respecting the ancient traditions associated with the instrument.

The harp is the national symbol of Ireland, found on all government correspondence and on our coinage. This reflects the importance of the harp in Ireland's musical history. The fact that Ireland is the only country in the world which has a musical instrument as its national emblem could be said to reflect the importance of music in Ireland from the earliest times right down to the present. See also **Belfast Harp Orchestra**; **Brittany**; **Galicia**; **Harpsichord**; **Harp Foundation, The**; **Isle of Man**; **Keyboard Instruments**; **Loughnane, Kathleen**; **Ó Riada, Seán**; **Renbourn, John**; **Wales**.

Harp Foundation, The Originally known as Cláirseoirí na hÉireann ('The Irish Harpers' Association'), which was established in 1986 under the auspices of **Na Píobairí Uilleann** in Dublin. Harpist **Janet Harbison** has been a major figure in the organisation since its foundation and in 1993 moved what became known as the Harp Foundation to Belfast. The **Belfast Harp Orchestra** was formed, but the foundation also runs harp classes, concerts, summer schools, festivals and tours for visiting artists who, along with beginners, can avail of a harp bank.

Harpsichord (*cruitchorda*) A keyboard instrument of importance from the 16th to the 18th century and still played. The strings are plucked rather than struck by hammers as in a piano, and the player cannot vary the loudness or softness of the tone by varying the pressure of the fingers. **Seán Ó Riada** believed that the harpsichord provided a closer parallel to the old metal-strung Bardic harp than the nylon or gut-string harps which were prevalent in his day. His last musical project was to record a selection of traditional music on an 18th-century upright harpsichord at Gareth Browne's home in Luggala, Co. Wicklow, just months before Ó Riada's death in 1972. The recordings were released by Browne's **Claddagh Records** as *Ó Riada's Farewell* (1972), which provides a fine example of how traditional music can be played on harpsichord, despite the age and imperfect condition of the instrument concerned. **Micheál Ó Súilleabháin** has also recorded traditional and original music on harpsichord. A number of the traditional tracks on *Micheál Ó Súilleabháin* (1976) are played on harpsichord, and on *Cry of the Mountain* (1981) the harpsichord features prominently on many tracks, both original and traditional. There are echoes of Ó Riada in the album's 'Concertino for Fiddle', an original piece composed around the traditional song air 'Seán Duibhir and Ghleanna' ('Seán O'Dwyer of the Glen'). This was the last track on *Ó Riada's Farewell*, and Ó Súilleabháin plays the air on harpsichord in the middle of his 'Concertino'.

Tríona Ní Dhomhnaill is also a fine harpsichord player, and the instrument was an integral part of the first, seminal **Bothy Band** album. Ní Dhomhnaill works the instrument into the band's arrangements of both songs and instrumentals with great artistry, sometimes accompanying, sometimes playing melody. On later Bothy Band albums she played other keyboard instruments, most notably **clavinet** and harmonium.

Although the use of the harpsichord in traditional music is by no means common, the instrument has an important place in the recent history of the music because of the innovative work of Ó Riada, Ó Súilleabháin and Ní Dhomhnaill. See also **Ceoltóirí Chualann**; **Keyboard Instruments**.

Harte, Frank (1933-2005) One of Ireland's finest traditional singers, from Chapelizod in Dublin. He was also a great collector of songs and had a vast repertoire stored on computer from a wide variety of sources. Some of these are in his collection *Songs of Dublin* (Dublin, 1978), published over a decade after his first album, *Dublin Street Songs* (1967). The capital city was also the focus of *Through Dublin City: Lyrical Ballads and Rebel Songs* (1973). His style and repertoire are a significant reminder of the wealth and depth of the English-language song tradition in Ireland. Much of his singing is unaccompanied. Although it is not highly ornamented like **sean-nós singing**, there is a particular beauty about the simplicity and directness of his style. On *And Listen to My Song* (1986), half the songs are unaccompanied and half are accompanied by bouzouki (**Dónal Lunny**), with concertina (Bertram Levy) on two of them. On the album sleeve Harte notes how Irish traditional song in English has been slighted in favour of song in Irish, 'as if somehow there was a conflict between them or that they came from a different race of people and were not created out of the same hardship, injustice, joy or sorrow'. It is a valid point that has seldom been articulated so clearly. Harte continues: 'I hold that in the tradition, the song of the Orangeman is as valid as that of the Fenian or that the song from the streets of Dublin has its place alongside the song from the wilds of Connemara.' Harte's repertoire certainly reflects the breadth of his views on traditional song and includes English **ballad**s such as 'Lord Randall' (on the 1967 album), as well as Dublin street songs such as 'Biddy Mulligan' and Dicey Riley' (both on the 1986 album), humorous songs, love songs and historical/political songs. Songs of the latter type are the focus of *1798: The First Year of Liberty* (1998), with Dónal Lunny. It includes songs from 1798 as well as later songs by **Thomas Davis** and songs written to commemorate the first centenary (1898) of the rebellion. Harte and Lunny followed this with *My Name Is Napoleon Bonaparte: Traditional Songs on Napoleon Bonaparte* (2001), a double CD with 26 songs dealing with **Napoleon Bonaparte**. This is a fine collection with an excellent booklet giving the background to the songs and epitomises the great work Harte did as a collector, singer and researcher. The approach is similar for another excellent collaboration with Lunny, *The Hungry Voice: The Song Legacy of Ireland's Great Hunger (2004)*, a collection of songs dealing with the **Great Famine** and its many effects on Ireland and her people. The album *Daybreak and a Candle-End*, originally released in 1987, was re-released on CD in 2002. See also **Nationalist/ Republican Song**; **Orange/Loyalist Song**; **Rebel Song**.

Hay Sometimes spelled 'hey', this was a **round dance** frequently mentioned in Anglo-Irish and English sources of the 16th century. One after another the dancers would weave in and out of the circle they formed. The French *haie*, meaning the stakes in a fence or row, was used to describe a line of soldiers or a line of dancers. The Irish hay was said to be similar to the Scottish rinky, a round field dance popular in the time of Mary, Queen of Scots (1542-1587).

Hayden, Cathal Fiddler from Pomeroy, Co. Tyrone who plays with **Four Men and a Dog**. Hayden has also recorded as a solo artist and on his second solo CD, simply titled *Cathal Hayden* (1999), is accompanied by **Arty McGlynn** (guitar) and Brian McGrath (keyboards). Although he is renowned primarily for his fiddling, this CD also includes six tracks on which Hayden plays the tenor banjo, including 'The Connachtman's Rambles' and 'The Dublin Reel'. See also **Mad for Trad**.

Hayes, Martin (b. 1962) From Maghera, near Feakle, Co. Clare, son of **P. J. Hayes** and one of the finest and most innovative traditional fiddlers. He won the **All-Ireland** Fiddle Championship six times and played regularly with the Tulla Céilí Band from the age of thirteen or fourteen. In 1985 he moved to the **US** and settled in Chicago where he listens to and is influenced by many different styles of music, including jazz and Estonian music. The music he plays, however, is firmly rooted in the Irish – or more specifically the Clare – tradition. His first solo album, *Martin Hayes* (1993) was followed by *Under the Moon* (1995) and *The Lonesome Touch*

Martin Hayes
(photo: Philippe Delagrange)

(1997), and *Live in Seattle* (1999) with guitarist Dennis Cahill. Hayes and Cahill were also involved in recording music to accompany four stories set in the West of Ireland and read by Eddie Stack, released on CD as *West* (2002).

Hayes has developed a delicate style, and much of the dance music is played at a slower pace than is usual today. This is perhaps best exemplified on *The Lonesome Touch*, an album which Hayes himself describes as a duo rather than a solo album. It features a unique style of guitar accompaniment by Cahill that blends elements of jazz, classical and traditional styles. The same is true of Hayes' playing, which has an almost hypnotic effect (see **Draíocht**). This style may not be to everyone's taste but although it often sounds sparse, his feel for ornamentation and variation is superb and the music shows a depth of feeling and an expressiveness often lacking in fast, technically brilliant renditions of Irish tunes. Website: www.martinhayes. com.

Hayes, P. J. (1921-2001)   East Clare Fiddler and leader of the Tulla Céilí Band, which he joined in 1946. The Tulla celebrated its 50th anniversary in 1997 when Hayes was 75. He toured in the **US** and Britain with the Tulla and recorded with the band and with his son, **Martin Hayes**. He was also a member of one of Clare's most famous trios, with **Paddy Canny** and **Peadar O'Loughlin**, who recorded the influential album *All-Ireland Champions: Violin* (1959) together.

Hayes, Tommy   One of Ireland's most accomplished bodhrán players. Born in Kildimo, Co. Limerick, he began to play bodhrán in 1975 and won the **All-Ireland** in the same year. He performed with **Stockton's Wing** from 1977 to 1983 and played solos in the middle of songs or instrumental sets. He subsequently played jazz with the group Puck Fair. He has made a video on how to play bodhrán, bones and spoons for traditional music and has appeared as a guest musician on many albums. On his first album, *An Rás* (*The Race*, 1991) he plays bodhrán, **Jew's harp**, **bones**, **djembe**, and a variety of other percussion instruments. The title track features poet Nuala Ní Dhomhnaill reading a poem in Irish with Hayes backing her on percussion. The music includes Irish traditional tunes (many played in a jazzy, improvisational style), some jazz, an original piece by jazz flautist Brian Dunning, 'Chanela' by flamenco guitarist Paco De Lucia and a percussion solo, 'Jimdance', composed by Hayes. There are substantial contributions from **Micheál Ó Súilleabháin**, **Kieran Hanrahan**, **Micheál Ó Domhnaill**, jazz guitarist Tommy Halferty (see **Khanda**), Brian Dunning (alto flute, concert flute, tin whistle) and Alasdair Fraser (fiddle). In 1997 Hayes released another album, *A Room in the North*, on which he again plays a variety of percussion instruments. The flute and whistle playing of **Ronan Browne** features strongly, with Kenneth Edge playing saxophone and the American Julie Haines on harp. Hayes' aunt, Meta Costelloe, also lilts on the album. Hayes' percussion is a major aspect of each track, with musical influences from such diverse sources as Ireland, Tibet, India and 14th-century Spain. It is Hayes at his adventurous best. See also **Hughes, Brian**.

Healy, James N. Cork-based actor, writer, ballad collector and singer. Although Healy made some commercial recordings of his ballad singing and poetry readings, his chief contribution was in the publication of ballad collections. Healy published many ballads for the first time, and his collections have excellent introductions and notes on the historical background to the ballads. From 1967 to 1969 he published four volumes of *The Mercier Book of Old Irish Street Ballads*, adding to his earlier collections of ballads (1955, 1962 and 1965) published by Mercier. He also published *Irish Ballads and Songs of the Sea* (Cork, 1967), which includes sea shanties (see **Sea Shanty**), songs on sailors and their loves, wrecks, 'Spanish Wine and Wild Geese' and other subjects relating to the sea. His publications include a collection of **Percy French** songs and *Love Songs of the Irish* (Dublin, 1977).

Heaney, Joe See **Ó Héanaí, Seosamh**.

Henebry, Richard (1863-1916) Fiddler, piper, scholar and ethnomusicologist born in Portlaw, Co. Waterford. He became Professor of Gaelic at Georgetown University, Washington DC and was a good friend of **Francis O'Neill**. The latter wrote in his *Irish Minstrels and Musicians* (1913), p. 178: 'Among the happiest days of our life were those in which the genial doctor [Henebry] favoured us with his music at our residence in Chicago in 1901, playing solo or in concert with the Irish-American pipers, fiddlers and fluters whom he subsequently immortalised in current literature.' Henebry published a treatise on Irish music entitled *Irish Music: Being an Examination of the Matter of Scales, Modes and Keys, with Practical Instructions and Examples for Players* (Dublin, 1903) and his *Handbook of Irish Music* (Cork, 1928) was published posthumously. In 1904 he met the piper and flute player, James Byrne (born at the foot of the Hill of Tara, Co. Meath) at Mooncoin, Co. Kilkenny and recorded him on an Edison phonograph playing the reel 'Rakish Paddy'. Three years later Francis O'Neill sent Henebry a series of wax cylinders which he had recorded himself in Chicago before 1905. These recordings are now housed in University College Cork, where Henebry was Professor of Gaelic from 1909 to 1916. They included recordings of the famous piper **Patrick J. Touhey** (1865-1923), some of which were used on the cassette *The Piping of Patsy Tuohey* (1986). Also housed in UCC are cylinders recorded by Henebry himself while he was there. Most of the material was recorded in the Déise region of Waterford and, although the cylinders are in a poor condition today, they are among the earliest field recordings of traditional music to be made in Ireland. Henebry also passed on the art of piping to a number of musicians, one of them a man called Walsh, who in turn taught the contemporary Waterford piper Tommy Kearney, from whom **Tommy Keane** learned to play.

Henry VIII King of **England** (1509-1547) and Ireland (1540-1547). Despite introducing legislation against Gaelic Irish musicians and poets, he used Irish kern or mercenary foot soldiers, accompanied by pipers, in his wars with Scotland and France. One contemporary painting of the siege of Boulogne (1544) shows the Irish kern, led by a piper, returning to camp after a cattle raid. Legislation against musicians and poets also formed part of the attempts made by his daughter **Elizabeth I** to complete the conquest of Ireland. See also **War Pipes, Irish; Bard**.

Henry, Sam (1878-1952) Customs official and pensions officer from Co. Derry who was also a song collector. From 1923 to 1939, he ran a series called 'Songs of the People' in the Coleraine weekly newspaper, *The Northern Constitution*. Henry tried to have the collection published as a book but failed and instead put together three 'official' sets of 'Songs of the People'. He gave one to Belfast Free Library, one to the Library of Congress in Washington DC and one to the National Library of Ireland in Dublin. In 1979 John Moulden, a local singer, educator and folklorist, published *Songs of the People: Selections from the Sam Henry Collection, 1*, which contained 100 of the songs with comments and background to the overall collection. Further volumes were never published, but the full collection of almost 690 songs was published in the **US** as *Sam Henry's Songs of the People* (1990, Athens, Georgia). This edition is edited, transcribed and annotated by the New England-based teacher and song collector Gale Huntington, with revisions, additions and indexes by another American with an interest in folk music, Lani Herrman. It includes an extensive bibliography, discography and various indexes, including a geographical index compiled with the aid of John Moulden.

Although Henry originally used tonic sol-fa notation for the melodies of the songs, the 1990 edition provides musical notation for all of the songs. Sources for the songs (where known) are given, as well as relevant historical background and comments from readers of the *Northern Constitution* that Henry invited at the original time of publication. It is a superb work of scholarship, containing songs of both local and national interest. Henry has been criticised for not preserving songs exactly as he received them, matching airs he considered appropriate to words for which he had no music and compiling 'ideal' versions of songs when faced with a number of different versions. Unfortunately he did not retain the original material from which he compiled his versions of songs. His aim, however, was not to work as a historian or folklorist but to put the songs in the mouths of the people again.

Sam Henry's Songs of the People contains many love songs as well as some old Presbyterian hymns, lullabies, children's games, songs on animals, hunting, racing, war, celebrations, the sea, crime and emigration. Issues that were likely to arouse controversy were avoided by Henry, so there are no famine songs, almost no songs referring to political events and only the mildest of 'blue' or bawdy songs. Nonetheless it is the largest single-volume collection of Irish folk songs and contains much that is of interest to the singer and the historian of Irish song.

Hernon, P. J. Button accordion player born in Connemara, Co. Galway who now lives in Co. Sligo. He was influenced by the playing of the innovative **Paddy O'Brien (Tipperary)** and won the **All-Ireland** two-row accordion title in 1973. In the 1970s he also played with the group Shaskeen, recording two albums with them, and made his first solo album, *P. J. Hernon*, in 1978 and a second, *First House in*

Connacht, in 1985. He also recorded two albums with his brother Marcus (flute). Hernon has taught button accordion since 1982 and made a video tutor, *Learn to Play the B and C Button Accordion*, in 1996.

Hey See **Hay**.

Highland or Highland Fling (*flaing* or *flaing Albanach*) The term used in Donegal for the **schottische**.

Hill, Noel (b. 1958) Concertina player from Caherea, near Ennis, Co. Clare, regarded as the 'King of Concertina'. He came from a family that included many concertina players and early influences included his parents, his uncle Paddy Hill and Paddy Murphy (all concertina players). In the late 1970s and early 80s he formed a duo with fiddler **Tony Linnane**, recording the classic *Noel Hill and Tony Linnane* (1979) album. Hill played a superb rendition of the hornpipe 'Johnny Cope' on the album, with some accompaniment by **Micheál Ó Domhnaill** on church harmonium. Since the early 1980s, Hill has pursued a solo career in music, one of the few concertina players to do so successfully. Before his first solo album, *The Irish Concertina* (1988), however, he made another highly acclaimed duo album, this time with accordionist **Tony MacMahon**. *I gCnoc na Graí* (1985) was recorded with a group of set dancers in Dan O'Connell's pub, Knocknagree, in the **Sliabh Luachra** district. Hill's first solo album includes many fine renditions of some of the great traditional tunes, including 'The Gold Ring' and 'The Drunken Sailor'. Two further solo albums followed, as well as *Aislingí Ceoil: Music of Dreams* (1993) with Tony MacMahon and sean-nós singer **Iarla Ó Lionáird**. See also **Planxty**.

Holmes, Joe (1906-1979) Traditional singer and fiddler from Ballymoney, Co. Antrim, who had a great repertoire of **come-all-ye**s, as well as some old **ballad**s. He recorded two albums with **Len Graham**, *Chaste Muses, Bards and Sages* (1976) and *After Dawning: Traditional Songs, Ballads and Lilts from Northern Ireland* (1979). Both albums feature solos and duets, as well as fiddling by Holmes.

Horns See **Bronze Age Horns**.

Hornpipe (*cornphíopa*) A dance of English origin, popular from the 16th to the 19th century and originally in three meters, 3/2, 2/4 and 4/4. 'Double-hornpipes' in 9/4 time were also played in **England** in the late 19th and early 20th centuries. Hornpipes became popular in Ireland during the late 18th and 19th centuries when they were usually played in 4/4 time. The hornpipe was sometimes used (as early as the 18th century) for group country dances. It is more widely known as a solo dance, and along with the jig and the reel it is a common form of **step-dancing**. In the past it was usually danced by the man alone, as the steps were thought to require a vigour and sound which only a man could bring to them. The structure is similar to a reel but the hornpipe is played more slowly with the first and third beats of each measure accented. Hornpipes are not as numerous as reels and jigs, but most traditional musicians play them. Among the most commonly heard are 'The

The Tailor's Twist (hornpipe)

Plains of Boyle', 'The Harvest Home', 'The Belfast Hornpipe', 'The Stack of Barley' and 'The Rights of Man'. Although many have just two sections, longer hornpipes can be heard. 'The Groves Hornpipe', for instance, has five sections and 'O'Dwyer's Hornpipe' has four. See also **Dance Music**.

Horslips The first band to successfully merge traditional Irish music with rock, seen as the founders of 'Celtic Rock'. Their first album, *Happy to Meet, Sorry to Part* was released in 1972 with its famous concertina record sleeve. The line-up was Barry Devlin (bass, vocals), Jim Lockhart (keyboards, flute), Eamonn Carr (drums, percussion), Charles O'Connor (fiddle, mandolin, concertina, Northumbrian pipes, vocals) and Johnny Fean (guitar, vocals, fiddle, mandolin, banjo). Their imaginative arrangements of traditional songs and instrumentals mixed acoustic and electric instruments with ease. They also worked old traditional melodies into what were essentially rock songs, often starting with the traditional melody (i.e. 'Brian Boru's March') and working it into the song ('Trouble with a Capital T') as a riff. One of their most famous songs in this style was 'An Dearg Doom', which used the traditional 'O'Neill's March' as an electric guitar riff. The themes for some of their original songs were loosely based in Celtic mythology, and they used coloured projections and Celtic style sets for their live performances. Between 1972 and 1980, they released ten albums and toured in Ireland, Britain, Europe and the **US**. Some purists were horrified at the Horslips approach to traditional music, but they attracted the interest of many young people who later went on to listen to more conventional forms. There is a unique sense of fun about much of their music and they remain one of the most interesting 'hybrid' traditional groups in Irish music. Many of their albums have been remastered by the band themselves and re-issued on CD.

Arguably the best of these albums in terms of fusing the traditional and rock influences are *The Táin* (originally 1973, remastered CD 2000) and *The Book of Invasions: A Celtic Symphony* (originally 1976, remastered CD 2000).

For *Rollback* (2004), the five original members of Horslips re-recorded 15 classic tracks from their repertoire in a quieter, more acoustic style. The album includes

Horslips today

'Trouble (With a Capital "T")', 'The Man Who Built America' and 'Cúchulainn's Lament'. The songs sound very different in these new acoustic/folk settings as opposed to the original electric/rock style. Three of the fifteen tracks are instrumentals, all traditional tunes played superbly on guitar by Charles O'Connor (two tracks) and Johnny Fean (one track). Website: www.horslips.ie. See also **Fusions**.

Hot Press Fortnightly Irish magazine, mainly focussed on contemporary rock/pop music but also dealing with current affairs and other musical forms, including Irish traditional. There are occasional interviews with traditional musicians or singers, reviews of traditional CDs and gig listings for venues in Ireland. Website: www.hotpress.com.

Hughes, Brian (b. 1970) Whistle player and uilleann piper born in Athy, Co. Kildare who has carried out an in-depth study of piping styles. His album *Whistle Stop* (1997), on which he plays the whistle only, is one of the finest of its kind. His whistle playing is flowing and delicately ornamented, and the arrangements are imaginative but subtle, adding to the light and shade of the whistle playing. He plays jigs, reels (including three of his own), polkas, slides, slow airs, hornpipes and a waltz. The percussion of **Tommy Hayes** and the keyboards, guitar and mandocello of Garry Ó Briain feature strongly on the album.

Hummingbird Productions Irish-based company established in 1987 by **Philip King** and Nuala O'Connor that specialises in producing programmes on traditional music. Their most notable documentaries to date have been ***Bringing It All Back Home*** and *A **River of Sound***, two ambitious television series dealing with historical and contemporary aspects of traditional music and song from different perspectives. The associated company Hummingbird Records also produced CDs of music featured on the documentaries and CDs arising from the music session series **Sult** and the documentary *Meitheal: Cooney and Begley*, the latter originally produced for TnaG (see **TG4**) in Irish with English subtitles. Hummingbird Productions has worked closely with TG4, **RTÉ**, the **BBC** and television networks in the **US** to bring its programmes to a wide audience at home and abroad. It has been nominated for a Grammy Award and won an Emmy for *Irish Music and America: A Musical Migration* in 1994. The documentaries certainly represent a new departure in traditional music, employing high standards of research and presentation and often ranging beyond Ireland to explore various aspects of the music. The recording company has also released CDs by a number of traditional artists, including Dermot Byrne of **Altan** and **Dónal Lunny**. In 2003 the company produced a new series for television, *The Raw Bar*, about the people and musicians who breathe life into Ireland's musical tradition. Website: www.hummingbird.ie.

Hurdy-Gurdy A stringed instrument bowed by a rosined wheel that is turned by a crank. A series of rods connected to a keyboard produce different notes when the various keys are depressed. The player usually turns the crank with the right hand and plays the keyboard with the left. The instrument can have just one melody string, or a pair tuned in unison, as well as three or four bass strings that sound continuously as a drone. It was popular throughout the Middle Ages, and in the 18th century such composers as de Boismortier (1689-1755), Haydn (1732-1809) and Mozart (1756-1791) all wrote pieces for the hurdy-gurdy or similar instruments. It has survived into the 20th century as a folk instrument and, although its use in Irish music is extremely rare, **Andy Irvine** has played it in live performance and recordings over the years. It is popular in **Galicia**, where it is called the *zanfona*.

I

IMRO (Irish Music Rights Organisation/*Eagras um Chearta Cheolta*) Organisation formed in 1989 whose membership is made up of composers, songwriters and music publishers, including those involved in traditional music. It collects and distributes the public performance rights due to its members for copyright material. It is a non-profit organisation which is run by an internally elected board and is affiliated to similar organisations in other countries. It is also involved in the sponsorship and promotion of music in Ireland. Song contests, seminars, workshops, research projects, showcase performances and music festivals are among the events which IMRO sponsors every year. In conjunction with *Irish Music* magazine and HMV it sponsors the annual '*Irish Music* Magazine Awards'. Another major annual award in which it is involved is the IMRO/**TG4** traditional music awards. Website www.imro.ie.

Irish Bouzouki See **Bouzouki** and **Cittern**.

Irish Folklore Commission (*Coimisiún Bhéaloideas Éireann*) A state-funded body formed in 1935, the commission gathered together a rich collection of folklore through collectors working all around Ireland until its archive was transferred to the **Irish Folklore Department, University College Dublin** in 1972. Its first director, Séamus Ó Duilearga, recruited **Séamus Ennis** as a collector in 1942. Aodh Ó Domhnaill, father of **Tríona and Maighréad Ní Dhómhnaill**, also worked with the Commission, bringing his young daughters with him on field trips. Ethnologist Kevin Danaher's work with the Irish Folklore Commission in the late 1940s included the earliest recordings of **John Doherty** and **Johnny Doran** and a trip to the **Isle of Man** to record some of the surviving speakers of native Manx. The commission gathered much valuable material, including stories, songs and tunes. In the early days wax cylinders were used to record in the field. The material was later transcribed and shaved off the cylinders, which were re-dipped for use again in order to save costs. Although this happened regularly with cylinders of stories and songs, a number of cylinders with tunes have survived. See also **Cronin, Elizabeth (Bess)**; **Recording**.

Irish Folklore Department, University College Dublin Took over the work and archive of the **Irish Folklore Commission** in 1972. **Breandán Breathnach** directed the music section, located in Earlsfort Terrace, for many years. **Micheál Ó Domhnaill** and Seán Corcoran (see **Cran 2**) are among the people who have worked as collectors on a temporary basis. The Folklore Council of Ireland (*Comhairle Bhéaloideas Éireann*) was also established in 1972 to index and publish material from the department's collection. Some recordings have been released, including one of piper **Johnny Doran** and another of fiddler Mickey Doherty (see **Doherty, John**). A few collections of songs have also been published, including a collection of the songs of **Tom Lenihan** (which includes both a book and recordings made by **Tom Munnelly**).

Irish Music Monthly magazine first issued in August 1995. It is the first widely available monthly magazine devoted exclusively to Irish traditional music and song and has made an important contribution to publicising the work of many musicians. Its first editor, Ronan Nolan, was replaced by Seán Laffey in June 1997. The magazine includes interviews with musicians and groups, articles on famous musicians of the past, published collections of music and occasional special supplements. There are regular reviews of gigs, books, CDs and general developments in traditional music, and tunes are sometimes published. It includes news and gig lists for Britain, Europe and North America, as well as Ireland. The magazine is available at many Irish newsagents and by subscription to anywhere in the world.

The magazine ran readers' polls in its early years but from 1999 started the '*Irish Music* Magazine Awards'. This is based on a poll in which readers vote for awards in various categories. An awards ceremony, at which some of the finest traditional artists perform, is held each year. Co-sponsors have varied, but have included HMV, **IMRO** and **RTÉ**, among others. In 2002 the publishers of *Irish Music* also started to bring out an annual **Traditional and Folk Music Directory**. Website: mag.irish-music.net.

Irish Music Rights Organisation See **IMRO**.

Irish Traditional Music Archive (*Taisce Cheol Dúchas Éireann*) An archive and resource centre for the traditional song, music and dance of Ireland, located at 63 Merrion Square, Dublin 2. It was established in 1987 by the Arts Council/*An Chomhairle Ealaíon* and is also supported by the Arts Council of Northern Ireland. It is grant-aided by the Arts Council but also invites donations to assist its wide-ranging work, which includes a 'repatriation programme' copying music materials held in archives outside Ireland.

The great piper and collector **Breandán Breathnach** had attempted to establish a traditional music archive in his lifetime, and after his death in 1985 his own collection formed the core of the present one. To this the Archive has constantly added new material, including sound recordings, books, manuscripts, sheet music, periodicals, films, videos, musical instruments and photographs. All information is classified, catalogued and indexed through a specially devised computer system, and there are public rooms for the study of materials. The Archive is also involved with **RTÉ** in making radio and television recordings available for public consultation. It provides an information and advice service and is cooperating with research projects being carried out by other bodies in Ireland and abroad. It is directed by **Nicholas Carolan**. Website: www.itma.ie. See also **Bunting, Edward**; **Goodman, James**.

Irish War Pipes See **War Pipes, Irish**.

Irish World Music Centre See **University of Limerick**

Irvine, Andy (b. 1942) Singer/songwriter and multi-instrumentalist who was born in London to parents of Scottish and Irish ancestry. He moved to Ireland in the early 1960s and has played with **Sweeney's Men**, **Planxty**, **De Dannan** and **Patrick Street**. He was a major influence in developing the Irish **bouzouki** and also plays **mandolin**, **mandola**, **guitar**, guitar-bouzouki, harmonium, **hurdy-gurdy** and **harmonica**. He is, in many ways, a unique talent in Irish music. He has designed his own bouzoukis with instrument makers such as the English-based Sobel and has an extraordinary ability to accompany his own singing with delicate counter-melodies and rhythms. In groups such as Sweeney's Men and Planxty and his work with fellow bouzouki players **Johnny Moynihan** and **Dónal Lunny**, he has created a unique and intricate accompaniment for both songs and instrumental music. He travelled in Eastern Europe at several different stages in his life and introduced Bulgarian music into his own work (*Rainy Sundays, Windy Dreams*, 1980) and that of Planxty, as well as recording *East Wind* (1992), a fine album of Eastern European Music, with piper **Davy Spillane**.

Andy Irvine (photo: Shigeru Suzuki)

Irvine's own songs are a mixture of contemporary and folk styles. Many of them reveal a deep interest in historical and human rights issues. He has written about the 1798 rebel leader Michael Dwyer and the 19th-century Irish land rights campaigner Michael Davitt ('A Forgotten Hero') and put new music to a traditional song about the socialist James Connolly (1868-1916). He ranges well beyond Ireland, writing songs about the Swede Raoul Wallenberg (who saved many Jews from the Nazi concentration camps), the Mexican revolutionary Emiliano Zapata and Irvine's hero **Woody Guthrie**. He has even written an extraordinarily atmospheric song about a failed Antarctic expedition ('Douglas Mawson'). Many of these songs are on his solo album *Rude Awakening* (1991), largely consisting of original material. In addition to his group and solo albums, he recorded two classic albums with singer/guitarists,

Andy Irvine/Paul Brady (1976) and *Parallel Lines* (1981) with **Dick Gaughan**. Further solo albums, *Rain on the Roof* (1998) and *Way Out Yonder* (2000), which includes songs from or dealing with **Australia** and New Zealand, have strengthened Irvine's reputation as a songwriter and a balladeer who continues to explore love, history and politics in Ireland and beyond through his music. His most recent venture is a band called Mozaik which plays music from Ireland, the **US** (old timey music) and Eastern Europe. The band first formed in Australia in 2002 and recorded an album, *Live in the Powerhouse* (2004) in Brisbane. The line-up includes Irvine (vocals, bouzouki, mandolin, harmonica) and Dónal Lunny (bouzouki, guitar, bodhrán, backing vocals); Dutchman Rens Van Der Zalm (backing vocals, guitar, fiddle, mandolin); the Hungarian Nikola Parov (gadulka, kaval, gaida – all Bulgarian instruments – as well as tin whistle, clarinet, guitar) and the American Bruce Molsky (vocals, fiddle, five-string banjo). Mozaik have also performed in Ireland with their unique musical mix which crosses many genres. Website: www.andyirvine.com.

Isle of Man Island of 220 square miles located 27 miles from **England** (Cumbria) and Ireland (Co. Down). Its name may be derived from the Irish sea and sun god, Manannán Mac Lir, who in oral tradition had three legs on which he rolled along on land like a wheel. The Isle of Man symbol to this day is a wheel with three legs. The Manx language is part of the same sub-group of Celtic languages as Irish and Scots Gaelic, and there is evidence of Irish involvement in the affairs of the island from the 6th century. During the Viking period, from the 9th to the 12th century, there were close relations between the Isle of Man and Dublin, but political contacts diminished after Man was annexed by England in the 14th century. For some time after this, there were significant ecclesiastical and trade links between the Isle of Man and Ireland, and in the 21st century tourism and the financial services sector maintain contacts.

Manx was the everyday language of the islanders until the 18th century when English began to replace it. In the 19th and 20th centuries a number of dedicated enthusiasts have kept the Manx language alive, and it is now officially taught in the island's schools. Many Manx language enthusiasts were also involved in preserving other aspects of Manx culture, including its music. Nineteenth-century collectors gathered together songs and tunes forming the basis of Manx traditional music today. Although some of the material collected in the 19th century remains unpublished, published collections such as A. W. Moore's *Manx Ballads and Music* (1896) and W. H. Gill's *Manx National Songs* (1896) were influential. Gill's collection has proved particularly popular and durable. A number of language and music enthusiasts carried the revival into the 20th century, most significantly Mona Douglas, who revived the annual competitive festival, *Yn Chruinnaght*, in the 1970s. The festival is still held in Ramsey, usually in the second half of July, and, in addition to most of the native players and singers, attracts musicians from **Brittany**, Cornwall, **Wales**, Ireland and **Scotland**. The annual Inter-Celtic festival, which celebrated its 21st year in 1998, attracts a similarly diverse array of musicians and listeners.

In recent years the work of revivalists such as Mona Douglas has been continued and further developed by Fenella Crowe Bazin. The latter produced the first coherent history of Manx music (up to 1896) as a Ph.D. thesis in 1995, much of this going into her book *Much Inclin'd to Music: The Manx and Their Music up to 1918* (Isle of Man, 1997), the first published work to deal comprehensively with the history of Manx music. Bazin works at the Centre for Manx Studies, which is under the auspices of the University of Liverpool but based in Douglas on the Isle of Man. The Centre has its own museum, Manx National Heritage, which also sells recent tune collections, recordings and other publications relating to the music of the island.

Bazin's work has identified Gaelic, Scandinavian, English and Scottish/Irish influences in Manx traditional music. Jigs and reels of Scottish or Irish origin came into the Isle of Man through the playing of 18th-century fiddlers, as did other forms of dance music, including *port y beayl*, the Manx equivalent of Scottish **mouth music**. Most dance music was sung or played on the fiddle, a popular instrument from at least the 17th century into the 19th century. Fiddlers often played alone for weddings and other special occasions, but would sometimes be accompanied by a piper or a clarinet player. Traditional Manx fiddling survived into the early 20th century, when it went into decline, although the late 20th century has seen a successful revival. Most dancing today is accompanied by solo fiddle or a group of musicians. One unusual dance which is still accompanied in the old style by voice is 'Reeaghyn Vannin' ('Kings of Man'), a sword dance said to date back to the times of the Norse kingdom. Although Manx music has absorbed a variety of influences, it has adapted them to its own style, and there are many tunes in Manx traditional music that are unique to the island.

Among the most prominent performers in the Manx revival since the 1970s have been the harpers Charles Guard and Emma Christian. Guard has been a central figure in Manx music since the 1970s, branching out into the related musical traditions of Ireland and Scotland. Guard lived in Dublin for several years, studying the Irish Harp with **Gráinne Yeats**. He performed with the largely Scottish group the Whistlebinkies, recording with them on their first album in 1977 and in the same year recorded his album *Avenging and Bright* (since 1991 available on a **Shanachie** CD) in Dublin. On the latter album Guard plays both steel and gut-string harps, and the material includes Irish, Manx and Scottish tunes. A more recent Manx artist, Emma Christian, sings and plays recorder as well as playing the harp. Her *Ta'n Dooid Cheet/Beneath the Twilight* (1994) is a fine collection of traditional Manx songs and instrumentals, with valuable notes explaining the background to the island's history, musical history and the individual pieces. It includes a beautifully performed version of 'Oikan ayns Bethlehem/Birth in Bethlehem', a traditional Manx carval. The carval, derived from the medieval **carol**, is a uniquely Manx form, a religious song traditionally sung after the parson had left the church at the end of the *Oie'll Voirrey* (Christmas Eve) celebrations. Christian's album also includes traditional Manx invocations to the Irish saints Colmcille (521-97) and Brigid (late 5th-6th centuries) as well as the traditional tune 'Mylecharaine's March', upon which the Manx national anthem is based.

Although the Manx traditional repertoire consists of only about 300 pieces, there is considerable variety in both songs and instrumentals. The Folktrax cassette *Reeaghyn dy Vannin: Songs in Manx Gaelic* (n.d.) is an interesting selection of material collected by Mona Douglas, although the title is somewhat misleading as there are a considerable number of instrumental tracks (mostly dance tunes) on the tape, and some of the songs are in English. There are also spoken introductions in English to many of the tracks, giving background information or stories. The instrumental tracks are played on harmonica by Joe Woods and include 'The Fairy Reel' (also recorded by Charles Guard) and wedding dances such as 'Peter O Tavey' and 'The Manx Wedding Reel'. It is obvious from the song *'Helg yn Dreean*/Hunt the Wren' that the Manx have a tradition similar to that of the Irish **wren-boys**. The song finishes with the words:

> The wren, the wren is king of the birds,
> St. Stephen's Day is caught in the furze,
> Although he is little his family's great,
> We pray you good people to give us a treat.

The story which tells of the origins of the custom on the Isle of Man, however, is quite different to any of the stories told in Ireland: Hundreds of years ago there was a beautiful white witch and all the men on the island were madly in love with her. She led all the men into the sea and the enraged women chased her until she turned into a wren. The women persisted in chasing the wren and managed to trap her, stoning and clubbing her to death in a furze bush. The wren was still pursued in this way until recent decades, not only by women but also by boys, who were seen to be avenging the deaths of their fathers. Hunting the wren is strictly peaceful nowadays, the bird being represented by a bunch of feathers.

A considerable number of recordings of Manx music have been made in the last decade. One that provides an excellent introduction to the variety of styles and artists is *The Best That's In It* (1996), released by the Manx Heritage Foundation, a government body that promotes Manx culture. The Foundation also released *The Light House*, a tape capturing the work of some of the fine young fiddlers who are part of a recent revival in Manx fiddling. At the start of the new millennium, Manx music is very much alive and benefits from the support and enthusiasm of a new, young generation of musicians. The Centre for Manx Studies has brought the academic study of Manx music to a new level and continues to explore new fields through original research. Some artists have recorded Manx music as part of a broader repertoire of music from Celtic countries. Singer/harper/guitarist Jill Rogoff's *The Celtic Cradle* (1994) includes four Manx songs as well as songs from Wales, Scotland, Brittany, Cornwall and Corsica. Musicians such as **Alan Stivell** and the Irish-American group **Solas** have also recorded the occasional Manx tune. See also **English Folk Dance and Song Society**; **Irish Folklore Commission**.

Ivers, Eileen (b. 1965) Innovative fiddler born to Irish parents in the Bronx, New York. She started to play the fiddle at the age of eight, the tenor banjo at ten, and was influenced from an early age by the great fiddle teacher **Brendan Mulvihill**, who guided her through eight successive **All-Ireland** titles on the fiddle, culminating in her 1984 senior title. She has performed with **Mick Moloney**, **Robbie O'Connell** and **Séamus Egan** in the group the Green Fields of America, with whom she recorded a live album in 1988. She was also a founder member of the Irish-American all-female group **Cherish the Ladies** and has been involved with many other groups, including (1991) rock stars Daryl Hall and John Oates, with whom she toured for almost a year in the **US**, **Australia** and Asia. She performed regularly with accordionist **John Whelan**, making the album *Fresh Takes* with him in 1986.

Eileen Ivers (photo: Robert Corwin)

Her first solo recording, *Eileen Ivers* (1994), is a remarkable display of her virtuosity and adventurous approach to playing traditional Irish and Cape Breton music (see **Nova Scotia**). She is accompanied by a fine array of musicians, including John Doyle (see **Solas**), **Tommy Hayes** and African percussionist Kimati Dinizulu. In the opening track – starting with the hornpipe 'The Flowing Tide', changing tempo for 'The Crock of Gold' (reel) and continuing with a fine version of 'Julia Delaney' (reel) – Ivers plays lively, jazz-style variations which still manage to keep in touch with the basic melody. Another fine track displaying her innovative approach is 'Pachelbel's Frolics'. Based on the famous canon by German composer Johann Pachelbel (ca. 1653-1706), it begins in recognisably classical form but gradually increases in tempo, Ivers improvising on the theme, and ends up being played almost as a traditional tune.

Ivers' performances with the **Riverdance** orchestra from 1995 brought her worldwide exposure. She subsequently released a second solo album, *Wild Blue* (1996), with John Doyle and Kimati Dinzulu again featuring strongly in the arrangements. It is similar in style to the first album, but the overall sound is somewhat different (drums and bass featuring strongly on many tracks) and Ivers is even more imaginative in her interpretation of classic traditional reels like 'Jenny's Chickens', 'The Pinch of Snuff' and 'The Star of Munster'. There is a playful, jazzy rendition of the hornpipe 'The Rights of Man' with drums, organ, bass and guitar accompanying, as well as a track of French-style tunes, one of them Breton.

With her next album, *Crossing the Bridge* (1999), Ivers explored a variety of musical styles, playing music from all over the world as well as six original compositions (by Ivers and musician/producer Brian Keane), which themselves incorporate a diverse range of musical influences, including African, Spanish and jazz. *Immigrant Soul* (2003) also incorporated diverse influences, with Emedin Rivera's Latin/Caribbean-style percussion and Bakithi Kumalo's South African bass playing often providing the backing for what are essentially Irish traditional or traditional-style tunes, as in the track 'Afro Jig'.

In addition to her solo work, Ivers has recorded and toured with numerous musicians, including Tommy Sands (see **Sands Family**) and the **Chieftains**. While her style might not be to the taste of all traditional music listeners, she is undoubtedly one of the most original and innovative players of recent years and has influenced a considerable number of the younger traditional fiddlers in Ireland and elsewhere. Website: www.eileenivers.com.

J

Jackson, Walker (d. 1798) Famous piper and composer of tunes in the traditional style who came from Ballingarry, Co. Limerick and is wrongly called 'Walter' by some 19th- and early 20th-century writers. **Edward Bunting**, **Francis O'Neill** and others confused him with another Jackson from Co. Monaghan. O'Neill seems to have been correct, however, in describing him (*Irish Minstrels and Musicians*, p. 182) as 'the most celebrated piper of the 18th century, or perhaps of any age' and was also accurate in asserting (p. 133) that Jackson's compositions were published in his lifetime. Thirteen of the piper's tunes were published in *Jackson's Celebrated Irish Tunes* (Dublin,1790, a reprint of an earlier edition) and six of these tunes are still known traditionally (where relevant, titles by which the tunes might be better known today are given in brackets): 'Cossey's Jigg' ('Molly Brallaghan'), 'Jackson's Humour's of Panteen', 'Jackson's Morning Brush', 'Jackson's Night Cap'('Strike the Gay Harp'), 'Humours of Listivain' ('Humours of Bandon') and 'Cummilum' ('Drops of Brandy').

Breandán Breathnach published an excellent article on 'Piper Jackson' in 1976, which is also available in *The Man and His Music: An Anthology of the Writings of Brendán Breathnach* (Dublin, 1996). Breathnach pointed out that 'Cummilum' predated Jackson's time by many years and thought it unlikely that the piper composed the 'Humours of Listivain'. There appears to be no reason to doubt that Jackson composed the other eleven tunes in the book. Over 60 other tunes are also credited to him in oral tradition, including 'Jackson's Drowsy Maggie' and 'Jackson's Delight', the latter identical with the famous jig 'The Irish Washerwoman'. With many of the tunes which bear his name, however, there is simply no evidence available to prove or disprove that Jackson himself composed them. What is certain is that he composed some of the tunes which bear his name and, given the fact that no other early traditional musician has had so many tunes named after him, he was a hugely influential figure.

Jacobite Song 'Jacobites' is a term used to describe supporters of King James II (King of England, Scotland and Ireland, 1685-1688) and his heirs. The Catholic James was deposed by the Protestant William of Orange (who became King William III) in 1688 and launched a bid to regain his crown through Ireland in 1689 (see **Orange/Loyalist Song**). James' defeat at the Battle of the Boyne (1690) led to his flight into exile, and he died in France in 1701. In Ireland his army fought on but was defeated at the Battle of Aughrim (1691) and subsequently surrendered at Limerick. Jacobite supporters in Ireland were numerous among the largely Catholic and Gaelic-speaking population, but they were soon subject to strict Penal Laws by the new Protestant rulers. Support for James II and his heirs (James Edward Stuart, the 'old pretender', and his son Charles Edward Stuart, the 'young pretender') was, therefore, the great hope for a release from the oppressions of the Protestant Ascendancy in Ireland during the 18th century.

The **aisling** of this period was one of the most popular types of Jacobite song, certainly in Munster. Other Jacobite songs survive, most of them in Irish and, like the aislings, derived from poetry. The most notable of these songs is 'Mo Ghile Mear' ('My Living Brightness'), the lyrics of which were written by the Cork poet Seán Clárach Mac Dónaill (1691-1754). One early **come-all-ye** (written in English) called 'The Blackbird' appeared as a London **broadside** around 1718, just three years after an unsuccessful Jacobite rising in Scotland. In the song a woman laments the flight of a bird that represents the unsuccessful James II. **Hugh Shields** has compared this song to the Irish aisling, and has made a good case for its author being Irish. A version of 'The Blackbird' was published by **Colm O Lochlainn** in *More Irish Street Ballads* (1st ed. Dublin, 1965; no. 78). The tune is commonly played as a set-dance and was also played as a reel by Donegal fiddler **Johnny Doherty**. One of the most interesting recordings of 'The Blackbird' appears on the **Bothy Band**'s *Out of the Wind, Into the Sun* (1977), where the tune is played as a slow air, a set dance and a reel. Another tune which survives from this period is the march, 'The Battle of Aughrim', which commemorates the Jacobite defeat in 1691. Na Casadaigh, the family group from Gweedore, Co. Donegal, released a concept album called *1691* (1992) to mark the 300th anniversary of the Treaty of Limerick. The event is also commemorated in the traditional air, 'Limerick's Lamentation'.

In **Scotland** there were three Jacobite risings in the 60 years between 1688 and 1747. The first, a Highland rising in support of James II, collapsed after the battle of Kiliecrankie (1689), when James himself was fighting in Ireland. Further rebellions in support of the 'old pretender' (1715-1716) and the 'young pretender' (1745-1746) also ended in defeat, but many Jacobite songs are still sung in Scotland. *The King Has Landed: Songs of the Jacobite Risings* (2002) is a compilation of popular Jacobite songs by various artists, including the Corries, the Whistlebinkies, **Ewan MacColl** and Brian McNeill. For a different perspective on the Jacobite cause, see **Dick Gaughan**. See also **Davey, Shaun**; **Political Song**.

James I King of Scotland (1567-1625) and of **England** and Ireland (1603-1625). He retained the Irish harper of Queen **Elizabeth I**, Cormac McDermot, at the English court. McDermot's name appears in a list of court musicians receiving annuities and fees from the Crown ca. 1607. Queen Anne, the consort of James I, also had an Irish harper, Dónal Dubh O Cahill, in her service.

Jew's Harp (*trumpa béil*) Also called the 'jaw harp' or 'trump', this is a small instrument comprising a flexible metal tongue or 'lamella' attached at one end to a stirrup-shaped frame. The narrow end of the frame is held loosely between the player's teeth and the plucking of the metal tongue causes it to vibrate, producing a twangy sound. Although only one basic pitch can be played, different harmonics or overtones can be produced by changing the position of the cheeks, lips and tongue.

The origins of the term 'Jew's harp' are obscure, as the instrument appears to have no historical connection with the Jews. Possibly coming to Europe from Asia in ancient times, it reached a peak of popularity in Europe (including Ireland) in the 19th century, when it was eclipsed in many places by the **harmonica**. Older fiddlers in Donegal remember the Jew's harp surviving as a popular instrument into the early 20th century. The continuous drone-like sound of the instrument was part of its appeal, and the famous Donegal fiddler, **John Doherty**, learned 'The Loughside Hornpipe' from the McMonagle family of Tievelough, by Lough Ea in Co. Donegal, a family renowned for their excellent Jew's harp playing (see Caoimhín Mac Aoidh, *Between the Jigs and the Reels*, p. 47). The **Flanagan Brothers**, one of the earliest Irish groups to record commercially in the **US**, used the instrument occasionally in performance and recording during the 1920s and early 30s, an interesting example being their rendition of the jigs 'Tobin's Favourite' and 'The Frost Is all Over', recorded in 1928 (see *The Tunes We Like to Play on Paddy's Day*, 1996, track 13). The instrument is only rarely heard in Irish traditional music nowadays, one of the few players being percussionist **Tommy Hayes**.

Jig (*Port*) A dance popular in Ireland and England from the 16th century and later adopted in continental Europe. The tune that went with the dance was also called a jig. **Breandán Breathnach** believed that the jig was the oldest form of Irish dance music still surviving and that some of the older jigs could have come from ancient clan marches, songs or dances. The vast majority, however, were composed by the pipers and fiddlers of the 18th and 19th centuries.

The Tenpenny Bit (double or common jig)

Three types of jig survive today: the double or common jig in 6/8 time (usually referred to simply as a 'jig'), the hop or slip jig in 9/8 time and the single jig (see **Slide**) in 6/8 or sometimes 12/8 time. The names for the different jigs derive from the different dances involved in each case. Various types of shuffling, grinding and battering steps are used in dancing jigs. The double jig (*port dúbalta*) uses what is called 'double battering' whereas the single jig (*port singil*), which is usually faster, uses only 'single battering' steps. The hop or slip jig (*port luascach*) derives its name from the light hopping, sliding and skipping movements associated with it.

Like most dance music, the typical jig has two parts, each part being played twice. There are, however, some notable exceptions to this. The popular slip jig 'The Kid on the Mountain' has five parts and there are a number of double jigs with up to seven parts. 'The Gold Ring', for instance, is a seven-part double jig and a favourite with uilleann pipers.

As with reels, new jigs are continually added to the 'traditional' repertoire by composer/musicians. 'The Mist Covered Mountains', for example, was composed by the Clare fiddler **Junior (Martin) Crehan**, who died in 1998. 'The Butterfly', a widely-known slip jig, was apparently composed by Dublin fiddler **Tommy Potts**, who died in 1988, but is noted in some published collections and recordings as 'traditional'. Fiddler **Máire Breatnach** has also composed some fine jigs, including 'Ben Gulban' and 'Oisín', tunes inspired by Celtic Mythology. Other modern composers of jigs include Paddy O'Brien from Offaly (see **O'Brien, Paddy 1**),

Hardiman the Fiddler (hop or slip jig)

Smash the Windows (single jig)

Paddy Keenan, **Bill Whelan**, **Eamonn Galldubh**, **Darach De Brún**, **Liz Carroll** and members of **Kíla**, to name but a few.

JMI (Journal of Music in Ireland) Magazine covering traditional, classical and jazz music in Ireland. First published in November/December 2000, the magazine is published six times a year. It aims to provide a critical and analytic perspective on music in contemporary Ireland, and each issue carries album and book reviews as well as interviews and articles. The JMI has published some excellent articles on aspects of traditional music, some of them covering broad topics, others focusing on individual musicians or singers. The articles and editorials often pose questions about major topics in traditional music such as commercialism, education and the development of traditional music in modern Ireland. The *Journal* has encouraged lively debate on many subjects relating to traditional music (see, for example, under **sean-nós singing**). Website: www.thejmi.com.

Johnstons, The One of the most distinctive groups who came to prominence during the **ballad boom**. In addition to singers Adrienne and Lucy Johnston, **Mick Moloney** (guitar, mandolin, banjo) and **Paul Brady** (guitar, dulcimer) also shared vocals. The Johnstons formed in 1967 and broke up in 1974. Based in England for three years, they had considerable success with a mixture of Irish, American and contemporary folk. All members of the group often sang together, in unison or in harmony. Sometimes the singers would alternate as the verses changed. They occasionally played instrumentals, recording a fine rendition of 'Carolan's Concerto' on two guitars. Their song arrangements included strong instrumental and vocal sections. **Ewan MacColl**'s 'The Travelling People' was one of their hits and they were one of the first groups to record Joni Mitchell's 'Both Sides Now'. They recorded many albums but *The Johnstons Sampler* (1970), a compilation, provides a good introduction to their style and repertoire. More recently two of their early albums, *The Johnstons* (1968), and *The Barleycorn* (1969) were released on a CD simply entitled *The Johnstons* (1996).

Journal of Music in Ireland See **JMI, The**.

Joyce, Patrick Weston (1827-1914) Collector of Irish music, historian and linguist born in Ballyorgan, Co. Limerick who completed a Doctorate in Literature (L.L.D.) at Trinity College, Dublin. He grew up in a musical environment, his father singing many airs and songs, and learned to play the fiddle. He began to write down tunes he had heard from his father and also started to collect tunes from the peasantry of the area around Ballyorgan. Through the Society for the Preservation and Publication of the Melodies of Ireland, he met **George Petrie**. The latter included much of Joyce's material in his own collection, gratefully acknowledging his indebtedness to the Limerick man.

After the death of Petrie in 1866, Joyce decided to publish his own collection. *Ancient Irish Music* (Dublin, 1873). It contained 100 airs, previously unpublished, with piano accompaniment, notes on sources and lore relating to the tunes. The book included the first published version of 'Fáinne Geal an Lae' or 'The Dawning of the Day', a tune still popular today. Joyce went on to publish *Irish Music and Song* (Dublin, 1888), the first collection of songs (twenty of them) in Irish to have the words set carefully under the appropriate musical note. His major collection, *Old Irish Music and Folk Songs* (Dublin, 1909), contained 842 airs and songs which had never been published before. Much of the material had either been collected by Joyce himself or sent to him by people interested in preserving the music. Irish folk songs in the English language were included, some from broadsheets and manuscript sources, others from Joyce's own memory. There was also material from the manuscripts of **James Goodman**, **William Forde** and **John Edward Pigot**.

Breandán Breathnach has pointed out that while Joyce's music is much closer to the native setting than that of either **Edward Bunting** or Petrie, his settings of dance music were skeletal and he was also prone to altering the notation of the tunes. Breathnach also criticised his 'false respectability' and 'literary snobbishness' in deeming some of the songs too coarse for publication. Song texts were often altered or had the original words substituted in places by verses composed by the collector's brother. Joyce himself also published a collection of seven 'peasant songs' with English words which he put to old Irish airs. In addition to his works on music, he published a *Grammar of the Irish Language* (1878) and *Old Celtic Romances* (1879), a collection of English translations of old Irish sagas. His *Irish Names of Places* (1869) is a classic study of the lore and history behind place names in Ireland. He was, like Petrie, a man with an extraordinary depth and breadth of scholarly knowledge. While his work on traditional music and song has been justifiably criticised by modern experts, the value of his contribution in this and other areas cannot be denied. The CD *Re-Joyce: Tunes and Songs from the Joyce Collection* (2003) includes reels, jigs, hornpipes, airs, a waltz and four songs in English played by fiddlers Máire O'Keeffe and Donal O'Connor, accordionist **Jackie Daly** and John Faulkner, who sings and plays bouzouki and guitar.

P. W. Joyce

K

Keane Family Famous musical family from Caherlistrane, in east Co. Galway. In the 1950s the family of four brothers and four sisters (including Sarah on fiddle and Rita on accordion) formed the Keane Céilí Band. They played all over Ireland, but Sarah and Rita are also well known as singers who have a great store of songs. Many of their songs do not appear in published collections and the Keane home was visited by many singers and collectors during the 1950s and 60s. Sarah and Rita are unusual among traditional singers in that they sing in unison, solo singing being much more common. They can be heard on *Once I Loved* (1968) and *At the Setting of the Sun* (1994), and Sarah sings with her niece, Dolores (b. 1953) on *Sáil Óg Rua* (1983). They also featured on the series ***Bringing It All Back Home***.

Dolores, a fine singer and flute player, was the first singer with **De Dannan** (1974-75), as well as the first singer to record with the **Chieftains** (on their 1976 album *Bonaparte's Retreat*). She made her first album, *There Was a Maid* (1978), with the group Reel Union and guest musicians Peadar Mercier (bodhrán) and Máirtín Byrnes (fiddle). The album features Keane singing unaccompanied and accompanied (mostly in English, one song in Irish), playing jigs and reels on flute with the group, and the slow air 'Lament for Owen Roe O'Neill' as a flute solo. She has recorded many albums (mostly singing) since, drawing on the repertoire of her aunts Sarah and Rita, among others, for traditional songs. In 1980 she recorded The Beatles' 'Hey Jude' with De Dannan, and has since mixed contemporary with traditional songs on her solo recordings. She recorded for *Bringing It All Back Home* with husband John Faulkner and sister Catherine as well as in a trio with **Mary Black** and American country singer Emmylou Harris.

Her brother Seán, who performed for some time with Dolores in Reel Union, is also a successful singer. He attended the **Fleadh Cheoil** regularly when younger, entering various music and singing competitions, sometimes with other members of his family. The whole family, including Matt (father of Seán and Dolores), recorded an album for **Gael-Linn**, *Muintir Chatháin: The Keane Family*, in 1985. Seán has had a successful career as a solo singer since the 1990s and has also performed with his brothers Pat, Noel and Matt, who made the album *Citizens Keane* (2002). Like Seán's own repertoire, the album is a mixture of different types of song, including some traditional and contemporary folk.

Keane, James (b. 1948) Button accordion player originally from Dublin. He won four **All-Ireland** titles in a row (1963-66) on button accordion and a further title in the céilí band category with the Castle Céilí Band, which he founded with his brother **Seán Keane**. He played with many famous musicians around Dublin during the revival in the 1960s, including **Dónal Lunny**, **Paul Brady** and **Liam**

James Keane
(photo: R. L. Geyer / Aesthetic Endeavors)

O'Flynn. After being invited to play in the **US** for the second time in 1968, he set-tled there and has become one of the most highly regarded box players in Ireland and the US. He has recorded with the **Chieftains**, **Kevin Conneff**, **Paddy Glackin**, **Matt Molloy**, Garry Ó Briain (of **Skylark** and **Buttons and Bows**), Liam O'Flynn and **Tommy Peoples**, and has also made a number of solo albums. Website: wwwjameskeane.com.

Keane, Seán (b. 1946) Fiddler born in Dublin to parents who both played the fiddle. Originally trained as a classical violinist, he was only fourteen years old when he formed the Castle Céilí Band with his brother, **James Keane**. He was an original member of the **Chieftains**, recording the first of many albums with them in 1963. He joined **Ceoltóirí Chualann** in 1965, staying with them for five years. He is still a member of the Chieftains, but has also performed and recorded with other artists over the years. He and fellow Chieftain **Michael Tubridy** were part of *The Castle Céilí Band* album (1973). He has made three solo albums, *Gusty's Frolics* (1975), *Jig It in Style* (1977) and *Seán Keane* (1981). He featured on *Roll Away the Reel World* (1980), his brother James' album, and he recorded an excellent album with **Matt Molloy** and **Arty McGlynn** (*Contentment Is Wealth*, 1985). This was followed by *The Fire Aflame* (1988), with **Liam O'Flynn** and Matt Molloy.

Keane, Tommy (b. 1953) A native of Waterford who plays uilleann pipes, tin whistle, mandolin, bouzouki and tenor banjo. He learned uilleann pipes from Tommy Kearney, a well-known piper in the Southeast, and recorded *Óró*

Domhnaigh (1977) with **Micheál Ó Súilleabháin**, **Noirín Ní Riain** and other musicians. In 1979 he formed The Bread and Beer Band with **Robbie O'Connell**, **Martin Murray** and guitarist Paul Grant. Although the group never released an album, Keane and O'Connell subsequently recorded much of their repertoire on the latter's first solo album, *Close to the Bone* (1982). Keane spent several years in London during the 1980s, returning to Ireland and settling in Co. Galway with his wife, concertina player Jacqueline McCarthy (see **McCarthy Family**) in 1987. His solo album, *The Piper's Apron* (1991) features some fine, unaccompanied piping as well as tracks that feature his wife, Paul Grant (guitar), Brendan O'Regan (bouzouki, guitar, synthesiser), Henry Benagh (fiddle), **Tommy Hayes** (bodhrán) and Michael Hynes (flute). Keane's tin whistle playing is also exceptional, especially on 'The Boys of the 25/The Hare's Paw/The Pinch of Snuff' (reels). *The Wind among the Reeds* (1995) features both Keane and his wife (with accompaniment by **Alec Finn** on bouzouki and guitar). The album is remarkable for the beautiful combination of two very different reed instruments in the uilleann pipes/concertina duets. There are also fine tracks featuring concertina, pipes or whistle as the only melody instrument. Keane has also recorded with artists as varied as the **Pogues**, **Clannad** and Ralph McTell.

Keenan, Johnny (1946-2000)   Talented multi-instrumentalist born into the musical Keenan family, older brother of **Paddy Keenan**. He started to play music at an early age, his first instrument being the uilleann pipes. He also played fiddle, low whistle and guitar but was best known as a banjo player. He played both the five-string and tenor banjo, but was a master of picking fast dance tunes on the tenor banjo. He and his father, John, pioneered the art of thimble-picking on the banjo, using a homemade thimble instead of the plectrum used by most banjo players. Johnny played with some of Ireland's finest musicians, busking with Ted and Paul Furey as a young man, travelling around Ireland with **Davy Spillane** and touring with the **Furey Brothers** in the 1960s. With his father and his brother, Paddy, he formed the group The Pavees who, in the 1970s, performed regularly in Slattery's of Capel Street, Dublin. Their guests included **Christy Moore**, **Paddy Glackin** and other members of the Glackin family and the Black Family (see **Mary Black**). The Pavees had various line-ups, which included, at different stages, George and Paul Furey, Sean Garvey and **Liam Weldon**. Johnny was later to form the group Tipsy Sailor, which included singer/songwriter Kieran Halpin in its line-up.

Johnny toured extensively in the UK, Europe and the **US** in his life-time. Unfortunately, he never made a solo album, although he featured on brother Paddy's first solo album, simply titled *Paddy Keenan* (1975). Here he played superb solo renditions (on banjo) of the reels 'Tarbolton/Longford Collector' and the long dance 'The Job of Journeywork'. He also made an album with Patrick (harp) and Frank Cassidy (mandolin, guitar) in the mid-1980s, playing banjo, fiddle and low whistle, but the album, made in Wales, was never released in Ireland. He is remembered annually in the Johnny Keenan Banjo Festival, first held in Longford town in the year 2002. Organised by his wife Chris, the festival includes concerts, workshops and pub sessions and embraces American Bluegrass as well as Irish traditional music. Website: www.johnnykeenan.com.

Keenan, Paddy (b. 1950) Uilleann piper, tin whistle and low whistle player born in Trim, Co. Meath. Although they eventually settled in Ballyfermot, Dublin, the Keenan family were **travellers** steeped in traditional music for generations. Paddy's father, grandfather and great-grandfather all played the pipes. His father, John, started to teach Paddy to play the pipes at the age of ten, and although Paddy's flowing, open-fingered style is often compared to that of the famous travelling piper **Johnny Doran**, it was his father who most directly influenced his playing initially.

Paddy Keenen

In his late teens, Paddy became more interested in blues and guitar and almost stopped playing the pipes altogether. In the early 1970s, however, he returned to Ireland after a spell in England and eventually joined the **Bothy Band**. By the time they broke up in 1979, Paddy Keenan's reputation as one of the finest uilleann pipers in the world was well established. His remarkable passion for music, his ability to improvise and his technical mastery of the pipes continue to astound audiences wherever he plays. Keenan has toured throughout Ireland and the **US**, where he settled in 1992.

His first solo album, *Paddy Keenan* (1975), features guest performances by his brothers Thomas (whistle) and Johnny (1946-2000, banjo), as well as fiddler **Paddy Glackin**. The album is rightly regarded as a landmark in piping recordings. He made *Port an Phíobaire* (1982) with **Arty McGlynn**, and *Na Keen Affair* (1997) features guest musicians from **Newfoundland** and Ireland. The latter album includes a set of traditional polkas from Newfoundland and two tunes composed by Keenan himself. **Tommy Peoples** is among the guest musicians and some of the tracks have a sound and style similar to that of the Bothy Band. Guitarist Tommy O'Sullivan also played on *Na Keen Affair* and went on to make *The Long Grazing Acre* (2001) with Keenan. O'Sullivan sings as well as playing guitar on the album and contributed an original composition, an unusual instrumental called 'Jutland'. Keenan also plays a number of his own compositions on the album, including a slow air dedicated to his mother and a jig for his brother, Johnny. Another brother, Brendan, is also an accomplished whistle player and piper and recorded an album, *Brendan Keenan* (1984), which features some superb whistle playing. Paddy Keenan was the **TG4** Traditional Musician of the Year in 2002. Website: www.paddykeenan.com. See also **Ó Canainn, Tomás**.

Kelly, Alan (b. 1972)   Piano accordion player from Roscommon town whose album *Out of the Blue* was released in 1997. Arguably the most interesting player of the piano accordion to emerge in many years, he has a light touch, rare on this instrument, and a tasteful and skilful way with ornamentation. *Out of the Blue* features a wide range of traditional music from Ireland, **Scotland**, Cape Breton (see **Nova Scotia**) and French **Canada**. His *Mosaic* (2000) pushes the boundaries of Irish piano accordion playing even further and features diverse musicians including **Arty McGlynn** (guitar), **Seán Smyth** (fiddle), Richie Buckley (saxophone), Daniel Healy (trumpet), Damian Evans (bass) and Liam Kilkelly (guitar). The album features three of Kelly's own compositions and original compositions by other musicians, including the 'Salamanca Samba', an evocative piece with accordion and brass composed by Arty McGlynn. Kelly's brother, John (flute) also appears as a guest on *Mosaic*, and the two brothers together recorded a more traditional album, *Fourmilehouse* (2002). Website: www.blackboxmusic.ie.

Kelly, James and John   Both fiddlers, sons of Clare musician John Kelly (see below). James played with **Ceoltóirí Laigheann**, and the two brothers also played together around Dublin during the 1970s. Both were featured on the album *Irish Traditional Music* (1980). James emigrated from Ireland to the US in 1979 and has toured or recorded with many musicians, including **Paddy O'Brien**, **Planxty** and **Patrick Street**. His solo albums include *Capel Street* (1989), *The Ring Sessions* (1995) and *James Kelly* (1996). John is not a professional musician but still plays extensively, mostly around Dublin, and has recorded with a number of musicians, including the 1980s group Bakerswell.

Kelly, John (1912-1987)   Fiddler and concertina player from Loop Head, Co. Clare. He came from a musical family and settled in Dublin in the late 1940s, buying a shop in Capel Street that was renowned for its music sessions. The Horse Shoe shop was visited by many famous musicians, including **Tommy Potts** and **Johnny**

Doran. Kelly met **Seán Ó Riada** in 1960 and played in **Ceoltóirí Chualann** and the Castle Céilí Band. He was recorded on *Seoda Ceol 1* (*Musical Treasures 1*, 1968), which also included **Willie Clancy**'s playing. He taught at the **Willie Clancy Summer School** and played with another Clare fiddler, John Ryan, for many years, mostly in O'Donoghue's pub in Dublin. Both were recorded on *Ceol an Chláir Vol. 1* (*Music of Clare Vol. 1*, 1979) with **Junior Crehan** and **Bobby Casey**. All five of his children play fiddle, but James and John Junior (see above) are the best known.

Kelly, Laoise (b. 1972)   Young harper from Westport, Co. Mayo who plays dance music on the **harp** with extraordinary vigour and style. She featured in the series and CD, *A River of Sound* and **Charlie Lennon**'s *Flight from the Hungry Land* (1996); she is also a member of the **Bumble Bees**. Her first solo album, *Just Harp* (1999), displays her mastery of the instrument and includes Carolan music as well as original pieces (including her own) and traditional dance tunes.

Kelly, Luke (1940-1984) Singer and five-string banjo player whose extraordinary voice had a passionate intensity and an earthiness which was instantly recognisable. He was undoubtedly one of the finest folk singers of the 20th century. Born and reared in Dublin's docklands, he left school at the age of twelve and in 1957 emigrated from Ireland to **England**. He became involved in the folk music scene in

Luke Kelly

cities such as Newcastle, Manchester and Birmingham. He also developed an interest in left-wing politics, joining the Communist Party and the Campaign for Nuclear Disarmament and stunning early audiences with his rendition of Ian Campbell's anti-nuclear song 'The Sun is Burning'. In the early 60s, Kelly moved back and forth between England and Ireland, but his involvement with **Ewan MacColl**'s circle of left-wing actors, singers and intellectuals, the Critics, had a profound influence. Kelly never failed to acknowledge MacColl as the greatest single influence on his musical development, and songs like 'Dirty Old Town', written by MacColl, became a regular part of Kelly's repertoire. MacColl and Peggy Seeger made their singing debut in Ireland at the St. Stephen's Green cinema, Dublin, in a programme with Luke Kelly and Liam Clancy (see **Clancy Brothers and Tommy Makem**). In the early 70s, Luke sang **Phil Coulter**'s song, 'Free the People', which was a reaction to the introduction of internment in Northern Ireland (1971). With the **Dubliners**, he performed at the Free the People

Rally in Dublin's National Stadium in 1971. He also attended the funerals of the victims of Bloody Sunday (1972).

Although he made his name as a singer with the Dubliners rather than as a solo artist, Kelly's individual talent always shone through, and since his death several compilations of his singing have been released. The double CD *Luke Kelly: The Collection* (1994) has 36 songs, including his superb renditions of Patrick Kavanagh's 'Raglan Road', and Phil Coulter's 'Scorn Not His Simplicity' and 'The Town I Loved so Well'. His repertoire reflects his broad concern with humanitarian issues, and one of the finest songs in the *Collection* is 'Springhill Mining Disaster', about a fatal mining accident in Nova Scotia. The latter song was also included on *Songs of the Workers* (1998), released by **Outlet Records**. *Thank You for the Day* (1999) is an album of nine recently discovered tracks.

Kelly's career was tragically cut short by cancer. Some, including Peggy Seeger and **Christy Moore**, felt that his success with the Dubliners and the hard drinking involved had a negative effect on his singing. Nonetheless, Luke Kelly remains a hero to many for giving his unique voice to social, humanitarian and political concerns. Dublin politician and trade unionist Des Geraghty was a personal friend of Kelly's and wrote *Luke Kelly: A Memoir* (Dublin, 1994). **RTÉ** broadcast a fine documentary about the singer, simply titled *Luke* (1999).

Kennedy, Frankie See **Altan**.

Keyboard Instruments A general term for instruments which use a series of levers arranged in a row to produce sound, including **harpsichord**, **piano** and **synthesiser**. These three instruments have all been used in the playing of traditional music, often in the work of innovators who bring various outside influences to the music through their style of playing. **Micheál Ó Súilleabháin**'s first solo album explored the possibilities offered by various keyboard instruments for playing traditional music, including pedal organ and clavichord as well as piano, harpsichord and synthesiser. **Tríona Ní Dhomhnaill**, who plays **clavinet** and harmonium as well as other keyboard instruments, is another prominent player.

The use of keyboards is not widespread in traditional sessions, a fact owing largely to the problem of portability presented by large instruments such as piano. In some venues where the piano is a permanent fixture, such as the Dublin headquarters of **Comhaltas Ceoltóirí Éireann**, it can, however, be a regular feature. Keyboards in general have, despite their relative rarity in sessions, been central to the work of some of the most innovative individuals and groups recording or performing in more formal settings. See also **Afro Celts**; **Bothy Band, The**; **Breschi, Antonio**; **Clannad**; **Glackin, Paddy**; **Ó Riada, Seán**.

Khanda Khanda (Sanskrit for 'five') is a Dublin-based group made up of musicians from different musical backgrounds, including traditional uilleann piper/whistle player Martin Nolan, classically trained Ellen Cranitch (flutes, whistle, zils) and jazz musicians Tommy Halferty (guitar), Ronan Guilfoyle (bass, saz, def) and Conor

Guilfoyle (drums, tablas, dumbek). Their instruments, like their influences, come from diverse traditions: zils are finger cymbals from the Turkish/Arab tradition, the def a North African frame-drum similar to a bodhrán, the dumbek an hourglass-shaped Arab drum. They released an album, *Khanda* (1997), with special guest Ramesh Shotam, a German-based musician from Madras in southern India. He plays a number of percussion instruments (including thavil, ghatam and dumbek) and is steeped in the south Indian classical tradition. He also sings on one of the album's most interesting tracks, 'Konnekol Reels'. *Konnekol* is rhythmic singing used in south Indian music like a drum language to teach all aspects of rhythm (percussion, drums, choreography). The track starts with Ramesh Shotam's unaccompanied singing and then moves into traditional reels played on uilleann pipes, initially with just percussion backing. Drums, bass and guitar (playing dissonant chords) come in for the second reel and there is an improvisation on flute before the set turns into the last reel, 'The Star of Munster'. The use of dissonant chords is highly unusual, but certainly casts the traditional melodies in a different light.

Khanda's non-Irish music shows the versatility of Irish traditional instruments such as uilleann pipes and (in the use of drones, percussion and *konnekol*, which can be seen as a type of **lilting**) establishes interesting musical links between the traditions of Ireland and India. Purists may not find the music to their taste, but Khanda have simply tried to bring a different sound to the traditional music they play, breaking with the guitar/bouzouki/bodhrán accompaniments that have become almost standard in Irish traditional group playing. In 2001 they toured in India with a line-up that included button accordion player Peter Browne, the tour resulting in a CD/DVD entitled *Five Cities*. Browne and Nolan were also involved in Ronan Guilfoyle's album, *Exit* (2003), along with Tanya Kalmanovitch (violin, viola), Julian Argüelles (saxophone), Rick Peckham (guitar) and Tom Rainey (drums). On *Exit*, Guilfoyle's jazz compositions are based around traditional tunes, sometimes starting with a traditional tune played in its normal structure and developing into improvisation which interweaves sections of the traditional tune with jazz.

Kíla One of the most interesting young Irish groups to emerge in the last twenty years, formed in 1987. Although they use many Irish traditional instruments and tra-ditional dance forms, their music is original. The seven members of the band are: the three Ó Snodaigh brothers Rossa (low whistle, tin whistle, bouzouki, mandolin, guitars, clarinet, percussion, vocals), Ronán (bodhrán, djembe, congas, percussion, backing vocals) and Colm (flute, tin whistle, clarinet, saxophone, guitar); the Hogan brothers, Brian (bass guitar, guitars, backing vocals) and Lance (guitars, bass guitar, hammer dulcimer, bass drum, djembe, percussion, vocals); Eoin Dillon (uilleann pipes, low whistle, tin whistle) and Dee Armstrong (fiddle, hammer dulcimer, accor-dion). Even this account of the instruments they play is simplified. They use a huge range of percussion instruments of various kinds and are known for swapping instruments in concerts. While many of their songs (mostly written by Ronán Ó Snodaigh) have Irish lyrics the vocal style and percussion make some of them sound like African tribal songs. Many of their instrumentals (composed mostly by Dee

Armstrong and Rossa Ó Snodaigh) have the form and sound of traditional Irish tunes, but the instrumental music is difficult to classify. Some of it sounds like Mediterranean or even gypsy music, with the use of brass instruments adding yet another dimension. Perhaps their finest album, *Tóg É Go Bog É* (1997) presents a mixture of different styles, with instrumental tracks such as 'Rusty Nails' sounding like a more broadly European ethnic music while developing a strong Irish flavour as it proceeds. A similar mix of styles is found on *Lemonade and Buns* (2000) and *Luna Park* (2003), the latter including lyrics by the poet Máirtín Ó Direáin put to music by Colm Ó Snodaigh, as well as original songs and instrumentals. *Live in Dublin* (2004) was mostly recorded in the Olympia Theatre and Vicar Street, Dublin, with one track recorded in France and one in Australia.

Kíla

Kíla have been compared by some critics to **Moving Hearts**, and their music is certainly not for the purist. Their live performances are famously energetic and the music very danceable. They have experimented with film, slides, overhead projectors, dancers, unicyclists, fire jugglers and stilt walkers in their live shows and hope to do more of this in the future. They have performed all over the world, including the **US** and Japan. Ronán Ó Snodaigh made a solo album, *Tip Toe* (2001), of his own songs, all in English. Website: www.kila.ie.

Kilduff, Vinny Primarily a whistle player, Kilduff also plays mandolin, keyboards and slide guitar on his album *The Boys from the Blue Hill* (1990). The album is an interesting, often playful collection of tunes that features many well-known guest musicians, including **Charlie Lennon**, **Steve Cooney** and **Tommy Hayes**. In addition to traditional material there are two jigs composed by Lennon. Cooney also composed two beautiful and unusual tracks, 'Andes (Llama)' and 'With a Love that's True', with Kilduff playing a wooden whistle on both. Kilduff has also made a video tutor for the tin whistle and worked as a producer with a number of different musicians, including **Seán Smyth**.

Killoran, Paddy (1904-1965) Fiddler from Ballymote, Co. Sligo who emigrated from Ireland to the **US** in 1922. Along with other Sligo fiddlers **Michael Coleman** and **James Morrison** (who taught him), Killoran was a big name in Irish music in America from the 1920s, and right up to the 50s his recordings in the US had a profound impact on traditional players in Ireland. He played in a lightly ornamented, up-tempo style and was famous for his fiddle duets with another Sligo man, Paddy Sweeny. A collection of his recordings, *Paddy Killoran's Back in Town*, was released in 1977 by **Shanachie Records**.

Kilmore Carols See **Wexford Carols**.

King, Philip (b. 1952) Singer/songwriter and harmonica player born in Cork who first came to prominence as a singer with the group **Scullion**. He sings and writes lyrics in both Irish and English and as well as his recordings with Scullion made two albums with **Peter Browne** – *Rince Gréagach* (*Greek Dance*, 1981) and *Seacht Nóiméad chun a Seacht* (*Seven Minutes to Seven*, 1983) – that combine traditional and original material, often in an innovative style. The title track of *Rince Gréagach*, for example, combines the Irish lyrics (by King and poet Liam Ó Muirthile) with the sounds of uilleann pipes, flute, guitar and a subtle and unusual piano. King also works as a broadcaster with **RTÉ** and in 1987 set up **Hummingbird Productions** with Nuala O'Connor, producing such notable TV series as ***Bringing It All Back Home*** and *A **River of Sound***.

Kings Galliard Dutch group that played Irish traditional music and won the award for best act at the Letterkenny Folk Festival in 1976. They were all students of classical music in The Hague. One of them, Kate Wilson (harp, vocals) was English, the rest of the band Dutch. They were Lenneke Williams (fiddle), Jan Erik Noske (flute, whistles), Jorn Plas (virginal, uilleann pipes) and Frank van Meeteren (mandolin, bouzouki, bodhrán, spoons). They released an album, *The Morning Dew*, in 1976. It has many interesting arrangements of traditional Irish tunes as well as an unusual reel composed by Jan Erik Noske ('Jan's Favourite') and a piece from the *Battle Suite* of **William Byrd**.

Kinsella, Mick (b. 1956) Harmonica and percussion player born in Tullow, Co. Carlow. Although Kinsella played drums in the Tullow Marching Band and a variety of showbands over the years, he took up the harmonica in 1980. Initially concentrating on blues, he became interested in playing traditional music on harmonica in the late 1980s through his involvement in sessions in Waterford with musicians such as Pat O'Brien (banjo) and **Martin Murray**. He began to learn through the Murphys (see **Murphy, Phil, John and Pip**) and **Eddie Clarke**, whose style of playing chromatic harmonica influenced him greatly in his own playing of traditional tunes. Kinsella has guested on almost 50 other albums with a wide range of musicians, including, **Martin Murray**, Phil Callery of the **Voice Squad**, **Cormac Breatnach** of **Deiseal**, **Antonio Breschi**, **Altan** and bouzouki player Brendan O'Regan. He has also performed with **Brendan Power**, recording a double harmonica track, 'The Real Blues Reel' with him for *A **River of Sound***.

Kinsella's first solo album, *Harmonica* (2000), on which he performs in a variety of styles on both chromatic and diatonic harmonicas, has added to his growing reputation as the most innovative contemporary Irish harmonica player. The album includes Kinsella's own compositions, some in the style of Irish traditional tunes ('Rosaleen's Children/The Spanncomp Jig'), others, such as 'Lip My Reeds', tending more towards blues. There is a diversity of musical styles on the album, including the most unusual 'Tango Ala Turk', a set of traditional Balkan tunes and four tracks of traditional Irish tunes. Kinsella also plays harmonica and concertina together on three tracks. The main accompanist on *Harmonica* is Cork guitarist Martin Dunlea, and the guest musicians include the group Whirlygig, **Emer Mayock**, Peter Browne (accordion), Dermot Byrne of Altan, Donal Siggins (tenor banjo), Niall O'Brien (violin, string arrangement) and Niall O'Callaghan of Deiseal. Kinsella released the album himself, but it is distributed by **Claddagh Records**.

L

Lá Lugh Group centred on **Gerry O'Connor** (fiddle) and **Eithne Ní Uallacháin** (vocals, flute, whistle), who made one album together, *Cosa gan Bhróga* (*Feet Without Shoes,* 1987), before their first album as Lá Lugh ('The Day of Lugh'). The name is derived from the ancient pagan god Lugh Lámhfhada ('Long-handed Lugh'), who gave his name to the modern Co. Louth. Lugh was the father of Cúchulainn, hero of the great Ulster epic *Táin Bó Cuailnge* (*The Cattle Raid of Cooley*). The group's repertoire draws attention to the rich tradition of music and song (in both English and Irish) in Ulster, of which Co. Louth was originally a part. Its sound is centred on O'Connor's fiddling and Ní Uallacháin's vocals, but other musicians who have recorded or toured with the group have made important contributions. The guitar and piano of Garry Ó Briain and the cello of Neil Martin are integral to most of the arrangements on *Lá Lugh* (1991), which also features the playing of **Máirtín O'Connor** on accordion and Ray Gallen on bodhrán. The album opens with a beautiful rendition of the Ulster song 'Mál Bhán Ní Chuilleannáin' ('Fair Molly Hollywood'), sung to an original air composed by Ní Uallacháin, with the slow reel 'The Destitution' incorporated into the arrangement. There are many fine songs in Irish and English on the album, most of them traditional Ulster songs, along with a range of instrumentals, including hornpipes, jigs, reels, a Shetland waltz, a Scottish highland and 'The Mummer's March', the latter derived from a dance performed by six **mummers** which became progressively more complex and assumed the appearance of a battle.

Lá Lugh was followed by *Brighid's Kiss* (1996) and *Senex Puer* (loosely meaning 'old and young', 1998), the latter largely a compilation of the first two albums. *Brighid's Kiss* won ***Irish Music*** magazine's 'Best Album of the Year' award. Martin and Ó Briain again feature strongly on both albums, as well as Angolan percussionist Mario N'Gomo, Breton guitarist Gilles Le Bigot (who also played on one track on the 1991 album), Shaun Wallace (keyboards, programming, guitar) Martin O'Hare (bodhrán) and Séanie McPhail (guitar). *Brighid's Kiss* represents a remarkable synthesis of old and new, Ní Uallacháin again providing new melodies for old songs. The song 'Brighid's Kiss', with verses in English and Irish, is at once ancient and modern in its music and lyrics, inspired by a belief in the modern relevance of the pagan goddess/Early Christian saint Brighid. The title track of *Senex Puer* combines Latin, Irish and English lyrics and starts out in the style of monastic chant but becomes more modern as synthesiser, cello, fiddle, drums and percussion are added. It is an extraordinary piece of work, combining (like 'Brighid's Kiss') ancient and modern in both lyrical and musical terms. Lá Lugh have made an original contribution to Irish traditional music and song, their music clearly rooted in the Ulster tradition but incorporating influences from further afield, their original lyrics inspired by a desire to bring together past and present.

Lambeg Drum A large, loud, two-headed drum which developed in the 18th and 19th centuries and is played with fife or flute in competitions and festivals or marches organised by the Orange Order. Over a metre in diameter and about 70 millimetres wide, it is usually made of oak and goatskin and is played with two canes. It is largely confined to Northern Ireland and even in recent times has been an important symbol of the Orange or Loyalist community in the North.

Interestingly, the lambeg as a political symbol has been used by some people in recent years to represent, along with the **bodhrán**, the aspiration for peace and harmony between the Protestant and Catholic communities in Northern Ireland. Singer/songwriter **Tommy Sands** went with a bodhrán player, a lambeg player (for both see **Different Drums of Ireland**) and a group of 30-40 school-

Lambeg Drum in action

children (Protestant and Catholic) to the gates of Stormont Castle at a very delicate stage in the Northern Ireland Peace Talks, just before the Good Friday Agreement was signed in April 1998. He wrote a simple song, 'Carry On', to encourage all of those involved in the talks to keep going. He felt he needed both the lambeg and the bodhrán to attract the attention of the representatives of both the Unionist/Loyalist and the Nationalist/Republican communities. Inside Stormont Castle, Séamus Mallon, one of the major participants in the talks, heard the music coming from outside. He told Tommy Sands afterwards that it was a defining moment in the peace process, that he knew the talks had to succeed.

In Dublin the following year, the biggest drum in the world was played by Brian Fleming. It was a two-headed drum designed to look like a lambeg on one side and a bodhrán on the other (see **De Jimbe**).

Lancer See **Quadrilles**.

Lay (*laoi* or *laoidh*) A type of heroic song, comparable to the heroic song of medieval France, which was sung in Ireland from the 12th century or earlier and continued to be sung up the 1940s. Many lays are concerned with the heroic deeds of the mythological Fionn Mac Cumhaill and the Fianna, his band of warriors, as recounted by Oisín (a survivor of the Fianna) to St. Patrick. The society which these

Fenian lays depict is pre-Christian and the themes are magical or romantic, with Fionn often playing the role of a god, poet or seer. They are narrative songs about invasions (often of Vikings), elopements, the slaying of monsters or encounters with supernatural beings. In lays which tell of invasions, the Fianna are portrayed as the defenders of Ireland's sovereignty, but there are also lays which describe them at more leisurely pursuits such as hunting, drinking or playing the ancient Irish game *fidcell* (a boardgame like chess). Some lays do not deal with Fionn and the Fianna but have a similar heroic style, as in 'Laoi an Amadáin Mhóir' ('Lay of the Big Fool'). The latter has a uniquely Arthurian ambience for an Irish lay and may well have been influenced by stories or songs of King Arthur in the late Middle Ages. It was popular up to the 19th and early 20th centuries and in 1911 was published in a small, 48-page edition, with notes and vocabulary.

Another popular lay of more recent times, 'Laoi na Mná Móire' ('Lay of the Big Woman') tells of an invading Greek princess who uses magic and military force against Fionn and the Fianna but is ultimately defeated. This lay was noted in Co. Waterford in 1936 and is documented from other parts of Ireland, with numerous prose versions of the tale also surviving. In the 1940s two brothers, Micheál and Séamus Ó hIghne, were recorded at Glencolumkille, Co. Donegal, singing versions of the lay. Micheál sang only a few lines while Séamus sang a complete but con-densed version. The recordings of these brothers (made in 1945 and 1949) were the first Irish sound recordings made of the singing of lays; unfortunately, they will probably be the last. Although lays are still sung in Scotland, they have disappeared from the traditional singer's repertoire in Ireland.

Lays were chanted rather then sung, with some historians comparing their style to plainchant or a priest 'singing' mass. Performers might have spoken some of the lay in verse or prose and there was generally no measured tempo but rather a free and wandering rhythm. They were evidently performed by one singer, although the possibility that the singer was, in the style of bardic poetry, accompanied by the harp cannot be ruled out. In their formal complexity, the lays share features of the scholarly poetry of medieval Ireland. In theory they had quatrains of seven-syllable lines and rhyming was quite regular, with the even lines (as in **ballad**s) rhyming or having assonance. Internal assonance is also a marked feature. Although this is the usual quatrain form of the later Fenian lays, some are in a metre called *deibhí*, which uses couplet rhymes and no internal assonance.

Although the lays were popular at all levels of society, they relate the deeds and values of the nobility. They could be considered 'folk songs' because they survived so long 'in the mouths of the people', but **Hugh Shields** has argued that the term is not appropriate because of the unique features of the genre. They are static in a temporal sense, situating history in relation to a Golden Age, a marked contrast with the old ballads, which use dialogue and refrain to link the past with a timeless present. The stories that the lays tell, as well as the manner in which those stories are told, are also markedly different to the ballads. However, the habits of versified story-telling which the lays formed in their composers and performers undoubtedly had an influence on the more recent Irish tradition of popular song, and the lays do share some common formal features with ballads, including the use of the quatrain form in words and music.

Although ballads became popular throughout Europe (including Britain) in the Late Middle Ages, they do not appear to have achieved the same level of popularity in Ireland until much later. Gaelic civilisation was largely rural and had a 'heroic' society long after other parts of Europe were developing along more modern lines. The lays, therefore, remained popular in Ireland for centuries, while the European ballads were longer in taking root and becoming widespread.

Leahy Canadian group originally consisting of five sisters and four brothers. Reared in the Ottawa valley, which forms the boundary between Ontario and Québec, their father's family emigrated from Ireland in the 19th century while their mother comes from a Cape Breton family of Scots ancestry. Their repertoire includes Irish, Scots and French-Canadian traditional music, but they also stray at times into other types, including ragtime and Hungarian music. French-Canadian step-dancing is a vital part of their live shows. Fiddles feature strongly in their line-up and their overall sound is often rock influenced, with drums and bass providing strong backing, along with guitar and keyboards. Their debut, *Leahy* (1997), was entirely instrumental and featured their own version of the famous **Moving Hearts** tune 'McBride's', composed by **Dónal Lunny** and Declan Sinnott. The album brought the group international attention and they played with the **Chieftains** in the **Gael Force** series of concerts in Dublin in 1997. They have since begun to include songs as well as instrumentals in their repertoire, and their live performances are energetic and visually impressive, with band members often playing and dancing at the same time. On their third album, *In All Things* (2004), four of the ten tracks are songs, all written by the band themselves and encompassing a wide range of influences. Website: www.leahymusic.com.

Ledrede, Richard (Bishop of Ossory, ca. 1319-1361) A Franciscan who migrated from London to take up the post of Bishop of Ossory in 1317 and in the 1320s composed a number of Latin hymns to try to entice his clergy away from their interest in 'vile secular songs'. His manuscript survives in *The Red Book of Ossory*, preserved in the episcopal palace, Kilkenny. Ledrede used short lyrical fragments of eight of the 'vile secular songs' to indicate the air to which his new, sacred songs should be sung. The fragments (two in French and six in English) consist of a few lines from the beginning of each song. The songs were love lyrics that Ledrede must have used because their airs were popular on the streets of Kilkenny. These medieval street songs could have been composed in Kilkenny, although **Hugh Shields** suggests that they came from Britain. Although there are no complete secular songs in the manuscript, the fragments give some indication of the type of song that was popular in the 14th-century Anglo-Norman colony in Ireland. Ledrede is also famous for his ruthless pursuit of the celebrated Dame Alice Kytler on charges of witchcraft.

Lenihan, Tom (1905-1990)   Singer, lilter and storyteller from Knockbrack, Miltown Malbay, Co. Clare. He spent his whole life working as a farmer, but had a large repertoire of songs, many of them learned orally but some learned from other sources such as **ballad sheets**, songbooks and gramophone recordings. He grew up in a musical household, his mother a singer and concertina player, his father a whistle player and all nine of his brothers and sisters playing musical instruments. His repertoire included **Child ballads**, local songs, political songs and dance-hall songs. He sang unaccompanied in English, but performed some English-language versions of famous Irish songs such as 'Ar Éirinn Ní Neosfainn Cé Hí' ('For Ireland I'd Not Tell Her Name'). As well as singing at house gatherings and sessions, he constantly sang at home while going about his daily work. There are many interesting songs in his repertoire, including one on the Lusitania, the ocean liner sunk by a German torpedo off the Old Head of Kinsale, Co. Cork on May 7th, 1915. The cleverly rhymed lyrics of 'Paddy's Panacea', a song in praise of whiskey, were learned from a book the singer received from his sister in the **US**. He used the tune of the jig 'Larry O'Gaff' for the song, which has become famous as 'Stick to the Craytur'. Like many of the old Clare singers, Linehan did not use dynamics for dramatic effect and used very little ornamentation.

The folk revival beginning in the 1960s brought many song collectors and folklorists to Knockbrack. These included **Tony MacMahon** and **Tom Munnelly**, who recorded Lenihan on numerous occasions between 1972 and 1988. Thirty-three selections from Munnelly's recordings (songs, lilting, comments), along with transcriptions of 50 songs with a jig and a reel which Lenihan used to lilt, were published as *The Mount Callan Garland: Songs from the Repertoire of Tom Lenihan* (cassettes and book, Dublin, 1994), edited by Munnelly. The book includes an excellent introduction covering the history of Irish and English in Co. Clare, a description of the Mount Callan area and a fine pen portrait of Lenihan. The song transcriptions are accompanied by additional information on sources, history and other relevant background material. The book gives a detailed insight into the life and songs of a man who lived through the most significant changes in Irish traditional music of the last century. Lenihan also recorded an album, *Paddy's Panacea* (1978), which includes five songs not on *The Mount Callan Garland* tapes. From the 1970s, he featured on many radio programmes and sang throughout the country. Despite receiving visitors from all over the world and several offers to go to the US and Britain, he never left Ireland. Lenihan was an important contributor to the **Willie Clancy Summer School** until the time of his death and also contributed, through Tom Munnelly, much material on local history, farming lore and cures for animal diseases to the Department of Folklore in University College Dublin.

Lennon, Charlie (b. 1938)   Musician and composer from Killyclougher, Co. Leitrim. Formally trained on piano and violin from an early age, he played in many bands in his youth and, after moving to Liverpool to study in 1961, played with the Liverpool Céilí Band. In 1969 Lennon returned to Ireland and lived in Dublin for many years. He initially made his name as an accompanist playing piano, recording with **Joe Burke** in 1971, but was more to the foreground in *Lucky in Love* (1981, with Mick O'Connor). *The Emigrant Suite*, his first solo album, featured his own compositions, some of which were taken up by **De Dannan**. *Island Wedding* (1990), a composition in sixteen movements for traditional ensemble and orchestra, features the playing of **Liam O'Flynn**, **Frankie Gavin** and Deirbhile Ní Bhrolcháin. He again blended traditional and classical idioms in *Flight from the Hungry Land* (CD, 1996), which was premiered in the National Concert Hall, Dublin in 1995. This three-part suite for traditional ensemble and orchestra was also performed as part of the 150th anniversary commemorations of the **Great Famine** at Lincoln Centre, New York in 1997. Lennon retired to Spiddal, Co. Galway in 1998 where he opened a state-of-the-art recording studio and technology centre with his daughter Eilis, a classical violinist.

Levey, Richard Michael (1811-1899) Classical violinist and collector of traditional music born in Dublin. He joined the Theatre Royal orchestra at the age of fifteen, later becoming its musical director. His real name was O'Shaughnessy but, according to **Francis O'Neill** (*Irish Minstrels and Musicians*, p. 141), he changed it to Levey after his first visit to London. He had arrived there to enrol for a music festival and gave his name to the official as 'Richard Michael O'Shaughnessy':

> 'Richard Michael O'Whatnessy?' echoed the astonished official.
> 'O'Shaughnessy', repeated the bewildered violinist.
> 'My friend,' volunteered his questioner, 'You can never hope to make a success in professional life with an unpronounceable name like that. By the way what was your mother's maiden name?' When told it was Leavy he wrote down Levey and announced to the abashed musician, 'Hereafter you will be known as R. M. Levey in this establishment.'

Levey composed over fifty overtures and arranged music for numerous pantomimes. He was a founder of the Royal Irish Academy of Music, where he became professor of violin. He had a life-long interest in traditional music and wrote down tunes from the playing of fiddlers and flautists in Dublin and London. Most importantly, he published the first ever collection devoted exclusively to Irish dance music, *The Dance Music of Ireland* (2 vols, London, 1858 and 1873; new ed. Dublin, 2003), each volume containing over a hundred tunes of many types, with basic piano accompaniments. Levey wrote that in only one case did he alter the music as it was played, making the collection an important resource on traditional music in his day.

Lilting (*portaireacht* or *portaíl*) A form of singing that uses vocables or 'nonsense' words, also known as 'puss-music' or 'dydling'. In the past, a lilter was often used to provide music for dancers when a musician was not available. Lilting (or singing) also had an important role to play in relieving the tedium of work. In recent decades it has been presented as an art form in its own right by professional and non-professional performers and is now included as a category in competitions at

Fleadh Cheoil Na hÉireann. Professional performers, including **Len Graham**, **Bobby Gardiner** and Tim Lyons, as well as non-professionals such as **Tom Lenihan**, have all made recordings that include lilting. Bobby Clancy (see **Clancy Brothers and Tommy Makem**) used to regularly perform a dance tune partly played on harmonica and partly lilted, while simultaneously accompanying himself on bodhrán. A favourite was the slide 'The Dingle Regatta', for which he used vocables that began 'diden-dee-ya-dan-diden-dee-ya-dan-da-diden-dee-i-dan-da'. Other lilters might use different vocables; Tom Linehan, for example, begins his lilting of 'The Colliers Reel' with 'daddle-diddle-do-rowdle-diddle-a-dee-idle-diddly.' Brendan Monaghan has recorded a fine track of lilting with **Different Drums of Ireland** which is initially unaccompanied but, as it develops, is accompanied by percussion on various instruments and interspersed with uilleann pipes and whistle.

Traditional music is often pejoratively referred to as 'diddly-i music', a term which undoubtedly derives from the vocables some lilters use. Lilting is also used frequently by musicians to remind each other of tunes or to teach each other tunes. A comparable use of some form of lilting for teaching tunes or rhythms can be found in many other cultures, and an interesting example of this, south Indian 'konnekol' can be heard combined with Irish traditional reels in the playing of **Khanda**. There are many fine examples of lilting on the album *Cavan's Lilter* (2003) by Séamus Fay. See also **McDermott, Josie**; **Mouth Music**; **Tunney, Paddy.**

Linnane, Tony Fiddler from Corofin, Co. Clare, whose early musical influences included his father (who played the whistle), his fiddle teacher Frank Custy (see **Custy Family**) and Donegal fiddler **Tommy Peoples**. He formed a duo with **Noel Hill**, touring and recording in the late 1970s and early 80s. Linnane and Hill were renowned for their unique blending of concertina and fiddle, and formed a group with **Kieran Hanrahan** (banjo) and Tony Callinan (guitar, vocals) in the late 1970s. They recorded one album (now unavailable) before splitting up in 1978. Hanrahan and Callinan went on to form **Stockton's Wing**, while the fiddle/concertina duo made the classic *Noel Hill and Tony Linnane* (1979). The album featured some fine tracks of the duo playing without accompaniment but also included tracks with **Alec Finn** (bouzouki, mandocello), **Matt Molloy** (flute) and **Micheál Ó Domhnaill** (church harmonium). They also recorded with **Christy Moore** (*The Iron Behind the Velvet*, 1978) and **Planxty** (*The Woman I Loved So Well*, 1980) before Linnane gave up working as a professional musician. He lives and works in Clare, where he still plays in local sessions.

Lisdoonvarna Small town in west Clare which hosted a famous music festival from 1979 to 1984, immortalised in the famous song by **Christy Moore**. The first festival was headlined by Moore himself and the **Chieftains**, and although the music became more international in subsequent years, there was always a strong representation of Irish bands, both traditional and rock. **Planxty**, **Moving Hearts**, **Andy Irvine**, **Clannad** and **Luka Bloom** all played Lisdoonvarna and all have tracks on *Donal Lunny's Definitive Lisdoonvarna* (2003). There are also tracks by

Jackson Browne, Van Morrison, Phil Lynott and other rock, folk and country artists. The original headliners, the Chieftains and Christy Moore, are also represented, the latter singing his own song, 'Lisdoonvarna'. An attempt to revive the festival in 2003 ran into difficulties and the Lisdoonvarna festival was actually held in Dublin's RDS that year.

Lomax, Alan (1915-2002) American ethnomusicologist, writer, promoter and record producer born in Austin, Texas. He was a major figure in the revival of interest in folk music in the **US** in the 1940s, 50s and 60s (see **American Folk Song**). His father, John (1867-1948), was also a musicologist and although Alan studied philosophy (University of Texas) and anthropology (Columbia University, New York), his main pursuit in his late teens and twenties was helping his father. In 1932 father and son undertook a major musical field trip in the southern US, sponsored by the Library of Congress. They recorded over 3,000 songs during the next eight years, including Cajun, gospel, jazz, voodoo music, blues and protest music inspired by the Great Depression. In 1934 they discovered the unknown genius of black singer/songwriter and guitarist Huddie Ledbetter (known as Leadbelly). Alan later secured Ledbetter's parole from a Louisiana jail and produced a collection of Leadbelly songs that had a profound influence on later folk and blues musicians. Alan also played a major role in documenting and bringing to public attention the work of blues guitarist Muddy Waters, pianist and composer Jelly Roll Morton and singer/songwriter **Woody Guthrie**. Together the Lomaxes wrote the major studies *American Ballads and Folk Songs* (1934) and *Our Singing Country* (1941). Alan eventually took over his father's post as curator of the American Archive of Folk Song and became director of folk music at Decca Records.

Alan Lomax also worked in radio, producing a weekly educational show on 'Columbia School of the Air' (CBS) in 1939 and hosting 'Back Where I Came From' (also on CBS) in the early 1940s. Both programmes were important in bringing Woody Guthrie to a wider audience and Lomax also recorded Guthrie at the Library of Congress in three marathon sessions in March 1940. These recordings were released on a three-record set in the mid 1960s.

From the 1950s, Alan Lomax began researching European folk music. He visited Spain, Italy, Scotland, Britain and Ireland and worked with **Séamus Ennis**. He recorded many traditional singers and musicians in Ireland, including the singer **Elizabeth (Bess) Cronin**, recorded on a trip to Ireland in 1951. He also recorded **sean-nós singing** in Connemara and Donegal and the street singer **Margaret Barry**, whom he met in Dundalk. His Irish volume of recordings appeared as *Columbia World Library of Folk and Primitive Music 1* (1955).

The work of Alan Lomax has been recognised by many as having a major influence on the development of folk and popular music in the US, and in Ireland his work is also recognised by musicians and collectors. Musician and producer **Philip King** remarked on Irish radio after Lomax's death that, to anyone involved in folk music he was 'The Man', giving voice to the 'little people', to the poor, to black musicians and others. Although his direct involvement in collecting and recording in Ireland was limited, he is still a major figure of inspiration to musicians and collectors in Ireland and elsewhere. **Nicholas Carolan** is working on a new volume of Lomax's Irish recordings for commercial release.

Long Dance See **Set Dance 2** and **Rince Fada.**

Lord of the Dance Stage show and video created and choreographed by **Michael Flatley** in 1996, after he left *Riverdance*. Although similar to *Riverdance*, *Lord of the Dance* is different in a number of ways. There is a storyline in which Michael Flatley plays the Lord of the Dance, battling to retain supremacy against Don Dorcha, the Dark Lord, and his masked dancers. Flatley also woos Saoirse (Irish for 'freedom') the Irish Colleen and Erin the Goddess, despite the attentions of Morrigan (an Irish war goddess) the Temptress. The dancing in the show is technically brilliant and more focussed on Irish step dancing than *Riverdance*, although many of the dance sequences involving the men are highly militaristic in style. The female dancers are, by contrast, more genteel and graceful in their dancing and their costumes are more colourful than the black of the men. Spectacular effects are used, with Flatley sinking into the stage in a puff of smoke and cameras under the stage being used to show his feet from a different angle. One of the most interesting dance sequences involves Morrigan dancing steps that are Irish in style but using her hands and body more in the style of a Spanish dancer. Ronan Hardiman composed the music for the show, incorporating Irish traditional tunes as well as original material. Although there is no denying Flatley's brilliance as a dancer, the show received mixed reviews when it opened in London in July 1996. Nonetheless, it has, like *Riverdance*, generated much interest in Irish dancing internationally. Website: www.lordofthedance.com.

Loughnane, Kathleen Harpist and member of the group **Dordán**, born in Nenagh, Co. Tipperary but living in Galway since 1982. She has published two books of slow airs, early harping tunes and dance music for the harp, entitled *Harping On* (Galway, 1995) and *Affairs of the Harp* (Galway, 1998). All of the tunes in the second book can be heard on the album of the same name. Her work has also been published by the organisation Cáirde na Cruite ('Friends of the Harp') in their *Sounding Harps* collections (Vols. 2 and 3) and included in the examination syllabus of the Royal Irish Academy of Music.

Love Song As in the folk music of other countries, love songs make up the majority of Irish folk song repertory. Love **songs in Irish** are, in many cases, distinct in form and style to those in English. In both cases there are many examples of songs written in Ireland that show a marked French influence in form and style (see **France**). A number of old English love **ballad**s have been sung in Ireland for so long now that they have been accepted as part of the national repertory. Overall there is a great variety in style and tone, ranging from the bitter and intense sense of loss expressed in 'Dónal Óg' ('Young Dónal') to the light playfulness of 'The Spanish

Lady'. Some love songs are closely bound with emigration (see **Emigration Song**), war, politics (see **Aisling**) and other subjects. The wealth of variety in types of love song can be seen by looking, for instance, at the **Sam Henry** collection, where there are twelve distinct sections (classified by theme) of love songs. These include 'Praise of a Girl', 'Courtship and Dalliance', 'Faithful Farewells', 'Disguises', 'Love Unrequited', 'Love Unfaithful', 'Deadly Love', 'Despite Relatives' and 'Domesticity'.

Although it is not possible to examine love songs in detail here, a few points are worth noting. Love songs in Irish are particularly notable for their lyric, rather then narrative, qualities and are often highly impressionistic and metaphorical. Folk poetry and song in Irish is also distinct from that of most European countries in the great number of men's love songs that exist. The decline of the Irish language has meant that many love songs are now more frequently heard as slow airs than songs (see **Air**). Many of the older traditional love songs in English are more narrative than lyrical in style, but there are exceptions, such as 'The Rose of Tralee', written by William P. Mulchinok (1820-1864) and 'Danny Boy', the most popular version of which was written by Fred E. Weatherly (1848-1929) in 1913. Some of the most famous Irish love songs, such as 'Down by the Sally Gardens' (see **Yeats, W. B.**) and 'She Moved Through the Fair' (see **Colum, Padraig**) are 20th-century versions of older, anonymous traditional songs. 'The Curragh of Kildare', a popular love song since the 1960s, was published (entitled 'The Winter It Is Past') in the collected works of the Scottish poet **Robert Burns** (1759-1796), but was arranged in the form now popular in Ireland by **Christy Moore** and **Dónal Lunny** around 1962.

A considerable number of love songs sung in Ireland are light-hearted or even bawdy. The night-visit or *pastourelle* type songs (see **France**) are often playful in their depictions of brief sexual encounters, while the popular 'The Old Woman from Wexford' (known in numerous versions in Ireland and beyond) is more ribald in style. New love songs are constantly being added to the repertoire of Irish folk singers, with some, such as **Jimmy MacCarthy**'s 'Ride On', achieving great popularity among folk and popular singers. See also **Comic Songs**; **Planxty**; **Spillane, John**.

Low Whistle (*feadóg mhór*) An instrument like a large tin **whistle** which is most commonly found pitched in 'D', a full octave below a tin whistle. It uses the same

Low Whistle

fingering system and forms of ornamentation as the tin whistle. The earliest examples made by Overton of England were made of a single piece of aluminium tubing with an aluminium fipple. Low whistles began to be played in Irish traditional music in the 1960s. 'The Lonesome Boatman', recorded by Finbar and Eddie Furey (see **Furey Brothers**) in the late 1960s, was one of the first tunes that many people heard played on a low whistle, and it is still strongly associated with the instrument.

Low whistles are perceived by some traditional musicians as merely a pale imitation of a 'real' flute, and some players find the spacing of the holes too awkward for the effective playing of fast dance tunes. Nonetheless, many fine players have emerged in the 1980s and 90s, among them Joe McKenna (see **McKenna, Joe and Antoinette**), **Davy Spillane**, **Cormac Breatnach** of **Deiseal**, **Michael McGoldrick** and **James McNally** of the **Afro Celts**. The recording and performance work of these musicians has established the low whistle as an important instrument in its own right. The Dublin-born uilleann piper and low whistle player, Eoin Duignan, deliberately chose to confine himself to the low whistle for his third album, *Lumina* (2004). Living in the heart of west Kerry for 25 years, Duignan was inspired in recent years by the Harry Clarke stained-glass windows in Dísert Chapel, Dingle. He composed a six-part suite of music for the low whistle, composing tunes for each of the stained-glass windows. In an interview in the *Irish Times* (30 July 2004), Duignan spoke about the reasons why he chose the low whistle for *Lumina*: 'The low whistle is played from low down, in the diaphragm', he says. 'You can get a lot of emotion into it. You can get a lot of feeling and you can tell a story very easily from deep down.' He talks about how different whistles in different keys hit 'different emotional spots' and how he used them in the recording *Lumina*. In the hands of such players, the low whistle (played by most in a variety of different pitches that also have different tones) can be used to produce unusual sounds and a range of effects that cannot be executed in quite the same way on any other instrument.

Aluminium low whistles are still manufactured by Overton (since 1999 based in Germany) and now also by Chieftain. Both companies make whistles in a variety of pitches. Other types are also available in a limited range of pitches, including the Shaw, a lighter, conical bore low whistle. Howard also makes a low whistle, cylindrical with a plastic mouthpiece, and the US-based Susato make fully plastic, tuneable low whistles. Other varieties of the instrument can be seen occasionally, usually custom-made.

Loyalist Song See **Orange/Loyalist Song**.

Lúnasa Instrumental group ('Lúnasa' is the Irish month of August, as well a harvest festival that takes place then) whose original line-up was **Seán Smyth** (fiddle), **Michael McGoldrick** (flute and low whistle), **John McSherry** (uilleann pipes and low whistle), also a member of **Tamalin**, Donagh Hennessy (guitar) and Trevor Hutchinson (bass). Their first album, *Lúnasa* (1998), includes traditional Irish, Breton (see **Brittany**) and original tunes. The sound is lively and varied in style, with many **set**s made up of tunes in different rhythms. Comparisons have been made to the **Bothy Band** and, like the latter group, Lúnasa's arrangements combine strong solos with dynamic group-playing in which harmony and a full, rich backing are important elements. Although Kevin Crawford (flute) and Cillian Vallely (uilleann pipes) eventually took over from McGoldrick and McSherry, the latter two musicians feature on the group's second album *Otherworld* (1999). By the time of the third album, *The Merry Sisters of Fate* (2001), the line-up of the band included the three original members Smyth, Hennessy and Hutchinson, along with Crawford and Vallely. The album is a mixture of traditional and original tunes (by Hennessy and McGoldrick) and includes Breton music and a track of tunes from **Asturias** and **Galicia** in northern Spain. *Redwood* (2003) again includes music from Brittany (composed by Breton musicians Christian Lamaitre and Nicolas Quemenar) as well as original compositions by (Martin) **Junior Crehan** and members of the band. After a legal dispute with **Green Linnet** over their *Redwood* album, they released *The Kinnity Sessions* (2004) with the US-based company, Compass Records. This is a live album recorded over three nights at Kinnity Castle, County Offaly. Website: www.lunasa.ie.

Lúnasa

Lunny, Dónal (b. 1947) Composer and bouzouki, guitar, keyboard and bodhrán player, an extraordinarily influential figure in traditional music since the 1960s. Born in Tullamore, Co. Offaly, he moved to Newbridge, Co. Kildare at a young age. His first success was with the group **Emmet Spiceland**, and he went on to be a central figure in **Planxty**, the **Bothy Band** and **Moving Hearts**. He initially played guitar, but after receiving a Greek **bouzouki** from **Andy Irvine** in 1970, this became, in various forms, his main instrument. He found the round back of the Greek bouzouki quite awkward and came up with a flat-backed design that has virtually become his trademark. In the late 1970s he also began to play a larger-bodied ten-string bouzouki called the **blarge**, and with Moving Hearts played a solid-body electric bouzouki. His playing with Planxty was lighter and involved more counter-melody than with the Bothy Band or Moving Hearts, where he still played counter-melodies but also powerful, often syncopated rhythms. His work as an arranger and producer with these groups has led to his being hailed as a major innovator in Irish traditional music. One of the most interesting projects he was involved in was 'Timedance', a suite which was commissioned by **RTÉ** as a centrepiece for their presentation of the Eurovision Song Contest in 1981. It consisted of one traditional tune and two original pieces, composed by **Bill Whelan** and Lunny, which were played by Planxty and a string ensemble. An original and evocative contemporary/ballet style dance was performed to the music, and the entire presentation was visually and musically striking.

Lunny has also produced numerous albums for other groups and solo artists, including **Christy Moore**, **Altan** and **Sharon Shannon**. With Moving Hearts he performed and recorded some of his own compositions, and has continued to do so since the band broke up. Between 1986 and 2001 he made a series of excellent albums with Dublin singer **Frank Harte**, underlining his talent for providing tasteful and subtle backings for traditional singers. In 1987 he released a short album (*Dónal Lunny*) which was recorded live and included a mixture of traditional and original material performed by a group which included **Nollaig Ní Chathasaigh**, **Cormac Breatnach**, **Arty McGlynn**, **Seán Óg Potts** and Dónal's brother Manus Lunny. Some of the original tunes sound traditional in style but have unusual rhythms, such as the jig 'Across the Hill' and the 'Tolka Polka'. Also included is Lunny's tribute to the Dublin musician Declan McNeilis (d. 1987), a beautiful air simply titled 'Declan'. Lunny wrote the theme music for the 1995 television series *A **River of Sound*** with **Micheál Ó Súilleabháin**, and produced the CD of music for the series.

His album *Coolfin* (1998) was acclaimed as another milestone in traditional music and features guest appearances by a number of well-known artists, including **Tríona and Maighréad Ní Dhomhnaill**, Marta Sebestyén (who sings on 'Moldavian Triptych'), Eddi Reader of Fairground Attraction, Sharon Shannon and Jean Butler of ***Riverdance***. The band Coolfin includes Nollaig Ní Chathasaigh and Máiréad Nesbitt on fiddles and **John McSherry** of **Tamalin** and **Lúnasa** on uilleann pipes. The music is an interesting mixture of traditional and original material, the rhythms generally more subtle and less driving than in other bands Lunny has worked with. In 1999 he released *This Is My Father: Original Soundtrack*, music from a film made by the Quinn brothers. *Journey: The Best of Dónal Lunny* (2000) is a compilation of his work with various musicians from the days of the Bothy Band and Planxty right through to Coolfin and features seven previously unreleased tracks under the title 'The Millennium Suite'. The sleeve notes, by Lunny himself, are full of interesting comments and insights. See also **Burns, Robbie**; **Faulkner, Jimmy**; **Sult**.

Macalla All-female traditional group formed on International Women's Day, 1984. The members of the group were mostly female traditional musicians based in the Dublin area. Initially there were 29 musicians, including **Seosaimhín Ní Bheaglaoich**, Mairéad Ní Mhaonaigh of **Altan** and **Catherine McEvoy**. Their sound on instrumentals was similar to that of a **céilí band**, with nine fiddles, three flutes, a concertina, a bodhrán, a harp and a piano in their initial line-up. They also performed traditional songs from Donegal, Wexford, Westmeath, Cúil Aodha and West Kerry. They made two albums, *Mná na hÉireann* (1985) and *Macalla 2* (1987), both of which were re-released on CD by **Gael-Linn** in 2004. Macalla toured sporadically between 1984 and 1988. Despite their popularity, they stopped performing together in the late 1980s. Since the turn of the century, the group has performed a number of times, including a reunion concert in Ennis, Co. Clare in November 2002 and on a special 'Céilí House' programme on **RTÉ** radio to mark their 20th anniversary in March 2004. They also performed a special 20th anniversary concert in Liberty Hall in May 2004.

Macaronic Song Songs consisting of phrases, lines, couplets or verses alternating between the Irish and English languages. Many of them date from the 19th century, when the Irish language had begun to decline but many people were bilingual. A considerable number of the **ballad sheet**s that appear in Ireland from the 1850s on have macaronic texts, and in some cases the English portions were translations from the Irish. In other cases, the Irish and English portions are different, the former sometimes ridiculing the laudatory sentiments expressed in English. Many of the macaronic songs are light-hearted in tone, often taking the form of a dialogue between a courting boy and girl. Some are more serious, such as the popular and enduring 'Siúil a Rún' ('Walk, My Dear'). This song is a woman's lament for the loss of her lover, one of the 'Wild Geese' who left Ireland after the Williamite War (1691; see **Jacobite Song**) to serve in the French army. The verses, in English, end with a refrain in Irish, and the chorus is in Irish. The song has been recorded by **Clannad** and, more recently, **Solas**. See also **Ó Héanaí, Seosamh**.

MacCarthy, Jimmy (b. 1953) Singer/songwriter born in Cork. One of the best known writers of contemporary songs in Ireland, he has described his own songs as 'folk pop' or 'Irish pop' in an *Irish Times* interview (5 February 1998). Many folk/traditional artists have recorded his songs, including **Moving Hearts**, Sliabh Notes (see **Cranitch, Matt**), **Mary Black** and **Christy Moore**, whose rendition of MacCarthy's 'Ride On' in 1984 gave the songwriter his first big breakthrough. Since then MacCarthy, who also plays guitar and keyboards, has recorded three albums of

225

his own, *The Song of the Singing Horseman* (1990), *The Dreamer* (1994) and *The Moment* (2002) and participated in the album *Warmer for the Spark: The Songs of Jimmy MacCarthy* (1998), on which various singers perform. The title of the album comes from the lyrics of one of MacCarthy's most famous songs, 'No Frontiers'. *No Frontiers: The Jimmy MacCarthy Songbook* (2000) is the first sheet-music collection of his best-known songs. *Ride On: Jimmy MacCarthy in Song and Story* (2002) is a collection of 53 song lyrics with a background to each song written by MacCarthy himself.

MacColl, Ewan (1915-1989) Singer, songwriter, collector, broadcaster and playwright, a major figure in the British folk revival who first came to prominence in the late 1950s and early 60s. Born to Scots parents, he grew up in the English industrial town of Salford, Greater Manchester. His father was a political radical involved in the workers' movement; his mother was a singer from whom Ewan learned many songs. He was active in reviving street theatre and forming the experimental Theatre Workshop in the 1940s. From 1957 he was involved in the BBC radio series *Radio Ballads*, which combined traditional songs recorded in the field with his own compositions. Some of MacColl's ballads from this series have become part of the standard folk repertoire in Britain and Ireland, including 'The Shoals of Herring' (recorded by the **Clancy Brothers and Tommy Makem**), 'The Travelling People' (a hit for the **Johnstons**) and 'Dirty Old Town' (also sung by the Clancys and later the **Pogues**). Other Irish singers have recorded his songs, and both **Luke Kelly** and **Christy Moore** spent time with him in England early in their careers.

MacColl was a passionate believer in the social and political power of folk song and through his own songs commented on many contemporary social, political and economic subjects. With his wife, Peggy Seeger (sister of **Pete Seeger**, who has made numerous albums of her own), he published collections of songs and folklore and recorded many albums. His song for her, 'The First Time Ever I Saw Your Face', was recorded by Elvis Presley and was also a hit in the **US** for Roberta Flack. His albums include *Bothy Ballads of Scotland* (1961), three volumes of *English and Scottish Popular Ballads (Child Ballads)* (Vol. 1, 1961; Vols. 2 and 3, 1962) and *The Singing Streets: Childhood Memories of Ireland and Scotland* (1958) with **Dominic Behan**. In October 1989 MacColl and Seeger recorded *Naming of Names* (released 1990), a collection of original, mainly anti-Thatcherite songs, some of which use traditional tunes, most of them blackly humorous. The album includes MacColl's 'The Island', a song about Ireland's struggle against successive invaders from the Vikings onwards. His autobiography, *Journeyman* (London, 1990), was published the year after his death.

MacColl had an enormous impact on a number of folk singers in Ireland, Britain and elsewhere since the 1960s. His daughter, Kirsty (1959-2000), a fine singer/songwriter, recorded the hit single 'Fairytale of New York' with the Pogues in 1987. She recorded with many rock bands, including Simple Minds, the Smiths and Talking Heads, and her solo albums *Kite* (1989) and *Tropical Brainstorm* (2000) revealed her talent as a songwriter. Other members of the MacColl family are also musicians and Ewan's multi-instrumentalist son, Neill, has performed and recorded some of his own songs with **Eleanor Shanley**. Scots singer/guitarist **Dick Gaughan** is very much in the MacColl tradition, combining traditional and contemporary folk with a strong emphasis on radical politics. He also has recorded some of MacColl's songs. *Paddy Reilly Sings the Songs of Ewan MacColl* (2000) features the Dubin singer, backed by members of the **Voice Squad**, singing a fine selection of MacColl songs, including 'School Days Over' (also recorded by **Mary Black**), 'The Ballad of Springhill', 'Sweet Thames Flow Softly', 'Dirty Old Town', 'Moving on Song', 'The Shoals of Herring', 'Go Down You Murderers', 'Free Born Man' and 'The First Time Ever I Saw Your Face'. See also **Political Song** and **Scotland**.

Ewan MacColl
(photo: Peggy Seeger)

MacDonncha, Seán (Name often spelt 'Seán 'ac Donncha') (1919-1996) **Sean-nós** singer from Carna in Connemara, Co. Galway who spent most of his life working as a primary school teacher but still made a number of recordings and sang in **Scotland**, **Brittany** and the **US**. He won the **Oireachtas** sean-nós competition in the 1950s and in 1959 was involved in making the earliest 78 rpm records with **Gael-Linn**. He went on to make albums with other record companies, including *An Aill Bhán* ('The White Cliff'; 1971) with **Claddagh Records**. He was a close friend of piper **Willie Clancy** and **Seosamh Ó Héanaí** (also from Carna).

MacGabhann, Antóin (b. 1945) Fiddler from Mullahoran, Co. Cavan who has won **All-Ireland** and **Oireachtas** titles and has been involved in **Comhaltas Ceoltóirí Éireann** for many years. He worked on the first **Fleadh Nua** in Dublin in 1970 with Father Pat Ahearn. In the late 1960s and early 1970s he played with the Green Linnet Céilí Band and subsequently with the Castle Céilí Band, along with **Leo Rowsome** and **Tommy Peoples**. His wife, Bernie, is from Co. Clare and together they have been involved in **set dancing** for many years. The **RTÉ** radio programme *Céilí House* has been broadcast from their home in Co. Meath on a number of occasions and they have been major figures in the revival of house sessions. Antóin has played in the **US** and **Cape Breton** (see **Nova Scotia**). His album *Ar Aon Bhuille: Matching Beats* (1994) was made in Cape Breton with pianist and step-dancer Hilda Chiasson and includes four compositions by **Vincent Broderick**.

MacGowan, Shane (b. 1957) Singer/songwriter born in Kent, England to Irish parents. He lived in Co. Tipperary up to the age of six, and then moved to England with his parents. His mother was an Irish traditional singer, his father an avid reader, and from an early age Shane read widely such authors as Graham Greene, Joseph Heller, John Steinbeck, James Joyce, **W. B. Yeats**, J. P. Donleavy and **Brendan Behan**. In his early years MacGowan also developed a love of traditional music and song, listening to the **Dubliners** and the **Clancy Brothers and Tommy Makem**. His abilities were recognised at the age of twelve when he started attending the prestigious Westminster School in London, although he was expelled after being arrested for possession of drugs in 1971.

Shane MacGowan (photo: Josie Monserrat)

Growing up in London, he was influenced by the punk rock of the 1970s, especially the music of the Sex Pistols. In 1977 he formed his own punk band, the Nipple Erectors (shortened to the Nips), who released a few singles and one album (*Only Happy at the Beginning*, 1980) before breaking up late in 1980. In 1982-83 the New Republicans (later the **Pogues**), who mixed Irish traditional music and song with punk, were formed. MacGowan's songwriting and singing were central to the success of the Pogues and the group were not the same after he left them in 1991. In 1993 he formed Shane MacGowan and the Popes with Paul McGuinness (guitars, vocals), Bernie 'the Undertaker' France (bass, vocals), Danny Pope (drums, percussion), Tom McAnimal (tenor banjo), Kieran Mo O'Hagan (guitars, vocals) and Colm O'Maonlai (whistles). Their first album, *Snake* (1994) had three traditional songs, including a version of the 1798 ballad 'Roddy McCorley', with most of the other material original songs by MacGowan. Their second album, *The Crock of Gold* (1997), is a mixture of Irish traditional, country and 1950s rock 'n' roll.

Through his work with the Pogues and the Popes, MacGowan has brought traditional music and song to a wider audience as well as penning classic songs, some of which have grown in popularity since their release. 'A Fairytale of New York' provides the most obvious example of the latter, a song which is widely known and has been covered by a number of artists, including **Christy Moore** and **Phil Coulter**. From his great drinking songs like 'Sally McLennane' through love songs like 'Broad Majestic Shannon' and political songs like 'Birmingham Six', MacGowan's lyrics have covered a broad range of themes. His work has also breathed new life into much of the old traditional material, often using sections of traditional tunes as riffs in song arrangements or giving a more contemporary, punk feel to old songs. Although his work has been uneven, the Pogues' albums *Red Roses for Me* (1984), *Rum, Sodomy and the Lash* (1985) and *If I Should Fall from Grace with God* (1988) represent MacGowan at his best in terms of singing, songwriting and new interpretations of traditional material. Even since his heyday with the Pogues, MacGowan has retained his lyrical powers and can still write witty and poignant songs, as, for example, in 'St. John of God's' on his album with the Popes, *The Crock of Gold* (1997). His own book with Victoria Mary Clarke, *A Drink with Shane MacGowan* (London, 2001) provides unique insights into the man and his work. Largely consisting of a series of interviews taped in different places and different times by Clarke, the book reveals MacGowan's honesty and intelligence and many of his comments on music, literature and life display a devious sense of humour.

MacGowan has also been the subject of books and documentaries by others, Joe Merrick's book *London Irish Punk Life and Music...Shane MacGowan* (London, New York, Sydney, 2001) provides discographies and descriptions of his work. The **BBC** broadcast a TV documentary about his life, *The Great Hunger* (first broadcast 1998) and another documentary focused exclusively on the song 'A Fairytale of New York'. A feature-length documentary, *If I Should Fall from Grace: The Shane MacGowan Story* (2001), directed by Sarah Share, had a limited run in cinemas in Ireland and was later televised. Website: www.shanemacgowan.com. See also **England**.

MacMahon, Tony (b. 1939) Accordion player, TV producer and archivist from Turnpike, Ennis, Co. Clare who has played accordion since childhood and was strongly influenced by **Joe Cooley**, a regular visitor to the family home. In the 1960s he played with many fine musicians, including **Séamus Ennis** and **Bobby Casey**, with whom he and others recorded the album *Paddy in the Smoke* (1968). In the late 1960s he began working as a freelance presenter of traditional music programmes for **RTÉ**. After joining the RTÉ staff in 1974 he made a particularly valuable contribution to the broadcasting of traditional music, initiating the radio series *The Long Note*. *The Green Linnet* (1974), produced by MacMahon, was a radio programme dealing with references to **Napoleon Bonaparte** in Irish music and song. *The Green Linnet* (1978) was also used as the title for a memorable TV series in which MacMahon and **Barney McKenna** travelled around Europe together playing music. He was later involved in the TV series *The Pure Drop* and *Come West*

Along the Road, a fascinating collection of material on traditional music from the television archives. He recorded a solo album, *Tony MacMahon* (1972), as well as *I gCnoc na Graí* (1985) with **Noel Hill** and a further album with Hill and **sean-nós** singer **Iarla Ó Lionáird**, *Aislingí Ceoil: Music of Dreams* (1993). He is a particularly fine player of traditional slow airs and has recorded a special free reed version (with piano and chamber orchestra) of **Micheál Ó Súilleabháin**'s 'Ah, Sweet Dancer', which can be heard on the latter's *Oileán/Island* (1989). *MacMahon from Clare* (2000) also includes some fine slow airs, among them superb renditions of 'Port na bPúcaí' ('Music of the Ghosts') and 'An Buachaillín Bán' ('The Little Fair-Haired Boy'). The recordings on the album span four decades, and it includes duets with Joe Cooley, Barney McKenna, Peadar Mercier (see **Chieftains**) and others. In an era when jigs and reels tend to be dominant on many traditional recordings, it is refreshing to find an album on which marches, slow airs and set dances make up more than half the tracks. 'Music is the language of passion' is printed on the back of the CD cover, and MacMahon's passion certainly comes through in every note.

MacMahon has been a passionate and articulate commentator on many developments in traditional music since the 1960s and is sceptical about the effects of commercialism and **fusions** with other forms of music. His comments in an RTÉ *Late Late Show* special on the **River of Sound** series led to his delivering a keynote address to a major conference on 'Tradition and Change in Irish Traditional Music', the first **Crossroads Conference** (1996). In his address he posed many relevant questions about the way in which traditional music is being exploited commercially. He was also critical of some aspects of Micheál Ó Súilleabháin's interpretations of traditional music, illustrating his points with an extract from *A River of Sound*. Although retired from RTÉ since 1998, MacMahon still works on television projects related to traditional music. He also (with John Comiskey) devised a unique show called *The Well*, which was performed as part of the Dublin Theatre Festival 2000. Exploring the sources of the shared musical and literary traditions of Ireland, **Scotland**, the **US** and **Canada**, the show featured musicians, singers and dancers from all four countries as well as readings of poetry on themes such as emigration, childhood, slavery and war. See also **Topic Records**.

Mac Mathúna, Ciarán (b. 1925) Influential collector who, in 1955, was appointed a producer in Raidió Éireann (see **RTÉ**) with special responsibility for traditional music, song and folklore. Born in Limerick, he received a Masters degree from University College Dublin with a thesis on Gaelic folksong. Since 1955, he has been central to the revival of traditional Irish music through his broadcasts and his collection of rare recordings. He has travelled extensively around Ireland, recording many musicians and singers who might otherwise have never been heard. His work as a collector has not been confined to Ireland and has taken him around the world to places which have connections with Irish music. In 1997-98, for example, he visited and produced excellent radio programmes on the folk music of **Newfoundland**.

His earliest series of radio programmes on traditional music were *Ceolta Tíre* and *A Job of Journeywork*; both programmes played a vital role in bringing new music and musicians to people all over the country at a time when traditional music was quite localised. He later produced a TV series called *The Humours of Donnybrook* but he is best known in more recent decades for his regular Sunday morning programme, *Mo Cheol Thú*, which has run continuously since 1970 and mixes music, song and poetry with Mac Mathúna's quiet presentation, often including anecdotes about well-known (or little-known!) musicians. While a portion of the material comes from easily obtained recordings, some is also from the RTÉ archive, to which Mac Mathúna himself has been a vital contributor. RTÉ released a CD of music, poetry and song from the programme to mark its 25th anniversary in 1995 (*The Touch of the Master's Hand – Mo Cheol Thú – Ciarán Mac Mathúna*). In 1990 Mac Mathúna was awarded an honorary doctorate by the National University at University College Galway for his work in traditional music and folklore. He has also received two Jacob's Awards for his work in radio and television.

Mac Mathúna, Pádraig (b. 1956) Uilleann piper and flautist, son of **Ciarán Mac Mathúna**. A solo album, *Blas Na Meala: Hives of Honeyed Sound* (1992), included a selection of reels, jigs, hornpipes, slow airs and a waltz. This album has an added attraction in the fact that most of the music is played on a boxwood B♭ set of pipes, with both the wood used and the pitch producing a mellower sound than the normal D pipes, which are also played.

Madden, Joannie (b. 1967) Whistle and flute player from the Bronx, New York whose father, Joe, was a button accordion player from Galway. She won the Senior **All-Ireland** Tin Whistle Championship in 1986 and is a founder member of the group **Cherish the Ladies**. She has also released two solo albums, *A Whistle in the Wind* (1994) and *Song of the Irish Whistle* (1996). The latter includes compositions by **Turlough O'Carolan**, **Seán Ó Riada**, **Paddy Fahy** and Madden herself, as well as traditional tunes.

Mad for Trad Website put together by Frank Torpey and Ciaran O'Connell which sells tutorial CD-ROMs for a range of traditional instruments. The tutorials cater for all levels from beginner to advanced and each CD-ROM provides video, texts, photographs and music notation. Many well-known traditional musicians have made tutorial CD-ROMs with Mad For Trad, including **Cathal Hayden** (fiddle), **Seamus Egan** (flute), Seán Óg Potts (uilleann pipes; see **Potts, Seán**), Brian Finnegan of **Flook!** (tin whistle), Frank Torpey of **Nomos** (bodhrán), Niall Vallely of Nomos (concertina), Karen Tweed (piano accordion; see **England**), Derek Hickey (button accordion; see **De Dannan**), **Karan Casey** (traditional singing), **Lills Ó Laoire** (sean-nós singing) and John Doyle (guitar; **Eileen Ivers** Band and formerly **Solas**). Like **Scoiltrad**, Mad For Trad aims to exploit modern technology in the teaching of Irish traditional music. The website also includes a CD shop which carries a wide range of Irish traditional music albums. Website: www.madfortrad.com.

Maguire, Seán (or McGuire, 1927-2005)   Musician and composer from a musical Co. Cavan family. He played a number of instruments, including the uilleann pipes, but is most famous for his fiddle playing. He was classically trained but played in his father's céilí band from the age of twenty. His style was unique, using a great deal of ornamentation and variation; he often changed the rhythm playfully for a bar or two in the middle of a tune, and employed short stops in the most unexpected places. His playing of the reel 'The Mason's Apron' became famous for the extraordinary variations he played on it.

Maguire learned to play uilleann pipes at the Belfast School of Uilleann Piping. He won many titles for playing music and received an unheard-of 100% mark from all four judges in the 1949 **Oireachtas**. He travelled extensively, playing in the **US** in the 1950s, and was a major figure on the Irish traditional music scene in 60s London. He made numerous solo albums (often with piano accompaniment) as well as recording with many traditional musicians, including **Joe Burke**. Teaching was a great passion for many years, one of his most famous pupils being **Kevin Burke**. On the album *Hawks and Doves of Irish Culture* (1996), Maguire plays uilleann pipes and fiddle, with his pupils playing on nine of the sixteen tracks.

Makem, Sarah (ca. 1898-1985)   Singer from Keady, Co. Armagh who had an extraordinary repertoire of songs, many of them rare folk songs but also popular songs. She first came to widespread public attention through the work of the **BBC** in Ireland during the 1940s and 50s, and her singing of the song 'As I Roved Out' became the signature tune for the famous BBC radio series of the same name. BBC Belfast also made a short film on her life and song, and she was visited by many enthusiastic song collectors from Ireland and further afield, including the Appalachian singer/researcher **Jean Ritchie** (see **Appalachians**). In 1968 she recorded an album, *Sarah Makem: Ulster Ballad Singer*. Much of her repertoire has been sung by her son, Tommy (see **Clancy Brothers and Tommy Makem**), who has also written a number of famous songs, including 'Four Green Fields' (see **Aisling**).

Mandocello   Originally called 'mandolincello', a member of the **mandolin** family developed at the same time as the **mandola**. It is usually bigger than the mandola and is tuned c-g-d-a an octave below it, just as the cello is tuned an octave below the viola. In Irish traditional music it is frequently played by mandolin or **bouzouki** players, but its strings, being lower in pitch, are heavier than those of the bouzouki. Garry Ó Briain of **Buttons and Bows** and **Skylark**, John Doyle of **Solas** and Gerry McKee of **Nomos** all play mandocello. Some beautiful mandocello accompaniments by Garry Ó Briain can be heard on **Brian Hughes**' solo album *Whistlestop* (1997) and the singer **Seán Tyrrell** regularly uses it to accompany his singing.

Mandola (*mandóla*)   An instrument of the **mandolin** family which, along with the **mandocello** and the bass mandolin (a three-stringed instrument with a spike for resting on the floor), was developed in the second half of the 19th century for playing in mandolin orchestras. It has a larger body and a longer neck than the mandolin and is normally tuned the same as a viola, c-g-d-a. Irish traditional players often tune the 'a' string down to 'g' for accompaniment (as opposed to melody playing). Mandola is often played by bouzouki or mandolin players such as **Andy Irvine** and **Alec Finn** and can be heard at its best in the playing of Brian McDonagh of the group **Dervish**. See also **Seán Tyrrell**.

Mandolin (*maindilín*) A small, stringed instrument closely related to the lute. It has four pairs of strings, tuned the same way as a fiddle (g-d-a-e). The mandolin is descended from the mandora, a 16th-century lute, and was first made in the 18th century. Mandolins of varying shapes and stringing were made in Italy in the 18th and 19th centuries, the Neapolitan type being the most common today. This originally had a pear-shaped, wooden body, a fretted neck and four pairs of steel strings played with a plectrum. This type of mandolin quickly became popular beyond Naples and by the late 19th century, Neapolitan mandolins were being mass-produced in Italian and German factories. During the 20th century the mandolin became a common folk instrument, played in Italy, the **US**, Ireland and other countries. Although instruments of a type almost identical to the 18th-century Neapolitan mandolin

Traditional Mandolin

Irish (Flat-Backed) Mandolin

are played by Irish traditional musicians today, the 'flat-backed' variety has also become very popular.

It is assumed that some mandolins were played in Ireland by the first decades of the 20th century, but their early history in traditional music has not been traced in detail. The banjo-mandolin (see **Banjo**) was certainly used in céilí bands from the 1930s. The mandolin has been popular with traditional musicians since the 1970s, a development closely associated with the introduction of the **bouzouki** to Irish music. Other related instruments, such as the **mandola, mandocello** and **cittern**, have risen in popularity with the bouzouki and the mandolin over the last two decades. The finest Irish maker of these instruments in recent decades is Joe Foley of Rathfarnham, Co. Dublin. Although the mandolin is sometimes used for rhythmic accompaniment to dance tunes, it is more commonly played as a melody instrument. Mike Flanagan of the **Flanagan Brothers** became famous in the 1920s and 30s mainly as a banjo player, but started on the mandolin like many banjo players of the time. Accomplished players such as Paul Kelly, **Mick Moloney**, **Jimmy**

Crowley, **Martin Murray** and Liam Kennedy of the Tallafornia Mandolin Band, can play beautiful renditions of Irish dance tunes on the mandolin. Eugene Sands of the **Sands Family**, who died in 1975, was also a fine player. The instrument has also been popular with ballad groups such as The **Wolfe Tones** and has been effectively used by younger bands such as **Solas** and **Kíla**. An electric version is often played for 'plugged in' (as opposed to acoustic) sessions. Pádraig Carroll's tutor *The Irish Mandolin* (Dublin, 1991) is accompanied by a CD.

Maoin Cheoil an Chláir **(Clare Music Education Centre)** Set up in 1993 and based in Erasmus Smith House in Ennis, Co. Clare, the centre offers over thirty courses of study on classical and traditional music. It was financed by LEADER, a European Community project for the combat of rural decline, and is run as a limited company and a registered charity. Its four shareholders are Rural Resource Development Ltd., Co. Clare Vocational Education Committee, the Sisters of Mercy and Clare County Council. As well as providing a wide range of lessons on traditional and classical instruments, the centre runs a traditional music recital series and has entered prize-winning groups in national music competitions. Its students have also achieved high results in the Leaving Certificate and other music examinations. The first director of the school was Andrew Robinson (1993-98), who was succeeded by Collette Moloney. Website: homepage.tinet.ie/~mcac.

March (*Máirseáil*) Marches are among the oldest forms of traditional music, and although it is difficult to date the earliest of them accurately, some could date from the late 16th and early 17th centuries or earlier. The tune to which P. J. McCall put his lyrics 'Follow Me up to Carlow' is traditionally held to have been the clan march of the O'Byrnes of Gabhaill Ragnaill, first performed in the time of Fiach MacHugh O'Byrne (d. 1597). Other marches, such as 'Allisdrum's March' and 'The Battle of Aughrim' commemorate events in the 17th century (1647 and 1691 respectively), and there is little reason to doubt that they were composed around the time of the

The Fingal March (slow march)

events that they commemorate. The latter two marches, in fact, were played by pipers of the 19th century as elaborate descriptive pieces incorporating depictions of various stages of battle, including the sounds of battle and laments for the slain. 'Brian Boru's March' is reported to have been played in a similarly dramatic and evocative style by the harper, Patrick Byrne (d. 1863). A detailed description, published in *The Emerald* of New York in 1870, can be read in **Francis O'Neill**'s *Irish Minstrels and Musicians* (1913, pp. 81-82).

Irish Marches are found in a variety of time signatures; 2/4, 4/4 and 6/8 are the most common, but examples can also be found in 3/4 and 9/8. **Breandán Breathnach** noted that a number of Irish marches were adapted as dance tunes, pointing to 'O'Sullivan's March' and 'Allisdrum's March' as tunes which can still be heard played as jigs in Munster. Although they are not commonly heard in sessions, marches continue to be recorded by some groups and individual musicians, including **Horslips**, whose reworking of 'O'Neill's March' into the rock song 'An Dearg Doom' was a hit in the 1970s. Some traditional musicians still compose marches for special ceremonies, one example being 'The Walk of the Fiddler's Bride', a wedding march composed by **Darach de Brún** and recorded by him on **Oisín**'s first album in 1976.

Masterson, Declan Dublin-born multi-instrumentalist who played uilleann pipes with **Moving Hearts** and **Patrick Street** and has also made three solo albums. On his 1993 album, *Tropical Trad*, he plays uilleann pipes, low whistles, tin whistle, bouzouki, guitar, keyboards, bodhrán and percussion. The material on the album is a mixture of traditional and original material, including Masterson's 'Tropical Trad', which uses samba rhythms. His 'Full Moon, Trail of Tears and Keep Her Going' is an evocative piece dedicated to the Choctaw Indian nation of North America, who sent money to alleviate the suffering of the Irish during the **Great Famine**. The album fully displays Masterson's talents as a multi-instrumentalist, arranger and composer.

Mayock, Emer Young flautist, whistle and uilleann pipes player born in Ross West, Co. Mayo. On her solo album, *Merry Bits of Timber* (1996), she plays flute and tin whistle and is accompanied by Donal Siggins (mandola, guitar), Kevin O'Connor (fiddle), Eamonn O'Leary (guitar), Robert Harris (bodhrán, djembe) and **Mick Kinsella** (harmonica). The album consists of a mixture of traditional and original tracks, most of the latter composed by Mayock herself. More recently she has performed with the **Afro**

Emer Mayock

Celts, and released her second solo album, *Playground* (2001), on which she plays flute, whistle, uilleann pipes, fiddle and cello. The majority of the tunes are her own compositions, wonderfully arranged with fine accompaniments by Donal Siggins (guitar, bouzouki, mandola, harmonium) and Robert Harris (percussion). There are also guest performances by Aidan Brennan (guitar), Mick Kinsella (harmonica, concertina) and Greg Anderson (bass). Mayock's original music shows great talent as a composer, and there are also two original tunes by Donal Siggins, two by Grey Larsen, three traditional tunes and a Breton set (see **Brittany**) made up of a composition by flute player Jean-Michel Veillon and a Breton tune of unknown origin. Website: www.emermayock.com.

Mazurka (*Masúrca*) A dance in 3/4 time that originated in Poland and spread throughout Europe around the mid-18th century, becoming immensely popular. In the 19th century mazurkas were composed by some classical composers (including Chopin) and became popular in Ireland. The rise in popularity of the mazurka in Ireland seems to be closely associated with the spread of **set dancing** from the early 19th century. 'The Mazurka Set' was a universally popular dance, and although it was probably danced to mazurkas (in 3/4 time) originally, it is now danced to reels (in 4/4 time) or jigs (in 6/8 time). It is known as the 'mazolka' in Monaghan, the 'mazorka' or 'mazourka' in Donegal, the 'myserks' in Clare and the 'mesarts' in Kerry. The mazurka, although similar to the **waltz**, differs from the latter in having a strong accent on the second or third beat of each measure. In a waltz, the emphasis is on the first beat. Well-known Irish mazurkas include 'Sonny's Mazurka', **'Charlie Lennon**'s Mazurka' and '**John Doherty**'s Mazurka', the latter two named after traditional fiddlers. The great Clare piper **Willie Clancy** recorded 'Garret Barry's Mazurka', named after a 19th-century piper (see **Barry, Garret**). Mazurkas make up a very small proportion of the contemporary traditional repertoire but can still be heard occasionally. Today the mazurka survives as a couple dance rather than a set; the tune type is particularly popular with some Donegal fiddlers.

Garret Barry's (mazurka)

McCall, Patrick Joseph (1861-1919) Dublin-born merchant and poet whose lyrics often reflect an interest in the south Leinster region from where his family came. He wrote the lyrics of many famous ballads, including 'The Marching Song of Feagh McHugh' (better known as 'Follow Me up to Carlow', recorded by **Planxty**), 'Boolavogue', 'The Lowlands Low' and 'Kelly of Killane'. His father, John (1822-1902), collected many ballads (words but not music) in the Carlow-Wexford region in the late 19th century and probably began the collection of fourteen volumes of **broadside**s under Patrick Joseph's name in the National Library, Dublin.

McCann, Jim (b. 1944) One of Ireland's longest-standing folk singers who gave up his studies in medicine in the early 1960s to travel as a musician. He initially performed as a solo singer on the folk club circuit in Britain in 1964. On returning to Ireland in 1965, he joined the Ludlow Trio, one of Ireland's top acts during the **Ballad Boom**. In 1966 they had a hit with a **Dominic Behan** song, 'The Sea Around Us', which reached number one in Ireland. After the trio broke up in 1967, McCann embarked on musicals and had his own television series, 'The McCann Man', as well as touring Ireland and Britain. He joined the **Dubliners** in 1973, initially as a temporary member. He toured and made many albums with the Dubliners but resumed his individual pursuits in 1979. Throughout the 1980s and 90s he recorded many singles (including 'Grace', which stayed in the Irish charts for 36 weeks) and albums and made regular television appearances. In 2002 McCann was invited to tour Europe with the Dubliners, who were celebrating 40 years on the road. Later that year he was diagnosed with throat cancer, which sadly brought a premature end to his singing career. He subsequently released *Seems Like a Long Time* (2004), a compilation of sixteen tracks taken from the albums *McCann* (1971) and *McCanned* (1972), which include a broad range of folk, rock and blues songs. Website: www.jimmccann.ie.

McCarthy, Timmy 'The Brit' Dancing master (he also plays melodeon and accordion) born in London whose grandfather was Irish. He moved to Cork in the mid-1960s at the age of 21 and became involved in organising the Folk Club circuit, through which he met many of the finest traditional musicians from all over Ireland. After meeting Dan O'Connell, owner of a famous music/set dancing pub in Knocknagree, **Sliabh Luachra**, McCarthy became a regular visitor to Sliabh Luachra and developed a great love of **set dancing**. He began to piece together various set dances from the Cork/Kerry area by talking to people who knew the old dances and was soon teaching set dancing throughout Cork and Kerry. He preferred the old-style approach to dance music that he found in the region, with just one or two musicians playing for the sets rather than a **céilí band**. Widely regarded as a major figure in the revival of set dancing, McCarthy still teaches in the Cork/Kerry area where he lives, but has taught set dancing all over the world and is a regular visitor to France and Germany. He was the first secretary/director of the Cork Folk Festival. *Timmy 'The Brit' McCarthy's Set Dances of Cork and Kerry* (2002) is a special CD of tunes for set dancers played by the Donncha Lynch Band.

McCarthy Family   Tommy McCarthy (1929-2000) from Kilmihil, Co. Clare played concertina, whistle, uilleann pipes and fiddle. He started to play tin whistle at the age of nine and subsequently took up the fiddle and the concertina, visiting the home of the famous **Elizabeth Crotty** in his teens. He purchased his first set of uilleann pipes in Dublin from **Leo Rowsome** before emigrating with his family to London (where he worked as a carpenter) in 1952. He played with many of the most famous traditional musicians in London, including **Bobby Casey**, **Felix Doran**, **Willie Clancy** and **Micho Russell**. He toured in Britain and the US as well as playing on a number of film scores. He was also a co-founder of the London Piper's Club in 1980. McCarthy released a solo album, *Sporting Nell,* in 1997 on which he plays concertina, whistle and uilleann pipes. His daughters Jacqueline (concertina; see **Keane, Tommy**), Marion (tin whistle, uilleann pipes) and Bernadette (fiddle, piano) and son Tommy (fiddle) are all accomplished musicians. All of the family moved back to the west of Ireland at different stages in the late 1980s and 90s, with the exception of Tommy junior, who runs a music pub in Boston. Jacqueline, Marion, Bernadette and Tommy junior made *The Family Album* together in 2002. Undoubtedly among the most talented of traditional music families, all four of the McCarthys are also married to musicians.

McConnell, Cathal (b. 1944)   Flute and whistle player and singer from Ballinaleck, Co. Fermanagh, brother of **Mickey McConnell** and a founder member of the Scottish group the **Boys of the Lough** in 1967. He also played whistle and flute on the album *For the Sake of Old Decency* (1993) with singer **Len Graham** and has produced a CD tutor for the tin whistle. Although it took many years for him to make a solo album, it finally arrived in 2000, appropriately titled *Long Expectant Comes at Last*, and includes both original and traditional material.

McConnell, Mickey (b. 1947)   Singer/songwriter who has written many perceptive songs on contemporary issues. These include 'Only Our Rivers Run Free' (recorded by a number of people, most notably **Planxty**) and 'Peter Pan and Me' (title track on his own 1991 album), portraying the ideology of the late 1960s Civil Rights Movement in Northern Ireland. A brother of **Cathal McConnell**, he also plays guitar, mandolin and banjo and has lived in Listowel, Co. Kerry for some years. His second album, *Joined Up Writing* (2000), includes 'Absent Friends', which completes the trilogy begun with 'Only Our Rivers' and continued with 'Peter Pan and Me'. His songs have been recorded by many artists, including **Mick Moloney** and **Robbie O'Connell**, **Niamh Parsons** and Ben Sands (see **Sands Family**).

McDermott, Josie (1925-1992)   Flute and whistle player from Coolmeen, near Ballyfarnon, Co. Sligo, close to the Roscommon border. McDermott also sang, lilted and played saxophone and in the 1960s and 70s won **All-Ireland** titles on whistle, alto sax, lilting and flute. He composed a number of tunes, some of which have been recorded by **Marcas Ó Murchú** and **Catherine McEvoy**, and also wrote songs about the countryside around Lough Arrow and Lough Kee. His only recording is the album *Darby's Farewell* (1977).

McEvoy, Catherine (b. 1956) Flute player born in Birmingham, **England**, to parents who had emigrated from Roscommon in the 1940s. She started to learn accordion at the age of thirteen and while still in her teens joined the Birmingham Céilí Band, with whom she initially played piano. Taking up the flute in the early 1970s, she continued to play with the Birmingham Céilí Band all over Ireland and Britain until 1977, when she decided to return to Ireland. From 1984 to 1988 she was a member of **Macalla** and in 1996 released her first solo album, *Catherine McEvoy with Felix Dolan: Traditional Flute Music in the Sligo-Roscommon Style*. The album includes traditional jigs, hornpipes, reels, marches, airs and a fling. There are also original compositions by a number of traditional musicians, including **Vincent Broderick**, **Josie McDermott** and McEvoy herself. The piano accompaniment by American Felix Dolan, who plays on the majority of the tracks, is in the vamping, céilí band style.

McGann, Andy (b. 1928) Fiddler from New York whose parents came from Co. Sligo. McGann learned from and played with **Michael Coleman** and became famous for his own Sligo-style fiddling. One of the most important Irish-American fiddlers of the 20th century, McGann has recorded with a number of different musicians including fiddler Paddy Reynolds, guitarist **Paul Brady** (with whom he made two albums), box player **Joe Burke** and pianist Felix Dolan. His classic tribute to Michael Coleman with Burke and Dolan was re-released on CD as *A Tribute to Michael Coleman* (1994).

McGlynn, Arty Guitarist from Northern Ireland whose seminal *McGlynn's Fancy* (1980) was the first Irish traditional album to focus on the guitar as a melody instrument. McGlynn plays jigs, reels, slow airs and Carolan tunes in a style that makes the guitar sound perfectly natural as a melody instrument. It is perhaps an indication of McGlynn's exceptional talent that this album is still the finest example of 'traditional' guitar-playing available from an Irish player. He also made two innovative albums with **Nollaig Ní Chathasaigh** featuring fine melody playing and accompaniment on electric and acoustic guitars. McGlynn has toured and recorded with some of the finest

Arty McGlynn & Nollaig Ní Chathasaigh

Irish musicians of the past 30 years, including **Paddy Keenan**, **Cathal Hayden**, **Dónal Lunny**, **Matt Molloy**, **Liam O'Flynn**, **Four Men and a Dog** and **Seán Keane**. He was also a founder-member of the group **Patrick Street**. See also **Guitar**.

McGoldrick, Michael (b. 1972)   Manchester-born musician/composer of Irish parentage who plays tin whistle, bodhrán, flute, low whistle, uilleann pipes and guitar. In addition to winning numerous **All-Ireland** championships, McGoldrick won the coveted BBC Radio Two Young Tradition award in 1995. He has recorded a number of albums with various artists including **Dezi Donnelly**, **Arcady**, **Flook!**, **Cappercaillie** and **Lúnasa**. He has also toured with the RTÉ Concert Orchestra, performing excerpts from composer **Shaun Davey**'s *The Brendan Voyage*. His acclaimed first solo album, *Morning Rory* (1996), comprises a combination of traditional and original instrumentals, augmenting McGoldrick's reputation as a musician and composer of new tunes in traditional forms. On his second solo album, *Fused* (2000), he experimented with more modern and, in terms of instrumentation, more diverse arrangements of original as well as traditional music. Among the many guests on the album are Donald Shaw (keyboards, programming, producer) of Cappercaillie, Che Beresford (drums), Ewan Vernal (bass), John Saich (bass), Neil Yates (trumpets), Andy Jones (electric guitar), James Grant (electric guitar), James Mackintosh (drums and percussion) and Johnny Kalsi (tablas). Traditional musicians include Manus Lunny, Dezi Donnelly and **Alan Kelly**, with singers Karen Matheson and **Karan Casey** also contributing. After the innovative approach on *Fused*, McGoldrick returned to a more basic, traditional style with piper **John McSherry** on *At First Light* (2001), although the album includes original music by a number of composers (including McGoldrick and McSherry) as well a traditional tunes. See also **England**.

McGrattan, Paul (b. 1967)   One of Ireland's finest flute players, he was encouraged to take up tin whistle at the age of seven, and later flute, by his uncle Paddy Tracey, a flute player from Co. Galway. He grew up surrounded by musicians, including the **Potts** family and John Egan, the famous Sligo flute player from whom he learned many tunes. *The Frost Is All Over* (1992) features McGrattan playing a fine selection of tunes from a variety of sources, including a set of polkas from the Sligo-Leitrim area, Kerry slides and reels from Donegal. Among others, **Arty McGlynn** (guitar), Noel O'Grady (bouzouki) and Noreen O'Donoghue (piano) accompany McGrattan on the album. Tunes from Donegal feature strongly on the album *Within a Mile of Dublin* (1995), a duo with fiddler **Paul O'Shaughnessy**. A superb second solo album, *Keelwest*, was released in early 2003 and again features Arty McGlynn on guitar with fiddler **Paddy Glackin**, **Gavin Ralston** (keyboards), Noel O'Grady (bouzouki) and **Colm Murphy** (bodhrán) also guesting. McGrattan, O'Shaughnessy, Ralston and O'Grady are all members of the group **Beginish.** McGrattan is also Course Director of the **Ceoltóir** project and has taught with the internet school **Scoiltrad**.

McGuire, Seán See **Maguire, Seán**.

McKenna, Barney (b. 1939) Tenor **banjo** player from a musical family in Trim, Co. Meath. He started to learn the mandolin at the age of five from his uncle Jim. Affectionately known as 'Banjo Barney from Donnycarney', he was the first player of the tenor banjo in the 1960s to bring the instrument to prominence in the playing of Irish dance music. His banjo playing was a central element of the **Dubliners**' sound, especially in their instrumental numbers. He made a memorable TV series with **Tony MacMahon** called *The Green Linnet* (1978), in which the duo travelled around Europe playing music. Tony MacMahon's album *MacMahon from Clare* (2000) includes three tracks with Barney McKenna.

McKenna, Joe and Antoinette Husband-and-wife duo from Dublin. Antoinette, who plays the harp and sings, is a sister of **Mary Bergin**, with whom she and Joe tour regularly. Joe, who plays uilleann pipes as well as tin whistle, low whistle and accordion, grew up in Thomas Street, where the **Dublin Pipers' Club** was located, and was a pupil of **Leo Rowsome**. Both of the McKennas have also composed original music, Joe winning the 'New Irish Music Composer' award in 1993. Since 1976, when they were asked by **Shanachie Records** to record and tour in the **US**, the McKennas have recorded a number of albums and toured extensively, including periods in Europe and **Australia**. Joe also played with **De Dannan** for about eight months. Most of their early material is purely traditional in style and arrangement.

After 1989, when they recorded *Magenta Music*, a more experimental album of contemporary and traditional music, they formed a group called Slua Nua. Originally called Sean Nua, the group (who made one album) also included Gerry O'Donnell (flute, whistle, clarinet, backing vocals), Joe McHugh (bouzouki, uilleann pipes, keyboards, backing vocals), Joe Partridge (guitar, backing vocals) and Mario n'Gomo (percussion). Since 1996, Joe has been Shanachie Records' representative in Ireland, scouting for new talent and playing an important role in the promotion and production of CDs for new names, most notably the group **Danú**. He is widely acknowledged as one of the finest uilleann pipers of his generation, although his album, *The Irish Low Whistle* (2001), demonstrates a natural talent for that instrument as well. It is a fine collection of traditional and original tunes on which Joe is accompanied by Antoinette (harp), John Doyle (guitar, see **Solas** and **Eileen Ivers**), Donnachadh Gough of Danú (bodhrán) and Trevor Hutchinson of **Lúnasa** (bass), among others. The tracks on which he is joined by Mary Bergin on tin whistle are gems of recorded whistle music, the two whistles beautifully interwoven on tunes such as 'Contentment Is Wealth/The Mooncoin Jig'. *The Best of Joe and Antoinette McKenna* was released in 1997 and the couple, who live in Roundwood, Co. Wicklow, have a long-standing involvement with teaching and performing sessions with local children. Joe is also a pipe maker, and initially learned his craft from Matt Kiernan in Dublin. For many years he and others members of his family made pipes in Thomas Street, and Joe plays a set of pipes which he made himself.

McKenna, John (1880-1947) Co. Leitrim-born flute player who made commercial recordings in the **US** during the 1920s and 30s. He stands out as a commercially successful flute player in an era dominated by other instruments, especially the fiddle. McKenna's style was breathy and deliberately accentuated, with sparing use of **rolls**. His tune sets, like those of his contemporary **Michael Coleman**, became part of the standard repertoire. His duets with the fiddler **James Morrison** are considered to be among the best musical collaborations of the period. He can be heard on *John McKenna: His Original Recordings* (1986), produced by **Harry Bradshaw** and **Nicholas Carolan**.

McKeown, Susan (b. 1969) Singer/songwriter from Brittas, Co. Dublin who studied English and philosophy at University College Dublin. She has lived in New York since 1990. A fine singer of traditional songs, she also writes her own songs,

Susan McKeown

which she has performed and recorded with her band, the Chanting House. Much of the original material veers more towards rock than traditional, although McKeown is at home singing in different styles and her arrangements of traditional songs show a taste for innovation and experimentation.

On her album *Prophecy* (2002) with the Chanting House she is joined by singer Natalie Merchant on a couple of tracks, one of which is McKeown's setting to music of the Emily Dickinson poem 'Because I Could Not Stop for Death'. The Chanting House share Mc Keown's versatility, and toured in 2000 playing a mixture of original rock songs and material from the singer's almost exclusively traditional album, *Lowlands* (2000). The album features guest musicians from Ireland, **England**, China, India, Mali, Norway, Iceland and the **US**. Three of the songs are in Irish, and there are traditional songs in English which come from Ireland, **Scotland** and England. The only non-traditional song on the album is **Liam Weldon**'s searing 'Dark Horse on the Wind', sung with great strength and passion by an unaccompanied McKeown. There is a version of the epic 'Lord Baker' which features atmospheric percussion as well as delicately interwoven accompaniment and instrumental breaks on kora (a West African harp-lute, played by Mamadou Diabate), clarinet and a variety of other instruments. Another unusual arrangement is 'The

Lowlands of Holland', with a sparse and high-pitched accompaniment on banjo (Eamonn O'Leary) tastefully combined with the sound of the erhu (a Chinese fiddle, played by Wang Guowei). On other tracks there are contributions from **Joannie Madden**, **Lúnasa** and, among others, Scottish fiddler John Cunningham.

McKeown toured the US with Cunningham, and their album, *A Winter Talisman* (2001), features a mixture of songs in English and Scots Gaelic as well as original tunes and poetry by Cunningham. They are accompanied by Aidan Brennan on guitar, and the album further displays McKeown's versatility. She has also composed, with Lúnasa, music for a US production of the Marina Carr play, *The Bog of Cats*. It is perhaps a significant indication of her standing in New York that she was asked to sing a lament for the *New York Times* documentary, *Portraits of Grief* (2002), which marked the first anniversary of the September 11th attacks on the US. *Sweet Liberty* (2004) is sparser in its arrangements than much of the earlier material and includes collaborations with musicians from Northern Mali (who accompany an English traveller song 'Eggs in Her Basket') and a Mexican mariachi band (on call and response songs from both the Irish and the Mexican traditions). Other guests include Joannie Madden, **Flook** and fiddler Dee Armstong of **Kíla**, and the material is mostly traditional songs from Ireland, including 'Sweet Liberty' (usually called 'The Emigrant's Farewell'), 'The Winter It Is Past' (see **Burns, Robbie**) and 'Fair Annie', learned from the singing of **Paddy Tunney**. Website: www.house-of-music.com/susan.

McNally, James English-born low whistle, bodhrán and accordion player who has won many **All-Ireland** titles and recorded with the **Pogues** and the **Afro Celts**. He also released a solo album, *Everybreath* (1996), on which he mainly plays low whistle. The title of the album comes from the Sting song 'Every Breath You Take', which is played as an instrumental piece on the album. The album consists largely of song airs (both traditional and contemporary) but there are four original pieces as well. Synthesisers and programmed drums are widely used in the arrangements. There are also fine renditions of 'Black Is the Colour' and the **Finbar Furey** classic 'The Lonesome Boatman', demonstrating McNally's ability to improvise and get a range of different sounds from the low whistle. See also **England**.

McPeakes, The Family of Belfast musicians. Francis J. McPeake (b. 1885) appears in a photograph of uilleann pipers taken at the 1912 **Oireachtas** competition in Dublin (**Francis O'Neill**'s *Irish Minstrels and Musicians*, p. 345). He won first prize in the uilleann pipes learners competition and O'Neill notes: 'The singing of the young man from the north to the accompaniment of his pipe music was a performance highly appreciated' (p. 346). His son Francis (uilleann pipes) and grandson James (harp, fiddle, accordion) formed the core of the family trio the McPeakes, whose recordings include the albums *The McPeake Family* (1962), *Introducing the McPeake Family* (1965) and *Jug of Punch* (1975). The family are well known and highly regarded as teachers of traditional music in Belfast, and have taught and influenced many musicians, including **Seán Maguire**.

McQuaid, Sarah (b. 1966) Music journalist, guitarist and singer. Born in Spain and raised in Chicago, she moved to Ireland in 1994 after many years of visiting and touring here, in the **US** and in France with groups playing traditional music. She published *The Irish DADGAD Guitar Book* (Cork, 1995; see **DADGAD**), an excellent tutor on accompaniment and playing melody. Her solo album, *When Two Lovers Meet* (1997), is a collection of songs (in Irish and English) and instrumentals that reflect her talents as both singer and guitarist.

McSherry, John (b. 1970) Highly talented uilleann piper born in Belfast who, under the influence of groups like **Planxty** and the **Bothy Band**, started playing the pipes at the age of eleven. By the time he was fifteen McSherry had won two **All-Ireland** titles. He became the youngest ever winner of the senior **Oireachtas** piping competition

John McSherry

at at the age of eighteen and went on to headline the Festival Interceltique at Lorient, Brittany. He formed the group **Tamalin** with his brothers and sisters, touring extensively in Europe and the **US** and releasing an unusual and critically acclaimed album with them in 1997. He was a founder-member of **Lúnasa**, recording two fine albums with them in 1998 and 1999, but left to record and tour with **Dónal Lunny**'s band, Coolfin. With **Michael McGoldrick** he returned to more traditional roots for *At First Light* (2001), which also includes original compositions by both musicians. McSherry has recorded with many other musicians, including **Clannad**, Nancy Griffiths, **Sharon Shannon** and Rod Stewart. Website: www.johnmcsherry.com.

Melodeon (*Mileoidean*) See **Accordion**.

Midnight Court, The An exuberant comic poem written in Irish by Brian Merriman (ca. 1749-1805) from Co. Clare in the late 1700s. Merriman, the illegitimate son of a country gentleman, was both a poet and a musician. His poem, over a thousand lines long, is an often bawdy celebration of love and sexuality. It has long been regarded as one of the great works to survive from that period and has been translated into English many times. The contemporary singer/composer **Seán Tyrrell** was for many years fascinated by the poem and, inspired by the musicality of its metre, set the entire poem to traditional-style music. Tyrrell's 'traditional opera' *The Midnight Court* was first staged by the Druid Theatre during the Galway Arts Festival, 1992. In addition to Tyrrell's own singing and playing it featured a number of singers, male and female, from Galway, Fermanagh and Leitrim. Some were singers in the traditional style but others, such as Bernie Mahony, were country singers; the show also featured singer and flute player Seán Keane (see **Keane Family**). *The Midnight Court* was highly successful and was subsequently performed in other parts of Ireland during 1992 and 1993.

Milwaukee Irish Fest Irish cultural festival held annually during the third weekend of August. With a wide range of activities and an annual attendance of over 125,000 people, it is renowned as the world's largest Irish cultural festival. The first Irish Fest was held in 1981 under the direction of Ed Ward, a central figure in the foundation and development of the festival. Since 1987, the Irish Fest Summer School has provided a week of courses in music, song, dance, Irish language, culture and arts and crafts. The Summer School runs for a week before the festival at the University of Wisconsin-Milwaukee. While the majority of classes and workshops are in musical instruments, dance and song, other subjects covered include genealogy, archaeology and Irish language. Top class teachers from Ireland and the **US** are employed in the Summer School and there is a selection of courses available for children. One of the children's courses involves the rehearsal of a drama which is presented at the Irish Fest.

The Irish Fest takes place on a large (85-acre) and scenic permanent festival site on the shores of Lake Michigan. The site has fifteen stages of various sizes, and from Thursday evening through to Sunday night there is a continuous programme of music and dance on each stage. Performers have included **Danú**, **Sliabh Notes**, **Different Drums of Ireland**, the **John Whelan** Band, the **Darach De Brún** Band and **Kíla**. There is also a **Gaeltacht**/Cultural Village area which includes an archive, a genealogy tent, a cinema and tents for **Waltons**, the Dublin-based music company, and *Irish Music* magazine. There is a special Children's Stage and a Children's Area where various activities, including crafts, take place. There is also a retail area, and food and drink are available on the site. Sports activities include rugby, hurling, currach racing and Gaelic football. The Irish Fest also hosts the US Tug of War championships. A special Sunday Liturgy for Peace and Justice is attended by more than 10,000 worshippers annually. The Irish Fest is truly a family event, with activities and entertainment for all ages throughout each day and night. Although a full-time executive director, Jane Anderson, has been employed by the festival since 1992, all others who work in the festival are volunteers, and whole families from the Milwaukee area can be found working in the festival every year.

Irish Festivals Inc., which runs the Milwaukee Irish Fest, also opened the Irish Fest Center in 1998. The Center houses the John J. Ward Irish Music Archives, a collection of more than 30,000 sound recordings and other music items related to Irish and Irish-American music. The Center also provides a year-round facility dedicated to Irish-related activities, including concerts, workshops, rehearsals and Irish language lessons. In 1993, the Irish Fest Foundation was established, providing grants to organisations and individuals to promote the development of community service, excellence in Irish music and drama, and to support the needs of the Irish community in the US and Ireland. The Foundation is financed by a portion of the festival's revenues. In 2001 Galway became a sister city of Milwaukee, with the Irish Fest of that year hosting over 70 representatives from Galway, including those involved in government, business and tourism. Website: www.irishfest.com.

Minstrels From the 12th to 17th centuries, a general name for various professional entertainers which often referred to secular musicians but could also cover jugglers, acrobats and storytellers. Some minstrels performed songs, often of their own composition, or dance music, but very little minstrel music has survived from the Middle Ages as most of it was transmitted orally. The English word 'minstrel' is derived from the Old French *menestral* or *ministral*, and one of the most interesting references to minstrels in medieval Ireland comes from the Statutes of Kilkenny (1366), the original texts of which were in French. These notorious statutes, which attempted to keep the English and Irish races in Ireland separate, have been described as a form of apartheid (all quotes from the statutes are taken from *Irish Historical Documents* edited by W. Curtis and R. B. McDowell, London 1943, pp. 55-56). Irish minstrels were forbidden to 'come among the English' and no English were allowed to 'receive or make gift to them'. Any English person who broke this law was to be imprisoned and fined at the King's will; Irish minstrels who broke it were to be imprisoned, fined and have 'the instruments of their minstrelry forfeited to the King'. The reason given for introducing these laws was that 'the Irish minstrels coming among the English spy out the secrets, customs and policies of the English whereby great evils have often happened'. While the document uses the general term 'minstrels' throughout, a more specific definition of the different types of performer who are covered by the term 'Irish minstrels' is provided: '…Irish minstrels, that is to say tympanours, poets, story-tellers, babblers, rymours, harpers or any other Irish minstrels…'. (For 'tympanours' see **Timpán**; for poets see **Bard**; for harpers see **Harp**.)

Irish poets, harpers and pipers were targeted by further legislation during the reign of Queen **Elizabeth I** (1533-1603), but the Gaelic social system which supported these minstrels collapsed in the wake of the English army's victory at the Battle of Kinsale (1601). In the 19th century, the term minstrel was used in the **US** for a member of a troupe of entertainers, usually white men made up as blacks, that presented songs, dances, jokes and comic skits. Many of the 19th-century US minstrels were Irish, or had Irish ancestors. They included Joel Walker Sweeny, who was born in Virginia to a family which traced its roots to Co. Mayo. Sweeny greatly increased the popularity of the **banjo** in the US and Europe and has been controversially associated with the addition of the fifth string to the banjo.

Modes Modes, often referred to as church modes, make up a system of scales that were used in all church music and in most secular music during the Middle Ages. They were supposed to be based on the scales used by the ancient Greeks and, although these were misunderstood, the modes still retain their Greek names. There were twelve modes in use by the 16th century, and the Ionian and Aeolian modes became the modern classical major and minor scales respectively. Between 1600 and 1800, the major and minor scales took over from the church modes in classical music but most folk music continued to be played in other modes. Although the original modes were all based around the eight notes that make up the present scale of C major, modes as they appear in Irish traditional and other forms of music can be transposed into any key.

In each of the groups below the top stave shows the modes in the pitches in which they were originally played with the interval for each mode marked. The pairs of staves below show the transposed modes which are most commonly found in Irish music. (T=tone S=semitone)

Phrygian

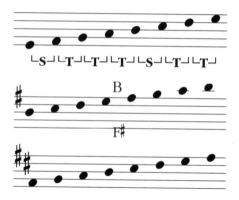

The modern major scale, which corresponds to the Ionian mode, is a heptaton-ic scale (having seven notes within the octave), where the intervals between the notes are T-T-S-T-T-T-S (T=tone, S=semitone). The Aeolian mode differs from the modern harmonic minor scale only in having its seventh note a semitone lower. The intervals in the Aeolian mode are T-S-T-T-S-T-T.

Breandán Breathnach estimated that over 60% of Irish traditional tunes and song airs used the Ionian mode, while only a small amount of tunes in the Aeolian mode exist. Traditional music also uses two of the other modes of the Middle Ages, the Dorian (over 10% of traditional tunes according to Breathnach) and the Mixolydian (15%). The intervals of the Dorian are T-S-T-T-T-S-T, the Mixolydian T-T-S-T-T-S-T. Examples of traditional tunes in the Dorian mode are 'Morrison's Jig' and 'Drowsy Maggie'. Examples of tunes in the Mixolydian mode are 'The Swaggering Jig' and 'Famous Ballymote'.

These modes are often explained in terms of the notes of the C major scale, itself the same as the Ionian mode. Using the notes that make up the C major scale, start-ing on A and finishing on A' (an octave above) gives the Aeolian mode, playing D to D' gives the Dorian mode and G to G' gives the Mixolydian mode. The tone inter-vals in each case correspond to those given above for each mode. This is the way the modes were played originally (using only the notes of the C major scale), but is not very useful when trying to relate to the modes most commonly used in Irish music. The latter are fully illustrated above, including the intervals for each mode and the original modes using C major. The tunes usually range beyond the one octave shown here, but a tune in E Dorian will usually end on E, a tune in D Mixolydian will usually end on D, and so on.

The modal nature of Irish music is better appreciated now than it was 30 years ago; this is especially evident in accompaniment instruments such as bouzouki and guitar. On guitar, for example, many musicians find that **DADGAD**, dropped D (see **Guitar**) and other 'alternative' tunings are better suited to traditional music than standard guitar tuning.

A relatively small number of Irish traditional tunes use a hexatonic (six notes to the octave) or pentatonic (five notes to the octave) scale. They differ from the heptatonic scale in missing its seventh note (hexatonic) or its fourth and seventh notes (pentatonic). 'The Cliffs of Dooneen' is in the hexatonic scale; 'The Dawning of the Day' is in the pentatonic scale.

Molloy, Matt (b. 1947) Master flute player from Ballaghadereen, Co. Roscommon who, in addition to playing with the **Bothy Band**, **Planxty** and the **Chieftains**, has made a number of superb solo albums. He started playing the fife in a local marching band while still at school and was initially taught dance music by his father. His Irish teacher, Paddy Noone, was also an early influence. Molloy went to Dublin to study after secondary school and met many of the musicians with whom he would later tour and record. *Matt Molloy* (1976), his first solo album, is still one of his best. It displays his remarkable skill with breathing and elaborate ornamentation, including **cran**s, a type of ornament normally used by pipers. In 1978 the *Matt Molloy - Paul Brady - Tommy Peoples* album was released and is one of the great traditional albums of recent decades. He has recorded four other solo albums, one in his pub in Westport, Co. Mayo. *Shadows on Stone* (1997) features some of his own compositions as well as a Chinese piece and Irish traditional tunes. Molloy won the **TG4** 'Traditional Musician of the Year' award in 1999. Website: www.mattmolloy.com.

Moloney, Mick (b. 1944) Traditional musician, researcher and university lecturer who grew up in Castletroy, Co. Limerick but has been based in the **US** since 1973. He became interested in folk and Irish traditional music in the 1960s through groups such as the Weavers (see **Seeger, Pete**) and the **Clancy Brothers and Tommy Makem**, and began playing jigs and reels on guitar and the rare six-string tenor banjo. He was a member of the Emmet Folk Group, a predecessor of **Emmet Spiceland**, before joining the **Johnstons**. In 1973 he studied folklore at the University of Philadelphia where he was ultimately awarded a Ph.D., writing a dissertation entitled *Irish Music in America: Continuity and Change*. He has lectured all over the US and **Canada** and has taught as visiting professor at a number of universities, including New York University (2002). He has been involved in the production of many radio and television programmes on Irish music in the US and played an important role in the television series ***Bringing It All Back Home***, for which he performed and was interviewed, as well as acting as consultant. Moloney continues to perform, playing with many famous Irish musicians in America (especially with the group the Green Fields of America) and has recorded many albums, including the solo *Strings Attached* (1980) as well as *There Were Roses* (1985) and *Kilkelly* with **Robbie O'Connell** and Jimmy Keane. His CD *Far from the Shamrock Shore: The Irish-American Experience in Song* (2002) brings together the fruits of Moloney's research and his musicianship. The first of a projected series of albums on Irish-American music, it has seventeen songs with extensive notes on the historical context of each song. An illustrated companion book, *Far from the Shamrock Shore*, detailing the history of Irish immigration, was published concurrently. Website: www.mickmoloney.com. See also **Burns, Robbie**.

Moloney, Paddy (b. 1938) Uilleann piper, tin whistle player and composer born in Donnycarney, Co. Dublin. He is best known as the leader of the **Chieftains**, but has been involved in many other major developments in traditional music. He started on tin whistle but then took up the uilleann pipes under the tutelage of **Leo Rowsome**. In 1951 he attended the first **Fleadh Cheoil** in Mullingar as part of Rowsome's group of fourteen students and in 1952 won his first **All-Ireland** medal. Involved in the founding of the Shannonside and Loch Gamhna Céilí Bands in the 1950s, he also played washboard and ukulele in a skiffle/country/traditional band called the Three Squares. In 1955, he won an **Oireachtas** competition with Barney McKenna (banjo), later to become famous with the **Dubliners**. From its beginnings in 1959, Moloney played an important role in **Ceoltóirí Chualann**, having a tense but fruitful relationship with **Seán Ó Riada**.

In 1956 he met Garech Browne of the Guinness family for the first time. Browne's company **Claddagh Records** played an essential role in the Chieftains' success in their early years, with Moloney becoming the full-time managing director of the company in 1968. The group, together and individually, recorded many albums with Claddagh. Moloney also produced albums by other traditional players, including *Ó Riada's Farewell* (1971) and the classic *The Liffey Banks* (1972) by Dublin fiddler **Tommy Potts**. He was also a founding member of **Na Píobairí Uilleann** in 1968.

Moloney's flair for composition and arrangement (including an Oscar-winning film score) found its greatest expressions through his work with the Chieftains, but he has also done much recording without the group. He plays a number of solo tracks on the piping album *The Drones and the Chanter* (1971) and made the classic *Tin Whistles* (1975) album with **Seán Potts**. He also contributed to Mike Oldfield's *Ommadawn* (1975) and *Five Miles Out* (1982). Apart from collaborations made with the Chieftains, Moloney himself has recorded with the Galician group Milladoiro (1982) (see **Galicia**), Eagles star Don Henley (1982, also with **Derek Bell**), Gary Moore (1988), Mick Jagger (1988) and Van Morrison (1997). He was awarded an honorary doctorate in music by Trinity College Dublin in 1988.

Monroe A group centred around **Mick Hanly** and **Micheál Ó Domhnaill**, formed after the break up of **Skara Brae**. They recorded one album, the excellent *Celtic Folkweave* (1974), which drew heavily on material collected by Micheál from his aunt Néilí of Rann na Feirsde, Co. Donegal and, like *Skara Brae*, was notable for its intricate guitar work. It also featured a fine rendition of a song by **Pentangle** and 'Breton Dances' beautifully played on guitars with simple bass and bodhrán backing. The line-up of musicians on this album included everyone (with the exception of **Paddy Keenan**) who, in 1975, would record the legendary first **Bothy Band** album. Indeed 'An Bothán a Bha'ig Fionnghuala' appeared on *Celtic Folkweave* as Monroe's most popular number before it was made famous by the Bothy Band.

Moore, Barry See **Bloom, Luka**.

Moore, Christy (b. 1945) Singer/songwriter, guitarist and bodhrán player born in Newbridge, Co. Kildare. Although initially interested in rock music, Moore became more interested in folk when he heard Liam Clancy and, subsequently, the **Clancy Brothers and Tommy Makem**. In his mid teens he was singing the Clancys' songs and at the age of sixteen or seventeen met the Co. Roscommon singer John Reilly (see **Travellers**), who introduced him to a wide variety of traditional songs. He worked briefly as a bank clerk, but a bank strike in 1966 forced him to go to England to seek work. He took many different jobs but also became a regular performer on the English folk club circuit and met many Irish, Scottish and English singers, including **Margaret Barry**, **Luke Kelly**, **Ewan MacColl**, **Martin Carthy**, the **Watersons** and Nic Jones. During this period he recorded his first album, *Paddy on the Road* (1969) in London. The album included traditional songs such as 'Tipping it up to Nancy' and 'The Spanish Lady'. Political songs, which were to be an important part of Moore's repertoire throughout his career, were also featured, including 'Avondale' (about Charles Stewart Parnell), 'The Ballad of Jim Larkin' and a Republican song, 'The Belfast Brigade'.

Moore returned to Ireland in 1971 and gathered together some of the finest traditional musicians for the album ***Prosperous*** (1972). The album's success led to the founding of **Planxty**, in which Moore played a central role right up to their re-formation in 2004. He was also a founding member of the traditional/jazz/rock band **Moving Hearts** in 1981, and recorded two albums with them. Between the various periods he spent with these groups, Moore continued to perform and record as a solo artist and after leaving Moving Hearts in 1982 was highly successful in his solo career. He has always shown an interest in political and social developments in Ireland and abroad, supporting the anti-nuclear movement and the IRA H-Block prisoners' demands for political status in 1980-81. As well as publicising the plight of Republican prisoners in such songs as 'Ninety Miles From Dublin', 'On the Blanket' and 'No Time for Love' (on *Moving Hearts*, 1981), he visited the H-Blocks and played many support gigs for the hunger strikers. *Ride On* (1984), one of his best solo albums, included two songs written by Bobby Sands, the first of the ten hunger strikers to die in 1981. Moore has supported many other causes over the years, including travellers' rights and the campaigns to release Nicky Kelly and the Birmingham Six (imprisoned for alleged terrorist activities). He stopped supporting the Provisional IRA's armed strategy after eleven people were killed on Remembrance Sunday, 1987 by an IRA bomb.

Moore's political interests were never confined to Ireland, however, and he is as famous for his sense of humour and his comic songs as for his political views. Indeed *Ride On* provides a good example of the diversity of styles and subject matter in his repertoire. In addition to the two songs by Sands (one of which is a humorous tale of a famous poitín maker, 'McIlhatton') there are songs about John Lennon's ideals for world peace, the contemporary war in El Salvador, the Spanish Civil War (1936-9) and emigration to the **US** during the **Great Famine**. One of Moore's most famous 'talking songs', the blackly humorous 'Lisdoonvarna', is also featured and the fine song from which the album takes its title, 'Ride On', is an evocative portrayal of a person torn between love and serving a cause, written by **Jimmy MacCarthy**. He also recorded a version of the **W. B. Yeats** poem 'The Song of the Wandering Aengus', for which he wrote the melody himself. There is, in fact, little that is 'traditional' about *Ride On*. It is really contemporary folk music but underlines the extent to which many Irish folk singers sing new songs that reflect a concern for contemporary developments, even if their style owes much to older forms.

While Moore's earlier albums include more traditional songs, his interest in contemporary songwriters and arrangements has been evident from the earliest days. *Prosperous*, for instance, features songs by Moore himself, his hero **Woody Guthrie** and contemporary playwright Patrick Galvin alongside the traditional songs. On *Whatever Tickles Your Fancy* (1975) there are contemporary, electric arrangements of traditional songs such as 'Van Diemen's Land', which features Robbie Brennan (drums), **Jimmy Faulkner** (electric guitar), Declan McNelis (bass) and **Kevin Burke** (fiddle). On *Christy Moore* (1976) two African drummers play on Moore's arrangement of the traditional song 'The Limerick Rake'. On *The Iron Behind the Velvet* (1978) the majority of the songs are by contemporary writers, although there are also fine renditions of the traditional songs 'Dunlavin Green' (about the 1798 rebellion) and 'Morrissey and the Russian Sailor'. In 1978 Moore also released *Live in Dublin* with **Dónal Lunny** and guitarist Jimmy Faulkner (both of whom played integral roles on a number of the singer's 'solo' recordings), providing unique backing and solo breaks. Their contributions, as well as the 'live' recording and the choice of songs, make this one of Moore's best albums. There are fine renditions of 'Black Is the Colour', 'Clyde's Bonny Banks' (about a mining disaster), 'Hey Sandy' (about the death of an anti-Vietnam War protester) and 'The Crack Was Ninety in the Isle of Man'.

Moore's next solo album, *The Spirit of Freedom* (1983) is highly political, with many of the songs reflecting Moore's concerns with the deaths of the ten hunger-strikers two years earlier. *The Time Has Come* (1983), *Ride On* (1984), *Ordinary Man* (1985) and *Unfinished Revolution* (1987) all combine songs on social or political issues with love songs and comic songs. After a heart attack in 1987, Moore began to take life a little easier, and his album *The Voyage* (1989) reflects, especially in its title song, a more reflective attitude. *Smoke and Strong Whiskey* (1991), *King Puck* (1993), *Live at the Point* (1995) and *Graffiti Tongue* (1996) all display a continued interest in political issues, with the latter including songs on the Holocaust, Bloody Sunday, the meat industry and the environment. In April 1998 Moore's manager announced the singer's retirement due to illness.

Although he doesn't tour solo on a regular basis anymore, he does the occasional concerts or concert series and has been quite productive since 1998. He recorded a whole series of programmes for **RTÉ** called *Moore Uncovered* (2001), in which he played and spoke about his songs, regularly accompanied by Dónal Lunny and Declan Sinnott. There were guest appearances by various members of his family as well as a host of other musicians, including **Shane MacGowan** and Jimmy Faulkner. His CD *Traveller* (1999) experimented with electronic sounds, using the talents of Leo Pearson, who played keyboards and did programming, mixing, engineering and production for the album. The cover of *Traveller* featured a picture of the singer John Reilly, a great influence on Moore. Moore returned to a more acoustic sound for *This Is the Day* (2001) and *Live at Vicar Street* (2002, with Dónal Lunny and Declan Sinnott). His book, *One Voice: My Life in Song* (London, 2000) takes an interesting approach to what could loosely be termed autobiography. The book contains the lyrics of over 200 songs (traditional and original). Alongside the songs are Moore's reminiscences on the songs themselves, his life, his music, songwriters, social and political events and other subjects. The book is full of insights into Moore, his music and his influences.

Christy Moore

The Box Set 1964-2004 (2004) has over 100 songs selected and annotated by Moore from 40 years of recordings. This is an extraordinary piece of work and is not simply a compilation of previous recordings. Many of the pieces (which include spoken comments on subjects as diverse as Margaret Thatcher, poitín and **Pierce Turner**) have not been released before. Of the songs which were previously released, there are different recordings or different versions. There are many gems here, including a spoken piece entitled 'I Love the Way Pierce Turner Sings' and a version of Turner's 'Among the Wicklow Hills' which, unlike the version Moore recorded on *Ride On*, sticks faithfully to Turner's original lyrics. There is a recitation of Samuel Beckett's 'Poor Old Earth' which starts and finishes with a sung verse of 'Love Is Pleasing', the melody of which is played throughout the recitation. There are many songs of social and political comment, including Moore's song about the Stardust Tragedy, 'They Never Came Home' (which was banned and withdrawn in

1986) and a live recording of 'No Time for Love' which is much longer than the version released on the first Moving Hearts album.

The Irish Recorded Music Association (IRMA) honoured Christy Moore in February 2004 with an award for his remarkable achievements and contribution to Irish music over the last 40 years. In 2004 and 2005 he performed a number of concerts with the reformed Planxty. Website: www.christymoore.com. See also **Burns, Robbie**.

Moore, Thomas (1779-1852) Dublin-born poet and one of few Catholics to be educated at Trinity College Dublin, where he befriended Robert Emmet, a hero of the 1798 Rebellion. In 1808 he published the first volume of his *Irish Melodies*, which appeared between 1808 and 1834 in ten successive volumes. Moore was a friend of **George Petrie** and used many of the melodies published by **Edward Bunting** for his songs, 124 in all. He was accused of tampering with the airs that Bunting had collected from Irish harpers, but justified this by saying that some changes were essential in changing a harp air into a song. He also argued that many of Bunting's airs would not have become so widely known and appreciated if they had not been used for his songs. Although Moore has been criticised in recent times for his appropriation of traditional material, he was regarded by many in his time as Ireland's national poet and played an important role in forging an Irish national identity in the 19th century. He lived in England from 1800 until his death and, through his songs, brought Irish music to a much broader audience. Many of his songs – including 'The Minstrel Boy', 'Believe Me If All Those Endearing Young Charms', 'The Last Rose of Summer' and 'The Harp that Once Through Tara's Halls' – remain popular today. See also **Behan, Dominic** and **Nationalist/ Republican Song**.

Morrison, James (1893-1947) Fiddler from Co. Sligo who emigrated to Boston in 1915, after an early career as a dancing and Irish language instructor for the Gaelic League. There he became famous for his recordings of traditional music, and in a career that lasted from 1921 to 1936, he was involved in numerous solo, duet and group recordings. He was one of the most technically brilliant and innovative fiddlers of his time, and is still held in high regard by traditional musicians such as Frankie Gavin of **De Dannan**. Along with **Michael Coleman**, also

James Morrison

a Sligo-born fiddler, Morrison had an enormous influence on fiddling and the development of Irish traditional music in the first half of the last century. *James Morrison: The Professor* (1989) is a double cassette of reissues of Morrison's original 78s (recorded 1921-36), remastered by **Harry Bradshaw**. A website dedicated to Morrison, www.morrison.ie, was created and is maintained by the Riverstown, Co. Sligo branch of **Comhaltas Ceoltóirí Eireann**, which also hosts the annual James Morrison Traditional Music Festival.

Mouth Music Mouth music or, in Scots Gaelic, *puirt a beul*, is a form of singing which, like Irish **lilting**, can use vocables or nonsense words; unlike Irish lilting, however, these are usually interspersed with recognisable lyrics. It is used to provide music for dancing and for teaching tunes. One of the most famous recordings made by the **Bothy Band** is a beautifully harmonised version of 'Fionnghuala', a piece of mouth music from the Hebrides, off the west coast of Scotland. The contemporary Scottish group **Cappercaillie** draw their inspiration from *puirt a beul* and have recorded a considerable amount of mouth music over the years.

The duo Talitha MacKenzie (vocals) and Martin Swan (instruments and arrangements) released an album entitled *Mouth Music* (1990) which consists mostly of traditional Scottish *puirt a beul* songs arranged in a highly unusual style. The sources of all the traditional songs are acknowledged and lyrics (with English translations) are given, making the content more accessible for those who do not understand Scots Gaelic. See also **Scotland**.

Mouth-Organ (*orgán béil*) See **Harmonica**.

Moving Hearts It is difficult to fully capture the sense of anticipation and excitement in the Irish music community during the first half of 1981, as rumours circulated about the formation of a new trad/rock band involving **Christy Moore** (vocals, guitar, bodhrán), **Dónal Lunny** (electric and acoustic bouzoukis, synthesiser, vocals) and **Davy Spillane** (uilleann pipes, low whistle), among others. When the album *Moving Hearts* was finally released later in the year, it entered the Irish charts at No. 1. In addition to the three musicians mentioned above, the original line-up included Declan Sinnott (lead and acoustic guitars, vocals), Keith Donald (saxophones), Eoghan O'Neill (bass, vocals) and Brian Calnan (drums, percussion). Their songs are generally rock in style, often with jazzy instrumental breaks on saxophone or uilleann pipes, and largely deal with political and social issues. The three instrumentals on the first album ('McBride's', 'Category' and 'Lake of Shadows) display the ability of Lunny, Sinnott and O'Neill to create a new music that is not simply traditional with a rock or jazz-rock backing, but a unique blend of styles.

Moving Hearts were often overtly political; the threat of a nuclear power station in Co. Wexford, rising unemployment and the deepening tensions over Northern Ireland were all confronted. A reduced rate of admission for the unemployed to their weekly gigs in the Baggot Inn indicated that their politics was not empty ideology. With ten I.R.A. hunger strikers dying in the H-Blocks in 1981, their song

'No Time for Love' (on *Moving Hearts*) became almost an anthem for those who were sympathetic to the hunger strikers. They had their critics, and many fans were uncomfortable with their open sympathies for the H-Block prisoners, but they certainly captured the spirit of a traumatic time in Irish politics.

By the time *Dark End of the Street* (1982) was recorded, Matt Kelleghan had replaced Calnan on drums. This second album again shows a concern with political and social issues in Ireland and further afield, including 'Allende', a song about the democratically elected President of Chile, killed in a bloody American-backed coup in 1974. 'What Will You Do About Me' raised a range of issues, including the environment, politics and the media, unemployment, internment without trial and the use of plastic bullets in Northern Ireland. There are also two love songs, one ('Let Somebody Know') written by Declan Sinnott, and two instrumental tracks, including Spillane's 'Downtown'. The 1983 album *Live Hearts* includes live recordings of material from the earlier albums, with a particularly fine version of 'McBride's'. There are also three new songs, with Mick Hanly replacing Christy Moore on lead vocals. One of these, 'Open Those Gates' (which deals with the Nicky Kelly case), reflects a continuing interest in controversial political issues. Flo McSweeny became lead vocalist with the Hearts after this, but never recorded an album with them.

In September 1984 Moving Hearts decided to disband. Despite their popularity in Ireland and Europe, they were unable to survive economically. Their farewell concert, 'The Last Reel', in the National Stadium in Dublin was an extraordinary night, with all three lead singers taking part and Declan Masterson playing a second set of uilleann pipes. The Hot Press/Stag Awards recognised the band's achievement

Moving Hearts

by giving them a special award 'For Brilliant Musicianship, for Live Performances of Extraordinary Intensity and for Giving Their All'. But there was more to come. *The Storm*, a purely instrumental album, with Greg Boland on guitar, Noel Eccles on percussion and both Spillane and Masterson playing pipes, was released in 1985. It was a seminal album that received great critical acclaim. The opening track, 'The Lark', consists of a mixture of seven traditional and original tunes played as one set lasting for 13 minutes. There are original compositions by Spillane, Lunny and O'Neill, and much of the material has unusual, syncopated rhythms. Moving Hearts did perform the occasional big concert in subsequent years, for example in College Green in 1994 as the final act for Dublin's celebration of the first May Day Public Holiday. In 2003 they released a 13-track compilation entitled *Donal Lunny's Definitive Moving Hearts*, which includes 'McBride's', 'Allende', 'Hiroshima, Nagasaki, Russian Roulette' and other previously released material, as well as two previously unreleased instrumental tracks recorded in 1985.

The group has influenced many young musicians, composers and songwriters. Cork singer/songwriter **John Spillane** and the innovative band **Kíla** are among the many who acknowledge this influence. Although much of their music was not traditional, there can be no doubt that traditional elements formed an integral part of Moving Hearts' sound. They also stimulated a great interest in traditional music, especially piping, among young people. Finally their songs are a testament to a difficult period in Irish history, a time of great social and political upheaval.

Moynihan, Johnny The man who introduced the **bouzouki** into Irish music in the late 1960s, a multi-instrumentalist (he also plays whistle, harmonium and fiddle) and singer/songwriter. He was a founder-member of **Sweeney's Men** and later played with **Planxty** and **De Dannan**. He has toured as a solo artist and with others in Ireland, Europe, America and Africa.

Mulqueen, Ann (b. 1945) Singer born in Castleconnell, Co. Limerick who comes from a long line of singers on her mother's side. She won the senior song competition at the **All-Ireland** Fleadh in 1959, 1960 and 1961. She sang all over Ireland and for two years in England during the 1960s. In 1969 she moved to the **Gaeltacht** area of Ring in Co. Waterford. The local singer **Nioclás Tóibín** and other members of his family had a strong influence on her singing. Her first solo album, *Kerry's 25th* (1979) was followed by *Mo Ghrása Thall na Déise* (1992) and *Briseann an Dúchas* (2001). The latter includes the singing of her daughters Odi and Sorcha. There are three songs in English and eleven in Irish, and eight of the songs are accompanied. The guest musicians include Garry Ó Briain (guitar, mandolin, mandocello, keyboards), Bruno Staehelin (percussion) and **Danú** members Tom Doorley (flute and whistle) and Ciarán Ó Gealbháin (accordion). Mulqueen has been involved in radio and television for many years and presents her own weekly programme, 'The Open Door' on the local radio station WLR FM.

Mulvihill, Brendan (b. 1954)   Fiddler born in Northampton, England who moved to the **US** with his family, settling in Washington DC. He played with a trio called the Irish Tradition for a number of years, making three albums with them. In 1979, *The Flax in Bloom,* a solo album (on which he was accompanied by **Mick Moloney**), met with critical acclaim. Mulvihill subsequently teamed up with Donna Long (piano); together they made *The Steeplechase* (1989) and *The Morning Dew* (1993) and have toured extensively. Mulvihill is renowned for his technical mastery of the fiddle and his creative approach to traditional music. His father, **Martin Mulvihill**, was also a renowned fiddler. Website: www.brendanmulvihill.com.

Mulvihill, Martin (1919-1987)   Fiddler from Glin, Co. Limerick who emigrated with his family, first to England and in 1965 to the **US**. He also composed many tunes and taught some famous Irish-American fiddlers, including **Eileen Ivers**. The Martin Mulvihill School of Music in New York, which he established, is highly acclaimed for the quality of its teaching. He published over 500 traditional dance tunes as *The Martin Mulvihill Collection* (New York, 1986).

Mummers   The term 'mummer' is derived from the Old French *momeur,* 'to act in a dumb show' and is also related to the Middle German *mummen,* 'a mask, disguise'. Mummers' plays are folk plays which, in the past, were known throughout Europe and are still performed in northern and eastern parts of Ireland around Christmas. Mummers' plays appear to have originated in the Medieval period; King Henry II was entertained by mummers when he spent the Christmas of 1171 in Dublin. In the 17th century mummers were associated with English settlers coming to Ireland during the plantations. The tradition gradually spread among the Gaelic Irish and Ulster Scots population and is still strong in Ulster as well as parts of north Co. Dublin and south Co. Wexford. The mummers would go from house to house and it was believed that they brought good luck with them as they went.

   The mummers' play lasts about ten minutes and involves a mock fight between two heroes, one of whom dies and is resurrected. In Ireland, St. George and St. Patrick are most commonly the heroes who do combat, but sometimes it is St. George and the Turkish or Turkey Champion. This echoes the medieval Crusades to the Holy Land, when Christian armies fought the Turks and other 'infidels'. St. George, the patron saint of England, was said to have come to the assistance of the Crusaders at Antioch in 1098. Sometimes the central heroes vary, with one version of the mummers play in north Co. Donegal using Adolf Hitler and Winston Churchill as the central characters. This play, scripted in 1942, also features Joseph Goebbels (the Nazi propaganda minister), who walks on to revive Hitler when he is slain, with smaller parts for Stalin and Gandhi. This particular mummers' play is, however, an unusual example. In most places, the traditional rhymes and characters are used and the additional characters (usually no more than twelve) often have strange or comic names such as Fiddle Funny, Beelzebub, Dandy Dick or Devil Doubt. Each mummer dresses up and plays the part of a specific character. Historical figures like **Napoleon Bonaparte** and other heroes of Irish history can also be used.

The play itself is usually in verse (hence the term 'rhymers' for the mummers in some places) and can be followed by song, music or dance. In Wexford the mummers do a sword or stick dance believed to have originated in Cornwall. The mummers traditionally visited houses in their area but in recent years can also be seen performing in pubs.

A conference on mummers was hosted by the Academy for Irish Cultural Heritages at the Magee Campus, University of Ulster, Derry in June 2003. Speakers from Ireland and other countries (Britain, France, Finland and Sweden) which have similar traditions addressed the conference. Some traditional musicians have recorded tunes associated with the mummers, 'The Mummers Jigs', for example, recorded by the Murphys of Wexford (see **Murphy, Phil, John and Pip**) and 'The Mummer's March', recorded by **Lá Lugh**. The mummers are sometimes confused with the **Wren-Boys** and the **Strawboys**. Although mummers and wren-boys operate independently and at different times in many places, there is some overlap in parts of Ireland. The Fingal Mummers in north Co. Dublin, for example, have often performed during wren-boy celebrations on St. Stephen's Day, and typical mummers outfits would be used by some wren-boys in other places. See also **Biddy Boys**.

Munnelly, Tom (b. 1944)   Song collector born in Dublin who has made an invaluable contribution to the collection and study of Irish folk song. Since 1970 he has contributed around 1500 tapes to the **Irish Folklore Department, University College Dublin**, most of them consisting of songs or commentaries on song from various singers around Ireland. He has also published a considerable number of articles on various aspects of song, including the singing tradition of **travellers**, **sea songs**, narrative songs in West Clare and the manuscript songbook of John McCall, father of **Patrick Joseph McCall**. He published jointly and edited recordings with **Hugh Shields**. Perhaps his most widely known work is the excellent 1994 book/cassette of Miltown Malbay singer **Tom Lenihan**.

Murphy, Bill   **Sliabh Luachra** fiddler, father of **Denis Murphy** and **Julia Clifford**. He was also known as 'Bill the Weaver' because his father and mother were both weavers. He played the flute and the tin whistle and passed a wealth of music on to other Sliabh Luachra musicians, including his son, his daughter and **Johnny O'Leary**. A number of tunes are named after him and O'Leary comments that he learnt five or six jigs from him which nobody else knew.

Murphy, Colm   Bodhrán player who grew up in Cork and did one of his earliest recordings with **Jackie Daly** and Séamus Creagh. He is now best known for his playing with **De Dannan**. In 1996 he released *An Bodhrán: The Irish Drum*, on which he plays bodhrán with a number of guest musicians, including **Eoin Ó Riabhaigh**, Conal Ó Grada (flute) **Seán Ryan** and members of De Dannan, collectively and individually. He was the first guest teacher in the innovative internet music school, **Scoiltrad**.

Murphy, Delia (1902-1971) Singer who, through her numerous recordings, did much to popularise Irish ballads in English. Along with **Margaret Barry**, she was one of the first Irish female folk singers to have a successful musical career. Born at Ardoe, Claremorris, Co. Mayo, she attended University College, Galway, later marrying diplomat Tom Kiernan, whom she followed to London, Rome, Canberra, Bonn and Ottawa. While in London she made the first of many 78rpm recordings for HMV in 1938. Later she adapted and recorded a number of ballads for Martin Walton's Glenside record label (see **Waltons**), including the 'The Spinning Wheel', 'Three Lovely Lassies from Bannion' and 'Dan O'Hara'. She is commemorated by a memorial near her childhood home, simply inscribed 'Delia Murphy, Ballad Queen'.

Murphy, Denis (1910-1974) **Sliabh Luachra** fiddler, son of **Bill Murphy** and brother of **Julia Clifford**, one of the most famous pupils of **Pádraig O'Keeffe**. He had a great repertoire of Sliabh Luachra music and a number of slides and polkas are named after him. He played for almost forty years with the box player **Johnny O'Leary**, and the duo gave a number of polkas and slides to the **Chieftains**. The album *Kerry Fiddles, Vol. 1* (1977) features the playing of Pádraig O'Keeffe, Julia Clifford and Denis Murphy. (The latter two fiddlers had previously recorded their own album, *The Star Above the Garter*, in 1969.) *Denis Murphy: Music from Sliabh Luachra* (1995), compiled by **Peter Browne**, collects recordings made between 1948 and 1969.

Murphy, Phil, John and Pip Father and two sons, renowned harmonica players from Ballygow, Bannow, Co. Wexford. Phil Murphy (1917-1989) started to play at the age of eight and developed a range of playing techniques that gave the harmonica a new status in Irish traditional music. He was much in demand for sessions and house dances and among **mummers** in south Wexford, and he won the **All-Ireland** three years in a row (1969-71). He also taught his sons John and Pip to play harmonica and the trio became famous in the 1970s and 80s for their unique style. John (1973) and Pip (twice in the 1980s) also won All-Ireland titles. The trio can be heard on *The Trip to Cullenstown* (1991), which includes some guitar accompaniment but consists mainly of harmonicas playing both melody and accompaniment. The recording of the album was completed just three weeks before Phil's death on July 23rd, 1989. Phil played tremolo harmonica, but also experimented with the chromatic and was famous for his vamping style on faster tunes, which can be heard on his playing of his own 'Ballygow Reel' on *The Trip to Cullenstown*. Playing with his sons, he often used the chromatic to play an octave lower than them, as on the jigs 'Kitty Come Over/The Mug of Brown Ale' and the album's title tune, 'The Trip to Cullenstown', using his vamping technique to provide a rhythmic accompaniment. The overall sound of all three playing together like this is somewhat reminiscent of an accordion player using the bass keys for accompaniment. When playing solo, John often uses the 10-hole diatonic harmonica (the type favoured by blues players, sometimes called the 'blues harp'), as on his playing of three reels, 'The Congress/The Heather Breeze/The Earl's Chair'. On 'The

Shepherd's Love Dream' (waltz), Phil (playing chromatic) uses his vamping technique to create the impression of two harmonicas (one melody and one accompaniment) playing together. The Murphys also guested on **Kevin Burke**'s solo album *Up Close* (1984) and on a compilation album of music from south Wexford. *The Trip to Cullenstown* is, however, their definitive work and a milestone in Irish traditional harmonica recording.

Murphy, Tom Billy (1879-1944) Fiddler from **Sliabh Luachra**, who, like his contemporary **Pádraig O'Keeffe** also taught fiddle. He was renowned as a musician for his huge repertoire of tunes, many of them unknown to others. **Johnny O'Leary** reckoned that O'Keeffe got all of his tunes from Tom Billy Murphy. A number of Sliabh Luachra tunes are named after him.

Murray, Martin (b. 1955) Banjo, mandolin and fiddle player from Carrick-on-Suir, Co. Tipperary who played with **Robbie O'Connell**, **Tommy Keane** and guitarist Paul Grant in the Bread and Beer Band in the late 1970s. A fine player on all three instruments, Murray has played and recorded with many of the finest traditional musicians and also engineered or produced many traditional albums at his Beau Street Studios in Waterford. His own album, *Dark Horse* (1993) features Cork-born fiddler John Dwyer (an early influence on Murray), **Frankie Gavin** and **Mick Kinsella**. The album is a mixture of traditional and non-traditional music, and includes a fine mandolin concerto.

Music Notation The earliest written musical notation in Ireland dates from the late 12th century, and staff notation has been available in publications since the 18th century. It is really only since the publication of **Francis O'Neill**'s collections in the early 20th century, however, that the use of music notation in learning traditional music has been in any sense widespread. Many traditional musicians today can read staff notation, and **Breandán Breathnach**'s collection *Ceol Rince na hÉireann* (Vol. 1 1963) enhanced the practical use of staff notation for traditional musicians by including not just the basic melody but symbols to indicate various forms of **ornamentation**. Symbols for ornamentation have subsequently been used by other music publishers, with collections like Anthony Sullivan's *Session Tunes* and various publications by **Waltons** (many of which include the tunes on CD) proving popular with musicians, especially learners. For most musicians staff notation, where it is used, is simply a guide to the tune. Individual musicians will use their own ornamentation and often change even the basic melody of the tune as notated.

It is important to realise that for centuries traditional music was passed on orally. Many of the subtleties of the music, such as variations in melody, timing and ornamentation, are difficult to capture comprehensively through notation. Many musicians who learn new tunes from staff notation would still learn a lot of tunes by ear as well. In cases where teachers use notation, it is still vital for the pupil to hear the tune played. Some individual teachers or organisations involved in teaching encourage learners to avoid or minimise the use of any form of notation and learn largely or solely by ear. **Na Píobairí Uilleann**, for example, encourages learning by ear, with teachers going through a tune in sections for the pupil, who plays the tune back to the teacher. Pupils might record the teacher playing the tune, but they are still learning essentially by ear.

Alternative systems of notation have been developed for different instruments. Charts showing the fingerings for different notes are often used, for example, in teaching the tin whistle, flute or uilleann pipes. In the case of the tin whistle or flute, these charts can be simplified to a numbers system that is often found to be very useful for beginners. Instruments such as the button accordion or concertina are often taught using a simple system of indicating whether the button for a particular note is used on the press or on the draw. The **Sliabh Luachra** fiddle master, **Pádraig O'Keeffe** (1887-1963), used a system of tablature for teaching fiddle where the four spaces between five lines were used to represent the strings, with numbers in these spaces indicating the fingers for the left hand. Smaller numbers were used to indicate ornamentation and strokes above the numbers showed groups of notes to be played together as well as the correct bowing.

A completely new system of music notation has also been developed by **Steve Cooney**. This system is based on a tonal 'mandala' showing the twelve points of the chromatic scale. Melodic spirals moving anti-clockwise indicate the melody is travelling upwards in pitch, moving clockwise the spirals show the melody moving downwards in pitch. A system of dots or buttons is used to indicate rhythm and sections of melody notated using this system have the appearance of representations of star systems or complex chemistry diagrams. Although Cooney's notation is not in widespread general use, he has used it with great success in his own teaching and composition.

Na Píobairí Uilleann See **Píobairí Uilleann, Na**.

Napoleon Bonaparte (1769-1821)   Also known as Napoleon I, Emperor of the French 1804-1815. The revolutionary and Napoleonic wars (1793-1802, 1803-1815) fought between England and France inspired great hope among Irish republicans, who sought and (in 1796 and 1798) gained support against the English from France. Although the French expeditions of 1796 and 1798 ultimately failed, Napoleon Bonaparte remained the great hope of Irish republicans, and the United Irishmen remained active in France until Bonaparte fell.

A considerable number of Irish traditional tunes and songs relate to the revolutionary and Napoleonic period. The hornpipe 'The Rights of Man' is probably named after the revolutionary book *The Rights of Man* by Tom Paine, which was very popular in Ireland, running to seven editions between 1791 and 1792. 'The Salamanca Reel' suggests a commemoration of the 1812 battle fought at the Spanish city between England and France during the Spanish uprising against Napoleon (1808-1814). A number of set dances and marches are directly associated with Napoleon, including 'Bonaparte's Retreat', 'Bonaparte's Advance', 'Madame Bonaparte', 'The Downfall of Paris', 'Bonaparte Crossing the Rhine', 'The Grand March' and 'Boney Crossing the Alps'. These tunes are still played in Ireland, and a number of Napoleonic songs are also sung, the most famous being 'The Green Linnet' and 'The Bonny Bunch of Roses-O'. 'The Isle of St. Helena' laments Napoleon's deportation to the island after his defeat at Waterloo (1815). 'Napoleon Bonaparte', recorded by **Frank Harte**, relates the 'deeds of great Napoleon', lamenting the 'fatal June at Waterloo' when 'he was forced to yield or run away' and recounts how the ashes of his heart were brought back to Paris after his death on St. Helena. Harte has released a double CD of Napoleonic material, *My Name Is Napoleon Bonaparte: Traditional Songs on Napoleon Bonaparte* (2001). The CDs are accompanied by an excellent booklet giving historical background to the 26 songs which Harte sings, many of them unaccompanied. The songs include 'The Isle of St. Helena', 'The Wounded Hussar' and 'The Love Token', among others, some well known, others more rarely heard. Harte's work is a major contribution to our appreciation and understanding of Napoleonic song and an excellent companion to his *The First Year of Liberty* (1998), a collection of songs of the 1798 rebellion.

While Napoleon enshrined the hopes of many in Ireland for liberation from English rule, many Irishmen also fought against him in the English army. Indeed Napoleon's vanquisher at Salamanca and Waterloo, the Duke of Wellington, grew up in Trim, Co. Meath where a column erected to his memory in 1817 still stands. The **Sam Henry** collection contains a number of Napoleonic songs in which women lament their lovers' deaths in battle against the Emperor of the French. Some of these, such as 'The Bonny Light Horseman' and 'The Drummer Boy at Waterloo', lament the deaths of Englishmen but obviously struck a chord among those in Ireland. Others, like 'The Plains of Waterloo', simply recount the events which led to the death of a lover (whose nationality is not specified) fighting against Napoleon. The Henry collection contains two versions of this song and another version has been recorded by Frank Harte. Some of these songs undoubtedly originated in England but enjoyed considerable popularity in Ireland.

A number of other singers and musicians have recorded Napoleonic tunes and songs, including **Willie Clancy** (air of 'The Bonny Bunch of Roses-O'), Dolores Keane (see **Keane Family**; song of 'The Bonny Bunch of Roses-O') and the group **General Humbert** ('Napoleon's Retreat', 'The Isle of St. Helena'). General Humbert took its name from a French general of the revolutionary period who landed at Killala Bay, Co. Mayo after the 1798 rebellion and routed English troops at 'the races of Castlebar'. In 1974 **Tony MacMahon** produced a programme for RTÉ radio called *The Green Linnet*, which dealt with references to Napoleon in Irish music and song. Some of the music from the programme can be found on **Micheál Ó Súilleabháin**'s album *Cry of the Mountain* (1981). MacMahon later made a television series, also titled *The Green Linnet* (1978) in which he travelled around Europe playing music with **Barney McKenna**. The **Chieftains**' album *Bonaparte's Retreat* (1976) sought to commemorate Ireland's role in supporting Napoleon. 'It's my tone poem', says **Paddy Moloney**, 'which was inspired by reading the history books and seeing the Irish connection with the French. It's about how the Irish asked for Napoleon's help and how they went over to help him out with our common problems with the neighbours' (John Glatt, *The Chieftains: The Authorised Biography*, London, 1997, p. 136).

A wealth of songs, poems and tunes from this period are found in Terry Moylan's book *The Age of Revolution in the Irish Song Tradition, 1776-1815* (Dublin, 2000). See also **France**; **Nationalist/Republican Song**.

Nation, The A weekly newspaper founded in 1842 to promote the political and cultural ideas of the nationalist **Young Ireland** movement. It was owned and edited by Charles Gavin Duffy (1816-1903) in collaboration with Thomas Davis (1814-1845) and John Blake Dillon (1814-1866). Ballads played an important role in the newspaper's attempt to create a coherent nationalist view of Irish history and culture. The Young Irelanders' ballads often caused controversy, stirring up public opinion with the doctrinaire nationalism of Davis and the other contributors. The paper claimed a readership of over 250,000. It was suppressed in 1848 but revived by Duffy in 1849 and continued until 1897. It made an important contribution to the development of **Nationalist/Republican Song**, and ballads from it were published separately as *The Spirit of the Nation* in 1843 and 1845. Many of the most famous nationalist songs, such as M. J. McCann's 'O'Donnell Abu', appeared first in the *Nation* and are still sung today. Thomas Davis was himself the author of a number of ballads, the most famous being 'A Nation Once Again'. See also **Political Song**.

Nationalist/Republican Song The association of musicians and songwriters/poets with nationalist politics has a long tradition in Ireland, stretching right back to the Elizabethan Conquest (see **Elizabeth I**) and the Middle Ages, when Gaelic harpers (see **Harp**), **minstrels** and poets (see **Bard**) were legislated against and persecuted by the English administration in Ireland. 'Republicanism', in an Irish context, is derived from 18th-century American and French political ideology but, during the 19th and 20th centuries was closely associated with a more general Catholic Nationalism. The earliest Republican Irish songs date from the 1790s, when the United Irishmen organised a mass political movement to fight, with French assistance, for an Irish Republic independent of Britain (see **Napoleon Bonaparte**). Among the most famous of these songs are 'Roddy McCorley' and 'The Croppy Boy'. Although both of these songs had later versions with different melodies, the oldest versions appeared during the 1798 period. Like many popular political songs, they personalise their subject, preferring the hero to the ideals for which he fought. Another song composed in the same period as the events it relates is 'Dunlavin Green', about the execution – on the green in Dunlavin, Co. Wicklow in May 1798 – of thirty men who took no part in the rising.

There are many other Republican songs about the 1798 rebellion, some of them written by nationalist or republican writers of the 19th or 20th centuries. 'The Rising of the Moon', for example, was composed by the Fenian John Keegan Casey almost sixty years after the events of 1798. The writing of political ballads was so popular throughout the 19th century that they can be used to provide a running commentary on political developments in Ireland. Wolfe Tone (1763-1798), Robert Emmet (1778-1803) and Charles Stuart Parnell (1846-1891) were among the many nationalist heroes frequently eulogised. A 1984 study of folklore about Daniel O'Connell (1775-1847) found a total of 226 songs (90 of them in Irish) which dealt with him. From 1798 onwards, there is considerable evidence of ballad-sellers being arrested for singing 'seditious' songs, indicating how seriously the authorities viewed the singing of political songs.

In the 1840s the **Young Ireland** movement played an important role in stirring up public opinion with new nationalist songs through its newspaper the *Nation*. An even more violent strain of balladry was published in the newspapers *United Irishman* (from 1848) and *The Irish People* (the Fenian weekly, 1863-1865). The songs of **Thomas Moore** also contributed to nationalist sentiment, but he remained independent of nationalist revolutionary organisations. From the middle of the 19th century onwards large numbers of ballad collections, many containing newly composed nationalist/republican songs, were published in Ireland and the **US**; some were new lyrics put to old melodies, but new melodies were also composed. Many of the authors were themselves committed to nationalist or republican movements. Some of the most famous nationalist/republican songs of the 19th and 20th centuries were, therefore, written by known authors and initially disseminated through **ballad sheets**, **chapbooks**, or more substantial printed collections. Although many were subsequently passed on orally, the role of literary composition and printed works in spreading the popularity of political ballads was clearly significant in the 19th and 20th centuries.

The revival of interest in traditional music and song, which began in the late 1950s and the 60s, was marked by a new interest in nationalist/republican song. The **Clancy Brothers and Tommy Makem**, a seminal influence in the early years of the revival, devoted their first album, *The Rising of the Moon* (1956), entirely to Irish songs of rebellion. In the **Ballad Boom** following their initial success, nationalist or republican songs were an important part of the repertoire of many groups, most notably the **Wolfe Tones**. The eruption of political violence in Northern Ireland in 1968 gave new significance to the place of nationalist/republican song in the revival. New songs were written and many of the old songs (often referred to as 'rebel songs') were performed and recorded time and again by various groups. The revival of interest in both traditional song and instrumental music was seen by many as integral to the republican political movement. In the case of instrumental music, the open support of republicanism by **Comhaltas Ceoltóirí Éireann** served to strengthen the perception that traditional music and republican politics were closely bound together. This not only alienated many members of the Northern Protestant community from traditional music (see **Orange/Loyalist Song**), but also alienated many musicians in both parts of Ireland who did not feel comfortable with the 'republican' image of traditional music.

Despite the associations between instrumental traditional music and republicanism in recent decades, many musicians do not see a political link in playing traditional music. Indeed there are musicians with Orange or Protestant backgrounds playing traditional music today who say that religion or politics never prevented them from doing so. In the case of song, the situation is more polarised. Just as there are Orange or Loyalist political songs inextricably bound to the Northern Ireland political situation of the last few decades, so there are also songs that are clearly nationalist or republican. Singer/songwriters such as **Christy Moore** ('Ninety Miles from Dublin'), **Mick Hanly** ('On the Blanket') and **Barry Moore** ('Section 31') have written and performed newly composed songs about contemporary events relating to the Northern Ireland 'Troubles' and taken a firmly committed position on many issues. Other artists like **Phil Coulter**, **Luke Kelly**, **Moving Hearts** and the **Pogues** have also performed contemporary songs on the Troubles. The extent to which contemporary songs dealing with Northern Ireland were proscribed by the media in the United Kingdom and the Republic of Ireland is a subject yet to be properly researched. That political songs were censored is beyond doubt (see **Section 31**), but the precise details remain somewhat obscure.

The bicentenary commemorations of the 1798 rebellion raised interesting questions about the history of republicanism in Ireland. Many of the leaders of the 1798 rebellion had been Protestants or Presbyterians who espoused a non-sectarian, democratic philosophy based on the principles of civil, political and religious freedom (see **Drennan, William**). The Official 1798 Bicentenary Commemorative Album, *Who Fears To Speak* (1997) included contributions from the Northern Ireland singer **Len Graham**, 'an Irish democratic agnostic of Presbyterian stock'

(Graham's own words in *Irish Music*, December 1997/January 1998, p. 8). Graham's involvement, and the interview in *Irish Music*, drew attention to the non-sectarian ideals of the early republicans, generally forgotten amidst the sectarianism that has frequently dominated Irish political life during the 19th and 20th centuries. Another excellent collection of songs released in the bicentenary year was **Frank Harte**'s *The First Year of Liberty* (1998). In the wake of the bicentenary, Terry Moylan published his book *The Age of Revolution in the Irish Song Tradition, 1776-1815* (Dublin, 2000). Rich in background information and the historical events of the time, the book also contains the lyrics and tunes of 157 songs as well as 25 poems and 25 tunes.

Since 1926 the Irish national anthem has been the nationalist 'Amhrán na bhFiann' or 'The Soldier's Song', written by Peadar Kearney (1883-1942) and Patrick Heeny (d. 1911). First published in 1912, it was used as a marching song by the Irish Volunteers, who were involved in the 1916 rising. From the late 1960s and the 'Troubles', many have expressed reservations about the militarism of the national anthem, and there have been appeals that it be changed. See also the **Sands Family**; **Zimmerman, Georges Denis**.

Neale, John and William This father and son ran a music business in Christ Church Yard, Dublin in the 18th century and published the first wholly Irish collection of music, *A Collection of the Most Celebrated Irish Tunes,* which appeared in 1724 and contained 49 airs. The only surviving original copy is among the **Bunting** papers in Queen's University, Belfast. A facsimile edition was published in 1986 by **Nicholas Carolan**. The Neales also published a collection of tunes composed by the harper **Turlough O'Carolan**, and *A Choice Collection of Country Dances* (ca. 1726). John was also Chairman of the Charitable Music Society, builders of the New Music Hall in Fishamble Street, where the first public performances of Handel's *Messiah* took place in 1742.

Neff Brothers Duo of talented brothers from near Blarney, Co. Cork. Eoghan (fiddle) and Flaithrí (uilleann pipes) have numerous awards (including **All-Ireland** titles) between them. At the time of their first album, *Soundpost and Bridle* (2000) they were aged only 19 and 21 respectively and were both studying music at **University College Cork**. They are joined on the album by their mother, Muireann (bodhrán, percussion) and father, Éibhear (mandola), with whom they perform gigs as Teaghlach. Their second album, *Ar Scáth A Chéile/Each Other's Shadow* (2003) has further enhanced their reputation as one of the most talented

Eoghan and Flaithrí Neff

young duos to emerge in recent years. The album is more experimental than the first and includes some fine original compositions.

Newfoundland Province of Canada consisting of Labrador (the mainland area) and the island of Newfoundland. It is a rugged area with a severe climate in which fishing is a major industry. The Irish St. Brendan (484-577) may have sailed there in the 6th century. Historians are somewhat sceptical, but a voyage in 1976/77 by Tim Severin, recounted in his book *The Brendan Voyage* (London, 1978), proved that it would certainly have been possible for the Irish saint to reach North America. Composer **Shaun Davey** composed a suite of music inspired by Severin's book, ending with Brendan's arrival in Newfoundland.

During the second half of the 17th century and throughout the 18th century, migrant fishermen established strong links between Ireland and Newfoundland. Sir Arthur Young wrote in his *A Tour in Ireland* (Cambridge, 1925) on July 12th, 1776, at Wexford, that 'Many lads go to Newfoundland in May and come home in October' (p. 26). A few months later, at Waterford (15 October 1776), Young wrote: 'Emigrations from this part of Ireland principally to Newfoundland, for a season; they have £18 or £20 for their pay, and are maintained, but do not bring home more than £7 to £11. Some of them stay and settle' (p. 135). 'The staple trade of the place', he wrote of Waterford, 'is the Newfoundland trade.... The number of people who go as passengers is amazing; from 60 to 80 ships, and from 3,000 to 5,000 [people] annually. They come from most parts of Ireland, Cork, Kerry etc.' (p. 137). St. John's (named after a Waterford city parish), the capital of Newfoundland, had a population which by 1784 was made up of 85% migrant fishery workers, many of them Irish, who also settled in more isolated communities on the southern shore of Newfoundland island. By 1820 it is estimated that up to 33,000 people from Waterford and its hinterland had settled in Newfoundland. **Gearóid Ó hAllmhuráin** has a short section on Irish music in Newfoundland in his 1998 *Pocket History of Irish Traditional Music*, where he notes a number of interesting details. The Irish-speaking population of Newfoundland had become so large in the 1780s that priests who spoke Irish were being requested from Ireland. The Clare-born poet Donncha Rua MacConmara, whose 'Bán Chnuic Éireann Ó' ('The Fair Hills of Ireland') is still sung, spent the years 1745-1756 in Newfoundland. Ó hAllmhuráin also notes that lancer set dances (still found in parts of Waterford, Kilkenny and Tipperary) are still danced in Newfoundland, and until recently the wren (see **Wren-Boys**) was hunted on St. Stephen's Day.

Waterford names like Walsh, McGrath, Phelan, Coady and Power are still found in Newfoundland, where there is a vibrant, living tradition of Irish music. The jig 'Bruacha Talaimh an Éisc' ('The Banks of Newfoundland') takes its name from the Irish for Newfoundland, *Talamh an Éisc*, literally 'Land of Fish'. Aidan O'Hara, a song collector, has pointed out (*Irish Music,* October 1997, pp. 31-32) that about one third of the population of the island of Newfoundland today is of Irish descent, the other two thirds coming originally from the English West Country. O'Hara helped to found the Newfoundland Folk Festival in 1977 and points out that over a thousand of the island's folk songs were published for collector Kenneth Peacock by the National Museum of Canada in 1965. This collection constitutes just over half of the museum's rich collection of Newfoundland folk songs.

Many Irish musicians have had connections with Newfoundland in recent decades, including Westmeath-born fiddler, **Séamus Creagh**. He went to St. John's in 1988 and spent over five years in Newfoundland collecting tunes and songs on a grant from the Irish Department of Foreign Affairs. Dolores Keane (see **Keane Family**) has performed there and recorded the Newfoundland traditional song 'The Sweet Forget-Me-Not'. **Christy Moore** is one of a number of artists to record the contemporary folk song 'Sonny' or 'Sonny's Dream' by Newfoundlander Ron Hynes. **Paddy Keenan**'s 1998 CD *Na Keen Affair* involved five Newfoundland musicians and was recorded in Newfoundland and Ireland. It includes 'Kelldevil Air', named after a town in Newfoundland and composed by Newfoundlander Gerry Strong, and (in the sleeve-notes) the poem 'Land of Fish/Talaimh an Éisc', written for Keenan by Des Walsh. The album *Island to Island* (2003) brings together eight Irish and Newfoundland musicians to play music shared by both traditions. Among the Irish musicians are Séamus Creagh (fiddle) and Aidan Coffey (accordion), and the Newfoundlanders include Graham Wells (accordion) and Colin Carrigan (fiddle).

Young musicians in Newfoundland have shown a great interest in their traditional music and song, tracing it back to its origins in Ireland. Among the recent groups to emerge are the Irish Descendants, the Masterless Men, the Punters and the Fine Crowd. Singer Anita Best has recorded unaccompanied traditional Newfoundland songs from the Irish, English and French traditions.

Waterford city was recently twinned with St. John's, Newfoundland and in June 2004 a permanent exhibition on Newfoundland opened in Waterford city's Museum of Treasures. It includes photographs, documents and artefacts which provide fascinating evidence of the history shared by Waterford and Newfoundland. The exhibition is sponsored by the state-funded Ireland/Newfoundland partnership.

Newgrange Passage-tomb and stone circle in Co. Meath, dated to around 3,200 BC. The tomb was cleverly constructed to allow sunlight to enter the central chamber at dawn around the winter solstice. The site has attracted the attention of astronomers, mystics, poets and songwriters, notably Ciarán Ó Braonáin of **Clannad**. His song, 'Newgrange', appeared on the group's 1983 album *Magical Ring*, the album taking its title from a line in the song: 'Mysterious ring, magical ring, forgotten is the race that no-one knows'. The poet Paul Durcan wrote an extraordinary poem about Newgrange, 'A Snail in My Prime' (published in a book of the same title, 1993) which he performed with a group of musicians playing music composed and conducted by Michael Holohan. The work was first performed in the Brú na Bóinne Visitor Centre near Newgrange and was recorded by **RTÉ** radio, first broadcast on Christmas Day 2001. It is a unique piece of work which features the singing of Melanie O'Reilly, the uilleann pipes of **Peter Browne**, **Bronze Age horns** and Iron Age horns (played by Siomon Ó Duibhir, Colin Blakey, John Purser and Maria Cullen), marimbas (Catríona Smith), cello (John Purser), bass flute (Colin Blakey) and percussion (Michael Holohan, John Purser, Colin Blakey and Catríona Smith). O'Reilly's voice and the various instruments are used to great effect, working around the poet's voice to produce an ambience that in some ways resembles ancient Greek drama. Indeed Holohan himself compared the repeated use of certain lines from the poem to the use of a chorus in Greek tragedy and compared the work overall to a type of mass, with the repetition of certain 'ritual chants' binding the piece together. This musical performance of 'A Snail in My Prime' deserves to be more widely heard and recognised, especially for the collaboration of poet, composer and musicians. Durcan himself studied archaeology, and while the poem is full of humour and innuendo, it also has many accurate references to the archaeology of the Newgrange monument. The uilleann pipes and horns of the Bronze and Iron Ages are particularly effective in evoking an otherworld atmosphere, and Melanie O'Reilly's vocals are a stunning contrast to the poet's voice. The Durkan/Holohan performance of 'A Snail in My Prime' won the Celtic music award at the Celtic Film, Television and Radio Festival Quimper, **Brittany**, in March 2002.

Ní Bheaglaoich, Seosaimhín   Singer from Baile na bPoc, on the Dingle peninsula, Co. Kerry who grew up in a musical family, learning to sing in traditional Corca Dhuibhne style from her parents. She can be heard singing in both Irish and English on *Taobh na Gréine: Under the Sun* (1994). The album also features Australian **Steve Cooney**, her son **Gavin Ralston** and her brother **Séamus Begley** and was produced by **Dónal Lunny**. She has also presented traditional music programmes for **RTÉ** television, including *The Mountain Lark*, a series that originally ran from 1985 to 1987. The series was subsequently repeated and gave many traditional musicians their first public broadcast. Australian Steve Cooney claims that the series made him a household name among traditional music listeners. Ní Bheaglaoich also broadcasts with **Raidió na Gaeltachta** and was a founder member of the group **Macalla**, with whom she made two albums. Her sisters Eilín, Caitlín and Máire are also accomplished singers who have recorded, Máire also playing accordion on her album with brother Séamus Begley, *Plansctaí Bhaile na Buc* (1989). Seosaimhín's son, Gavin Ralston, is an accomplished guitarist and producer and another brother, **Brendan Begley**, is a fine accordion player.

Ní Bhraonáin, Eithne   See **Enya**.

Ní Bhraonáin, Máire (Máire/Moya Brennan)   Lead singer and harpist with **Clannad**, who has also pursued a career with her own group, the Moya Brennan Band, in which she performs a mixture of traditional and contemporary material. Between 1992 and 2003 she made five albums, the first simply titled *Máire* (1992). She followed this with *Misty-Eyed Adventures* (1994), *Perfect Time* (1998) and *Whisper to the Wild Water* (1999). She describes herself as a Celtic Christian and her 1998 album, *Perfect Time*, is essentially a series of personal religious songs. The final track is a reworking of Psalm 67 and features the Bunbeg Parish Choir. *Two Horizons* (2003) explores themes connected with the legendary harp of Tara, site of the ancient high kings of Ireland. Her autobiography, *The Other Side of the Rainbow: The Autobiography of the Voice of Clannad* (London, 2001) is of great interest in charting the career of Brennan and the family group, Clannad. She won 'Best Contemporary Female' in the ***Irish Music*** magazine awards in 2000 and 2001 and remains one of the most innovative artists in Irish music. Website: www.moyabrennan.com.

Ní Chathasaigh, Máire (b. 1956) Harpist and singer born in Bandon, Co. Cork who developed new techniques for playing Irish traditional dance music on the harp. During the 1970s, while in her teens and early twenties, she won several national and international harp competitions as well as touring and

Máire Ní Bhraonáin / Moya Brennan
(photo: Peer Lindgreen)

recording with **Comhaltas Ceoltóirí Éireann**. At that time, most Irish harpists were playing the harp simply to accompany songs or play slow melodies. One of the few players of the Celtic harp who was playing Irish dance music was Breton musician **Alan Stivell**. Ní Chathasaigh developed new techniques for playing dance tunes on the harp, and her first solo album *The New Strung Harp* (1985) broke new ground in Irish harping.

In 1987 she formed a duo with the talented guitarist Chris Newman (see **Guitar**) from England, and with him recorded an innovative album, *The Living Wood* (1988). Never before had harp and guitar been used so effectively together for playing Irish dance music and Carolan tunes (see **O'Carolan, Turlough**). The guitar is played superbly as both a lead and accompanying instrument, and both harp and guitar play bluegrass tunes normally associated with American fiddlers and banjo players. There are also three songs on the album, one of which runs into a traditional Basque waltz, and tunes from **Scotland** and Cape Breton (see **Nova Scotia**). Newman plays mandolin, electric bass and percussion, with Ní Chathasaigh adding synthesiser and piano on some tracks. The duo have since toured extensively and recorded more albums. *Out of Court* (1991) includes Máire's sisters Maighréad (harp and fiddle) and **Nollaig Ní Chathasaigh** as well as **Liam O'Flynn**. It was followed by *The Carolan Albums* (1994), devoted exclusively to the music of **Turlough O'Carolan**, and *Live in the Highlands* (1995). *Agallaimh/Dialogues* (2001) again included Nollaig (fiddle, viola) as well as guest performances by Scottish fiddler Ian MacFarlane, Simon Mayor (mandolin), Roy Dodds (percussion) and Liz Hanks (cello). The album is similar to *The Living Wood* and *Out of Court* in its inclusion of tunes from different musical traditions, including Irish, Scottish, bluegrass and jazz.

Máire Ní Chathasaigh

There are also original compositions by both Newman and Ní Chathasaigh. The latter has published two collections of her harp arrangements in *The Irish Harper Vol. 1* (Yorkshire, 1991) and *The Irish Harper Vol. 2* (Yorkshire, 2001). She won the **TG4** 'Traditional Musician of the Year' award in 2001. Website: www.irishharper.com. See also **Burke**, **Joe**.

Ní Chathasaigh, Nollaig Fiddler from Bandon, Co. Cork who grew up with both classical and traditional music. In her early teens she attended the **Cork Pipers' Club** and went to **Fleadh Cheoil na hÉireann** regularly with her family. She studied music at **University College Cork** and played violin with a number orchestras, including the **RTÉ** Symphony Orchestra. Since 1980, when she joined the reformed **Planxty**, she has performed and recorded with many other traditional artists including the **Dónal Lunny** band, her sister **Máire Ní Chathasaigh**, **Dick Gaughan** and **Andy Irvine**. She has also performed with Tommy Makem and Liam Clancy, with the Clancy Brothers on their reunion tour in 1983 (see **Clancy Brothers and Tommy Makem**) and with *Riverdance*. Under her English name, Nollaig Casey, she made two albums with her husband **Arty McGlynn**, *Lead the Knave* (1989) and *Causeway* (1995), both notable not only for their fine fiddling but also for the excellent fiddle/guitar interplay and innovative, modern arrangements.

O'Stravaganza (2001) was another innovative project in which Casey was involved. Recorded in Italy, the album brings together Irish traditional music and **Turlough O'Carolan** tunes with Italian Baroque music. Other Irish musicians included **Emer Mayock** (uilleann pipes, flute, whistle), Donal Siggins (mandolin, bouzouki), Ronan Le Bar (uilleann pipes) and Robert Harris (bodhrán, bones). The Italian Baroque ensemble Le Orfanelle della Pietà perform with the Irish musicians on fourteen tracks of subtly interwoven Baroque and Irish themes. The concept of amalgamating Baroque and Irish music came from the producer Hughes de Courson, who worked closely on the project with Breton composer Youenn Le Berre. Casey was also a regular member of the house band for the television series **Sult** and was a member of the Coolfin band, led by Dónal Lunny, which emerged from the series.

Ní Chathasaigh's first solo album, *The Music of What Happened* (2004) features six of her own instrumental compositions as well as traditional instrumentals (one from **Galicia**) and songs (in Irish and English). Her evocative composition 'The Last

Lord of Beare' is a tribute to Dónal O'Sullivan Beare (ca. 1560-1618), the chief of the O'Sullivans of Beare, Co. Cork. It marks the 400th anniversary of the chief's exile to La Coruña in Galicia (1604). There are other fine tunes dedicated to her children and her father, including the 'Two Sisters Set', where she is joined by her sister Máire on harp. Arty McGlynn arranged, accompanied and produced the album.

Ní Dhomhnaill, Maighréad and Tríona Singers whose family originally came from Rann na Feirsde, Co. Donegal but moved to Kells, Co. Meath as part of Eamonn De Valera's attempt to establish the Irish language on the east coast of Ireland (see **Gaeltacht**). Their aunt, Neilí, was a famous traditional singer who had a huge repertoire of folk songs, in both Irish and English. Conall Ó Domhnaill, their uncle, was also an accomplished singer and a songwriter who worked all of his life to promote Irish culture and the Irish language.Their father, Aodh, was a well-known collector of Irish songs who worked with the **Irish Folklore Commission**. He was a singer himself and also played flute and accordion. The family spent their summers in the Donegal **Gaeltacht** and the rest of the year at their home in Kells, Co. Meath. Exposed to **sean-nós singing** as well as classical piano from an early age, Maighréad, Tríona and their brother **Micheál Ó Domhnaill** recorded their first album together as **Skara Brae** when the girls were still at school. Tríona became a professional musician from that time onwards, touring and recording with many groups, most notably the **Bothy Band**, **Relativity** and **Nightnoise**. Her voice is one of the most distinctive in Irish music, undoubtedly influenced by sean-nós singing, although she sings traditional songs in both Irish and English as well as composing her own in more recent years.

Maighréad and Tríona Ní Dhomhnaill

She also plays a variety of keyboard instruments, including the **clavinet**, harpsichord, harmonium and piano (see **Keyboard Instruments**) and her playing of both lead and accompaniment has been an integral part of the sound of the bands in which she has played. Maighréad never opted for a professional career in music but has nonetheless recorded two fine solo albums (1976 and 1991) and is well known in traditional circles. Both sisters appear as guests on **Dónal Lunny**'s *Coolfin* (1998), singing two traditional songs. Together they made the album *Idir dhá Sholas/Between Two Lights* (1999), on which they sing in both Irish and English.

Ní Dhonnchadha, Máire Áine (1919-1991) Sean-nós singer (see **Sean-nós Singing**) from Cois Fharraige, Connemara, Co. Galway. On her album *Deora Aille*

('Teardrops of the Cliff', 1970) she sings unaccompanied songs in Irish, including the classics 'Úna Bhán' ('Fair Úna') and 'Dónal Óg' ('Young Donal'). She also sings two interesting **occupational songs** in dance rhythms, 'An Faoitín' ('The Whiting') and 'Sambó Éara' (nonsense words), displaying a fine mastery over more light-hearted songs as well as the tragic love songs. The album is also notable for its excellent sleeve-notes (by **Seán O'Boyle**) and a beautifully produced booklet with the lyrics in Irish (using the old Irish letter types) and English translation (printed by **Colm O Lochlainn**'s Three Candles Press). The cover is designed by Louis Le Brocquy. Like many Connemara sean-nós singers, Ní Dhonnchadha also sings in English (on the compilation *Traditional Music of Ireland 1*, 1962).

Ní Ghráda, Máire (b. 1959) Tin whistle player and uilleann piper from Cork. She started to play whistle at the age of ten and two years later was attending piping classes at the **Cork Pipers' Club**, learning to play from Micheál Ó Riabhaigh, father of **Eoin Ó Riabhaigh**. Along with the latter and five other young uilleann pipers, she recorded two tracks on the album *The Piper's Rock: A Compilation of Young Uilleann Pipers* (1978). Her piping is greatly influenced by that of **Séamus Ennis** and **Liam O'Flynn**. She has played in Germany and all over Ireland and has appeared on a number of radio and television programmes, including the traditional music series **Sult**.

Nightnoise Group formed in 1986 with **Micheál Ó Domhnaill** (guitar, keyboards, whistles), **Tríona Ní Dhomhnaill** (keyboards, vocals, whistle, accordion) and Brian Dunning (flute, pan pipes). Scots fiddler John Cunningham was also a member of the group, and Bill Oskay (viola, violin, keyboards) joined them for a while. They played original music, mostly instrumental, which is sometimes described as a traditional/jazz fusion. Some elements of both traditional and jazz are to be found in the group's style, as in the up-tempo 'At the Races' on *At the*

End of the Evening (1988), although much of their music shows little obvious influence from either traditional or jazz. Nightnoise released eight albums between 1986 and 1997 and were well known in the **US**.

Ní Riain, Nóirín (b. 1951) Classically trained singer born in Caherconlish, Co. Limerick. She studied music at **University College Cork** (where she met her husband, **Micheál Ó Súilleabháin**) and has done extensive research into Irish song and Gregorian chant. She made her recording debut in 1977 on the album *Óró Damhnaigh*, a collection of songs and tunes that also featured Ó Súilleabháin (piano), **Tommy Keane**

Nóirín Ní Riain

(whistle), Tommy Kearney (uilleann pipes), Matt Fahy (flute) and John Dwyer (fiddle). Her first solo album, *Seinn Aililiú* ('Sing Hallelujah', 1978), was a collection of Irish songs with backing from traditional, classical and jazz players. There followed a trilogy of albums recorded with Benedictine monks in Glenstall Abbey, Co. Limerick: *Caoineadh na Maighidine* ('Lament of the Virgin, 1979), *Good People All* (1986, a recording of the **Wexford Carols**) and *Vox de Nube* ('A Voice from the Cloud', 1989). This trilogy established Ní Riain as an international name in the singing of Irish and European spiritual songs, and she has explored the world of spiritual music further on *Gregorian Chant Experience* (1997). Ní Riain has also recorded the works of the Benedictine abbess Hildegard of Bingen (1098-1179) and a number of secular albums. She published collections of songs in Irish in 1987 and 1988.

Ní Uallacháin, Eithne (d. 1999) Singer, flute and whistle player who was also a talented songwriter. A native Irish speaker, she moved from Donegal to Louth as a child and learned many songs from her father, Paddy. She entered the Irish Studies programme at the University of Ulster in Coleraine, where she got to know some of the great Ulster singers, including **Joe Holmes**, **Eddie Butcher** and **Len Graham**, guesting with the latter and husband **Gerry O'Connor** on **Skylark**'s album *All of It* (1989). She sang in Irish and English, her voice clear and soft, her diction nearly always perfect. Her love of Irish mythology, history and language came through in the work she did with Gerry O'Connor, first on the album *Cosa gan Bhróga* ('Feet without Shoes') and then on three fine albums as **Lá Lugh**. Her sudden death in May 1999 was a great loss to her family and friends and traditional music generally.

Ní Uallacháin, Pádraigín (b. 1950) Singer and native Irish speaker born in Co. Louth, sister of **Eithne Ní Uallacháin** who, like the latter, learned many songs from her father and went on to study **sean-nós singing** in Dublin and Irish Studies at the University of Ulster in Coleraine. In the late 1970s and early 80s she worked with **RTÉ**, researching and presenting the radio series *Reels of Memory* between 1979 and 1981. She writes her own songs, some of which can be heard with unaccompanied sean-nós songs on *An Dara Craiceann/Beneath the Surface* (1995). She has also recorded two collections of children's songs, *A Stór 's Stóirín* (1994) and *When I Was Young* (1996) with her

Len Graham and Pádraigín Ní Uallacháin

husband, **Len Graham**. *An Irish Lullaby: Suantraí* (2000) is a fine collection of traditional lullabies in Irish and English as well as original lullabies in traditional style by Ní Uallacháin herself and her version of the **W. B. Yeats** poem 'The Faery Song' (which she calls 'The Sleeping Lover'). Some of the tracks on *An Irish Lullaby* were originally recorded for the 1994 and 1996 albums.

Ní Uallacháin has worked closely with accompanist and arranger Garry Ó Briain (mandocello, keyboards, guitar), who also produced the 1994 and 1996 albums. She has done extensive research into the Gaelic songs of the ancient kingdom of Oriel in southeast Ulster, and unaccompanied singing of previously unrecorded songs from the area can be heard on *The Gaelic Songs of South Ulster* (2000). *A Hidden Ulster: People, Songs and Traditions of Oriel* (Dublin, 2003) is the first major study of the Gaelic song tradition of an area which, from the late 17th to the mid-19th century, was a vital centre of literature in Ireland. It includes the texts, source music and translations of 54 songs and facsimile copies of unpublished dance tunes. *An Dealg Óir/The Golden Thorn* (2002) has fourteen of the 54 songs from *A Hidden Ulster* arranged with subtle accompaniments by a number of musicians, including **Steve Cooney**, **Liam O'Flynn** and **Laoise Kelly**.

Nomos   Cork-based quintet originally made up of Niall Vallely (concertina, low whistle), **Liz Doherty** (fiddle), Gerry McKee (mandocello), Frank Torpey (bodhrán), and **John Spillane** (vocals, acoustic guitar, electric fretless bass). Their first album, *I Won't Be Afraid Any More* was released in 1995, with the second, *Set You Free* coming out in 1997. On the second album, Liz Doherty was replaced on fiddle by Vince Milne. The group's instrumentals come from a diverse range of sources, including traditional tunes from Ireland, **Scotland**, Cape Breton (see **Nova Scotia**) and Québec (see **Canada**), as well as recently composed material. Some of the songs are traditional, but the majority are written by John Spillane in his own unique style. Spillane left the group in 1998 to pursue a solo career.

North Cregg   Cork-based band formed in 1996 by Christy Leahy (button accordion), Caoimhín Vallely (fiddle, piano), John Neville (vocals, guitar) and Ciarán Coughlan (piano). By the time of their first album, *And They Danced All Night* (1999), the line-up included Martin Leahy (percussion) and guest Paul Meehan (banjo). The band mix instrumental music with a strong **Sliabh Luachra** influence and songs, many of which are original. On their first album there are four songs by John Neville, a traditional song from the **US**, traditional jigs, reels, and polkas, and original tunes by **Ed Reavy** and Shetland's Ronnie Cooper. The same line-up is featured on *mi.Da.Za* (2001), with Paul Meehan by then a full member and playing mandolin and bouzouki as well as banjo. The unusual title is Cork slang, a phrase which means 'that's good' or 'that's great'. The clarinet player Bernard Subert from Brittany guests on the album, adding a distinctive sound to much of the music. There are more original songs (by Neville, Steve Tilston and Paul Metzer) and a fine interpretation of the traditional ballad 'Lord Franklin' (see **Ó Domhnaill, Micheál**). The instrumentals include slides and an unusual piano duet by Coughlan and

Vallely, 'Hornpipes for Four Hands'. *Summer at My Feet* (2003) saw one change in line-up, with vocalist Fiona Kelleher replacing Neville. The album has five songs (including the title track by Cork songwriter Ger Wolfe) and instrumental sets of jigs, reels, slides and hornpipes. While Niall Vallely was involved as producer on the first two albums, the third is produced by Donald Shaw of **Cappercaillie** and is North Cregg's first album on the Scottish Greentrax label. The band have toured extensively in Ireland, Britain and continental Europe and are renowned for their energetic live performances. They won the 'Best Trad Newcomers' award in *Irish Music* magazine reader's poll for 2000. Website: www.northcregg.com.

North Cregg (photo: Louis De Carlo)

Northumbrian Pipes See **Bagpipes**; **England**.

Nova Scotia Literally 'New Scotland', maritime province in eastern **Canada** first colonised by the French in the early 17th century but passed to **England** in 1621. In 1821 it was united with the island of **Cape Breton**. There is a strong Scottish, and some Irish, influence in Cape Breton (where 30% of the population are Irish) and Nova Scotia. In the late 18th and early 19th centuries many Scots immigrants arrived after being driven out of **Scotland** in the wake of the defeat at the Battle of Culloden (1746) and the Highland Clearances. A strong tradition of **step dancing**, **set dancing**, dance music and songs (sung in Scots Gaelic, English and sometimes French) survives throughout Nova Scotia. Fiddling is particularly strong in Cape Breton, where fiddlers have developed their own unique style.

The Cape Breton Fiddlers' Association, founded in the early 1970s, held their first fiddlers' festival in 1973. It is now an annual two-day event attracting thousands and has strengthened the fiddling tradition of the island. The Cape Breton repertoire includes jigs, reels, hornpipes and strathspeys, and its musical influence has been felt in Irish America in cities such as Boston through the interaction of Irish-American and Cape Breton musicians.

In recent years, Nova Scotia and Cape Breton musicians such as fiddler Jerry Holland (who also composes), harmonica player Tommy Basker and fiddler/dancer Natalie McMaster have become well known internationally. A number of Scottish, Irish and Irish-American artists include Cape Breton music in their repertoire, including **Cappercaillie**, **Alan Kelly**, **Solas**, **Eileen Ivers** and **Nomos**. Donegal fiddler **Liz Doherty**, in addition to recording Cape Breton music, wrote a Ph.D. thesis (1996) on the Cape Breton fiddle tradition and has published and lectured on the subject. Songs relating to Nova Scotia are occasionally heard in the Irish repertoire; the group **Oisín**, for example, recorded 'Farewell to Nova Scotia' on their first album. Halifax, the capital of Nova Scotia, played host to the first Fiddles of the World festival for five days in July 1999, presenting a series of workshops and seminars on all aspects of the fiddle, including the diversity of international playing styles. Among the many fiddlers who took part were Natalie McMaster and **Kevin Burke**. The Celtic Colours International Festival, held annually (since 1997) on Cape Breton for a week in October, plays host to a wide range of top artists from Canada, Ireland, Scotland and the **US**. In 2002 Rounder Records released the first two volumes in a planned four-volume CD collection, *Traditional Fiddle Music of Cape Breton*.

O

O'Boyle, Seán (1908-1979)   Song collector born in Belfast and educated in Queen's University, Belfast. He did extensive research on Irish music and song and taught Irish music in Rannafast, Co. Donegal (1947-1944). *Cnuasacht de Cheoltaí Uladh* (Newry, 1944) was a collection of 25 songs in Irish (words and music) most of which were collected in the Rosses, Co. Donegal. From 1952 to 1954 he did a recording survey of Ulster folk music for the **BBC** and used much of the material in the radio series *As I Roved Out*, one of several series that he made. *The Irish Song Tradition* (Dublin, 1976) has the words and music of 25 Ulster songs in Irish and English. The collection includes notes to all of the songs, and in his introduction, entitled 'The Origins and Nature of Irish Songs', O'Boyle makes some interesting comments on the problems of collecting and other subjects.

Ó Briain, Donncha (1960-1990)   Dublin-born tin whistle player and teacher. He was encouraged to play traditional music by his father, Dinny, who played button accordion. Donncha took up the whistle at the age of six and won many **All-Ireland**, **Slógadh** and **Oireachtas** competitions for his playing. He toured Europe extensively and was a popular teacher at **Comhaltas Ceoltóirí Éireann** in Clontarf. The latter organisation published his collection of tunes, *The Golden Eagle* (Dublin, 1988; 2nd edition Dublin, 1993). He was among the whistle players whose versions of tunes were published in Tommy Walsh's *Irish Tin Whistle Legends* (Dublin, 1989). One of the finest whistle players of his generation, his playing can be heard on the album *Donncha Ó Briain* (1979).

O'Brien, Paddy 1 (b. 1945) Button accordion player and collector born in Birr, Co. Offaly, who won the **Oireachtas** four times and the **All-Ireland** Senior Championship twice. He was a member of **Ceoltóirí Laigheann** and also recorded with fiddler **James Kelly**. He emigrated to the **US** in the late 1970s, releasing his first solo album *Stranger at the Gate* in 1988. He has collected over 3,000 traditional tunes and issued a collection (originally on twelve cassettes, now also on ten CDs) with a book called *The Paddy O'Brien Tune Collection: A Personal Treasury of Jigs and Reels* (1995). Twenty of his notations of traditional tunes appeared in

Paddy O'Brien

Breandán Breathnach's *Ceol Rince na hÉireann* (vols. 2 & 3). In the late 1990s his group, Chulrua, won great critical acclaim in the US with their mixture of traditional songs and instrumentals. O'Brien's recordings with Chulrua include *Down The Back Lane* (2003), and although the group's line-up has changed a little over the years it still includes O'Brien and fellow founder-member Pat Egan (guitar, vocals), along with fiddler Patrick Ourceau, originally from France. Website: www.chulrua.com.

O'Brien, Paddy 2 (1922-1991) Button accordion and fiddle player from Newtown, near Nenagh, Co. Tipperary. He came from a great family of fiddle and concertina players, but although fiddle was his first instrument, it was for his accordion playing that he became best known. In the 1950s he was renowned for developing a new style of playing the B/C accordion, a style which influenced many players, most notably **Joe Burke** and, in his early playing career, **Séamus Begley**. O'Brien played in a number of céilí bands in both Ireland and the **US**, where he lived from 1954 to 1962. He made numerous recordings and also composed many tunes, a selection of which was published as *The Compositions of Paddy O'Brien* (Ayrshire, 1992).

Ó Canainn, Tomás (b. 1930) Uilleann piper, accordion player, lecturer and writer from Derry. Ó Canainn went to Liverpool to study Electrical Engineering in the late 1950s and was a founder member of the Liverpool Céilí Band. From 1961 he lectured in Electrical Engineering at **University College Cork** and also lectured in music, taking over from **Seán Ó Riada** after the latter's death in 1971. He was a founder member and played with **Na Filí** (1968-1979) and published *Traditional Music in Ireland* (London, 1978), a book which included detailed analyses of structure, style, **sean-nós singing**, the uilleann pipes, the fiddle and the music of **Paddy Keenan**, **Matt Cranitch** and **Diarmuid Ó Súilleabháin**. A man of many talents, Ó Canainn has also published poetry, an autobiography and a collection of Irish slow airs (with an accompanying recording). He has released three solo albums, including *The Pennyburn Piper Presents Uilleann Pipes* (1998). Website: http:// homepage.tinet.ie/~tocanainn.

O'Carolan, Turlough (1670-1738) In Irish Toirdhealbhach Ó Cearbhalláin, generally referred to as 'Carolan', born near Nobber, Co. Meath. Itinerant harper and composer whose compositions form a distinct branch of the 'traditional' repertoire. He lived in a time of great change, the great Gaelic patrons of the harpers having seen their whole way of life disappear in the wake of the Elizabethan (see **Elizabeth I**) and Cromwellian conquests. When Turlough was about fourteen, his father moved to Roscommon, where he went to work for the MacDermott Roe family of Alderford House. Turlough was blinded by smallpox at the age of eighteen, but Mrs. MacDermott Roe (who remained his most important patron throughout his life) arranged for him to be taught the harp. After learning the brass-strung harp for three years, Carolan embarked on a career as an itinerant harper, travelling mostly around Connacht for the rest of his life. Many of the old harpers were blind; travelling from house to house and playing, teaching, or composing on the harp was one of the few ways for a blind person to make a living.

Carolan was not, by all accounts, a good player, but found his true strength in composition. 'Sí Bheag, Sí Mhór', based on a legend about a war between two armies of the Otherworld, was said to have been his first composition. Throughout his life he composed numerous pieces, the majority of them for his patrons (or their relatives); among whom was Jonathan Swift, Dean of St. Patrick's Cathedral, Dublin and author of *Gulliver's Travels*. Carolan also wrote a substantial amount of poetry, some of which he used as the lyrics for songs sung to his own melodies. (His poetry has been published in the original Irish by the Irish Texts Society but is generally of poor quality.)

His compositions display three different stylistic influences, those of folk music, European art music and the music of the old Gaelic harpers. Of the three, the influence of folk music is the weakest but is found in a few tunes such as 'Elizabeth McDermott Roe'. The influence of the Gaelic harping tradition can be heard in pieces such as 'Dr. John Hart' and 'Sir Arthur Shaen'. The strongest influence, however, was that of contemporary Italian composers such as Vivaldi, Corelli and Geminiani. The famous 'Carolan's Concerto' was said to have been composed as part of a musical competition between Carolan and Geminiani when both were guests of Lord Mayo. In

Turlough O'Carolan

its imitation of Italian musical forms it is typical of the Irish harper and, according to some stories, is derived from part of Vivaldi's *The Four Seasons*. Carolan may well have invented the term **Planxty**, which is used of a cheerful, lively piece, often in **jig** time. While the origins of the word are obscure, it undoubtedly signified some form of dedication or toast to a particular person. Carolan uses the term at the start of many tune titles, following it with the name of the person to whom it is dedicated, as in 'Planxty Irwin', 'Planxty Hugh O'Donnell' or 'Planxty Kelly'.

Carolan married Mary Maguire at the age of 50 and began farming at Mosshill, Co. Leitrim. After her death in 1733, however, he took to the road again, although the loss of his wife left him severely depressed and he drank heavily. Five years after the death of his wife, Turlough himself died at the home of his chief patrons, the McDermott Roes of Alderford. He was buried in their family plot in the grave of

Kilronan, near Keadue, Co. Roscommon. He had six daughters and a son who published a collection of Carolan tunes in 1747, although this book did not survive. Collectors like **John and William Neale**, **Edward Bunting**, **George Petrie**, **Patrick Weston Joyce** and others played a major role in preserving and publishing the music of Carolan after his death.

Carolan composed over 200 pieces that survive today, a remarkable achievement for a man who had no formal training in composition and could neither read nor write music. His music today is regarded by many musicians as a distinct part of the traditional repertoire, although some musicians play few if any of his pieces, regarding them to be outside the tradition. Before **Seán Ó Riada** began to include Carolan pieces in the repertoire of his group, **Ceoltóirí Chualann**, very little Carolan music was played by traditional musicians. Turlough O'Carolan's life and work have been extensively studied by **Donal O'Sullivan** in *Carolan: The Life, Times and Music of an Irish Harper* (2 vols, London, 1958). The second volume of this work contains notations of all of Carolan's musical compositions, which were republished as a separate volume, *The Complete Works of O'Carolan, Irish Harper and Composer* (Cork, 1989). O'Sullivan's 1958 work was republished in a single volume by Ossian Publications, Cork (2001), with extra notes, an appendix and newly discovered tunes by harper Bonnie Shaljean. Harper **Gráinne Yeats** has done much to bring Carolan's lesser-known works to public attention through her research and playing; Michael O'Connor has published over 200 of the harper's compositions in one volume, and Waltons has published 110 in one volume of their *Ireland's Best* series, with arrangements suitable for most traditional instruments. There are also a number of more specialised published collections of Carolan tunes, arranged for guitar or harp. Carolan is the subject of a novel by Brian Keenan, *Turlough* (2000), which does not attempt to provide a historically accurate biography but a series of different perspectives on the harper/poet's work and life. See also **Bell, Derek**; **Feely John**; **Taylor, Simon**.

Ó Catháin, Darach (1922-1987)   **Sean-nós** singer whose family originally came from Connemara, Co. Galway, but moved to the newly created **Gaeltacht** area of Rathcairn, Co. Meath in 1935. Ó Catháin recorded a number of songs on the first **Ceoltóirí Chualann** album in 1962, and subsequently released a solo album *Darach Ó Catháin* (1975).

Ó Catháin, Ruairí Dall (ca. 1570-1650)   Harper from Co. Derry who made many visits to Scotland. He is credited with the composition of a number of tunes, most famously 'Tabhair dom do Láimh' ('Give Me Your Hand'), composed to mark a reconciliation with Lady Eglinton of Eglinton Castle, Ayrshire, Scotland. The tune is widely played and has been recorded by a number of musicians and groups, most famously **Planxty**. Brian Warfield of the **Wolfe Tones** put lyrics to the melody. See also **Scotland**.

Occupational Song Songs which have rhythms to match the work for which they are sung are rare in Ireland, in sharp contrast to Scotland where there are numerous waulking songs (see **Cappercaillie**) and boat songs. There are some spinning songs in Irish and in English, such as "Sambó éara', 'Mailero léró is ím bó néro' (both nonsense word titles) and 'The Spinning Wheel', composed by John Francis Waller (1809-1894). **George Petrie** included spinning and weaving tunes as well 'plough whistles' in his collection. The **sea shanty**, a unique form of occupational song sung by groups of seamen, was sung by Irish sailors, but many sea shanties were universal. 'Paddy Works on the Railway' is an interesting example of an occupational song sung by Irish immigrants to the **US** around the middle of the 19th century and has been recorded by **Mick Moloney**.

Although **pantomimic dances** that related to work did formerly exist in Ireland, it is difficult to judge how widespread work songs may have been in the past. **Gearóid Ó hAllmhuráin** is of the opinion that the 'cataclysm' of the **Great Famine** 'exacted a cruel toll from a once thriving tradition of work songs' (*A Pocket History of Irish Traditional Music*, p. 75). **Breandán Breathnach**, on the other hand, does not believe that such songs were once plentiful but died out with the activities that they accompanied. He points to the fact that, although hand spinning and weaving survived into the 20th century in **Gaeltacht** districts, no songs survived with them (*Folk Music and Dances of Ireland*, pp. 27-28). Part of the problem with a largely oral tradition of song such as this lies in securing sources which can help in evaluating how extensive or otherwise a tradition now lost may have been. **Hugh Shields** (*Narrative Singing in Ireland*, pp. 151-52) points to some interesting examples of songs sung during certain activities that were not necessarily related to the activity itself. It may have been the case that, while many people sang as they worked, they did not necessarily sing occupational songs in the strict sense of songs which, lyrically and rhythmically, were related to the work they were doing. Clearly, the subject of occupational songs in Ireland invites more comprehensive research.

O'Connell, Robbie (b. 1950) Singer, songwriter and guitarist, originally from Waterford city. His mother, Cait, was a sister of the Clancy Brothers (see **Clancy Brothers and Tommy Makem**), and Mount Richard (the family-run guesthouse in Carrick-on-Suir, Co. Tipperary) was visited by many famous musicians in the late 1950s and 60s. After moving to the **US** in 1972, O'Connell's interest in Irish folksong and traditional music deepened. He began to tour with the Clancys in the US and recorded with them. After his mother's death in 1976, he returned to Carrick-on-Suir to help his father run the family business, the Tinvane Hotel. He formed a group with **Tommy Keane**, **Martin Murray** and Paul Grant called the Bread and Beer Band, but they broke up in 1979 when O'Connell returned to the US. By this time he was writing his own songs in a folk, often mock-heroic style, and three of these were featured on his first solo album *Close to the Bone* (1982). The album also featured Tommy Keane and a selection of songs and tunes that had been part of the Bread and Beer Band's repertoire.

O'Connell settled in Massachusetts and recorded *There Were Roses* (1985) with **Mick Moloney**, piano accordion player Jimmy Keane and fiddler **Liz Carroll**. There are traditional instrumental sets, traditional songs and two classics from the **Sands Family**, Colum's 'In Almost Every Circumstance' and Tommy's 'There Were Roses'. With Moloney and Keane, O'Connell made another fine album, *Kilkelly* (1987). The title track is an unusual and moving portrait of the loneliness of emigration derived from a series of letters written between 1860 and 1890. Half of the album is taken up with the 'operetta' *The Green Fields of America*, a mixture of songs and instrumentals related to the experience of Irish immigrants to America. There is also a fine rendition of **Mickey McConnell**'s 'Peter Pan and Me'.

Robbie O'Connell

O'Connell's next album, *The Love of the Land* (1989), again featured Moloney and Keane but also included **Eileen Ivers**, **Séamus Egan** and uilleann piper Tim Britton. There is a fine version of the traditional song 'The Keg of Brandy' (learned from Annie Roche and Bobby Clancy in Carrick-on-Suir), for which O'Connell wrote a new verse melody. He also wrote all other songs on the album. O'Connell's songs cover a wide range of themes, including emigration and Irish identity ('The Land of Liberty', 'You're Not Irish' and 'Two Nations') and what O'Connell himself describes playfully as an anthem of Celtic Zen, 'Early Riser'. 'The Road to Dunmore' and 'Love of the Land' hark back to life in Ireland, and there is a song about the Dublin street singer **Zozimus**. *Never Learned to Dance* (1992) was produced by Scottish fiddler John Cunningham, who also played on the album. All of the songs are written by O'Connell, and while the line-up again includes Keane, Egan and Britton, some of the material marks a new departure in style. John Sands (drums), Ruth Rothstein (French horn), Brian O'Neill (keyboards) and Billy Novick (saxophone, clarinet) give a more rock-style sound to tracks such as 'American Lives' and 'When the Moon Is Full'). *Never Learned to Dance* again shows O'Connell's concern with themes like love, justice, emigration and war, although a sense of humour is also an important part of his work.

In addition to his solo work, O'Connell has played for many years in the group the Green Fields of America with Moloney, Ivers, Egan and others. More recently he has played with Liam Clancy and his son Dónal, with whom he released albums in 1997 and 1998. He also released *Humorous Songs Live* in 1998. A welcome addition to O'Connell's work is the compilation *Recollections Vol. 1* (2002), which includes a selection of his finest recordings made between 1981 and 1996. Five of the album's fifteen tracks include the fine harmony vocals of his wife Roxanne, and a 1996 recording of the song 'If Wishes Were Horses', originally written by O'Connell for his wife in the 1970s, is also included. Website: www.robbieoconnell.com.

O'Connor, Gerry 1 Musician from Garrykennedy, Co. Tipperary, one of the finest players of Irish traditional music on the tenor banjo. He also plays fiddle and guitar. He toured with traditional groups in the late 1970s and 80s and also played cabaret, rock and country music on the fiddle for a few years. Between 1982 and 1988 he recorded and toured extensively with **Four Men and a Dog**. He returned to playing banjo in 1990, recording a solo album, *Time to Time*. One of the tracks, 'Lumela Lesotho', combines African singing and the Irish traditional 'Kilfenora Jig' and was inspired by a lecture O'Connor had heard about the African origins of the banjo. *Time to Time* added to O'Connor's reputation as a fine player of traditional music comfortable with playing and composing in

Gerry O'Connor

other styles. Other original pieces in the album include 'Funk the Cajun Blues' and the title track, 'Time to Time'. A second solo album, *Myriad* (1998) again features a wide range of styles, including traditional, and again there are a number of tracks composed by O'Connor himself. His brother Michael (accordion) and father Liam (fiddle) join him on 'The Garrykennedy Set'. *No Place Like Home* (2004) marks a return to Irish traditional roots, although there is one American old timey tune on the album. In additional to the Irish traditional music, the album includes original compositions by a number of composers of traditional style tunes, including O'Connor himself, who also plays fiddle on the album.

O'Connor, Gerry 2 Fiddler from Dundalk, Co. Louth. He learned to play fiddle as a child from his mother, Rose, who taught the instrument for over three decades. He has performed with many of the finest traditional musicians and singers and was a founder member of **Skylark** in 1987. He also recorded four distinctive albums with his wife, **Eithne Ní Uallacháin**, three of these under the group name **Lá Lugh**. His first solo album, *Journeyman* (2004) was co-produced by his son, Dónal, and includes accompaniment by Paul McSherry (guitar, piano) and Martin O'Hare (bodhrán). It is a fine collection of both standard session tunes and more unusual traditional music. Website: www.gerryoconnor.net.

O'Connor, Máirtín (b. 1955) Button accordion player and composer born in Barna, Co. Galway. One of the finest living button accordion players, he has performed with many great traditional groups, including Reel Union with Dolores Keane (see **Keane Family**), **De Dannan** and **Skylark**. He has also recorded a number of solo albums. The first was *The Connachtman's Rambles* (1979), an album of traditional Irish tunes, most of them based on the collections of **Francis O'Neill** and **Breandán Breathnach**. A second solo album, *Perpetual Motion* (1990), contained no Irish traditional music, the title track a version of 'Moto Perpetuo' by the legendary Italian violinist and composer Niccolò Paganini (1782-1840) and the rest a mixture of American old time music (see **Appalachians**), Italian, French, Cajun, Ukrainian, Bulgarian and American ragtime tunes. One track, 'Emerald Blues', was composed by O'Connor himself. On his next album, *Chatterbox* (1993), which contained all original material, O'Connor displayed his ability to compose in a variety of styles.

Máirtín O'Connor

While pieces like the air 'Annaghdown Pier' and the jig 'Solid Ground' are Irish in style, others, such as 'Lucca's Waltz' and 'Amelan Waltz' display O'Connor's ability to compose in a more classical style. The superb 'Maam Turk', composed for an Irish-language version of the García Lorca play *Yerma*, has a Middle Eastern flavour. *The Road West* (2001) is a further collection of original tunes, although much of the music is more traditional in style than that on *Perpetual Motion* or *Chatterbox*. O'Connor composed a suite of music for the St. Patrick's Day Festival fireworks display in Dublin in 2003, and this music formed the core of the album *Rain of Light* (2003). Guests on the album include Kenneth Edge (saxophone, clarinet) and Garry Ó Briain (mandocello and keyboards). O'Connor has also played with the **Riverdance** Orchestra. Website: www.mairtinoconnor.com. See also **Argentina**; **Faulkner, Jimmy**; **Four Men and a Dog**.

O'Curry, Eugene (1796-1862) Historian, scholar of Irish and one of the most important ethnomusicologists of the 19th century, born in Carrigholt, Co. Clare. In the years 1834-1837 he worked for the historical and topographical section of the Ordnance Survey under **George Petrie**. He became an expert in Gaelic manuscripts, researching and cataloguing them at the Royal Irish Academy and the British Museum. He edited and published Gaelic legal texts, legends and poetry and became Professor of Irish History and Archaeology at the Catholic University (now University College Dublin) in 1854. He reconstructed the life and customs of the ancient and medieval Irish from manuscript sources, publishing two major works,

Lectures on the Manuscript Materials of Ancient Irish History (Dublin, 1861) and *On the Manners and Customs of the Ancient Irish* (Dublin, 1873). The latter included a section on 'Musical Instruments of the Ancient Irish', a major contribution to the subject. He also collected music and songs with George Petrie in the Aran Islands which the latter published in his *Ancient Music of Ireland 1* (Dublin, 1855).

Ó Domhnaill, Micheál   One of the finest contemporary singers of traditional songs (in both Irish and English) as well as a gifted guitarist. A brother of **Maighréad and Tríona Ní Dhomhnaill**, he grew up in the Donegal Gaeltacht and in Kells, Co. Meath. He took up the piano at the age of four and, under the influence of the American folk revival of the 1960s, started to play guitar at thirteen. From 1969 he took Celtic Studies at University College Dublin and later collected a vast repertoire of songs from his aunt Néilí. His first venture into recording in 1971 involved his two sisters and Dáithí Spról playing as **Skara Brae**. When they broke up, he formed **Monroe** and released the fine album *Celtic Folkweave* in 1974. The following year saw the release of the first of four classic albums Micheál and Tríona made as members of the **Bothy Band**. After the group disbanded in 1979, Micheál moved to the **US**, forming a duo with fiddler **Kevin Burke**. Their first album, *Promenade* (1979), is still regarded as a classic, and features a marvellous rendition of the song 'Lord Franklin', telling the tale of the English explorer's fatal expedition to the Arctic in 1847. Ó Domhnaill and Burke made another fine album together, *Portland* (1982). Micheál and Tríona again teamed up to form half of the dynamic Irish/Scots band **Relativity** in the 1980s and played together for over a decade with a jazz/traditional fusion group, **Nightnoise**. After returning to live in Ireland, Ó Domhnaill got together with fiddler **Paddy Glackin** and made the album *Athcuairt/Reprise* (2000). See also **Pentangle**.

O'Donnell, Joe (b. 1947)   Fiddle player, fiddle maker and composer born in Limerick who started to learn classical violin at the age of twelve. In the late 1960s he won two scholarships to the Royal Irish Academy of Music, where he studied orchestral work. He emigrated to London in 1971, where he played with the Woods Band, formed by Gay Woods and Terry Woods, later of Steeleye Span and the **Pogues**. He started making electric violins, including an 8-string violin, for his own use. He composed and recorded the unusual and much neglected album, *Gaodhal's Vision*, in 1977. The album is an eclectic 'symphony' (entirely instrumental) which traces the mythical origin of the Milesians in Egypt, their exodus with their leader Gaodhal, their rise to power in Ireland and the evolution of a new society in Ireland centred on the royal seat at Tara. The story seems to be based on the version of early Irish history which medieval 'synthetic historians' elaborated, linking the story of Celtic Ireland to events and characters in the Bible. The themes of the second half are loosely based on a picture of Irish society in the Iron Age, centred in some cases on specific parts of the historic site of Tara, including 'The Great Banqueting Hall'. O'Donnell plays acoustic fiddle and 8-string electric fiddle throughout, with 1970s rock/blues star Rory Gallagher playing guitar. Other musicians include Bill Smith (bass), Theodore Thunder (drums), David Lennox (keyboards) and Jon Field (flute). The music is an unusual mixture of styles. Much of it is in the style of 1970s Celtic rock, electric fiddles and guitars frequently playing lead to a drum, bass and keyboard backing, but at points the music exhibits eastern and classical flavours. The fiddling on *Gaodhal's Vision* is not traditional in style, yet manages to create an Irish ambience in this musical exploration of the early story of the Celts. Changes in style, tempo and instrumentation are the most striking characteristics of this album, which is an interesting piece of work and deserves more attention in the context of the various forms of experimentation that took place in Irish music during the 1970s. Perhaps more people will discover its delights and eccentricities through the re-released CD version of 2004.

After *Gaodhal's Vision* O'Donnell played the festival circuit for some time and worked as a session musician in London. He moved to Guernsey during the 1980s, where he lived for fourteen years, playing with different groups but moving back to the British mainland in the late 1990s to relaunch his musical career. His first album for 23 years, *Schkayla* (2000), is a mixture of traditional style acoustic tracks and the electric folk/rock style explored on *Gaodhal's Vision*. O'Donnell also sings traditional and original songs, and there are some tunes from **Brittany**. O'Donnell plays a number of different instruments on the album, including a unique ceramic violin made by John Stevens, a model maker from Kent.

O'Donovan, Joe and Siobhán

O'Donovan, Joe and Siobhán Husband-and-wife team of **set dancing** teachers who have played an important role in the revival of interest in set dancing. An **All-Ireland** dance champion at the age of fourteen, Joe O'Donovan was a founder member of the Cork branch of **Comhaltas Ceoltóirí Éireann** and is Director of Dance at the **Willie Clancy Summer School**. He is regarded by many as *the* master dancer of the 20th century. His video, *Old Style Traditional Step Dancing, 1700-1930* was commissioned by **Comhaltas Ceoltóirí Éireann** and released in 1997. It is both a tutor for aspiring dancers and a history of the subject.

Ó Drisceoil, Con

Ó Drisceoil, Con Button accordion player, pianist and singer/songwriter from west Cork who has lived for many years in Cork city. He played in the Phoenix Céilí Band and the Four Star Trio as well as the short-lived Irish Parlour Trio with **Colin 'Hammy' Hamilton** and **Paul McGrattan**. He writes his own humorous songs, and his first song to reach widespread public attention was 'The Pool Song' in the 1970s, made famous by **Jimmy Crowley**. He also wrote a song called 'King Lear', a hilarious reworking of William Shakespeare's classic play. Another of his songs, 'The Probation Act', deals with events surrounding a raid during a session in a bar in Milltown Malbay, Co. Clare during the **Willie Clancy Summer School**. He can be heard playing the box and singing 'King Lear' and 'The Spoons Murder' on *It's No Secret* (2001) with **Séamus Creagh** and Hammy Hamilton.

O'Farrell

O'Farrell (First name uncertain, possibly Patrick) Clonmel-born uilleann piper and collector of Irish music who made a considerable name for himself in London during the late 18th and early 19th centuries. He published the first known book on how to play the uilleann pipes, *O'Farrell's Collection of National Irish Music for the Union Pipes* (London, 1804; reproduction by Patrick Sky, Chapel Hill, North Carolina, 1995), which includes 'a treatise with the most perfect instructions ever yet published for the pipes'. The title page of the book shows the author playing the uil-

leann pipes 'in the favourite pantomime of Oscar and Malvina' (in which another Irish uilleann piper, Patrick Gaynor, also performed). O'Farrell himself states in his introduction that the pipes are 'an instrument now so much improved as renders it able to play any kind of music', and he gives a fully chromatic fingering chart. All of these notable details from O'Farrell's book, as well as the fact that fully keyed chromatic chanters survive from this period, have led Ciaran Carson to suggest (*Irish Traditional Music*, pp. 13-14) that the pipes may have been developed for the playing of non-Irish music. *O'Farrell's Pocket Companion for the Union Pipes* was published in London in four volumes. Although the dates of publication are uncertain, it seems that the four volumes were published between ca. 1805 and 1810. All four were republished by Patrick Sky in the **US** (Chapel Hill, North Carolina, 1999). The *Pocket Companion* contained an early version of the descriptive piece called 'The Foxhunt', attributed to the blind piper Edward Keating Hyland. It also included some of O'Farrell's own compositions, including 'The Waterford Waltz' and 'O'Farrell's Welcome to Limerick'.

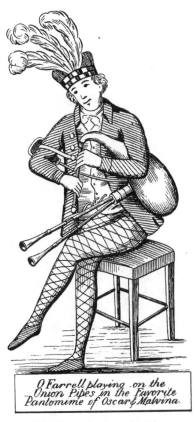

O'Farrell (illustration from the title page of *O'Farrell's Collection of National Irish Music for the Union Pipes*)

Ó Fátharta, Meatí Jó Shéamuis (b. 1947)

Sean-nós singer, flautist, uilleann piper, whistle player, collector and broadcaster from Cois Fharraige, Connemara, Co. Galway. His mother was also a fine sean-nós singer and Meatí Jó has a deep knowledge of sean-nós songs. A full-time broadcaster with **Raidió na Gaeltachta**, he has also taught at the Milwaukee Summer School and broadcast from the **Milwaukee Irish Fest**. On his album *Bóithríní an Locháin* (2003) he sings sean-nós songs from Connemara as well as lilting and playing flute and uilleann pipes.

O'Flynn, Liam (Liam Óg) (b. 1945)

Uilleann piper and whistle player born in Kill, Co. Kildare. His mother, Maisie Scanlan, played piano and was a cousin of

Junior Crehan. His father, also Liam, played the fiddle and moved from his native Kerry to Kildare when Liam Óg was about six years old. Liam Óg started learning the whistle at the age of six and the pipes from **Leo Rowsome** at age twelve. In the 1960s he won first prize at the **Oireachtas** piping competition on three occasions, and was also **All-Ireland** champion at the **Fleadh Cheoil**. His piping was influenced by that of **Willie Clancy** and **Séamus Ennis** (who shared a flat with O'Flynn in Dublin during the 1970s and left his pipes to the young Kildare piper), as well as by Rowsome. Following the success of **Christy Moore**'s album **Prosperous**, O'Flynn became a founding member of the group **Planxty**, with whom he recorded seven albums between 1972 and 1983.

In 1980, O'Flynn performed and recorded *The Brendan Suite*, composed for

Liam O'Flynn

uilleann pipes and orchestra by **Shaun Davey**, the first of a number of collaborations of this kind. In 1988 he released *The Fire Aflame* with **Seán Keane** and **Matt Molloy** and his first solo album, simply titled *Liam O'Flynn*. There are guest appearances by Seán Keane, **Dónal Lunny** and others, including Séamus Ennis's daughter Catherine, who accompanies the uilleann pipes on Church organ for the slow air 'Easter Snow'. Further solo albums followed, including *The Fine Art of Piping* (1989) and *The Piper's Call* (1998). Among the greatest of uilleann pipers, he has also worked with many non-traditional musicians, including rock singer Kate Bush, avant-garde composer John Cage and Dire Straits' guitarist Mark Knopfler, whose music he performed for the film *Cal* (CD 1984). He has also performed Galician music with the piper Carlos Nuñez (see **Galicia**). In 1999, he collaborated with poet Seamus Heaney, making a film together entitled *Making Time*, and giving some stage performances, one of which was broadcast on radio as *The Poet and the Piper* (1999). One of the pieces which O'Flynn played with Heaney was the slow air 'Port na bPúcaí' ('Music of the Ghosts'), which inspired Heaney's poem 'The Given Note', the latter being used by O'Flynn as a title for his 1995 solo album. **Claddagh Records** released a CD of Heaney and O'Flynn in 2003, also under the title *The Poet and the Piper*.

Ó hAllmhuráin, Gearóid (b. 1955)   Concertina player, uilleann piper, historian and anthropologist from Ennis, Co. Clare. He played with the Kilfenora Céilí Band and was awarded a Ph.D. by Queen's University, Belfast in 1990 for a thesis entitled *The Concertina in the Traditional Music of Clare*. He is now based in the **US**, where he tours and lectures. Since 2000 he has been Jefferson Smurfit Corporation Professor of Irish Studies at the University of Missouri-St. Louis. He released a solo CD, *Traditional Music from Clare and Beyond* (1996) on the Celtic Crossings label and wrote *A Pocket History of Irish Traditional Music* (Dublin, 1998), which traces traditional music and song through Ireland's history, from earliest times up to the present. The book is particularly interesting on the subject of the early history of Irish emigration to **Canada** (including **Newfoundland** and **Nova Scotia**) and the US. Ó hAllmhuráin has toured extensively with French-born fiddler Patrick Ourceau, and the two released *Tracin': Traditional Music from the West of Ireland* in 1999, also on the Celtic Crossings label.

Ó Héanaí, Seosamh (1920-1984)   Also known as Seosamh Ó Héiniú or Joe Heaney; **sean-nós** singer born to Irish-speaking parents from Carna in Connemara, Co. Galway. He was the first sean-nós singer to attract widespread attention and publicity during the revival in the 1960s and 70s. He lived in London before emigrating to the **US**, where he spent over twenty years working in Brooklyn, New York as an elevator operator and, during the 1960s and 70s, appeared in some of the big American folk festivals alongside such artists as the **Clancy Brothers and Tommy Makem**, **Jean Ritchie** and **Bob Dylan**. Before his death he worked as artist-in-residence at the University of Washington, Seattle, where he left a considerable collection of song and folklore. *An Index to the Songs and Stories in the Joe Heaney Collection* was edited by Seán Williams and published by the University of Washington in 1985 and 1991.

Although he says he never sang until he was about twenty years old, Ó Héanaí had a remarkable mastery of the difficult ornamentation and phrasing of sean-nós singing. He played an important role in popularising many songs that might otherwise have been lost, and his influence has been acknowledged by many Irish singers, including Liam Clancy and **Christy Moore**.

Ó Héanaí's voice has been captured on several albums. The first, *Irish Traditional Songs in Gaelic and English* (1963, re-released 1989), includes the popular 'Tighearna Randall', an adaptation of the English 'Lord Randall' (see **Child Ballads**) and one of the few old ballads that passed from the English into the Irish language. The album also includes the **chantefable** 'Peigín is Peadar', in which Ó Héanaí gives the background to the song in English and then proceeds to sing the song in Irish. There is also an Irish version of the light-hearted 'Cúnnla' (later made famous in an English version by **Planxty**) and the **macaronic song** 'One Morning in June', as well as sean-nós classics such as 'Caoineadh na dTrí Muire' ('The Lament of the Three Marys'; see **Religious Songs**) and 'Casadh an tSúgáin' ('The Twisting of the Rope').

Ó Héanaí had a remarkably rich repertoire of songs, some learned from his father in Carna, others learned from singers in other parts of Ireland. *Seosamh Ó*

Héanaí (1971) has songs in Irish only and includes 'Eanach Dhúin' ('Annaghdown'), a lament composed on the occasion of a tragic drowning of nineteen people from Annaghdown, Co. Galway. *Joe Heaney* (1975) includes songs in English as well as Irish, the classic 'Róisín Dubh' ('Little Black Rose'; see **Aisling**) among the latter. On *Ó Mo Dhúcas* ('From My Tradition', 1976, re-released on CD 1997) the material is all in Irish, including two chantefables, 'Seachrán Chearbhaill' ('Carroll's Wandering') and 'Peigín is Peadar', which on this album has both the spoken story and the song in Irish. Ó Héanaí's versions of the classic Irish love songs 'Dónal Óg' ('Young Donal') and 'Úna Bhán' ('Fair Úna') are also on this album. *The Road from Connemara* (2000), a double CD released by **Cló Iar-Chonnachta**, has 41 tracks of songs and stories as told to **Ewan MacColl** and Peggy Seeger in 1964. The album includes songs of love, rebellion, the sea, drinking songs and commentaries on the history and context of the material. An acclaimed documentary, *Sing the Dark Away*, about the life and work of the Carna singer was produced for **RTÉ** television by Michael Davitt and was first shown in January 1996.

Oireachtas, An t   The Oireachtas (literally 'the assembly') was founded by **Conradh na Gaeilge** (the Gaelic League) in 1897 and is Ireland's longest running annual cultural festival. There was a break from 1923 to 1939 and when the festival was revived it was held every year in the Mansion House, Dublin. From 1974, however, it reverted to the original idea of a varied venue. It is now a ten-day event that includes a major art exhibition as well as 150 competitions in literature, composition and performance arts, including traditional music, dance, singing, drama and story-telling. The **sean-nós singing** competitions are a major attraction and the final competition in late October (for the *Corn Uí Riada*, named after **Seán Ó Riada**) is broadcast live by **Raidio Na Gaeltachta**. **Sean-nós dancing** became part of the event's competitive structure in 1977.

Oisín   Dublin-based traditional group whose original line-up consisted of Geraldine McGowan (vocals, recorder, bodhrán), Tom McDonagh (bouzouki), Mick Davies (fiddle, vocals), Brian McDonagh (mandolin) and Seamus McGowan (guitar, vocals). Their first album, *Oisín* (1976) was produced by **Paul Brady**, who also played guitar on some tracks. It featured guest musician **Darach de Brún** (whistle, uilleann pipes), who also composed some of the material, 'The Maple Leaf/The Man of Aran' (reels) and 'The Walk of the Fiddler's Bride' (march') and 'Terry's Travels' (reel). The group had a distinctive blend of instruments, with the bouzouki and mandolin being used effectively for both melody and accompaniment. A good example is provided by the jigs with which they open their first album, 'Doherty's Jig/Donnybrook Fair', beginning with a fine mandolin/bouzouki duet that gradually builds to include the other instruments. Geraldine McGowan's strong vocals were always central to the group's sound as well, and she and Séamus, as well as Mick Davies, remained with the group through various changes in line-up. Among the considerable number of musicians who played with Oisín are Gerry Phelan (flute), Anne Conroy (accordion), Micheál Ó Briain (uilleann pipes), **Steve Cooney** and

Davy Spillane. They released numerous albums between 1972 and 1987 and toured extensively in Europe. Geraldine and Shay McGowan have been based in Germany since the group broke up. Brian McDonagh was a founder member of **Dervish**, whose use of stringed instruments is similar in style to that of Oisín.

O'Keeffe, Pádraig (1887-1963) Last of the travelling fiddle masters from the **Sliabh Luachra** area, born at Gleanntán, Cordal, Castleisland. His mother, Margaret O'Callaghan, played fiddle and concertina and his uncle, fiddler Callaghan O'Callaghan, was a major influence. He trained as a schoolteacher but was never fully committed to teaching and left his job as principal of Gleanntán School in 1920. Eventually he started to work as a travelling fiddle master, writing tunes for pupils for which he was paid. He could read and write standard musical notation but preferred to use his own system of tablature, specially devised for teaching the fiddle easily (see **Music Notation**). Although he composed many slides and polkas because there was a demand for them in the area, he preferred playing reels, hornpipes and jigs. Many tunes, especially slides and polkas, still bear his name in their title. **Séamus Ennis**, who became a close friend of O'Keeffe's and learned many tunes from him, described the fiddler's style as 'a light, agile flowing style with a wonderful, pulsating vigour in the dance rhythms with a tendency to gay, wild abandon in the slides and polkas' (*Ceol na hÉireann,* No. 2, 1994, p. 68). O'Keeffe spent his life travelling the mountainous countryside of Sliabh Luachra, teaching and playing sessions in the pubs of villages such as Scartaglen, Castleisland, Brosna and Ballydesmond. He appears to have had a huge repertoire of tunes, many of them from memory only, which he had learned from older musicians, books such as the **O'Neill** collection and the radio. Among his many pupils was **Denis Murphy**.

O'Keeffe travelled little outside Sliabh Luachra in his lifetime, during which he had only one track on a commercial recording, *The Lark in the Morning* (1955). Since his death, *Kerry Fiddles, Vol. 1* (1977, from recordings made by Séamus Ennis in 1952) was released, with solos by O'Keeffe and duets and trios with **Julia Clifford** and Denis Murphy. *The Sliabh Luachra Fiddle Master* (1993) consists of over an hour of music recorded by Ennis in 1948-49. The **RTÉ** Archive has tapes of radio programmes about O'Keeffe, including four programmes made by Peter Browne in 1993. Browne reports, in a fine article about O'Keeffe, that the latter was not particularly religious. He used to say that when he died he would not go to heaven or hell but to 'Fiddler's Green'. This, said O'Keeffe, was eight miles below hell and 'you'd need all steel strings on the fiddle as any other strings wouldn't be able to stand up to the heat' (quoted in Browne's 'The Sliabh Luachra Fiddle Master Pádraig O'Keeffe [1887-1963]' in *Ceol na hÉireann* No. 2, 1994, p. 78). Dermot Hanafin has published a book *Pádraig O'Keeffe: The Man and His Music* (Castleisland, 1995). A bust of O'Keeffe now stands in the village square at Scartaglen, and a Pádraig O'Keefe Festival is held annually in Castleisland

Ó Laoire, Lillis (b. 1961) Sean-nós singer, lecturer, researcher and writer from Gort a' Choirce in the Donegal **Gaeltacht**. He became interested in **sean-nós**

singing while studying Irish at University College Galway and went on to win the *Corn Uí Riada* in 1991 and 1994. He can be heard singing on *Bláth Gach Géag dá dTtig* (1992). During the 1990s he undertook research on the traditional song, music and dance of Tory Island, off the coast of Donegal. The work was for a Ph.D. thesis at the University of Limerick, but he also received a scholarship from the University of California, Los Angeles in 1996-97. The fruits of his research were published by **Cló Iar-Chonnachta** as *Ar Chreag I Lár na Farraige* (2002), a publication which includes 80 photographs and a companion CD. Ó Laoire sings eight of the tracks on the CD himself, the remainder coming from recordings made by **RTÉ**, **Raidió na Gaeltachta** and **Séamus Ennis**. See also **Mad for Trad**.

O'Leary, Johnny (1923-2004) Box player from **Sliabh Luachra** who played in the 'press-and-draw' style (see **Accordion**). From Maulykeavane, between Gneevgullia and Killarney, he started to play the melodeon when he was only five years old and went on to the two-row button accordion. From the age of thirteen he was performing in the local hall with **Denis Murphy**. Their partnership lasted almost 40 years. O'Leary is noted for the speed and vigour of his style, which part-ly derived from his regular playing for dancers. He recorded three albums, *Music for the Set* (1977), *The Trooper / An Calmfhear* (1989) and *Johnny O'Leary of Sliabh Luachra: Dance music from the Cork/Kerry Border*, recorded in December 1995 in Dan O'Connell's pub in Knocknagree.

Breandán Breathnach recognised that O'Leary's playing preserved the tradi-tional style and repertoire of Sliabh Luachra and began to compile a collection of his tunes. Breathnach died before the project was completed and the work was taken up by piper Terry Moylan, who edited and published *Johnny O'Leary of Sliabh Luachra: Dance Music from the Cork-Kerry Border* (Dublin, 1994). It is in many ways a seminal work, with careful transcriptions, interesting notes on the tunes and musicians of Sliabh Luachra, some of O'Leary's stories about the tunes and analysis of style and repertoire. O'Leary spent over half of his time playing polkas and slides, and great work went into finding proper names for many of these tunes. The 1995 album of the same title is intended to complement the book.

O'Leary's repertoire of tunes was vast and many of them were performed and recorded by groups such as **Planxty**, the **Bothy Band**, **Sliabh Notes** and **Beginish**. He won awards from the **Willie Clancy Week** Festival (2001), the **Padraig O'Keefe** Festival (2003) and the **TG4** 'Gradam Saoil/Lifetime Achievement' award in 2003.

Ó Lionáird, Iarla (b. 1964) Sean-nós singer born in the **Gaeltacht** area of Cúil Aodha in West Cork, a nephew of the singer **Elizabeth Cronin**. He sang on radio at the age of seven and won many **Slógadh** competitions up to the age of fifteen. He was also a member of **Seán Ó Riada**'s Cór Chúil Aodha. He recorded *Aislingí Ceoil: Music of Dreams* (1993) with **Noel Hill** and **Tony MacMahon**. He has per-formed on numerous compilations, including *A River of Sound* and *Sult* and is a member of **Afro Celts**. His work with the latter group and his solo album *Seven*

Steps to Mercy (1997) has brought **sean-nós singing** into a more modern, 'world music' context. *Seven Steps to Mercy* was produced by the Canadian experimental guitarist Michael Brooke, who also plays on the album. Uilleann piper **Ronan Browne**, the only additional musician, features on just one track. Brooke's special guitar effects are a perfect compliment to the haunting vocals. One track, 'Aisling Gheal' ('Bright Vision'), was recorded when Ó Lionáird was only fourteen, and 'Abha' ('River') has an introduction which includes the voice of the poet Dónal Lihane and the singer's own moth-

Iarla Ó Lionáird

er talking about the river in Cúil Aodha in 1932. Overall, the album has a uniquely modern sound and yet brings out the best in the singer's voice and style. This is perhaps the most unusual album of sean-nós singing ever made and has already stimulated a new interest in the 'old style'. Ó Lionáird also recorded music for the film *I Could Read the Sky*, which was released on CD in 2000.

O Lochlainn, Colm (1892-1972) Ballad singer, ballad maker, collector and publisher. A later collector, **James N. Healy**, dedicated his *The Mercier Book of Irish Street Ballads, Vol. 3* (Cork, 1969) with the words: 'To Colm O Lochlainn who did so much for ballad collections in Ireland in darker days'. O Lochlainn founded the Three Candles Press (1926-1989) in Dublin and was noted for the quality of his typography. His *Irish Street Ballads* (1939) and *More Irish Street Ballads* (1965) were originally published by Three Candles Press, beautifully produced with full musical notation for all songs and illustrated with woodcuts from various sources. He also provided notes on all of the ballads in both collections, which were republished in a single volume as *The Complete Irish Street Ballads* by Pan Books in 1984. O Lochlainn also wrote *Songwriters in Ireland in the English Tongue* (Dublin, 1967).

O'Loughlin, Peadar (b. 1929) Fiddler, uilleann piper and flautist from Cullen, Kilmaley, Co. Clare, six miles from Ennis. His father was a well-known concertina player and during the 1940s, 50s and 60s O'Loughlin played with some of the finest traditional musicians, including **Joe Cooley**, **Willie Clancy**, **Elizabeth Crotty** and **Tommy Potts**. He joined the Fiach Rua Céilí Band in 1948 and subsequently played with the Tulla and Kilfenora **Céilí Band**s. He recorded *All-Ireland Champions: Violin* (1959) with fellow fiddlers **Paddy Canny** and **P. J. Hayes** and piano player Bridie Lafferty. In the 1950s he played extensively with local concertina player Paddy Murphy and in more recent decades has performed with Paddy Canny. O'Loughlin has made two excellent albums with **Ronan Browne**, *The South West Wind* (1988) and *Touch Me If You Dare* (2002). *The Thing Itself* (2004) is a duet album with fiddler Maeve Donnelly (accompanied on piano by Geraldine Cotter). Ronan Browne guests on flute and whistle, and there are excellent sleeve notes by piper Pat Mitchell.

Ó Murchú, Marcas (b. 1961) Flute player from Belfast. Family connections with the Sligo-Leitrim area led Ó Murchú to explore the flute playing of North Connacht, and he got to know many of the older players of this region. His album *Ó Bhéal go Béal* (1997) is in many ways a personal tribute to the old-style players of North Connacht, although there are tunes from Munster and Ulster as well. The range of different tune types on the album is unusually broad – including jigs, reels, hornpipes, polkas, highland schottisches, planxties and slow airs – and he also sings three songs in Irish. There is a mixture of traditional and more recently composed material, by **Paddy O'Brien** (Tipperary), **Cathal McConnell** of the **Boys of the Lough** and the Roscommon flute player **Josie McDermott**. Ó Murchú's unusual phrasing often varies markedly within the same tune. He sometimes uses long notes in the dance tunes to emphasise the rhythm, and the tone overall is delicate and often wavering. The album has been praised as providing 'an immensely valuable unbroken link with the past' (*Irish Music*, November 1997, p. 39) because of the attention paid to the old North Connacht style, and it has won critical acclaim as 'pure' traditional music. Some of the tracks are unaccompanied, but others feature accompaniment by Eoghan O'Brien of Déanta (guitar, harp), Seamus O'Kane (bodhrán) or Bríd McNally (piano), with Maurice Bradley (fiddle) and Peter Gallagher (accordion) also guesting. The accompanying booklet provides excellent notes on the tunes and songs and is notable for the recognition given to all composers of new tunes. It underlines the extent to which the traditional repertoire is constantly expanded by new compositions, an aspect of the music often neglected. Ó Murchú's playing is technically accomplished and, without straying from the main lines of the melodies, he varies them imaginatively in a manner that encourages close listening.

O'Neill, Francis (1848-1936) The most famous and influential collector of traditional Irish music. Born in Tralibane, near Bantry in Co. Cork, during the **Great Famine**, O'Neill grew up in an environment where he was surrounded by traditional dance music and songs, and learned to play the traditional flute at an early age from a local gentleman farmer. He was an outstanding pupil in mathematics, Latin and Greek, and was nicknamed 'Philosopher' by one teacher. His parents hoped he would become a priest or Christian Brother, but at the age of sixteen he ran away to sea. In his late teens and early twenties, he sailed to various parts of the world, including Russia, Egypt, Japan and the Americas. In the late 1860s he was shipwrecked in the mid-Pacific and rescued with his fellow crewmen in a half-starved condition. After this, he had another brief spell at sea and also sailed on the Great Lakes in 1870, basing himself in Chicago. By the age of 24, O'Neill had worked not only as a sailor but also as a shepherd, a teacher, a railroad labourer and a lumberyard supervisor. In autumn 1870, he married Anna Rogers in Bloomington, Illinois. She was an emigrant from Feakle, Co. Clare, whom O'Neill had met on his first voyage to the **US** in 1866.

In July 1873 the adventurous young Irishman finally settled on a career, joining the Chicago police force. By 1901 his bravery, honesty and good standard of education earned him the position of General Superintendent or Chief of the Chicago police, a position he held until his resignation in 1905. He was one of the few superintendents in the history of the Chicago police force who was untainted by corruption, and he appointed the first African-American policeman in the US to be promoted above the rank of patrolman.

O'Neill used every opportunity, in his working and private life, to discover Irish musicians and collect new tunes. Emigrant musicians from all counties of Ireland were living in the area around Chicago and there was a constant stream of musicians passing through. He was assisted in his collecting and transcribing of tunes by James O'Neill (1863-1949, no relation), a fiddler from Co. Down. Although 'the Chief' did develop some degree of musical literacy in his later years, he did not have the ability to write down tunes quickly and accurately from the playing of others, and in this James provided crucial assistance. 'The Chief' got his namesake into the police force, and they collaborated in the production of the first three O'Neill collections. *O'Neill's Music of Ireland*, the largest collection of Irish music ever printed, was published in 1903 and contains a total of 1850 tunes, classified

Francis O'Neill

under Airs (625), **Turlough O'Carolan** compositions (75), Double Jigs (415), Slip Jigs (60), Reels (380), Hornpipes (225), Long Dances (20) and Marches and Miscellaneous (55). Although it was greeted with praise in many quarters, it was harshly criticised by some. Arthur Griffith's periodical, the *Nationalist*, accused O'Neill, among other things, of padding out his book with dozens of English airs and ballad tunes. No criticisms could detract, however from the enormity of O'Neill's achievement, and he soon produced a cheaper book for musicians who were interested only in the dance music. *The Dance Music of Ireland* was published in 1907 and contains 1001 jigs, reels, hornpipes and special dance tunes. This overlapped to a considerable degree with the dance music in the earlier collection, but included an additional 140 tunes.

The Dance Music of Ireland proved so valuable to musicians and circulated so widely that it became known simply as 'the book', a virtual bible for many traditional players (it is available today in a facsimile edition from **Waltons**). The book was produced to meet a particular demand from musicians, as was O'Neill's next collection, *O'Neill's Irish Music: 250 Choice Selections Arranged for Piano and Violin – First Series* (1908). As with the two earlier volumes, James O'Neill arranged all of the material, but the piano arrangements were criticised and no further volumes in the planned series appeared.

Arrangements for the collections, *Popular Selections from O'Neill's Dance Music of Ireland* (1910) and *Waifs and Strays of Gaelic Melody* (1922 and 1924), were done by Selena O'Neill (again no relation), a young violinist trained at Chicago Music College. The 1922 edition of *Waifs and Strays* consists of 335 Irish and Scottish melodies with historical and descriptive notes, while the 1924 edition has 365 melodies. Francis O'Neill also produced a semi-autobiographical book, which dealt as well with aspects of the history of Irish music and musical instruments, under the title *Irish Folk Music: A Fascinating Hobby* (1910). Three years later he published *Irish Minstrels and Musicians*, a fascinating account of Irish musicians, historical and contemporary, with many digressions on other aspects of Irish music history.

In addition to playing the flute, O'Neill played the uilleann pipes, the Scottish Lowland pipes, the Scottish Highland pipes, the fiddle and the tin whistle. He was still publishing articles on Irish music at the age of 84, and died of heart failure at his home in Chicago on 28 January 1936. His collections have appeared in many different editions since his death and his influence on the evolution of traditional Irish dance music is felt right down to the present day. **Nicholas Carolan**'s *A Harvest Saved: Francis O'Neill and Irish Music in Chicago*, an excellent account of O'Neill's colourful life and his work, was published in 1997. It was published by **Ossian Publications** as an introduction to a new, complete O'Neill collection, which is being worked on at the **Irish Traditional Music Archive**. This is a combined edition of all O'Neill's substantial collections. All the tunes are being reset and the collection will include four comprehensive indexes which contain all primary and secondary tune titles and a coded thematic index.

Orange/Loyalist Song

A type of **political song** that, in contrast to **Jacobite song** or **Nationalist/Republican song**, espouses the views of the Irish Protestant community loyal to the English Crown. One of the earliest Orange songs was 'Boyne Water', celebrating the Protestant William of Orange's victory over the Jacobites at the Battle of the Boyne in 1690. Although the date of the song is uncertain, it did serve as a stylistic prototype for the orange songs of celebration and confrontation that began to appear during the politically polarised 1790s. In that decade, the first popular Orange or Loyalist anthologies were published in Dublin and Cork, reflecting the fact that the tradition of this type of political song extended throughout the whole of Ireland. One of the songs emerging from this period was 'Lisnagade', which commemorated the 1791 clash between 'Protestant Rights' and 'Popery' at an anniversary celebration of the Battle of the Boyne in Co. Down.

Throughout the 19th century, Orange/Loyalist and Nationalist/Republican songs were important expressions of opposing political viewpoints. These political songs could also play their own role in events, often stirring up crowds or swaying people towards political action as effectively as the most gifted orators. One of the best known Orange songs to emerge from this period was 'Dolly's Brae', dated to 1849. 'Lillibulero' (an anti-Jacobite parody issued in the late 1680s), 'The Protestant Boys' and 'The Old Orange Flute' are all still sung today. *On Boyne's Shore. Historical Folk Songs of Ulster* (1978), released on **Outlet** is a selection of Orange songs sung by the folk group Houl Yer Whist, of which Bobby Hanvey is a member. Hanvey, although born into a Nationalist family, has collected a substantial body of Orange/Loyalist music and song. The Swiss scholar **Georges Denis Zimmerman** included eight Orange songs in his *Irish Songs of Rebellion* (originally published 1966), along with an excellent short essay on the history of orange songs and ballads. Two more recently composed Orange songs were collected by **Hugh Shields** at Annalong, Co. Down in 1955. They both commemorate Orange parades passing through a Catholic neighbourhood, one in 1933 and another in 1955.

The political turmoil that engulfed Northern Ireland from 1968 has had its effect on the tradition of Orange/Loyalist song. The most famous Orange song of recent decades, 'The Sash My Father Wore', is strongly associated with the often contentious Twelfth of July (anniversary of the Battle of the Boyne) Orange marches. Benedict Kiely, in a recent book on Irish poetry and ballads, commented: 'There was a time when, without offence and in mixed (sectarian, not sexual) company, it was possible to sing 'The Sash My Father Wore'. This may no longer be advisable. But the magic flute [i.e., 'The Old Orange Flute'] may, because of its very intractability, retain a heavenly neutrality' (*And as I Rode by Granard Moat*, Dublin, 1996, p. 14). There is a perception, bolstered by some political and cultural organisations, that traditional song and music are products of Republicanism and therefore hold little interest for the Northern Irish Orange/Loyalist community. Many Loyalist songs from the recent 'Troubles' use non-traditional texts as models and appear overall to be less traditional in style than earlier Loyalist political song.

Ó Riabhaigh, Eoin (b. 1959) Uilleann piper born in Dublin who moved to Cork while still a child. Son of Micheál Ó Riabhaigh (d. 1976), who revived the **Cork Pipers' Club** in 1963. He plays a mixture of the 'open' and 'close' fingering styles, reflecting his interest in the piping techniques of **Leo Rowsome**, **Patsy Tuohey** and **Wille Clancy**. He recorded the descriptive piece 'The Foxchase' and the reel 'Colonel Frazer' on the album *The Piper's Rock: A Compilation of Young Uilleann Pipers* (1978). The album also featured tracks by **Máire Ní Ghráda**, **Davy Spillane**, **Robbie Hannan** and others. On that album Ó Riabhaigh played a set of Taylor pipes made in Philadelphia ca. 1890, the famous **Phair's Pipes** which his father owned before him.

From 1977 he played and recorded with the group Stoker's Lodge, fronted by **Jimmy Crowley**. Around the late 1970s/early 1980s he also perfomed with **Mary Black** in the group General Humbert. He played a mixture of Irish traditional and bluegrass with the Steampacket Company and made an album with the American songwriter Tom Russell in Norway, a mixture of American country, Irish traditional and Norwegian music. Ó Riabhaigh also recorded on the album *Tideland* (1996) with the Norwegian singer Rita Erikson and **Dolores Keane** and has recorded with a wide range of Irish traditional musicians. His first solo album, *Tiomnacht: Handed On* (2000), is dedicated to his father. Ó Riabhaigh plays some classic piping tunes on the album (including 'The Gold Ring' and the two tunes he had recorded in 1978) as well as some beautiful renditions of traditional slow airs ('The Cuilin' and 'Bean Dubh a' Ghleanna'/'Dark Woman of the Glen') and even some bluegrass tunes. One track features seven uilleann pipers and a snare drum playing two marches. Ó Riabhaigh was a co-founder of the innovative **Scoiltrad**, a traditional music school on the internet, with fiddler Kevin Glackin (see **Glackin**, **Paddy**) and flautist Conal Ó Gráda.

Ó Riada, Seán (1931-1971)   Composer, musician, scholar and broadcaster of traditional music who was highly influential in developing ensemble playing in traditional music through the group **Ceoltóirí Chualann**. He was born in Cork and brought up in Bruff, Co. Limerick, where he learned to play traditional fiddle. He also learned piano in his youth and studied music (as part of an Arts degree) with **Aloys Fleischmann** at **University College Cork**. On graduating with honours in 1952 he was appointed Assistant Director of Music in Raidió Éireann (see **RTÉ**) but resigned within two years and went to Paris to study music. He was influenced by the work of Arnold Schoenberg and was also closely involved with many jazz and Greek musicians, including Mikis Theodorakis. On his return to Ireland, he was appointed Musical Director of the Abbey Theatre and also returned to work with Raidió Éireann.

Ó Riada first came to prominence in 1959 when he was commissioned by **Gael-Linn** to write the music for George Morrison's feature-length film on Ireland's struggle for political freedom, *Mise Éire/I Am Ireland*. Ó Riada's score used traditional Irish airs arranged for full orchestra. His friend the poet Thomas Kinsella described how 'Ó Riada wrung from his basic theme, in full Mahlerian and Sibelian harmonies, every emotional possibility.' Ó Riada became a national celebrity and with this, and subsequent work took Irish traditional music in new directions, both in terms of arrangement and audiences. Two further scores for films dealing with Ireland's history followed, *Saoirse/Freedom* (George Morrison, 1960) and *An Tine Bheo/The Living Fire* (Louis Marcus, 1966). Music from all three documentaries, performed by the RTÉ Symphony Orchestra, was released as *Mise Éire* in 1979.

Ó Riada's work with the group Ceoltóirí Chualann (1959-1970) developed a new approach to the ensemble playing of Irish traditional music. The group revolutionised the arrangement and performance of the music and also played an important role in the radio programmes that Ó Riada made. They formed an integral part of the two series *Reacaireacht an Riadaigh* and *Fleadh Cheoil an Raidió* during the 1960s, playing music from the standard traditional repertoire and also seeking to highlight **sean-nós singing** and the rarely heard compositions of **Turlough O'Carolan**.

Ó Riada also made a seminal radio series, *Our Musical Heritage* (1962), which explored the history of traditional music and song. The series provided an important framework for the discussion of traditional music, particularly in its identification of **regional styles** of fiddling and sean-nós singing. Although reaction to it was mixed (Ó Riada's criticisms of accordion players and **céilí band**s aroused the anger of many musicians), the majority welcomed it as providing rare insights into traditional music. A booklet edited from the original series, along with a selection of the recordings Ó Riada had played as examples of his various subjects, was released in 1982 as *Our Musical Heritage*. The booklet has valuable introductions about the man and his work written by the poet Thomas Kinsella (editor of the booklet) and the musician and former pupil of Ó Riada, **Tomás Ó Canainn** (music editor). It is a valuable collection of recordings, including many solo pieces by players from throughout the country, and the booklet provides (in addition to historical background) an interesting critique of traditional Irish music in the 1950s and 60s.

In 1963, Ó Riada took up a post lecturing in music in University College Cork and soon afterwards moved to the West Cork **Gaeltacht** village of Cúil Aodha or Coolea. He composed a number of liturgical works that are still performed by the choir he founded in Cúil Aodha. His classical compositions, produced between 1957 and the mid 60s, include *Hercules Dux Ferrarie (Nomos No. 1)* and *Five Greek Epigrams (Nomos No. 2)*, a cycle based on poems by the Greek dramatist Sophocles. He also wrote settings of a number of songs by the German poet Hölderlin (1770-1843).

Seán Ó Riada

Ó Riada continued to lecture in Cork until his death in 1971. Just a few months before he died, he recorded fourteen pieces of traditional music on Garech Browne's (see **Claddagh Records**) antique harpsichord at Luggala, Co. Wicklow. **Paddy Moloney** brought the tapes to London to mix them and Ó Riada heard and approved the edited tapes just a few days before he died, in London, on October 3rd. These recordings were released posthumously as *Ó Riada's Farewell*. Ó Riada was buried at the little church in Cúil Aodha to the sound of the traditional song 'Mo Ghile Mear' ('My Living Brightness').

Ó Riada's early death was a tragedy not just for traditional music but for Irish music as a whole. There can be no doubt about the role he played in bringing Irish traditional music to a much broader audience. His development of ensemble playing inspired many groups that followed and lives on more directly in the **Chieftains**, described by Ó Riada himself as a 'subsection' of his own group, Ceoltóirí Chualann. Ó Riada, however, was a complex character and some friends and music critics believe that his greatest tragedy was a failure to fulfil his potential as a classical composer. One friend, the poet John Montague, has said: 'He burned out. What do you do if you are a composer and your works are only performed once and respectfully buried? Frustration's not the word for it' (See J. Glatt, *The Chieftains*, p. 76). Music historian Harry White goes even further in his book *The Keeper's Recital: Music and Cultural History in Ireland, 1770-1970*, arguing that Ó Riada's career represents a broader conflict between Irish traditional music and European 'Art' music. White sees Ó Riada's interest in traditional music as ultimately leading him away from original composition. The nationalist politics of music, which dictated that traditional Irish music and classical music were in opposing camps, caused an artistic paralysis within Ó Riada which prevented him from integrating both styles. Thus, in White's argument, Ó Riada never fulfilled his potential as an original composer. Whatever the cost may have been, Ó Riada's contribution to traditional music has been crucial to developments since the 1960s. He was a controversial figure in his own lifetime and interpretations of his significance as a composer continue to spark heated debate. **Tomás Ó Canainn** has written biographies of Ó Riada in Irish and in English, *Seán Ó Riada: A Shaol agus a Shaothar* (Dublin, 1993) and *Seán Ó Riada: His Life and Work* (Cork, 2003). See also **Ó Súilleabháin, Micheál**; **Whelan, Bill**.

Ornamentation A general term used to describe various embellishments to the main melody of an instrumental piece or a song. The term is mostly used in relation to instrumental music but, in the case of **sean-nós singing** especially, can be used in relation to song. The use of ornamentation varies from player to player, and many musicians will vary their use in a particular tune as the mood suits them. Along with other factors such as speed, tone, melodic variation and phrasing, the way ornamentation is used contributes significantly to the style of an individual or region (see **Regional Styles**). The terms used for the different forms of ornamentation can vary from one region to another, or from player to player, but the main types are **cut**s, **casadh**s, **roll**s, **triplet**s, **double-stop**s and **cran**s. **Slur**s and **vibrato** are generally considered forms of articulation rather than ornamentation, as they relate to the manner in which individual notes or pairs of notes are played, but these techniques are used to achieve the same effects as ornamentation in embellishing or decorating a tune. The forms of ornamentation listed here will not necessarily suit all the instruments on which traditional music is played, nor is the list exhaustive. Some players have devised their own unique forms of ornamentation.

O'Shaughnessy, Paul Fiddler from Artane, Co. Dublin, who initially learned fiddle from his mother, Pearl, and later from Co. Cavan fiddler Antóin MacGabhainn. His mother passed him on many tunes from the repertoire of Sligo flute player John Egan, and from his late teens O'Shaughnessy also developed a great interest in Donegal music. He toured and recorded with **Altan**, making three albums with them between 1989 and 1992. The influence of Egan and Donegal fiddlers is apparent on his duo album with **Paul McGrattan**, *Within a Mile of Dublin* (1995), which includes barndances and flings as well as jigs, reels, hornpipes and airs. Accompaniment is provided by Seánie McPhail (guitar), Noel O'Grady (bouzouki) and **Colm Murphy** (bodhrán). Donegal repertoire and styles are also apparent on O'Shaughnessy's first solo album, *Stay Another While* (1999, with Frankie Lane on guitars, dobro, mandolin, bass). In his sleeve-notes to *Stay Another While*, O'Shaughnessy remarks on southwest Donegal: 'The music or musics of this region, because there are as many styles of playing as there are players, continue to have a great influence on the music I play.' The view that Donegal has many styles of playing, and not just one, is an accurate assessment (see **Regional Styles**). O'Shaughnessy also plays with **Beginish**, along with McGrattan and O'Grady.

Ossian Publications   Cork-based company founded in 1979 which initially concentrated on the publication of books dealing with all aspects of Irish traditional music. They have published tutors on various traditional instruments as well as tune collections (including a reprint of **Francis Roche**'s 1920s collection) and special studies such as **Nicholas Carolan**'s excellent 1997 book on **Francis O'Neill**. The latter is an introduction to a newly edited O'Neill collection which is being worked on in conjunction with the **Irish Traditional Music Archive**. In 2002 they republished **Dónal O'Sullivan's** definitive work on **Turlough O'Carolan**. In the early 1980s they began to release recordings, concentrating first on archive recordings made originally made by **Topic Records** and Folkways. The recording side of Ossian's productions gradually expanded to include Scottish material (especially the work of **Ewan MacColl**) and new recordings of local traditional musicians including the groups **Sliabh Notes** and Calico and the duo **Séamus Creagh** and Aidan Coffey. The archive recordings include valuable field recordings made by noted collectors such as **Séamus Ennis**, **Alan Lomax** and **Jean Ritchie**, whose field recordings from Ireland, originally released by Smithsonian Folkways in the **US** in 1960, were reissued by Ossian in 1990. Website: www.ossian.ie.

Ó Súilleabháin, Diarmuid (1947-1991)   **Sean-nós** singer from Cúil Aodha in West Cork who was a member Cór Cúil Aodha (Coolea Choir), directed by **Seán Ó Riada** and later by his son, Peadar. A teacher by profession, Ó Súilleabháin moved on to work in radio, ultimately for **Raidió na Gaeltachta**, but he also recorded with **Ceoltóirí Laigheann**. He was killed tragically in an accident but a collection of his songs was posthumously released as *Bruach na Carraige Báine* (1995). Éigse Dhiarmuid Uí Shúilleabháin, a weekend of traditional music in honour of the singer, is held every year in Cúil Aodha early in December. See also **Ó Canainn, Tomás**.

Ó Súilleabháin, Micheál (b. 1950)   Academic, composer and pianist. Ó Súilleabháin spent 25 years in the Music Department at **University College Cork**, first as a student of **Seán Ó Riada** and **Aloys Fleischmann**, then as a lecturer. In 1994 he moved to the new **University of Limerick**, where he holds the Chair of Music and played a key role in establishing the Irish World Music

Centre. In the same year he was involved in devising, writing and presenting *A **River of Sound***, a major television series on the changing course of Irish traditional music.

Like Ó Riada, Ó Súilleabháin has also done innovative work as a performer, arranger and composer. His approach is evident from his first solo album, *Micheál Ó Súilleabháin* (1976), on which he explores the possibilities of playing traditional music on various keyboard instruments. The album includes music of the 17th- and 18th-century harpers as well as dance music and slow airs played on **piano, harp-**

Micheál Ó Súilleabháin
(photo: Christy McNamara)

sichord, clavichord, pedal organ and mini-moog **synthesiser**. Since the 1970s he has also been involved as musician, arranger or producer in a number of projects with his wife, **Noirín Ní Riain**, including a group album, *Óró Damhnaigh* (1977), her first solo album and her recordings with the monks of Glenstal Abbey. In 1981 Ó Súilleabháin released *Cry of the Mountain*, which brings together music recorded for radio and films between 1974 and 1978. It features music from the radio programme *The Green Linnet* (see **Napoleon Bonaparte**), a concertino for fiddle and two interesting collages which combine elements of Irish, Oriental and South American music.

Through the late 1980s and 90s, Ó Súilleabháin developed a unique approach to playing Irish music on piano, taking traditional tunes and improvising on them in a style that has been called 'Hiberno-Jazz'. A good example is 'Oíche Nollag/ Christmas Eve' from his album *The Dolphin's Way* (1987). On 'Brian Boru', from *Casadh/Turning* (1990), he uses the traditional 'Brian Boru's March', playing it first in a reasonably straight manner, but gradually varying the melody, tempo and rhythm of the original tune to create different shades and moods. While much of his work from this period consists of solo piano playing, or piano accompanied by percussion, he has also done a great deal of ensemble work with the Irish Chamber Orchestra and traditional musicians, blending elements of jazz, traditional and classical music. *Oileán/Island* (1989) combines orchestral arrangements of tunes from the repertoire of traditional flute player **Matt Molloy** and original sequences composed by Ó Súilleabháin. The album also features 'Idir Eatarthu/Between Worlds' based on an English song melody ('Jockey to the Fair') which came into Irish music as a single jig. The tune is played on piano as both a jig and a hornpipe, and combines the classical approach of the Irish Chamber Orchestra with the traditional rhythms of bones and bodhrán.

Ó Súilleabháin also composed the 1995 Eurovision centrepiece *Lumen*, an elaborate work for choir, solo voices, orchestra and traditional instruments. With **Dónal**

Lunny, he composed the theme for *A River of Sound*, using players and instruments from other musical traditions. Both pieces appear in *Between Worlds* (1995), which also includes pieces from the 1987-1995 albums as well as from *Gaiseadh/Flowing* (1992). *Becoming* (1998) features a work for piano and orchestra based on music composed for the Irish silent film, *Irish Destiny* (1925). It incorporates explorations of the melody of the Irish national anthem and shades of Seán Ó Riada's *Mise Éire*. The influence of Ó Riada is also apparent on *Templum* (2001) which fuses elements from traditional, classical and religious music. One of the eleven tracks, 'Aisling Gheal' ('Bright Vision'), is dedicated to Ó Riada and the album features the Irish Chamber Orchestra and the National Chamber Choir.

Ó Súilleabháin has made major contributions to the development of traditional music in a number of different areas. His playing and compositions have blended traditional music with other idioms in a unique way. His work in the universities has given traditional music an unprecedented place in the academic sphere, while his television work has served to stimulate the (often heated) debate on current developments in traditional music. See also **Crossroads Conference**.

O'Sullivan, Donal (1893-1973)   Collector and researcher born in Liverpool to parents from Co. Kerry. He worked in the civil service in London but was transferred to Ireland after World War I. Despite working at a number of different jobs over the years (including clerk in the Senate and lecturer in foreign affairs at Trinity College, Dublin), he found time to carry out extensive research on Irish music. He published an edition of **Edward Bunting**'s collection in six parts in London between 1927 and 1939. He also published articles in many academic journals and a collection of his own translations of some of the greatest Irish language songs, *Songs of the Irish* (Cork, 1960). His finest work, however, was the two-volume *Carolan: The Life, Times and Music of an Irish Harper* (London, 1958), recently republished in a single volume by **Ossian Publications** (see **Turlough O'Carolan**). O'Sullivan also wrote the entry on Irish music in *Grove's Dictionary of Music and Musicians* (1954).

Outlet Records   Belfast-based record company founded in 1966 by Billy McBurney which specialises in the production and distribution of albums by Irish-based artists. Outlet advertises as the largest independent Irish music retailer in the world and over the years has produced and distributed a wide variety of genres, including traditional, country, contemporary folk, gospel, Republican (see **Nationalist/Republican song**) and Orange (see **Orange/Loyalist song**) music. The company's recording division includes music and video products on the Homespun, Chime and Outlet labels. **Seán Maguire**, **Séamus Tansey**, **Joe Burke**, **Margaret Barry** and **Luke Kelly** are among the traditional and folk artists who have been released on Outlet. The company has had its own studio in Belfast since its foundation, and its back catalogue has over 3,000 original recordings. While many of the releases of recent years have been re-masters of older material, Outlet is now looking for new artists to record and promote. Although Billy McBurney is now retired, his daughters Audrey and Ciarna are still involved in the company. In 2002 Canice McGarry became a large shareholder and Managing Director and has set about reorganizing the company. A new website, www.soundsirish.com, was launched in 2002 and McGarry has also set about expanding the company's Dublin operation, which previously served only as a distribution point.

P

Pantomimic Dance A dance in which particular actions are imitated. In Connacht, for example, there used to be a solo dance called *Maide na bPlanndaí*, in which the tilling, planting and digging of the potato was imitated. Only a few of these types of dances have survived into recent years, the most popular being *Rince an Chlaidhimh* or sword dance. It is known by different names in different parts of the country, and sweeping brushes, spades, sticks or other implements are used instead of swords.

Parsons, Niamh Singer from Dublin who sang and recorded with **Arcady**. She also sings unaccompanied traditional songs and on her album with the Loose Connections, *Loosen Up* (1997) sings songs written by her husband, Dee Moore, arranged in a variety of styles. Some of the songs, although recently composed, have a marked traditional style, while others use unusual combinations of traditional and non-traditional instruments. More traditional in material and style is the album *Blackbirds and Thrushes* (1999), with some of the songs unaccompanied and others quite sparsely accompanied. Two of the twelve songs are in Irish ('Droimeann Donn Dílis'/'Beloved Brown White-Backed Cow' and 'Fear a Bháta'/'The Boatman'), and the album confirmed Parson's reputation as one of the finest

Niamh Parsons
(photo: Mike Mulcaire)

young traditional singers in Ireland. She followed it with two further albums of beautifully sung and subtly arranged traditional songs, *In My Prime* (2000) and *My Heart's Desire* (2002).

Patrick Street Group formed in 1985 by **Andy Irvine** (vocals, mandolin, bouzouki and harmonica), **Jackie Daly** (accordion), **Kevin Burke** (fiddle) and **Arty McGlynn** (guitar). A top-class combination of musicians in which Irvine's songwriting talents have come to the fore in a way they did not with **Planxty**. The group also play traditional songs, but historical/political songs from Irvine such as 'Facing the Chair' and 'A Forgotten Hero' mark a distinctive contribution. The group's instrumental sets are a fine mixture of solo virtuosity and strong accompaniment. For their album, *Irish Times* (1990), they had three new members: **Declan Masterson** (uilleann pipes), James Kelly (fiddle) and Gerry O'Beirne (guitar). Between 1987 and 1993 they released three albums and the issue of a compilation, *The Best of Patrick Street* (1995) seemed to signal the unlikelihood of the group continuing. In 1996-97, however, they toured Europe and the **US** and recorded a further album (*Cornerboys*, 1996) in Cork, with Ged Foley replacing Arty McGlynn. This was followed by *Made in Cork* (1997), and with the same line-up they released *Live from Patrick Street* (1999), a mixture of material from other albums and some new tracks recorded on their tour of Ireland and the UK in winter 1998-99. *Compendium: The Best of Patrick Street* (2001) has fourteen tracks, most of them taken from seven earlier albums, two of them previously unreleased.

Patrick Street

Pentangle Folk group of the 1960s from **England** with Jacqui McShee (vocals), Bert Jansch (guitar, vocals), John Renbourn (guitar, vocals), Danny Thompson (bass) and Terry Cox (drums). Well known and popular in Ireland, Pentangle's songs remind us that many 'Irish' **ballad**s have their origins in English folk song. Pentangle were also remarkable for their arrangements, often featuring intricate guitar playing by Jansch and Renbourn. Their style of guitar accompaniment had some influence in Ireland, most notably in the case of **Micheál Ó Domhnaill** and **Mick Hanley**, whose album *Celtic Folkweave* (1974, see **Monroe**) features the Pentangle song 'No Love Is Sorrow'. The ***Skara Brae*** (1974) album also displays the influence of Pentangle in the style of guitar accompaniment used. Renbourn has more recently explored Irish connections in some of his own compositions for guitar, including 'Clarsach', 'The Nine Maidens' and 'The Fiddler' (which adapts tunes such as 'The

Musical Priest' and 'The Battle of Aughrim'). Bert Jansch and the story of the British Folk revival are the subject of an interesting book by Colin Harper, *Dazzling Stranger: Bert Jansch and the British Folk and Blues Revival* (London, 2000).

Peoples, Tommy (b. 1948)   Fiddler born in Letterkenny, Co. Donegal. He grew up in Killycally, St. Johnston, Co. Donegal but lived in Toonagh, Co. Clare from the 1970s until 2002, when he moved to the **US**. He learned partly from his father but started lessons with his cousin Joe Cassidy at the age of seven. He developed his own techniques of bowing from early in his playing career and is one of the most inventive and imaginative of traditional fiddlers. A move to Dublin led to his involvement in the foundation of The Green Linnet Céilí Band and, in 1974, to a brief spell with the group 1691 (see **Weldon, Liam**). He replaced the original fiddler, **Paddy Glackin**, in the legendary **Bothy Band**, with which he recorded just one album in 1975. In the late 1970s he played for a time with the Kilfenora Céilí Band but was always happier in small sessions rather than stage performances. One of the most memorable traditional albums of this period is *Matt Molloy, Paul Brady, Tommy Peoples* (1978), notable for the great passion and energy of all three players' performances.

Peoples has released a number of solo albums including *The High Part of the Road* (1976), on which he was accompanied by **Paul Brady**. Throughout the 1980s and 90s he played small sessions, many of them around Co. Clare. *The Quiet Glen/An Gleann Ciúin* was released in 1998, with Alph Duggan on guitar, and has strengthened Peoples' standing as one of the all-time greats of traditional fiddling. Mic Moroney summed up his review of the album by writing: 'Call them irrational forces, but it's often hard to know where the endless variations of Peoples' fiddle-playing are taking you. If it's really music you're after, this is a piece of rare beauty.' (*Irish Times*, 31 July 1998) Peoples is certainly a unique stylist, but *The Quiet Glen* also reveals his brilliance as a composer (17 of the 28 tunes are his own). In 1998, he won the first TnaG/IMRO National Traditional Music Award. He subsequently moved to the US, where he

Tommy Peoples

released *Waiting for a Call* (2003) with **Shanachie Records**, most of which (eleven of the sixteen tracks) was recorded in 1985 with **Alec Finn** (bouzouki) and **Donál Lunny** (bodhrán). Five additional tracks were newly recorded with John Doyle (guitar). Peoples' daughter, Siobhán, is also a fine fiddler and recorded the album *Time on Our Hands* (2002) with box player Murty Ryan. The album features original tunes by Siobhán and Tommy Peoples as well as traditional tunes. Website: http://homepage.tinet.ie/~logo/tommy.htm.

Petrie, George (1789-1866) Irish music collector of Scots ancestry, also an antiquarian and artist. The Royal Irish Academy awarded him a Gold Medal for his extensive essay, *The Origins and Uses of the Round Towers of Ireland*, the first major attempt to understand the functions and date of Irish round towers. With **Eugene O'Curry** and John O'Donovan, two outstanding Gaelic scholars of the time, Petrie worked for the Ordnance Survey Office, travelling the entire country and making detailed notes on historical and archaeological sites. He also used the opportunity to take down tunes from traditional musicians throughout Ireland. He was a founding member (in 1851) of the Society for the Preservation of the Melodies of Ireland, the first organisation to concern itself with Irish music. The society's only publication was Petrie's *Ancient Music of Ireland* (1855). This was published (with the posthumously published *Ancient Music of Ireland, Volume 2*, 1882) in a new edition as *The Petrie Collection of the Ancient Music of Ireland* (edited by David Cooper) in 2003. It contains almost 200 airs, many with extensive descriptive and historical notes, and texts of songs in Irish and English.

George Petrie

Petrie criticised the careless manner in which **Edward Bunting** had collected his melodies, and was himself criticised for manipulating the original notations of airs to meet notions of harmony which were not applicable to traditional music. Like Bunting, he came to Irish music as an outsider. The most famous collector of traditional Irish music, **Francis O'Neill**, had the distinct advantage of being a traditional musician himself and thus had a greater understanding of the music he collected than either Bunting or Petrie. Petrie's contribution to Irish music was, nonetheless, enormous, especially with the completion of his work by Sir Charles

Stanford. Stanford edited Petrie's manuscript collection of 2,148 pieces down to 1,578 tunes and published them as *The Complete Collection of Irish Music as Noted by Petrie* in 1902-1905. This collection contains dance tunes, marches, songs, plough whistles, spinning and weaving tunes, laments, hymns and lullabies arranged in sections under those without titles, those with English titles and those with Irish titles. A facsimile reprint of Stanford's Petrie (which includes Petrie's own introduction to the 1855 collection) was published in three volumes by Lanerch Publishers, Felinfach in 1994 and 1995. See also **Burns, Robbie**.

Phair's Pipes A set of **uilleann pipes** made ca. 1890 by the Taylor brothers of Philadelphia. They were originally owned by a renowned piper and scholar from Dingle, Co. Kerry, Canon **James Goodman** (1828-1896), who stipulated in his will that the pipes be buried with him. This was done after he died on January 18th, 1896, but the pipes were dug up again as it had not been stated that this could not be done. They came into the possession of Alderman William Phair (d. 1912), a popular public representative in Cork city and a founder (in 1898) and first president of the **Cork Pipers' Club**. They remained with the Phair family until about 1963, when they were donated to Micheál Ó Riabhaigh after he had revived the Cork Pipers' Club. When Micheál died in 1976, Phair's Pipes passed on to his son **Eoin Ó Riabhaigh**.

Piano (*Pianó*) A keyboard instrument with a range of about seven octaves in which the keys cause hammers to strike the strings, causing them to sound. The player can produce louder or softer tones by varying the finger pressure on the keys, a feature not available on the **harpsichord**, which preceded the piano.

In the 18th century, the decline of the Irish **harp** was paralleled by a rise in the popularity of the piano. When **Edward Bunting** transcribed the music of the old harpers and published his three collections, he arranged the music for piano, the most popular instrument of the time, in an attempt to appeal to a wider audience. Other 19th-century collectors of traditional music, including the piper **O'Farrell**, included piano in their published arrangements of traditional music, and in the early 20th century **Francis O'Neill** published special collections with piano arrangements. These published collections may not reflect a widespread use of the piano among traditional musicians in the 19th and early 20th centuries, but they do provide evidence that the piano was used in some circles for playing traditional music before the first commercial recordings appeared.

Many of the earliest commercial recordings of traditional players, such as those of **Michael Coleman**, did have piano accompaniment as a regular feature. **Seán Ó Riada** abhorred the way the piano was used on these early recordings, putting it down to a national inferiority complex and the attempt to make Irish music as 'respectable' as classical music. He particularly commented on the case of Coleman: 'The piano accompaniments on his records, far from enhancing his playing, are a blotch and blemish on it' (*Our Musical Heritage*, Portlaoise, 1982, p. 59). **Seán O'Boyle** made similar comments about the desire of song collectors to 'lend a social status to a music hitherto neglected or despised' (*The Irish Song Tradition*, Dublin, 1976) by publishing songs with piano accompaniment.

Piano accompaniments like those of Coleman and others, often described as 'vamping' or 'driving', are still to be heard on more recent recordings, especially by older fiddlers, accordionists and, to a lesser extent, flute players. **Catherine McEvoy** (flute) provides a recent example, using the American pianist Felix Dolan on her *Traditional Music in the Sligo-Roscommon Style* (1996). Dolan has played with many of the great traditional musicians, including **Seán Maguire**, **Bobby Gardiner** and **Joe Derrane**, a reminder of how popular the old-style piano accompaniment can be. Another development that took place early in the 20th century and is still widespread is the use of piano 'vamping' by **céilí bands**. The first Irish piano tutor, entitled *Seinn an Piano: Playing the Piano Irish Style* and written by Geraldine Cotter, was published in 1996.

Since the 1970s a few pianists have approached the performance of Irish traditional music in a very different way. Among these are **Micheál Ó Súilleabháin**, who has developed a unique style, influenced by jazz and classical music, and **Antonio Breschi,** who accompanies Irish songs and plays Irish instrumentals in a bluesy style. Pádraig O'Reilly, a young pianist from Corofin, Co. Clare, plays straight traditional melodies and accompaniment on his ground-breaking album *Down the Ivory Stairs* (2001). See also **Ceoltóirí Chualann**; **Ó Riada, Seán**; **Keyboard Instruments**.

Piano Accordion See **Accordion**.

Pigot, John Edward (d. 1853)

Pigot, John Edward (d. 1853) Music collector, composer and songwriter. He gave some of the traditional tunes he had collected to **George Petrie**, who acknowledged individually the tunes Pigot had given him in his published collection. **William Forde**'s unpublished collection of traditional music came into Pigot's hand after Forde's death in 1845. Pigot also wrote some songs, which were published in the *Nation*. The Pigot and Forde collections are both held in the Royal Irish Academy, Dublin and material from both collectors was published by **Patrick Weston Joyce**.

Píob Mór See **War Pipes, Irish**.

Píobairí Uilleann, Na (The Pipers' Club)

Píobairí Uilleann, Na (The Pipers' Club) Organisation founded at a famous *tionól* (assembly) of uilleann pipers at Bettystown, Co. Meath in April 1968, attended by **Breandán Breathnach**, **Séamus Ennis**, **Leo Rowsome** and other great pipers. With only five uilleann pipe makers left in Ireland and the instrument facing possible extinction, 'The Pipers' Club' (as it is known to many) faced considerable difficulties in attempting to revive interest in this most famous of Irish instruments. They immediately faced pressure from the president of **Comhaltas Ceoltóirí Éireann** to disband and work as individuals within the CCÉ network. The pipers, however, resisted and through the efforts of many, but especially Breandán

Breathnach, went on to establish a highly successful organisation which has clubs in Europe, the **US**, **Australia** and New Zealand. In addition to running lessons on the uilleann pipes, they also give reed-making classes, hold recitals and an annual concert in the National Concert Hall and operate a pipes loan scheme for beginners. They have issued three volumes of a tutor CD called *The Art of Uilleann Piping*, the third volume of which (released in 2000) features the playing of Gay McKeon and Nollaig Mac Carthaigh. They also bring out *An Píobaire*, a monthly magazine for members, and have published a number of books on traditional music, song and dance. The Dublin club is located in a beautiful Georgian house, No. 15 Henrietta St., Dublin 1. In addition to teaching the pipes, the club also has lessons in other traditional instruments and holds sessions with the **Brooks Academy of Dancing** as well as **sean-nós** singers. There is an excellent archive of sound, photographic and recorded material run by Terry Moylan. They receive an annual grant from the Arts Council and also receive donations from other patrons. Na Píobairí Uilleann has been crucial in rescuing the uilleann pipes from oblivion and restoring them to a central role in Irish traditional music. Website: www.pipers.ie.

Pipes See **Bagpipes**; **Uilleann Pipes**; **War Pipes, Irish**.

Planxty 1 A type of tune played by harpers of the 17th and 18th centuries, many of which **Turlough O'Carolan** composed. Most of O'Carolan's planxties were in 6/8 time. The word 'planxty' is also thought to have indicated some kind of a toast, usually in praise of a particular person. The origin of the word is obscure, although it may be derived from the Irish toast *sláinte*, meaning 'health'.

Planxty 2 Renowned group of the 1970s and early 80s. The group was formed in 1972 after **Christy Moore** gathered together a number of musicians to record his album ***Prosperous***. Four of the musicians involved in *Prosperous* went on to form Planxty, whose first album, simply called *Planxty* but often referred to as 'The Black Album', was released in 1973. The original line-up was Christy Moore (guitar, vocals), **Andy Irvine** (mandola, vocals), **Dónal Lunny** (bouzouki, bodhrán, vocals) and **Liam O'Flynn** (uilleann pipes, whistles).

Further albums followed in 1973 (*The Well Below the Valley*, which featured the arrangement from *Prosperous* of the song 'The Raggle Taggle Gypsy' changing time into the instrumental 'Tabhair Dom Do Láimh') and 1974 (*Cold Blow and the Rainy Night*). Mandola and bouzouki feature prominently in many of the group's arrangements, both as melody and accompanying instruments, and are tastefully blended with the uilleann pipes, bouzouki and mandola often playing intricate harmonies or counter-melodies. **Sweeney's Men** had played in a similar style in the late 1960s, but played little dance music. In the early days instrumentals formed about a third of Planxty's repertoire, but they often went from a song straight into an instrumental, sometimes changing rhythm from one to the other. Frequently the songs concerned devious or adulterous lovers, but political and historical songs were also featured. The wit and humour of the group was a marked feature of their live performances and the often long and rambling introductions could be as entertaining as the music itself. They had the appearance and relaxed attitude of a rock band, in contrast to the formality of the other prominent stage performers of dance music at the time, such as the **céilí bands** and even **Ó Riada**'s **Ceoltóirí Chualann**.

Dónal Lunny left Planxty in 1973, to be replaced by **Johnny Moynihan**, and Christy Moore left soon afterwards. **Paul Brady** joined the group in 1974, but they broke up in 1975. After the demise of the **Bothy Band** in 1979, Planxty re-formed with the four original members and **Matt Molloy**. With this line-up they recorded *After the Break* (1979). **P. J. Curtis** has written of the re-formed Planxty: 'For many the group's old magic had dissipated somewhat' (*Notes From the Heart*, p. 29), but *After the Break* is one of Planxty's finest albums. There is not one weak track and songs such as 'The Good Ship Kangaroo' and 'The Pursuit of Farmer Michael' are classics of arrangement. Matt Molloy added to the sound, especially on the instrumental tracks, and Dónal Lunny was by this time playing the **blarge** or 10-string bouzouki, adding more depth to many of the rhythm accompaniments. This and the group's following two albums have a higher proportion of instrumentals (50/50) than the earlier albums, and *After the Break* includes a stunning arrangement of 'Smeceno Horo', a Bulgarian dance tune.

Shortly after the release of *After the Break*, Planxty did a memorable series of concerts in the Olympia Theatre, Dublin. Andy Irvine, Liam O'Flynn (with Dónal Lunny) and Christy Moore all did 'solo' slots at the start of the concert. The four then played together and gradually other musicians joined them on stage, including Matt Molloy and **Nollaig Ní Chathasaigh**. This unusual concert format displayed the array of both individual and group talent. Matt Molloy joined the **Chieftains** later in 1979 but guested on *The Woman I Loved so Well* (1980) along with **Noel Hill** (concertina), **Tony Linnane** (fiddle) and **Bill Whelan** (keyboards). This was another fine selection of subtly arranged instrumentals and songs, including the epic song from Moore, 'Little Musgrave'. *Words and Music* (1983) was also recorded with the original four members and a few guests, and featured 'Lord Baker', another epic song from Moore (see **Child Ballads**). Also included were 'The Irish Marche', composed by the 16th-century composer **William Byrd**, and 'I Pity the Poor Emigrant', written by Bob Dylan.

The 1970s and early 80s were an exciting time for Irish music, with **Supergroups** such as Planxty, the Bothy Band and the Chieftains bringing traditional music and song to a wider audience than ever before. Planxty and the Bothy Band in particular made the music more appealing and accessible to many listeners in Ireland and abroad through their innovative arrangements and an approach demonstrating that the music was something more than a local curiosity. That line-ups and arrangement styles similar to Planxty and the Bothy Band have in many ways become 'standard' (see **Altan**, **Nomos**, **Solas**), shows the wide appeal of their approach to Irish traditional music. The line-up on Paul Brady's *The Missing Liberty Tapes* (2001) includes Planxty members Andy Irvine, Dónal Lunny, Liam O'Flynn and Brady himself, as well as Noel Hill and Paddy Glackin. It was recorded in 1978. **RTÉ** broadcast an excellent documentary on Planxty in their *No Disco* television series (first broadcast March 2003).

In 2004 a reformed Planxty, featuring O'Flynn, Moore, Irvine and Lunny, performed a series of concerts in Ennis, Co. Clare and at Dublin's Vicar Street, which were also recorded for a new CD, video and DVD, all entitled *Planxty Live 2004*. The concerts showed that Planxty have not lost their passion and mastery, and their comments between the songs, always a feature of their performances, were as sharp and entertaining as ever. They have continued to perform into 2005.

Planxty, 1979

Pogues, The London-Irish band with a style that mixed influences from Irish traditional music and ballad singing with punk rock. Their original line-up included **Shane MacGowan** (lead vocals, guitar), Jem Finer (banjo, mandola, saxophone), James Fearnley (accordion, piano, mandolin, dulcimer, guitar, cello, percussion), Cáit O'Riordan (bass, vocals), Spider Stacey (tin whistle, vocals) and Andrew Rankin (drums, percussion, vocals, harmonica). Initially called the New Republicans, they changed their name to the Pogue Mahones (an anglicised spelling of the Irish for 'kiss my arse') and released a single, 'The Dark Streets of London', in 1983. This was followed by their first album, *Red Roses for Me* (1984) under the name the Pogues. The album was a mixture of original songs by Shane MacGowan and folk songs, as well as **Brendan Behan**'s 'The Auld Triangle' and the traditional dance tune 'Dingle Regatta'. A second album, *Rum, Sodomy and the Lash* (1985), with Philip Chevron playing guitar and mandolin and sharing vocals, included the single 'A Pair of Brown Eyes' and other songs written by MacGowan, as well as **Ewan MacColl**'s 'Dirty Old Town', Eric Bogle's classic World War I song 'And the Band Played Waltzing Matilda' and a couple of traditional songs. In 1987 their single with the

Dubliners, 'The Irish Rover', hit No. 1 in Ireland and No. 8 in the UK, leading to the Pogues' first appearance on 'Top of the Pops'. Later the same year MacGowan's classic Christmas song, 'Fairytale of New York' (on which he shared the lead vocals with Kirsty MacColl) reached No. 2 in the UK charts. By the time of their third album, *If I Should Fall from Grace with God* (1988), Cáit O'Riordan had left and there were two new members, Daryl Hunt (bass, percussion, vocals) and Terry Woods (cittern, concertina, mandolin, tenor banjo, dulcimer, guitar, vocals). With this new line-up they also made *Peace and Love* (1989) and *Hell's Ditch* (1990), Shane MacGowan's last album with the group.

The Pogues developed a reputation for hard drinking and wild behaviour and outraged many purists with their irreverent, raucous versions of folk classics like 'The Wild Rover' and 'South Australia'. Their wild, energetic live performances, however, delighted younger audiences in Britain, Ireland and the **US**, and there was a wealth of talent in the group. Songwriters Philip Chevron, Terry Woods and especially Shane MacGowan penned lyrics which captured the sensibilities of Irish emigrants and dealt with contemporary political and social issues. Even the great drinking songs ('The Sick Bed of Cúchulainn', 'The Old Main Drag', 'Sally McLennane', all by MacGowan) abound in references to social and historical issues. Just as the ballads of the 19th century provided a commentary on the political and social developments of that era, so the Pogues' original songs evoked the concerns and feelings of many, especially emigrants, in the 1980s and early 90s. Songs like Chevron's 'Thousands Are Sailing' and MacGowan's 'Fairytale of New York' uniquely capture both the dreams and reality of an emigrant's life. 'Streets of Sorrow/Birmingham Six' (Woods/MacGowan) combines a quiet, anguished song with a more up-tempo, angry swipe at imperialism and the framing of Irishmen in Britain. The song was initially banned in Britain, although the ban was lifted in 1991 after the Birmingham Six and the Guildford Four had their original convictions quashed by the courts. MacGowan has also written some fine love songs ('A Rainy Night in Soho') and has an exceptional talent for capturing loneliness and confusion ('Lullaby of London').

After MacGowan parted company with the group, two compilations were released, *The Best of the Pogues* (1991) and *The Best of the Rest* (1992). The group continued to perform, with Spider Stacey taking over on lead vocals after a short period when Joe Strummer of the Clash filled the slot. After their first album without MacGowan, *Waiting for Herb* (1993), Woods, Fearnley and Chevron left. Stacey, Finer, Hunt and Rankin were then joined by Jamie Clarke (guitar, bass guitar, backing vocals), **James McNally** (accordion, whistle, uilleann pipes, piano), Stephen Warbeck (accordion, mandolin, piano) and David Coulter (baritone ukulele, mandolin, tambourine). The band made *Pogue Mahone* (1995), with songs written by Finer, Rankin, Hunt, McNally, Stacey and others. For many fans of the Pogues, however, MacGowan was central to the group and without his songwriting skills, and those of Chevron and Woods, the Pogues would never be the same. After a gig at the Montreux Jazz Festival in July 1996, the Pogues announced that they were finally disbanding. They have, however, played the odd gig at Dublin's Point Depot including one in June 2002 with the classic line-up of MacGowan, Finer,

Rankin, Stacey, Hunt, Chevron, Woods and Fearnley. See also **England**.

Political Song The tradition of political involvement of musicians, poets and bards has a long history in Ireland, stretching back to the reign of **Elizabeth I** and before that to the Middle Ages (see **Harp**). Nevertheless, political songs make up less than ten percent of the traditional or folk song repertoire, although many of them are well known and widely sung and recorded. The **aisling** and other types of **Jacobite song** of the 18th century are among the earliest political songs that can still be heard in Ireland today. Traditions of **Orange/Loyalist Song** and **Nationalist/Republican Song** developed rapidly in the 1790s. The writing of new popular political **ballad**s played an important role in the development of Nationalism in the 19th and 20th centuries. Political groups such as the **Young Ireland** movement (initially through their newspaper the *Nation*) and individuals like **M. J. McCann** and **P. J. McCall** promoted a new sense of Irish national identity through their ballads, many of them dealing with historical subjects.

Although political divisions along Orange or Loyalist and Nationalist or Republican lines have tended to dominate Irish politics (and therefore political song), other types of political song do exist. **Hugh Shields** has argued that songs of outlawry and desertion or resistance to enlistment should really be considered as extensions of political song. Examples of outlawry are 'Brennan on the Moor' and 'The Wild Colonial Boy', recorded by the **Clancy Brothers and Tommy Makem** among others. Perhaps the most famous song of desertion or resistance is 'Arthur McBride' (recorded by **Planxty** and **Paul Brady**). Irish folk singers have also, since the 1960s, shown a broader interest in social and political issues beyond Ireland. This has been partly due to the influence of **American Folk Song**, particularly that of such American singer/songwriters as **Woody Guthrie** and **Pete Seeger**. Radical British singers/collectors like A. L. Lloyd and **Ewan MacColl** have also been important influences since the late 1950s. Scotsman **Dick Gaughan**, who made a memorable album with Andy Irvine, has written songs about a wide range of issues, including several relating to Ireland. Irish groups such as the **Dubliners**, the **Sands Family** and **Moving Hearts**, and solo performers like **Christy Moore**, **Mickey McConnell** and **Andy Irvine** have all performed and recorded songs about a wide range of social and political issues. These include a Canadian mining disaster (the Dubliners), modern warfare (Moving Hearts), the Mexican Revolution (Andy Irvine), the East/West divide in Europe (Colum Sands) and the Spanish Civil War (Christy Moore). See also **Section 31**.

Polka (*Polca*) A lively dance in 2/4 time with a distinct rhythm in which the third quaver (eighth note) of each bar is usually emphasised. It originated as a folk dance, probably in Bohemia (in the modern Czech Republic), during the early 19th century, becoming one of the most popular ballroom dances of the period; it is still danced throughout Europe in places as diverse as Ireland and the Ukraine. Within Ireland, polkas seem to have appeared in ballrooms from the 1840s, gradually moving to the countryside through the work of the **Dancing Masters**. They became especially popular in Kerry (as did **slides**), Cork and to a lesser extent Tipperary, Waterford, Limerick and Clare; they are particularly associated with the **Sliabh Luachra** district. Their rise in popularity in Ireland seems to be closely related to the spread of **set dancing**, and older tunes known as 'single reels' (see **Reel**) or 'dancing master reels' were identical in tempo and rhythm to polkas. One emigrant travelling from Queenstown, Co. Cork to New York in 1881 compared the style of dancing the relatively new '**German**' with the more familiar Irish style of dancing polkas.

Polkas are usually only played for dancing a **set** (as opposed to solo dancing), with two to four pairs dancing together. Although polkas are played outside the six counties mentioned above, they are not as commonly heard as jigs and reels. As with all such regional patterns, however, there are exceptions. **Pádraig O'Keeffe** (1887-1963), the Sliabh Luachra fiddle master, is said to have written polkas and slides only because of demand in the area. He seldom played polkas and slides for his own pleasure, preferring reels, hornpipes and jigs. Although the southwestern counties of Munster still retain a particular fondness for polkas, sets are also danced to polkas further east and north in, for example, Kilkenny, Kildare, Dublin, Roscommon, Fermanagh, Down and Armagh. In the north of Ireland the polka is also popular as a couple dance. Altough polkas are played in a very fast tempo most places, musicians in west Clare often played them at a slower tempo, as suited the old time set dancing in that area. **Micho Russell**, for example, played slow polkas and Bill Ochs notes of his playing of 'The Steamroller McTeige's Polka' that slow polkas such as this sometimes substituted the **hornpipe** for the last figure of the Caledonian set. See also **Regional Styles**.

Carroll's Polka

Potts, Seán (b. 1930) Tin whistle player from one of Ireland's most famous musical families of the 20th century. His grandfather, John, was a legendary figure in traditional music during the 1940s. John Potts, originally from Co. Wexford, had moved to Dublin where his home in Crumlin became an important centre for teaching and sessions. He was an authority on the uilleann pipes and taught many, including **Breandán Breathnach**. His sons Tommy (see below) and Eddie played fiddle and pipes respectively. He gave a set of pipes to his grandson, Seán, when he was ten years old, but Seán never mastered them. Seán received his grandfather's repertoire largely through his father (also John) and became famous as a whistle player. The family home in Dublin's Liberties was often visited by musicians from different parts of the country, giving Seán the chance to expand his repertoire. His fame came mostly through his membership of **Ceoltóirí Chualann** and the **Chieftains**, whom he left in 1979. He formed the group Bakerswell with his son Seán Óg (uilleann pipes), Kevin Glackin (fiddle, see **Glackin, Paddy**), John Kelly Jnr. (fiddle), John McEvoy (fiddle), Mick Hand (flute) and Noirín O'Donoghue (harp). They made one album together, *Bakerswell* (1988), a wonderful collection of instrumental music (airs, marches, dance tunes and a tune by **Turlough O'Carolan**) beautifully played and subtly arranged.

Potts also made a seminal album with **Paddy Moloney**, *Tin Whistles* (1975). The album combines tin whistle duets with the occasional solo. Apart from interspersed bodhrán from another Chieftain, Peadar Mercier, there is no accompaniment. Both whistle players perform superbly, however, and on some tracks shift between unison and harmony playing in a striking manner. Although a number of tin whistle players have recorded fine solo albums since, this one remains unique.

Seán Potts has done fund-raising for and been Chairman of **Na Píobairí Uilleann** and has edited its monthly magazine for a number of years. His son, Seán Óg, plays the uilleann pipes and has recorded with many artists, including **Dónal Lunny**. On his first solo album, *Seán Potts* (2002), he is accompanied by **Gavin Ralston** (guitar).

Potts, Tommy (1912-1988) Dublin fiddler, uncle of **Seán Potts**, renowned for his innovative style of fiddling. He was born into a family steeped in traditional music and started to play at the age of fifteen. He found the 'sheer precision and stereotyped settings' of traditional playing did not satisfy him fully. He began to experiment with playing tunes in different keys, varying melodies and rhythms in a style that was most unusual among traditional players. His album *The Liffey Banks* (1972) is still regarded as a classic by many, with Potts displaying a unique talent for ornamentation and improvisation, as well as an extraordinary use of off-beat rhythms which many would not associate with traditional dance tunes at all. Many of the tunes on the album are played in unusual keys, 'The Drunken Sailor' (in B♭ minor) and 'The Star of Munster' (in F major). **Séamus Ennis** wrote on the sleevenotes for *The Liffey Banks* that 'individualistic' was the term for Tommy's playing and continues '...he is the only person I know who takes a melody and sees in his mind's eye its main trend, together with all its moods, side-tracks and tendencies, and succeeds in portraying the entire composite in his performance'. **Micheál Ó Súilleabháin** did an in-depth study of Potts' music for his Ph.D. thesis, 'Innovation and Tradition in the Music of Tommy Potts' (Queen's University, Belfast, 1987), using much of this material for his address to the 1996 **Crossroads Conference**.

Power, Brendan Harmonica player born in Mombasa, Kenya whose parents moved to New Zealand when he was nine. His grandfather on his father's side had emigrated from Waterford to South Africa in the 1920s. He has incorporated much of the technique and style of jazz/blues **harmonica** into his playing of Irish traditional music. His album *New Irish Harmonica* (1994), with guitarist Chris Newman, broke new ground in Irish harmonica playing. Although he plays some tunes on the diatonic harmonica, he generally uses the chromatic. The album includes reels, jigs,

Brendan Power

hornpipes, slow airs and Carolan tunes (see **O'Carolan, Turlough**). His use of ornamentation is superb, and on some of the tracks there are introductions, breaks or endings incorporating jazzy improvisations on traditional melodies. Power wrote and performed the soundtrack for the Irish film *Guilttrip*, releasing much of it on the album *Blow In* (1995), which is even more varied in style and material than *New Irish Harmonica*. It includes two tracks on which Power plays mandolin, some 'mood pieces' by Power from the film soundtrack, his own three-part jig, 'Jig Jazz', two completely different versions of the traditional set dance 'The King of the Fairies', two fine tracks with **Cormac Breatnach** and a Japanese folk tune. Power released *Jig Jazz* (with Mayo-born guitarist Frank Kilkelly) in 1996, combining traditional and original material. He has also performed with the **Riverdance** Orchestra, and has released his own CD of music from *Riverdance*. Power often performs with leading Irish harmonica player **Mick Kinsella**. Website: www.brendan-power. com.

Press and Draw Style A style of playing the button accordion. See **Accordion**.

Prosperous A village near Newbridge, Co. Kildare from which **Christy Moore** took the name of his seminal album *Prosperous* (1972). After his return from England in 1971, Moore began to play sessions in Dowling's pub in Prosperous. Through these sessions he gathered a line-up of musicians which included **Liam O'Flynn** (uilleann pipes/whistle), **Andy Irvine** (bouzouki/ mandola/vocals), **Dónal Lunny** (bouzouki/bodhrán/vocals), **Kevin Conneff** (later of the **Chieftains**, bodhrán), Clive Collins (fiddle) and Moore himself singing and playing guitar. *Prosperous* marked the dawning of a new era in traditional music, but some of its stylistic innovations were natural progressions from the earlier work of the musicians involved. The mixture of Irish folk songs with more contemporary folk material had been part of Moore's repertoire since the 1960s. The arrangements, in which stringed instruments such as bouzouki and mandola feature strongly, echo the work that Lunny had done with **Emmet Spiceland** and Irvine with **Sweeney's Men**.

Prosperous did, however, mark a new stage in the development of group playing of traditional song and music. The combination of Lunny and Irvine, providing intricately woven backings to the songs on the album, as well as Moore and Irvine's singing and the use made of the uilleann pipes are all factors which make this album special. Dónal Lunny later remembered 'The Cliffs of Dooneen' as one of the most important tracks on the album because of the prominence of the uilleann pipes in the arrangement. The arrangement of 'The Raggle Taggle Gypsy', which led directly into the 17th-century air 'Tabhair dom do Láimh' ('Give Me Your Hand'), was also a major innovation in the way it married song and instrumental music. *Prosperous* 'brought traditional music to the attention of Irish people in a completely different way', wrote Dónal Lunny, adding that 'the effect of this album is still reverberating through Irish music today' (*The Christy Moore Songbook*, Dingle, 1984, pp. 5-6).

The group **Planxty** (originally made up of Moore, Irvine, Lunny and O'Flynn) emerged as a direct result of the success of *Prosperous* and took their unique style of traditional music and song to a much broader national and international audience than ever before. Some of the songs that later became Planxty classics, including 'The Raggle Taggle Gypsy' and 'The Cliffs of Dooneen', appeared first on *Prosperous*. The album marked the emergence of the innovative style that was so successfully explored by Planxty in subsequent years.

Push and Pull Style Also called 'press and draw', a style of button accordion playing. See **Accordion**.

Public Dance Hall Act (1935) Draconian legislation attempting to control public morality by tightening the licensing, control and supervision of places used for dancing. The Act was introduced by the Fianna Fáil government of Eamonn De Valera at a time when the clergy, judges and police were all calling for restrictions. It was believed that unsupervised dances held in dancehalls, houses, crossroads and other places were encouraging excessive drinking and sexual license. It was also claimed that money raised at house dances was being used to fund subversive organisations. The Public Dance Hall Act, however, was in line with other restrictive legislation and attitudes towards jazz, modern cinema, art and literature. Under the Act, any dance which was open to the public had to be licensed by a court, and strict conditions were laid down.

The Gárda Síochána (police) or any individual could oppose the granting of a license. Although there are doubts about how far this legislation was intended to stretch, the clergy and the police used it effectively to put an end to house dances. It had a drastic effect on social life, especially in rural Ireland. New parochial halls sprang up in towns and villages all over Ireland after 1935, with the clergy exercising considerable control over the dances held in them. **Céilí dancing**, as opposed to

set dancing, was generally preferred because of its modesty and formality, and the **céilí bands** received an enormous boost. However, many Irish musicians found the halls cold, unnatural and unsuitable for traditional music, dancing and storytelling. See also **Dancing Commission**; **Crehan, Junior (Martin)**; **Gaelic League**.

Quadrille (*Cuadraill*)   A French country dance, originally performed by sets of four, six or eight couples. It developed from the **cotillion** in the early 19th century and arrived in Ireland around 1816, although it does not seem to have spread to some parts (including Clare and Kerry) until the 1880s and 90s. It was adapted by the **dancing masters** to suit the capabilities and tastes of their pupils and in most places was danced to traditional Irish tunes which were popular in that particular locality. The French term is derived from the Italian *quadrigalia*, a troop of horsemen who formed a square when taking part in a tournament. These dances were brought to most parts of Europe by military personnel, diplomats and travellers. Many could have come to Ireland through **England** (as suggested by the names of dances, such as 'The Lancers' or 'The Victoria') or directly from **France** ('The Paris Set'). In Ireland, they formed the basis of **set dancing** and many still survive.

Generally, the figures or different stages of the dances became fixed in certain combinations, or 'Sets of Quadrilles'. Three of these can still be recognised in Ireland today, obviously in a form that has been adapted to Irish and even local circumstances: 1) 'The First Set of Quadrilles', also known simply as 'The Quadrilles', originally the most popular set with early 19th-century dancers in Paris; 2) 'The Lancers', said by one source to have been composed by a French dancing-master at the request of a lancer regiment based in Dublin in 1817. Other sources place its origin in France. Its movements are said to reflect drills and formations familiar to the military; 3) 'The Caledonians', possibly originating in **Scotland** and described in dancing manuals dating from the end of the 19th century. See also **Reel**.

Ragús 'Ragús' is an Irish word meaning 'a strong urge or desire' and is the name used for a show of traditional song, music and dance from the Aran Islands, off the Galway coast. The show was founded by the **sean-nós** singer and button accordion player Fergal Ó Murchú, a native of Moygownagh, Co. Mayo. It started in July 1999 on Inishmore, the largest of the Aran Islands, where it still runs every summer. In 2001 the show also ran in Dublin's Vicar Street during July and August, moving to the larger Olympia Theatre in Dublin for summer runs in 2002 and 2003. Dancer Michael Ryan from Co. Tipperary is responsible for the show's choreography and Maurice Lennon (formerly of **Stockton's Wing**) is musical advisor and has also performed with the show. A first CD, simply titled *Ragús*, was released by **Gael-Linn** in 2001, and a second CD came out in 2003. Website: www.ragusonlinesales.com.

Raidió na Gaeltachta Connemara-based Irish-language radio station that was set up by the government and began broadcasting on April 2nd, 1972. It aims primarily to serve **Gaeltacht** areas, but can be received all over Ireland and is listened to by many people outside the Gaeltacht. There is a special emphasis placed on traditional music, which is played for 14-15 hours (out of a total of 84 hours) a week, about a quarter of the material played having been collected by the station itself. Many staff members are traditional musicians or singers. The station has also released a number of CDs and annually broadcasts live the final of the *Corn Uí Riada*, a **sean-nós singing** competition in the **Oireachtas**. The station has played an important role in establishing communication between the isolated Gaeltacht areas of Ireland and also links up with the Scottish station *Radio nan Gaidheal* (see **Scotland**). Many of the station's staff also work with **TG4** and both are under the **RTÉ** Authority.

Raidió Teilifís Éireann See **RTÉ**.

Ralston, Gavin (b. 1970) One of Ireland's finest young guitarists, born in Dublin, son of **Seosaimhín Ní Bheaglaoich** from the Dingle **Gaeltacht**. He has toured with **Sharon Shannon**, **Arcady**, and the **Waterboys,** and has recorded three albums with **Niamh Parsons**. He has also performed with **Anúna** and **Máire Breatnach** and is a regular performer with the group **Beginish**. His video tutor, *Irish Traditional Guitar Accompaniment* (1997), provides an excellent guide to techniques and styles of accompaniment for Irish traditional music. In 1997 he also published a book of the same title. He uses various tunings but favours a 'dropped D' tuning for playing traditional music. He runs a studio in Co. Wicklow and in 2001 produced an excellent solo album by his uncle, **Brendan Begley**, with whom he tours regularly. Ralston's playing can be heard on the album *Michelle O'Brien, Aogán Lynch and Gavin Ralston* (2003). Aogán Lynch (concertina), Ralston's cousin, also plays with the group **Slide**, and Michelle O'Brien (from Co. Clare) is one of the most talented young fiddlers to emerge in recent years. The album is a mixture of traditional and original tunes (including a waltz by **Tommy Peoples** and two jigs by **Liz Carroll**), and there is one song sung by Aogán's mother Caitlín Ní Bheaglaoich.

Reavy, Ed (1899-1988)   Irish fiddler and prolific composer of traditional style tunes. Born in Co. Cavan, but emigrated to the **US** as a boy, settling in Philadelphia. Reavy was an accomplished fiddler who played from the 1920s on, and began composing his own tunes in the 1940s. He wrote around 400 tunes, including 'The Hunter's House', a reel popularised by **Seán Maguire** in the 1950s. Many of these tunes were well established in the 'traditional' repertoire before their composer died, and numerous musicians have recorded Reavy tunes, including **Mick Moloney**, **Eileen Ivers** and **Solas**. *The Collected Compositions of Ed Reavy*, edited by Joseph M. Reavy (Drumshambo, 1984), was reprinted in 1996 and has an accompanying cassette. In 2001 it was announced that Ed Reavy Jnr. was working closely with the US Library of Congress to convert Ed Reavy's home recordings onto CD issues for the public, a major project which it is hoped will be completed in two to three years.

Rebel Song   A term used, sometimes pejoratively, for **Nationalist/Republican song**. During the **Ballad Boom**, many rebel songs were overplayed and often performed badly. This, as well as the association of rebel songs with support or sympathy for the violent Republicanism of the 1970s, 80s and 90s, led to disdain in many quarters for this type of song. Many rebel songs, however, are not only historically accurate but give voice to the feelings or political viewpoint of people who are otherwise under-represented in standard historical works. They are important historical documents in themselves and, even when written after events they describe, can tell us much about how events in one era can be remoulded to suit the political ideals of a later time. See **Section 31**; **Zimmerman, Georges Denis**.

Recording   The American Thomas Edison invented the phonograph, a forerunner of the gramophone, in 1877. Initially the phonograph recorded sound onto a metal foil coated cylinder, but wax cylinders were used from 1887. The first recordings of Irish traditional music were made on wax cylinders in the earliest years of the **Feis Ceoil**, 1897-1900. Forty-six cylinders from the recordings made at the unpublished airs competition survived and were donated to the **Irish Folklore Commission** in 1955. Twenty-three of these were audible and suitable for dubbing, seventeen were audible but not suitable for dubbing and the remainder were inaudible. In the **US**, commercial recordings of Irish traditional music were made by the Edison Company as early as 1899 and uilleann piper **Patsy Touhey** bought his own Edison phonograph and recorded his playing onto cylinders that he sold by mail order.

The gramophone, which used a flat disc instead of a cylinder, was invented by the German Emile Berliner and began to be manufactured on a small scale by 1894. The flat disc or record gradually took over from the wax cylinder, and artists such as German-American accordionist John Kimmel made recordings on both cylinder and disc. Kimmel, whose recording career spanned the years 1904-1920, was one of a number of non-Irish musicians who recorded Irish traditional music at this time. Unlike most others, however, he had a good understanding of the music and was a fine stylist. The first commercial disc recording of Irish musicians playing traditional music featured the banjo/accordion duo of Eddie Hebron and John Whelan and was made by Columbia Records in New York in 1916.

This was the beginning of a new era for Irish traditional music. One of the main advantages of the 78 rpm disc over the cylinder was that many copies could be made from a master recording, while cylinders could only be recorded one at a time. The commercial recording industry in the US had great success with Irish traditional musicians such as **Michael Coleman**, **James Morrison**, **John McKenna**, **Paddy Killoran**, the **Flanagan Brothers** and others during the 1920s and 30s. All of these artists, as well as Patsy Touhey, Packie Dolan (fiddle), Michael Gaffney (banjo), Peter Conlon (button accordion) and Tom Ennis (uilleann pipes) can be heard on the **Shanachie Records** collection, *The Wheels of the World: Early Irish-American Music* (2 CDs, 1996), which also has excellent background information and photographs. The 78 rpm records of players such as Coleman and Morrison had an enormous impact in Ireland, and many musicians adopted their repertoire, style or tune settings, contributing to the process of standardisation in traditional music that had begun with **Francis O'Neill**'s published collections. Recording did play a role in weakening **regional styles** from the 1920s right up to the present.

Tape recorders came into use in the 1940s and were important to collectors of folk and traditional music in Ireland. In the 1950s American collectors like **Alan Lomax** and **Jean Ritchie** often used more up-to-date recording technology than previous collectors working in Ireland and therefore produced higher quality recordings. Raidió Éireann (see **RTÉ**) got their first magnetic tape recorders in 1952 and later in the 1950s home recorders became available to the general public. Some singer/collectors, such as Bobby Clancy (see **Clancy Brothers and Tommy Makem)**, used these to great effect in building up their own collections of traditional songs. Although the majority of 78 rpm recordings of traditional music and song were made in the US, one Irish company, **Gael-Linn**, did produce some 78s of traditional singers and musicians in the late 1950s, at the very end of the 78 rpm era. In terms of commercial recordings, the use of vinyl as a material for making records allowed for a finer groove than the 78, providing better sound quality and opening the way for long-playing records or LPs. These could take up to twenty minutes of music on each side, compared to about three minutes for each side on the 78s. The first LPs of Irish folk and traditional music appeared in the second half of the 1950s, **Margaret Barry** being among the earliest Irish artists to record an LP in Ireland. In the US, the Clancy Brothers and Tommy Makem made their first LP in

1956. Gael-Linn and **Claddagh Records**, two important Irish recording companies, were set up in the 1950s, both contributing enormously to the release of LPs by folk and traditional artists who might not have been considered by the more commercially minded record companies. The English record company **Topic** and American labels such as Tradition and Folkways also played significant roles in recording Irish traditional music and song in the 1950s and 60s. From the 1960s many albums were released on cassette tapes, and the availability of small, inexpensive cassette recorders made them an invaluable tool through which musicians and singers passed on tunes and songs to each other.

In the early 1980s Compact Discs or CDs were introduced, and they gradually eclipsed the use of vinyl LPs. One of Claddagh Records' last vinyl LPs was Robbie Hannan's *Traditional Irish Music on the Uilleann Pipes*, released in 1990. The production of vinyl records was a more complex and expensive process than the production of CDs, and since the 1990s there has been prodigious growth in the number of independently produced albums by traditional musicians. There has also been growth in the number of recording studios in Ireland, making it easier for traditional musicians to record and control what happens to the recorded product. A far greater amount of 'traditional' material is now being released than ever before. See also **Cló Iar-Chonnachta**; **Ossian Publications**; **Outlet Records**.

Reel (*Cor, Ríl*) Along with the **jig**, the reel (or double reel) is the most popular type of dance tune played in Irish traditional music today. It is used for solo **step dancing** and various group dances, including **set dancing** and older group dances such as the four- or eight-hand reel. It is Scottish in origin, and the earliest reference to the dancing of reels comes from 1580, although the dance itself is thought to be of much greater antiquity. The music is in 4/4 time and is usually played in a fast, free-flowing style. The reel seems to have become popular in Ireland from the late 18th century and the earliest reels, many of which are still played today, can be traced to **Scotland**, some to particular Scottish composers. 'Bonnie Kate', for instance, was composed by Daniel Dow, a fiddler from Perthshire, and was originally published under the title 'The Bonny Lass of Fisherrow' around 1760. Another 18th-century Scots fiddler, William Marshall, was the original composer of 'The Duke of Gordon's Rant', known in Ireland as 'Lord Gordon's Reel'. Among the numerous other examples of reels popular in Ireland that **Breandán Breathnach** traced to Scottish origins are 'The Boyne Hunt', 'The Fairy Reel', 'Rakish Paddy', 'Creig's Pipes', 'Lucy Campbell' and 'The Flogging Reel'. Breathnach estimated in 1981 (*The Man and His Music: An Anthology of the Writings of Breandán Breathnach*, Dublin, 1996, p. 151) that most of the reels found in Ireland can be allocated to the period 1780-1880, with little fresh material being added in the century following. Certainly in the past three decades, however, a considerable number of new reels have been composed by Irish musicians, and some of these tunes have already been accepted as part of the 'traditional' repertoire. A good example is the pair of reels called 'The Maple Leaf' and 'The Man of Aran', composed by **Darach de Brún** in 1975 and 1976 respectively. These two reels are played by many traditional musicians and have been recorded, separately or together, on at least a dozen albums. While it is impossible to quantify the number of new reels composed in recent years, there appears to be an increasing amount of new material being written by musicians of all ages. Among the many talented composer/musicians of recent years are **Paddy Fahy**, Paddy O'Brien from Offaly (see **O'Brien, Paddy 1**), **Paddy Keenan**, Eamonn **Galldubh** and **Liz Carroll**.

In the past there were a considerable number of 'single reels', usually in 2/4 time (although Breathnach notes that they could also be in 4/4 time), associated with early set dancing in Ireland. They had a strongly accented rhythm, identical to the **polka**, and were used to teach the basic steps to dancers. Volumes 2 and 3 of the *Roche Collection*, which date from the early decades of the 20th century (see **Roche, Francis**), have sections described as 'Old "Set" Tunes' and 'Quadrilles' (see **Quadrilles**). Roughly half of these tunes are in 6/8 time and half are in 2/4 time, the latter presumably being the tunes referred to elsewhere as single reels. Some older musicians refer to these tunes as 'old dancing master reels', and Breathnach collected one such tune in Listowel, Co. Kerry in 1968 that bore the title 'The Dancing Master's Reel' (see *Ceol Rince na hÉireann 2*, No. 126). The dominance of polkas in the set dancing of southwest Ireland may reflect the former popularity of single reels, which are basically the same type of tune. Although musicians today never use the term 'single reel', some of the tunes played as polkas could be old single reels. See also **Broderick, Vincent**; **Reavy, Ed**.

Geehan's Reel

Regional Styles The term 'regional styles' is used by some musicians and commentators to refer to a particular style of singing or playing which has characteristics that are shared by the singers or musicians of a certain geographical area. The characteristics involved can include phrasing, articulation, tone, speed, ornamentation, variation (melodic or rhythmic) or the use of special performance techniques. Before the era of popular published collections (like **Francis O'Neill**'s) and media such as radio, television and commercial **recording**s, regional styles appear to have been more pronounced. At a time when most musicians travelled little beyond their own district and the occasional travelling musician was all they heard of music from beyond their area, local versions and stylistic features in music and song would certainly have been more marked. This was the situation that prevailed throughout Ireland until the early decades of the 20th century. In some parts of the country change came slowly, and even in the early 1960s **Seán Ó Riada** identified regional characteristics in the singing and instrumental music of certain areas. In **sean-nós singing**, for instance, Ó Riada found that Connacht (especially Connemara) singers generally sang within a narrower range (just over one octave) than Munster singers. The Munster songs also tended to be longer, having an average four-line unit as opposed to the average eight-line unit in Connemara songs. He also noted differences in the ways in which the melodies of songs were varied, West Munster singers, for example, using more rhythmic variation than other regions. Since Ó Riada's time singers like **Lillis Ó Laoire** and **Pádraigín Ní Uallacháin** have done much through their research to highlight the unique significance of the musical (especially sean-nós singing) traditions of Tory Island and southeast Ulster respectively.

Ó Riada also identified certain regional characteristics in fiddling (see **Fiddle**) and flute playing (see **Flute**). Although he was not the first person to notice regional characteristics in Irish music, he brought them to the attention of a wider audience than ever before through his radio series *Our Musical Heritage* in 1962. At the time, some singers and musicians did not agree with his views on regional styles, but many found his analysis illuminating. Ó Riada also pointed out that in some areas styles were disappearing or being diluted, and this process continued in many areas through the 1970s and 80s.

In recent years there has been a notable resurgence in the emphasis placed on regional styles in some parts of the country. Groups like **Altan** (Donegal) take pride in the style and repertoire of their county. Solo musicians like Birmingham-born flute player **Catherine McEvoy** pay homage to particular regional styles, in this case flute music in the Sligo-Roscommon style. The **Willie Clancy Summer School** now runs workshops on West *and* East Clare fiddling styles. A number of books and albums concentrating on regional styles or repertoire have been released in recent years, including *The Trip to Sligo* (originally published 1990, 2nd edition 1998, Boyle), a book by Bernard Flaherty which has extensive notes on the topography, musicial style and musicians of the Sligo area as well as being a collection of music from the Sligo repertoire. Another fine collection is *Hidden Fermanagh* (2003), a CD and book (which contains tunes and some songs) put together by brothers **Cathal McConnell** and **Mickey McConnell** and flautist Cyril Maguire. A second CD, *Hidden Fermanagh, Vol. 2* (2004), also accompanies the book. Many of these developments seem to be partly a reaction to the standardisation or dilution of regional styles. There is a sense of musicians delighting in what is distinctive about the style or repertoire of a particular area. It is certainly a positive development that diversity and uniqueness in traditional music are recognised and cherished. The extent to which regional styles encompass whole areas in a clearly identifiable, naturally occurring way is, however, open to question.

What is clear is that in a few parts of the country there are certain types of tunes that are favoured more by musicians than others. In **Sliabh Luachra** and the Dingle peninsula, for example, **polka**s and **slide**s make up a far greater proportion of the dance music than elsewhere. In northern counties like Donegal and Tyrone, musicians play a larger number of **strathspey**s, **highland**s, **barndance**s and **mazurka**s than elsewhere. Some of these types originally became popular through strong historical links with **Scotland**. For many years, however, northern musicians have been composing their own tunes in these forms.

In terms of style, as opposed to repertoire, what is heard through travel, radio, television or commercial recordings can influence a singer or musician as much as the music in his/her immediate vicinity. It must also be accepted that many musicians develop a style that is entirely their own. Categorising styles by region can be misleading in the sense that when the characteristics of that style are described, exceptions can always be found among individual players. In his study of the Donegal fiddle tradition, Caoimhín MacAoidh describes a general preference among Donegal fiddlers for a staccato style of bowing with a notable use of **triplet**s in ornamenting tunes. He also stresses that there are exceptions to this generalisation within the Donegal tradition (*Between the Jigs and the Reels*, Manorhamilton, 1994, p. 52). What emerges most strongly from MacAoidh's work is that, while certain stylistic characteristics may be shared by some players from Donegal, there is also a huge variety of local and individual styles within the county (see also **O'Shaughnessy, Paul**). The misconception that **Johnny Doherty**'s style is *the* Donegal style has been pointed out by **Tommy Peoples** as well as MacAoidh.

What is true of Donegal is true of other regions as well. Certain characteristics may be shared by a considerable number of musicians in a certain area, but there will usually be individual stylistic features as well. In many areas there will be musicians whose style simply can't be described by regional characteristics. Perhaps it would be more accurate to speak in terms of 'regional *tendencies*' and accept that such tendencies are not shared by all. Exceptional individual musicians do inspire pupils or imitators, as in the case of Johnny Doherty, but this does not mean that the style is a regional one. Clare fiddler **Martin Hayes** has been described as having a 'Neo-East Clare' style; this seems a convoluted way to define a style that is very much his own.

Whole conferences have been devoted to debating the subject of regional styles, and there is considerable disagreement about whether or not they exist at all. The ease of travelling in the late 20th century and the massive changes brought about by modern media have undoubtedly diluted regional styles; the recent resurgence of interest can be seen as a resistance to standardisation in traditional music. One wonders, however, if there is a danger that individual styles are not seen by some as having the same legitimacy as certain regional styles. For many musicians, stylistic labels don't matter at all; they simply want to play from the heart, adding their own touches as imagination or technique permit.

Relativity Scots-Irish group who played traditional music and song with great flair and passion. The Scots members were brothers Phil (piano accordion, keyboards, whistle, bodhrán) and John (fiddle) Cunningham. The Irish half was made up by **Micheál Ó Domhnaill** (vocals, guitar, keyboards) and his sister **Tríona Ní Dhomhnaill** (vocals, clavinet). Their material was a powerfully arranged mixture of Scottish and Irish instrumentals and songs (sung in both Irish and English). Some of the material was original. Although they did play in Ireland, they toured far more in the **US**. They made two excellent albums, *Relativity* (1986) and *Gathering Pace* (1987).

Religious Songs Religious songs, of which there are very few surviving in the Irish tradition, are strongly associated with female singers. The pagan ritual of keening, or wailing lamentations for the dead, was usually carried out by women. Despite its non-Christian origins, keening influenced Christian religious songs in Ireland, and the central role played by women may explain keening's strong association with religious song in general. Although keening declined during the **Great Famine**, it was noted in the early 20th century on the Aran Islands, Co. Galway. One of the most popular of the surviving religious songs is 'Caoineadh na dTrí Muire' ('Lament of the Three Marys'). Many versions of this song are found in Ireland, some bearing the title 'Caoineadh na Páise' ('Lament of the Passion') or 'Caoineadh na Maighdine' ('Lament of the Virgin'). Its popularity in the 19th century is indicated by the fact that it was one of the few songs in Irish to appear on a ballad sheet (around 1850) as 'Ceeny na Dree Virow'. This *caoineadh* (lament) also provides a rare example of a song composed in Irish that imitates the form and style of a **ballad**. Its refrain ('ochón agus ochón ó') was typical of the vocables of lament used by keening women.

'Seacht nDólás na Maighdine Muire' ('The Seven Sorrows of the Virgin Mary') and 'Seacht Suáilce na Maighdine Muire' ('The Seven Joys of the Virgin Mary') are medieval **carol**s possibly introduced into Ireland as early as the 13th century by the Franciscans (see **Ledrede, Richard**). 'Muire agus Naomh Ioseph' ('Mary and St. Joseph') is an Irish version of the old English ballad 'The Cherry Tree' (Child 54, see **Child Ballads**). It is associated with the Christmas season, but is also known in an Easter version entitled 'Hymn Dhomnach Cásca' ('Hymn for Easter Sunday').

Collectors such as **George Petrie** and Úna Ní Ógáin made important contributions to the preservation of Irish religious songs. **Noirín Ní Riain** has studied and published extensively on the subject, as well as recording religious songs from Ireland and Europe. The **sean-nós** singer **Seosamh Ó Heanaí** is one of the few male singers of recent decades who was noted for singing religious songs. The only full-length study of the genre is *'Caoineadh na dTrí Muire': Téama Páise i bhFilíocht na Gaeilge* (Dublin, 1983) by Angela Partridge (Bourke). Hector Zazou's *Lights in the Dark* (1998) is an extraordinary album of Irish religious songs. It features the Irish singers Lasairfhíona Ní Chonala, Breda Mayock and Katie McMahon (also of **Anúna** and *Riverdance*), with contributions from a number of musicians of other nationalities including Carlos Nuñez (flute, ocarina), Mark Isham (trumpet),

Ryuichi Sakamoto (piano) and Peter Gabriel (vocals). The arrangements, by Zazou himself (who also produced and performed on the album) are imaginative and daring, creating soundscapes at once modern and ancient. It includes most of the songs mentioned above, including two versions of 'Caoineadh na dTrí Muire'. **Micheál Ó Súilleabháin** has also recorded some religious music, most notably on his album *Templum* (2001).

Republican Song See **Nationalist/Republican Song**.

Rince Fada ('Long Dance')

A processional dance popular in Ireland in the 17th and 18th centuries. It involved couples following a leading group of three people, all holding white handkerchiefs, in what started as a procession to slow music. The music would speed up as the couples passed under the handkerchief of the leaders and danced a variety of lively movements before resuming their original positions. The *rince fada* was danced in honour of King **James II** on his arrival at Kinsale in 1689. It remained popular well into the 18th century, when it was usually danced at the end of private and public balls. In the second half of the 18th century the **cotillion** and later the **quadrille** gradually replaced the old long dance. **Breandán Breathnach** has compared the *rince fada* with the present-day dance called 'The Bridge of Athlone'.

Rince Mór ('Big Dance')

Often referred to as the 'trenchmore'. Mentioned in the 17th century as a **long dance** for as many people as wanted to take part.

Ritchie, Jean (b. 1922)

Singer, songwriter, collector and **dulcimer** player from Viper, Kentucky who has researched extensively and published on the music of the **Appalachians**. She came from a family of singers who rose to prominence in the late 1940s and 50s when there was a new interest in folk music in the **US**. One of her first big appearances as a singer and dulcimer player was in the late 1940s at a festival run by **Alan Lomax** at Columbia University. Photographer George Pickow was sent to Kentucky to photograph the famous Ritchie singing family and fell in love with Jean. They married and moved to Port Washington. Pickow accompanied her on many of her collecting trips, and they collected in Britain and Ireland as well as in the US.

Ritchie was interested in tracing the Irish and British origins of the many songs which her family sang. She won a Fulbright Scholarship to pursue this work and in 1952 she and George Pickow visited Ireland. They had the latest in recording technology, the first portable reel-to-reel tape recorder, and made very high quality recordings. The artists they recorded in Ireland included **Elizabeth Cronin**, **Sarah Makem**, **Séamus Ennis** and others. Ritchie and Pickow subsequently released the album *As I Roved Out: Field Recordings from Ireland* (1960) in the US. The album was reissued by **Ossian Publications** in 1990. They also released an album of songs from **England**, **Scotland** and Ireland and Ritchie published a book, *From Fair to Fair: Folk Songs of the British Isles* (New York, 1966). Pickow also produced some wonderful photographs of the Irish musicians. These photographs and the tapes are now in the Ritchie-Pickow Archive at the National University of Ireland, Galway.

Ritchie is also a singer who made many recordings of her own singing. In the 1950s she performed at concerts in New York which were organised by the **Clancy Brothers and Tommy Makem** and was an inspiration and mentor to collector Diane Hamilton. Hamilton played a major role in launching the singing career of the Clancys and Tommy Makem in the late 1950s. Although Ritchie sang many traditional songs she is also a songwriter of considerable talent, and her album *None but One* (1977) won the *Rolling Stone* Critic's Award. Her song 'One I Love' was recorded by the Irish singer **Karan Casey**. Website: www.jeanritchie.com.

Jean Ritchie with Séamus Ennis, 1952 (photo: George Pickow)

Riverdance   Dance show that began as a seven-minute interlude in the Eurovision Song Contest in Dublin (1994). It featured music by **Bill Whelan**, the singing of the group **Anúna** and the Irish-style step-dancing of Americans **Michael Flatley** and Jean Butler. The Eurovision interlude was so successful that producer Moya Doherty and director John McColgan developed it as a full stage show, bringing in musicians and dancers (Russian, Spanish and American tap) from other traditions. Much of the dancing is based around Irish step-dancing, but it is presented in

a more modern style. Spectacular lighting, visual images and costumes are all important elements in the presentation, and a more liberal use is made of arm movements
than is usual in Irish dancing (with the exception of some **sean-nós dancing**).
Many initially responded to *Riverdance* as 'sexy Irish dancing', and the costumes
and style of the dancing itself suggest that this image was deliberately developed by
the producers. Bill Whelan's music for the show often uses traditional forms (such
as the slip jig in the original dance sequence) but also employs more irregular time
structures not found in traditional music. The music is performed by the *Riverdance*
Orchestra, which has featured many of the finest contemporary Irish traditional
musicians, including **Davy Spillane**, **Máire Breathnach**, **Máirtín O'Connor**,
Eileen Ivers and **Brendan Power**. The video *Riverdance: The Show* (1995) is an
international spectacle, featuring performances by Spanish dancer Maria Pages, the
Russian Moiseyev Dance Company, the Harlem Tappers and the American Gospel
singers James Bignon and the Deliverance Ensemble. Further videos, *Riverdance:
The New Show* and *Riverdance: A Journey* (which tells the story of the production
of *Riverdance*) have, like the first, been best-sellers.

The *Riverdance* stage show has been so successful that a number of different
dance troupes and orchestras now tour simultaneously in different parts of the
world. It is constantly changing; one American production, for example, featured
poetry by Theo Dorgan spoken by the actor John Kavanagh and a dance sequence
in which American tap dancers imitate and mock the Irish dancers, deriding their
'arms straight down by the sides' and serious facial expressions. The show has provided an unprecedented level of professional work for Irish dancers and musicians
and has contributed to an explosion of interest in Irish dancing worldwide. Despite
the loss of Flatley, who went on to produce his own show, ***Lord of the Dance***, the
Riverdance stage show continues to be enormously successful internationally.

River of Sound, A Major television series by Hummingbird Productions,
broadcast by **RTÉ** and the **BBC** in 1995. Subtitled 'The Changing Course of Irish
Traditional Music', it examined the development of Irish traditional music, dance
and song, with an emphasis on the contemporary interaction between tradition and
innovation. The series was written, devised and presented by **Micheál Ó
Súilleabháin**, produced by Nuala O'Connor and directed by Philip King. 130 musicians, including some of the best traditional musicians of the 1990s, took part in the
series, and a selection of the music was released on the CD *A River of Sound* (1995).
The series was received with great interest by the media and general public and was
the subject of a special *Late Late Show* on RTÉ. It was criticised by some for not featuring enough of the older traditional musicians and for other aspects, including
having a theme tune that was not traditional. The heated debate which broke out on
the *Late Late Show* about what, precisely, constituted traditional music reflected a
more general, ongoing tension between 'preservation' and 'innovation', with some
arguing that commercial appeal and **fusions** with other forms of music could ultimately destroy what is most unique about Irish traditional music. **Tony MacMahon**
(one of the main critics of *A River of Sound* on the *Late Late Show*) and Ó

Súilleabháin were subsequently invited to deliver keynote addresses at a major conference '*Crosbhealach an Cheoil* /Music at the Crossroads: Tradition and Change in Irish Traditional Music' (see **Crossroads Conference**). See also ***Bringing It All Back Home***.

Roche, Francis (1866-1961) Dancing master, fiddler and collector from Co. Limerick who published a two-volume collection of Irish traditional music in 1911, adding a third volume in 1927. A number of aspects of Roche's collection are of special interest. In addition to airs, marches, double jigs, reels and hornpipes, Roche included a considerable number of single jigs, hop or slip jigs and set dances in his collection. Most significantly, he did not exclude other types of tunes that were popular at the time, or had been popular in the past. In Volume 2, for instance, he has whole sections devoted to flings, long dances (country dances), quadrilles and old set tunes. Volume 3 also has a section of old set tunes, and as in Volume 2 they are all untitled tunes which presumably were used for various figures used for **set dancing**. In addition, Volume 3 contains a selection of 'Old Dances' (not Irish by origin) that includes waltzes, schottisches, polkas, barndances and mazurkas.

Although a member of the **Gaelic League**, Roche did not agree with their policy of banning set dancing in favour of **céilí dancing**. In his introduction to Volume 1, Roche defended his inclusion of what some would consider 'matter foreign to a collection of Irish music, such as Quadrilles, or "Sets", as they are popularly called, and other dance tunes also', by suggesting that the tunes had become 'Irish by association'. He continued: '[S]o long as people dance Sets, etc., it is better that they should do so to the old tunes in which their parents delighted, rather than be left depending on those books from across the water containing the most hackneyed of Moore's melodies mixed up with music hall trash, and, perhaps, a few faked reels and jigs thrown in by way of padding.' Roche's introduction to Volume 3 has a fascinating 'Note on Irish Dancing' that indicates the variety of dances to be found in Ireland at the time. Some of the settings of tunes are unusual and Roche attempted to notate the 'glide' or 'sliding' ornamentation used by fiddlers, explaining the technique in detail in Volume 1. All three volumes were republished in one volume as *The Roche Collection of Traditional Irish Music* (Cork, 1982; new edition 1993).

Roinn Bhéaloideas Éireann See **Irish Folklore Department**, **University College Dublin**.

Roll A form of **ornamentation** played in two ways, the long roll and the short roll. In the long roll, the main note is played first, then 'cut' by a grace note that is higher. After returning to the main note, the player then 'tips' a grace note below it, returning rapidly to the main note (see below). A long roll usually takes place in the time value of a dotted crotchet (quarter note). It can also be used to replace a sequence of three notes where the first and last notes of the sequence are the same and the middle note is just above or below them. The short roll can involve exactly the same sequence of notes played within the time value of a crotchet (quarter note) only, but the way it is played can vary according to the instrument or the player (see below). Instead of the five distinct notes described above for the long roll, the short roll can be reduced to four. The precise grace notes used in playing both types of roll, and the way they are fingered, can vary greatly. Rolls can provide great rhythmic drive to a tune and can also be used to vary melody or accentuation.

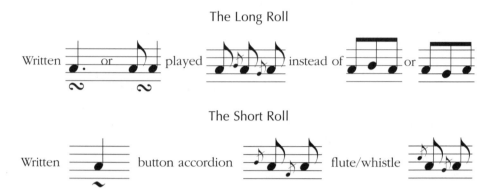

The Long Roll

The Short Roll

Round, The A 32-bar formula to which much **dance music** is played. It is made up of two eight-bar parts or strains, each of which is repeated. This 32-bar sequence makes up the tune and is normally played at least twice. There are dance tunes that have more than two parts, and some tunes vary from this pattern in other ways (see, for example, under **Set Dance**).

Round Dance A general term used to describe any group dance in which the dancers (usually couples) form themselves in a line or circle. The earliest known round dance in Ireland was the **carol**, introduced in the Middle Ages. Another form of round dance, mentioned from the 16th century, was the Irish **hay**. Round dances were still popular in Ireland in the 17th and 18th centuries and continue to form the basis for most of the traditional dancing found in **Brittany**. The **dancing masters**, from around the mid-18th century, devised round dances for social occasions and taught them to their pupils, who would have known the steps for the jig, reel and hornpipe. The **céilí dancing** of today owes much to these earlier forms of round dance.

Rowsome, Leo (1903-1970) Uilleann piper, pipe maker and teacher whose enormous influence requires fuller recognition. He came from a family whose fame as uilleann pipers goes right back to before the **Great Famine**. His father, William, was a piper and violinist who moved from his native Co. Wexford to Dublin, where he soon established himself as an instrument maker at the start of the 20th century. Leo took over the pipe-making business at a time when pipes were going into serious decline. In 1934 he re-established the old **Dublin Pipers' Club** and was also involved with his brother Tom in the founding of **Comhaltas Ceoltóirí Éireann** in 1951. Leo was also a fine piper and won first prize in the Dublin **Feis Ceoil** piping competition in 1924. He performed all over the world, playing Carnegie Hall in New York in the 1960s to an audience of 6,000. He made many recordings, initially on 78 rpm records and later on LP records, most notably *Rí na bPíobairí (The King of the Pipers,* 1959), the first ever record made by **Claddagh Records**. Two records of remastered 78 rpm recordings, originally made between 1926 and 1948, were released by **Topic Records** in the 1970s and are available on CD as *Classics of Irish Piping* (1993). Rowsome was famous for his ability to write tunes down rapidly and was highly regarded as a teacher, publishing an excellent tutor for the pipes in 1936. **Liam O'Flynn** and **Joe McKenna** are among the most famous of his many pupils. He collapsed and died while adjudicating in the Fiddler of Dooney competition at Riverstown Hall in Co. Sligo in 1970. His brother Liam published a book about Leo, *The Man I Knew,* in 1996. His daughter Helena edited *The Leo Rowsome Collection of Irish Traditional Music* (2002), comprising over 400 jigs and reels that he had written down over the years, and including a substantial introduction on his life and work as well as a facsimile reprint of his 1936 tutor.

Many of Leo's children and grandchildren were – and are – also involved in music. His daughter Helena played tin whistle from an early age and was a founder member of the Clontarf Branch of Comhaltas Ceoltóirí Éireann. She made many recordings for **RTÉ**, UTV and **BBC** in the 1960s and taught the whistle for many

Leo Rowsome with Garech de Brún, founder of Claddagh Records, 1966

years at Craobh Chluain Tarbh. More recently she has taught at the Boston College Irish Studies week. Leo's son Leon (1936-1994), also an uilleann piper, recorded two albums and toured Europe, the **US** and **Canada**. He took over his father's teaching at the College of Music in Dublin where he had many pupils, including his own son Kevin. Kevin Rowsome is establishing a growing reputation as a player of the uilleann pipes, winning the **Oireachtas** in 1996 and recording an album, *The Rowsome Tradition: Five Generations of Uilleann Piping*, in 1999. He is also a pipe maker.

RTÉ (Raidió Teilifís Éireann) National radio and television company, supervised by a government-appointed body, the RTÉ Authority (established 1966). It was preceded by the Dublin Broadcasting Station (popularly known as 2RN), which began broadcasting in 1926, and Radio Athlone or Raidió Éireann, which superseded 2RN in 1933. RTÉ and its predecessors have played an important role in promoting traditional music and song, although it is not universally accepted that their role has always been a positive one.

The first director of 2RN, Séamus Clandillon, invited traditional musicians to play on the radio in the late 1920s. Among the earliest musicians to broadcast were Dick Smith's céilí trio (fiddle, flute, piano), which performed a series of weekly recitals in 1927, Leo Molloy's céilí band (1929), the Ballinakill Traditional Players (see **Céilí Bands**) and some solo performers. Some traditional songs were also broadcast, but until the 1950s they were rarely performed by traditional singers. The **BBC** initiated the first major field recording project in traditional music and song (in Britain and Ireland) in the late 1940s/early 1950s. Raidió Éireann soon had its own mobile recording unit, and collectors like **Séamus Ennis** and **Ciarán Mac Mathúna** played vital roles in building up a collection of field recordings from all over Ireland, the **US** and **Canada**. Radio programmes such as *Ceolta Tíre* and *A Job of Journeywork*, both presented by Mac Mathúna, made a significant contribution to spreading interest in and knowledge of traditional music in rural and urban Ireland from the mid-1950s.

The 1960s brought **Seán Ó Riada** to prominence, *Our Musical Heritage* (1962) and his broadcasts with **Ceoltóirí Chualann** generating widespread interest in traditional music. In the early 1970s the series *The Long Note* began, an excellent programme that had as presenters, among others, **Paddy Glackin** and **Peter Browne**. It ran into the 1990s, one of the longest running traditional music programmes ever. RTÉ Radio 1 continues to broadcast regular series on traditional music, including Mac Mathúna's *Mo Cheol Thú*, *Céilí House* with **Kieran Hanrahan** and the *The Late Session* with Áine Hennessy. Special documentaries or concert performances are also broadcast occasionally, and **Raidió na Gaeltachta** includes a significant proportion of traditional music and song. **Harry Bradshaw** has also been an important contributor to traditional music on the radio and the history of radio in Ireland.

Irish television began on 31 December 1961 with the first RTÉ broadcasts. From the earliest days there has tended to be an overlap with radio when it comes to presenters of traditional music programmes, Séamus Ennis and Paddy Glackin, for example, appearing on both. A number of important television series have been made over the years, including *The Pure Drop* and the more ambitious ***Bringing It All Back Home*** and *A **River of Sound***, both made for RTÉ and BBC by Hummingbird Productions. RTÉ television continues to broadcast traditional music and song, but **TG4** now has a greater range of programmes.

The late **Breandán Breathnach** accepted that Raidió Éireann's mobile recording unit from the 1950s to the 70s did important work in collecting genuine material at source, but he expressed reservations about the effect that radio and television had on traditional music. He was concerned about the standardisation of repertoire, the abandonment of local styles, and the mixture of genuine material with what he saw as 'spurious' (see **Regional Styles**). He doubted that the authorities in charge of radio and television were aware of the significance of their potential role in aiding the survival and renewal of traditional music. Perhaps Breathnach would be pleasantly surprised by some developments in recent decades, but a considerable number of musicians and music enthusiasts share the view that radio and television could do more for traditional music. RTÉ and its predecessors, however, have undoubtedly done invaluable work over the years, and the RTÉ archives contain much rare material. Constructive criticism of their work is essential, but should be balanced by an appreciation of their achievements. See also **Irish Traditional Music Archive**; **Section 31**.

Rua Duo of red-haired musicians Liz Madden (vocals) and Gloria Mulhall (keyboards, piano, violin) whose name, Rua, is the Irish word for 'red haired'. Madden writes lyrics for some of the duo's songs while Mulhall composes the music and arranges the material. Although their background is in pop and classical music, their first album, *Rua* (2001), had four tracks described as traditional, including 'She Moved Through the Fair' (see **Colum, Padraic**), 'Jail of Clonmel' and 'Fear an Bháta' ('The Boatman'). Traditional musicians on the album included uilleann pipers **Ronan Browne** and Tiarnán Ó Duinnchin, Fionán De Barra (guitar, also with **Máire Ní Bhraonáin** and **Galldubh**) and **Tommy Hayes** (bodhrán). They also perform original material, and their first single, 'Le Marais' (named after the district on the north bank of the Seine in Paris), was written by Madden and Mulhall. It can be heard on their second album, *Dream-Teller* (2003), which includes **Jimmy MacCarthy**'s 'Ride On', also released as a single. In addition to their own material, the album includes renditions of the traditional songs 'Carrickfergus' and 'Black Is the Colour'. The actor Gabriel Byrne also narrates the poem 'I Am of Ireland' by **W. B. Yeats** on the CD.

Russell, Micho (1915-1994) Tin whistle and flute player, lilter, story teller and singer from Doonagore, Doolin, Co. Clare who came to prominence in the 1960s. Micho started to play tin whistle at the age of eleven in an area where unadorned concertina-playing was a marked feature of traditional music. The subtlety of his sparsely ornamented style on the whistle won him many admirers. He also had many old stories connected with the tunes he played and is remembered for his geniality and humour as well as his playing and singing. **Breandán Breathnach**

transcribed hundreds of tunes from Russell's playing, some of which were published in his important collection *Ceol Rince na hÉireann* (Vol. II).

From the mid 1960s, when he first came to the attention of audiences beyond his native area, until the time of his tragic death after a car accident, Russell performed to audiences all over Ireland, Britain, Europe and the **US**. He recorded a number of albums, as a solo artist and with his family, including his brothers Packie (concertina) and Gussie (flute).

Micho Russell

One of the most interesting of his albums is the posthumously released *Ireland's Whistling Ambassador* (1995), which is accompanied by an excellent booklet written by Bill Ochs. It includes Russell's whistle playing, singing in English and Irish and, on some tracks, his talking about the background to tunes or songs. He also published *The Piper's Chair: A Collection of Tunes and Folklore* (Cork, 1989, reprint of 1980) and a collection of songs. He played an important role in attracting people to the tiny village of **Doolin**, which became a mecca for traditional musicians and enthusiasts from all over the world. His last recording was with Chicago-born **John Williams**. The poet Michael Coady from Carrick-on-Suir, Co. Tipperary, published a fine tribute to the Russells in *The Well of Spring Water: A Memoir of Packie and Micho Russell of Doolin* (Coady, 1996). Since his death, a Micho Russell Memorial weekend has been held annually at Doolin, and in 1999 the Micho Russell Memorial Centre was built in the village.

Ryan, Connie (1939-1997) Dancing master born in Clonoulty, Cashel, Co. Tipperary. His name is closely associated with the revival of **set dancing** in recent decades. Around 1977 he started to teach both set and **céilí dancing**. As the popularity of set dancing increased, he began to teach it exclusively and, although it was not his full-time profession, he taught throughout Ireland, Europe, **Australia** and the **US**. He also travelled around Ireland seeking to revive sets that, in many cases, had almost died out.

Ryan, Seán (b. 1949) Tin whistle player from Cashel, Co. Tipperary. He joined the Sam Dougherty Céilí Band at the age of fifteen for three years, later working in England and returning home in 1970. Although never a full member of the group, he also played and toured with **De Dannan**. *Súil Uait*, his first album, was released by **Gael Linn** in 1989, with *Cliaraí Ceoil: Minstrel's Fancy* following in 1994. He has toured Ireland, Europe and the **US**.

Ryan, William Bradbury (1831-1910) Collector and publisher born in Lyndon, Vermont. Having fought in the American Civil War he became a bandleader in Boston and later worked as an assistant to the publisher Elias Howe (1820-1895), who pioneered large collections of traditional music from the 1840s on. In 1883 he published, with Howe, *William Bradbury Ryan's Mammoth Collection of more than 1050 Reels and Jigs, Hornpipes, Clogs, Walk Arounds, Slip Jigs, Essences, Strathspeys, Highland Flings and Contra Dances, with Figures*. In addition to the large proportion of Irish tunes (approximately one third) in Ryan's collection, a quarter of the tunes are Scottish; there are also tunes such as clog dances from the American minstrel tradition (see **Minstrels**) and a few early ragtime tunes. About a tenth of the tunes include dancing instructions. Patrick Sky, a pupil of **Séamus Ennis** and Dublin piper Tommy Reck and founder of **Green Linnet** records, studied *Ryan's Mammoth Collection* for his Master's thesis in the US (1993) and edited a new edition for Mel Bay in 1995. Ryan's collection is significant in its own right and an important forerunner to **Francis O'Neill**'s first collection of 1903. O'Neill never mentioned Ryan's collection by name, despite the fact that it contained many of the dance tunes which appeared (some note for note) in his own collection.

Sam Henry Collection See **Henry, Sam**.

Sands Family, The Multi-talented family of musicians from Mayobridge, near Newry, Co. Down, many of them taught to play by their father, Mick Sands, a fiddler. Their mother played accordion. The five youngest members of the family entered a competition in the Old Sheiling, Raheny, Dublin, in the late 1960s, winning a three-week trip to play music in New York. Tommy (vocals, guitar), Colum (double bass, fiddle, sitar, viola, vocals), Eugene (vocals, guitar, bouzouki, mandolin, tin whistle), Anne (vocals, bodhrán) and part-time member Ben (vocals, fiddle, sitar, viola) went on to make five albums together as the Sands Family. They toured extensively in Europe and the **US** and were popular in East Germany. They sang and played a mixture of traditional songs in English and instrumentals, Tommy composing some songs of his own. His song 'All the Little Children', its lyrics grappling with the escalating political conflict in Northern Ireland, is a classic of modern Irish folk song. Like later songs by Tommy and Colum, 'All the Little Children' takes Irish political songs beyond the old Nationalist/Loyalist division. The song reached number one in East Berlin in 1974. 'All the Little Children' can be heard on the group's album *You'll Be Well Looked After* (1975), which has a fine collection of traditional songs and instrumentals and a second song by Tommy, 'Peter's Song'. The song is dedicated to fiddler Peter McArdle (d. 1974), and the group incorporates an archive recording of his playing at the end. The instrumental track 'The Battle of the Boyne' (see **Jacobite Song** and **Williamite Song**) is an interesting composite of traditional tunes and is explained in the sleeve-notes as follows: 'The slow air "Quiet Land of Erin" is disturbed by the war drums of William's March. The reaction, if you could call it that, came with James' "Jacket's Green". The "'Limerick Lament" which follows is not just lamenting the Boyne and broken treaty, but also the fact that the battle continues.'

In 1975 Eugene, affectionately known as Dino, was tragically killed. The other members of the family continued to perform and record, Tommy and Colum separately developing their unique songwriting talents. Colum has made three solo albums, *Unapproved Road* (1981), *The March Ditch* (1989) and *All My Winding Journeys* (1996). He also presents folk programmes on BBC Radio Ulster and as a producer has made many fine traditional albums at his studio in Rostrevor, Co. Down. One of his most interesting and innovative projects is the publication of a book, *Between the Earth and the Sky* (Donaghadee, 2000) with painter Colum McEvoy. McEvoy had painted an illustration for the cover of Sands' album *The March Ditch* and went on to illustrate all ten songs on the album. Sands and McEvoy subsequently did a successful concert/exhibition tour called *Songs on a Wall*.

Tommy has released five solo albums, including *Singing of the Times* (1989), *The Heart's a Wonder* (1995), *To Shorten the Winter* (2001) and an album of children's songs. On *Singing of the Times* he is accompanied by other members of the family group and friends, including **Arty McGlynn**, **Dónal Lunny** and **Nollaig Ní Chathasaigh**, among others. In his sleeve-notes to the album, **Pete Seeger** wrote that Tommy 'has achieved that difficult but wonderful balance between knowing and loving the traditions of his home and being concerned with the future of the whole world'. Tommy Sands' work has indeed taken him all over the world. He made an inspired and moving album, *Sarajevo/Belfast* (2001), with Sarajevo cellist Vedran Smailovic. The album includes contributions from Joan Baez, Pete Seeger (who sings 'The Music of Healing', co-written with Tommy Sands), Colum Sands, and a superb rendition of Seeger's 'Where Have All the Flowers Gone' by Dolores Keane and Tommy Sands. Tommy has also worked in Reno, Nevada, teaching songwriting to young prisoners and was awarded an honorary Doctorate by the University of Nevada, Reno in May 2002. Closer to home, he has always been closely involved with events in Northern Ireland and in 1998 put together a group of musicians and children to go to Stormont Castle and sing encouragement to those involved in the peace talks that

Tommy Sands

led to the Good Friday Agreement, 1998 (see **Lambeg Drum**). He has also worked as a radio presenter for Downtown Radio and written on folk music for a number of publications, including *Hibernia*. His moving song 'There Were Roses', which has been recorded by **Robbie O'Connell**, tells the story of two friends who died as a result of sectarian hatred in Northern Ireland.

Both Colum and Tommy Sands have demonstrated a flair for writing a wide range of contemporary folk songs which can be humorous or tragic, songs of the everyday or songs dealing with contemporary political issues. Ben is also a fine singer, songwriter and instrumentalist who has produced a number of solo albums. *Take Your Time* (1993) and *Roots and Branches* (1998) both mix traditional, original and cover songs. *Better Already* (2003) consists entirely of Ben's own compositions, mostly songs in a folk style but also including the fine instrumental 'Farewell to the Town'. The Sands' contribution to keeping Irish folk song alive and relevant to contemporary life is comparable to what Pete Seeger has done for American folk song and what his sister Peggy and **Ewan MacColl** have done for British folk. See also **Political Song**.

Scales See **Modes**.

Schottische (Derived from the German *der Schottische tanz*, 'the Scottish dance') A couple dance of German origin, like a **polka** but slower, played in 4/4 time. It was introduced into England in 1848 as the 'German Polka' and soon spread to **Scotland** where local Highland schottisches were composed. In the second half of the 19th century it was brought by migrant workers from Scotland to Donegal, where it is called simply a highland. In other counties of Ulster, the term is used interchangeably with 'highland', 'fling' and 'barndance'. It was known as the 'fling' in Clare and the 'highland fling' in Cork. Although both the dance and the tunes that went with it were originally found throughout Ireland, the schottische today is most commonly played in Ulster, where a number of different dances are performed to it. An unusual variant is the Irish highland, a dance performed not by a couple but by two women and a man. Versions of this dance have been collected in Fermanagh and Sligo but not further south. Fiddlers from Donegal and other northern counties composed some tunes of their own but also developed highlands by adapting

The Fermanagh Highland

strathspeys or converting **reel**s. They are played slightly faster than strathspeys but considerably slower than reels. The characteristic strings of triplets found in the original strathspeys are often simplified but not eliminated completely. The rhythm is usually dotted, played in a distinctive staccato style that is sometimes referred to as the 'Scots snap'. When a northern fiddler, therefore, turns a reel into a highland he is often said to have given it a 'Scots snap'.

Scoiltrad The first interactive music school on the internet. The project began when three traditional musicians, **Eoin Ó Riabhaigh** (uilleann pipes), Conal Ó Gráda (flute/whistle) and Kevin Glackin (see **Glackin, Paddy**) entered a competition to find a business idea that could make the best contribution to Irish music through the internet. The competition marked the new millennium and was run by

Údarás na Gaeltachta, the elected assembly for Irish-speaking areas (see **Gaeltacht**) in Ireland. The Scoiltrad project won the competition and set up their internet school at a base in the Gaeltacht of Múscraí or Muskerry in west Co. Cork in March 2001. The idea was to give learners all over the world access to expert tuition in traditional instruments at beginner, intermediate and advanced levels. Classes take the form of a downloadable multi-media package with audio or audio/video clips of tunes being played at different speeds, with ornamentation or with variations. Students can record their own playing of the tune and send it by e-mail to their tutor for assessment. Apart from a computer and a microphone, no additional hardware is required. The initial tutors were the three founders of the project with **Colm Murphy** (bodhrán) as their first guest tutor. In March 2002 Scoiltrad announced a series of masterclasses with fiddler **Tommy Peoples** as well as new banjo classes with **Kieran Hanrahan** and new button accordion classes with Aidan Coffey. Website: www.scoiltrad.com.

Scoil Samhraidh Willie Clancy See **Willie Clancy Summer School**.

Scotland The name 'Scotland' is derived from *Scotti*, the standard word for the people of Ireland in medieval Latin. Scotland, therefore, is literally 'Land of the Irish', and Ireland, especially Ulster, has had close connections with Scotland throughout recorded history. From the 3rd century AD the northern Irish kingdom of Dál Riata began to colonise considerable areas of Scotland, and from the 6th century Irish Christianity became widespread. By ca. 1000 Scots Gaelic, derived from the Irish language, was being spoken in many areas. Many Scottish place names have Irish origins, and the early folktales of Scotland suggest close links with Ulster.

Throughout the Middle Ages there were close military and political links between Ireland and Scotland, culminating in the Bruce Invasion of Ireland (1315-1318), when Edward Bruce, brother of Robert Bruce, King of Scots, attempted to overthrow the English in Ireland through an alliance with Gaelic Ireland. Although the invasion ultimately failed, the northern half of Ireland retained closer links with Scotland than with England up to the early 17th century. The plantation of Ulster (1605 and 1609) by Scots and English settlers established links of a very different nature between Scotland and Ireland. Tensions between Scots Presbyterian settlers and dispossessed (largely Gaelic-speaking and Catholic) natives became part of a major European war fought on Irish soil between 1689 and 1691 (see **Jacobite Song** and **Orange/Loyalist Song**). Despite the fact that the Presbyterians supported the Protestant king William III against the Catholic King James II in the war, they suffered a certain amount of religious persecution during the 18th century. Most of Ulster's Presbyterians were small tenant farmers who suffered increased economic hardship. In the 18th century, many of them emigrated from Ulster to the **Appalachians**, where they became known as the Scots-Irish. Some of those who remained joined the United Irishmen and played a leading role in the 1798 rebellion (see **Nationalist/Republican Song**).

The 19th-century Catholic Emancipation movement created a closer alliance between Presbyterians and Anglicans, and competition for jobs in industrialised Belfast added to sectarian tensions. With the advent of the **Great Famine**, many Irish people emigrated to Scottish cities like Glasgow, and Catholic/Protestant sectarian animosity became as much a feature of life in Scottish cities as it was in the north of Ireland. Sectarian hostility has continued in Northern Ireland, and to a lesser extent in Scotland, to the present day.

Apart from sharing political ideology and songs at certain points in history, there are numerous musical connections between Scotland and Ireland. Like Ireland, Scotland had a strong tradition of **harp** music from the Early Medieval period into Early Modern times. Depictions of triangular frame harps are found in Scotland in carvings from the 8th and 9th centuries, some three centuries earlier than in Ireland. Although Gerald of **Wales** wrote, in the 12th century, that both Scotland and Wales sought to imitate and emulate Ireland in music, many people believed in his time that Scotland had already exceeded Ireland, 'her instructor', in musical skill. There is evidence that Irish harpers performed in Scotland from the Late Medieval period to the 18th century (see, for example, **Ó Catháin, Ruairí Dall**), and Scottish harpers also visited Ireland. Scotland also has a strong tradition of lays or Ossianic ballads that have many features in common with the Irish **lay**s that became popular after James McPherson began to publish his versions in the 1760s. The Scots settlers who came to Ulster from the 17th century on had a profound influence on the development of **ballad** singing in Ireland (for Scottish ballads see **Child Ballads**, **Greig-Duncan Folk Song Collection** and **Bothy Ballads**). Lyrical **songs in Irish** are paralleled in the Scots-Gaelic lyrical song tradition, and there is much shared dance music, especially **reel**s. Regular seasonal migration of agricultural workers from Donegal to Scotland in recent centuries has meant that Donegal in particular shares much of the Scottish repertoire of dance music. **Strathspey**s and **schottische**s or highland flings are dance forms more popular in Donegal than elsewhere in Ireland because of the Scottish connection. Irish **céilí dancing** was also influenced by Scottish dancing through the involvement of Scottish members of the **Gaelic League** in the late 19th and early 20th centuries.

Musical forms and instruments unique to the Scottish tradition include the Scots Gaelic waulking songs (see **Cappercaillie**) and a rich tradition of **mouth music**, related yet distinct from the Irish tradition of **lilting**. The mouth-blown Highland pipes (see **Bagpipes**) are more prevalent in Scotland than in Ireland, where the bellows-blown **uilleann pipes** are more popular. The fiddle is also prominent in Scots traditional music, and the popularity of the fiddle in Donegal and other northern counties in Ireland is again partly due to Scottish influence.

The folk revival that began in the 1950s and 60s has seen a further strengthening of musical links between Scotland and Ireland. As early as 1955, the Irish singer Liam Clancy and American collector Diane Hamilton (see **Clancy Brothers and Tommy Makem**) did field-work in Scotland's Hebrides with Hamish Henderson (1919-2002), a major figure in the Scottish folk revival. Henderson was a folklorist, singer, translator, poet and songwriter, and Clancy and Hamilton went to the Hebrides with him to collect waulking songs and mouth music. The Clancys later sang Henderson's 'The 51st Highland Division's Farewell to Sicily', and Bobby Clancy used to perform a wonderful rendition of the song, preceded by **W. B. Yeats'** poem 'The Hosts of the Air'. The **Boys of the Lough** have had a mixture of Irish and Scots musicians since their inception, and their repertoire derives from Scotland and Ireland in almost equal measure. Likewise **Relativity**, an American-based group of the late 1980s, were a mixture of Scots and Irish musicians. Phil (piano accordion, keyboards) and John (fiddle) Cunningham (1957-2003), who were members of Relativity, had previously played in the group Silly Wizard who, along with groups like the Battlefield Band and Alba, raised the profile of Scottish music internationally in the 1970s. Both have become central figures in Scottish traditional music, and Phil performs regularly with Shetland fiddler Aly Bain, formerly of the Boys of the Lough and another major influence in Scottish music. Although influenced by Scottish accordion player Jimmy Shand, Phil Cunningham also acknowledges the huge influence of Irish music through players like **Joe Burke** and groups like **Planxty**.

Singer/songwriters such as **Ewan MacColl** (born in England to Scots parents) and **Dick Gaughan** have influenced a number of Irish singers. Gaughan, a former member of the Boys of the Lough, collaborated on an album with **Andy Irvine** in 1981 and has performed and recorded such Irish songs as 'Erin go Bragh' and Tommy Makem's 'Four Green Fields'. Likewise many Irish groups and singers include Scottish songs in their repertoire. The Clancy Brothers and Tommy Makem, for example, popularised songs like 'Go Lassie Go', 'Marie's Wedding' and 'Rohtsea-O' which, like other Scottish songs, are fully accepted as part of the Irish folk singer's repertoire. Modern Scottish groups like Cappercaillie (of which Irishman Manus Lunny is a member) and Run Rig, who blend Scottish traditional music and song with a more modern sound, have raised the profile of the music and the Scots-Gaelic language both at home and internationally.

There has also been a recent revival of interest in the harp in Scotland, and significant links have been established with Ireland. Savourna Stevenson, who plays a nylon-string harp, made the album *Calman the Dove* (1998) at **Davy Spillane**'s studio in west Clare, with Spillane producing and performing on the album. The music was composed by Stevenson who sought 'to celebrate the coming of Celtic Christianity to Iona and the parallel crossing of Irish culture and music, taking inspiration from the life and travels of Columba and the spiritual beauty of the islands' (sleeve-notes to *Calman the Dove*). St. Columba (ca. 521-597, also called Columcille or Calman) was born in Derry and founded an important monastery on the western Scottish island of Iona in 563. The wire-string harp has also been revived in Scotland, and in recent years some Irish harpers, such as the talented Mary Gregg of Dublin, have begun to play small, metal-strung harps made in Scotland.

The Scottish Traditional Music and Song Association, established in 1966, now receives some funding from the Scottish Arts Council and has a network of branches throughout Scotland. They hope in the future to establish a national archive along the lines of the **Irish Traditional Music Archive** in Dublin. With devolution and the opening of the new Scottish parliament in July 1999, Scottish culture, including traditional music and song, seems assured of greater public support. Although the area in which Scots-Gaelic is spoken has diminished in recent years, there is a Scots-Gaelic radio station, *Radio nan Gaidheal*, which has established links between Scots-Gaelic communities and the Irish **Gaeltacht** through **Raidió na Gaeltachta**. See also **Behan, Dominic**; **Burns, Robbie**; **Doherty, Liz**; **Canada**; **James I**; **Nova Scotia**.

Scots Snap See **Schottische**.

Scullion
Group whose original line-up was **Philip King** (vocals, harmonica), Sonny Condell (vocals, guitar, piano, saxophone, percussion), Greg Boland (vocals, guitar, percussion) and Jimmy O'Brien-Moran (uilleann pipes, whistle, recorder). Most of the music they played was contemporary folk, with many songs written by King and Condell, but there was initially a strong traditional influence. Their first album, *Scullion* (1979) is a brilliant mixture of traditional and contemporary styles. It opens with the jig-time song 'The Cat She Went a Hunting', in which the lyrics are interwoven with breaks on guitar, uilleann pipes and whistle. 'Educo', a song questioning the values of educators, is far more contemporary in style, with superb rhythm and lead acoustic guitar playing. 'The Fruit Smelling Shop' is an unusual musical adaptation by Condell of lyrics from James Joyce's *Ulysses*, with instrumental breaks on pipes and saxophone. Another adaptation is 'I Am Stretched on Your Grave', the lyrics a translation by Frank O'Connor of a haunting 18th-century poem in Irish, superbly sung by King with minimal backing, ending with the lonely sound of **Kevin Burke** playing the song's melody on fiddle. There is hardly a weak track on the album, from 'Flight of the Pretenders' (instrumental) to Scottish singer/songwriter John Martyn's 'John the Baptist', Condell's song about the struggles of 'The Kilkenny Miners' and King's strange 'Word about Colour' followed by a slow air by **Peter Browne**.

Jimmy O'Brien-Moran left Scullion shortly after the first album, but they continued as a trio, making four further albums and writing many fine songs in a contemporary folk style, the most famous of which is Condell's 'Down in the City'. They performed together occasionally in the 1990s, usually with Robbie Overson on guitar instead of Greg Boland. While Philip King has mainly been involved in television production (see **Hummingbird Productions**), Sonny Condell continues to perform and record as a solo artist.

Sean-nós
Irish-language term meaning 'old style', as in sean-nós dancing and sean-nós singing (see below).

Sean-nós Dancing
The term 'sean-nós dancing' appears to have been used for the first time in 1975 to describe the 'old-style' solo step dancing found mainly in the Connemara (Co. Galway) and Rathcairn (Co. Meath) **Gaeltacht**. The **dancing masters** of the 18th and 19th centuries appear to have had less influence in this area than they did in places like Munster. In the 20th century, the work of the

Dancing Commission in formalising and regulating Irish step dancing influenced dancers in Connemara, but the older, less formalised style of dancing also survived. Unrestrained by the regulations, bureaucracy and formal teaching structure of the *damhsa foghlamtha* ('learned dance'), taught nationwide by teachers following Dancing Commission rules, the sean-nós dancing of Connemara allowed much more room for personal creativity and individual freedom of expression. Although some steps are similar to those of the *damhsa foghlamtha*, one of the most distinctive of the sean-nós steps, called *timeáil* (a foot movement which produces a strong percussive effect by using the heel) has invited comparisons with Spanish flamenco rather then Irish dancing. Individual dancers also have much more freedom in choosing how they will use their body and arms in the dance. While some might choose a relatively restrained, arms-by-the-side approach, others might dance with their hands in their pockets or moving their arms up to shoulder height or even higher. Flamboyant arm movements are relatively rare and more commonly used by male than by female dancers. However, the dancer has the freedom to choose his/her own movements, unlike the *damhsa foghlamtha* practice of teaching dances in which every movement is fully mapped out in advance.

Sean-nós dancing was largely unrecognised beyond Connemara for many years and had no place in national dancing competitions until the 1970s. Gluaiseacht Síbhialta na Gaeltachta, the Gaeltacht civil rights organisation formed in the 1960s, sought to highlight the uniqueness of the traditions of Connemara when the **Oireachtas** was held there in 1975, and the organisation put on displays of what was termed local sean-nós dancing as a fringe event. By 1977, the Oireachtas included for the first time ever a national sean-nós dancing competition. The local Pléaráca Chonamara, a week-long festival of music, dance, song, story telling, drama and sport also hosts a major sean-nós dancing competition each year in September. A large number of younger people in both Connemara and Rathcairn have taken up sean-nós dancing, often mixing it with movements taken from jiving and other, more contemporary forms of dance. The style is also found in some other areas, such as the border of counties Cavan and Monaghan. Indeed it is even being taught now outside **Gaeltacht** areas, which would have been inconceivable twenty years ago. Sean-nós dancing, despite years of ignorance about it beyond Connemara and Rathcairn, is in a healthy state and with the influx of external influences from other dance traditions viewed as part of its development, is set to grow and develop further in the 21st century.

Sean-nós Singing

The term is associated with a particular style of singing found in the *Gaeltachtaí* or Irish-speaking areas of Ireland. The precise origins of the term are obscure, but it may have been invented by the **Gaelic League** to distinguish what they saw as 'old style' singing in Irish from singing in English. Sean-nós singing is generally unaccompanied and often highly ornamented. Variation in the use of ornamentation, in the melody or in the rhythm is used for dramatic effect. These variations may be very slight, but the best singers will rarely sing two verses of a song in the same way. Dynamics (the raising and lowering of the voice) are not generally used, but have been employed by some sean-nós singers, especially in the West Cork **Gaeltacht** of Cúil Aodha. Although sean-nós is usually thought of in relation to songs in Irish, many singers (see **Ó Héanaí, Seosamh** and **Ní Dhonnchadha, Máire Áine**) sing songs in English as well, often using the same, highly ornamented style.

Seán Ó Riada did much to broaden public interest in and appreciation of sean-nós singing through his radio series *Our Musical Heritage* in 1962. He analysed the different styles of singers from Connacht (**Seán Mac Dhonnacha** and **Darach Ó Catháin**), the Déise area in Co. Waterford (**Nioclás Tóibín**) and West Munster (Padraig Ó Tuama, Máire Ní Cheocháin of Cúil Aodha and **Seán De Hóra** of Dingle). Ó Riada also incorporated sean-nós singing into **Ceoltóirí Chualann**'s repertoire. At around the same time Seosamh Ó Héanaí was beginning to make a name for himself, bringing sean-nós singing to a wide audience in Britain and the **US** during the 1960s and 70s.

The Connemara Gaeltacht from which Ó Héanaí came continues to be the strongest area in Ireland for sean-nós. It has produced a host of singers including Seán Mac Donnacha, Seán Ó Conaire, Máire Áine Ní Dhonnchadha, Josie Sheáin Jeaic Mac Donncha, the **Griallais Family**, Vail Ó Flatharta, **Meatí Jó Shéamuis Ó Fátharta** and Dara Bán Mac Dhonnchadha. Among the most notable of the younger generation of singers from Connemara is Róisín Elsafty, who learned to sing from her mother, Treasa Ní Cheannabháin, a well-known singer and teacher of the form. Lasairfhíona Ní Chonaola from Inisheer, one of the Aran Islands, has a style of singing which is deeply rooted in sean-nós but has been influenced by a broad range of contemporary music. She recorded with Frenchman Hector Zazou on his album of Irish sacred music, *Lights in the Dark* (1998, see **Religious Songs**) and has also released a solo album, *An Raicín Álainn* (2002).

Younger singers have learned from older masters in other areas too, and the tradition is carried on in Dingle by Eibhlín and **Seosaimhín Ní Bheaglaoich**, among others. In Ring, Áine Uí Cheallaigh carries on the work of Nioclás Tóibín; both are included on *Cois Mara Thoir sa Rinn: The Musicians and Singers of the Rinn Gaeltacht in Co. Waterford* (1999), along with Tóibín's sister Eibhlís. Cúil Aodha, partly because of Ó Riada's activities, has also produced some fine singers, including **Diarmuid Ó Súilleabháin**, who recorded with **Ceoltóirí Laigheann**, and **Iarla Ó Lionáird**, who has taken sean-nós singing into new areas through his solo and group work (see **Afro Celts**).

Although Ó Riada did not include Donegal or other parts of Ulster within the scope of his work on sean-nós singing for *Our Musical Heritage*, the singing of Donegal singers (such as **Maighréad Ní Dhomhnaill** or **Lillis Ó Laoire**) is just as 'old-style' as that of the West or Southwest. Indeed Lillis Ó Laoire has done much to bring the sean-nós of Donegal, especially Tory Island, to wider public attention through his singing, publishing and broadcasting. Another Donegal singer, Mairéad Ní Mhaonaigh of **Altan**, sings many of the songs which would be sung by sean-nós singers, but with group arrangements. **Pádraigín Ní Uallacháin** has carried out major research on the sean-nós of southeast Ulster and north Leinster, an area where, although Irish is no longer an everyday language, there is a rich tradition of old poetry and song in Irish.

The Góilín Singers' Club, who meet regularly to share songs, and the annual festival Sean-nós Cois Life ('Sean-nós by the Liffey') in Dublin have gone from strength to strength in the last decade. This is indicative of a new interest in sean-nós in parts of the country not normally associated with this style of singing. The **Oireachtas** sean-nós singing competition, *Corn Uí Riada*, for years dominated by singers from the Connemara Gaeltacht, was won for the first time by a native Dubliner, Mairéad Ní Oistín, in 1995 and Lillis Ó Laoire has won it twice. The final of the competition is broadcast live on **Raidió na Gaeltachta**, which has also played an important role in the survival of sean-nós singing through its daily broadcasts. Record companies like **Cló Iar-Chonnachta** and annual events such as the **Willie Clancy Summer School** and **Fleadh Cheoil Na hÉireann** have helped to sustain and develop interest in the style.

The poet, playwright and critic Seán Ó Tuama has carried out detailed research on the origins of the songs sung by sean-nós singers. His major study of love in Irish folk song, *An Grá in Amhráin na nDaoine* (Dublin, 1960) analysed the influence of French forms of song (see **France**) in Ireland in the Middle Ages. He compared song types, themes and motifs from both Irish and French material and concluded that the Irish love song as it has survived down to the present substantially originated in the influence of French literature in 13th- and 14th-century Ireland. Ó Tuama's studies on this subject can also be found in a collection of his essays in English, *Repossessions: Selected Essays on the Irish Literary Heritage* (Cork, 1995). Ó Tuama also worked with Thomas Kinsella on *An Duanaire, 1600-1900: Poems of the Dispossessed* (Mountrath, 1981), an excellent dual-language edition of Irish poetry, including words of a number of famous songs in Irish.

Ó Tuama's work is of great interest in examining the origins of the themes and motifs found in the songs sung by sean-nós singers. **Ciarán Mac Mathúna**, Seoirse Bodley, Ríonach Uí Ógáin and others have also done important work in collecting and analysing examples of sean-nós singing. The precise origins and development of the style of this singing, however, remain uncertain. In *Our Musical Heritage* Ó Riada suggested that in sean-nós it is 'best to listen as if we were listening to the music for the first time, with a child's new mind; or to think of Indian music rather than European.' (*Our Musical Heritage*, Mountrath, 1982, p. 23) Although Ó Riada did not attempt to trace the origins of sean-nós to India, the suggestion of a style that is distinctly non-European has captured the imagination of many. Documentary maker Bob Quinn included an exploration of the origins of Connemara sean-nós singing in his three-part television series *Atlantean* (1983) and an additional programme, *Navigatio-Atlantean 2* (1998). In the initial series, he argued that Irish culture owed more to the influence of North Africa and the Middle East than to any mainstream European tradition. He used historical, archaeological, linguistic, religious, musical and other evidence from prehistory right up to the present. The sea, he argued, has been a major channel of communication since prehistory and links the cultures of Europe's periphery, including Ireland, Scotland, Wales, Brittany, northeast Spain, Morocco, Tunisia and Egypt. He suggested an affinity between the sean-nós singing of Connemara and styles of singing found in North African Mediterranean areas, Spain and **Brittany**. Quinn also published a book on the subject, *Atlantean: Ireland's North African and Maritime Heritage* (1986). In *Navigatio-Atlantean 2*, Quinn's focus was on the relationship between central Europe and its periphery, particularly in the Middle Ages. Sean-nós singing was again an important part of his thesis, as significant a cultural artefact of Ireland's Golden Age (ca. 600-1000 AD), he argued, as objects such as the Book of Kells.

Quinn's thesis is fascinating, and the young sean-nós singer Róisín Elsafty, whose father is Egyptian, sees much merit in the idea of a cultural link between North Africa and the west of Ireland. She points out that the singing style of one of the great Egyptian singers, Um Kasoum, is essentially sean-nós. The arguments put forward by Quinn, however, are not definitive and indeed were not presented as such. Quinn made it very clear that he was exploring possible connections and making suggestions rather than presenting a definitive case. The ideas he presented in *Atlantean* continue to provoke debate, but Quinn himself is not always acknowledged directly for his contribution.

Some scholars and singers are critical of the concept of a non-European influence in the development of sean-nós singing. **Hugh Shields** has written of the 'unusual interest' of the regional Western and South-Western style, 'which, if it has international links, is more likely to find them in Europe than in Africa or the Middle East (as it is sometimes suggested)' (*Narrative Singing in Ireland*, Blackrock, 1993, p. 124). Lillis Ó Laoire has also argued against what he calls the 'exoticisation' claimed for traditional Gaelic song. Reviewing a CD by three-times *Corn Uí Riada* winner Josie Sheáin Jeaic Mac Donncha, Ó Laoire describes as disturbing this 'insistent exoticisation' in the CD notes which likens Gaelic song to flamenco, North African, Asian or Indian singing. 'Such a strategy', he continues, 'is meant to be sympathetic, but it deliberately removes this kind of singing from the real, and places it in one hermetic, ahistorical, timeless, category, rendering it mysterious, eastern and non-European' (*Journal of Music in Ireland*, Jan./Feb. 2003, p. 27). He argues that these claims are highly exaggerated and are closely linked to fervent nationalism in the early 20th century and in the 1960s. He criticises Ó Riada's 'impressionistic overview' of Ireland's musical tradition in *Our Musical Heritage* and questions many of Ó Riada's ideas about sean-nós singing. While recognising the importance of Ó Riada's work in bringing traditional music and song to previously unsympathetic audiences, Ó Laoire calls for 'new and contemporary insights into the cultural dynamics of song and music' to build on the work done by Ó Riada (ibid., p. 28).

Ó Laoire himself has done valuable work in placing traditional singing in its social and historical context, especially in his study of Tory Island. His comments in *JMI* (*Journal of Music in Ireland*) provoked an interesting and somewhat heated debate in the pages of the *JMI*, which in March/April 2003 carried articles by Bob Quinn and Jean Yves Bériou, producer of the two CDs reviewed. While both were angered by inaccuracies and omissions in Ó Laoire's review, many interesting points on sean-nós singing emerged. Ó Laoire replied to Quinn and Bériou in the May/June edition of the *JMI*, and the series of articles should be read by anyone interested in the debate on sean-nós singing. The debate also points to the fact that, although much has been written and said about the origins and development of sean-nós singing, there is still no comprehensive study available. There is certainly a need for a review of the whole subject which addresses all the arguments about origins, influences and the development of sean-nós from the earliest times to the present, although it may prove extremely difficult or even impossible to make definitive statements because of a lack of evidence in historical records. See also **Regional Styles**.

Sea Shanties A unique type of **sea song** or **occupational song** sung by groups of seamen as they performed various tasks aboard ship. One man usually sang the verses, which generally consist of just one or two lines, while the rest of the crew sang the refrain. The rhythm made it easier for the men to pull ropes or turn the capstan, and each particular task had its own particular shanty to suit the rhythm required. A number of sea shanties date from the 1840s, a time when many Irish people undertook long sea journeys to the **US** and **Australia** before and during the **Great Famine**. From this period onwards, steamships began to take over from the old sailing ships and sea shanties gradually disappeared as occupational songs, but were still sung by traditional singers as entertainment. Irish seamen would have sung many 'international' shanties, such as 'South Australia', recorded by the **Clancy Brothers and Tommy Makem** on *The Boys Won't Leave the Girls Alone* (1962). This shanty was more recently recorded, along with two others ('Santy Ano' and 'Blood Red Roses'), by Clancy, O'Connell, Clancy with Warp Four (see **O'Connell, Robbie**) on *The Wild and Wasteful Ocean* (1998). Sea shanties with strong Irish connections include the exclusively Irish 'The Montague' and the Irish-American shanties 'Across the Western Ocean' and 'The Girls of Dublin Town'.

Sea Song Apart from **sea shanties**, a considerable number of Irish songs of the sea are known, especially from the 19th century, although most are not commonly heard today. Some of them are love songs (such as 'The Maid of Coolmore'), others tend to be bawdier, such as 'The Holy Ground', originally about Swansea, Wales, but very much associated with Cobh, Co. Cork. British ballads about female sailors who disguise themselves in order to accompany or rejoin their lovers were popular in Ireland and inspired some native imitations; 'William Taylor', recorded by **Andy Irvine** with the group **Patrick Street**, is a good example. There are songs about fishing, like the traditional 'Herring the King' or the more recent 'Shoals of Herring' (written by **Ewan MacColl**). Deliberate or accidental drownings ('The Two Sisters' and 'My Love Willie', respectively) also provide a common theme. Voyages of particular vessels can, in cases like 'The Irish Rover', be comic or bawdy songs. And shipwrecks have inspired many songs, including the wreck of the 'Titanic' (1912) and 'The Loss of the Evelyn Marie', about the wreck of a trawler off the Donegal coast in 1975. **James N. Healy**'s *Irish Ballads and Songs of the Sea* (Cork, 1967) is an excellent collection that encompasses the great diversity of this form. Another fine singer of sea-songs is **Jimmy Crowley**.

Section 31 Under Section 31 of the Broadcasting Act of 1960, Raidió Éireann was subject to directives from the Minister for Communications restricting the broadcasting of certain materials. With the escalation of the Northern Ireland 'Troubles' from the late 1960s, Section 31 was amended on a number of occasions to restrict representatives of organisations perceived as a threat to the State from being interviewed on radio and television. A 1976 amendment to the Act stated: 'Where the Minister is of the opinion that the broadcasting of a particular matter or any matter of a particular class would be likely to promote, or incite to, crime or would tend to undermine the authority of the State, he may by order direct the Authority to refrain from broadcasting the matter or any matter of the particular class, and the Authority shall comply with the order'. Orders issued under Section 31 had to be renewed every twelve months, and the principal order, made in 1983, directed the **RTÉ** Authority to refrain from broadcasting interviews or reporting interviews with spokesmen for various organisations, including the Irish Republican Army, Sinn Féin, the Irish National Liberation Army, the Ulster Defence Association and other organisations proscribed in Northern Ireland. Section 31 was always controversial but was renewed annually until 1994, when a Fianna Fáil/Labour government did not renew it. This was partly a response by Minister Michael D. Higgins to persistent criticism of the legislation by journalists, human rights groups and some musicians and other artists. It should also be viewed, however, in the context of the Northern Ireland Peace Process and undoubtedly assisted in the opening up of debate involving former paramilitaries and the political groups which represented them. Section 31 was not renewed again and was repealed by the Broadcasting Act (2001).

The effect of Section 31 on the broadcasting of traditional music, especially song, is difficult to gauge precisely. While music was not specifically censored under Section 31, it appears that RTÉ itself decided to operate its own censorship of songs in line with Section 31. At a 1991 conference organised by Co-Operation North, **Ciarán Mac Mathúna**, emphasising that he was not speaking for RTÉ officially, stated: 'There is no written rule and no list of songs which I know of that shouldn't be broadcast, but there is a guideline to the effect that you should not broadcast any material which is going to offend the sensibilities of people in this island, either politically or religiously.' (*Traditional Music: Whose Music?*, Belfast, 1992, p. 77) The effect was that few, if any, songs with Irish political themes, whether they were **Nationalist/Republican songs** or **Orange/Loyalist songs**, were broadcast on RTÉ radio or television while orders issued under Section 31 were in force.

Section 31 was the subject of almost constant, heated debate throughout the 1970s, 80s and early 90s. Singer **Christy Moore** regularly sang a song called 'Section 31', written by his brother Barry (see **Bloom, Luka**) as part of a campaign against the legislation, and Moore recorded the song on his album *The Time Has Come* (1983).

Seeger, Pete (b. 1919) American folk singer and songwriter, born in New York City, noted for his radical politics and protest songs. The latter include 'We Shall Overcome' (1960), 'Where Have All the Flowers Gone?' (1961) and 'Little Boxes'

(1962). From 1940 he sang with **Woody Guthrie** in the Almanac Singers, starting the contemporary folk protest movement. Seeger and his group the Weavers (popular in the 1950s and 60s) had a direct influence on the **Clancy Brothers and Tommy Makem**, especially the group's use of choral singing and accompaniment on guitar and five-string banjo. The Weavers were blacklisted for some time in the 1950s by the US House of Representatives Un-American Activities Committee, but re-emerged in 1958 without Seeger.

Seeger himself, whose great grandfather came from Belfast, plays some Irish tunes and has used Irish melodies with some of his own lyrics. His song 'Kisses Sweeter than Wine', for instance, uses the melody of the Irish song 'Droimeann Donn Dílís'. In the late 1940s he put together two almost identical Irish-American songs to make the song 'No Irish Need Apply'. Seeger is an important figure in a broader American tradition of protest song that has had a profound influence on a number of Irish folk singers since the 1960s. He has performed and recorded with Tommy Sands (see **Sands Family**), and together they wrote the song 'The Music of Healing'. In recent years he has become involved in the ecology or environmental movement. His songs have been recorded by many artists, including Peter, Paul and Mary and Joan Baez. *Where Have All The Flowers Gone: The Songs of Pete Seeger, Vol. 1* (1998) is a tribute album with a wide range of singers singing Pete Seeger songs, including Tommy Makem, **Dick Gaughan**, Bruce Springsteen, Jackson Browne, Billy

Pete Seeger (photo: Bud Schultz)

Bragg and the Indigo Girls. The third volume in the series, *Seeds: The Songs of Pete Seeger, Vol. 3* (2003) features Seeger himself on some tracks. His sister, Peggy Seeger, is also a renowned folk singer who married and recorded extensively with **Ewan MacColl**. See also **American Folk Song**.

Session (*Seisiún*) An informal gathering at which musicians play, usually in a pub but sometimes outdoors or in a person's home. Before the **Public Dance Hall Act**, 1935, gatherings at which people danced to the playing of one or more local musicians, told stories and often just chatted and played cards were commonplace in the countryside. The Act of 1935 effectively put an end to such gatherings, and sessions appear to have gradually evolved in response to the need for a more informal setting to that provided by the dance halls where 'legal' **céilí** dances took place from the late 1930s on. The history of precisely how and when pub sessions developed in different places is difficult to pinpoint precisely. **Colin 'Hammy' Hamilton** researched the subject in detail for an M.A. thesis titled 'The Session: A Socio-Musical Phenomenon in Irish Music' (Queen's University, Belfast, 1978). He concluded that while there was music in pubs by the late 1930s in some areas, such as **Sliabh Luachra**, the pub session was essentially a phenomenon of the revival in the 1950s and 60s. The idea of a session certainly gained momentum from the informal playing of musicians outside competitions during **Fleadh Cheoil Na hÉireann** from 1951. Sessions became more popular throughout the 1950s and 60s with the revival of interest in traditional music and song. Since the 1970s, sessions have gradually become more numerous and widespread around Ireland as the popularity of traditional music has spread. Although some pubs in Dublin, like O'Donoghue's in Merrion Row, have had sessions since the earliest days of the revival, the last decade has seen a phenomenal increase in the number of pub sessions in the Republic's capital, especially during the summer. As in other places around the country, many pubs now pay a core group of musicians to come and play regularly, but additional musicians will often turn up to join in or just play a few tunes. Musicians still play sessions without being paid, and annual events like the Fleadh and the **Willie Clancy Summer School** are still great occasions for informal sessions at which younger or less experienced musicians can participate with famous masters.

There are no formal rules for sessions, but it is understood that those attending the session will observe certain conventions. Usually the oldest or most experienced musicians are central to the way the session progresses, choosing the tunes to be played, starting off the sets, or inviting others to start a set, play a solo or sing a song. If you are not a regular at a session, you should wait to be asked before starting a set of tunes or playing a solo. Otherwise you simply play along with any tunes you know as they come up. The number of times a tune is played before changing into another tune can vary. The core musicians in a group will always know where to change, and in some sessions other musicians will be told, 'we play most tunes three times before we change' or whatever the case may be. You should listen for the changes, taking your cue from the core musicians.

Although many sessions are made up largely of dance tunes, songs are often sung as well, depending on the region and the musicians involved. A lot of conversation can take place between the tunes, with the musicians talking about the names of tunes, where they came from, or sometimes subjects unrelated to music. Although many pub owners appreciate this aspect of the session, in some pubs (especially where musicians are paid to play) long breaks between sets of tunes are discouraged. Story telling or the recitation of poetry can also be a feature of sessions, and a story, poem or song will often be performed because of something that arises in conversation. There is no set list for sessions, and the casual arrival can often influence the session to a considerable degree.

In the best sessions there is a sense of sharing, a sense of people making music and entertainment for one another. All participants are encouraged to contribute, not just those who are technically brilliant. There can, however, be a ferociously competitive element in sessions, especially if two or more virtuoso musicians try to outdo each other in speed-playing or the playing of unusual tunes that others might not know. Some people enjoy such musical showdowns, but they can destroy a session and leave many people out of it.

The wrong kind of percussion (on bodhrán, bones or other instruments) or rhythm accompaniment (guitar, bouzouki, etc.) can put musicians off. Many musicians only like a particular kind of accompaniment, some don't like any at all, and unless percussion and rhythm players are attuned to the music and to each others' playing, the music can suffer. In many sessions nowadays the playing is almost constantly fast and furious, which seems a great pity. There is a wealth of tune types and tempos in Irish music, but jigs and especially reels tend to predominate. Everyone's taste and repertoire differs, but it seems a shame that more slow airs are not played in sessions nowadays. They add another dimension to the session, bringing out more of the light and shade that exists in traditional music.

Many musicians will not take kindly to the taking of photographs, video footage or sound recordings at a session if their permission has not been asked. In pub sessions, people will often chat away while the music is being played, but those who want to listen will sit close to the musicians; seats are often reserved for them. Drinking tends to be a part of session culture, given the venue. Not all musicians drink, but sometimes an appreciative listener will buy a drink for the musicians and in some cases a few 'rounds on the house' can be part or all of the payment which the musicians receive.

Although sessions take place most frequently in pubs, some people have them at home, often casually after the pub closes or because somebody calls in. Others might invite friends and musicians to their home for a session. From time to time, weather permitting, musicians might head off to a pier, a hilltop or a riverside location to play until dawn.

Set 1 Although used as an adjective in the terms **set dancing** and **set dance**, 'set' is often used on its own as a noun to describe one of these dances (e.g., 'dancing a set'). A full set, as opposed to a **half set**, involves four couples.

Set 2 Musicians playing dance tunes solely for listening and not for dancing use 'set' in a different way. It is common practice to play a group of three or four dance tunes continuously as a single piece, often referred to as a 'set'. It is equally common, therefore, to hear musicians at a session refer to 'a set of jigs' or a 'set of reels'. Although the *type* of tunes played in such 'sets' is often the same, it has become more common in recent years for sets to be made up of different types of tunes. Thus the group **Lúnasa**, to take just one example, has a set consisting of a march, a Breton gavotte and a reel on their 1998 album.

Set Dance 1 Term used to describe one of the dances referred to here under the general heading of **set dancing**. These set dances derived from **cotillions** and **quadrilles**.

Set Dance 2 A solo dance, also called a long dance, which took a particular form and was danced to a particular tune of the same name. The tunes themselves are also termed 'set dances' and are now often played just for listening. Examples include 'The Blackbird', 'Bonaparte's Retreat' and 'St. Patrick's Day'. They have usually a jig or hornpipe rhythm and differ from the normal form of other types of **dance music** in having one part (usually the second) longer than the others. Sometimes the parts can also be in different times.

Set Dancing Irish set dancing was developed in the 18th and 19th centuries by the old itinerant **dancing masters**. Set dancing involves four couples who dance as partners, either face-to-face or side-by-side (see also **Half Set**). It was greatly influenced by French country dances such as the **cotillion** and the later **quadrille**. These dances, popular all over Europe, were originally adapted by the dancing masters at the behest of the upper classes, anxious to keep up with the latest fashions. In time, they were taught to others lower down the social scale and were danced at crossroads and house dances. The original term 'sets of quadrilles' was shortened to 'sets'.

In many cases, the Irish dancing masters retained the basic movements and figures of the original dances but simplified the often complex French steps. Irish tunes popular to the particular locality where the master was teaching were used. Set dances, usually named after the area where they evolved, consist of anything between two and nine figures or fixed patterns of dancing. Each figure is danced to a particular type of tune, with **reels, jigs, hornpipes, polkas** and **slides** being commonly used, flings (see **Schottische**), **barndances** and **marches** being used occasionally. Sometimes a set will use the same type of tune for all figures – as, for example in the 'Clare Lancers Set', where there are five figures, all danced to reels. Other sets use various tune types for the different figures. The 'Derrada Set' danced in Co. Mayo, for example, has three figures, the first danced to a jig, the second to a polka and the third to a reel.

Set dancing was widespread in Ireland during the 18th and 19th centuries and survived the Catholic Church's almost constant denunciations of dancing (see **Dancing and Religion**). The **Gaelic League** banned it in favour of **céilí dancing** but then attempted to revive many of the set dances through its **Dancing Commission**. The **Public Dance Hall Act** (1935) was used by the clergy to put an end to house dances, crossroads dances and other gatherings where dancing took place without a licence. This had a more drastic effect on set dancing than it had on the more formal céilí dancing, which tended to be favoured in the new, licensed dance halls. Set dancing, however, survived in many places, and recent decades have seen a remarkable revival. Modern dancing masters such as the late **Connie Ryan**, **Joe and Siobhán O'Donovan** and **Timmy 'The Brit' McCarthy** have collected a wide repertoire of sets from all over Ireland. The **Brooks Academy** in Dublin has also contributed to the revival. Pat Murphy's book *Toss the Feathers: Irish Set Dancing* (Cork and Dublin, 1995) details the remarkable history and precise movements of set dancing, describing its revival as having 'inspired one of the most successful social developments for generations.' He continues: 'When one considers that less than twenty years ago, very few sets were danced, or even heard of, outside their own locality, it is amazing to think that for many people of all ages, from all walks of life and diverse social backgrounds, set dancing has become almost a way of life.' See also **MacGabhann, Antóin; Sliabh Luachra**.

Shanachie Records American-based recording company founded in 1972 by Richard Nevins and Daniel Michael Collins. At the time, Nevins was compiling material from old 78 rpm recordings of **Michael Coleman** and **Patrick J. Touhey**, which were eventually released on the double-CD *The Wheels of the World* (1996; see **Recording**). Collins had been working on putting together an album of the music of Galway flute player, **Paddy Carthy**. Both were working on their separate projects essentially as a hobby but decided to work on the recordings together and Shanachie was formed. Founded in the Bronx and now based in Newton, New Jersey, early releases by Shanachie also included albums by **Tommy Peoples**, **Frankie Gavin** and **Alec Finn**, and the duo **Joe and Antoinette McKenna**. The company, now called Shanachie Entertainment, has played a major role in promoting Irish traditional music but also gradually became involved in reggae, Jewish music and other types of ethnic or world music. In addition to distributing much Irish material, Shanachie has released original recordings and albums initially released on other labels. Artists available on Shanachie include Tommy Makem, the Clancy Brothers (see **Clancy Brothers and Tommy Makem**), the **Furey Brothers**, John Kelly (see **Kelly, James and John**), **De Dannan**, the **Boys of the Lough**, Paddy O'Brien (see **O'Brien, Paddy 1**), **Pádraigín Ní Uallacháin**, **Phil Coulter**, **Matt Molloy** and **Mick Moloney**. The company has recorded and promoted the Irish-American group **Solas** as well as releasing solo albums by Solas members **Seamus Egan**, Winifred Horan and **Karan Casey** (no longer a member of Solas). Through Joe McKenna, their representative in Ireland, Shanachie also signed the young Irish group **Danú**, providing a major boost to the group's popularity in the **US**. Website: www.shanachie.com.

Shanley, Eleanor Singer from Co. Leitrim who first came to prominence as a member of **De Dannan** (1988-1993). Her mother, from whom she learned some of her first traditional songs, came from a family of singers. Since leaving De Dannan, Shanley has made a name for herself as one of the finest singers of traditional and contemporary folk songs, releasing two albums, *Eleanor Shanley* (1995) and *Desert Heart* (1997). The latter was produced by multi-instrumentalist Neill MacColl (son of **Ewan MacColl**), who also contributed two of his own compositions. Website: www.eleanorshanley.com.

Shannon, Sharon (b. 1968) A native of Corofin, Co. Clare, best known for her accordion playing but also plays fiddle, tin whistle and low whistle. Her grandparents, parents, brother and sisters were all musical, and Frank Custy (see **Custy Family**) was an important early influence. At the age of fourteen she was doing short **US** tours with Custy's Dísert Tola and in her late teens she played in **Doolin**. She provided music for Druid Theatre, Galway's production of *The Hostage* by **Brendan Behan** and played with **Arcady** and the **Waterboys**. Her first solo album, *Sharon Shannon* (1991), featured Portuguese, Cajun and French-Canadian as well as Irish music. **Dónal Lunny**, **Tommy Hayes**, Mike Scott of the Waterboys and Adam Clayton of U2 are among the musicians who play on the album, which has a very contemporary feel in terms of the arrangements and instrumentation. It was very successful in Ireland, reaching unprecedented sales for an exclusively instrumental album.

In 1992 the *Late Late Show* dedicated a whole programme to Sharon and her music, a rare tribute for one so young. Her subsequent albums, *Out the Gap* (1994), *Each Little Thing* (1997), and *Spellbound: The Best of Sharon Shannon* (1998; largely a compilation but with five new tracks), have seen her build on a reputation for a modern, progressive sound and a repertoire that includes music from many dif-

ferent traditions. In touring and recording, she has worked with a wide range of musicians, including **Steve Cooney**, Trevor Hutchinson (bass) and **John McSherry** (uilleann pipes) of **Lúnasa**, **Tommy Peoples**, **Gavin Ralston** and her sister Mary (banjo, bouzouki, whistle) of the **Bumble Bees**.

In the late 1990s Shannon toured extensively with Dónal Lunny's band and featured on his album *Coolfin* (1998). Her own *Diamond Mountain Sessions* (2000) featured guest performances by Lunny, Galician piper Carlos Nuñez, her sister Mary (banjo, mandolin), Liz and Yvonne Kane (fiddles) and many singers including Steve Earle, Jackson Browne and John Prine. *Libertango* (2003) also features a host of guest singers, including Sinéad O'Connor, Pauline Scanlon,

Sharon Shannon

Róisín Elsafty and the Elsafty Family, and Kirsty MacColl. MacColl sings the album's title track, originally recorded for *Each Little Thing* but now with extra fiddle and bass. The song is based on a tune by the bandoneon (a type of accordion) player Astor Piazzolla of **Argentina**, and Shannon's accordion plays a prominent part in the song's arrangement. There is a wide variety of traditional and original songs (including **John Spillane**'s 'All the Ways You Wander') and instrumental music on the album, including tunes from **Scotland** and **Canada**, and original compositions by Sharon and Mary Shannon, Jim Murray, Tommy Peoples and Peter Browne, a mandola player from Salthill, Co. Galway. Website: www.daisydiscs.com (the Daisy Label is an Irish-based record company established by Shannon and John Dunford).

Sheahan, John Dublin-born fiddler (classically trained) and composer who, in addition to his years of work with the **Dubliners** has composed a considerable amount of original material. His first big hit was 'The Marino Waltz', after which he released two albums with classical guitarist and co-writer, Michael Howard. More recently he has recorded his tune 'The Impish Hornpipe' with **Danú**.

Shields, Hugh (b. 1929) Lecturer in French at Trinity College Dublin, where he researches medieval and oral literature, and also a collector and scholar of Irish song and storytelling. In addition to numerous articles on folk song in Ireland, he has published *Shamrock and Thistle: Folk Singing in North Derry* (Belfast, 1981) and *Old Dublin Songs* (Dublin, 1988). His *Narrative Singing in Ireland: Lays, Ballads, Come-All-Ye's and Other Songs* (Dublin, 1993) is a masterly study of the origins and development of different forms of song and storytelling (in both Irish and English) in Ireland. He traces forms such as the **lay** and the **ballad** back to their medieval origins and examines such subjects as the social context in which singers perform, the effects of modern media on traditional singing and the manner in which traditional singers are often 'song makers' as well. The book is an outstanding contribution to the history of traditional song, complete with musical examples, a glossary, song index, singers index and general index – as well as an excellent bibliography and discography. While Shields does mention high-profile traditional groups of recent decades, he compares them to pop groups who usually enjoy short-lived success and concentrates on less commercially oriented, individual singers. Another major piece of work was the publication of *Tunes of the Munster Pipers: Irish Traditional Music from the James Goodman Manuscripts, 1* (1998), which Shields edited. See also **Goodman, James**.

Single Jig See **Jig**.

Single Reel See **Reel**.

Sirr Harp See **Harp**.

Skara Brae Short-lived but important group made up of Dáithí Spról (guitar, later of **Altan**), **Micheál Ó Domhnaill** (vocals, guitar), **Maighréad** (vocals, only age fifteen when their album was released) **and Tríona Ní Dhomhnaill** (keyboards and vocals). The group was formed when Spról, a visitor to the **Gaeltacht** who sang Beatles' songs, encouraged the others to develop a different approach to the traditional songs with which they had grown up. They recorded a seminal album, simply titled *Skara Brae* (1972), which featured songs in Irish with intricate guitar accompaniments (see **Pentangle**), and some fine harmony singing. The blending of traditional song with such relatively modern-sounding accompaniments, as well as the use made of harmony, were new at the time and heralded talents which would later mature in groups such as the **Bothy Band**, **Relativity** and Altan. The album also featured an interesting instrumental track entitled 'Angela', with the guitarists Spról and Ó Domhnaill working an original composition into a version of the traditional 'Exile's Jig'. The album was re-released in the late 1990s on CD, and Skara Brae performed in the Belfast Festival at Queen's in November 1998.

Skirm Singer/guitarist from Northern Ireland whose 1995 album with **Dezi Donnelly**, *Welcome*, is a fine mixture of traditional and contemporary songs and instrumentals. His strong, rhythmic accompaniments work brilliantly with Donnelly's wild and innovative style of fiddling. He also has a powerful and expressive voice and sings a fine version of 'Carrickfergus' as well as his own unique renditions of songs by contemporary writers such as **Paul Brady** and **John Spillane**.

Skylark Group formed by **Len Graham** (vocals), Dubliner Garry Ó Briain (mandocello, keyboards, guitar), **Gerry O'Connor** (fiddle, viola) and Clare man Andrew McNamara (button accordion). Their songs, sung in gentle, understated style by Graham, were sometimes unaccompanied but generally accompanied with a light backing. The backings were also light for the dance music the group played, bringing the fiddle and accordion playing to the fore. Their first album, *Skylark* (1987), consisted half of songs and half of instrumentals. Graham sang a number of rare or unusual versions of traditional songs with the group, many of them learned from older singers like **Eddie Butcher**. On the 1987 album, one of the finest tracks features Graham singing a version of 'The Parting Glass' which he learned from Antrim singer **Joe Holmes**, initially unaccompanied but joined in the second half by unobtrusive accordion and mandocello. Graham then lilts a schottische, 'The Peacock's Feather', with the mandocello playing melody, and then the group plays the reel 'Paddy Mill's Delight'. The track has the feel of a quiet, relaxed session in a pub, a style characteristic of much of Skylark's music.

Skylark went on to make three more albums over the next nine years. Graham, O'Connor and Ó Briain were with the group throughout, with **Eithne Ní Uallacháin** (vocals, flute, whistle) and Eilish O'Connor (fiddle) guesting on *All of It* (1989). McNamara had left the group by this time, but **Máirtín O'Connor** guested on accordion and was to become a full member of the group, recording *Light and Shade* (1992) and *Raining Bicycles* (1996) with them. The latter album features guest appearances by **Martin Murray** (mandolin, banjo) and James Blennerhasset (string bass, cello), among others.

Sliabh Luachra An upland district in Munster which has no specific boundaries but incorporates parts of east Kerry, north Cork and west Limerick. It was the birthplace of the famous **aisling** poets Aogán Ó Rathaille (ca. 1675-1729) and Eoghan Rua Ó Súilleabháin (1748-1784) and the priest Patrick Dinneen, whose *Irish-English Dictionary* was first published in 1904. Although Irish is no longer spoken as the everyday language in Sliabh Luachra, the area has retained a rich and unique body of traditional music. **Slide**s and **polka**s make up a huge proportion of the dance music played by local musicians, with many of these tunes being composed in the area. **Set dancing** has been popular in the district for many years, Dan O'Connell's famous pub in Knocknagree serving as a regular venue since 1965. Sliabh Luachra musicians are renowned for the strong rhythms and drive of their music, which is usually achieved without resorting to excessive speed. Both the late **Pádraig O'Keeffe** (fiddle) and **Johnny O'Leary** (button accordion) have been noted for these qualities in their playing and for their subtle use of ornamentation and variation. *Johnny O'Leary of Sliabh Luachra* (edited by Terry Moylan, Dublin, 1994) is the finest published collection of the area's music. O'Leary's playing has preserved the repertoire and style of Sliabh Luachra's music, and Moylan notes that approximately a quarter of his playing was devoted to polkas, a quarter to slides, and the rest of the time to jigs, reels and hornpipes. O'Leary and other local musicians such as **Denis Murphy** (fiddle) have been the source of tunes that have been adapted by groups such as the **Chieftains**, **Planxty** and **De Dannan**. Recordings of the aforementioned local musicians, as well as others by the Cliffords (see **Clifford, Julia**) and **Jackie Daly** (button accordion), have been released commercially. Donal Hickey's *Stone Mad for Music: The Sliabh Luachra Story* (Dublin, 1999) provides fine insights into the area's musical, dance and literary traditions. See also **Cranitch, Matt**; **Murphy, Tom Billy**; **North Cregg**; **Regional Styles**; **Sliabh Notes**.

Sliabh Notes Dynamic trio formed in 1994 who play mostly music from Sliabh Luachra, with a strong emphasis on dance tunes, including slides, polkas, jigs and reels. The line-up is **Matt Cranitch** (fiddle), Donal Murphy (button accordion) and Tommy O'Sullivan (guitar, vocals). **Steve Cooney** has sometimes stood in for Tommy O'Sullivan and has recorded with the group. There is a great energy and drive to their music, their playing of slides and polkas especially having a great lift. Their first album, *Sliabh Notes*, was released in 1995, followed by *Gleanntán* (1999) and *Along Blackwater's Banks* (2002). The last album features guest performances by **Kevin Burke**, **Matt Molloy**, Steve Cooney, **Colm Murphy** and others. While much of the music they play is instrumental, they also perform and have recorded several songs including **Jimmy MacCarthy**'s 'The People of West Cork and Kerry' on *Gleanntán* and a song from **Newfoundland** on *Along Blackwater's Banks*.

Sliabh Notes

Slide 1 (*Sleamhnán*) A form of **set dancing** and **dance music** especially popular in Kerry and Cork (see **Sliabh Luachra** above). Like the single **jig**, it is in 12/8 time and is usually played with great speed and vigour. Like the **polka**, which is also very popular in the southwest of Ireland, the slide is more directly associated with dancing than any other form of dance music. Slides have even been recorded by

Séamus Begley and **Steve Cooney**, as well as **Johnny O'Leary**, with the sound of dancers' steps in the background. Although they are particularly popular in the sets danced in Kerry and Cork, they are danced to a lesser extent in the neighbouring counties of Limerick and Tipperary. Even in Kildare there is a set consisting of five figures, three of which are slides, but it is rare to find this outside the southwest of Ireland.

The Star Above the Garter (slide)

Slide 2 Talented group of young musicians made up of Eamonn De Barra (flute, whistles, piano, vocals), Aogán Lynch (concertina, whistle), Daire Bracken (fiddle, guitar, vocals) and Mick Broderick (bouzouki). Although based in Dublin, Lynch comes from Ballincollig, West Cork. His father plays accordion and his mother is Caitlín Ní Bheaglaoich (see **Ní Bheaglaoich, Seosaimhín**; **Beg-ley, Brendan**; **Begley, Séamus**) from the famous Begley family of Dingle. He won the **TG4** 'Young Musician of the Year' award in 1999. The others all grew up in Dublin and are among the most talented young musicians to emerge in recent years. Their debut album, *The Flying Pig* (2001) won great critical acclaim and Slide won the 'Best Newcomers' award in the **Irish Music** magazine awards, 2001. Their second album, *Harmonic Motion* (2003), is notable for its inventive arrangements, sometimes mixing dance tunes in different time signatures on the same track, and some fine original songs. Website: www.slide.ie.

Slide

Slip Jig See **Jig**.

Slógadh See **Gael-Linn**.

Slow Air (*fonn mall*) See **Air**.

Slur Slurring is a form of articulation and involves sliding between one note and another. It is used by many players as a form of **ornamentation** and is especially effective in slow airs, where it can be used to create atmosphere. A slur is often indicated in notation by a line or an arrow above or below the two notes concerned.

Slur

Solas Irish-American group formed in 1995. Since the release of their first album *Solas* in 1996, they have rapidly become one of the most popular Irish traditional groups in the **US**, Ireland and other parts of the world. The original line-up was **Séamus Egan** (flute, tres, tin whistle, low whistle, uilleann pipes, guitar, bodhrán, backing vocals, banjo, mandolin), **John Williams** (button accordion, concertina, backing vocals), Winifred Horan (fiddle, backing vocals), John Doyle (guitar, mandocello, backing vocals) and **Karan Casey** (lead vocals).

Solas' first album has a mixture of traditional and original instrumentals (jigs, reels and airs) and traditional songs sung in Irish and English. The arrangements are tightly orchestrated, with dynamic, often percussive guitar accompaniments, and make full use of the various instruments in different combinations to change the texture of instrumental sets. Their second album, *Sunny Spells and Scattered Showers* (1997), has a similar range of material and also includes a Manx air and a barndance. The 1798 rebellion song 'The Wind That Shakes the Barley' has an unusual arrangement, with fast instrumental breaks between verses, which is almost Eastern European in style. There are many other fine arrangements of both songs and instrumental music. In the set which starts with 'The Big Reel of Ballynacally', instruments initially swap the lead and are then variously combined, with harmonies featuring strongly on the second tune and the guitar rhythms changing between the two parts of the last tune. The set is built up in a style reminiscent of some of the **Bothy Band**'s finest arrangements, although with different instrumentation. Along with the group's original line-up, percussionist John Anthony guested on the first two albums.

The musicianship of the individual players is excellent (Egan and Williams are both **All-Ireland** champions) and the vocals are top class. Solas have rightly won critical acclaim and a number of awards for their first two albums. John Williams left the group after the second album to be replaced by Mick McAuley (accordion, concertina, vocals). Their third album, *The Words That Remain* (1998) includes songs by Peggy Seeger and **Woody Guthrie**, and Solas won two *Irish Music* magazine awards in the year of its release, for 'Best Traditional Album' and 'Best Overseas Traditional Act'. Karan Casey left the group in May 1999 and was replaced initially by guest singer Sheila O'Leary, originally from Co. Kerry.

By the time of their fourth album, *The Hour Before Dawn* (2000), Deirdre Scanlon had taken over from O'Leary as the group's main vocalist. The album has more bass and percussion than the group had used before and includes original compositions by Egan and McAuley as well as a traditional Norwegian air. In August 2000 Dónal Clancy (guitar, bouzouki), formerly of **Eileen Ivers**' band, replaced John Doyle. *The Edge of Silence* (2002) saw further changes in style. Using keyboards, loops, strings and electric guitar solos, Solas moved towards a more rock-oriented sound. There are more songs (from a variety of songwriters, including one by Tom Waits) than instrumentals, although Egan, Horan and McAuley all provide some fine new instrumental compositions. Eamon McElholm (guitar, keyboards, vocals) joined the group in August 2002, taking the place of Dónal Clancy. Fiddler Winifred Horan can be heard playing her own diverse compositions (as well as one by Séamus Egan) on her solo album *Just One Wish* (2002). Her extraordinary ability to coax a wide variety of moods and tones from the fiddle is apparent on this album as it is in her work with Solas. Accordionist Mick McAuley also released a solo album, *An Ocean's Breadth* (2003), and in the same year Solas released *Another Day* (2003). In the wake of some unfavourable criticism of the band's change in style on *The Edge of Silence*, Solas sought to blend the old and the new styles on *Another Day*. The album includes contemporary songs (by Dan Fogelberg, Kieran Goss and Dougie McClean) as well as traditional songs. There is some electric guitar on the album, but it is far less prominent than on *The Edge of Silence*. Overall the

Solas

arrangements are simpler and the sound more acoustic than the 2002 album. *Another Day* confirms Solas' wealth of talent in performance, arrangement and composition, and nowhere is this more apparent than in Winnifred Horan's exotic and wonderfully arranged tune 'The Highlands of Holland'. Website: www.solasmusic.com. See also **Shanachie Records**.

Songs and Singers (general)

Songs and Singers (general) A variety of traditional Irish song forms exist today. These include the **aisling**; the **ballad** (see also **Child Ballads**), of which the **come-all-ye**'s are a particular variety; the **chantfable**, which was even less common in the late 20th century; and **songs in Irish**, the majority different in form and style from most traditional songs in English. The **carol** had a different form in the past to what it has now, and one form which died out in the 20th century is the **lay**. The **love song** is the most commonly found subject type, but there are also **comic songs**, **emigration songs**, **occupational songs**, **sea shanties**, **sea songs** and **sporting songs**. **Political songs** of a number of different kinds are also found, including **Jacobite song**, **Nationalist/Republican songs** (sometimes called **rebel songs**), **Orange/Loyalist songs** and songs relating to **Napoleon Bonaparte**. The influence of **American folk song** since the 1960s has been significant, especially through singers like **Woody Guthrie** and **Pete Seeger**. Closer to home, singer/songwriters **Ewan MacColl** and his wife Peggy Seeger were also an important influence on some Irish singers, **Luke Kelly** and **Christy Moore**, for example. These influences from the **US** and Britain have helped to shape a new kind of political, contemporary folk song which can be heard in the work of Moore, **Andy Irvine**, Colum and Tommy Sands (see **Sands Family**) and others.

Sean-nós singing is regarded by some as the only purely Irish form. It is usually unaccompanied, but singers like **Maighréad and Tríona Ní Dhomhnaill** and their brother **Micheál Ó Domhnaill** have, over the years, used elements of the sean-nós style in group settings (see **Bothy Band** and **Relativity**). More recently, sean-nós singer **Iarla Ó Lionáird** has recorded old songs in Irish with unusual accompaniments, and he performs original songs in the 'old style' with a contemporary group, the **Afro Celts**.

Important song collectors of the 20th century include **Séamus Ennis, J. N. Healy, Sam Henry, Ciarán Mac Mathúna, Tom Munnelly, Seán O'Boyle, Colm O Lochlainn** and **Hugh Shields**. Many of the older traditional singers of the last century, like **Sarah Makem, Elizabeth Cronin** and **Tom Linnane**, did little professional work as musicians, while others, like **Eddie Butcher**, made a number of recordings. Most of these singers sang solo, but among the older singers Sarah and Rita Keane (see **Keane Family**) are unusual for their traditional duet singing. All of these singers were also, perhaps unconsciously, collectors of songs in that they had rich repertoires of often rare traditional songs which had been passed on orally.

Many of the professional singers who emerged in the 1960s and 70s were also important collectors. Singers like Bobby and Liam Clancy (see **Clancy Brothers and Tommy Makem**) collected songs from various sources, often using portable tape recorders to record singers all over Ireland and in **Scotland**. Tommy Makem had a rich source of traditional songs in his own mother, Sarah Makem. Singers like **Paddy Tunney** and **Frank Harte** also collected many songs, Harte building up a vast personal archive of material which he has carefully indexed. The significance of these singer/collectors lies in their collecting, singing and often releasing the older songs on their own recordings. In this way they perpetuate a living tradition, singing and releasing the collected songs on a regular basis and thus providing greater accessibility to traditional material for those who are interested.

Many groups who play a mixture of traditional instrumental music and songs can have a very strong element of contemporary or non-traditional singing. Such groups include **Nomos, Kíla** (who sing original songs, mostly in Irish, but often with an African style of arrangement) and **Tamalin**. **Eithne Ní Uallacháin** of **Lá Lugh** had an exceptional talent for composing new melodies for old songs and entirely new songs that capture in a unique way the timelessness of many traditional songs. The **Pogues** blended punk rock versions of folk songs with more original material, much of it written by **Shane MacGowan**. In the 1970s and 80s groups such as **Horslips** and **Moving Hearts** combined elements of traditional music with what were essentially rock songs.

There are many fine contemporary Irish songwriters who were influenced in some way by traditional music and song. These include **Phil Coulter**, **Luka Bloom**, **Jimmy MacCarthy**, **Mickey McConnell**, **John Spillane**, **Robbie O'Connell** and **Pierce Turner**. In addition, poets and songwriters like **Padraig Colum**, **Percy French**, **Patrick Joseph McCall**, **Thomas Moore** and **W. B. Yeats** all made important contributions to the Irish song tradition. Dubliner Pete St. John has written a number of ballads which have become part of the modern folk repertoire, including 'The Fields of Athenry' and 'The Rare Ould Times'.

Most unusual in the Irish singing tradition was the singing trio, the **Voice Squad**, who sang unaccompanied, often using elaborate harmonies. They were influenced in their harmony singing by the Copper Family from **England**.

Two significant works which have appeared on songs and singers in recent years are Dáibhí Ó Cróinín's *The Songs of Elizabeth Cronin* (Dublin, 2000, see **Elizabeth Cronin**) and **Pádraigín Ní Uallacháin**'s *A Hidden Ulster: People, Songs and Traditions of Oriel* (Dublin, 2003). While the first book deals with the life and repertoire of a particular singer and the second deals with the songs and singers of a region, both share a high standard of research, with various versions of songs provided as well as ample background information. Benedict Kiely's *As I Rode by Granard Moat* (Dublin, 1996) is a very different type of book which has a unique charm and vitality. Kiely travelled around Ireland, recalling songs, ballads and poems associated with particular places as he went. The lyrics of numerous songs and ballads (some traditional, others with known authors) are a central part of the text, and the book is both a personal journey and a wonderful evocation of Ireland as an interwoven fabric of history, place, song and poetry.

Songs in Irish Most songs in the Irish language have a distinct style that is quite different to songs in English. While Irish songs in the English language are strongly influenced by the **ballad** form and are frequently written as straightforward narrative, songs in Irish are generally more lyrical and often only hint at a narrative background to the subject. This can be partly explained by the fact that songs in Irish have absorbed more stylistic features from the medieval court poetry of Europe, especially **France**, than most European folk song. In addition, early Irish poetry shows a tendency towards an impressionistic lyricism that carried into much of the later poetry and song.

Many songs in Irish are deliberately vague or even ambiguous. They may open with a question, as in 'A Bhuachaill an Chúil Dualaigh' ('You Long-Haired Boy'), which begins with the words 'A bhuachaill an chúil dualaigh, cár chodail mé aréir?' ('You long-haired boy, where did I sleep last night?'). The identities of the main people in the song may be confused and in many cases details of a relationship are not provided. First-person narration predominates, and the identity of the author of a song's lyrics can often be a matter of special interest to the audience. A good example is 'An Bonnán Buí' ('The Yellow Bittern'), written originally as a well-wrought literary poem by the South Ulster poet Cathal Buí Mac Giolla Ghunna (ca. 1680-1756). It is still sung today in various orally transmitted versions. In the original, the poet, who has a weakness for drink, laments the death of a bittern that apparently died by a frozen pool for want of a drink. The parallels between the bird and the author are clearly drawn in the original, but some versions of the song which survive in oral tradition appear to be about little more than a dead bird. The audience would need to have some knowledge of the author's background to realise fully the significance of the lyrics.

Allegorical songs are best exemplified by the **aisling**, but songs with double meanings outside this particular genre are also quite common. 'An Raibh Tú ag an gCarraig?' ('Were You at Carrick/the Rock?') appears to have been written originally as a love song but was interpreted in Penal times as making a veiled reference to a mass-rock (*an Carraig*), with the Church symbolised by the woman.

'Ca rabháis ar feadh an lae uaim' ('Where Were You All Day?'), an adaptation of the **Child ballad** (no. 12) 'Lord Randal', and 'Muire agus Naomh Ioseph' ('Mary and Saint Joseph' an Irish version of 'The Cherry Tree Carol', Child no. 54) are the only examples which **Hugh Shields** could trace of old English ballads going into Irish while retaining something of the ballad style. Likewise new ballads or **come-all-ye**s have had very little influence on songs in Irish, with 'Máire Ní Mhaoileoin' and 'An Rábaire' ('The Dashing Fellow') providing rare examples of songs in Irish which have fully developed sequential narratives similar to new ballads. Some popular songs in English have been translated into Irish, including 'Skibbereen', a ballad of the **Great Famine** and 'Down by the Sally Gardens' by **W. B. Yeats**, recently recorded in Irish by **Tamalin**.

In many parts of Ireland and abroad, what were known originally as songs in Irish are often simply played instrumentally as slow **air**s. This is partly due to the drastic decline in the Irish language that took place after the Great Famine. In many **Gaeltacht** areas the lyrics are still sung, however, and a number of singers since the 1960s have played an important role in promoting an international awareness of songs in Irish. These include **Seosamh Ó Héanaí**; **Máire Ní Bhraonáin** of Clannad; **Mairéad Ní Mhaonaigh** of **Altan**; **Iarla Ó Lionáird** of the **Afro Celts**; **Micheál Ó Domhnaill** and his sisters **Tríona and Maighréad Ní Dhomhnaill**. Aoife Ní Fhearraigh from Donegal and Lasairfhíona Ní Chonaola from Inisheer, one of the Aran Islands, are among the many fine young singers to emerge in recent years.

The Belfast-based Albert Fry recorded some fine renditions of songs in Irish which he had learned in Donegal on his album *Albert Fry* (1979). There are some traditional songs, but many are by Seán Bán Mac Grianna. There are also some fine reels, slides, jigs and slow airs. The album was notable not just for Fry's singing but for the quality of the arrangements, which were somewhat unusual for the time. They feature cello (Seosamh Ó Dubhghaill), harpsichord (Manus Ó Baoill) and guitar (Dónal O'Hanlon), as well as fiddle and flute played respectively by Máiréad Ní Mhaonaigh and Frankie Kennedy (who would later form the group Altan). The album was released by **Gael-Linn**, an organisation which has done much to record and promote singers of songs in Irish. More recently the publishing and recording company **Cló Iar-Chonnachta** has performed a similar function, producing many CDs of **sean-nós singing**.

The albums *Éist* (1999) and *Éist Arís* (2000) are compilations of songs sung in Irish by various singers, some of whom regularly sing in Irish, others (like Kate Bush, Paul Brady, Van Morrison and Brian Kennedy) who recorded in Irish especially for this project. It was initiated jointly by Dara Records and Bord na Gaeilge and had some success in raising the level of public interest in Irish-language songs. See also **Chantfable**; **Macaronic Song**; **Scotland**.

Sources of Irish Traditional Music Project See **Fleischmann, Aloys**.

Spillane, Davy (b. 1959) Uilleann piper, low whistle player and composer who grew up in Dublin listening to a wide variety of music, including jazz, swing and classical as well as traditional. He was playing the uilleann pipes as a teenager and in his twenties served a pipe-making apprenticeship with Johnny Burke in Bray, Co. Wicklow. He was a founding member of **Moving Hearts**, a band that brought Spillane fame as an innovator in piping. His playing with the group, in which traditional, jazz and rock styles were blended, brought the uilleann pipes beyond purely traditional style playing. Spillane continued to experiment with his own traditional/rock band, simply called the Davy Spillane Band, after Moving Hearts officially broke up in 1984. The regular line-up of Spillane (pipes, low whistle), Anthony Drennan (electric and acoustic guitars), James Delaney (keyboards), Paul Moran (drums, percussion) and Tony Molloy (bass) was augmented by guest musicians for recording and live performance. Guests as diverse in style as rock/blues guitarist Rory Gallagher and traditional box virtuoso **Máirtín O'Connor** are among the many who have recorded with the band. Much of their material was composed by Spillane, but traditional tunes were included as well. Their first album, *Atlantic Bridge* (1988) established the group as an exciting traditional/rock combination in which Spillane's playing on both uilleann pipes and low whistles is often far from traditional. This was followed by *Out of the Air* (1988), which includes a tribute to rock singer/guitarist Phil Lynott of **Thin Lizzy**, and *Shadow Hunter* (1989), arguably the finest of the band's albums. The title of the last album came from one of two highly evocative songs performed by guest singer **Seán Tyrrell**. Songs were a new departure for the band, having recorded purely instrumental material on their two earlier albums. Further albums followed, the instrumental *Pipedreams* (1991) and *A Place among the Stones* (1994).

Spillane has become a session musician with a considerable international reputation, recording as a guest on albums by Kate Bush, Elvis Costello and Baba Maal among others. He made a fine album of Eastern European music with **Andy Irvine** (*East Wind*, 1992) and guested on and produced the album *Calman the Dove* (1998) by Scottish harper/composer Savourna Stevenson. This is an interesting collection of original, acoustic music commissioned to commemorate the anniversary of the Irish-born St. Columcille (ca. 521-597), founder of the island monastery of Iona, Scotland.

Davy Spillane

Spillane's own album, *Sea of Dreams* (1998) features songs performed by Sinéad O'Connor, his own version of 'My Heart Will Go On' from the movie *Titanic* as well as new material and new recordings of some older pieces. In 1997 and 1998, Spillane played many purely traditional gigs and joked about becoming more conservative as he got older. His straight traditional album with fiddler Kevin Glackin (see **Glackin, Paddy**), *Forgotten Days* (2001), won an **Irish Music** magazine award for 'Best Traditional Album'. Whether experimenting with different styles of music or playing straight traditional, Spillane is a highly accomplished musician. He has contributed enormously to music in Ireland not just through his playing but also his compositions. He is one of the finest players of the relatively recent low

whistle and has probably done more than any other single piper to stimulate a new enthusiasm among the younger generation for uilleann piping. Website: www.davyspillane.com.

Spillane, John (b. 1961) Cork-born singer/songwriter who also plays guitar and bass. He has played with rock and jazz groups, including the Stargazers, but in 1994 joined the Cork-based traditional group, **Nomos**. After touring and recording with Nomos for a few years, he left in 1998 to pursue a solo career. His solo album *The Wells of the World* (1997) expresses, often with black humour, mixed feelings for his native Cork. Other Spillane songs have a beautiful, delicate and at times almost mystical lyricism, as in 'All the Ways You Wander', which he recorded on the first Nomos album. *Will We Be Brilliant or What?* (2002) is a second collection of original songs by Spillane.

Spoons Ordinary domestic soup spoons, dessert spoons or table spoons are often used to provide rhythmic accompaniment to traditional dance music. Sometimes the spoons have been 'customised' to suit the player's needs. Two spoons are held between the fingers of one hand and banged rapidly on the knee (or sometimes a table or other surface) to produce a clacking rhythm, not unlike the effect of the **bones**. The fingers of the free hand are often used to create additional rhythmic effects by breaking the passage of the spoons to the knee. They are a marvellous accompaniment in the hands of a skilful player, who will often vary the tone by banging the spoons off various parts of tables, chairs or even people sitting within range!

Sporting Songs Songs about sporting events have been popular in Ireland since the 18th century, with the horse-racing ballad 'Skewball' (1752) providing one of the earliest surviving examples of the **come-all-ye**. The song, which has survived orally, celebrates the famous victory of the horse Skewball over Miss Greisel at the Curragh races. **Andy Irvine** recorded this song as 'The Plains of Kildare', with new words and music. Another early sporting song is 'The Kilruddery Hunt' (1744), which describes a foxhunt south of Dublin and inspired a local English hunting song. One of the most famous sporting ballads is 'Master McGrath', which imitates the form and style of 'Skewball' in commemorating the great greyhound that won the Waterloo Cup in 1868, 1869 and 1871. Other old sporting songs can be found in *Sam Henry's Songs of the People* (see **Henry, Sam**), where songs about animals, hunting and racing are grouped together. Songs about local sporting events can also be found all over Ireland. They are often recently composed and are sometimes written in the style of a mock-heroic ballad.

Step Dancing This term is usually applied to solo dances, although various forms of group dancing would use steps similar to those used by solo dancers. Many of the step dances seem to have evolved around the late 18th century under the influence of the **dancing masters**. The principal steps were the **jig, reel** and

hornpipe, and there were also special set or figure dances (see **Set Dance** 2). Despite the speed and vigour of the footwork, the body was kept rigid above the waist with the arms held straight down by the sides. This, apparently, was the ideal form of dancing taught by the old dancing masters, who often taught deportment and social etiquette as well. It was said that a good dancer could hold a pan of water on his head without spilling a drop. The best solo dancers were honoured by having a door taken off its hinges or a table cleared to allow them to display their skills. Most of these features of step dancing survive to the present day, many of the steps having been formalised and regulated by the **Dancing Commission** from 1929 right down to the present. The Commission generally favoured the style of step dancing found in the southern province of Munster to the detriment of other regional styles such as those found in Connemara (see **Sean-nós Dancing**) and in the Northern part of the island (see **Clog Dancing**). The less formalised context in which the latter two styles of step dance were learned meant that there was more scope for individual expression, often resulting in dances which were less rigid than those favoured by the Commission, using body, arms and legs in a different way. New forms of step dancing have been explored in Tralee's Siamsa Tíre/National Folk Theatre, which produced **Bill Whelan**'s *Seville Suite,* performed at Expo '94 in Seville, Spain. Irish step dancing has also been presented in new forms through internationally acclaimed shows like *Riverdance* and *Lord of the Dance*. See also **O'Donovan, Joe and Siobhán**.

Stivell, Alan Harper, singer and composer from **Brittany** who has made numerous albums and been a vital figure in bringing Breton music to the attention of people in Ireland and elsewhere since the early 1970s. He has also consistently and successfully played a repertoire of music from all of the Celtic lands. Long before the subject was researched in depth for *Bringing It All Back Home*, Stivell voiced his belief that Celtic music played an important role in the evolution of American folk music and was the inspiration for much rock and pop music.

Stivell made his name initially as an innovator, playing music described by some as 'Celtic Pop' but which Stivell himself preferred to call 'ethnic modern'. He combined his own singing of traditional and original songs with his harp playing in a dynamic line-up which usually included organ, drums, bass and electric guitar as well as more traditional instruments such as tin whistle, flute, fiddle and **bombarde** (an instrument popular in Breton folk music). *Alan Stivell à l'Olympia* (1972) is a good example of Stivell's early 'ethnic modern' style. It includes his version of the Irish song 'The Foggy Dew', 'The Trees They Do Grow High' (a Hebridean folk song), a traditional South American Suite, Breton traditional songs and instrumentals and a rousing version of the set dance 'The King of the Fairies'. One of the most interesting tracks on the album is 'Pop Plinn', Stivell's arrangement of a traditional Breton tune which combines the use of electric guitar, harp and bombardes as melody instruments in a uniquely modern way.

The year after *Alan Stivell à l'Olympia* was released, Stivell brought out a very different kind of album, *Renaissance of the Celtic Harp* (1973). This album was

Alan Stivell

entirely instrumental and, while some tracks featured additional instruments, solo harping was the central feature. At a time when most Celtic or Irish harpers were playing the instrument simply to accompany songs, *Renaissance* was an extraordinary piece of work. It could truly be called a 'Celtic' album, as it included traditional music from **Wales**, Brittany, Ireland, **Scotland** and the **Isle of Man**. The album opens with the sound of the sea, which fades gradually as the harp is introduced and Stivell plays his own composition 'Ys', named after a legendary Breton city which disappeared beneath the sea. *Renaissance* was recently re-released on CD. Despite the number of fine harpists who have emerged playing instrumental music in recent years, Stivell's 1973 album is still unique, a classic of Celtic harping.

In 1984, Stivell released his *Tír na nÓg: Celtic Symphony*, a 90-minute composition in three movements involving 75 musicians from all over the world. He incorporated sung or spoken versions of ancient texts from Tibet, India, North Africa, Brittany, Ireland and Native North and South Americans. 'In this symphony', wrote Stivell in the sleeve-notes, 'I also wanted to include minority cultures whose closeness to the Celts goes back to antiquity, from the intervals in sound, our scales and our ways of thinking, our relationship with nature and the cosmos, from our hatred of the State'. The symphony incorporates a wide variety of influences, reflected in the composition of the orchestra, which includes some conventional orchestral instruments, many traditional instruments from all over the world and modern instruments like electric guitar, bass, drums and saxophone. Through the music, Stivell explores his musical ideas on a grander scale then ever before and incorporates ideas and symbolism from the modern and ancient worlds.

Stivell continues to perform and record, still bringing together music from Celtic lands and fusing it with modern music. A number of Irish musicians recorded with him on *Brian Boru* (1995), including **Máire Breatnach** and **Ronan Browne**. The album mixes traditional music and song from Brittany, Wales, Scotland and Ireland with original lyrics or music by Stivell, contemporary Irish poet Theo Dorgan, Scottish poet **Robert Burns** and others. The title track mixes the melody part of the Irish 'Brian Boru's March' with additional melody by Stivell, lyrics in Breton and Irish (sung by Stivell and Máire Breathnach), instrumental breaks on harp and uilleann pipes (Ronan Browne) and a modern backing on electric guitar and drums. It is an extraordinary fusion of different instruments, languages and styles of music.

Many critics are sceptical about the perceived unity of the culture of 'Celtic nations', pointing out, for example, that there is no direct historical link between the traditional music of Brittany and that of Ireland. However, Stivell has forged a unity between the music of the Celtic lands through his own work, and has brought together musicians from all around the world over the years.

Stockton's Wing One of Ireland's longest-running traditional groups, they have seen many changes in line-up and style. Stockton's Wing were formed in 1977 in Ennis, Co. Clare with Tony Callinan (guitar, vocals) and four **All-Ireland** champions in Paul Roche (flute, tin whistle, vocals), Maurice Lennon (fiddle, viola, vocals), **Tommy Hayes** (bodhrán) and **Kieran Hanrahan** (banjo). They recorded their first album, *Stockton's Wing*,

Stockton's Wing
(courtesy of Tara Music)

in 1978, playing a fast and fiery mixture of instrumental music and ballads. By the time of their second album, *Take a Chance* (1980), Mike Hanrahan had replaced Tony Callinan as lead singer/guitarist. Their live performances in these early years often featured extraordinary bodhrán solos from Tommy Hayes. The group changed direction in 1982 with the album *Light in the Western Sky*, with new member **Steve Cooney** playing bass and didgeridoo. The material was more contemporary, with Mike Hanrahan writing hit singles such as 'Beautiful Affair'. Tommy Hayes left in 1983, Fran Breen (drums) and Peter Keenan (keyboards) adding to a more Celtic rock/pop sound for the remainder of the 1980s.

Between 1984 and 1988, they released four albums and a number of singles and toured all over the world. Released in 1991, *The Stockton's Wing Collection* is a twenty-track compilation of their first three albums. Fran Breen and Steve Cooney left in 1991 and Dave McNevin (banjo, mandolin, guitar) replaced Kieran Hanrahan. These changes marked a return to an acoustic sound, with *The Crooked Rose* (1992) exemplifying the change in style. Their 1995 album *Letting Go* features Eamonn McElholm, a singer/songwriter with a background in rock music, who also plays guitar, keyboards and cello. Maurice Lennon has also made an ambitious album, *Brian Boru: The High King of Tara* (2002), released to commemorate the thousandth anniversary of Brian Boru (d. 1014) becoming High King of Ireland. Lennon assembled an impressive array of musicians to play on the album, including Seán

Keane (see **Keane Family**), **Dónal Lunny** and **Máirtín O'Connor**. Lennon's music portrays the epic life and times of one of Ireland's great historical figures.

Strathspey (*straithspé*) A slow type of Scottish **reel** that originated ca. 1750. It is in 4/4 time, has a distinct dotted rhythm and is often marked by long runs of triplets. In Ireland it is most common in Ulster, where it is especially favoured by many Donegal fiddlers. See also **Scotland**.

The Iron Man (strathspey)

Strawboys Like the **mummers** and **wren-boys**, the tradition of strawboys probably dates back to medieval or even prehistoric times. They wore straw masks and often straw capes or a complete straw outfit. Mummers and wren-boys sometimes wore straw hats or suits as well, but many accounts associate the strawboys particularly with weddings. They would arrive as uninvited guests at the dance that follows a wedding, the leader claiming the right to dance with the bride. According to one account the strawboys, arriving at sundown, danced with all at the wedding but never spoke and disappeared again after about an hour. Disguise was an important element in this ritual, which may originate in a form of fertility rite. See also **Biddy Boys**.

Sult *Sult* literally means 'fun' or 'pleasure' and is the name of a television programme hosted by **Dónal Lunny**, the initial series of which was made for the inaugural schedule of Teilifís Na Gaeilge (see **TG4**) in 1996. The thirteen programmes which made up the first series were recorded in Temple Bar Music Centre, Dublin, and comprised an interesting mixture of top-class traditional musicians and contemporary artists. The Sult house band, who performed with most of the guests, was made up of Lunny (bouzouki, keyboards), Pat Crowley (keyboards), **Nollaig Ní Chathasaigh** (fiddle, viola, vocals), Noel Bridgeman (drums, percussion, vocals) and **Steve Cooney** (bass, guitar, percussion, vocals). A CD of seventeen tracks from the first series was released as *Sult: Spirit of the Music* (1996) and featured

Matt Molloy, **Liam O'Flynn**, **Máirtín O'Connor**, Van Morrison, Mark Knopfler, **Paul Brady** and many other singers and musicians. A further series of Sult followed in 1997, and it presented an interesting combination of traditional and contemporary artists, with the house band providing dynamic, modern arrangements. It was produced by **Hummingbird Productions**.

Supergroups A term used in the 1970s and 80s to describe popular traditional Irish groups who recorded, toured extensively (usually in Ireland, Britain, Europe and the US) and had a status and an image which was close to that of pop or rock bands. Apart from **céilí bands** and the exceptional **Flanagan Brothers**, the playing of traditional music in groups or ensembles was not widespread before the 1960s. The emergence of groups like the **Clancy Brothers and Tommy Makem**, **Ceoltóirí Chualann**, the **Chieftains**, the **Dubliners**, the **Johnstons** and **Sweeney's Men** in the 1960s marked the beginning of a new era in traditional ensemble playing. These were really the earliest 'supergroups', although the term is usually applied to later groups such as **Clannad, Planxty, De Dannan**, the **Bothy Band, Moving Hearts, Patrick Street** and others. The idea of groups playing traditional music (often blended with other forms), touring internationally and recording many albums was so new that the term 'supergroups' seemed an apt description. In the 1990s, the phenomenon has continued with groups like **Altan, Dervish, Solas, Nomos, Lúnasa** and the **Afro Celts**, to name a few. The term 'supergroups' is not so commonly used to describe these later groups, however, as the phenomenon is accepted now as part of the traditional music scene.

The line-up and style of arrangement used in the early and mid-1970s by supergroups like Planxty, the Bothy Band and De Dannan was highly original then, but over the next two decades it became almost a formula for success. While there are unique aspects to the style and repertoire of groups like Altan, Dervish, Nomos and Solas, for example, they all share an overall style of arrangement. This style includes features such as the use of a strong, rhythmic guitar accompaniment; combinations of stringed instruments such as guitar, bouzouki and mandola to provide accompaniment; the use of bodhrán and/or a percussive style of rhythm accompaniment on stringed instruments (especially guitar); and the use of melody instruments in changing combinations within a set of tunes to change the texture of, and maintain interest in, the overall arrangement of the set. Some of these features of arrangement are found in all of the aforementioned groups and most can be traced back to the 1970s supergroups. Perhaps this style of arrangement is popular because it works so well in bringing the best out in the music. What was innovative and frowned upon by many purists in the 1970s is no longer original, and groups like the Afro Celts and **Khanda** (who have broken with this approach) are often criticised today in the same way that Planxty and the Bothy Band were criticised in the 70s.

Sweeney's Men One of the major groups of the **ballad boom** era who brought a new and more intricate style of arrangement into the Irish music scene in the late 1960s. The original line-up (1966), who played under the name 'The Sweeneys', was

Johnny Moynihan, **Andy Irvine** and Joe Dolan. Terry Woods (later of the **Pogues**) replaced Dolan in 1967. The following year Irvine (vocals, harmonica, mandolin, guitar), Moynihan (vocals, bouzouki, tin whistle) and Woods (vocals, six- and twelve-string guitars, five-string banjo, concertina) made the classic album *Sweeney's Men* (1968). They sing a wide range of material, including Irish, Scottish and American folk as well as original songs. Stringed instruments (mandolin, bouzouki, guitar) feature strongly in their arrangements, often playing in harmony on instrumental breaks in the songs. Whistle, harmonica and fiddle are also used in these instrumental breaks. The use made of stringed instruments and the arrangements were entirely new at the time. The Irvine/Moynihan combination was central to the group's sound, and when Irvine left in 1968 (to be replaced by rock guitarist Henry McCullough) it wasn't quite the same. Moynihan and Woods made a second album, *The Tracks of Sweeney's Men* (1969), but the group broke up later in the same year. Both albums were re-released on the CD *Sweeney's Men* (1996). The group **Planxty**, of which both Irvine and Moynihan were members, had many of the characteristics of Sweeney's Men but also developed their own unique style and approach.

Synthesiser An electronic instrument that is usually, but not always, in the form of a keyboard. Its development began in the 1950s, but its use in Irish music only began in the 1970s, when some Irish musicians, most notably **Micheál Ó Súilleabháin** and the **Bothy Band**, began to use it in a limited way. On the album, *Hidden Ground* (1980), multi-instrumentalist Jolyon Jackson used synthesisers extensively, playing both melody and accompaniment to **Paddy Glackin**'s fiddling. Synthesisers combined with multi-tracking techniques, whereby Jackson can be heard playing a number of different instruments on the one track, made this one of the most daring and innovative albums of the 1980s. It is remarkable that, despite the far more developed synthesisers available in the 1990s, there is still no album to compare with *Hidden Ground* in terms of the variety and effectiveness of synthesiser use. In the 1980s and 90s the instrument has been used by many musicians (including **Dónal Lunny**, **Declan Masterson** and **Steve Cooney**) to provide backing and create atmosphere. For the group **Clannad** and for **Enya**, the use of synthesisers with vocals has been central to creating a subtle, other-worldly atmosphere, perhaps best exemplified on the Clannad single 'Harry's Game' (on the album *Magical Ring*, 1983). In the 1990s, the **Afro Celts** used keyboard and drum synthesisers, often programmed by computer, to create a very modern blend of music played by Irish, Breton, African and English musicians. **Cappercaillie** also use keyboard and wind synthesisers to great effect, and Canadian Michael Brook uses guitar synthesisers on his album with **sean-nós** singer **Iarla Ó Lionáird**. The Breton innovator **Alan Stivell** has also used synthesisers.

T

Tamalin Belfast-based band with Tina McSherry (vocals and flute), **John Mc Sherry** (uilleann pipes and low whistle), Joanne McSherry (fiddle), Paul McSherry (acoustic guitar, Dobro) and Kevin Dorris (bouzouki and bodhrán). The band's first album, *Rhythm and Rhyme* (1997), consists of an eclectic collection of traditional songs and instrumentals, original compositions and cover versions of songs. Among the most interesting of the songs are an Irish version of **W. B. Yeats**' 'Down by the Sally Gardens', translated from English by Belfast poet Sean MacAindreasa, and a cover of Fairport Convention's (see **England**) 'Crazy Man Michael'. The music is energetic and exciting, the vocals tinged more with blues and rock than with traditional influences.

Tansey, Séamus (b. 1943) An **All-Ireland** champion flute player from Gurteen, Co. Sligo. His playing is highly ornamented and, like many of the older traditional players, he has amassed an extraordinary amount of history and folk tales related to the tunes that he plays. He is a colourful and often controversial commentator on traditional music, viewing many modern developments with scepticism. Since his first album, *Séamus Tansey and Eddie Corcoran* (1970), he has made many recordings, including *Easter Snow: Irish Traditional Flute Music* (1997) and, with Jim McKillop (fiddle), *To Hell with the Begrudgers* (1999). His triple CD *The Phantom Shadows of a Connacht Firelight* (2001) is an unusual mixture of music, songs, stories and recitations. Tansey plays flutes and whistles in different keys on the album, talking about the background to the different types of flute and the music played on them.

Tara Music Dublin-based recording company formed in 1972. Tara Records was originally a record shop run by Jack Fitzgerald in Dublin's Tara Street which specialised in American imports. Due to the demand for **Christy Moore**'s album *Prosperous*, originally released on the UK label, Leader, Jack Fitgerald bought the rights to the album in 1972 and released it on the Tara label. The recording company was then developed by John Cook (still its Managing Director), whose signing of the band **Planxty** as re-formed in 1978 marked a major development for the Tara label. Cook was born in Scotland and educated in England and Ireland, and had opened his own record shop in Rathfarnham, Dublin, in the late 1960s.

Planxty released two fine albums on the Tara label, *After the Break* (1979) and *The Woman I Loved So Well* (1980). Christy Moore also released two further albums on the label, the second, *Live in Dublin* (1978), one of his finest ever. Tara were involved in releasing some of the most innovative albums of this time, including **Clannad**'s *Fuaim* (1982) and *Magical Ring* (1983), the first three **Stockton's Wing** albums and the ground-breaking works of **Shaun Davey**, starting with *The Brendan Voyage* (1980). The label has also released albums by Rita Connolly, **Davy Spillane**, **Liam O'Flynn** and the duo **Nollaig Ní Chathasaigh** and **Arty McGlynn**. Tara's reputation for high-quality recordings by innovative musicians has continued right down to the present, their most recent release being Maurice Lennon's ambitious *Brian Boru: The High King of Tara* (2002, see under **Stockton's Wing**). The advent of digital technology has seen Tara re-master most of their catalogue for CD.

Taylor, Paddy (1914-1976) Flute player born in Loughill, Co. Limerick. He moved to London in the 1930s where he played in the famous Garryowen Irish Club (opened in the 1930s), which had its own **céilí band**. He became involved in early attempts by **Comhaltas Ceoltóirí Éireann** to set up sessions and their own branch in west London in the 1950s.

Taylor, Simon Dublin-born classical guitarist who has performed and recorded some fine arrangements of traditional music for classical guitar. Almost half of *The Irish Guitar: A Collection of Traditional Airs and Dance Tunes* (1985) is devoted to O'Carolan's music, but there are also other old harping tunes, slow airs, hornpipes a jig and a set dance. All the arrangements are by John Loesberg and are published in two volumes as *The Irish Collection* (Cork, 1981).

Teilifís Na Gaeilge (TnaG) See **TG4**.

Tenor Banjo See **Banjo**.

TG4 Television station set up by the government under the RTÉ Authority (see **RTÉ**) which began broadcasting as Teilifís na Gaeilge (TnaG) in 1996. In September 1999, it changed its name to TG4 in an attempt to boost its ratings. Based in Connemara, it aims primarily to serve **Gaeltacht** areas and broadcasts more traditional music programmes than any other television station available in Ireland.

Under *Ceannasaí* (Controller) Cathal Goan, TG4 has developed a variety of music programmes that are devoted to – or include – traditional music. *Geantraí* (Light Music), produced by the independent Forefront company, has had a number of series since the station opened, concentrating in each series on the music of a particular geographical area. The programme features local traditional musicians recorded in a local setting, and has been presented in recent years by **Brendan Begley**. *Síbín* (from the Irish word for an illegal drinking house or 'speak-easy') has a pub-style setting and features traditional music alongside other types of music. A twelve-part series called *Teach na Céibhe* takes its name from the Quays pub in Galway where groups including **Kíla**, **Cappercaillie**, **Altan** and **Tamalin** were recorded in concert. This and *Síbín* were produced by an independent company, Gaelmedia. Another independent company, **Hummingbird Productions**, produced the highly successful series ***Sult***. *'Sé Mo Laoch*, a series profiling some of the greatest living exponents of traditional music, began in 2001 and continued into

2002 and 2003. Another new series, *Flosc*, began in 2002, presenting contemporary traditional musicians in more modern stage settings or in specially made videos to accompany their music, a new departure in traditional music.

TG4 is also the main sponsor (with the Irish Music Rights Organisation, see **IMRO**) of the National Traditional Music Awards. In the first year (1998) the main award was won by **Tommy Peoples**, with flautist June Ní Chormaic winning the 'Young Musician' award. Subsequent winners of 'Musician of the Year' include **Matt Molloy, Mary Bergin, Máire Ní Chathasaigh, Paddy Keenan, John Carty.** and **Seán Keane** Since the awards began, the categories have expanded and now include 'Traditional Singer of the Year' and 'Composer of the Year'. Website: www.tg4.ie.

Tenor Banjo See **Banjo**.

Timpán The word *timpán* appears in medieval Irish sources with two different meanings, a 'tambourine' or 'drum' and a 'stringed instrument'. The timpán as a 'stringed instrument' was often played by harpers. Little is known in detail about it, but an Irish timpán player is illustrated in the margins of Gerald of Wales' *Topography of Ireland* (written 1185-88). It consists of a trapezoidal-shaped box with a sound-hole and eight pairs of strings, somewhat akin to a medieval **dulcimer** or psaltrey. The player is seated, with the instrument held upright and resting across the top of one knee and the inside of the other. There are sticks in each of the player's hands. It is difficult to tell whether or not these are being used as plectra (to pluck the strings) or hammers (to strike the strings), but they appear to be pointed, suggesting they served as plectra. The deaths of a number of timpánists are recorded in the medieval Irish annals and in some cases both the timpán and the harp were played by the same musician. The notorious Statutes of Kilkenny (1366) listed 'tympanours' among the different types of Irish **minstrels** who were legislated against as spies.

Derek Bell of the **Chieftains** started to play an instrument which he called a timpán in the 1970s, making his first recording with it in *Chieftains 5* (1975), on a track called 'Timpán Reel'. The instrument is like a hammer dulcimer and he continued to play it after 1975, using it, for example, on the opening sequence of the album *The Bells of Dublin* (1991), where it is used to produce bell-like sounds.

Tin Whistle See **Whistle**.

Tóibín, Nioclás (1928-1994) Sean-nós singer from the Co. Waterford **Gaeltacht** of An Rinn or Ring, near Dungarvan. He is regarded as one of the finest exponents of **sean-nós singing** in recent times, and one of his most famous songs was 'Na Connerys'. The Connerys were transported to New South Wales, **Australia** for allegedly stealing sheep, and the song curses the man who, by his lies, was the cause of their misfortune. *Nioclás Tóibín*, an album of songs sung in Irish, was released in 1977. Singer Áine Uí Cheallaigh and others, including Ciarán Ó Gealbháin (see **Danú**), have led something of a revival in singing in Ring since

Tóibín's death. The latter's voice, from a 1962 recording, features on a recent album *Cois Mara Thoir sa Rinn* (1999), along with Uí Cheallaigh, Liam Clancy, Nioclás' sister Eibhlís and other musicians from Ring. See also **Mulqueen, Ann**.

Topic Records English-based recording label which had its roots in the Workers' Music Association, founded in 1939. Topic's view of music as a tool for revolution and folk music in particular as the 'voice of the people' led to it being described as the 'little red label' in the 1950s. Many of Topic's early releases were influenced by the work of **Ewan MacColl** and the singer and historian A. L. Lloyd. The label also made the music of American folk singers **Woody Guthrie** and **Pete Seeger** more easily available in Britain and in the 1960s released many influential recordings, including those of the Spinners, the **Watersons**, uilleann piper **Leo Rowsome** and the Irish sean-nós singer **Seosamh Ó Heanaí**. More recently Topic worked with the Irish company **Cló Iar-Chonnachta** on the production of a double-CD of previously unissued Ó Heanaí material. In the late 1960s Topic also made the seminal album of London Irish music, *Paddy in the Smoke*, which included fiddlers **Bobby Casey**, **Julia Clifford**, Michael Gorman and accordionist **Tony MacMahon** among others. Later they released an album by the Irish singer **Margaret Barry** as well as albums by the Scottish singer/guitarist **Dick Gaughan**, including his instrumental album *Coppers and Brass* (1977). The company has released a number of compilation albums of Irish traditional music, including *Past Masters of Irish Dance Music* (2000) and *Past Masters of Irish Fiddle Music* (2001). They also released an ambitious twenty-volume anthology of traditional and folk music from **England**, **Scotland**, **Wales** and Ireland under the title *The Voice of the People*. Website: www.topicrecords.co.uk.

Patsy Touhey

Touhey, Patrick J. (Also known as 'Patsy', 1865-1923) Uilleann piper from Loughrea, Co. Galway who immigrated to the **US** with his family in 1868. He sold his own recordings on wax cylinder by mail order and also made 78 rpm disc recordings in the early 1900s, just before the **Coleman** and **Morrison** era. He was an exceptionally gifted piper and had a successful career as an entertainer, being renowned as much for his comic skills as he was for his piping. Touhey provided **Francis O'Neill** with much of the material for his collections. A collection of his 78 recordings was released on the cassette tape, *The Piping of Patsy Touhey*, which accompanied a book of the same title edited by Pat Mitchell and Jackie Small (Dublin, 1986). The book has details of his life, Touhey's tips for pipers and transcriptions of 58 of the tunes he played.

Traditional and Folk Music Directory An annual directory for musicians, suppliers to the industry and traditional music fans. It was first published in 2002 and contains a wide range of information on musicians, agents, broadcasting, recording studios, CD processing, festivals, venues, shops, recording companies and other information useful to people working in any area of traditional music. It is distributed free to key people in the industry and is also available for purchase in bookshops throughout Ireland and specialist shops around the world. It is published by the same company that publish *Irish Music* magazine and **IMRO** *News*.

Traditional Music Archive See **Irish Traditional Music Archive**.

Travellers Nomadic people also known as itinerants or tinkers. Unlike the European gypsies, they are genetically indistinguishable from the settled population in Ireland but are now recognised as being a distinct ethnic group with their own customs and identity. There is little definite evidence of their origins. It has been suggested that they are linked to a specialised class of wandering metalworkers in Early Medieval times or are descended from small farmers who were forced to leave their land at the time of Cromwell (1600-1658) or the **Great Famine** (1845-1849). It seems, however, that travellers existed in Ireland before the Great Famine as the Poor Inquiry of the 1830s distinguished between tinkers and other types of 'vagrants'. Although travellers today are English speaking, they also speak what linguists call Shelta. Travellers themselves use the terms Gammon and Cant, which are distinct but mutually intelligible dialects. Research suggests that much of the vocabulary used in Gammon and Cant is related to words from the Irish language.

Travellers have had a strong association with the **uilleann pipes** since the 19th century, and the Cash family of Co. Wexford were widely respected as pipers. John Cash (1832-1909) was a tin-smith and horse dealer but became famous as a piper, playing at fairs, races and other social gatherings around Co. Wexford and its adjoining counties. He had learned the pipes from an uncle, James Hanrahan, in Co. Tipperary and passed his knowledge of the instrument on to his son, James (1853-1890). James developed a reputation as a brilliant piper while still a boy and according to **Francis O'Neill** developed no other trade or calling, devoting himself exclusively to the pipes. As well as travelling around Leinster, Munster and Connacht to play, he also appeared in theatres and music halls. William Rowsome, the father of piper and pipe-maker **Leo Rowsome**, knew the Cash family and described James Cash as 'the star piper of all the globe' (quoted in Francis O'Neill, *Irish Minstrels and Musicians*, p. 260). The Dorans of Rathnew, Co. Wicklow were another great family of traveller musicians, and the marriage of John Doran and Margaret Cash produced two of the most famous and influential pipers of the 20th century, **Johnny Doran** and **Felix Doran**. Another great traveller piping family of the 19th century was the Byrnes of

Shangarry, Co. Carlow. Jemmy Byrne (who died around 1867) and his three sons Thomas, John and 'Young Jemmy' were all pipers. 'Young Jemmy' Byrne taught Samuel Rowsome, grandfather of Leo Rowsome, to play the uilleann pipes, and Samuel Rowsome also played with the above-mentioned John Cash. Pipers from traveller families thus had a profound influence on the development of piping in the 19th and 20th centuries through their own playing and their teaching of and influence on members of the 'settled' community, especially the Rowsome family. This influence is still very strong in the 21st century, with pipers **Paddy Keenan** and Finbar Furey (see **Furey Brothers**) both having learned from Paddy's father, Johnny Keenan, who came from a traveller family in which music had been passed on for many generations.

The Furey brothers' father, Ted, was a fiddler and music collector who also came from a traveller family. The influence of travellers on fiddling has been particularly marked in Donegal where families like the Gallaghers, the McSweenys, the McConnells and the Dohertys (see **John Doherty**) can trace their musical ancestry back to the 18th century. As in the case of pipers, the influence of fiddlers has spread far beyond the travelling community, and they have played a vital role in the development and passing on of traditional music. Donegal fiddler Ciaran Tourish of **Altan**, for example, remarked in an interview in the *Irish Times* (February 25, 2000) on the influence of street players and travellers in Inishowen, where he grew up. His teacher on the fiddle, Dinny McLoughlin, had learned to play from Pat Mulhearne, who in turn had learned from travelling musicians. Settled musicians living in isolated areas often depended on travellers for learning new tunes or techniques and for maintaining and repairing their instruments. Tin-smith travellers often made tin fiddles for musicians who couldn't obtain normal wooden fiddles for financial or other reasons. Simon Doherty (1916-1987) of Donegal, a brother of John Doherty, claimed that his granduncles were the first people to make tin fiddles, and he himself made some simple box-shaped tin fiddles.

The other instruments which are strongly associated with travellers are the harmonica, the tin whistle and the banjo. The most famous player of the banjo in recent years is 'Pecker' (Paddy) Dunne, who learned fiddle from his father and is also a guitarist and singer. He can be heard on *The Very Best of Pecker Dunne, Ireland's Legendary Street Singer* (2001). In 2002, Dunne became one of the artists-in-residence at the Irish World Music Centre, **University of Limerick**. His appointment was enabled by the NOMAD project, an initiative which aims to facilitate access to performing arts in a university environment for the travelling community. The project is funded by the Higher Education Authority, and its first major event was a concert at the University Concert Hall in Limerick which featured some of Ireland's most famous exponents of traveller music traditions, including 'Pecker' Dunne and Finbar Furey.

Many travellers are also fine lilters (see **Lilting**), who have a distinct style of ornamentation. Lilter travellers include Johnny Keenan of Ennis and Jim Donovan of Finglas. There are many fine singers in the travelling community, and their distinctive style of singing has been documented by **Tom Munnelly**. The style preferred by older traveller singers is generally high-pitched and nasal, and many travellers sing with greater strength and volume than settled singers. The songs are generally in English, although some are in cant or Shelta. The most famous traveller singer of recent generations was **Margaret Barry**, who also played guitar and banjo and made a number of albums. John Reilly (1926-1969), a traveller who settled in Boyle, Co. Roscommon, was also a fine singer who was recorded in 1969 by Tom Munnelly. Reilly was an important influence on **Christy Moore**, who recorded a number of songs from his repertoire; Moore's versions of 'The Raggle Taggle Gypsy', 'Tippin' It up to Nancy', 'The Well Below the Valley' and the epic 'Lord Baker' all came from Reilly. A number of Reilly's songs were rare survivors in the oral tradition, especially 'The Well Below the Valley', which was the first orally recorded version of a song which appeared in the **Child ballads** as 'The Maid and the Palmer'. Reilly himself can be heard on *The Bonny Green Tree: Songs of an Irish Traveller* (1978).

There are approximately 25,000 travellers in the Republic of Ireland. Some travellers settle in a particular location and lose the urge to move, but in 1995 the Department of the Environment estimated that there were about 8,000 travellers living on the side of the road. Government policy towards travellers has varied. The government-established Commission on Itinerancy (set up in 1960) issued a report in 1963 that suggested travellers presented an itinerant problem which should be solved through rehabilitation, assimilation and integration. This report had a profound influence on government, local authority, church and educational think-ing on travellers for many years. Travellers themselves have pointed out that the 1963 report did not acknowledge the distinct culture, identity, language, customs or values of the traveller community. Things have changed, however, partly as a result of a government task force report in 1995. Travellers are now recognised as having a unique identity under the Equal Status Act. The Pavee Point in North Great Georges Street, Dublin 1 serves as a centre for travellers studies, leadership courses and travellers' rights. A government-financed public awareness campaign in 1999-2002 called 'Citizen Traveller' tried to bridge the gap between traveller and settled communities. 'Citizen Traveller' ended amidst controversy in November 2002, after a Government-ordered review carried out in the wake of a hard-hitting outdoor advertising campaign which accused the authorities of criminalising travellers with 'racist' anti-trespass laws.

The tensions between the travelling community and the settled community, which 'Citizen Traveller' sought to bridge, have existed for many years. Some folk singers from the settled community have tried to spread an understanding and awareness of travellers' lifestyles and struggles through their songs. The **Johnstons** had a big hit in 1967 with 'The Travelling People', written by **Ewan MacColl**. The latter's 'Go, Move, Shift' was recorded in 1975 by Christy Moore, who has performed the song regularly over the years. He has also added a number of verses which record attacks on travellers in Ireland in recent years (see *One Voice: My Life in Song*, London, 2000, p. 85). Singer **Liam Weldon** developed a passionate interest in song partly through knowing travellers where he grew up in Dublin city. He championed the cause of travellers' rights through his singing and songwriting, most notably in 'The Blue Tar Road'.

In addition to recordings by the traveller musicians and singers mentioned above, *Songs of the Irish Travellers* (1983) is a good, representative compilation recorded and edited by Tom Munnelly. *Songs of the Travelling People* (1994) includes recordings by travellers from both Ireland and Britain. The Pavee Point released an interesting recording of the Cassidy family in Ballyfermot, Dublin entitled *Whisht...Irish Traveller Folktales and Songs*. Released in 2003, the recordings were originally made almost thirty years previously.

Treoir Quarterly magazine of **Comhaltas Ceoltóirí Éireann**, edited by Labhrás Ó Murchú since its first issue in 1968. It is available only by subscription and carries articles (mostly in English, some in Irish) relating to Comhaltas activities in traditional music, dance and song. Notations of tunes and songs which are not published anywhere else are also a regular feature, a valuable source for new tunes gathered through the vast Comhaltas branch network in Ireland and abroad.

Triplets A triplet is a group of three notes played in the time of (usually) two quavers. Although triplets may appear an integral part of a tune as a player learns it, they are really optional and are used as a form of **ornamentation**. Triplets are often used in hornpipes, but can be heard in most forms of dance music and in marches and slow airs.

Triplet

TTCT (Teastas I dTeagasc Ceolta Tíre) A week-long diploma course for teachers of traditional music which was initiated by **Comhaltas Ceoltóirí Éireann** in 1980. Around twenty people are selected from a growing pool of applicants each year.

Tubridy, Michael (b. 1935) Musician from Kilrush, Co. Clare who plays flute, tin whistle and concertina. He lived in England for a year in 1953, returning to Ireland to study engineering at University College Dublin. In Dublin, he became involved in **Ceoltóirí Chualann** and the Castle Céilí Band. He was a founding member of the **Chieftains**, with whom he stayed until 1979. The year before he left the group, he released a solo album, *The Eagle's Whistle* (1978). Tubridy still lives in Dublin, where he has been involved in the **set dancing** revival and is an authority on Clare set dancing.

Tunney, Paddy (1921-2002) Traditional singer, lilter and writer born in Glasgow who grew up in Co. Fermanagh. He learned many songs from his mother Bridget, herself a renowned singer. He usually sang or lilted without accompaniment and made eight solo albums, including *The Man of Songs* (1963; released as *Lough Erne Shore*, 1978) *A Wild Bee's Nest* (1965) and *The Mountain Streams Where Moorcocks Crow* (1975). He also made a double album with his mother, sons and daughter, *Where the Linnet Sings: Three Generations of the Tunney Family and their Songs*

(1993). In his late teens he joined the IRA and was arrested and sentenced to seven years imprisonment for possession of explosives in 1943. While in prison in Belfast he studied the Irish language and history and read widely. He was released after four and a half years and subsequently qualified from University College Dublin as a public health inspector. With his wife Síle he played a major role in bringing TB under control in Co. Donegal from 1955.

Ewan MacColl described Tunney as 'the greatest lyrical folk-singer in the English language', and it was at the invitation of MacColl and Peggy Seeger that Tunney began the first of many tours of Britain in 1967. He also toured the **US** in 1976 and 1981 and performed regularly at the Tradition Club in Dublin. Many tried to imitate his style, and singers such as **Robbie O'Connell** and **Frank Harte** did their own versions of songs from his repertoire. He influenced many other singers, including Dolores Keane (see **Keane Family**), **Andy Irvine** and **Dick Gaughan**. Tunney had a higher public profile than other traditional singers in the 1960s and 70s, with the exception of **Seosamh Ó Héanaí**. He also wrote the autobiographical *The Stone Fiddle: My Way to Traditional Song* (Belfast, 1991, reprint of 1979 edition) and a collection of songs and stories entitled *Where Songs Do Thunder: Travels in Traditional Song* (Belfast, 1991). The books provide a fascinating insight into Tunney's world, including anecdotes of other singers, musicians and poets, legend, history and numerous song lyrics. He also published a collection of Ulster folk stories for children and two volumes of poetry. In addition to broadcasting music programmes with **RTÉ** and the **BBC**, he wrote plays for radio.

Turner, Pierce (b. 1951) Uniquely talented singer, songwriter, guitarist and keyboard player born in Wexford town. Classically trained as a child, he sang at plainchant festivals, was a member of a traditional Irish tin whistle group at the age of seven and later played in a brass and reed orchestra and a pop show-band. He eventually went to live in New York, where he made his first album, *It's Only a Long Way Across* (1986), co-produced by avant-garde composer Philip Glass. His music is original and defies categorisation. His 'Wicklow Hills', from the first album, was recorded by **Christy Moore**, but Turner's own version has a very different feel to it, ending with a superb section of chanting, orchestrated with a modern backing of drums, synthesisers and electric guitars. On the television programme ***Bringing It All Back Home***, Turner cited plainchant and **Seán Ó Riada** as two major influences

Pierce Turner
(photo: Tom Le Goff)

and performed 'All Messed Up' (from his third album, *Now Is Heaven*, 1991). The lyrics were written by Turner himself, but the melody is a reworking of the traditional air 'Seán Ó Duibhir an Ghleanna' ('John O'Dwyer of the Glen'), the last track on Seán Ó Riada's last album, *Ó Riada's Farewell* (1971). The song 'You Can Never Know', from *The Sky and the Ground* (1989), incorporates the hymn 'Faith of Our Fathers' at the end of Turner's almost surreal lyrics about dreams and childhood memories.

Turner's music was described by music journalist Liam Fay as 'simultaneously universal and more intrinsically Irish than anything that has ever been conceived by the auld sod itself' (notes to the 1998 album *The Compilation: Pierce Turner*). The influence of Ó Riada and Irish traditional music is not immediately obvious in much of his material, but some of his work demonstrates how traditional or religious music can be successfully reworked in the hands of a talented artist. On *Mañana in Manhattan...Live* (recorded in 1994) Turner performs a rousing rendition of 'O'Carolan's Receipt', as well as **Ewan MacColl**'s 'Dirty Old Town'. Turner's lyrics for his song 'I Set You up to Shake' are sung to the melody of the traditional song 'The Death of Queen Jane'. Website: www.pierceturner.com.

Tyrrell, Seán (b. 1943)

Singer/songwriter and player of guitar, tenor banjo, mandola, mandocello and mandobass, born in Galway city. He started playing banjo at the age of 22 and in the 1960s played with a group called Freedom Folk (which included singer/songwriter Johnny Mulhern). From 1968 to 1975 he lived and played music in the **US**, where he performed in sessions with musicians such as **Joe Burke** and Andy McGann (fiddle) and was a founding member of a group called Apples in Winter. After his return to Ireland in 1975, Tyrell went to live in the Burren in Co. Clare, where he played regular sessions with the fiddler **Tommy Peoples** and other traditional musicians. He recorded two songs on **Davy Spillane**'s album *Shadow Hunter* (1989), both with lyrics by Irish poets put to music by Tyrrell. 'The Hosts of the Air' (lyrics by **W. B. Yeats**) and 'Walker of the Snows' (lyrics by C. D. Shanley, a 19th-century poet) are both beautifully arranged and sung, evoking a ghostly, otherworld atmosphere. Tyrrell's voice is rich and resonant with a distinctive, earthy quality. His great interest in poetry is evident in his selection of songs, many of which are poems set to Tyrrell's music. He also sings traditional material, writes his own songs and performs songs by contemporary songwriters. His first solo album, *Cry of a Dreamer* (1994), was received to great critical acclaim and is made up of a typically diverse range of material from different sources.

Tyrrell also composed and arranged music which transformed the 18th-century poem *The **Midnight Court*** into a traditional opera, first staged by the Druid Theatre in Galway in 1992 and subsequently toured around Ireland. This innovative marriage between poetry and music received an enthusiastic response from the critics and public during its original Irish tour and was staged in Ireland again in 1999.

A second solo album, *The Orchard*, was released in 1998. Tyrrell's interest in poetry is again apparent, with sung versions of lyrics by poets W. B. Yeats, Michael Hartnett, Charles Lever and others. There is an interesting version of 'The Rising of the Moon', using the melody of the old 1798 song but with new lyrics. There is also a fine version of **Liam Weldon**'s 'Dark Horse on the Wind', sensitively arranged and making sparse but effective use of accompaniment on mandocello, electric guitar, keyboards, drums, bass, viola, violin and low whistle. Tyrrell also plays two of his own compositions on the album (playing mandola), one dedicated to the victims of violence in Northern Ireland, the other to his daughter.

A third album, *Belladonna* (2002), takes its title from a poem by Michael Hartnett which Tyrrell set to music. Four of the eighteen tracks on the album are instrumental and include his own compositions as well as a reel by **Paddy Fahy** and a set of traditional jigs. The songs include 'John O' Dreams' and a version of the traditional song 'An Spailpín Fánach' to which Tyrrell has put his own melody. *Rising Tide: The Collection* (2004) is a compilation of ten tracks from his previous albums as well as seven new tracks. Website: www.seantyrrell.com.

Seán Tyrrell

Uilleann Pipes (*píb uilleann*) Referred to as 'Irish bagpipes' or 'union pipes' until the early 20th century. In 1903 Grattan Flood first used the term 'uilleann pipes' (from the Irish word *uille*, meaning 'elbow'), which only gradually became standard. The instrument developed in Ireland in the early 18th century, gradually superseding the earlier mouth-blown **bagpipes** that had been played here since medieval times. A full set of modern uilleann pipes consists of bellows, bag, chanter, drones and regulators (see illustration). A beginner can start on a 'practice set', which comprises the bellows, bag and chanter only. The drones can then be added to make up a 'half-set', with the addition of regulators making a 'full set'. One reason for building up a set of pipes gradually like this is the difficulty of mastering the instrument. Another reason, in many cases, is the high price of the instrument. It can be more effective for learning, as well as more financially practical, to build up a full set of pipes over a number of years.

A full set of uilleann pipes is expensive, difficult to play well and requires a good ear for pitch. It is also a complex instrument, and there are different tastes when it comes to deciding how best to use the drones and regulators. Two basic styles of piping can be distinguished: the staccato or close-fingering style and the legato or open-fingering style. In reality, most players use a combination of both styles, although close-fingering is often used for teaching beginners.

Any description of the instrument must begin with the chanter, which is fitted with a double reed (like that of an oboe) and sounds when air from the bag is supplied at the right pressure. This pressure is controlled by the player's left elbow. The bag is supplied with air by the bellows, which is strapped to the player's right arm, just above the elbow. The chanter has seven finger-holes in the front and a thumb hole at the back. It produces a range of two octaves, and the bottom note is usually tuned to D above middle C. In 'flat sets' the bottom note is tuned lower than D, to C♯, C, B or B♭. Bottom chanter notes higher than D can also be found (E♭ or E). Sometimes metal keys, which produce chromatic semitones, are also found on the chanter. For all except the bottom note, the chanter is closed off at its end by resting it on the knee. Many players use a 'popping strap', a piece of leather tied around the knee, to seal the end of the chanter more effectively.

The bag, into which the top of the chanter is fitted, can be made of leather, plastic or rubber. The main stock, through which the drones and regulators are supplied with air, is attached to the bag. A tube lying across the player's midriff carries air from the bellows to the bag.

There are three drones: tenor, baritone and bass. The tenor drone is tuned to the same note as the bottom note on the chanter, the baritone is an octave below that and the bass a further octave below the baritone. The drones are wooden pipes of cylindrical bore, each fitted with a single reed or quill. They sound continuously once they are switched on, but can be silenced by the use of a switch on the main stock.

There are also three regulators: tenor, baritone and bass. These are wooden pipes of conical bore with double reeds. Each regulator has four or five metal keys that produce individual notes when pressed. The regulators are set up to enable the player to play simple dominant or tonic chords with the wrist or heel of the lower hand while the melody is played on the chanter. Sometimes the fingers of a hand that is temporarily free of the chanter will play individual notes on the regulators. The regulators are only sometimes used by solo players and are rarely heard in group situations as the chord progressions provided could clash with other accompanying instruments.

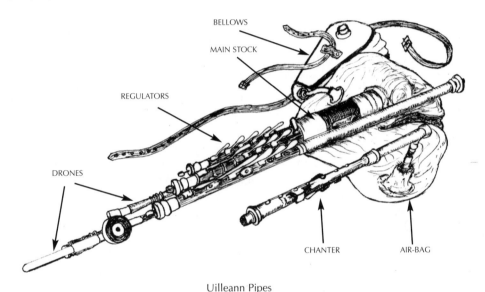

BELLOWS

MAIN STOCK

REGULATORS

DRONES

CHANTER

AIR-BAG

Uilleann Pipes

The development of the uilleann pipes to their present form has been a long and complex process. Many aspects of this process have yet to be fully understood, and it is far from certain that the modern pipes were developed for the playing of Irish traditional music. It appears that there were no regulators until the 1780s, when the tenor regulator was added to the already existing drones. In the 1790s, the instrument was called the 'union pipes', referring to the musical union of chanter, drones and regulator in the instrument as a whole or perhaps to the physical union of drones and regulator in the main stock.

Uilleann Piper Wilbert Garvin published an excellent book on *The Irish Bagpipes: Their Maintenance and Construction* (Belfast, 1st published 1973, 3rd revised and updated edition 2000). It is a practical guide to the construction and maintenance of the uilleann pipes with clear instructions for making a full set of pipes, including many precise diagrams.

The first known tutor for the pipes was **O'Farrell**'s *Collection of National Irish*

Music for the Union Pipes, published ca. 1800. This tutor refers only to the tenor regulator, additional regulators (up to five on 19th-century sets) being added in the first quarter of the 19th century. The front piece of O'Farrell's book shows the author playing the pipes in '[T]he favourite pantomime of Oscar and Malvina'. This, along with other factors, has led Carson (*Irish Traditional Music*, pp. 13-14) to argue that the playing of the pipes in opera and pantomime may have been a major influence on the development of the regulators. He argues that the kind of accompaniment provided by the regulators would have been more appropriate to opera or pantomime than to Irish traditional music. He also notes that O'Farrell gives fingering charts for a fully chromatic scale and that fully keyed chromatic chanters survive from this period. This supports the overall argument that the pipes were used for playing music other than Irish traditional, which only rarely uses accidentals.

Further important developments in pipe making took place in the **US** during the closing decades of the 19th century. William Taylor (born ca. 1830) and his stepbrother Charles emigrated from Drogheda, Co. Louth in the 1870s and eventually settled in Philadelphia. They were, like their father, pipers and pipe-makers, and they soon found that the usual 'flat sets' of pipes were too mild and quiet in tone to suit American stages and dance halls. They therefore developed the more high-pitched and compact pipes which are now standard (see **Phair's Pipes**). They are usually pitched in D, the chanter having larger finger-holes and a wider bore than the old 'flat sets', thus producing more volume. The great collector and historian of Irish music **Francis O'Neill**, a contemporary of the Taylors, wrote in 1913: 'So successful was it in meeting the popular demand that the Taylor type of Irish bagpipe has superseded the old mellow-toned parlor instrument almost altogether' (*Irish Minstrels and Musicians*, p. 161). Although uilleann pipes pitched in D are still the most common type today, there has been a revival of interest in the older 'flat sets' in recent years (see **Hannan, Robbie** and **Mac Mathúna, Pádraig**).

Pipers and piping were at a peak before the **Great Famine** (1845-1849). Although emigration, death and lack of patronage drastically reduced the number of traditional musicians in Ireland after the Famine, the decline of pipe music had, according to O'Neill, already set in. This was due partly to an increase in the number of brass bands and partly to the spread of the temperance movement, which suppressed many of the festivals at which pipers often played. The popularity of the mass-produced melodeon (see **Accordion**) and **concertina** in the second half of the 19th century contributed further to the decline of the pipes. Under the impetus of the **Gaelic League** (founded 1893), a revival took place; the **Cork Pipers' Club** and the **Dublin Pipers' Club** were founded in 1898 and 1900 respectively. The newly founded **Feis Ceoil** and **Oireachtas** organised piping competitions and old pipers passed on their art to the younger generation. The earliest recordings of Irish traditional music (on cylinder) come from these piping competitions. A lack of sustained public interest and the difficulty of obtaining a well-made set of pipes meant that this revival was short-lived, however, and the new pipers' clubs did not last long, although **Leo Rowsome** revived the Dublin club in 1934.

From the 1950s to the present the uilleann pipes have benefited greatly from the general revival of interest in Irish traditional music. The founding in 1968 of **Na Píobairí Uilleann** or the Pipers' Club (based in Dublin) has been a major factor in spreading the popularity of the pipes. The Cork Pipers' Club was also revived in 1963, and more recently the Thomond Pipers' Club in Limerick was revived after 100 years. Among those central to the revival of the Thomond club is Mickey Dunne, a piper and reed-maker from Caherconlish, Co. Limerick.

One of the most famous and influential pipers of the first half of the 20th century was **Johnny Doran**. He was born into a family of travelling musicians and spent most of his life travelling the country and playing music. Numerous pipers say they were influenced, directly or indirectly, by Doran. These include the famous Clare piper, **Willie Clancy**, as well as **Finbar Furey**, **Davy Spillane** and **Paddy Keenan**. The Dubliner Leo Rowsome was also very influential in the first half of this century, publishing an excellent tutor for the pipes (with **Waltons**) in 1936. He taught the instrument for many years, **Liam O'Flynn**, **Paddy Moloney** of the **Chieftains** and **Joe McKenna** being among his most famous pupils. **Séamus Ennis**, another Dubliner, was influential both as a piper and as a collector. Seán Seery (1926-2002) was taught to play pipes by Rowsome and later

The Piper, Tullamore
(Father Browne Collection)

(in the 1940s and 50s) played with Ennis, Willie Clancy and Jack Wade in the celebrated Leo Rowsome Quartet. Seery was a first-class piper and played an important role in the revival of piping and traditional music in general from the 1940s on. One of the earliest musicians to make commercial recordings was the American-based piper **Patrick J.** (or Patsy) **Touhey**.

Other famous pipers of recent years are Liam Walsh, Tommy Reck, Tommy Kearney, Robbie Hannan, **Tommy Keane**, **Peter Browne**, **Darach de Brún**, Brendan Ring, Martin Nolan of **Khanda**, Brian McNamara, Eoin Duignan (see **Low Whistle**), Gay McKeon, **Eoin Ó Riabhaigh**, **Máire Ní Ghráda**, **Ronan Browne** of the **Afro Celts, Declan Masterson** and Cillian Vallely of **Lúnasa**. **John McSherry** of Belfast is an exceptionally gifted piper who has also played with Lúnasa and with **Dónal Lunny**'s Coolfin. Young pipers of great promise include **Emer Mayock** and Louise Mulcahy (also a fine flute player), who has recorded with her sister Michelle (concertina, harp) and her father Mick (button accordion, tenor banjo). Brendan Monaghan from Banbridge, Co. Down (see **Different Drums of Ireland**) is an excellent uilleann piper but also plays a number of other instruments, including Scottish Highland pipes and Scottish small pipes. One of the finest recent releases on which to hear a full set of uilleann pipes played without any accompaniment is *The Leitrim Thrush* (1997), the second solo album by Neil Mulligan. Mulligan, from a famous musical family in Phibsboro, Dublin, plays a set of pipes in C♯ on the album, which also features an old recording of Neil's father, Tom (1915-1984), playing two reels on the fiddle. See also **Goodman, James**; **Henebry, Richard**; **Travellers**.

University College Cork (the National University of Ireland, Cork) UCC has had a long history of teaching traditional music, and many innovative musicians have studied there. **Carl Gilbert Hardebeck**, who held the Chair of Music from 1918-1923, was the first to introduce courses in traditional music as part of the Bachelor of Music degree. Since 1923 the traditional music curriculum has expanded and developed under a number of lecturers, including **Aloys Fleischmann**, **Seán Ó Riada**, **Tomás Ó Cannain**, **Micheál Ó Súilleabháin** and **Liz Doherty**. There is a wide range of courses on offer dealing with various aspects of traditional music, song and dance. The Irish Traditional Music Society is an active and important part of college life and the music scene generally in Cork. It has featured guest performances by musicians from all over Ireland as well as from **Scotland**, **Nova Scotia** and **Brittany**. The first Seán Ó Riada International Conference was held in 1996, and the annual Ó Riada Memorial Lecture is published jointly by the Irish Traditional Music Society and the traditional music archive, which is part of the Music Department and is open to the public. As well as forming a major part of the Bachelors Degrees in Music and Arts, traditional music can also be studied at Masters and Doctorate level. Among the musicians who have emerged from UCC are the band **Nomos** and the highly talented duo, the **Neff Brothers**.

University of Limerick (Irish World Music Centre) Established by **Micheál Ó Súilleabháin** at the University of Limerick in 1994, initially as a centre for research and innovation in Irish and Irish-related music worldwide. Since 1996, the centre has developed a number of postgraduate courses, including Master of Arts programmes in Ethnomusicology, Irish Traditional Music Performance, Dance Performance and Community Music. In 2002 the Paddy Clancy Memorial Scholarship Fund was established for students in Ireland and North America with an interest in pursuing study related to traditional singing. In the same year banjo player and singer Pecker (Paddy) Dunne (see **Travellers)** became one of the centre's musicians in residence under a special project designed to facilitate access of travellers to the university environment. Since 1997, the centre has run the annual **Blás** International Summer School of Traditional Irish Music and Dance. Students at the University of Limerick can study traditional music at Bachelor, Masters and Doctorate levels. Website: www.ul.ie/~iwmc.

US or USA (United States of America) The number of people of Irish descent currently living in the US is difficult to calculate, but it is at least 21 million and possibly over 40 million. Irish traditional music and song have been influenced by developments in the US in many significant ways, and an Irish influence can be found in many forms of music which have evolved in the complex, multiracial society of the US during the past 200 years.

A central figure in Irish-American music of the past twenty years is **Mick Moloney**, not only a fine musician and singer but a man who has contributed greatly to a deeper understanding of the social and cultural background to Irish music in America through his work as an academic. Moloney estimated that over 100,000 people, mostly Catholic men in their late teens and early twenties, emigrated to the US in the 17th century to escape poverty and social unrest. The mass emigration from Ireland that took place in 1700-1785, mainly to the **Appalachians** (the source of bluegrass and country music), was of a different kind, largely involving Ulster Presbyterians, known in the US as Scots-Irish. Since the foundation of the country in 1776, between 5.5 and 6 million Irish immigrants have left Ireland for the US. Harsh economic and social conditions in Ireland between 1820 and 1860, especially in the wake of the **Great Famine** (1845-1849), made this a major period for emigration. The Irish settled initially in large cities like Chicago and New York; by 1850 the population of these cities was up to 26% Irish-born. From before the Great Famine until around 1890, the Irish also worked on the railways that contributed to the westward expansion of the US. A number of railroad songs from this period with Irishmen as subject survive, and songs from Ireland such as 'Brennan on the Moor' and 'Siúil a Rún' ('Walk My Love') were collected in lumber camps. The Irish often suffered discrimination and violence in this period, with Protestants (who made up a large part of the US population) determined to drive the Catholics out of America. Although this Catholic/Protestant antagonism was partly a result of similar antagonisms which had existed in Ireland, in the US context many Americans saw Catholics, who vowed allegiance to the Pope, as threatening the separation of church and state enshrined in the American constitution. Violent incidents in which Irish Catholics lost their lives took place in the 1830s and 1840s, and the 1850s saw the emergence of the Know-Nothings, a loose federation of American Nativist secret societies who made no secret of their desire to rid America of Catholics. Anti-Irish sentiment is clearly demonstrated by the song 'No Irish Need Apply' which American singer **Pete Seeger** discovered through his research. Many versions of this song existed, and it was the most celebrated song among Irish Americans in the 1860s. Mick Moloney has recorded a version written by the popular New York songwriter, John Poole.

The Catholic Irish fought back against groups like the Know-Nothings, building communities and schools in American cities which helped them establish a firm foothold in American society. Loosely organised groups like the Molly Maguires (ten of whom were executed in 1877 after a rigged trial) fought against the oppressive practices of large companies like the Reading Railroad Corporation. The 'martyred

Mollies' were widely celebrated in song and were remembered as visionaries of the early American labour movement.

Around 200,000 Irish-born men fought in the American Civil War (1861-1865), the majority falling in behind the North and President Lincoln. The reasons for Irish enlistment in the 'Yankee' army were varied, and songs like 'Paddy's Lamentation' and 'Pat Murphy of the Irish Brigade' capture their responses to the war. David Kincaid, a musician and historian, has researched the subject of Irish Songs of the American Civil War and produced a CD, *The Irish Volunteers: Songs of the Irish Union Soldier, 1861-1865* (1998). The brave fighting and sacrifice of Irish lives in the Civil War helped to quell anti-Irish feeling and in the long run proved a major turning point for the Irish in America. As the 19th century drew to a close the Irish had established themselves in many sectors of American society, and the 20th century saw Irish Americans rise to positions of power and influence in politics and many others areas, culminating in the election of John F. Kennedy as President in 1961. America played a major role in the Peace Process in Northern Ireland in the 1990s, culminating in the signing of the Belfast Agreement (1998).

The story of Irish music in the US has been well treated in ***Bringing It All Back Home***, a television documentary series (with accompanying book) which traces the influence of Irish music in America from the 18th-century settlers in Appalachia to the early 1990s. It also explores the influence which developments in America have had on the evolution of traditional music in Ireland itself. The series deals in considerable detail with the period from the 1950s to 1990. It also includes musicians such as Bob Dylan, Van Morrison, Thin Lizzy and U2, and looks at the influence that Irish traditional music and song has had in shaping rock music as well as the evolution of traditional music itself from the time of the **Clancy Brothers and Tommy Makem**. In addition, **Gearóid Ó hAllmhuráin** includes in his book brief sections which cover the history of Irish music in America at different stages, from 18th-century settlers in the Appalachians to ***Riverdance***.

Francis O'Neill is still a major figure in the history of Irish traditional music in America, and his work as collector and publisher of Irish music in the US had a huge impact in Ireland. O'Neill's collections set standards in terms of repertoire and tune settings, and this process of standardisation was carried even further through developments in the **recording** of Irish traditional music in the US during the 1920s and 30s. The first truly professional Irish recording artists were American-based players such as **James Morrison** and **Michael Coleman**. Their recordings, especially those of Coleman, had an enormous influence in Ireland, setting standards of musicianship, style and repertoire to which many musicians still aspire. The use which many of these recordings made of **piano** accompaniment has also had an enduring effect in Ireland.

More recently the revival of interest in Irish traditional music and song which began in the late 1950s was in many ways influenced by the revival of **American folk song** which began in the 1930s and 40s and flowered in the following two decades. American collectors **Alan Lomax** and **Jean Ritchie** visited Ireland in the 1950s and recorded many traditional musicians and singers. American singers like

Woody Guthrie and Pete Seeger have perhaps been a more significant inspiration to singers in Ireland than has hitherto been recognised. Seeger and other figures of the American folk revival were clearly important in shaping the music of the Clancy Brothers and Tommy Makem, which marked a major turning point in the international popularity of Irish music. The influence of the US on the evolution and design of the **uilleann pipes** through the work of the Taylor brothers is another area where it is arguable that insufficient recognition has been given.

Irish influences can be found in much of the music and entertainment of the US from the early 1700s to the present. There are many organisations involved in traditional Irish music, song and dance throughout the country. Numerous major festivals are held every year which feature traditional musicians from Ireland and elsewhere, and many Irish groups and singers tour there regularly. Many, indeed, have moved permanently or temporarily to the US to work as musicians. Singer/songwriter Larry Kirwan and **Pierce Turner** emigrated from Wexford to the US in the Early 1980s, with Kirwan eventually forming the innovative band Black 47 with New York policeman Chris Byrne (uilleann pipes, whistle, bodhrán, vocals). Their unique mix of rock, reggae, ska and Irish music can be heard on *Trouble in the Land* (2000). Irish America has produced many fine young musicians, most recently **Séamus Egan** and **Liz Carroll**, **Solas**, **Eileen Ivers**, **Cherish the Ladies** and **Brendan Mulvihill**, to name a few. In addition to his solo work and research, Mick Moloney has made some fine recordings with Jimmy Keane and **Robbie O'Connell**. The latter, in addition to singing traditional songs, has composed many fine songs of his own, including 'You're Not Irish', which deals humorously with the problems encountered by an Irish folk singer facing an Irish-American audience: 'You're not Irish, you can't be Irish, you don't sing Danny Boy, or Toor-a-Loor-a-Loor-a, or even Irish Eyes.' The song highlights some differences between the Irish-American and the Irish perception of what Irish music is. The dance shows *Riverdance* and ***Lord of the Dance*** are very much in the tradition of American show business, taking something essentially Irish and building a large, spectacular show around it.

Although Irish traditional music in the US is frequently associated with a rural population, many of the most important developments of the 20th century have taken place in the urban centres. Urban settings continue to play a significant role in forging the musical identities of – and providing audiences for – Irish musicians (see, for example, **Martin Hayes**). The American city of Milwaukee hosts the biggest annual festival of Irish music and culture (see **Milwaukee Irish Fest**) and other urban centres in the US play host to annual festivals or summer schools of Irish music. See also **Banjo** and **Guitar**.

V

Vallely, Fintan (b. 1949) Flute player, songwriter, journalist, lecturer and writer, born in Tullygarron, Co. Armagh. He has made three solo albums, one of satirical songs (1988) and two of flute playing (1985, 1992), as well as two albums of satirical song with singer/songwriter Tim Lyons, most recently *Big Guns and Hairy Drums* (2001). He published the first tutor for traditional flute, originally published in Miltown Malbay (1986) and now available as *Timber: The Flute Tutor* (Dublin, 1987). Vallely has contributed articles on traditional music to a wide range of publications, including the *Irish Times*, ***Irish Music*** magazine and the *Sunday Tribune*. With Charlie Piggott he co-authored *Blooming Meadows: The World of Irish Traditional Musicians* (Dublin, 1998), with photographs by Belgian photographer Nutan. The book features 35 musicians, including **Micho Russell**, **Joe Burke**, **Len Graham**, **Pádraigín Ní Uallacháin**, **Mary Bergin**, Mairéad Ní Mhaonaigh of

Fintan Vallely

Altan and **Martin Hayes**. and provides interesting insights into the musicians' lives and their different views of the music they play. Vallely also edited *The Companion to Irish Traditional Music* (Cork, 1999), to which 108 experts contributed, an A-Z guide to all aspects of traditional music with an excellent bibliography and discography. He played a major role in the organisation of both **Crossroads Conference**s and is on the board of the **Irish Traditional Music Archive**.

Varsovienne A European couple dance which became popular in the ballrooms of Ireland around the 1850s and gradually spread to the countryside, where it was adapted to Irish dance steps and music. Often called the 'verse' in Ireland, its rhythm is closely related to that of both the **mazurka** and the **waltz**. A dance song was often used to accompany the dance, the song giving the dance its name. Examples include 'Shoe the Donkey' and 'Father Halpin's Top Coat'. The latter, described as 'The Versevianna', was published in Volume 3 (1927) of the **Roche Collection**, in a section of 'Old Dances (not Irish by origin)', which also included waltzes, mazurkas, **polka**s, **barndance**s and **schottische**s.

Vibrato A form of articulation that, like the various forms of **ornamentation**, is used to embellish or decorate a tune. It involves slightly wavering the pitch of a note, and is often used on long notes in slow airs. Some traditional players associate the use of vibrato with classical rather then traditional music, but if used subtly and sparingly, it can be highly effective.

Violin See **Fiddle**.

Voice Squad Trio who, most unusually in the Irish tradition, sing traditional songs in harmony, unaccompanied by any instruments. Gerry Cullen, Fran McPhail (both from Co. Louth) and Phil Callery (from Co. Cavan) made their first album, *Many's the Foolish Youth*, in 1987. In the same year, as the Dooli Gatecrashers they recorded two songs on *Ceoltóirí Chairbre*, an album of music and song from the famous Carberry's Pub in Drogheda. In the excellent sleeve-notes to *Many's the Foolish Youth*, Seán Corcoran explains how the folk tradition of unaccompanied harmony singing first came to light in the recordings of the Copper family of Sussex, **England**. The Coppers could trace this tradition, derived from village church singing, back 600 years. Cullen, McPhail and Callery, who sing two songs from the Coppers' repertoire on *Many's the Foolish Youth*, developed their own style of singing Irish traditional song in harmony. Their style and repertoire owe much to the great traditional singers of northern counties, including **Eddie Butcher**, **Paddy Tunney** and Geordie Hanna of Tyrone and, from Co. Louth, Pa Cassidy and Mary Ann Carolan. In addition to the Coppers' songs, *Many's the Foolish Youth* includes fine renditions of 'The Parting Glass', the classic Ulster ballad 'The Banks of the Bann', 'Ode to Autumn' by Scottish poet **Robert Burns** and 'Kilmore Carol' (see **Wexford Carols**). As the Voice Squad, the trio subsequently released *Holly Wood*, much of which was recorded in St. Kevin's Church, Hollywood, Co. Wicklow in 1991, and *Good People All*. *Many's the Foolish Youth* was remixed for a CD release in 1995. Phil Callery released a solo album, *From the Edge of Memory*, in 1999.

Wales Considered to be, like Ireland, a Celtic country, largely on the basis of language. Welsh and Irish, however, belong to two distinct branches of the Celtic language group. Welsh, along with Breton (see **Brittany**) and Cornish (which died out in the 18th century) are what linguists describe as 'P' Celtic, while Irish, Scots Gaelic and Manx are 'Q' Celtic. Both groups share common structures, but while an Irish speaker would understand a good proportion of Scots Gaelic, Welsh would not be comprehensible to either the Irish or the Scots Gaelic speaker.

Ireland may have been Christianised from Wales, and there were many political and cultural ties between southeast Ireland and Wales during the Early Medieval period. Both were colonised by England – Wales after the Norman invasion of 1066, Ireland from 1169 – and there are many parallels in the histories of Ireland and Wales into modern times. Nationalism in Wales, however, did not become the same political force that it was (and still is) in Ireland in the 19th and 20th centuries. Irish immigrants to Wales in the wake of the **Great Famine** (1845-1849) were generally viewed as suspect and threatening. This was partly because Wales, since the 18th century, had been largely shaped by Calvinism whereas most Irish immigrants were Catholics. The Irish also used English more than Welsh and were thus seen as a threat to the survival of the Welsh language.

The first outsider to write a general book about Ireland and her inhabitants was Giraldus Cambrensis, or Gerald of Wales, in the late 12th century. He praised the Irish for their musical skill (see **Harp**) and also noted that 'both Scotland and Wales try to imitate Ireland in music and strive in emulation. Ireland uses and delights in two instruments only, the harp, namely, and the tympanum. Wales uses the harp, the pipes and the crowd' (*Topography of Ireland*, translated by J. J. O'Meara, Dundalk, 1951, p. 88).

Wales, unlike Ireland and **Scotland**, has had an unbroken tradition of harp playing since medieval times. Although the metal-string harp is not in evidence as in Ireland, many different types of harp have been played in Wales at different times. One unique example is the *telyn* or triple harp, which is fully chromatic and has three rows of strings. It is still played and can be heard on the album *Telyn* (1997) and *Melangell* (2000) by Llio Rhydderch.

The Welsh pipes are mouth-blown **bagpipe**s similar to the gaita played in Spain (see **Galicia**) and the biniou of Brittany. Although they have not been played continuously since the 12th century, there are a number of contemporary Welsh pipers; Ceri Rhys Matthews (who plays with the group Fernhill) and John Shortland are among the best known.

The crowd or *crwth* mentioned by Gerald in the 12th century survived in Wales until the early 19th century and is currently being revived. In the form to which it had developed by the Late Medieval period, it was a bowed lyre with a rectangular wooden frame, a fingerboard and six strings, two of which ran to the side of the fingerboard and could be plucked or used to provide a drone. It went into decline around the 17th century, when the modern violin or fiddle began to take over. There are some signs of a revival in interest in the *crwth*, however, with the first solo album of *crwth* music released by Cass Meurig, simply entitled *Crwth* (2004).

In popular history the fiddle was brought to Wales by Abram Wood around 1700. Wood was the patriarch of the Welsh Romany families (Woods and Roberts) who carried Welsh fiddling well into the 20th century, playing more recent polkas and mazurkas as well as older music. Although Welsh fiddling was in serious decline at the start of the 20th century, not only has it survived but there are signs of a new awakening in Welsh music. One track of *crwth* playing by contemporary fiddler Robert Evans can be heard on the album *Ffidil* (1997), and the sound of the instrument is extraordinarily full and rich. Although it would have been good to hear more *crwth* playing, *Ffidil* is a fascinating album, encompassing a fine range of Welsh traditional hornpipes, reels, jigs, polkas and other tunes. There is no accompaniment on the album, but twelve of the eighteen tracks have two fiddles playing, either in unison or as melody and drone or harmony. The style is different to that of Irish fiddling, but several of the tunes closely resemble Irish music. Two of the fiddlers on the album, Bernard and Gerard Kilbride, can be heard playing with guitar and bass accompaniment on *Kilbride* (1997). Another Welsh instrument that had died out but has been revived in recent decades is the *pibgorn*, literally 'pipe-horn' or hornpipe, a mouth-blown reed instrument with a bell at the end. The music played on these instruments comes from a variety of sources. There is dance music originally played on the harp and *crwth*, some of which probably dates back to medieval times and some of it more recently composed. Some jigs, reels and hornpipes can also be heard, possibly through Irish and Scottish influence. Much of the music is played at a slower pace than Irish dance music.

The Welsh people are internationally renowned for their choral singing, but in addition to hymns and carols, ballads have also enjoyed some popularity. One unique aspect of the Welsh musical tradition is *cerdd dant*, which involves harp and song. *Cerd dant* originated with the bardic order of the Medieval period, when verses were sung or recited to a harp accompaniment. As in Ireland, the complex and formalised verse of the bardic order began to die out in the 16th and 17th centuries. Singing which took its lead from the harp melody, on which it often improvised, was later developed in Wales and, in the 20th century, the medieval term *cerd dant* has been used again for formalised harp and vocal performances which form an important part of Welsh music competitions. These music competitions form part of the annual *Eisteddfod* in Wales, a cultural festival that originated in the Middle Ages.

Although Welsh traditional musicians may not be as numerous as their Irish counterparts, and the musical tradition of Wales is not as popular or widely known as that of Ireland, recent decades have seen a considerable revival of interest in many areas of Welsh music. Young Welsh musicians have been influenced by Irish music since the 1970s, and the largest Welsh recording label, Sain, has done much to promote the work of Welsh artists (partly, though not exclusively, in the traditional arena) for over three decades. Fflach Tradd (founded in 1997), a Welsh recording company which released the *Ffidil*, *Telyn*, *Kilbride* and *Crwth* albums mentioned above, has added a new dimension to that country's traditional music scene. Other releases include an album by their traditional music director Ceri Matthews with Jonathan Shortland, *Pibau: Cerddoriaeth Gymraeq ar y Pipa cwd a'r Bombo: Welsh Bagpipe Music* (1999) and *Minka* (1999) by the new Welsh band the Rag Foundation. Fflach also released a compilation of Welsh accordion and concertina music, titled *Megin* (2000), which means 'bellows'. In 2001 they released the first album by the Swansea-based trio, Boys of the Hill, and *Perillan* (2001), from the established band Pigyn Clust. *Toreth* (2004) is a collection of traditional Welsh music played on fiddle and button accordion by Guto Dafis and Gareth Westacott.

With Wales getting more control over its own affairs since the turn of the century, there is some prospect of Welsh traditional music receiving more organisational and financial support from government in the future. The announcement in 2004 of a new initiative to support performing arts tours, touring exhibitions, co-productions and networking events in Ireland and Wales should help to develop the relationship between artists, including musicians, in both countries. The initiative, which runs until the end of 2006, is called CCAT (Cultural Co-operation and Touring @ Aberystwyth Arts Centre (Wales) and Temple Bar (Dublin).

Waltons Ireland's best-known music company, Waltons was founded by Martin Walton (1901-1981). Walton, a **Feis Ceoil** winner on violin, had been a member of na Fianna and at the age of fifteen had acted as a courier between the GPO and Jacob's Mill during the Easter Rising of 1916. During a period of internment at the Ballykinlar prison camp in 1919, he organised an orchestra there, in keeping with the Irish provisional government's emphasis on Irish culture and education. In 1924 he founded the Dublin College of Music in North Frederick Street. From there he developed a retail music shop, began manufacturing Irish harps and uilleann pipes, and set up a publications division specialising in Irish songs and ballads written or collected by Peadar Kearney (composer of the Irish national anthem), Leo Maguire, Joseph Crofts and **Delia Murphy**, among others, as well as publishing a tutor for **uilleann pipes** (by **Leo Rowsome**) and the **Edward Bunting** and **Francis O'Neill** collections. In 1952 Walton set up the Glenside Record Label, recording and publishing both original and traditional Irish songs and ballads, including 'Biddy Mulligan', 'Connemara Cradle Song', 'The Dacent Irish Boy (Patsy Fagan)', 'The Dublin Saunter', 'The Isle of Innisfree', 'Kevin Barry', 'Lough Sheelin', 'The Valley of Knockanure' and 'The Whistling Gypsy'.

Waltons' national reputation grew substantially during the period of the 'Waltons Radio Programme', a sponsored programme broadcast on Raidió Éireann (see **RTÉ**) from 1952-1981 and presented by Leo Maguire (1903-1985). Maguire, who began his singing career at a Citizen Army Rally he attended at the age of ten, worked as a music teacher, conductor of church and school choirs and broadcaster on 2RN from 1927. Broadcast on Saturday afternoons, the programme became a national institution, its slogans – including 'If you feel like singing, do sing an Irish song' and 'A weekly reminder of the grace and beauty that lie in our heritage of Irish song' – now embedded in the national collective memory.

Waltons' operations today encompass two Dublin retail music shops (supplying a range of Irish traditional instruments and publications); a manufacturing company (producing tin whistles and bodhráns, as well as traditional instrument tutors and Irish music collections); a wholesale and mail-order division; a publications division (holding copyright to many Irish songs and ballads, as well as arrangements of traditional material); a record label; and a school of music (see below). Website: www.waltons.ie.

Waltons New School of Music Founded in 1994 and located in Dublin city centre, the school was designed as a comprehensive music centre, with Irish traditional music as a core programme. Its current faculty comprises over fifty instrumental, voice and theory/musicianship teachers, and it provides tuition in the broadest range of instruments and styles (classical, Irish traditional, jazz, popular, world music) of any music school in Ireland. Its traditional music programme includes beginners' group courses in bodhrán, fiddle and tin whistle; private lessons in almost all Irish traditional instruments; and regular music sessions. A music technology programme offers courses in recording and production techniques of interest to traditional musicians. Two-hour summer 'crash courses' in bodhrán and tin whistle as well as two-hour 'intensive lessons' in other traditional instruments, designed for tourists and short-term visitors to Ireland, have attracted hundreds of participants from the **US**, Japan and many European countries. In-school and outreach workshops are scheduled throughout the year and conducted both in Dublin and around the country. These include introductions to Irish music for primary and secondary schools as well as specific topics of interest to intermediate and advanced musicians. Website: www.newschool.ie.

Waltz (*váls*) A couple dance in 3/4 time that originated in Austria and Germany in the late 18th century. It is thought to have begun as a peasant dance, but became one of the best known and universally loved dances of the 19th century. The waltz was considered daring, as it was one of the first dances to involve couples embracing one another. Numerous classical composers (including Schubert, Strauss and Tchaikovsky) wrote waltzes, and towards the end of the 19th century the waltz, along with other European dances (including the valeta, another waltz-type dance, and the **varsovienne** or verse), became popular in Ireland. The dance was adapted to Irish tunes and some Irish musicians began to compose their own waltzes. One of the earliest known examples of this is 'The Waterford Waltz', composed by the piper **O'Farrell** from Clonmel around 1800. Waltzes make up only a tiny proportion of the traditional repertoire today, although one example of a recently composed and very popular tune is 'The Marino Waltz' by **John Sheahan**, fiddler with the **Dubliners**. In many places the waltz is danced to popular ballads in 3/4 time. See also **Mazurka**.

The Waterford Waltz

War Pipes, Irish An Irish variety of **bagpipes**. Bagpipes were probably known in Ireland from the 11th century, although the first depictions of the instrument are found in the 15th and 16th centuries. From this period there is a carving in wood (kept at Woodstock Castle, Co. Kilkenny) and a drawing in a missal (owned by the abbey of Rosgall, Co. Kildare), both showing pipers with their instruments. In both cases the pipes comprise bag, chanter and two drones and are similar to the present *píob mór* or war pipes of Scotland. John Derricke's *Image of Ireland* (1581) shows a bagpiper leading Gaelic *kerne* or foot soldiers into battle. Pipers were part of the Gaelic Irish military establishment at this time, and are referred to a number of times during the reigns of **Henry VIII** and **Elizabeth I**. As in Derricke's illustration and the earlier depictions, Richard Stanihurst's description of the Irish bagpipes in his *On Ireland's Past: De Rebus in Hibernia Gestis* (1583) indicates that they had a chanter and two drones. In contrast to other early illustrations and descriptions, however, Stanihurst states that the pressure is applied to the air-filled bag by the elbow (rather than, as usual, by the forearm or wrist). This may represent a very early stage in the evolution of the **uilleann pipes**, for which the elbow is also used.

Stanihurst observed that: 'As other soldiers are roused for battle by the sound of the trumpets, so Irish soldiers are spurred on by the sound of the pipes.' (See Colm Lennon, *Richard Stanihurst, The Dubliner, 1547-1618*, Dublin, 1981, p. 151). The military associations of the war pipes are still pronounced in Ireland today, but even in earlier centuries they were also used at funerals, hurling matches and dances, just as the Scottish war pipes can still be heard on such occasions today. The latter normally have three drones, a development that took place in **Scotland** early in the last century.

Waterboys, The A group centred around Scotsman Mike Scott, the Waterboys has seen many changes in line-up, as well as considerable changes in style, since they were first formed in 1981. Although not an Irish traditional band, the rock sound of the Waterboys changed considerably after Scott moved to Dublin in the mid-80s, living first in Dublin and then in Galway. Their sound

Irish War Piper
(from Derricke's *Image of Ireland*)

became more acoustic, the music more like contemporary folk than rock, and a number of Irish musicians (traditional and non-traditional) recorded or toured with the band as guests in the late 1980s and early 90s. Steve Wickham (fiddle) and Trevor Hutchinson (bass; later with the **Sharon Shannon** Band and **Lúnasa**) were regular members in these years.

The first Waterboys album made in Ireland, *Fisherman's Blues* (1988), featured guest appearances by **Máirtín O'Connor**, **Alec Finn**, Brendan O'Regan (bouzouki) and **Charlie Lennon**, who wrote and played (on fiddle) the tune 'River Road Reel' for Scott's song 'When Ye Go Away.' The album is contemporary in style, but has an Irish influence that is more marked on some tracks than on others. Scott and Wickham adapted a traditional song, 'When Will We Be Married?', working part of the melody of the Irish jig 'The Tenpenny Bit' around the lyrics of the song. Original tunes like 'Jimmy Hickey's Waltz' and the jig 'Dunford's Fancy' have a strong traditional flavour. **W. B. Yeats**' poem 'The Stolen Child' is beautifully interpreted, with Scott singing some of the verses himself and with other verses spoken by Tomás McKeown, a traditional singer from Carraroe, Co. Galway. The album ends with a brief version of **Woody Guthrie**'s 'This Land Is Your Land', which replaces the American place-names of the original with Irish place-names.

Room to Roam (1990), the second album made in Ireland, featured Sharon Shannon, who toured extensively with the band and launched a highly successful solo career after her spell with the Waterboys. Like *Fisherman's Blues*, the album is a unique style of contemporary folk with a strong Irish influence, as on Scott's 'A Man Is in Love', which ends with a lively jig. The album also includes a version of 'The Raggle Taggle Gypsy', a folk song found in many different versions throughout Ireland and Europe.

Mike Scott at the Olympia Ballroom, Dublin, 1986 (photo: Colm Henry)

Scott moved to New York after Ireland, where he recorded *Dream Harder* (1993) with a new Waterboys line-up. The album is a return to rock music and very different to the Irish albums. Nevertheless Ireland, the traditional music of the country particularly, had a profound influence on Mike Scott's music. He seems to have understood the spirit in which traditional music is played, incorporating elements of Irish music into his own music and doing some highly original work with traditional musicians. He provides a good example of how an international artist can create tasteful, often strikingly original fusions with Irish traditional music. Website: www.mikescottwaterboys.com.

Watersons, The Family of singers from Yorkshire, **England**, who were influential in the folk music revival of the 1960s. Sisters Norma and Lal and their brother Mike started up the Folk Union One club (which continued into the mid-1990s) in Hull in the late 1950s. Together with various members of their extended family, they formed the Watersons, a harmony vocal group who sang traditional east Yorkshire songs. They were Britain's foremost harmony singing group in the 1960s and were joined by **Martin Carthy**, who married Norma in 1972. Mike and Lal (d. 1998) emerged as talented songwriters in the 1970s, Lal producing some of her best work on *Once in a Blue Moon* (1996) just two years before her death. Norma, who has recorded and performed extensively with her husband, made her first solo album, *Norma Waterson*, in 1996 and was runner-up (to the pop band Pulp) for the prestigious Mercury Music Prize in that year.

In the 1960s the Watersons toured the same folk circuit in England as did many Irish artists, including **Christy Moore**. Indeed Moore cites them (as well as Martin Carthy) among the singers and musicians who influenced his own music. He learned 'The Lakes of Ponchitrain' and 'Van Diemen's Land' from Mike Waterson on one of his visits to Hull and describes his first experience of hearing the Watersons sing as 'spellbinding' (see *One Voice: My Life in Song*, London, 2000, pp. 138-9). Website: www.watersoncarthy.com.

Weldon, Liam (1933-1995)   Singer, songwriter and collector born in Dublin. After six years in England during his late teens and early twenties, Weldon returned to Dublin to marry his teenage sweetheart, Nellie. She was also a fine singer and the inspiration for one of his best songs, 'Via Extasia'. Together they ran a number of famous folk clubs in the 1970s, including the Pavees Club in Slattery's of Capel Street, the Saturday Singer's Club in the Tailor's Hall (then a pub) and sessions in the Brazen Head pub and Mother Redcaps.

Weldon was a champion of the rights of the poor and the **travellers**, as reflected in songs such as 'The Blue Tar Road' and 'Dark Horse on the Wind'. He was a member of the short-lived but influential group 1691, a forerunner of the **Bothy Band** who made one album, *1691* (1974). In 1976 he recorded the album *Dark Horse on the Wind* (re-released on CD in 1999) and made further albums in 1984 and 1990 with the French flute player Paul Huellou. In a thought-provoking and moving tribute to Weldon, Fintan Vallely wrote: 'His integrity [was] too blunt a weapon for the prospects of a career in music, his loyalty to the people he was of [*sic*] too deep to betray them to the ambitions of another class' (*Irish Music*, Feb. '96). **Seán Tyrrell** and **Susan McKeown** have both recorded fine versions of his song 'Dark Horse on the Wind'.

Wexford Carols   A collection of 22 Christmas carols, the lyrics of which were mainly written by two Catholic clergymen in the late 17th and early 18th centuries. Some of these carols are still sung to traditional melodies in the parish of Kilmore, Co. Wexford every Christmas and are thus often referred to as the 'Kilmore Carols'. The lyrics of one, 'Song for Jerusalem', were written by an English Catholic priest and first published in 1601. Eleven of the lyrics were written by Luke Waddinge and were first published in Ghent in 1684. Waddinge was the Catholic Bishop of Ferns, Co. Wexford, and his 1684 book, *A Garland of Pious and Godly Songs*, also contained some religious posies and poems written for the disinherited gentry of Wexford. The Waddinges were one of the principal Anglo-Norman families of Wexford and had lost their lands in the Williamite Confiscation. Luke was banished twice from Ireland and suffered under the Penal Laws against the Catholic religion. His carols reflect the influence of the metaphysical poets and, in some cases, the religious persecution of the times. The remaining ten carols are believed to have been written by William Devereaux, parish priest of Drinagh, Co. Wexford. In 1728 he collected a number of carols into a manuscript entitled *A New Garland Containing Songs for Christmas*, which included the 'Song for Jerusalem' and the ten other carols of the Wexford collection. Although it is not certain that Devereaux wrote the lyrics of these ten carols, musical experts, as well as the people of Kilmore, believe this to be the case.

Some of the carols are still sung every Christmas in Kilmore by a choir of six men who divide into two groups to sing alternate verses. Only six of the traditional airs that were used survive, although some airs are used with the lyrics of more then one of the carols. Some of the carols have been recorded by **Dordán**, **Noirín Ní Riain** and the **Voice Squad**. They are published as *The Wexford Carols* (Portlaoise, 1982), with an excellent introduction by editor Diarmuid Ó Muirithe and music transcribed (with commentary) by Seoirse Bodley.

Whelan, Bill (b. 1950) Composer, keyboards player and producer born in Limerick. Although his background was not in traditional music, he has produced albums for many traditional musicians, including **Andy Irvine** and **Stockton's Wing**. He was also a member of **Planxty** in their latter years, and with them he played his piece *Timedance* as the centrepiece for the Eurovision song contest in Dublin in 1981. A modern ballet was performed to the music, which incorporated **Junior Crehan**'s 'The Humours of Barrack Street' as part of a sequence of tunes that changed in mood and rhythm, building up to a grand finale. There were some musical parallels with Whelan's later Eurovision centrepiece, *Riverdance* (1994), although the style of dancing was very different. Between *Timedance* and *Riverdance*, Whelan worked on an album of music from Macedonia and Bulgaria with Andy Irvine and **Davy Spillane**. *Eastwind* (1992) introduced Whelan to a whole new area of music and rhythm which was to be essential in the music he subsequently composed for *Riverdance*. Whelan's success in composing for the *Riverdance* shows following the Eurovision performance is his most notable achievement to date. The music incorporates a diverse range of influences, including that of Irish traditional music, East European and Spanish music. Whelan has also composed music for a number of films and was specially commissioned to compose *The Seville Suite* for Expo '92 in Seville, Spain and *The Spirit of Mayo* for the Mayo 5000 celebrations in 1993. He also performed with **Moving Hearts** in their early days, although he never recorded with them. He admires the work that **Seán Ó Riada** did in bringing Irish and classical music together and believes that Irish composers should look to traditional Irish music, rather than to European music, for inspiration. Website: www.billwhelan.com.

Whelan, John (b. 1959) Button accordion player and composer born near Luton, England to parents from Tipperary and Wexford. At the age of eleven he began learning from the London-based native of Co. Clare, Brendan Mulkere. Whelan won the **All-Ireland** seven times on the button accordion, recording an album, *The Pride of Wexford* after his 1974 All-Ireland win. In 1980 he moved to the **US** and, after playing in a showband for a few years, formed a partnership with **Eileen Ivers**. They played together for seven years and together recorded the album *Fresh Takes* (1986), in which they experimented with traditional, rock and jazz influences. Throughout the late 1980s and well into the 90s Whelan toured and recorded with the Kips Bay Céilí Band, mixing Irish, Scottish and American music, leaving the group in 1997 to form his own band. Whelan has also recorded several solo albums, including *From the Heart* (1990), *Celtic Reflections: Misty-Eyed Mornings* (1995), *Come to Dance* (recorded in a church in Whelan's home town of Milford, Connecticut in 1998) and *Spirit of Dance* (2002). He has also performed and composed for film soundtracks, and teaching has been a very important part of his career. A playful and entertaining performer, Whelan is very popular in the US and is one of the biggest selling traditional musicians of all time. Website: www.john-whelan.com.

Whistle (*feadóg*) Whistles of various types are found in most cultures, from ancient times to the present, and on every continent. In Ireland, the Brehon Laws mention whistle players as early as the 6th or 7th century, and there are numerous references to them in the earliest Irish literature. The earliest physical remains of whistles were found in Christchurch Place, Dublin. These date from the 13th century and are made of bird bone. The tin whistle is the most common type played in modern times, and is sometimes sold as a 'flageolet'. The term derived from a fipple flute similar to a tin whistle that was known in Europe from the late 16th century. It became popular in England and France in the 17th century, where it was used for playing classical music well into the 19th century. Most flageolets of this era, however, were more elaborate in design than the tin whistle and some even had keys instead of simple open holes.

Until recent decades, the English-made 'Clarke' tin whistle, first manufactured in 1843, was the standard type. Still played today, it consists of a cone-shaped piece of tin with a wooden fipple (a plug forming a flue) in the mouthpiece. In the past 30 years, cylindrical whistles made of brass (or nickel-plated brass) with plastic mouthpieces have become more common. The British-made 'Generation' was the first of this kind of whistle to be mass produced and Generation still make the widest variety of whistles in different pitches. Tin whistles are also made in Ireland now, most notably the 'Feadóg' (Irish for 'whistle') and 'Waltons' type. **Waltons** produce a variety of whistles with different tones by changing either the bore or the type of material used. American-

Whistles

made 'Susato' plastic whistles are also becoming popular, although the tone is not as sweet as the 'tin' whistle. Handmade wooden whistles can also be found.

Although fingering charts for a full chromatic scale often come with tin whistles, it is only by using half-covered holes that a player can play a chromatic scale. On the most commonly used whistle, pitched in 'D', a player can also get C natural without using half-covered holes. A G-major scale could thus be played easily on a 'D' whistle, and similarly whistles in other pitches can always be used to play in a second major scale without resorting to the use of half-covered holes. A good player can produce a whole range of complex forms of **ornamentation** on the whistle in a manner very similar to the flute.

Donncha Ó Briain, **Seán Potts**, **Micho Russell**, **Seán Ryan**, **Mary Bergin**, **Vinny Kilduff**, **Joannie Madden**, **Brian Hughes** and Conor Byrne are among the most famous tin whistle players of recent decades. Many uilleann pipers, such as Brendan Monaghan (formerly of **Different Drums of Ireland**), **Liam O'Flynn**, **Darach De Brún**, **Joe McKenna**, **Paddy Maloney**, **Paddy Keenan** and **Brendan Keenan** are also fine whistle players. Although the fingering system of the chanter on the uilleann pipes and the whistle are not identical, the way the fingers are used to produce ornamentation are similar, and some teachers of the pipes will recommend that a pupil play tin whistle for a year or so before starting the pipes. Some tin whistle players and pipers also play the **low whistle**. Two fine young whistle players who have released albums in recent years are Gavin Whelan and Breda Smyth.

Williams, John (b. 1967) Button accordion and concertina player born in Chicago who, in 1989, became the first American to win the Senior **All-Ireland** Concertina Championship. His father and grandfather (originally from **Doolin**, Co.

John Williams

Clare) both played accordion as well. He has worked on film soundtracks, including *The Brothers McMullen* (1994), which introduced him to other members of the band which later became **Solas**. His first album, *John Williams* (1995), was purely traditional in style, although Williams has played in other idioms. It features **Martin Hayes**, who lived in Chicago for seven years, as well as **Micho Russell**, and was the last recording Russell made before his death. In 1996 and '97 Williams recorded a further two albums, this time with Solas, but left the group in 1997. He continues to perform and released a second solo album, *Steam*, in 2001 with guests **Liz Carroll**, **Séamus Egan** and former Solas guitarist, John Doyle, among others. The album was nominated for a Grammy Award. Website: www.johnwilliamsmusic.com.

Willie Clancy Summer School Ireland's largest traditional music summer school, based in Miltown Malbay, Co. Clare. It has been held annually (during the first week of July) since 1973, in memory of the famous musician and singer **Willie Clancy**. Up to a thousand students from all over the world attend the daily classes in Irish music and dance every year; there is also a full programme of lectures, *céilithe* (see **Céilí**), recitals and exhibitions. The daily music classes, held every morning, are available in uilleann pipes, whistle, flute, fiddle, concertina, button accordion and traditional singing. Many of the teachers are famous traditional musicians who perform in the afternoon/evening recitals. **Na Píobairí Uilleann** (the Pipers' Club) provides the piping teachers and an annual lecture in honour of founding member **Breandán Breathnach**. A daily course introducing students to Irish traditional music is also available. For the first week of July, the pubs, halls and homes of Miltown Malbay are crammed with musicians and dancers. Apart from the organised classes and concerts, there are constant impromptu sessions where students can play with established musicians. School fees are reasonable, but anyone thinking of going to this famous summer school should, if possible, book accommodation well in advance! Tony Kearns and Barry Taylor's *A Touchstone for the Tradition: The Willie Clancy Summer School* (Cork, 2003) offers a detailed history of the school and gives a good insight into the daily classes there. Website: www.set-dancingnews.net/wcss.

Wolfe Tones, The Group that emerged during the **Ballad Boom**, naming themselves after the United Irishmen leader, Theobald Wolfe Tone (1763-1798), the father of Irish republicanism. Brian Warfield (tin whistle, harp, guitar, five-string banjo, backing vocals), Derek Warfield (mandolin, vocals), Noel Nagle (tin whistle, uilleann pipes) and Tommy Byrne (guitar, vocals) are all from Dublin and started to play together in 1964. They turned professional in the same year, and initially worked in **England**, where their first album *The Foggy Dew* was released. This was followed by *Up the Rebels* (1966) and the first of many trips to the **US**. They became enormously popular in Ireland, Britain, Europe and the US, where they played their first concert in Carnegie Hall, New York in 1976. Their repertoire reflects a strong sense of national identity and republican ideals (see **Nationalist/Republican Song**). They sing traditional songs, but also a considerable number of original songs, most of them written in ballad style by Brian Warfield. His 'Helicopter Song' (celebrating the mass escape of IRA prisoners) was a No. 1 hit in 1973, and he has written on a wide range of subjects, including love, politics and emigration. The Wolfe Tones have released about twenty albums, including a double to mark their 25th anniversary.

Derek Warfield left the band in January 2002, and *Irish Times* journalist Fintan O'Toole provoked controversy when he wrote an article titled 'Why the end of the Wolfe Tones is music to my ears' (*Irish Times*, January 12, 2002). O'Toole argued that the group had 'expressed hatred for all things English and whipped up support for violent nationalism'. He subsequently appeared on **RTÉ** television's *Late Late Show* to debate his views with members of the Wolfe Tones.

The trio, calling themselves 'Noel Nagle, Tommy Byrne and Brian Warfield of the Wolfe Tones', continued to perform and record together, with Derek Warfield forming his own group, Sons of Erin. Ironically, the nationalist ballad 'A Nation Once Again' as performed by the Wolfe Tones was voted the world's favourite song in a 2002 internet poll organised by the **BBC** World Service. The song was written by Thomas Davies of the **Young Ireland** movement in the 1840s, and canvassers encouraged people to register '800 years of oppression' as the reason they were nominating the song. The BBC reported intense on-line campaigns by supporters during the polls. Website: www.wolfetonesofficialsite.com.

Wren-Boys Sometimes confused with **mummers**, the wren-boys gather only on St. Stephen's Day (December 26th). The custom of 'hunting the wren' was also known in other parts of Europe. In the past, wren-boy ceremonies in Ireland involved much fertility symbolism, with men disguised as women, but this aspect seems to have died out. In Britain, St. Stephen's Day used to be called 'Wrenning Day' because in many villages a wren was stoned to death in commemoration of the stoning to death of St. Stephen (died ca. 35 AD), the first Christian martyr. A wren is said to have given away the saint's hiding place to Roman soldiers – although Lady Wilde noted that the Irish hatred of the bird derived from the fact that wrens had given away the position of Irish troops preparing to attack the army of Cromwell (1599-1658) by perching on their drums and making noise. 'So ever since', writes Wilde, 'the Irish hunt the wren on St. Stephen's Day, teach their children to run it through with thorns and kill it whenever it can be caught. A dead wren was also tied to a pole and carried from house to house by boys, who demanded money; if nothing was given the wren was buried on the door step, which was considered a great insult to the family and a degradation' (*Ancient Legends of Ireland*; London, 1888, p. 177). Although the wren-boys of today do not actually kill a wren as did those of the 19th century, the idea of asking for money to bury the wren is still common in the verses sung by wren-boys. One typical song sung around Waterford in the second half of the 20th century begins:

> The wren, the wren, the King of all Birds,
> St. Stephen's Day was caught in the furze.
> Roly-poly where's your nest?
> Up in the tree that I love best,
> Up in the holly and ivy tree
> Where all the birds follow me,
> Up with the kettle and down with the pan,
> Give me a penny to bury the wren.

Wren-boys still go out on St. Stephen's Day, especially in the south and west of Ireland, dressing up (sometimes in straw outfits, like **strawboys**) and blackening their faces. In many places the event is simply called 'the wren' (often pronounced 'ran'), and though still referred to as 'wren-boys', the groups involved usually include women as well. They visit homes or pubs, singing a verse like the above at each place they visit and staying a while, usually to play and sing, sometimes to dance. In some places, the money collected is now donated to charity, as in the case of the wren in Carrick-on-Suir, Co. Tipperary in the 1970s and 80s, where the money was usually donated to the local Meals-on-Wheels. The wren, revived in Glendalough, Co. Wicklow in the early 1990s, visited a circuit of pubs in the Wicklow Mountains and donated its collection to the local school fund. Wren-boys visiting homes in suburban Dublin were relatively common in the 1960s, and wren-boys can still be seen on St. Stephen's Day in some parts of the capital. In Dingle, Co. Kerry there are a number of groups of wren-boys, each named after a street in the town. In many of these places the tradition of the wren seems to be growing in popularity at the start of the third millennium.

The wren can be enacted by as few as one or two people, but many of the better-organised groups can be up to thirty or forty people, among them musicians and/or singers. Many instruments are played, but the **bodhrán** has particularly strong associations with the wren. Wren-boys in the **Isle of Man** sing a song finishing with a similar verse to that quoted above, but their story of how the custom originated is quite different to the Irish one. See also **Biddy Boys**; **Newfoundland**.

Wren-Boys

Yeats, Gráinne (b. 1925) Harpist, singer, pianist and researcher who sings and plays both classical and traditional music. She sings in Irish and in English and has

done some invaluable work on the music of the 17th- and 18th-century harpers. Her double CD *The Belfast Harp Festival/Féile Cruitirí Bhéal Feirste* (1992) is among the finest of her traditional releases. Half of it is devoted to the compositions of **Turlough O'Carolan** and half to the music composed or played by other 17th-and 18th-century harpers. She plays a number of different harps, including three that are strung with brass wire, two of which are replicas of 17th-century Irish harps. The CD contains two excellent booklets with information on the **Belfast Harp Festival** (1792), the harpers them-

Gráinne Yeats

selves and the music they played. It is a fine contribution, both in musical and in scholarly terms, to the appreciation of old harp music in Ireland. See also **Harp**.

Yeats, W. B. (1865-1939) Prolific poet, playwright, folklorist and critic born near Dublin who won the Nobel Prize for Literature in 1923. He was a central figure in the Irish literary revival and was a founder of Irish National Theatre Company at the Abbey Theatre, Dublin. A number of his poems are sung by Irish folk singers, perhaps most famously 'Down by the Sally Gardens'. The latter was an attempt to reconstruct an old song that Yeats had heard a peasant woman singing in Ballisodare, Co. Sligo. The Belfast group **Tamalin** recorded a version of the song in Irish in 1997. The original ballad still survives in a number of different versions and was recorded by **Robert Cinnamond** and **Planxty** as 'You Rambling Boys of Pleasure'.

In the past three decades a number of singers have put other Yeats poems to music, including 'The Song of the Wandering Aengus' (**Christy Moore**), 'The Stolen Child' (Mike Scott of the **Waterboys**) and 'The Hosts of the Air' (**Seán Tyrrell**). Liam and Bobby Clancy (see **Clancy Brothers and Tommy Makem**) have also incorporated recitations of Yeats' poems into their performances. Bobby Clancy's album *Make Me a Cup* (2000) has eight Yeats' poems wonderfully recited, some with sparse musical backing. It also has Yeats' 'Lake Isle of Innisfree' sung beautifully by **Aoife Clancy** to a melody she composed herself. Not to be confused with the song 'The Isle of Innisfree', Yeats' poem was inspired by Henry David Thoreau's *Walden* (1854). *Now and in Time to Be: A Musical Celebration of the Works of W.*

B. Yeats (1997) features performances by Christy Moore, **Shane MacGowan**, **Sharon Shannon**, Van Morrison and others. *Dancing in the Wind* (2000) is a collection of poems by Yeats set to music by Claire Roche. Yeats also wrote a collection of poems with the interesting title *Words for Music Perhaps* (1931), although the most famous of his 'songs' came from other collections. The structures and rhythms of much of the poet's work make it suitable for adaptation to song, and it seems likely that more of his verses will be set to music in the future. See also **Rua**.

Young Ireland A group of mainly middle-class romantic nationalists, both Catholic and Protestant, who were active in the period 1842-1848. Their initial leaders were Charles Gavin Duffy (1816-1903), Thomas Davis (1814-1845) and John Blake Dillon (1814-1866). They sought to promote a non-sectarian Irish national identity partly through writing and publishing new **ballad**s in their weekly newspaper the ***Nation***. While some of their ballads dealt with contemporary events or (like Davis' 'A Nation Once Again') promoted a poetic concept of Irish nationhood, others (such as 'O'Donnell Abu') portrayed events from Ireland's history in a strongly nationalistic light. Although the Young Ireland movement failed to achieve anything through their rebellion in 1848, the sense of romantic nationalism that they passed on to subsequent generations was arguably their major success. Their vision of nationalism has, through their ballads, survived right down to the present day, as well as inspiring later writers of **Nationalist/Republican song**. Ironically, Davies' 'A Nation Once Again' was voted the world's favourite song in an internet poll run by the BBC's World Service in 2002 (see **Wolfe Tones**). See also **Political Song**; **Great Famine, The**.

Z

Zimmerman, Georges Denis (b. 1930) Researcher and writer born in Lausanne, Switzerland who undertook Ph.D. studies in Geneva on the subject of Irish political ballads. He became a regular visitor to Ireland where he went through library collections of **broadside** ballads, doing similar research in Britain as well. *Irish Political Street Ballads* was published in 1966 in Switzerland and was reissued the following year as *Songs of Irish Rebellion* in Ireland and the **US**. In 2002 the Four Courts Press in Dublin published a second edition of the book under the title *Songs of Irish Rebellion: Irish Political Street Ballads and Rebel Songs, 1780-1900*. The book was divided into three parts, the first consisting of a series of essays on the background to the ballads, the second a collection of 92 political ballads (words and music) of the 18th and 19th centuries. The ballads in part two were those of the Nationalist/Republican view while in part three Zimmerman published eight Orange/Loyalist songs, preceded by a short essay on the background to these songs. See also **Nationalist/Republican Song**; **Orange/Loyalist Song**.

Zozimus (ca. 1793-1846) Famous blind ballad-maker and singer born in Dublin's Liberties. He used to sing and perform recitations in a limited area around old Dublin, including the quays around O'Connell Bridge, Patrick Street and Winetavern Street. His real name was Michael Moran, but he was named 'Zozimus' after an abbot who discovered St. Mary of Egypt doing penance in the desert. Moran, famed for his extraordinary ability to memorise or adapt what he heard, composed a recitation on the subject from a theological account by the Bishop of Raphoe. **Dominic Behan** reconstructed a number of songs by old Dublin ballad-makers, including Zozimus, recording the latter's 'The Twangman's Revenge' in 1956. The song was recorded later by the **Dubliners**. The most famous of Zozimus' songs was 'The Finding of Moses', a comic account of the biblical story set in ancient Egypt, and he is said to have written 'St. Patrick was a Gentleman' (recorded by **Christy Moore**). He often versified items from the news in a satirical style and was famed for his wit, presentation and voice. Dominic Behan described him as the 'greatest of ballad-singers'. **Robbie O'Connell**'s song 'The Last of the Gleemen' is based on an incident involving Zozimus which was recounted by **W. B. Yeats** in his *Mythologies* (1959). He was buried in Glasnevin, where a monument was unveiled in 1988.

Select Bibliography

History, Biography and Reference

Breathnach, Breandán. *Folk Music and Dances of Ireland*. Revised edition. Cork and Dublin: Mercier, 1977.

————. *The Man and His Music: An Anthology of the Writings of Breandán Breathnach*. Dublin: Na Píobairí Uilleann, 1996.

Brennan, Helen. *The Story of Irish Dance*. Dingle: Brandon Publications, 1999.

Carolan, Nicholas. *A Harvest Saved: Francis O'Neill and Irish Music in Chicago*. Cork: Ossian, 1997.

Carson, Ciaran. *Irish Traditional Music*. Belfast: Appletree, 1986.

Clancy, Liam. *Memoirs of an Irish Troubador*. London: Virgin Books, 2002.

Clarke, Victoria Mary and MacGowan, Shane. *A Drink with Shane MacGowan*. London: Pan Books, 2002 (first published by Sidgwick and Jackson, 2001).

Curtis, P. J. *Notes from the Heart: A Celebration of Traditional Irish Music*. Dublin: Torc, 1994.

Fleischmann, Aloys (ed.), Micheál Ó Súilleabháin (asst. ed.) and Paul McGettrick (assoc. ed.). *The Sources of Irish Traditional Music 1583-1855*, 1-2. New York and London: Garland, 1988.

MacAoidh, Caoimhín. *Between The Jigs and the Reels: The Donegal Fiddle Tradition*. Manorhamilton: Drumlin, 1994.

McNamee, Peter (ed.). *Traditional Music: Whose Music? Proceedings of Co-operation North Conference, 1991*. Belfast: Institute of Irish Studies, 1992.

Moore, Christy. *One Voice – My Life in Song*. London: Hodder and Stoughton, 2000.

Murphy, Pat. *Toss The Feathers: Irish Set Dancing*. Cork and Dublin: Mercier, 1995.

Ó Canainn, Tomás. *Traditional Music in Ireland*. London, Boston and Henley: Routledge, 1978.

O'Connor, Nuala. *Bringing It All Back Home*. London: BBC, 1991.

Ó hAllmhuráin, Gearóid. *A Pocket History of Irish Traditional Music*. Dublin: O'Brien Press, 1998.

O'Sullivan, Donal. *Carolan: The Life, Times and Music of an Irish Harper*. Cork: Ossian, 2001 (single volume edition of two volumes originally published in London, 1958).

O'Neill, Francis. *Irish Minstrels and Musicians*. Cork and Dublin: Mercier, 1987 (reprint of 1913 edition).

Shields, Hugh. *Narrative Singing in Ireland: Lays, Ballads, Come-all-yes and other Songs*. Dublin: Irish Academic Press, 1993.

Tunney, Paddy. *The Stone Fiddle: My Way to Traditional Song*. Dublin: Gilbert Dalton, 1979.

————. *Where Songs Do Thunder: Travels in Traditional Song*. Belfast: Appletree, 1991.

Vallely, Fintan (with Charlie Piggott, photographs by Nutan). *Blooming Meadows: The World of Irish Traditional Musicians*. Dublin: Townhouse, 1998.

—————— (ed.). *The Companion to Irish Traditional Music*. Cork: Cork University Press, 1999.

—————— (ed., with Hammy Hamilton, Eithne Vallely and Liz Doherty). *Crosbhealach an Cheoil/The Crossroads Conference, 1996: Tradition and Change in Irish Traditional Music*. Dublin: Whinstone Music, 1999.

Zimmerman, Georges Denis. *Song of Irish Rebellion: Irish Political Street Ballads and Rebel Songs, 1780-1900*. Dublin: Four Courts Press, 2002 (first edition published in Geneva, 1966).

Collections of Instrumental Music and Songs

Breathnach, Breandán. *Ceol Rince na hÉireann*, Vols. 1-5. Dublin: An Gúm, 1963-99.

Bunting, Edward. *The Ancient Music of Ireland: The Bunting Collections*. Dublin: Waltons Publishing, 2002 (single-volume, facsimile edition of collections originally published in 1796, 1809 and 1840).

Huntington, Gale (ed., with Lani Herrmann and Joth Moulden). *Sam Henry's Songs of the People*. Athens and London: University of Georgia Press, 1990.

Joyce, Patrick Weston. *Ancient Irish Music*. Dublin, 1873.

Mitchell, Pat. (ed.) *The Dance Music of Willie Clancy*. Cork: Ossian, 1991 (reprint of 1976 edition).

—————— with Jackie Small (eds). *The Piping of Patsy Touhey*. Dublin: Na Píobairí Uilleann, 1986 (book with cassette).

Moylan, Terry (ed.). *Johnny O'Leary of Sliabh Luachra: Dance Music from the Cork-Kerry Border*. Dublin: Lilliput Press, 1994.

—————— *The Age of Revolution: 1776 to 1815 in the Irish Song Tradition*. Dublin: Lilliput Press/Góilín Traditional Singers Club, 2000.

Munnelly, Tom (ed., with Marian Deasy). *The Mount Callan Garland: Songs from the Repertoire of Tom Lenihan of Knockbrack, Milltown Malbay, County Clare*. Dublin: Comhairle Bhéaloideas Éireann, 1994 (book and tapes).

Ó Cróinín, Dáibhí (ed.). *The Songs of Elizabeth Cronin*. Dublin: Four Courts Press, 2000 (book with 2 CDs).

Ó hEidhin, Micheál (ed.). *Cas Amhrán*. Indreabhán: Cló Iar Chonnachta Teo, 1990.

O Lochlainn, Colm (ed.). *Irish Street Ballads*. London and Sydney: Pan, 1978 (reprint of 1939 edition).

—————— *More Irish Street Ballads*. London and Sydney: Pan, 1978 (reprint of the original 1965 edition).

O'Neill, Francis. *O'Neill's Music of Ireland: Eighteen Hundred and Fifty Melodies*. Pacific, Missouri: Mel Bay, n.d.(facsimile of 1903 edition).

—————— *O'Neill's 1001: The Dance Music of Ireland*. Dublin: Waltons Publishing, 1999 (facsimile of 1907 edition).

Petrie, George. *The Complete Collection of Irish Music as noted by George Petrie (1789-1866)*. Edited from the original manuscripts by Charles Villiers Stanford. Felinfach, Wales: Lanerch Publishers, Part One and Part Two, 1994 and Part Three, 1995 (facsimile reprints).

————. *The Petrie Collection of the Ancient Music of Ireland*. Edited by David Cooper. Cork: Cork University Press, 2003 (new edition of Petrie's original 1855 publication).

Roche, Francis. *The Roche Collection of Traditional Irish Music*. Cork: Ossian, 1993 (1993 reprint of three original volumes, 1911-27).

Rowsome, Helena (ed.). *The Leo Rowsome Collection of Irish Music*. Dublin: Waltons Publishing, 2002.

Ryan, William. *Ryan's Mammoth Collection*. Pacific, Missouri: Mel Bay, 1995 (reprint of 1888 edition).

Shields, Hugh. *Tunes of the Munster Pipers*. Dublin: Irish Traditional Music Archive, 1998.

Select Discography

Solo Artists

Begley, Brendan. *Oíche go Maidean: It Could be a Good Night Yet.* Brendan Begley, no reference number.

Bergin, Mary. *Feadóga Stáin: Traditional Irish Music on the Tin Whistle.* Gael-Linn, CEFCD 071.

Clancy, Willie. *The Pipering of Willie Clancy* (2 vols.). Claddagh Records, CC32CD (Vol. 1), CC39CD (Vol. 2).

Coleman, Michael. *Michael Coleman 1891-1945* (double). Gael-Linn, CEFCD 161.

Doherty, John. *The Floating Bow.* Claddagh Records, CCF31CD.

Gaughan, Dick. *Coppers and Brass: Scots and Irish Dance Music on Guitar.* Topic, KTSC 315.

————. *Redwood Cathedral.* Green Trax, CDTRAX 158.

Heany, Joe. *Irish Traditional Songs in Gaelic and English.* Ossian, OSS 22.

Hill, Noel. *The Irish Concertina.* Claddagh Records, CCF21CD.

Keenan, Paddy. *Na Keen Affair.* Hot Conya Records, HCR O1 97.

Kelly, Alan. *Mosaic.* Tara, Tara CD 4010.

McGlynn, Arty. *McGlynn's Fancy.* Emerald Records, KBER 011.

McKenna, Joe. *The Irish Low Whistle.* Shanachie, Shanachie 78043.

McKeown, Susan. *Lowlands.* Green Linnet, GLCD 1205.

Molloy, Matt. *Matt Molloy.* Shanachie, Shanachie 79064.

Murphy, Colm. *An Bodhrán: The Irish Drum.* Gael-Linn, CEFCD 175.

O'Connell, Robbie. *Recollections Vol. 1.* Celtica, Celtica 2002-1.

O'Connor, Máirtín. *Chatterbox.* Dara, Dara CD 052.

O'Flynn, Liam. *The Given Note.* Tara, Tara CD 3031.

Ó Riada, Seán. *Ó Riada's Farewell.* Claddagh Records, CC12CD.

Peoples, Tommy. *The Quiet Glen/An Gleann Ciúin.* Tommy Peoples Publishing, TPCD 001.

Power, Brendan. *Blow In.* Hummingbird Records, HBCD0008.

Potts, Tommy. *The Lifffey Banks.* Claddagh Records, CC13CD.

Rowsome, Leo. *Rí na bPíobairí (King of the Pipers).* Claddagh Records, CC1.

Russell, Micho. *Ireland's Whistling Ambassador.* The Pennywhistler's Press, PWCD 80001.

Stivell, Alan. *Brian Boru.* Keltia III and Disques Dreyfus, FDM 36208-2.

Tyrrell, Seán. *The Orchard.* Longwalk Music, LM CD 002.

Groups and Other

Afro Celt Sound System. *Volume 1: Sound Magic.* Realworld, CDRW61.

Altan. *The First Ten Years, 1986-1995.* Green Linnet, GLCD 1153.

Arcady. *Many Happy Returns.* Dara, Dara CD 080.

Begley and Cooney. *Meitheal.* Hummingbird, HBCD 0004.

Bothy Band, The. *Out of the Wind, Into the Sun*. Mulligan, LUNCD 013 and Green Linnet, GLCD 3013.

Cappercaillie. *To the Moon*. Survival, SURCD 019.

Chieftains, The. *The Chieftains Live*. Claddagh Records, CC21CD.

Dervish. *Live in Palma* (double). Whirling Discs, WHRL 004.

Flanagan Brothers. *The Tunes We Like to Play on Paddy's Day*. Viva Voce, Viva Voce 007.

Glackin, Paddy and Jackson, Jolyon. *Hidden Ground*. Tara, 4TA 2009.

Hayes, Martin and Cahill, Denis. *The Lonesome Touch*. Green Linnet, GLCD 1181.

Irvine, Andy and Davy Spillane. *East Wind*. Tara, Tara CD 3027.

Keane, Tommy and Jacqueline McCarthy. *The Wind among the Reeds*. Maree Music, MMC CD51.

Kíla. *Tóg é Go Bog é*. Green Linnet, GLCD3128.

Lá Lugh. *Senex Puer*. Sony, SK 60385.

Lúnasa. *Lúnasa*. Lúnasa, LS001.

Molloy, Brady and Peoples. *Matt Molloy, Paul Brady, Tommy Peoples*. Mulligan, LUN 017.

Moore, Christy with Dónal Lunny and Jimmy Faulkner. *Live in Dublin*. Tara, Tara CD 4010.

Moving Hearts. *The Storm*. Tara, Tara CD 3014.

Murphy, Phil, John and Pip. *The Trip to Cullenstown*. Claddagh Records, CC55CD.

Ó Súilleabháin, Micheál. *Oileán/Island*. Virgin, CDVE40.

Planxty. *Planxty*. Shanachie, Shanachie 79009.

Pogues, The. *If I Should Fall from Grace with God*. WEA, 2292-44493-2.

Potts, Seán and Paddy Moloney. *Tin Whistles*. Claddagh Records, CC15CD.

Solas. *Sunny Spells and Scattered Showers*. Shanachie, Shanachie 78010.

Voice Squad, The. *Holly Wood*. Hummingbird, HBCD0002.

Wheels of the World: Early Irish-American Music, Classic Recordings from the 1920s and '30s (2 vols.). Yazoo, Yazoo 7008 (Vol. 1), Yazoo 7009 (Vol. 2).

Specialist Record Companies

Ceol Music Ltd., Unit 2 Benson Street, Enterprise Centre, Hanover Quay, Dublin 2. Company founded in 1996, specialising in Irish and Irish-American music. Has recorded artists such as Johnny McEvoy and the Fureys.

Claddagh Records Ltd., Teach an Dama, Sr. an Dama, Dublin 2. Along with Gael-Linn, has been recording traditional artists in Ireland since the 1950s. Has recorded many famous artists, including Leo Rowsome, Willie Clancy, the Chieftains, Dolores Keane and Skylark. In addition to releases by Irish traditional musicians and singers, Claddagh has also released some Scottish (the Whistlebinkies) and Manx (Charles Guard) musicians, as well as a considerable number of spoken arts recordings. Website: www.claddaghrecords.com.

Cló Iar-Chonnachta, Indreabhán, Co. na Gallaimhe, Éire/Ireland. Gaeltacht-based company that, since 1985, has produced an excellent selection of traditional musicians and singers. While many of the company's releases are of sean-nós singers such as Peadar Ceannabháin and Gearóidín Bhreathnach, it has also released many fine instrumentalists, including Johnny Connolly and his son Johnny Óg, Paddy Canny and Marcas Ó Murchú. Releases are always accompanied by excellent notes on the artists and the music, usually in both Irish and English. Website: www.cic.ie.

Gael-Linn Records, 26 Merrion Square, Dublin 2, Ireland. Like Claddagh Records, has made an important contribution to the recording of Irish traditional music since the 1950s, releasing major artists such as Seán Ó Riada, Clannad, Paddy Keenan, Dolores Keane, Dónal Lunny and many others. Releases always carry a strong Irish language element, with sleeve-notes, line-ups etc. usually appearing in Irish primarily, but often with English translations as well. Although the company is still involved in distribution, they ceased making their own recordings in 2001. Websites: www.gael-linn.ie / www.gael-linn.com.

Green Linnet Records, Danbury, Connecticut. American-based company that has recorded a vast array of Irish, Irish-American, Scottish, Breton and English artists since its foundation in the 1970s. Releases many major artists, including Séamus Ennis, James Keane, Buttons and Bows, Dolores Keane, Kevin Burke, Joe Burke, De Dannan, Robbie O'Connell, Niamh Parsons, Scottish group Silly Wizard, Dan ar Baz (Breton), the Bothy Band and Lúnasa. Website: www.greenlinnet.com.

Hummingbird Records, 76 Irishtown Road, Dublin 4. Branch of a major television production company founded by singer Philip King and researcher Nuala O'Connor. Has produced a number of albums from television series, including

Bringing It All Back Home, *A River of Sound* and *Sult*, as well as recording artists such as Begley and Cooney and De Dannan. Website: www.hummingbird.ie.

Ossian Publications, P.O. Box 84, Cork, Ireland. Major specialist recording and publications company that has released albums by Cork-based artists, including Séamus Creagh, Jackie Daly and Matt Cranitch; the group Oisín and other famous players such as Willie Clancy, Séamus Ennis, John Doherty and Joe Heany. Also has released albums of Scottish music, including a whole series of Ewan McColl albums. Also produces video tutors and music books, often accompanied by recordings. Websites: www.ossian.ie / www.ossianusa.com.

Outlet Recording Co. Ltd., 12/21 Gordon Street, Belfast BTI 2LG. Founded in 1966, Outlet is not exclusively a traditional music label, but has released some fine traditional artists over the years, including Joe Burke, Séamus Tansey and Luke Kelly. Website: outlet-music.com.

Shanachie Records. Shanachie Entertainment Corporation, 37 East Clinton Street, Newton, New Jersey 07860. For Ireland, Shanachie Ireland, c/o Joe McKenna, Moneystown North, Roundwood, Co. Wicklow. American-based company founded in 1972. Has many major artists, including Solas, Joe and Antoinette McKenna, Cathy Ryan and Karan Casey. Since 1996 Joe McKenna has been Shanachie's representative in Ireland, looking out for new and interesting talent in the traditional music world. Website: www.shanachie.com.

Tara Music Company Ltd., 4 Allen's Lane, Dublin 2, Ireland. Tara's first release was the famous Christy Moore album *Prosperous*, and the company subsequently released some of the biggest names in traditional music, including Planxty, Clannad, Shaun Davey, Davy Spillane, Stockton's Wing and Liam O'Flynn. Website: www.taramusic.com.

Torc Music Ltd., Units 3 and 4, Great Ship Street, Dublin 8, Ireland. Markets and distributes the Dara and Dolphin labels, releasing Irish traditional and contemporary artists such as Arcady, Ronnie Drew, Dolores Keane, Mary Black and Tommy Fleming as well as compilations like *A Woman's Heart* and *Éist*.

Festivals and Summer Schools

Note: The festivals listed below are mainly traditional music/song/dance or feature a considerable amount of Irish traditional music. In addition to those listed, the county and provincial heats of the Fleadh take place throughout May, June and July, culminating in the All-Ireland Fleadh in the last weekend of August. Festivals are in the Republic of Ireland unless otherwise stated.

Since contact details and website addresses are subject to change without notice, these are not listed here. They can generally be obtained from Irish music websites, or by internet search. This is by no means an exhaustive list of festivals and summer schools, and we would be happy to add any annual events that have taken place for at least three consecutive years prior to our next edition.

January
1st or 2nd weekend: Frankie Kennedy Winter School, Gweedore, Co. Donegal
Last 2 weeks: Celtic Connections Festival, Glasgow, Scotland

February
2nd weekend: Ballyvaughan Traditional Singers Weekend, Ballyvaughan, Co. Clare
Last weekend: Micho Russell Memorial Weekend, Doolin, Co. Clare

March
Week of March 17: St. Patrick's Day Festival, Dublin City
1st full weekend after St. Patrick's Day: Inishowen International Folk Song and Ballad Seminar, Buncrana, Co. Donegal
Weekend before Easter (if in March): Edinburgh International Harp Festival, Edinburgh, Scotland
Easter weekend (if in March): Traditional Music Weekend, Tory Island, Co. Donegal
Last week: Edinburgh Harp Festival, Edinburgh, Scotland
Last weekend: Ballad and Folksong Seminar, Inishowen, Co. Donegal
Last weekend: Galway Set Dancing Festival, Galway City

April
Weekend before Easter (if in April): Edinburgh International Harp Festival, Edinburgh, Scotland
Easter weekend (if in April): Traditional Music Weekend, Tory Island, Co. Donegal
1st week: Éigse na Laoi, Music Department, University College Cork
1st or 2nd weekend: Kilfenora Set Dancing Weekend, Kilfenora, Co. Clare
2nd or 3rd week: Pan-Celtic International Festival, Tralee, Co. Kerry
2nd or 3rd week: Cumar, Connemara, Co. Galway (different venue in Connemara each year)
Last week: Lahinch Folklore School, Lahinch, Co. Clare

Last week/1st week May: Féile na Déise, Dungarvan, Co. Waterford

Last week/1st week May: Féile na Bealtaine, Dingle, Co. Kerry

May

Last week April/1st week: Féile na Déise, Dungarvan, Co. Waterford

Last week April/1st week: Féile na Bealtaine, Dingle, Co. Kerry

1st weekend: Clare Festival of Traditional Singing, Milltown Malbay, Co. Clare

1st weekend: Bealtaine Festival, An Creagán Visitors Centre, Creggan, Omagh, Co. Tyrone, Northern Ireland

2nd weekend: Edward Bunting International Irish Harp and Singing Festival, Armagh City, Co. Armagh, Northern Ireland

2nd or 3rd weekend: Séamus O'Duggan Sean-nós singing weekend, Tory Island, Co. Donegal

3rd week: An t-Oireachtas, 6 Harcourt Street, Dublin 2

Last week: Avoca Melody Fair, Avoca, Co. Wicklow

Last weekend: Fleadh Nua, Ennis, Co. Clare

June

1st weekend: Ennistymon Festival of Traditional Singing, Ennistymon, Co. Clare

1st weekend: Alaska Irish Music Festival, Anchorage, Alaska, USA

2nd weekend: Mid-Ulster Folk Festival, Moneymore, Co. Derry

3rd weekend: An Creagán Midsummer Festival, An Creagán Visitors' Centre, Creggan, Omagh, Co. Tyrone

4th week: Gaelic Roots: A Music, Song and Dance Summer School, Boston College, Boston, USA

Last week: Kilfenora Music School, Kilfenora, Co. Clare

Last week: Tommy Makem International Festival of Music and Song, Co. Armagh, Northern Ireland (various venues)

July

1st week: Willie Clancy Summer School, Miltown Malbay, Co. Clare

1st week: Douglas Hyde Summer School of Traditional Irish Music and Dance, Ballaghaderreen, Co. Roscommon

2nd week: South Sligo Summer School, Tubbercurry, Co. Sligo

2nd weekend: James Morrison Traditional Weekend, Riverstown, Co. Sligo

2nd and 3rd week: Blás International Summer School of Irish Traditional Music and Dance, Irish World Music Centre, University of Limerick

2nd or 3rd week: Galway Arts Festival, Galway City

2nd or 3rd week: The Francis McPeake International Summer School, Belfast, Northern Ireland

2nd and 3rd week: Kilfenora Music School, Kilfenora, Co. Clare

3rd week: Joe Mooney Summer School, Drumshambo, Co. Leitrim

3rd or 4th week: Mallow Folk Festival, Mallow, Co. Cork

2nd-last weekend: Traditional Music weekend, Tory Island, Co. Donegal

Last week: Fiddler's Green International Festival, Rostrevor, Co. Down, Northern Ireland

Last weekend: Phil Murphy Weekend, Carrick-on-Bannow, Co. Wexford

Last weekend: Cleveland's Irish Cultural Festival, Cleveland, Ohio, USA

August

1st weekend: Le Chéile: Oldcastle Arts and Music Festival, Oldcastle, Co. Meath

1st weekend: Ballyshannon Folk and Traditional Music Festival, Ballyshannon, Co. Donegal

1st weekend: O'Carolan International Harp Festival, Keadue, Co. Roscommon

1st or 2nd week: Siamsa Sráide Swinford, Swinford, Co. Mayo

1st or 2nd weekend: Feakle Traditional Music Festival, Feakle, Co. Clare

2nd and 3rd week: Festival Interceltique, Lorient, Brittany, France

2nd week: Masters of Tradition Festival, Bantry House, Bantry, Co. Cork

2nd weekend: Seán McCarthy Memorial Weekend, Finuge, Lixnaw, Co. Kerry

2nd weekend: Granard Harp Festival, Granard, Co. Longford

2nd weekend: Celtic Fusion International Music Festival, Castlewellan, Co. Down, Northern Ireland

10th-12th: Puck Fair, Killorglin, Co. Kerry

Weekend closest to 15th: Traditional Music Festival, Tory Island, Co. Donegal.

Week around middle of month: ESB Beo Celtic Music Festival at the National Concert Hall, Dublin

2nd or 3rd week: Kilkenny Arts Festival, Kilkenny City

2nd and 3rd week: Festival Interceltique, Lorient, Brittany, France

2nd or 3rd weekend: Eigse Mrs Crotty, Kilrush, Co. Clare

3rd week: Milwaukee Irish Fest, Milwaukee, Wisconsin, USA

3rd weekend: Michael Shanley Traditional Weekend, Killyclogher, Co. Leitrim

2nd-last weekend: Festival of World Cultures, Dún Laoghaire, Co. Dublin

3rd or 4th week: Aonach Paddy O'Brien, Nenagh, Co. Tipperary

Last week: Tønder Festival, Tønder, Denmark

Last week and last weekend: Scoil Eigse and Fleadh Cheoil na hÉireann/All-Ireland Fleadh (venue varies)

September

1st weekend: Coleman Country Traditional Festival, Gurteen, Co. Sligo

1st weekend: Washington Irish Folk Festival, Washington DC, USA

Weekend after Labor Day: Pittsburgh Irish Festival, Pittsburgh, Pennsylvania, USA

1st or 2nd weekend: Cork Folk Festival, Cork City

2nd weekend: Chicago Celtic Fest, Chicago, Illinois, USA

3rd week: Music under the Mountains, Hollywood, Co. Wicklow

Last weekend: Johnny Keenan Banjo Festival, Longford Town, Co. Longford

October

1st weekend: Slieve Gullion Festival of Traditional Singing, Forkhill/Mullaghban, Co. Armagh

1st weekend: O'Carolan Harp and Cultural Festival, Nobber, Co. Meath

2nd week: Celtic Colours International Festival, Baddec, Canada

2nd weekend: Féile An Fhómhair of Traditional Irish Music, An Creagán Visitors Centre, Creggan, Co. Tyrone, Northern Ireland

Over 3 weekends, late October/early November: Donegal Fiddlers' Weekends, Glenties, Co. Donegal

Last week: Return to Camden Town, Festival of Irish Music, Song and Dance, London, England

Bank Holiday weekend: Scoil Shéamuis Ennis in Naul and District, Co. Dublin

Bank Holiday weekend: Pádraig O'Keefe Traditional Music Festival, Castleisland, Co. Kerry

Last weekend: Kilfenora October Festival, Kifenora, Co.Clare

Last weekend: The Táin Rhythm amd Roots Festival, Dundalk, Co. Louth

Last week (October) into 1st week (November): Belfast Festival at Queen's, Queen's University, Belfast, Northern Ireland

November

1st or 2nd weekend: Ennis Trad Festival, Ennis, Co. Clare

3rd week: William Kennedy International Piping Festival, Armagh, Northern Ireland

Last weekend: Drogheda Traditional Music Weekend, Drogheda, Co. Louth

Last weekend or 1st in December: Éigse Dhiarmuid Uí Shúilleabháin, Cúil Aodha, Co. Cork

December

Last weekend in November or 1st in December: Éigse Dhiarmuid Uí Shúilleabháin, Cúil Aodha, Co. Cork

26th-27th: Woodford Mummers Festival, Woodford, Co. Galway

Possibly starting last days of December: Frankie Kennedy Winter School, Gweedore, Co. Donegal